Accounting Theory and Practice

By the same authors
Accounting in a Changing Environment
(Pitman Publishing, 1974)

M. W. E. GLAUTIER
and B. UNDERDOWN

Accounting
Theory and Practice

Pitman

Pitman Publishing Limited
39 Parker Street, London WC2B 5PB

Associated Companies
Copp Clark Pitman, Toronto/Fearon-Pitman Publishers Inc, San Francisco/
Pitman Publishing New Zealand Ltd, Wellington/Pitman Publishing Pty
Ltd, Melbourne

© M.W.E. Glautier and B. Underdown 1976

First published in Great Britain 1976
Reprinted 1977, 1978

Printed by photolithography and bound in Great Britain
at The Pitman Press, Bath

ISBN 0 273 00705X

Contents*

Preface   vii

Acknowledgements   xi

Part 1   **A Theoretical Framework   xii**

Part 2   **Financial Accounting Information   45**
Section 1   Financial Accounting Method   55
Section 2   Periodic Measurement   111
Section 3   The Application of Financial Accounting Method to Corporate Enterprises   185

Part 3   **Planning and Control   247**
Section 1   A Framework for Planning and Control   259
Section 2   Planning   305
Section 3   Control   433
Section 4   The Design of Management Information Systems   509

Part 4   **Financial Reporting   527**
Section 1   Conceptual Considerations in Financial Reporting   535
Section 2   Value and Income Measurement   555
Section 3   Comparability and the Interpretation of Financial Reports   609
Section 4   Increasing Financial Information   651

Part 5   **Social Responsibility Accounting   669**

Index   735

* Contents in more detail appear at the beginning of each Part.

Preface

The tradition in accounting education has been to focus the teaching of accounting almost entirely upon procedures for processing financial data. The treatment of accounting as a skill, rather than as a body of knowledge, is based on the belief that 'accounting is what accountants do'. Whilst this assertion undoubtedly holds good as a statement of what accountants do, such a view of accounting has serious shortcomings as regards the educational qualities of accounting courses and the education of accountants. First, by restricting the nature and scope of accounting to an exposure of its procedures, it fails to provide an adequate understanding of these procedures in relation to the problems facing accountants. Second, it impedes the recognition of economic and social changes which bear directly on these problems. These changes have made many accounting practices redundant, and have called for a re-structuring of the accounting process. Third, it supports a conviction widespread among students and practitioners that what they have been taught is in the nature of an everlasting truth, or a collection of everlasting truths. Hence, it has hindered the development of accounting.

The most damaging factor as regards the teaching of accounting has been the absence of a theoretical framework to serve as a standard of reference for examining the validity of the assumptions held by accountants. As a result, accounting courses have sometimes tended to be virtually devoid of rigorous analysis, which is characterized by the uncritical acceptance of the assumptions reflected in accounting procedures. It is not surprising, therefore, that teachers of other subjects tend to regard accounting as being qualitatively inferior in the potential which it offers for the development of the mind and person.

This textbook is committed to a different view of accounting education in a number of important respects. First, as its title Accounting Theory and Practice implies, it attempts to provide a theoretical framework for the understanding of the nature of the accounting problem and an appreciation of the purpose of various accounting practices. This approach permits accounting practices to be exposed to critical analysis by means of which their usefulness and relevance may be assessed and their shortcomings exposed. Hence, it provides the teacher and the student with a means of overcoming the most serious criticism made about accounting education. Second, the nature and the scope of accounting is extended beyond accounting procedures by conceiving the essential function of accounting as facilitating socio-economic activities and decisions. Accordingly, we give a global and rounded view of accounting in which the emphasis is appropriately placed on the role of accounting as being the provision of information for decision-making. We examine both traditional and new problems, and bring to our analysis developments in other subject areas which are important to accounting. In so doing, we provide for the inter-disciplinary nature of accounting and hope to end its isolation as an esoteric collection of procedures. From this viewpoint, we believe that the traditional emphasis placed in first-year texts on the importance of financial accounting is misplaced.

We have emphasized the importance of the scientific method for the development of accounting. In terms of its ultimate objectives, ac-counting is as scientific as any other discipline. In terms of its ability to develop and apply empirically verified theories, it is far from being a mature science, but it is striving in this direction. We try to reflect this trend in this textbook.

Finally, we believe that accounting is a very important social science. We hope that our readers will develop insights into the social role of accounting at an early stage, and it is for this reason that we decided to adopt a global, rather than a narrow view of the accounting process.

We have interpreted the broad objectives of accounting as being to provide information for the following purposes:

(1) Decision-making regarding the use of limited resources, in-cluding the identification of crucial decision areas, and the determination of objectives and goals.
(2) Effectively directing and controlling human and material re-sources.
(3) Maintaining and reporting on the custodianship of resources.
(4) Facilitating social functions and controls.

The textbook is divided into five parts, as follows:

Part 1 A Theoretical Framework
Part 2 Financial Accounting Information
Part 3 Planning and Control
Part 4 Financial Reporting
Part 5 Social Responsibility Accounting

In Part 1, we discuss the nature and the importance of theory covering every aspect of accounting knowledge and incorporating this knowledge into a unified whole, the purpose of which is the provision of information for socio-economic decision-making.

Part 2 examines the traditional nature of accounting information and the conventions which illustrate the way of thinking underlying financial accounting practices.

Part 3 is addressed to the problem of the role of accounting information in organizational decision-making, and illustrates how the limitations of financial accounting have been overcome in the development of cost and management accounting practices.

Part 4 considers financial reporting, which is an important accounting responsibility in a traditional sense, for it is concerned with the supply of information to shareholders and investors, particularly information for the purpose of investment decision-making. It is a controversial area in accounting, and involves many points of current interest.

Finally, Part 5 is devoted to a brief analysis of social responsibility accounting, which is a new development reflecting the changing nature of the accounting problem. In our view, social responsibility accounting may well be a watershed in the development of accounting, for not only does it imply an extension of accounting beyond traditional confines, but also the addition of non-monetary measurements to the traditional monetary measurements which have been the hallmark of accounting.

We would emphasize that although this textbook is divided into five parts, each addressed to a special aspect of accounting, they are nevertheless linked by the provision of a theoretical framework which brings them together and establishes their purposes in the provision of information for decision-making.

The reader will notice that this book contains no questions or exercises. These, in fact, will be included in support material to accompany this text in the form of a workbook, a solutions manual and a book of readings. Therefore, although this book is entirely self-contained, we regard it also as part of a comprehensive programme to develop students' understanding of the theory and practice of accounting.

We believe that this book will be suitable for the following uses:

(1) University and Polytechnic first- and second-year degree courses in Accounting;
(2) First-year MBA courses in Business Schools;
(3) Professional examinations;
(4) Practising accountants who wish to acquire a broader viewpoint of the accounting process.

As a guide to a possible teaching programme, it is suggested that the sequence of chapters set out below may well serve the purpose of satisfying those courses which demand concurrent consideration of the underlying theoretical approach and of the experience of practical applications. The subject matter in the text pursues a logical sequence as we see it but this does not preclude other valid progressions using alternative sequences.

We believe that the following sequence could be adopted and that it would give students a sufficient grasp of techniques whilst not sacrificing the more rigorous analysis of underlying principles which we deem to be the essence of our approach to accounting.

Part 1

Chapter 1 (10 pages)

Chapter 2 ⎱ Part 1
Chapter 3 ⎰ 46 pages

Chapter 1 ⎱
  „ 2 ⎱ Part 4
  „ 3 ⎰ 50 pages
  „ 4 ⎰

Chapter 1 ⎱
  „ 2 ⎪
  „ 3 ⎪
  „ 4 ⎪ Part 2
  „ 5 ⎰ 153 pages
  „ 6 ⎪
  „ 7 ⎪
  „ 8 ⎰

The student at this point would have been introduced to the environment of accounting, a consideration of the foundation of the economic determination of income, and to the general principles of the double entry system of book-keeping.

Several of our examples in the text up to this point have concurred, in part, the affairs of limited companies without dwelling on the distinctive nature of such organisations or their specific accounting requirements.

The next sequence is suggested to enable the student to become acquainted with the corporate structure and the implications which flow from its concept. Not only has the corporate sector become the dominant business section in most advanced national economics but it has also acted as a focal point for practical applications of all those complementary disciplines which now form the accepted corpus of knowledge for our accountant.

Part 2

Chapter 9 ⎱
  „ 10 ⎰ 75 pages
  „ 11 ⎰

Part 4

```
Chapter  5 ⎫
  „      6 ⎪
  „      7 ⎬ 92 pages
  „      8 ⎪
  „      9 ⎪
  „     10 ⎭
```

Part 3 can be utilized as a complete section which covers the managerial view of accounting and Part V is an attempt to indicate the way accountants may have to widen the present perception of their role in the light of more recent insights into the interaction between economic activity and society at large.

Acknowledgements

We wish to place on record our gratitude to colleagues and friends for the advice and help which they have given us in the course of writing this text. We owe a particular debt to Professor W. Rotch of the Colgate Darden Graduate School of Business Administration, University of Virginia, and Charles Clark, Principal Lecturer in Accounting, Manchester Polytechnic, who have both been closely associated with every aspect of the book and who have helped us unstintingly, as well as Professor T. A. Lee of Edinburgh University, Professor R. H. Parker of Exeter University, Dr Anthony Hopwood of the Oxford Centre for Management Studies, C. P. Rickwood of Birmingham University, Geoffrey J. Harris of Melbourne University and Dr H. C. Dekker of Amsterdam University.

Our very good friend E. C. Johnson, Senior Lecturer in Accounting, University of Hull, contributed two chapters on Accounting for Acquisitions and Mergers (Part 2, chapters 10 and 11), whilst C. Burke and O. A. Bello, both of Southampton University, and P. J. Taylor of the University College of North Wales read and commented in detail on several chapters.

We have been privileged as authors to have had so much support from our publishers Pitman Publishing Ltd, and this book is indeed the outcome of a close partnership between authors and publishers. We wish to thank all those members of the Pitman staff who have worked with us, particularly Navin Sullivan, Managing Director, and Martin Marix Evans and James Shepherd of the University and College Department. James Shepherd deserves special mention for his patience, tact and above all for the hard work which he has put into this book.

Dr Ken Watkins of Sheffield University was one of the original instigators of this book, and we owe much to his friendship.

We would also like to express our gratitude to the Quaker Oats Company and The R. G. Barry Corporation for permission to reproduce their published financial reports in Part 5, to Greenall Whitley and Co. for allowing us to publish the cash-flow analysis of their accounts for 1972 to 1975, and to S. A. Dixon, a post-graduate student of Manchester University who prepared the statement and gave his consent to its use in this book. We both are fortunate to have wives who have encouraged us to work, and who have made the many sacrificies which wives of authors have to make. We dedicate this book with our love to Christianne and Anne.

A Theoretical Framework

Part 1 A THEORETICAL FRAMEWORK

1 Scope and Method   1
The scope of accounting   1
The emerging role of accounting as a social science   2
The difficulties facing the accountant   7
Summary   8
References   9

2 Accounting as an Information System   10
The boundaries of an information system   11
The output of an information system   13
    The information needs of management   14
    The information needs of shareholders and investors   14
    The information needs of employees   15
    The information needs of governments   16
    The information needs of creditors   16
    The information needs of other groups   17
Accounting information and the allocation of resources   19
Behavioural aspects of decision-making   20
A systems approach to the study of accounting   21
Summary   23

3 The Foundations of Accounting Theory   25
The nature of theory   25
    Logic and theory   26
    The development of empirical theories   26
    The scientific method and the social sciences   28
The roots of accounting theory   30
Decision theory   30
  Decision-making and problem solving   30
    Decision-making and prediction   31
    Decision theory and the use of models   32
    Models and the accountant   33
Measurement theory   33
    The object of measurement   34
    The standard of measurement   35
    The dimensions of the unit of measurement   35
    Valuation and measurement   36
Information theory   37
    The production of information   37
    Valuing information   39
Summary   39
References   40
Selected further readings   41
    Accounting history   41
    Accounting theory   41

1
Scope and Method

The scope of accounting

Accounting is in an age of rapid transition; its environment has undergone vast changes in the last two decades and an accelerating rate of change is in prospect for the future. Much of what is accepted as accounting today would not have been recognized as such 50 years ago, and one may safely predict that in 50 years' time the subject will bear little resemblance to what it is today.

Changing social attitudes combine with developments in information technology, quantitative methods and the behavioural sciences to affect radically the environment in which accounting operates today, thereby creating the need to re-evaluate the objectives of accounting in a wide perspective. Accounting is moving away from its traditional procedural base, encompassing record-keeping and such related work as the preparation of budgets and final accounts, towards the adoption of a role which emphasizes its social importance.

The changing environment has extended the boundaries of accounting and has created a problem in defining the scope of the subject. There is a need for a definition which is broad enough to delineate its boundaries, whilst at the same time being sufficiently precise as a statement of its essential nature. It is interesting to contrast definitions which were accepted a little time ago with more recent statements. According to a definition made in 1953,

'the central purpose of accounting is to make possible the periodic matching of costs (efforts) and revenues (accomplishments). This concept is the nucleus of accounting theory, and a benchmark that affords a fixed point of reference for accounting discussions' (Littleton, 1953).

The Committee on Terminology of the American Institute of Certified Public Accountants formulated the following definition in 1961:

'Accounting is the art of recording, classifying and summarising in a significant manner and in terms of money, transactions and

1

events which are, in part at least, of a financial character, and interpreting the result thereof' (A.I.C.P.A., 1961).

A more recent definition is less restrictive and interprets accounting as

'the process of identifying, measuring and communicating economic information to permit informed judgements and decisions by the users of the information.' (A.A.A., 1966).

This definition comes closer to our own interpretation of the scope of accounting, and the manner in which we should like to treat its subject matter, but we would add the rider that accounting is moving rapidly now towards the objective of providing 'socio-economic' information for decision-making. The rapidity with which this change is occurring has created a gulf between conventional business accounting based on the profit concept and social responsibility accounting which is concerned with the social role of business organizations and views profit as only one of their objectives. The humanization and the democratization of work which is now at the fore of political and industrial debate reflect a radical shift in the nature of society from a capitalistic basis to a broader democratic basis. The transition from profitability accounting to social responsibility accounting is part of a historic process, however, and should be judged in that context.

The emerging role of accounting as a social science

The social sciences study man as a member of society; they share a concern about social processes, and the results and consequences of social relationships. In this respect, the usefulness of accounting as a social science depends on the benefits which it may bring to society, rather than on the advantages which it may confer to its individual members. We would say, therefore, that although an individual businessman may benefit from the availability of accounting information, what is much more important is that society as a whole should benefit from the fact that its individual members use accounting information for the solution of business problems.

The history of accounting reflects the evolutionary pattern of social developments and in this respect, illustrates how much accounting is a product of its environment and at the same time a force for changing it. There is, therefore, an evolutionary pattern which reflects changing socio-economic conditions and the changing purposes to which accounting is applied. From today's perspective, we may distinguish four phases which may be said to correspond with its developing social role.

(1) Stewardship accounting has its origins in the function which accounting served from the earliest times in the history of our society of providing the owners of wealth with a means of safeguarding it from theft and embezzlement. The title 'stewardship' accounting also has its origins in the fact that wealthy men employed 'stewards' to manage their property. These stewards rendered an account periodically of their stewardship, and this notion still lies at the root of financial reporting today. Essentially, stewardship accounting involved the orderly recording of business transactions, and although accounting records of this type date back to as early as 4500 B.C., the method of keeping these records, known as 'book-keeping', remained primitive until fairly recent times. Indeed, the accounting concepts and procedures in use today for the orderly recording of business transactions have their origin in the practices employed by the merchants of the Italian City States during the early part of the Renaissance. The main principles of the Italian Method, as it was then known, were set out by Luca Pacioli in his famous treatise *Summa de Arithmetica, Geometrica, Proportioni et Proportionalita* which was published in Venice in 1494. The Italian Method, which became known subsequently as 'double-entry book-keeping' was not generally used in Western Europe until the early part of the 19th century. Whether or not businessmen kept their accounts on the single-entry or the double-entry principle, stewardship accounting played an important social role during the period of commercial expansion in Western Europe, which followed the Renaissance and characterized that phase of Capitalism known as Commercial Capitalism. Stewardship accounting is associated, therefore, with the need of businessmen to keep records of their transactions, the manner in which they had invested their wealth and the debts owed to them and by them.

(2) Financial accounting has a much more recent origin, and dates from the development of large scale businesses which were made possible by the Industrial Revolution. Indeed, the new technology not only destroyed the existing social framework, but altered completely the method by which business was to be financed. The industrial expansion in the early part of the 19th century necessitated access to large supplies of capital. This led to the advent of the Joint Stock Company, which is a form of business which enables the public to participate in providing capital in return for 'shares' in the assets and the profits of the company. An earlier experience of the Joint Stock form of trading which had resulted in a frantic boom in company flotations, culminating in the South Sea Bubble of 1720, had instilled

public suspicion of this form of trading. Reflecting this mood, Adam Smith, himself, questioned the ability of the directors of such companies to administer honestly and well any of the most routine and easily checked business, for

'... being the Managers rather of other people's money than of their own, it cannot well be expected that they should look over it with the same anxious vigilance with which the partners of a private copartnery frequently watch over their own ... Negligence and profusion ... must always prevail, more or less, in the management of the affairs of such a company'. (Smith, 1904 edition).

Nevertheless, the Joint Stock Companies Act, 1844 permitted the incorporation of such companies by registration without the necessity of obtaining a Royal Charter or a special Act of Parliament. It was not until 1855, however, that the Limited Liability Act permitted such companies to limit the liability of their members to the nominal value of their shares. This meant that the liability of shareholders for the financial debts of the company was limited to the amount which they had agreed to subscribe. In effect, in subscribing for a £1 share, a shareholder agreed to pay £1, and once he had paid that £1, he was not liable to make any further contribution on the event of the company's insolvency.

The concept of limited liability was a contentious point in the politics of the mid-19th century. The Limited Liability Act 1855 was passed in the teeth of bitter opposition, and one Member of Parliament described the Act as a 'rogues' charter'. Mindful of the potential for abuse which lay within this legislation, and mindful too of the necessity to safeguard the interests of shareholders and investors in these companies, Parliament eventually restated the doctrine of stewardship in a legal form. It made the disclosure of information to shareholders a condition attached to the privilege of Joint Stock status and of Limited Liability. This information was required to be in the form of annual Income Statements and Balance Sheets. We may say briefly, however, that the former is a statement of the profit or loss made during the year of the report, and the balance sheet indicates the assets held by the firm and the monetary claims against the firm.

Financial accounting is concerned with the emergence of these two accounting statements as vehicles for the disclosure of information to shareholders in Joint Stock companies. The unwillingness of company directors to disclose more than the minimum information required by law, and growing public disquiet as to the usefulness of the information contained in financial accounts culminated in the extension of disclosure requirement in the United Kingdom by means of the Companies Act, 1967. It is evident that the 1967 Act will be but one step in the history of public involvement in this problem which effectively began in 1844, and which has conferred upon accounting information an important social role.

Parallel developments have taken place also in the United States, where since the early 1930s there has been a continuous discussion on ways to improve the disclosure of information. The Securities and Exchange Commission has been concerned with the problem of the sufficiency of information disclosed at the time when new issues are sold to the public, and together with the Stock Exchanges and the accounting profession via the Financial Accounting Standards Board, it has been concerned with the adequacy of financial information regularly disclosed by companies. For some years, also, the European Economic Community has been trying to move towards a standardization of accounting practices both as regards disclosure and consistency of practices as an important aspect of the problem of facilitating trade between the member nations.

The legal importance attached to financial accounting statements stems directly from the need of a capitalist society to mobilize savings and direct them into profitable investments. Investors, be they large or small, must be provided with reliable and sufficient information in order to be able to make efficient investment decisions. Herein lies one of the most significant social purposes of financial accounting reports. In a changing society, increased recognition that employees have a legitimate right to financial information is evident in the legislation passed or proposed in several European countries. After the failure of a large private firm in Germany in the early 1970s, for example, there was consternation that most employees had no idea that the firm was so fragile. A more important influence in the demand for the disclosure of financial information to employees stems from the growing strength of the worker participation or co-determination movement. This aspect of social responsibility accounting will be examined in Part 5.

(3) Management accounting is also associated with the advent of Industrial Capitalism, for the Industrial Revolution of the 18th century presented a challenge to the development of accounting as a tool of industrial management. In isolated cases there were some, notably Josiah Wedgwood, who developed costing techniques as guides to management decisions. But the practice of using accounting information as a direct aid to management was not one of the achievements of the Industrial Revolution: this new role for accounting really belongs to the 20th century.

Certainly, the genesis of modern management with its emphasis on detailed information for decision-making provided a tremendous impetus to the development of management accounting in the early decades of this century, and in so doing considerably extended the boundaries of accounting. Management accounting shifted the focus of accounting from recording and analysing financial transactions to using information for decisions affecting the future. In so doing, it represented the biggest surge forward in seven centuries.

The advent of management accounting demonstrated once more the ability and capacity of accounting to develop and meet changing socio-economic needs. Management accounting has contributed in a most significant way to the success with which modern capitalism has succeeded in expanding the scale of production and raising standards of living.

(4) Social responsibility accounting is an entirely new phase in accounting development which owes its birth to the social revolution which has been underway in the Western world in the last few years. Social responsibility accounting widens the scope of accounting by considering the social effects of business decisions as well as their economic effects. The demand for social responsibility accounting stems from an increasing social awareness of the undesirable by-products of economic activities, and in this connection, one may point to the public attention which has been given to environmental problems over the last few years. Increasingly, management is being held responsible not only for the efficient conduct of business as expressed in profitability, but also for what they do about an endless number of social problems. Hence, with changing attitudes, the time-honoured standards by which performance is measured have come into disrepute. There is a growing consensus that the concepts of growth and profit as measured in traditional Balance Sheets and Income Statements are too narrow to reflect what many companies are trying, or are supposed to be trying to achieve.

In the fullness of time, therefore, we may expect that accounting statements will indicate the social and economic benefits created by the enterprise, and the social and economic costs incurred. In this way, they may disclose the total contribution which the firm is making towards solving the problems of society.

Already in this generation, accounting is beginning to play an important role in the activities of Government Agencies which are concerned with some of the serious social problems such as urban congestion, poverty, pollution and crime (Estes, 1973). Accounting plays an important role in measuring national economic health, and has the potential to contribute to the development of national measures of the quality of life (Terleckyj, 1973). Social responsibility accounting reveals many new vistas, and offers the possibility of many new exciting developments in accounting.

The difficulties facing the accountant

The process of change has created a number of problems for the accountant in adapting to a new social role. Some of these problems affect the very nature of the accounting process, and the function of the accountant in that process. We may identify these fundamental problems as follows:

(1) In recent times, the changing environment has shifted the focus of interest towards decision-making. Since there are different aspects of decision-making—economic, behavioural, sociological and quantitative, accounting has become an inter-disciplinary subject. The accountant has to be knowledgeable over a broad area if he is to be efficient in providing information which is relevant and useful for decision-making. The education of the accountant has tended to be traditional and to have had a narrow focus on gaining a knowledge of accounting methods. Hence, many accountants were not educated to cope with the problems of change, and in particular were not able to integrate their own skills with the knowledge relevant to decision-making.

(2) Traditional accounting areas are being invaded by experts in cognate areas, such as systems analysts, computer programmers and operations research specialists, who bring with them new knowledge and different skills. As a result, the traditional status and role of the accountant is being threatened.

(3) Accounting is not an exact science, though it is a social science. As is the case in other social sciences, accounting concepts do not rest on universal truths or general laws. Hence, value judgements are applied to the interpretation of economic and social events. The subjective nature of these values implies that the measurement process in accounting is not exact, and there is ample opportunity for controversy as to how events should be measured.

(4) In particular, the nature of external financial reporting has caused much concern in recent years. The status of the accounting profession has depended to some extent on its monopoly of the auditing and external financial reporting function. Not only has it become more generally recognized that these financial reports have a limited usefulness for decision-making, but public attention has also been drawn to the fact that accountants are able to produce significantly different statements of the financial results of a particular firm for

a given year, whilst still complying with accepted accounting conventions. This situation has been succintly stated as follows:

'The principles of accounting are a sturdy set of tools, but they are deteriorating rapidly under the impact of radical changes taking place in the nature of business operations. Principles that were satisfactory during the 1930s are no longer adequate today, and unless we begin bringing them up to date we will soon reach a state of affairs in which income and other data of financial statements produced with the tools of the 1930s will leave the reader of financial statements completely misinformed.' (Gordon, 1967).

Three major consequences have resulted from the difficulties which face the accountant at the present time, as follows:

(1) The accountant in management does not exist in isolation. He should be regarded as a member of the management team. We discuss this point further in the next chapter, and we suggest that this difficulty may be resolved by adopting a 'systems approach' to the study of accounting.

(2) There is a need to establish a theoretical framework for validating external financial reporting practices in terms of their perceived objectives, and to enable future development to take place in accordance with those objectives. We may note, in this connection, that the lack of comparability between financial statements issued by different firms has provided the impetus for the development of accounting theory.

(3) Finally, the transition from profitability accounting to social responsibility accounting imposes new information objectives for accountants and these new objectives will require a new accounting methodology. At this point in time, we are able to discuss only the information objectives, though some countries, particularly France, are already legislating for this new accounting development.

Summary

In this chapter, we have examined the development of accounting from its earliest form as a recording activity to its present-day importance which stems from its objective of providing socio-economic information for decision-making.

The history of accounting development reflects an ability to respond to changing social needs. Today, changing social attitudes combine with developments in information technology, quantitative methods and the behavioural sciences to radically affect the environment in which accounting operates. These changes have created a number of problems for the accountant. It is with these problems that this book is concerned.

References

1. A.A.A., *A Statement of Basic Accounting Theory*, p. 1, 1966.

2. A.I.C.P.A., *Committee on Terminology*, p. 9, American Institute Publishing Co. New. York, 1961.

3. Estes, R. W., *Accounting and Society*, Melville Publishing Co., New York 1973.

4. Gordon, M. J., An Economist's View of Profit Measurement, in *Profit in the Modern Economy* Stephenson, H. W. & Nelson, J. R. (eds) 1967, p. 71, Minneapolis, University of Minnesota Press.

5. Littleton, A. C., *The Structure of Accounting Theory*, A.A.A. Monograph No. 5, 1953, p. 30.

6. Smith, A., *Wealth of Nations*, pp. 233, 246, (Cannon edn) Volume 2 1904.

7. Terleckyj, N. E., Measuring Progress Towards Social Goals, *Management Science*, August, 1973.

2
Accounting as an Information System

The term 'system' is commonly used today, and we read much about environmental systems, ecological systems, economic systems and political systems. Indeed, we live in the age of systems. Reduced to its utmost simplicity, a system is a set of elements which operate together in order to attain a goal. The following are examples of systems analysed in this manner:

System	Elements	Basic goal
Social club	Members	Recreation
School	Teachers, students, textbooks, buildings	Education
Police	Men, equipment, communication network, buildings	Crime control

From the foregoing illustrations, we may see that systems vary considerably in their appearance, their attributes, their elements and their basic goals. They have certain characteristics in common, however, for they consist of parts which interact together to achieve one or a number of objectives. Systems, therefore, do not consist of random sets of elements, but of elements which may be identified as belonging together because of a common goal.

A system may also be seen as consisting of three activities: input, processing of input, and output. Sometimes, one hears references to closed systems and open systems, and these terms refer to the nature of the relationship between these systems and their environment. An open system is one which interacts with its environment, and a closed system is one which does not. We may classify a business organization as open system which has a dynamic interplay with its environment from which it draws resources and to which it consigns its products and services. An example of a closed system is a chemical reaction in a sealed container. The important distinction between an open and a

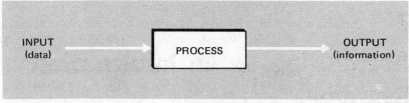

Fig. 1.1

closed system is that the former is constantly rejuvenated by its environment, whereas the latter tends to run down through loss of energy which is not replaced from the environment.

We stated in chapter 1 that the objective of accounting is to provide socio-economic information for decision-making. This objective is often analysed as a series of activities which are linked and form a progression of steps, beginning with observing, then collecting, recording, analysing and finally communicating information to its users. We may say, therefore, that *accounting information* has a special meaning in that it is data organized for a special purpose, that is, decision-making. The task of the accountant is to transform raw data into information. Of itself, data is simply a collection of facts expressed as symbols and characters which have no meaning, and are unable to influence decisions until transformed into information. We shall see in Part 2 how conventions existing among accountants for the treatment of data gives accounting information a distinctive character.

Accounting is a social science which lends itself easily to its analysis as an information system, for it has all the attributes of a system. It has a basic goal, which is to provide information, and it has clear and well-defined elements in the form of men and equipment. Moreover, accounting has the typical activities of systems, consisting of input, process and output, as shown in Fig. 1.1.

The application of systems analysis to the treatment of accounting facilitates our study of accounting as a social science, and enables us to examine its various activities in terms of the relevance of its output for decision-making purposes.

The boundaries of an information system

An important aspect of the study of accounting as an information system is the definition of its boundaries. A system exists as an independent entity in an environment, and the nature of its relationship with that environment is clearly very important. We have already made reference to the distinction which exists between 'open' and 'closed' systems. We must now turn our attention to a closer examination of the boundaries of a system, by which we mean identifying a system in such a way that we are able to distinguish it from its environment.

In the previous section, we mentioned that the accountant selected from raw data that data which is relevant to his purpose. The filtering process by which he selects accounting data is provided by the conventions of accounting, which play a deterministic role in defining accounting information. This filtering process may be taken as one boundary between the accounting system and its environment; that point at which raw data becomes input data. The data which is so selected forms, as we have seen, the input into the processing system which produces accounting information. The information output is used by a group of decision-makers, which we are able to identify, and it is evident that a decision-oriented information system should produce information which meets the needs of its users. Clearly, these needs should be specified in accordance with a theory of users' requirements. We may say, therefore, that the other boundary to an accounting information system is established by the specific information needs of its users. We may establish these boundaries diagramatically as in Fig. 1.2.

This analysis of accounting as an information system enables us to make some important deductions. Firstly, the goal of the system is to provide information which meets the needs of its users. If we can sufficiently and correctly identify these needs, we are then able to specify the nature and character of the output of the system. Secondly, the output requirements should determine, therefore, the type of data which is selected as the input for processing into information output. Thirdly, we are able to apply rigorous criteria to the selection of data and in this way examine accounting methods in terms of a theoretical framework which relies upon the scientific method. Fourthly, we are

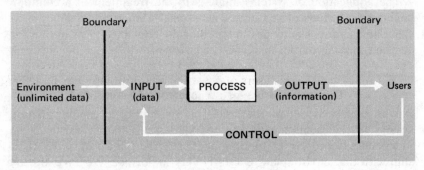

Fig. 1.2

able to understand how the theoretical foundations of accounting which are discussed in chapter 3 are integrated in an information system: decision theory provides a means of examining the output requirements of the system, measurement theory specifies the items to be measured and the value to be attached to them and information theory enables us to consider the optimal level of information supply by measuring the costs of information supply in relation to its benefits to users. In this connection, the idea of *control* which has been indicated on the diagram above shows that users' needs not only should determine the nature of data input but that the extent of the data input should be determined by a cost-benefit analysis related to users' needs.

An important application of the concept of an information system's boundaries will be seen in Part 4 where we examine the problems of financial reporting in the context of investors' needs for information which is not really provided by the accountant. By ignoring users' needs, accounting information is deprived of the objectives which otherwise would enable us to validate accounting practices in the area in terms of the decision theory framework which we have adopted.

The output of an information system

The foregoing discussion has served to indicate how important are the needs of users of accounting information, for they determine the goals of an accounting information system.

There are several groups of people who have vested interests in a business organization—managers, shareholders, employees, customers and creditors. Additionally, the community at large has economic and social interests in the activities of business organizations. This interest is expressed at national level by the concern of government in various aspects of firms' activities, such as their economic well-being, their contribution to welfare, their part in the growth of the national product, to mention but a few obvious examples; and at local level by the concern of local authorities and bodies in the direct socio-economic impact of the activities of local businesses.

It is quite evident that an examination of the types of decisions usually made by various users of accounting information may be taken as a basis for stipulating the goals of an accounting information system, and therefore, for evolving a normative theory of accounting by which to judge the relevance and usefulness of the information produced by accountants. The study of accounting as a social science requires, therefore, that we begin by stating the general nature of the needs of information users.

The information needs of management

Organizations may be considered as falling into two broad classes: those having profit or business objectives, and those having welfare objectives. In this book, we are concerned mainly with business organizations, but it should be remembered that many of the accounting methods employed in business organizations are equally employed by welfare or non-profit organizations. As regards the management of organizations, little difference exists between the information needs of managers of business organizations and those of welfare organizations.

The management process may be analysed into three major functions—planning, organizing and controlling the activities of the organization. Planning involves setting objectives for the organization, and devising strategies to attain those objectives. Organizing means establishing the administrative structure for implementing plans. Controlling is the process of observing and measuring actual performance so that it conforms with the planned and required performance. Thus, controlling means identifying deviations from planned performance, and taking such corrective action as may be necessary.

These various management functions have one thing in common: they are all concerned with making decisions, which have their own specific information requirements. Planning decisions, for example, are directed towards realizing broad goals which, in addition to the organization's survival and its profitability, usually include the intention to grow and to capture a large share of the market for its products. Other goals often include product leadership, increased productivity and improved industrial relations. There is an element of conflict between various organizational goals, and it is the function of management to reconcile them through the planning process.

We devote Part 3 of this book to the examination of the accounting information needs of management, and the manner in which these needs are met. The scientific management of organizations has considerably extended the demand for accounting information, and the nature of the accounting problem. As we shall see, the influence of the behavioural sciences and the need for more information generally has created measurement problems as well. As far as possible, we shall discuss some of these new problems in Part 3, but we deal with some special topics of interest, such as human resource accounting and social responsibility accounting in Part 5.

The information needs of shareholders and investors

Historically, business accounting developed to supply information to those who had invested their wealth in business ventures. As we saw in chapter 1, financial accounting, as it is now known, emerged in the 19th century as a result of the need to protect investors in Joint Stock Companies trading under limited liability. It has been evident for a long time that the information needs of investors are not adequately met by published Balance Sheets and Income Statements. In Part 2, we shall examine the nature of the information disclosed to shareholders and investors, and in Part 4, we shall subject traditional financial accounting practice considered in Part 2 to a critical analysis based on the question "what information should be provided to investors?" To answer this question, we begin our discussion in Part 4 with an inquiry into the objectives of shareholders in business corporations. By stating that they are concerned with the value of their investment and the income which they expect to derive from their shareholding we are able to enquire into the nature of the information which they need in order to make rational decisions.

The information needs of employees

It is a popular view that the interests of employees are in direct conflict with those of the firm, and in particular with those of management. Unless employees are able to share in the profits of business organizations, they are effectively dissociated from their activities if we suppose that the objective of business organizations is to maximize profits and maximize returns to shareholders. This classical concept of the objective of business enterprises is being replaced as a result of the social changes taking place in our society, and there is a broadening view of the social and economic responsibilities of management. It is recognized that employees have a vested interest in the outcome of management decisions of every kind. Improvements in industrial democracy through employee participation in management decisions have important implications for the supply of information to employees. A number of firms are already investigating this question. As regards the settlement of wage disputes, the question of profit sharing between employees, shareholders and management can only properly be settled on the basis of a full disclosure of the relevant facts.

The immense importance of good industrial relations, of harmony between management and employees, is acknowledged already in the literature of management science. It is quite evident that there must be eventually a symmetry of treatment between shareholders, management and employees in respect of the accounting information which each group requires and receives. We may say therefore, that the economic and social role of accounting in this particular context has not yet been properly explored. We touch upon these issues in Part 5.

The information needs of governments

To a greater or lesser degree, all Western governments intervene in the activities of business organizations in the process of managing what is known as a 'mixed economy', that is, an economic system consisting of both State-controlled and privately-controlled business organizations. Government Agencies, such as Central Statistical Services, Ministries of Commerce, Industry, Employment etc., all collect information about the various aspects of the activities of business organizations. Much of this information is a direct output of the accounting system, for example, levels of sales activity, profits, investments, stocks, liquidity, dividend levels, proportion of profits absorbed by taxation etc. This information is very important in evolving policies for managing the economy.

Governments, in addition, can compel the disclosure of information which is not otherwise made available to the public, such as future investment plans, expected future profits and so on.

By and large, however, governments tend to expect accounting information to be presented in a uniform manner, so that the rules applying to accounting methods and the preparation of accounting reports for government use are the same as those which govern the nature of accounting information disclosed to investors and shareholders. If governments base policy decisions on accounting information which distorts the true position, it is evident that the ill-effects of such decisions will be widely felt. The failure to adjust for the effect of inflation, for example, not only gives an excessive view of company profits but may lead the government to believe that company profits are running at a sufficiently high level to enable firms to finance investments and provide an adequate return to shareholders. We may say, therefore, that all parties having an interest in business organizations should be concerned with the quality of the accounting information produced, as well as the relevance of that information to their own needs. It is for this reason, that we devote chapter 1 of Part 2 to a thorough examination of the conventions which govern the nature of financial accounting information.

The information needs of creditors

We may define as creditors all those who have provided goods, money or services to business organizations and have accepted a delay in payment or repayment. In a sense, therefore, they are short-term investors. Creditors include suppliers of materials and goods, normally described as trade creditors, credit institutions such as bankers and hire-purchase firms who lend money for interest on a relatively short-term basis, and those who have provided services and are awaiting payment, for example, employees, outside contractors who have made repairs, electricity and gas undertakings who have presented accounts and have not yet been paid. There are very few groups of people who deal with business organizations who are not, at some time, creditors.

The main concern of creditors is whether or not the organization is credit-worthy, that is, will it be able to meet its financial obligations? They are interested in the organization's profitability only insofar as it affects its ability to pay its debts. On the other hand, creditors are very concerned with the firm's liquidity, that is, those cash or near-cash resources which may be mobilized to pay them, as well as the willingness of banks and other creditors to act like them in being willing to await payment. Creditors react quickly to changes of opinion about a firm's credit-worthiness, and if there is any doubt that a firm may not be able to pay, they will press for immediate settlement of debts owing and probably drive into bankruptcy a firm whose prospects in the medium and longer term are not necessarily bad.

Creditors are interested, therefore, mainly in financial accounting information which deals with solvency, liquidity and profitability, that is, with obtaining reports which will describe a firm's financial standing. We shall consider these aspects of financial reporting in Part 4, and in particular, we shall examine the adequacy of criteria applied to the analysis of financial statements, such as solvency, liquidity and profitability ratios.

The information needs of other groups

We have dealt so far with the information needs of four major groups which have vested interests in business organizations, and we have discussed the nature of their information requirements. How far and how adequately their information needs are suitably satisfied depends largely upon the pressure which these groups may exert upon the accountant to produce information tailored to these needs. How well they are able to articulate their information needs, how well accountants are able to understand the reasons why the information is needed and how willing and able accountants are to provide that information will be the theme of much of this book. We may say, for example, that the information needs of management are more adequately met than those of employees, shareholders, creditors and also the governments. But there are two further groups in society who are interested in the activities of business organizations, and who are pretty well excluded from receiving information: the local community and customers.

(a) *The information needs of the local community*

Local communities are very dependent on local industries, not only because they provide employment, but also because they affect directly the entire socio-economic structure of the environment. Firms provide employment, they create a demand for local services, they cause an expansion in commercial activities, as well as extensions in the provision of welfare services as the economic well-being of the community improves. Large firms, in particular, are able to exert a dominating influence on the local social framework which often is reflected in the corporate personality of the inhabitants. Miners, steelworkers, shipbuilders and workers in the motor industry do have styles of living and attitudes forged to some extent by the industries in which they work and live.

Local industries have positive and negative influences on the locality. Pollution, despoilation, congestion are all negative aspects of their activities which constitute external direct and indirect social and economic costs, which are borne by the community.

The local community has an interest in the activities of local industries, and evidently requires much more information of social benefits and costs than the public relation-type information which is presently disclosed. The social audit points to a possible remedy for the lack of objectivity in the information presently disclosed.

(b) *The information needs of customers*

Of recent years, Consumers Councils and other bodies have been formed in order to restore in some measure the disproportionate balance of power which has appeared in our society between the large and powerful producers of consumer goods and the voiceless masses of our population, who subjected to sublimal advertising, monopoly practices and suffering from ignorance have been at the former's mercy. In a few instances, the Monopolies Commission have acted to protect consumers, but their power to intervene is based upon law.

Customers may well have little influence in markets increasingly dominated by large business organizations, and it is difficult at this stage to see how, even if more information were made available, the balance might be redressed. Certainly, one may suggest that customers are interested in information indicating the fairness of pricing policies, such as the relative proportion of unit price which consists of costs, profits and taxes, as well as the differential costs between one product and another product produced by the same firm at a different price. For example, why should one electric shaver cost £10 more than another, and in what ways is this difference value for money? Clearly, there will be many more social changes in our society before questions of this sort will be loudly heard and answers demanded.

Accounting information and the allocation of resources

The various groups of information users which we have just discussed share a common concern, which is to make decisions about the allocation of scarce resources between competing ends. Students of economics will find such a statement echoes a popular definition of the subject matter of economics. The importance of accounting information is that it makes such an allocation possible in a market economy, where individuals and organizations are largely free to allocate the resources which they control between competing ends. Therefore, the theoretical objective of an accounting information system is to permit information users to make optimal decisions, that is, to make the best allocation of the resources which they control. As we have seen, optimal decision-making may only be understood in relation to the objectives of decision-makers, so that the various groups of information users whose information needs we have just discussed may be said to have quite different and occasionally competing decision objectives. Optimal decision-making also means that the results of decisions should have a certain quality: optimal means that they should be the best possible results which could have been achieved under given circumstances, and implies a standard against which actual results may be compared.

We are stating, therefore, that the objective of accounting information systems is to enable decision-makers to attempt to optimize the allocation of the resources which they control, and to assess the actual results of their decisions against the forecast results, so that a measure of the efficiency of the decision-making process is the extent to which the actual result compares to the optimal result. In this connection, the terms 'efficiency' and 'effectiveness' are used in the literature in a special sense. The term 'efficiency' is usually reserved for the analysis of input-output relationships, so that the 'efficiency' of a factory production process may refer to the degree of technical skill with which inputs of production factors are transformed into finished goods, as well as to the success with which input factors values in monetary terms are transformed into outputs also valued in monetary terms. By contrast the term 'effectiveness' is reserved for the analysis of the success with which policy objectives are attained. Thus, we may talk of 'organizational effectiveness' in discussing how well management decisions lead to the attainment of organizational objectives.

Consequently, we may say that the 'effectiveness' of an accounting information system is the extent to which it enables its users to make optimal decisions. By examining the different objectives which we assume they have, we are able to judge the 'effectiveness' of accounting information by reference to the relevance of that information to the types of decisions which they wish to make. Management makes decisions about the allocation of men, materials, machines and money in such a way that the firm's objectives may be reached. As we shall see in Part 3 chapter 1, firms have different objectives, and income is one of these objectives. Often, it is thought that the size of the firm's income reflects the 'efficiency' of management in transforming inputs of factors of production into sales of finished goods. It is evident, however, that in our analysis income figures, though important, should not be confused with 'managerial effectiveness'.

We devote two Parts of this book (Part 3 and Part 4) to an analysis of the effectiveness of accounting information systems in meeting the needs of management and shareholders. As we have already indicated, social responsibility accounting widens the scope of accounting to include the information needs of the other groups of interested persons mentioned in this chapter. By devoting only Part 5 to this aspect of accounting we may appear to be attributing less importance to this area of accounting than it deserves. Indeed, our view is that social change will establish the overall importance of social responsibility accounting in future years. At the moment, however, the state of the art requires us to meet our readers' needs by concentrating on the problems of conventional accounting.

Behavioural aspects of decision-making

It does not follow that the availability of the right information will necessarily lead its users to make optimal decisions regarding the allocation of resources. The behavioural aspects of decision-making have now assumed a major importance in the eyes of those concerned with management decision-making. In Part 3, we shall consider the behavioural aspects of decision-making in business organizations, and their implications for accountants. In this connection, we may say that accountants have traditionally tended to regard organizations from a technical viewpoint, treating men as adjuncts to or as substitutes for machines, to be hired and employed for the purpose of maximizing productivity and profits. As a result, accountants have tended to place a heavy emphasis on the value of economic rewards and penalties as a means of controlling the performance of labour, and have ignored other factors which affect behaviour.

Behavioural considerations are of the utmost importance for the designer of management information systems, for having stated that, from a management point of view, the purpose of accounting information is to enable the organization to attain its goals, it must follow that the effectiveness of accounting information is evidenced in the manner in which it affects behaviour. In this sense, we may say that unless accounting information serves to produce the desired action, it has served no purpose at all. Research has shown, for example, that even when managers have all the information which they need, they do not always make the right decisions. Hence, the human process which leads managers to recognize or fail to recognize the significance of accounting information deserves a better understanding, and accountants need to be aware of the role of accounting information in enabling managers to identify their mistakes and to learn from them. Feedback information, for example, plays an important part in this process.

Moreover, an information system can only function effectively where there exists a satisfactory organizational structure, within which managerial roles are properly defined, and where the style of management favours the free flow of information. Indeed, one of the most important purposes of an organizational structure is to define managerial roles so as to facilitate the flow of information to and from decision-makers in the organization. In this sense, management may be considered as the process of converting information into action. As a consequence, organizational structures should be designed around information flows. Information will not flow freely through an information system, however, if the style of management prevailing in the organization inhibits individuals from communicating information.

A systems approach to the study of accounting

The study of the firm as an organization consisting of several systems, for example, an operating system, a financial system, a personnel system and a marketing system, enables one to see the accounting system as one element of an interacting whole. This manner of seeing the nature of the various elements of an organization is known as the systems approach.

The accounting system is the most important element of an organization's information system, for the following reasons:

(1) The accounting information system is the only one which enables management and external information users to get a picture of the whole organization. How adequate is this picture is the subject matter of Part 4.

(2) The accounting information system links other important information systems such as marketing information, personnel, research and development and production information, in that the information which is produced by these other systems may ultimately be expressed in financial terms in planning strategy to attain organizational goals.

Moreover the systems approach to the study of accounting permits the integration of accounting into a coherent framework in which, in accordance with our thesis, its role is concerned with the provision of information for decision-making.

The systems approach also enables us to integrate modern technological developments into the study of accounting. With the development of the computer, for example, rapid advances have been made in electronic data processing. These advances have affected accounting in a number of ways. Firstly, information systems have been formalized, so that information may be fed directly from the computer to decision-makers without the intervention of accountants. Secondly, computers have made possible the merger of accounting and non-accounting information, leading to the centralization of information services and reductions in duplication and hence information costs. Thirdly, there has been an increase in the accuracy of the information provided resulting directly from the reduction of duplication. Fourthly, the ability of computers to integrate information of different forms has brought into view the possibility of a 'total system' as the means of meeting the information needs of decision-makers, which suggests that the entire information system of an organization, regardless of its size, could be integrated or combined into one giant system from which one person, or each level of management in each function, may obtain all the information which could be required whenever it is needed. The enormous complexity of such a system, and the difficulty of seeing how data required for such decisions as strategic planning could be provided by a computerized system, without human intervention, has led many to believe that a 'total systems approach' to the provision of information may never be realized. Nevertheless, the systems approach is invaluable in the sense that it enables one to visualize an information system as a collection of sub-systems having a high degree of integration.

Finally, the systems approach widens the possible applications of information. Thus, one of the developments which has influenced management decision-making in recent years is operational research, which is concerned with the study of the behaviour of the various parts or sub-systems of an organization in such a way that all its activities may be analysed as a whole. Operational research uses mathematical techniques for solving business problems, and its growing importance is reflected in the increasing use of management decision models which attempt to predict and compare the predicted outcome of alternative strategies. Traditionally, mathematicians have specialized in the expression and the solution of complex logical problems, and although the techniques which they had evolved had a potential use for decision-making in organizations, they were not employed in business situations because of the time-lag which existed in the processing of data. The advent of the computer has closed the technological gap, and has greatly contributed to the increased importance of quantitative methods in management. The information required for operational research studies is often not the type which is handled by traditional accounting systems. The systems approach, therefore, not only coincides with the manner of studying organizations by operational research scientists, but by encouraging the integration of accounting and non-accounting information into integrated information systems, it increases the range of applications of the information produced by such systems. In this connection, the need for non-financial measures in such areas of accounting as social responsibility and human resource accounting may be met by integrated information systems whereas, of course, such measures would not be made available by conventional accounting systems. We will discuss these points in Part 5.

Summary

We began this chapter with an examination of accounting as an information system consisting of three activities—input, processing and output. The systems characteristic of accounting suggests that the systems approach is the ideal way of studying the subject. It is not sufficient, however, to view accounting purely as an operating system, for its relevance and usefulness may only be judged by the degree with which its output meets the needs of the users of accounting information. By identifying the basic goal of an accounting information system as being the provision of information for decision-making, we provide a framework by which to judge the effectiveness of that system.

There are many approaches to the study of decision-making—economic, behavioural and quantitative, and the inter-disciplinary nature of decision theory has the inevitable consequence that accounting has also become an inter-disciplinary subject. The systems approach facilitates an inter-disciplinary study of accounting because it requires that it be viewed, not in isolation, but as one element in an interacting operating system, which is the nature of a business organization. Indeed, the systems approach provides a better picture of the network of organizational sub-systems and the way in which they are inter-related to form a complex whole.

Finally, the systems approach allows for the proper development of accounting in a number of ways. Firstly, it makes fuller use of the potential of computers in allowing the integration of accounting and non-accounting information, thereby heightening the significance of accounting as the major link in an information system. Secondly, it enables an integrated information system to have a greater flexibility of purpose, such as providing information for operational research studies which form part of decision-making in organizations. Lastly, it allows accounting to consider the development of non-financial measurements for such new areas of accounting as social responsibility and human resource accounting.

3
The Foundations of Accounting Theory

In this chapter, we discuss the theoretical foundations of accounting theory from two viewpoints:

(a) The nature of theory in itself, and its implications for the expansion of accounting knowledge. This analysis involves examining the relevance of the scientific method for evolving theory.

(b) The roots of accounting theory insofar as they stem from decision theory, measurement theory, and information theory.

The nature of theory

One of the major obstacles to the development of accounting theory has been the accountant's own concept of theory and its relevance to his problems. In spite of well-established concepts of theory in the physical and social sciences, accountants have regarded theorizing as a process which should follow rather than precede practice. Some writers have attempted to relate the practices of accountants to a generalized statement of theory. In their view, accounting theory is to be discovered by examining the practices of accountants because "accounting theory is primarily a concentrate distilled from experience ... it is experience intelligently analysed that produces logical explanation ... and ... illuminates the practices from which it springs." (Littleton & Zimmerman, 1962).

The role which theory plays in other subjects has useful lessons for the role which theory could perform in the development of accounting knowledge. By analogy with these other subjects, the concept of theory may be adapted to different purposes. A theory which attempts to explain how financial information is collected, analysed and communicated is called a *positive* or *descriptive* theory. A theory which attempts to state what financial information should be collected, analysed and communicated is called a *normative theory*. A positive theory of accounting is concerned with *what is*, and a normative theory of accounting with *what ought to be*. It is evident that the growth of knowledge in the natural sciences is expressed in positive theory, whereas a great deal of research effort in the social sciences appears in the formulation of normative theories. Normative theories depend upon our judgement of what is good and what is bad, so that the need for a normative theory of accounting is self-evident if we wish to test the validity of accounting practices.

Judging from the debates which have been raging for several years about the quality of accounting information, it appears that the most important function which accounting theory could perform is the provision of a coherent set of logical principles which would form a general frame of reference for the evaluation of sound accounting practices (Hendriksen, 1970). Indeed, a statement by the American Accounting Association reached the same conclusion by saying that "the purpose of developing a theory of accounting is to establish standards for judging the acceptability of accounting methods" (A.A.A., 1966). The call, therefore, is for a normative theory of accounting, which would not only permit the evaluation of existing and proposed practices, but would also focus attention on areas of the subject where further research is needed. Moreover, it would provide a rational basis for the study of accounting. One cannot separate entirely the normative from the positive in a philosophical sense, for any normative statement is ultimately derived from a belief of what really is. This point in itself reinforces the importance of developing a normative theory of accounting as a means of clarifying in our minds the nature of accounting.

Logic and theory

It is evident from the foregoing discussion that, if theory has an important role to play in the development of accounting knowledge, we should be acquainted with the methods of reasoning employed by theorists. The study of logic is an important aspect of philosophy, but for the purposes of this book we must be content with a brief mention of the two methods of logic known respectively as *inductive* and *deductive* logic.

Inductive logic is a process of reasoning which allows a general proposition to be derived from a particular case. Thus, if every kangaroo which we have observed eats grass, by induction we may induce that, therefore, all kangaroos eat grass. Deductive logic, however, begins with a general proposition which, by deduction, may be applied to a particular case. For example, from the general proposition that all kangaroos eat grass we may, by deduction, infer that some kangaroos eat grass.

We may say, therefore, that an inductive approach to accounting theory is one which relies on a particular proposition as a basis for making a general statement. The danger with the process of inductive logic is that the premises contained in the original proposition may not be sufficient to guarantee the conclusion. This approach has encouraged the erroneous conclusion which we mentioned earlier that accounting is what accountants do, and that, therefore, a theory of accounting may be extracted from the practices of accountants.

In recent years, some accounting theorists have adopted a deductive approach to the formulation of accounting theory, beginning with certain general propositions about accounting from which they have attempted to define its particular features. According to them, it is possible to build a theory of accounting without reference to the practices of accountants. In other words, a deductive approach to the formulation of accounting theory makes possible the construction of a normative theory of accounting, the need for which we discussed earlier.

The truth is that the formulation of scientific theories requires both inductive and deductive logic. Thus, by a process of inductive logic Newton's observations of falling objects led to the theory of gravity, whereas Einstein evolved his theory of matter by a process of deductive logic. As is well known, Einstein's theory assumed a relationship between matter and energy expressed in this famous equation $E = mc^2$ (Energy = mass × the square of the speed of light), before this relationship could be proved. The success of nuclear fission later proved that this theory was correct.

Likewise, the formulation of accounting theories involves the use of both inductive and deductive logic. There are theories of accounting which are descriptive and which were evolved by induction from observations of what accountants did. The theory of double-entry, for example, which relates to the manner in which accountants process financial data (see Part 2), was formulated from observations of how Italian businessmen began to keep their records in the 14th and 15th centuries. By contrast, the present debate among accountants about accounting principles is an attempt to construct normative theories which, by the process of deduction, may be used as a basis for developing accounting practice.

The development of empirical theories

Empirism is extremely important to the development of accounting theory. Empirical research relies on actual data to test rigorously hypotheses or beliefs. Normative theories are subjective because they depend upon our judgement of what is good and what is bad. If normative theories are to be validated as theories which are generally acceptable, they must be tested and proved by empirical research. The scientific method provides the means for testing and validating theories. The scientific method involves the following steps.

(a) Observation
The scientific method begins with the observation of the phenomenon or problem under scrutiny. For this purpose a system of classification (taxonomy) is needed in order to determine areas of observation.

(b) Definition of the problem
The critical issues must be determined with care and exactitude, so as to avoid wasting time and money on solving the wrong problem. Therefore, factors which are irrelevant to the problem must be eliminated in the process of clarifying and defining the problem. It is at this stage that one is concerned with the problem of measurement.

(c) Formulation of hypothesis
Once the problem has been defined, a careful analysis enables a hypothesis to be formulated. A hypothesis is a solution to the problem, and it predicts the outcome of the relationship between the variables envisaged by the hypothesis. A hypothesis is a view, therefore, of the underlying relationships involved in the problem and often takes the form of a model.

(d) Experimentation
Once established the hypothesis must be tested. One is concerned at this stage, therefore, with selecting appropriate methods of testing the validity of the hypothesis.

(e) Verification
This last stage is the most important one for it involves the confirmation or rejection of the hypothesis. By subjecting the hypothesis to experimentation, its verification is made possible by means of an independent process. It is important, therefore, that the method selected for verifying a hypothesis should be appropriate and that it should be free from bias.

The scientific method and the social sciences
From the foregoing, we may say that science is concerned with explanations, which result from the search for understanding, and with predictions which are founded on the validity of hypotheses which have been properly tested. By defining science in this manner, it is clear that the natural sciences and the social sciences differ only as regards their subject matter. It may be argued, however, that this

definition overlooks certain features which do make these branches of knowledge significantly different from each other. There are three areas of difference which demand our attention. Firstly, the testing of hypotheses is easier in the natural sciences than in the social sciences where it is difficult, if not impossible, to conduct controlled and reproducible experiments. Secondly, as the social sciences are concerned with social behaviour, the presence of the human element is said to affect the predictive ability of their theories. Thirdly, the social sciences are concerned with value judgements, which by their nature are subjective. Let us, therefore, consider these three points.

(a) Testing hypotheses

To a greater or lesser extent, all theories are concerned both with explanation and prediction. Explanation by itself is rare, and its more usual purpose is to lend substance to prediction. The' laws of physics, for example, do explain various physical phenomena, but their essential purpose is to predict what will happen under certain defined conditions. Hypotheses which explain phenomena may be tested under laboratory conditions which reproduce the conditions to which they relate. Therefore, not only can experiments be controlled, but they may also be reproduced at any time. By contrast, hypotheses about human behaviour are not readily testable under laboratory conditions. Moreover, human behaviour is extremely complex, and it has not the stability required for laboratory experiments. It must be admitted, therefore, that the hypotheses of social scientists cannot be tested in the same rigorous manner as those of natural scientists. This does not imply, however, that the scientific method is not an appropriate method for the social sciences, where hypotheses are tested by events and circumstances of the real world, which provides in a sense a rough and ready laboratory.

(b) Predictive ability

It must be emphasized that the main reason why social scientists develop theories is to help them to make predictions about social behaviour. In this regard, they are less interested in individual behaviour than in group behaviour, so that the mathematical law of large numbers reduces the uncertainty which is present in hypotheses about individual behaviour. It is possible to say, for example, that on a hot summer's day, the sale of ice cream to the public will be higher than on a cold day. It is not possible to say, however, that one particular individual will consume more ice cream on a hot day than on a cold day. Relying upon the law of large numbers to reduce the variability of individual behaviour, social science theories are able to predict with some measure of accuracy the behaviour of groups of individuals.

(c) Value judgements
The problem of value has special importance in accounting and presents difficult problems of measurement. We shall discuss these points more fully in Part 4 chapter 3.

The roots of accounting theory
In our introduction to this chapter, we identified the roots of accounting theory as being in decision theory, measurement theory and information theory. Accounting theory has been and continues to be influenced by developments in other fields, such as economics and the behavioural sciences. We shall assess the relative contribution of these other sciences as we proceed with our study of accounting. At this stage, however, a closer examination of the roots of accounting theory is needed.

Decision theory
Traditionally, the focus of attention among accountants has been the measurement of profits, or as it is more usually known, the measurement of income. In the last 20 years, however, changing social attitudes, the developments in information technology, quantitative methods and the behavioural sciences have all combined to shift the focus of attention in accounting away from income theory towards decision theory.

Decision theory is partly descriptive in that it attempts to explain how decisions are actually made. It is also partly normative in that it attempts to throw light on how decisions ought to be made, that is, it is concerned with establishing standards for the best, or optimal, decisions. Decision theory is of major importance to accounting for we believe that a proper understanding of accounting may be obtained only by seeing its essential purpose as providing information for decision-making.

Decision-making and problem-solving
To many people the terms 'decision-making' and 'problem-solving' are doubtless synonymous, and we would concede that it is difficult to imagine the one without the other. Indeed, it is only when a problem has been properly understood and its causes established, that a decision may be made regarding the action which should be taken. It follows that there is an important distinction between the two terms.

Problem-solving may be defined as the questioning process, which seeks to establish the causal factors of a problem. Decision-making may be defined as the termination of the questioning process with the aim of taking action to remove the problem.

The decision-making process may be viewed as a logical sequence of events which may be analysed into the following stages:

(1) Recognition of a problem or the need for a decision.
(2) Defining all the alternative solutions to the problem.
(3) Gathering all the information relevant to those alternative solutions.
(4) Assessing and ranking the merits of the alternative solutions.
(5) Deciding upon the best alternative solution by selecting that one which is most highly ranked.
(6) Validating the decision by means of information feedback.

Decisions which result from this process express rationality in seeking the best or optimal solutions to problems.

It is clear from the foregoing that information is required at every stage of the decision-making process. It is evident also that there are two ways in which the quality of decisions may be improved. The first way is to improve the quality of the information supplied, and the second is to improve the use made of the information.

Decision-making and prediction

Decisions are always addressed to the future, even though that future may be just seconds away. By definition, decisions are concerned with shaping the course of future events, and they are essentially reactions to views about the future which we may term 'predictions' of the future. We are using the term 'prediction' in a vastly different meaning from that associated with the concentrated peering into crystal balls. By eliminating in this way what we may describe as 'irrational predictions' we are left with rational predictions, that is, those which are based on information.

In a world characterized by constant change and a great deal of uncertainty, it is very important that predictions about the future should be based on information which is as reliable and as accurate as possible. The importance of information in this context is that although it does not eliminate uncertainty, it does reduce it. The value of information may be assessed in terms of its success in this role.

It is evident from our analysis of the various stages in the decision-making process that it requires decisions at every stage, and furthermore that each such decision be made on some prediction of the future. For example, the definition of objectives depends upon a prediction about the future, and the selection of one of several possible alternative courses of action in a rational manner must be made on the basis of predictions about each alternative and its predicted result.

Decision theory and the use of models

We stated in chapter 1 that the role of theory is to bring together existing knowledge as a means of explaining events or relationships, and in this way making predictions about the future. In the social sciences, the term 'theory' is not always distinguished from the term 'model', the reason being that models are developed from theories. A model may be defined, therefore, as a device for expressing a theory clearly and cogently. It is really a deliberate simplification designed to make it easier to understand complex relationships and structures by isolating aspects of primary importance to the problem under examination. Models have become essential tools of analysis for getting to grips with the complexities of the real world.

The advent of management science and the increasing use of quantitative methods have emphasized the utility of models, for not only is the human mind incapable of grasping or understanding without aid the complexities of a decision problem but it is incapable of performing all the calculations involved in the solution of a complex decision problem. By simplifying the complexities of real-life in such a way that the human mind can grasp the significance of at least the most important inter-relationships, models clarify the type of questions which must be answered. Thus, they offer scope for improving the quality of predictions by posing such questions as "if this occurs what will follow?". Hence, they also offer scope for improving the quality of information used in decision-making by defining more precisely the type of information which is required. Once the information inputs and outputs have been precisely defined, models become susceptible to quantitative analysis and computers may be applied to the solution of the quantitative problems involved in such analysis.

Model building facilitates the application of the scientific method, which we mentioned in the previous chapter, to the study of decision-making. The formulation of a hypothesis, which is a central feature of the scientific method, takes the form of a model which assumes certain relationships between action and reaction. Once the model has been constructed, it may be validated in accordance with the procedures of the scientific method. The models used in management decision-making are less reliable than those used in the natural sciences because they cannot be rigorously tested in 'laboratory' conditions. Moreover, the elements of management decision-models are less stable through time, and hence one has less confidence in the conclusions indicated by these models.

Models and the accountant

Models are not new to accountants, who have practised model building for centuries. Indeed, the entire structure of accounting is a model for describing in money terms the operations of a business. As a result of the changing focus of accounting away from income measurement towards the supply of information for decision-making, mathematical decision-models have assumed a growing importance for the accountant for the undermentioned reasons:

(1) The accountant supplies the information input for the various models employed by decision-makers.

(2) Some decision models, for example inventory models, which can be entirely programmed are an integral part of the information system. As a designer of the information system, the accountant must be familiar with such models.

(3) The accountant may himself employ decision models when he acts as a decision-maker, for example in financial planning and in designing an information system.

(4) If he is to attempt to construct an optimal information system, that is one which relates the value of information to its cost, the accountant should be sufficiently acquainted with decision models so as to be able to assess the impact of changes in information supplied.

Measurement theory

Rational decision-making depends upon information, or data, the significance of which has been accurately represented. Measurement theory is of great importance to the accountant, therefore, because it deals with the problem of assessing or evaluating data so that its significance is correctly stated. Since the person concerned with making decisions expects accounting measurements to represent the truth of a situation, event or phenomenom, it befalls the accountant to devise measures which will satisfy this criterion.

Measurement has been defined as the "assignment of numbers to objects and events according to rules specifying the property to be measured, the scale to be used and the dimensions of the unit". (Chambers, 1966). This definition, therefore, sets out the measurement problem as follows:

(1) What events or objects should be measured?

(2) What standard or scale should be used?

(3) What should be the dimension of the unit of measurement?

The object of measurement

Having specified that the objective of accounting is to provide information for decision-making, it follows that the nature of particular decisions will determine what objects or events are to be measured. Moreover, the measurement of objects or events is not restricted on a time basis: decision-makers may need information about past, present or future events or objects. It is evident that there is more difficulty in measuring an event which has not yet happened than in measuring one that has already occurred. Thus, if one had to measure the price of acquiring a house, the immediate question which one would ask is "when?". It is easy to measure the price of acquistion of a house which one has already acquired in terms of what one has paid, but it is a different matter to attempt to measure the price of acquiring that same house if one were considering its acquistion next year. Since all measures of future events are subjective estimates, they are much less reliable than measures of past events of which there are objective standards, such as what one has paid.

The foregoing discussion leads us to the next point, that is, that different types of decisions require information which is measured on an appropriate basis. The decision to sell a house which one has already acquired obviously requires a measure of its present value in order that a pricing decision may be made. Unless there were urgent reasons for selling, one would not sell a house at a loss, but one would be encouraged to sell by the size of the expected profit if a tentative decision to sell had already been taken. A property dealer considering the purchase of a house requires a measurement of its present and future value in order to determine whether to buy the house and to estimate the date when he should resell it.

These simple examples contain important lessons about the purpose of measurement in management decision-making. Measurements are required not only to express objectives as clearly defined targets about which decisions must be made, but they are also required to control and to assess the results of the activities involved in reaching those targets. The profit objective of a business organization for example, is usually stated in the form of a 'return on capital employed' which is a measure of the profit earned as a percentage of the capital employed in the business. It is the expression, therefore, of that profit target which is considered reasonable and which should be reached. At the same time, it imposes a standard of performance for assessing the efficiency of the firm and its management.

The necessity for suitable and effective measures for expressing organizational objectives as targets and for expressing results as standards of performance in relation to those targets is illustrated by the

well-known example of a Soviet Nail Factory. The factory's objective
was stated in terms of weight of nail output. Employees and management soon learned to maximize this output by producing only huge
spikes. Once the authorities realized that such spikes were being
produced in over-abundance and that there was a widespread shortage of other nails, the measure of the factory's effectiveness was
changed to the number of nails produced. Whereupon, employees and
management learnt to maximize this new measure of effectiveness by
devoting its whole production to very small tacks! (Niskasen, 1967).

We may conclude from this amusing example that the objects or
events selected for measurement should reflect the objectives of business decisions clearly and without the possibility of ambiguity.

The standard of measurement

In accounting, the standard of measurement is the monetary unit. In
Britain, the pound sterling (£) is used, in the United States the dollar
($), in France the franc (Fr.) and in Germany the deutschmark (DM),
so that measurements are expressed in the relevant monetary unit.
Unlike weights and physical measures, money measurements provide a
useful means of attaching a common significance to very diverse
objects and events about which business decisions are made. Traditionally, the accountant has been strictly concerned with financial measures. Therefore, his role has been to provide information for financial
decisions.

Unfortunately, the use of a money standard of measurement has its
disadvantages. To begin with, some organization objectives are more
easily expressed in money terms than others—for example, the profit
objectives may be readily quantified in the form of a money target, but
the wish to have an efficient human organization cannot be expressed
as a measured target of employee morale, skills, loyalty etc. As a
result, organizational objectives which may be expressed clearly as
financial targets are much more likely to be attained than those which
may not be so defined. We shall examine later on the many problems
which stem from the need to use money measures in accounting.

The dimensions of the unit of measurement

The accuracy and reliability of standards of measurements, be they
weights, distances, liquid measures or money standards, depends upon
the stability of the unit of measurement. Thus, whatever standard of
measurement may be appropriate an essential requirement is that the
dimensions of the unit of measurement should remain constant. Unfortunately, the monetary unit of measurement decreases in value because
its purchasing power falls according to the degree of inflation. This

problem is not limited to any one country in the world, but it is common to all countries which are suffering the effects of inflation.

The consequences of the instability in the dimensions of the unit of measurement in accounting is that objects and events which were measured in one period of time cannot be compared with similar goods and events which were measured in a subsequent period. Since the "operations of addition, subtraction and relation necessary in any form of summarization can only be performed validly if the separate items are valued on a uniform basis", (Chambers, 1969) it is now admitted that a correction is needed to the unit of measurement if accurate measurements and comparisons are to be made. This, too, is a problem which we shall discuss later in this book.

Valuation and measurement

'Value' is a term which occurs frequently in accounting. Indeed, it may be said that valuation lies at the heart of measurement, and that the accountant is concerned essentially with measuring values.

Numerous concepts of value are to be found in the literature of accounting and economics, so that there are many different ways in which value may be measured. The quintessence of the concept of value is to be found in expected benefits. Thus, an 'asset' is considered to be valuable because of its service potential. Take, for example, the manner in which a person values a car. The value of the car will be related to two factors: firstly, the value of the services which that person expects to derive from its future use, and secondly, the sum of money which he could presently obtain from its sale. The value of that sum of money is related, of course, to the benefits he may be able to obtain from other goods or assets which he is able to acquire. Hence, however one likes to value the car, its value is related to future expected benefits.

Valuation presents a major measurement problem in accounting because it is a subjective and personal estimate of the worth of future expectations. The tradition in accounting has been to seek objective measures, that is, measures which are relatively free from the bias of personal judgements. In the search for objectivity, accountants have tended to equate verifiability with objectivity. In accounting, therefore, objectivity is found in the cost of acquistion of assets, and consequently, cost-based valuation models tend to be preferred. Another major problem stems from the view widely held among accountants, and best expressed by G. O. May, that "accounting is not essentially a process of valuation .... Primarily accounting is historical in its approach, with valuation entering into it as a safeguard. The emphasis is on cost . . ." (May, 1936). In the past, accountants have been mainly concerned with the process of stewardship accounting, and the attitudes which this process engendered remain very influential today. Accountants are still unwilling to provide information to external users which relates to the future, who therefore have to be content with past information for making predictions. To date, they have not been prepared to consider providing information about future expectations which would be useful for decision-making, since this would mean abandoning a tradition based on objectivity, as understood in accounting. Such a step would undermine the reliability of measurements, but as we saw earlier, the effect of inflation on the monetary unit of measurement is such as to make cost-based measurements unreliable even for short-term predictions.

The development of accounting as an information science concerned with the needs of decision-makers requires measurements which are relevant and useful for these needs. In particular, such measurements should possess a high degree of predictive ability. Accounting tradition, therefore, poses serious obstacles at present to progress. We shall see in Part 3, however, the manner in which accounting has responded to the pressure for management information.

Information theory

The literature of economics and accounting recognizes the importance of information as an organization resource, and information theory now has become an important subject in its own right. The purpose of information is to enable an organization to reach its objectives by the efficient use of its other resources, that is, men, materials, machines and other assets and money. Since information is also a resource, information theory considers the problems of its efficient use.

In a very broad sense, the idea of efficiency is expressed in the relationship of inputs to outputs. The efficiency of a transformer, for example, may be measured by comparing the power output as against the power input. Similarly, we may consider the problem of assessing the efficiency of the utilization of information as a resource by attempting to match the costs associated with the production of information against the benefits derived from its use.

The production of information

The costs associated with the production of information are those involved in collecting and processing data and distributing the information output. The total costs of producing information increase directly with the volume of information distributed, and, moreover, they tend to increase at an accelerating rate. This is because extending the information supply means acquiring more staff, and beyond a certain point, installing expensive data processing equipment. We may say, therefore, that the marginal costs of producing information tends to increase with the volume of information output.

Clearly, one important implication of the relationship between the marginal cost of information and its volume stems from the accountant's role in controlling and minimizing costs. From his point of view, therefore, it may be argued that since additional information involves proportionately greater increases in cost, the output of information should be kept to a minimum. Another important implication lies in the relationship between the marginal cost of information and its marginal value, that is, its marginal utility. We may note in this connection that the marginal utility of information tends to behave in the same way as the marginal utility of goods, for it tends to decrease as the volume of information expands. The more information is produced, the less is the additional benefit which is derived from it. The various relationships which we have discussed above may be illustrated in Fig. 1.3. Figure 1.3 indicates that at the intersection of

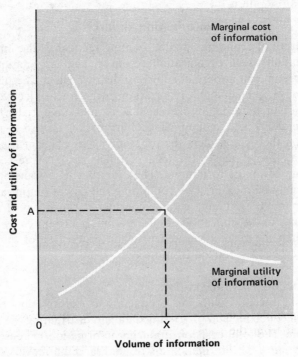

Fig. 1.3

the two curves, the marginal cost of producing information is equal to the marginal utility of information at that point. The optimum volume of information production, therefore, is indicated by OX and its total cost will be OA.

The foregoing analysis suggests that as regards the production of information, the accountant should be less concerned with minimizing the cost of information and more concerned with discovering the optimum level of information production. In theory, therefore, the economics of an optimal management information system is a relatively simple matter of equalizing the marginal utility with the marginal cost of producing information. In practice, however, although it is possible to measure the cost of information with some degree of accuracy, it is a much more difficult task to attempt to measure its utility.

Valuing information

The value of information lies in its end use, that is, its intelligibility to persons making decisions, and its relevance to those decisions. One of the techniques which have been evolved in recent years to measure the value of information is based on the reduction of uncertainty resulting from information. This method makes use of measures of expectations and probabilities, for example, if a manager is 95% sure that he understands a given situation, any additional information is of less value to him than if he were, say, only 70% sure. In more technical language, the greater the probabilities or expectations attached to the occurrence of an event, the smaller is the value of any information about that event. The significance of this method for the accountant is that it implies that the volume of information which he supplies should be determined by its effectiveness in reducing uncertainty in decision-making, thereby offering an opportunity for improving the quality of decisions.

We may conclude by saying that information theory implies that the production of information should be determined by cost-benefit analysis by means of which the benefits resulting from the supply of information are measured against its costs of production.

Summary

We may conclude, therefore, that the natural sciences should not be distinguished from the social sciences because their hypotheses may not be tested in the same way, and that the predictive ability of social science theories is subject to the constraint which we have mentioned.

According to Rudner, there are not two different logical systems of inquiry in science for:

> 'The method of science is, indeed, the rationale on which it bases its acceptance or rejection of hypotheses or theories. Accordingly, to hold that the social sciences are methodologically distinct from the non-social sciences is to hold not merely (or perhaps at all) the banal view that the social sciences employ different techniques of inquiry, but rather the startling view that the social sciences require a different logic of inquiry. To hold such a view, moreover, is to deny that all science is characterized by a common logic of justification in its acceptance or rejection of hypotheses or theories.' (Rudner, 1966).

Accounting is very closely associated with the scientific management of human and non-human resources by virtue of its concern with the provision of information which is used in that process. It is possible, therefore, to construct scientific theories of accounting, which do not necessarily describe what accountants do presently, but which may serve as standards by which accounting practices may be judged. The development of normative theories of accounting is certainly one aspect of our study which we should bear in mind. Furthermore, such normative theories may be developed independently of the practices of accounting.

Our study of accounting would be incomplete and would certainly lack realism if we did not gain a knowledge of the nature of accounting practice. This knowledge is contained in the descriptive theories of accounting, and much of this book will be devoted to discovering the nature of accounting practices. The usefulness of normative theories, therefore, is to provide a yardstick against which to judge the relevance of descriptive theories. We shall note, as we go along, that much of what accountants do does not conform with any normative theory of what they should do. Indeed, as G. O. May, a very distinguished accountant, has pointed out accounting practices are the product of experience rather than the product of logic (May, 1946). Moreover, such is the diversity of practices permitted under the 'generally accepted principles of accounting' which guide accountants, that some have suggested that they may be appropriately defined as an art form rather than a science.

References

1. A.A.A., *A Statement of Basic Accounting Theory*, p. 6, 1966.

2. Chambers, R. J., *Accounting, Evaluation and Economic Behaviour*, p. 10, Prentice Hall, Englewood Cliffs, N.J., 1966.

3. Chambers, R. J., *Accounting and Financial Management*, p. 554, Butterworths, Sydney, 1969.

4. Hendriksen, E. S., *Accounting Theory*, Richard D. Irwin, Homewood, Illinois, 1970.

5. Littleton, A. C. & Zimmerman, V. K., *Accounting Theory : Continuity and Change*, Prentice Hall, Englewood Cliffs, N.J., 1962.

6. May, G. O., *Twenty-Five Years of Accounting Responsibility 1911-1936*, American Institute of Accountants, New York, 1936.

7. May, G. O., *Financial Accounting*, Macmillan, New York, 1946.

8. Niskasen, W. A., *Measures of Effectiveness in Cost Effectiveness Analysis*, Goldman, T. A. (ed.), Frederick A. Praeger, New York, 1967.

9. Rudner, R. S., *Philosophy of Social Science*, p. 5, Prentice Hall, Englewood Cliffs, N.J., 1966.

Selected further readings

Accounting history
Brown, R. G. & Johnston, K. S., *Paciolo on Accounting*, McGraw-Hill, New York, 1963.

DeRoover, R., New Perspectives on the History of Accounting, *Accounting Review* July, 1955.

Glautier, M. W. E., The Idea of Accounting: a Historical Perspective, *Accountants' Magazine*, August, 1973.

Glautier, M. W. E., Roman Accounting: the Influence of Socio-Economic Factors on the Development of Accounting Concepts, *International Journal of Accounting Education and Research*, Volume 8, No. 2 Spring, 1973.

Littleton, A. C., *Accounting Evoluting to 1900*, American Institute Publishing Co., 1933.

Littleton, A. C. & Yamey, B. S., *Studies in Accounting History*, Sweet and Maxwell, London, 1956.

McKendrick, N., Josiah Wedgwood and Cost Accounting in the Industrial Revolution, *Economic History Review*, 2 SER Volume 23, 1970.

Most, K. S., Sombart's Propositions Revisited, *Accounting Review*, October, 1972.

Pollard, S., *The Genesis of Modern Management* (chapter 6, Accounting and Management) Pelican Library, Penguin Books Ltd, 1968.

Yamey, B. S., Accounting and the Rise of Capitalism: Further Notes on a Theme by Sombart, *Journal of Accounting Research* Volume 1-2, 1963-64.

Accounting theory
A.A.A., Jaedicke, R. K., Ijiri, Y. & Nielsen, O. (eds) *Research in Accounting Measurement*, 1966.

A.A.A., Studies in Accounting Research No. 2 Baruch Lev, *Accounting and Information Theory*, 1969.

A.A.A., Report of the Committee on Accounting and Information Systems in the Supplement to the *Accounting Review* Volume 46, 1971.

A.A.A., Report of the Committee on Foundations of Accounting Measurement in the Supplement to the *Accounting Review* Volume 46, 1971.

A.A.A., Report of the Committee on Theory Construction in the Supplement to the *Accounting Review* Volume 46, 1971.

A.A.A., Report of the Committee on Research Methodology in Accounting in the Supplement to the *Accounting Review* Volume 47, 1972.

A.A.A., Studies in Accounting Research No. 5. Feltham, G. A., *Information Evaluation*, 1972.

Buckley, J. W., Kircher, P. & Mathews, R. L., Methodology in Accounting Theory, *Accounting Review*, April, 1968.

Caplan, E. H., Relevance: 'A Will o' the Wisp', *Abacus*, September, 1969.

Chambers, R. J., Blueprint for a Theory of Accounting, *Journal of Accounting Research*, Volume VI January, 1955.

Chambers, R. J., Details for a Blueprint, *Accounting Review*, Volume 32 April, 1957.

Chambers, R. J., The Conditions of Research in Accounting, *Journal of Accountancy*, December, 1960.

Churchill, N. C., Kempster, J. H. & Uretsky, M., *Computer-Based Information Systems for Management: A Survey*, Research No. 1 in Management Planning and Control, National Association of Accountants, New York, 1969.

Churchman, C. W., *The Systems Approach*, Dell Publishing Co., New York, 1968.

Glautier, M. W. E. & Underdown, B., *Accounting in a Changing Environment*, Pitman Publishing, London, 1974.

Godfrey, J. T. & Prince T. R., The Accounting Model from an Information Systems Perspective, *Accounting Review*, January, 1971.

Hendriksen, E. S., *Accounting Theory*, revised edition, Richard D. Irwin, Homewood, Ill., 1970.

Ijiri, Y., *The Foundations of Accounting Measurement*, Prentice Hall, Englewood Cliffs, N.J., 1967.

Imke, F. J., Relationships in Accounting Theory, *Accounting Review*, April, 1966.

Iselin, E. R., The Objectives of Accounting in an Accounting Theory Based on Deductive Methodology, Ph.D. thesis published by the University of Queensland, Australia, 1972.

Johnson, R. A., Kast, F. E. & Rosenzweig, J. E., *The Theory and Management of Systems*, McGraw-Hill, New York, 1963.

Kam, V., Judgement and the Scientific Trend in Accounting, *Journal of Accountancy*, February, 1973.

Mattessich, R., Methodological Preconditions and Problems of a General Theory of Accounting, *Accounting Review*, July, 1972.

Murdick, R. G. & Ross, J. E., *Information Systems for Modern Management*, Prentice Hall, Englewood Cliffs, N.J., 1971.

Prince, T. R., *Extension of the Boundaries of Accounting Theory*, South-Western Publishing Co., Cincinnati, 1963.

Rappaport, A., (ed.), *Information for Decision-Making*, Prentice Hall, Englewood Cliffs, N.J., 1975.

Simon, H. A., A Behavioural Model of Rational Choice, *Quarterly Journal of Economics*, February, 1955.

Sterling, R. R., Theory Construction and Verification, *Accounting Review*, July, 1970.

Tilley, I., Accounting as a Scientific Endeavour: Some Questions the American Theorists Tend to Leave Unanswered, *Accounting and Business Research*, Autumn, 1972.

Wheeler, J. T., Accounting Theory and Research in Perspective, *Accounting Review*, January, 1970.

Williams, T. H. & Griffen, G. H., On the Nature of Empirical Verification in Accounting, *Abacus*, Winter 1969.

Zani, W., Blueprint for MIS, *Harvard Business Review*, November–December, 1970.

Part 2

Financial Accounting Information

Part 2   FINANCIAL ACCOUNTING INFORMATION

Introduction   51

Section 1   **Financial Accounting Method**

1 Financial Accounting Conventions   56
The nature of financial accounting conventions   56
Types of financial accounting conventions   57
Fundamental conventions   58
Procedural conventions   62
Summary   76
References   77

2 The Generation of Financial Accounting Data   78
An outline of the information generation process   78
Source documents   79
   Source documents related to sales   81
   Source documents related to purchases   82
   Source documents related to the receipt of goods   83
The entry of basic data in the subsidiary books   83
   The day books   85
   The cash book   86
The development of data processing systems   87
   The write-it-once principle   88
   The mechanization of accounting   89
Summary   95
Reference   95
Further readings   95

3 Data Processing and Double-Entry Book-keeping   97
The meaning of book-keeping   97
The origin of double-entry book-keeping   98
The nature of double-entry book-keeping   99
Double-entry book-keeping as a 'closed' system   102
Accounts as descriptions of transactions   104
The mathematical implications of double-entry book-
   keeping   105
The trial balance 107
Summary   108

Section 2   **Periodic Measurement**

4 Double-Entry Book-keeping and Periodic
   Measurement   112
Problems in periodic measurement   112
Identifying the revenues and expenses of the period   113
The meaning of revenue and expense   114
Periodic measurement and the accrual convention   115
The accrual of income   116
The accrual of expenses   117
The results of the accrual adjustments   121

The matching of revenues and expenses   123
Inventory adjustments   123
Summary   125

5 Losses in Asset Values and Periodic Measurement   127
The treatment of losses in asset values   127
Losses in the value of fixed assets   128
The nature of depreciation   128
   Depreciation as a fall in price   128
   Depreciation as physical deterioration   128
   Depreciation as a fall in value   129
   Depreciation as cost allocation   129
The accounting concept of depreciation   130
   Depreciable and non-depreciable fixed assets   131
   Factors in the measurement of depreciation   131
   Identifying the cost of the asset   132
   Ascertaining the useful life of an asset   132
   Determining the expected residual value   133
   Selecting the method of depreciation   134
   Depreciation and total asset costs   137
Accounting for depreciation   138
Accounting for the sale or disposal of assets   140
Losses through defaulting debtors   141
   The treatment of bad debts   143
   The treatment of doubtful debts   144
Summary   145
References   146

6 Preparing an Income Statement and a Balance Sheet   147
Preparing an Income Statement   147
   Adjusting for accruals   149
   Adjusting for inventories   150
   Adjusting for the loss in asset values   150
   Calculating the periodic income   151
The formal presentation of the Income Statement   154
Preparing a Balance Sheet   155
   Collecting and classifying balances   156
   Verifying balances   157
   Bank reconciliation statement   157
The formal presentation of the Balance Sheet   158
Summary   160

7 The Valuation of Recorded Assets and Liabilities   161
The valuation of assets   162
The valuation of fixed assets   163
   The valuation of land   163
   The valuation of buildings   163
   The valuation of plant and machinery and other
      fixed assets   164
   The valuation of natural resources   164

The valuation of current assets 164
    The valuation of inventories 165
    The 'lower of cost or market rule' (LCM) 166
    Different meanings of 'market rule' 167
    General criticism of the LCM rule 168
    The valuation of debtors 168
The valuation of other assets 169
    Investments 169
    Intangible assets 169
The valuation of liabilities 172
    The valuation problem 173
    Contingent liabilities 174
    Deferred liabilities 174
The valuation of shareholders' equity 175
Summary 176
References 176

8 Cash-Flow and Funds-Flow Statements 177
Cash-flow statements 177
    Form and content of cash-flow statements 178
    Financial analysis by cash-flow statement 178
Funds-flow statements 179
    Form and content of funds-flow statements 180
Summary 184
Reference 184

**Section 3 The Application of Financial Accounting
Method to Corporate Enterprises**

**9 Financial Accounting Information for
Corporate Enterprises 186**
The nature of corporate enterprises 187
Financial accounting implications of corporate status 189
The capital structure 190
Gearing and the capital structure 192
Accounting procedures applied to the capital structure 194
    The share capital 194
    Loan capital 199
Accounting procedures applied to periodic income 200
Accounting procedures for the payment of dividends 202
Published financial accounting statements 203
Summary 206

10 Financial Accounting for Groups of Companies 208
Legal obligation to disclose financial accounting information 209
The definition of a subsidiary company 210
The obligation to disclose information concerning subsidiaries 211
Consolidated accounts 212
    Problems in the consolidation of Group accounts 214

The treatment of dividends   218
   Dividend paid by Parent Ltd   218
   Dividend paid by Subsidiary Ltd   218
   Dividends paid out of pre-acquisition income   219
The treatment of minority shareholders   221
   Acquisitions and the creation of minority interests   222
Summary   226
Reference   227

11 Problems in the Preparation of Consolidated Finan-
   cial Statements   228
Consolidating the financial statements of multiple sub-
   sidiaries   228
The acquisition of a subsidiary at less than book value   228
The treatment of losses made by subsidiaries   229
Consolidating subsidiaries having complex capital struc-
   tures   230
Subsidiaries acquired during an accounting period   231
Consolidation and inter-group transactions   231
Consolidated Income Statements   234
The sub-subsidiary relationship   236
Merger or acquisition?   240
Summary   245

Introduction

In Part 1 we defined accounting as the "process of identifying, measuring and communicating socio-economic information to permit informed judgements and decisions by the users of the information". From this definition, we may deduce that accounting is concerned with the following process:

(a) identifying and selecting the information which intended users will need;
(b) evaluating that information in the manner which is most useful to the intended users;
(c) communicating the information selected and processed in the form most appropriate to the requirements of its users.

From a theoretical point of view, these three areas define the scope and boundaries of the subject-matter of accounting, and the social role of accountants as information scientists. Insofar as business firms are concerned, a distinction is normally made between *financial accounting* which is the activity of recording and analysing the financial results of transactions as a means of arriving at a measure of the firm's success and financial soundness, and *management accounting* which is the activity of providing information to enable management to make efficient decisions as regards the use and allocation of the firm's resources. As yet, the hallmark of business efficiency is financial success, and this emphasis may be seen in the critical importance which is attached to financial results. As we shall see in Part 5, socio-economic measures of efficiency are still in their infancy, and we have some considerable way to go before the wider social purposes of business firms are reflected in accounting and management practices.

The purpose of this Part is to examine the nature and the methods of financial accounting which is concerned with the following activities:

(a) recording financial transactions;
(b) summarizing and presenting financial information in reports.

Financial accounting information is used by a variety of interested parties. Managers require financial information so as to evaluate the financial results of past decisions, for the evaluation of past performance is an important part of management decision-making. Shareholders and investors need financial information which will enable them to predict both their income from the firm and the value of their investment. Hence, shareholders and investors require financial accounting information for the purpose of making decisions about their investment in the firm. Besides shareholders and investors, there are other external users of financial information, notably the Inland Revenue which requires a firm to submit financial accounts for the purpose of assessing its tax liability, and Trade Unions and employees who have a vested interest in the size of a firm's income.

The nature and methods of financial accounting are determined to a considerable extent by the conventions which exist among accountants for identifying, evaluating and communicating financial information. This is particularly true of the information which is provided for external users such as shareholders and investors. It is evident that unless accountants obey the same rules as regards selecting, measuring and communicating information to external users, the latter will be placed at a great disadvantage in respect of the reliance which may be attached to the information they receive. The usefulness of accounting conventions lies in the uniformity and comparability of information which is made possible thereby, though as we shall see in Part 4, the conventions themselves permit a variety of different practices which nullify to some extent the comparability of accounting statements as between different companies. Accounting conventions do secure for external users a much greater degree of comparability in the information emanating from the same firm over a period of years. Accountants do not attempt, however, to meet the specific information needs of external users, and the information which they do provide is dictated by the conventions which they have followed for a very long time, rather than the information needs of external users.

The users of external reports have no control, therefore, over their content. We may contrast Fig. 2.1 below, which illustrates the boundaries of the financial accounting system for external users, against the user-oriented model shown on page 12 of Part 1 (Fig. 1.2). In this case, there is no control by the user over the final output. Hence, it may be suggested the information system for external decision-makers is not user-oriented. The output, and therefore also the input into this system is determined by conventions which are embodied in accounting tradition and in law. External users are provided with reports on a take-it-or-leave-it basis, although more useful information could be provided for them without imposing additional costs on the firm. However, in view of the broad objectives and definition of accounting as an

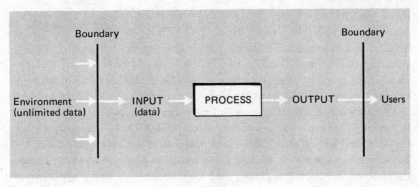

Fig. 2.1

information system, which we adopted in Part 1, we would expect to find inherent limitations in current external reporting practices. We shall discuss these limitations in Part 4.

A basic assumption underlying communication theory is that there is a clear separation between the transmitter and the receiver of information. This is acknowledged also in financial accounting theory in the distinction which is drawn between the function of the accountant as the transmitter of information and the external user as the receiver of information. The external user relies upon the accountant to provide him with a significant supply of information for making economic decisions. It is for each user to evaluate and interpret this information in the course of formulating decisions which only he may make. It is not the objective of either the accountant or of financial reports to make such evaluations and draw conclusions for the external user. Consequently, it is not the function of the accountant to value a firm for the external user: on the contrary, it is for the investor to establish the value of the firm as an investment and to bear the risk involved in acting on such a valuation. The function of the accountant in this analysis is to assist the external user in valuing the firm by the provision of such information as is necessary for that purpose.

In line with this reasoning, we consider in this Part the problems associated with the production of financial accounting information. We examine how data is selected from the environment, and the manner in which it becomes an input into the financial accounting system. We discuss also the manner in which the output of the financial accounting system is formulated as financial reports. We shall examine in Part 4 the relevance of these reports to the decisions which shareholders and investors wish to make.

We have limited our analysis of financial accounting information to those aspects which we consider important and relevant to the text-book as a whole. We have divided this Part into three sections. In Section 1, we examine financial accounting method to gain an understanding of its nature and of the principles underlying its procedures. In Section 2, we analyse the process of periodic measurement, which is one of its main applications. In Section 3, we select for closer analysis the application of financial accounting procedures to the production of financial statements for corporate enterprises. There are two reasons for this feature of this Part. First, corporate activity constitutes the most important area of interest to students of accounting and management science generally. Hence, we believe that an early exposure to some of the accounting problems involved in corporate activity is desirable. Second, we have devoted Part 4 to an analysis of financial reporting, which is an area in which many controversial problems exist. We have found it necessary, therefore, to deal with the procedural foundations of financial reporting in this Part. The tendency for corporations to grow by merger and acquisition of other corporations is recognized in chapters 9 and 10, and the accounting problems resulting therefrom are examined.

One important application of financial accounting method relates to the use of accounting records for the day to day control of assets and liabilities. These technical aspects of control are treated as a 'background subject' in this text, so as not to detract from the important theoretical and practical aspects of the accountant's role in providing information for decision-making purposes.

Section 1

Financial Accounting Method

1
Financial Accounting Conventions

We mentioned in the Introduction to this Part that the nature of financial information was dictated not by the needs of external users, but rather was determined to a considerable extent by the conventions existing among accountants for identifying, evaluating and communicating financial information. As regards the provision of financial information for management purposes, the same does not apply since accountants are more concerned in this case with identifying and meeting the information needs of management rather than strictly observing accounting conventions. For example, if management wished to know the impact of inflation on the recorded value of fixed assets, the accountant would attempt to produce an inflation-adjusted statement of the value of fixed assets, whereas as regards financial accounting information prepared for external users, he would abide by the historic cost convention of valuation. Most countries in Europe are now considering the problem of inflation, but as yet, few have abandoned the historic cost convention as a basic accounting rule.

Nevertheless, even as regards the provision of financial information for management, it is true to say that accountants may hesitate to depart from established conventions. Moreover, the nature of the financial information supplied to external users is important to management in that this information is utilized by external users in evaluating the firm and its management. Financial accounting conventions are important, therefore, because of the influence they bear on the nature of the information supplied and used in one way or another in evaluating the firm.

Figure 2.2 below illustrates the manner in which financial accounting conventions act as filters in selecting data as input into the processing system and as output of information for users.

The nature of financial accounting conventions

Textbooks refer variously to 'accounting principles', 'postulates of accounting', 'accounting concepts', and 'accounting standards' to describe those basic points of agreement on which financial accounting theory and practice are founded. We prefer to use the term 'accounting

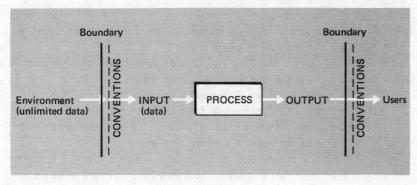

Fig. 2.2

conventions' so as to stress that the ground rules of financial accounting are not the subject of immutable law, but are based on consensus.
If accountants as a group wish to change some of their conventions,
they are free to do so. Indeed, accounting bodies in Britain and in the
United States are engaged in the review of their conventions and
practices, and for this purpose, the Financial Accounting Standards
Board was established in the United States in 1973 (replacing the
Accounting Principles Board) and in the United Kingdom the Accounting Standards Steering Committee was established in 1971 with
similar objectives.

The term 'accounting conventions' serves in another sense to underline the freedom which accountants have enjoyed in determining their
own rules. There is no tradition of State interference in the USA and
UK, for example, as regards the practice of accounting. Such laws as
are to be found are contained in statutes dealing with the activities of
corporate bodies, such as the Companies Acts which specify the nature
of the accounting information that must be disclosed to shareholders,
and the Income Tax and Corporation Tax Acts which impose a duty on
business firms to submit accounting information for the purpose of
assessing the liability to tax. So far, neither Parliament nor the Courts
have issued directives to the accounting profession as regards the
conventions which they should observe. In France, by contrast, there is
a different political tradition, and there is legislation dealing with
accounting practices and they are detailed in the *Plan Comptable*, which
is an edict issued by the French Government detailing the manner in
which accounting statements should be prepared.

Types of financial accounting conventions

We may classify accounting conventions into two broad groups—those
which may be said to go to the very roots of financial accounting,

which we shall call 'fundamental conventions', and those which bear directly on the quality of financial accounting information, which we shall describe as 'procedural conventions'.

In our view, there are only two 'fundamental conventions' which may be said to characterize financial accounting:

> (a) the entity convention which states that financial accounting information relates to the activities of a business entity only, and not to the activities of its owners;
> (b) the money measurement convention which limits the recognition of activities to those which can be expressed in monetary terms.

The alteration of either of these two conventions would change the entire nature of financial accounting.

There are several 'procedural conventions', which though of great importance, affect the manner in which financial accounting information is selected, analysed and communicated. Some of these conventions are the subject of criticism, for example, the realization convention which holds that a gain in value may only result from a transaction. The following conventions are generally regarded as the most important conventions in this group:

> (a) the going concern convention
> (b) the cost convention
> (c) the realization convention
> (d) the acrrual convention
> (e) the matching convention
>
> (f) the convention of periodicity
> (g) the convention of consistency
> (h) the convention of conservatism.

Fundamental Conventions

(a) The entity convention
The practice of distinguishing the affairs of the business from the personal affairs of its owner originated in the early days of double-entry book-keeping some 400 years ago. Accounting has a history which reaches back to the beginning of civilization, and archaeologists have found accounting records which date as far back as 4000 B.C., well before the invention of money. Nevertheless, it was not until the 15th century that the separation of the owner's wealth from the wealth invested in a business venture was recognized as necessary. This arose from the habit of employing managers or stewards to run a business and to require them to render accounts of their stewardship of the

funds and assets entrusted to them. Consequently, the 'capital' invested in the business represented at once not only the initial assets of the business but a measure of its indebtedness to the owner. This principle remains enshrined in modern financial accounting, and the owner is shown as entitled to both the 'capital' which he has invested in the business, and also the profits which have been made during the year. The accounting and legal relationship between the business and its owner is shown on the Balance Sheet, which states the firm's assets and liabilities and hence indicates its financial position and financial well-being.

Example

J. Soap has recently inherited £30,000 and decides that the moment is opportune for him to realize his life-time ambition and open up a hairdressing salon. Accordingly, he makes all the necessary arrangements to begin on the 1st April, 19X0, under the name 'J. Soap—Ladies Hairdresser', and commits £10,000 of his money to that business. He will, therefore, open another account at his bank under the name 'J. Soap—Ladies Hairdresser', or he may simply call it the 'No. 2 account'.

As a result, the financial position of the firm on the 1st April, 19X0, from an accounting point of view will appear as follows:

J. Soap—Ladies Hairdresser
Balance Sheet as at the 1st April, 19X0

Capital account	£10,000	Cash at bank	£10,000

The business is shown as having £10,000 in cash as its asset at that date, and as owing J. Soap £10,000, that is, recognizing its indebtedness to him in respect of the capital he has invested.

The accounting effect of the entity convention is to make a clear distinction between J. Soap's private affairs and his business affairs: what he does with his remaining £20,000 is of no concern to the accountant, but what happens to the £10,000 invested in the business is the subject-matter of accounting.

The interesting aspect of the entity convention is that it establishes a fictional distinction between J. Soap and the business which is not recognized at law: he remains legally liable at law for the debts of the business, and should the business fail, he will have to pay the creditors out of his private funds.

In the case of corporations, there is a legal distinction between the owners, that is, the shareholders and the business, so that the shareholders are not liable for the corporation's debts beyond the capital which they have agreed to invest. The accounting treatment of the relationship between the shareholders and the corporation is no different to that accorded to the sole trader and his business, except of course that the capital of the corporation is divided into a number of shares.

Example

Multiform Toys Limited is registered on the 1st April, 19X0 as a public company, the objectives being to manufacture a wide range of children's toys. The promoters of the company need £100,000 to launch the company. They decide to offer for sale 100,000 Ordinary Shares of £1 each to the public, and the promoters themselves will subscribe for 25,000 of these shares.

If we assume that all the shares have been taken up and paid for on the 1st May, 19X0, the Balance Sheet of the company will be as follows:

Multiform Toys Limited
Balance Sheet as at 1st May, 19X0

Share Capital	£100,000	Cash at bank	£100,000

The promoters have become shareholders, along with the members of the public who have subscribed for the shares. The liability of the company to the shareholders amounts to £100,000, and the company has £100,000 in cash by means of which it may pursue its objectives.

The effect of the entity convention in the case of incorporated business is to recognize the separate identity of the company from that of its shareholders. The shareholders themselves are not liable for the debts of the company, and their total liability is limited to the £100,000 which they have subscribed. We shall discuss full implications of incorporation from an accounting point of view in chapter 9.

(b) The money measurement convention

Both trade and accounting existed before the invention of money, which we know began to circulate in the 6th century B.C. Its role as a common denominator by which the value of assets of different kinds could be compared encouraged the extension of trade. By Roman times, money had become the language of commerce, and accounts were kept in money terms. Hence, there is an accounting tradition which dates back some 2000 years of keeping the records of valuable assets and of transactions in monetary terms. It should not appear surprising, therefore, that accounting information today reflects the time-hallowed practice of dealing only with those facts which are capable of expression in money.

The money measurement convention sets an absolute limit to the type of information which may be selected and measured by accountants, and hence limits the type of information which accountants may communicate about a business enterprise.

Example

The Solidex Engineering Co. Ltd, is an old-fashioned company which specializes in the production of a single component used in the manufacture of mining gear. The Balance Sheet of the company as at 31st December 19X0 reveals the following position:

The Solidex Engineering Company Ltd.
Balance Sheet as at 31st December, 19X0

	£		£
Share capital	100,000	Land and Buildings	30,000
		Equipment	25,000
		Inventories	30,000
		Cash	15,000
	100,000		100,000

For some time, it has been known that a competitor has developed a better product, and that the company is likely to lose its market. The Managing Director is ill, the Production Manager and the Accountant are not on speaking terms and the labour force is resentful about the deterioration in working conditions in the factory. The buildings are dilapidated, but the land itself is valuable. The equipment is old and needs a great deal of maintenance, and as a result, there is a considerable wastage of labour hours owing to machinery breakdown.

It is clear from the foregoing example that the most significant information of interest to shareholders is not what is contained in the Balance Sheet but the information which is left out of it, and which is much more relevant to an understanding of the firm's position. Yet, the accountant is unable to measure and communicate that information to shareholders directly in money terms, although all these facts may explain poor income figures. The reader of a financial accounting report should not expect, therefore, that all or perhaps even the most important facts about the business will be disclosed, and this is why there is such a premium on 'inside' information in order to make correct assessments of the firm's true position. One of the major problems of accounting today is to find means of solving the measurement problem: how to extend the quality and the coverage of information in a way which is meaningful. The advantage of money, of course, is that people are able to grasp the meaning of facts which are stated in money, and it remains the most obvious standard of measurement in accounting.

There are futher problems associated with the practice of using money as a standard of measurement in accounting. Money does not have a constant value through time, nor does the value of specific assets remain the same in relation to money. Until recently, accountants turned a blind eye to this problem by assuming that the money standard did have a constant value. The rising rates of inflation in the 1960s and 1970s destroyed this fiction, but any solution for dealing with the instability of the money standard will have its own problems.

Financial accounting records serve two distinct and important purposes. First, they provide evidence of the financial dimensions of rights and obligations resulting from legal contracts. For this purpose these records must be kept in the form of unadjusted money measurements. Second, they are used as a basis for providing financial information for shareholders, investors and a variety of users who need such information for decision-making. For this purpose, the money measurements must reflect the economic reality of business transactions and for this reason must be adjusted for changes in price levels. In this Part, we shall discuss the first purpose of financial accounting records, and in Part 4, we shall discuss the second purpose.

It is clear from our discussion so far that the abandonment of either of the two conventions which we have examined would alter the nature of financial accounting completely. Communicating information about a business entity in money terms is the basis of modern financial accounting theory and practice. The conventions which we shall now discuss relate to the treatment of data.

Procedural conventions

(a) The going-concern convention

The valuation of assets used in a business is based on the assumption that the business is a continuing business and not one on the verge of cessation. This convention is important: many assets derive their value from their employment in the firm, and should the firm cease to operate the value which could be obtained for these assets on a closing-down sale would be much less probably than their book value.

Example

The Zimbabwe Gold Mining Company Ltd, has been mining gold for many years in Southern Africa. The assets of the company consist of a mineshaft half a mile deep which enables the company to reach the gold reef, small gauge railway tracks and truck within the mine, lifting gear, conveyor belts, crushing plant and sundry equipment. The Balance Sheet of the company at the 1st April, 19X0 shows the following position:

The Zimbabwe Gold Mining Company Ltd
Balance Sheet as at 1st April, 19X0

	£		£
Share Capital	500,000	Mineshaft	500,000
Retained income	300,000	Land and Building	25,000
		Plant and Equipment	200,000
		Tools	15,000
		Gold in transit	50,000
		Cash at bank	10,000
	800,000		800,000

The mineshaft was sunk originally with the money raised by the issue of shares, and the other assets were financed out of loans which were repaid out of income, which was not distributed to shareholders. In terms of the entity convention the total liability of the company to shareholders is, therefore, £800,000—which is the amount which they might expect to receive if the company ceased to operate. For the time being, apart from £60,000 in gold or cash, the balance of their interest is substantially the mineshaft and the plant and equipment amounting to £700,000. If the gold reef ceased to be economically workable and the mine had to be abandoned, the mineshaft, being purely a hole in the ground would become valueless, and so would much of the plant. Hence, it is unlikely that shareholders would get back even a fraction of their investments.

The going-concern convention indicates the need to relate the value of assets to the future profits which they will make possible. This convention opens the way for the method favoured by economists of finding the present value of an asset by reference to the discounted value of future returns which are expected to be derived from the use of that asset.

(b) The cost convention

By convention, however, accountants determine the value of an asset by reference to the cost of its acquisition, and not by reference to value of the returns which are expected to be realized. Hence, the 'value in use' of assets which the going concern convention maintains is the cost of acquisition. To the accountant, the difference between the value in use and the cost of acquisition of an asset is income:

$$\text{Value in use} - \text{Cost of acquisition} = \text{Income}$$

Example

W. E. Audent & Son is a professional firm of chartered accountants with a large auditing practice. Its major asset is the staff of audit clerks. The value in use of the staff may be calculated by reference to the hourly rate at which their services may be charged out to clients: the cost of securing their services to the firm is represented by their salaries: and the annual profit of the firm is in substance the difference less, of course, the administrative expenses of running the firm.

In accounting, cost is used as a measure of the financial 'effort' exerted in gaining access to the resources which will be deployed in earning revenues. Since these resources are secured through financial transactions, the financial effort is measured at the time of acquisition, which coincides, of course, with the legal obligation to pay for those resources in money. The cost convention raises the following problems:

(a) The historic cost of acquisition of assets is not a dependable guide to their current value because it fails to reflect:

(i) changes in the general purchasing power of money,
(ii) changes in the specific value of individual assets in relation to money.

(b) The historic cost of acquisition of assets used up in the activity of earning income does not form a dependable basis for calculating income.

Example

John Smith is a dealer in hides. He obtains his yearly supplies from Canada in the autumn, and sells them in the United Kingdom during the ensuing 12 months. In October, 19X0 he bought

20,000 hides at an average cost of $20 Canadian, equivalent to, let us say £10, and by September, 19X1 had sold them all at an average price of £20, making an overall profit of £20,000. Meanwhile, the posted price of Canadian hides has increased by 50% so that to replace inventory which he has sold during the year he will now have to pay an average of £15 a hide. Hence, the income of £20,000 is overstated by £10,000 because the hides sold have been valued at £10 instead of £15 each—which is their current value in Canada.

(c) The accounting practice of writing off the cost of certain assets as depreciation against income means that it is possible to remove the cost of these assets from the accounts altogether. For a long time, for example, it was the practice of banks to reduce the value of land and buildings to £1 and so create secret reserves.

(d) Since incurring a cost depends upon a financial transaction, there are assets which create income for the firm which can never appear as such in the accounts. Often the major asset of a highly successful firm is the knowledge and the skill created as a result of teamwork and good organization. This asset will not appear in the accounts, since the firm has paid nothing for it, except in terms of salaries which have been written off against yearly profits. Allied to this problem is the failure in making any mention in the Balance Sheet of the value of the human assets of the firm. Long ago, the economist Alfred Marshall stated that "the most valuable of all capital is that invested in human beings" (Marshall, 1964, 8th edn), and it is universally recognized that the firm's human assets are its chief source of wealth. Yet, it is only recently that accountants have begun to recognize this fact, and efforts are now being made to find ways in which information on the value of human assets may be most appropriately presented. Other important assets of which no mention is made in financial accounting statements are, for example, the value to the firm of its hold on the market which may be a very valuable asset if the firm enjoys a monopoly position, and the value of the firm's own information system which will affect the quality of its decisions.

Many of the most controversial issues in financial accounting theory and practice revolve around the cost convention. External users of financial statements basically wish to have information of the current worth of the firm on the basis of which they may make investment decisions. Accountants argue that there must be an objective basis to the information which they provide, and to them 'objectivity' means being able to verify information from the results of transactions which create legal rights and obligations. Accountants feel that to depart from the cost convention would open the way to fraudulent practices for in the absence of a transaction to test the value of an asset, its value is merely a matter of opinion.

(c) The realization convention

The realization convention is also closely related to the cost convention, for as the recorded value of an asset to the firm is determined by the transaction which was necessary to acquire it, so any change in its value may only be recognized at the moment the firm realizes or disposes of that asset. The realization convention reflects totally the historical origin of accounting as a method for recording the results of transactions. To an accountant there is no certainty of income until a sale has been made: hence, increases in value which have not been realized are not recorded.

The realization convention is strongly criticized by economists. They argue that if an asset has increased in value then it is irrelevant that it has not been sold. For economists, it is sufficient that the gain in value could be realized for that gain to be recognized. The realization convention, it is true, may lead to absurd conclusions.

Example

William James and George Lloyd have bought a pair of dilapidated cottages in Gwynedd for £5000. They spend £2000 on restoring the cottages, so that their total cost amounts to £7000. Both cottages are identical and form part of one unit, that is, they are semi-detached. The cottages were bought as part of a speculative venture to make profit out of the popularity of Welsh cottages as holiday homes. A businessman from Manchester offers to buy both cottages for £10,000 each, but the partners decide to sell only one of the cottages and to retain the other for sale at a higher price in the future.

From an accounting point of view, the cottage which is sold is recognized as being worth £10,000, and the difference of £6500 between the accounting cost and the sale price is the realized income. The second cottage, which could also have been sold for £10,000 to the same man, is recorded as being worth only £3500—being the costs associated with acquiring and restoring it.

Unrealized gains in value are widely recognized by non-accountants. Bankers, who are perhaps the most cautious of men, are prepared to lend money on unrealized values: businessmen reckon as income increases in the value of assets even though they are unsold—yet accountants will not do so unless and until a contract of sale has taken place which creates a legal right to receive the agreed value of the asset sold.

As a result of the realization convention, two classes of gains may be distinguished—'holding gains' which are increases in value resulting from holding an asset, and 'trading or operating gains' which are gains realized as a result of selling assets. 'Holding gains' are not recorded, but 'operating gains' are reported. The realization convention means, in effect, that the reported income of a business is a part only of the total increases in value which accrue to a firm during an accounting period.

The realization convention does not require the accountant to await the receipt of cash before recording a transaction. Indeed, in many cases the delivery of goods and the receipt of cash occur after the legal agreement which determines the timing of the transaction.

Example

On the 1st January, 19X0, Midlands Motor Engineers receive an order from one of their accredited dealers for five tractor engines each costing £400. The engines are despatched on the 10th January, and on the 5th February, a cheque for £2000 is received in payment.

From a legal point of view, the acceptance of the order on the 1st January marks the timing of the sale, and the creation of the contractual obligation to deliver the engines as well as the contractual right to receive payment. Accounting follows the law in this respect, and it is common practice to write to confirm the receipt of an order and its acceptance, so as to leave no doubt as to the legal and accounting position.

On occasions, however, when a contract is for work which cannot be completed for a long period of time, the contract may stipulate when rights to payment arise. This is particularly the case as regards large civil engineering contracts, shipbuilding contracts, and large Government contracts. In these situations, accounting practices once more follow the law, and the timing of the right to receive cash is determined by the contract.

Example

Westlands Civil Engineering Co. Ltd, is awarded a Government contract for the building of a 50-mile section of a motorway. The work is required to be completed in three years. Payments are to be made by the Government on the basis of the work completed in each three monthly period. It is agreed that an independent firm of quantity surveyors will certify the volume of work completed in each period, and that these certificates will form the basis for calculating the period payments to the company on the 'percentage-of-completion' method.

In accordance with this contract, the timing of the realizations will depend upon the issue of the certificates by the quantity surveyors.

(d) The accrual convention

The realization convention which asserts that gains in value may not be recognized until the occurrence of a transaction is reinforced by the accrual convention, which applies equally to revenues and expenses.

The accrual convention makes the distinction between the receipt of cash and the right to receive cash, and the payment of cash and the legal obligation to pay cash, for in accounting practice there is usually no exact coincidence in time between cash movements and the legal obligations to which they relate.

Let us examine, firstly, the manner in which the accrual convention applies to revenues. Revenue may be defined as the right to receive cash, and accountants are concerned with recording these rights. Cash receipts may occur instantaneously and also as follows:

(a) before a right to receive arises;
(b) after the right to receive has been created;
(c) cash may be received in error.

The accrual convention provides a guideline to the accountant as to how to treat these cash receipts and the rights related thereto.

Example

Mrs Smith is an old lady who occupies a flat owned by Mereworth Properties Ltd. The rent is payable monthly in advance on the 1st day of each month, and amounts to £25 a month. She is very forgetful, and rarely does a month pass without some complication in the payment of her rent.

On the 1st January, she sends her cheque for £25 in respect of the rent due for January. This rent is due and payable to the company, and must be included in its revenue for that month. On the 10th January, Mrs Smith sends another cheque for £25, thinking that she had not paid her rent for January. This is a cash receipt to which the company is not presently entitled, and it must either be returned to Mrs Smith, or it may be kept on her behalf as a payment in advance of her February rent—but only if she agrees. The accountant returns her cheque saying that she has already paid her rent for January, and she receives this letter on the 20th January. She forgets to pay her rent on the 1st February. The accountant is obliged to include the rent due in February in the revenue for that month, even though it is only ultimately paid on the 15th March. Until Mrs Smith has paid her rent for February, she will be a debtor of the company for the rent owing.

Similar rules apply to the treatment of expenses incurred by the firm. Expenses may be defined as legal obligations incurred by the firm to pay in money or money's worth for the benefit of goods or services which it has received. Cash payments may occur instantaneously and as follows:

(a) before they are due for payment;
(b) after due date for payment;
(c) cash may be paid in error.

The accrual convention requires the accountant to treat as expenses only those sums which are due and payable. If a payment is made in advance, it must not be treated as an expense, and the recipient is a debtor until his right to receive the cash matures. Cash paid in error is never an expense, and until it is recovered the person to whom it was paid is also a debtor. Where an expense had been incurred, however, and no payment has been made, the expense must be recorded, and the person to whom the payment should have been made is shown as a creditor.

We shall see in chapter 6 the importance of the accrual convention as regard record-keeping and the presentation of financial accounting statements.

(e) The matching convention

One of the important purposes of financial accounting is to calculate income resulting from transactions. This means identifying the gains resulting from transactions and setting off against those gains the expenses which are related to those transactions. The realization convention identifies the timing of gains, and the accrual convention enables the accountant properly to record revenues and expenses: neither, however, helps the accountant to calculate income. The matching convention links revenues with their relevant expenses.

Example

On the 1st April, Cash and Carry Ltd, purchase for resale 2000 tins of beans at a cost of 5p a tin. The selling price is 8p a tin. During the month of April, 1000 tins are sold. What is the profit for the month which is attributable to this line of goods?

We know that the expenses are $2000 \times 5p = £100$, and that the revenues are $1000 \times 8p = £80$. On the face of it, therefore, Cash and Carry Ltd have made a loss of £100 less £80, that is, £20. This conclusion is nonsense, because we are setting off against the sale proceeds of 1000 tins the cost of acquiring 2000 tins.

In accordance with the matching convention, the accountant establishes the income for the month of April by calculating the cost of purchasing 1000 tins of beans and setting this expense against the revenue realized from the sale of these tins:

Sales revenue	1000 tins @ 8p = £80
Cost of sales	1000 tins @ 5p = £50
Income from Sales	£30

The 1000 tins remaining unsold remain in the accounting records as assets, and when they are eventually sold the income from sales will be calculated by deducting the cost of acquisition against the sales revenue which are realized.

The matching of revenues and expenses is very often a most difficult problem in accounting, and many types of expenses are not easily identifiable with revenues.

Example

Bloxwich Pharmaceutical Co. Ltd, manufactures and sells pharmaceutical products. Its major activity is the manufacture of antibiotics, which accounts for 80% of its sales revenue. The remaining 20% of its sales is derived from beauty creams. Its expenses for the year 19X0 are as follows:

Manufacturing costs of antibiotics	£500,000
Manufacturing costs of beauty creams	20,000
Administrative costs	100,000
Selling and financial costs	50,000
Research and development costs	150,000
Total expenses for the year	£820,000

In the same year, the total revenue from sales of both antibiotics and beauty creams amounts to £1,000,000. Calculate the income on the antibiotic side of the business.

We can begin to answer this problem as follows:

Sales revenue from antibiotics (80% of total)	£800,000
Manufacturing costs of antibiotics	500,000
	300,000
Other expenses	?
Income in respect of antibiotics	?

Clearly, we should need to have more information in order to allocate the administrative, selling and financial costs as between the antibiotics and the beauty creams. It is unlikely that an exact allocation could be made, and in the end, an estimate would be made.

As regards the research and development costs, which are concerned with developing new antibiotics and beauty creams, there is an even more difficult problem. Strictly speaking, we should not set these costs against the revenues of the year, since the benefits of this expenditure will not occur in this year. Much of this expenditure, however, may not lead to new products. Therefore, if we ignore this expenditure, the company's reported income will be inflated and unrealistic.

From the foregong example, it is seen that the exact matching of revenues and expenses will often be impossible. Accountants do try, however, to make estimates of appropriate expenses so as to produce income figures which are sufficiently reliable as a guide to the firm's financial performance.

(f) *The convention of periodicity*

It may safely be assumed that the custom of making periodic reports to the owner of a business dates from the time when wealthy men employed servants to manage and oversee their affairs. Periodic accounting has its origin in the idea of control, therefore, and company law to this day sees the role of financial accounting reports as being essentially the communication of financial information from the managers of the business, that is the Directors, to the owners of the business, that is the Shareholders. However much as we may disagree with this view of the relationship of Directors and Shareholders as being unrealistic, we must accept that there is an element of shareholder control over company directors which stems from the legal duty laid on the latter to issue financial reports on their stewardship of the firm's assets.

The convention of periodicity is now established by law as regards certain types of reports such as Balance Sheets and Profit and Loss Accounts. The Companies Act requires yearly reports to shareholders, and the Income Tax Acts require accounts for all businesses to be submitted yearly. There is no reason, however, to prevent companies, if they so wish, to provide financial information at more frequent intervals to investors.

The idea of making yearly reports has grown out of custom, and many would question the wisdom of selecting an arbitrary period of 12 months as a basis for reporting upon the activities of a business. The idea of yearly reporting is strongly entrenched, and even the Government runs its business on a yearly basis and budgets for one year, although many of its activities are continuing ones which cannot be seen correctly in the perspective of 12 months. This is equally true for all large companies, and many smaller businesses.

Example

Universal Chemicals Ltd manufactures a wide range of chemical products and has factories throughout the country. Owing to unusually difficult labour relations, Government control on prices, rising raw material costs and stiffening competition, its reported income for the year ended 31st December, 19X0 has decreased by 10% over the previous year. Its borrowings, however, have increased by 20% due to an enlarged capital investment programme which is designed to add substantially to income in about five years' time.

Clearly, in this case the reader of the report for the year 19X0 should consider the report in its proper context, and look to the long-term trend of income and to the better financial position which is expected in the future.

The convention of periodicity as expressed in yearly accounting fails to make the important distinction between the long-term trend and the short-term position. Hence, it places limits on the usefulness of the information communicated to shareholders and investors.

Together with the matching convention, the convention of periodicity seeks to relate all the transactions of one particular year with the expenses attributable to those transactions. From a practical point of view, accountants are compelled to carry forward expenses until they can be identified with the revenues of a particular year, and to carry forward receipts until they can be regarded as the revenues of a particular year in accordance with the realization convention. Since all assets are 'costs' in accounting, the convention of periodicity creates difficulties for accountants as regards the allocation of fixed assets as the expenses of particular years. We shall examine this problem when we come to discuss depreciation in chapter 5 (see p. 127).

So far we have mentioned the effect of the convention of periodicity on the usefulness of the information communicated to external users, but we should say a word about its effect on income measurement. The majority of economists treat accounting income as the 'income' of a business, and hence as a measure of the income which investors and shareholders derive from their investment in the firm. As a result, they impose the economic criteria appropriate to the measurement of economic income to accounting income and are very dissatisfied with shortcomings of accounting income which they see as stemming from accounting conventions for calculating periodic income. Ideally, of course, an accurate measurement of the income or loss of a business can only be made after the business has ceased operating, sold off all its assets and paid off all its liabilities. The net income accruing to investors would then be the difference between the sum total of all their receipts, either as dividends or capital repayments, and their initial investment. It is clear, however, that accounting income is merely the result of completed transactions during a stated period: the convention of periodicity is a statement of this view. We shall discuss the nature of business income in Part 4.

(g) *The convention of consistency*

The usefulness of financial accounting information lies to a considerable extent in the conclusions which may be drawn from the comparison of the financial statements of one year with that of a preceding year, and the financial reports of one company with those of another company. It is in this way that we may deduce some of the most important information for decision-making, such as an indication that there has been an improvement in income since last year and that therefore it is worth buying more shares, or the income of Company A is better than those of Company B and given current shares prices one should switch from holding shares in Company B and buy those of Company A.

The comparability of financial statements depends largely upon the choice of accounting methods and the consistency with which they are applied. A change in the basis on which a firm values inventory, for example, may result in an income figure different from that which would have been computed had the accountant adhered to a consistent basis of valuation. If firms wish to change their method for treating a particular problem, such as the valuation of inventory or the value attached to a particular asset, they may do so, but they should mention the effect on the reported income of the change in accounting methods.

Comparing the accounts of different companies is altogether more difficult, and unfortunately the accounting methods of individual firms are not the same. There is no uniformity of accounting method which would provide the consistency of treatment of information necessary for the comparison of the accounts of different companies. Whereas the accounting convention of consistency is generally followed by individual firms, there is no agreement at all that different firms should use the same accounting methods. Hence, the needs of investors for greater comparability of information between companies is frustrated by accounting conventions which insist on the one hand on consistency, but allow on the other hand different methods of measurement and treatment which cannot yield comparable results. The Accounting Standards Steering Committee is charged with the task of trying to secure agreement on appropriate accounting methods which will ensure a higher degree of comparability of accounting information, and we shall examine some of its achievements so far in Part 4. It is clear that European integration will hasten progress towards uniformity in accounting standards.

(h) *The convention of conservatism*
The convention of conservatism reflects the accountant's view of his social role and his responsibilities towards those for whom he provides information. It is seen at work in some of the conventions which we have examined in this chapter, for example, the realization convention which requires the realization of a gain before it may be recognized, and the cost convention which holds that the value of an asset is the cost of acquisition.

There are two principle rules which stem directly from the convention of conservatism:

(1) the accountant should not anticipate income and should provide for all possible losses;
(2) faced with a choice between two methods of valuing an asset, the accountant should choose the method which leads to the lesser value.

These two rules contravene some of the conventions of accounting, for example, the cost convention, for if the market value of trading inventory has fallen below the cost of acquisition it must be valued at the market value. Equally, the logic which underlies the realization convention as regards gains, that is, that there is no certainty of receiving a gain until there is a sale, does not extend to the treatment of anticipated losses. Thus, accountants are willing to accrue losses in value which are sufficiently foreseeable to make them a present reality, and in the accountant's mind to ignore such losses might mislead the user of accounting information. The policy of conservatism has been explained by G. O. May, as follows:

'.. the great majority of ventures fail, and the fact that enterprises nevertheless continue is attributable to the incurable optimism (often dissociated from experience) as well as to the courage of mankind. In my experience, also, losses from unsound accounting have most commonly resulted from the hopes rather than the achievements of management being allowed to influence accounting dispositions. To me, conservatism is still the first virtue of accounting, and I am wholly unable to agree with those who would bar it from the books of accounts and statements prepared therefrom and would relegate it to footnotes' (May, 1946).

The caution of the accountant may well be a foil for the optimism of businessmen, but although it may be highly desirable for the accountant to be conservative in the estimates which he makes, the selection of accounting methods for recording and presenting information on the basis that they understate assets or earnings should not be an overriding principle. Investors and shareholders need reliable and useful information: to understate is as bad as to overstate—investment in a business may be discouraged if it appears to be less valuable than it really is. Users of accounting information, as all others who are faced with making decisions, look for guidance on the lowest value, the highest value and the probable value. In restricting accounting information to the statement of the lowest value, the accountant is prevented from fulfilling the social role expected of him as a supplier of comprehensive financial information.

The convention of conservatism has also frustrated the evolution of accounting methods which are more appropriate to modern needs. One of the most outspoken critics of this convention has called it 'the most objectionable and obstructive tradition in accounting' because 'any proposal seeking to broaden the horizons of accounting is effectively squashed if excuse be found for referring to its nonconservatism'. (Paton, 1965).

Summary

The conventions of accounting serve as guide-posts, but they do tend to emphasize the reliability of information rather than its usefulness. The conflict between reliability and usefulness has caused controversy in accounting. At one extreme, there are accountants who contend that if a measurement is useful, further justification is unnecessary. At the other extreme, others hold that the reliability of accounting information is the most important criterion, and will ultimately determine the extent to which external users will accept accounting statements for the purpose of making investment decisions.

The effect of accounting conventions on financial reporting may be criticized for three reasons:

(a) They prevent change, for the fact that conventions have to be generally agreed prevents new conventions being adopted. Thus, the Accounting Principles Board of the American Institute of Certified Public Accountants rejected a recommendation for a new development with the words '. . . while these studies are a valuable contribution to accounting studies they are too radically different from present generally accepted accounting principles for acceptance at this time' (Sprouse & Moonitz, 1963).

(b) Generally accepted practice does not necessarily provide the most useful information for decision-making, because 'general acceptance suggests a rut. What is done is not necessarily right just because it is done' (Cowan, 1965).

(c) Accounting conventions do not create uniformity. A classic example of this point is the large number of methods permitted for the valuation of inventory, which is an important influence in the measurement of income. One authority has calculated that there are 108 methods of valuing inventory, each of which is likely to produce a different income figure (Chambers, 1965).

The effect of generally accepted accounting conventions on external financial reports is to create a degree of diversity which is at variance with the objective of efficient resource allocation. In this connection, and by way of conclusion, one commentator has suggested that accounting is an art form, and that two firms of accountants looking at the same figures are quite capable of turning up income figures as far apart as a Rubens is from a Rembrant (Bambridge, 1969).

References

1. Bambridge, A., in *The Observer* 19th October, 1969.

2. Chambers, R. J., Financial Information and the Securities Market, *Abacus*, September, 1965.

3. Cowan, T. K., A Resource Theory of Accounting, *Accounting Review*, January, 1965.

4. Marshall, Alfred, *Principles of Economics*, Macmillan, London, 1964, 8th edn.

5. May, G. O., *Financial Accounting: A Distillation of Experience*, Macmillan, New York, 1946.

6. Sprouse, R. T. & Moonitz, M., Comments on 'A Tentative Set of Broad Principles for Business Enterprise, *Journal of Accountancy*, April, 1963.

7. Paton, W. A., Accounting Procedures and Private Enterprises, in *"Significant Accounting Essays"* Moonitz, M. & Littleton, A. C. (eds), Prentice Hall, Englewood Cliffs, N.J., 1965.

2
The Generation of Financial Accounting Data

In the previous chapter, we examined the nature and the boundaries of the financial accounting system. We noted that the conventions of financial accounting constituted one of the boundaries insofar as they act as a filtering process for the data which is fed into the financial accounting system. We concluded that these conventions played a crucial role in determining the nature of financial accounting information.

The purpose of this chapter is to examine the processes involved in the generation of financial accounting data prior to its transformation into financial accounting information.

An outline of the information generation process

The generation of financial accounting information is the result of a process involving the following stages:

(a) the preparation of source documents;
(b) the entry of basic data into subsidiary records;
(c) the posting of data from the subsidiary records into the Ledger, which is the formal record of data.

The production of financial accounting information in the form of financial reports may be illustrated as in Fig. 2.3.

Although the principles underlying the financial accounting system have remained unchanged, its processes have undergone and are still undergoing modification and improvement. In particular, technological change has dramatically affected these processes. The advent of electronic data processing (EDP) has considerably speeded up and streamlined the data recording process, and indeed, as we shall see, has permitted the integration of several stages of this process into one single operation.

In this chapter, we shall be concerned with an analysis of the traditional data recording practices relating to source documents and subsidiary books, and we shall examine the impact of recent changes

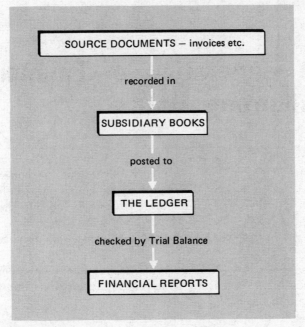

Fig. 2.3

on these practices. We shall examine the process of preparing financial reports in subsequent chapters.

Source documents

As we explained in chapter 1, financial accounting data originates in financial transactions. Source documents are designed to capture the details of these accounting events. Source documents also have a very important functional purpose as regards the activities of an enterprise.

Data flows generated within a business may be classified according to their sources. (i) Financial accounting data flows are generated from activities conducted between the firm and external groups such as customers and suppliers of materials, goods, services and finance. (ii) Data flows generated for the internal purposes of the business constitute a substantial volume of the total information flows. These flows are generated and channelled through a Management Information System (MIS) whose function it is to meet the information needs of management for the purposes of management planning and control. Since the firm is an open system, it is clear that the initial impetus for any activity stems from some agent in the firm's environment. The relationship between external and internal data flows and the complexity of

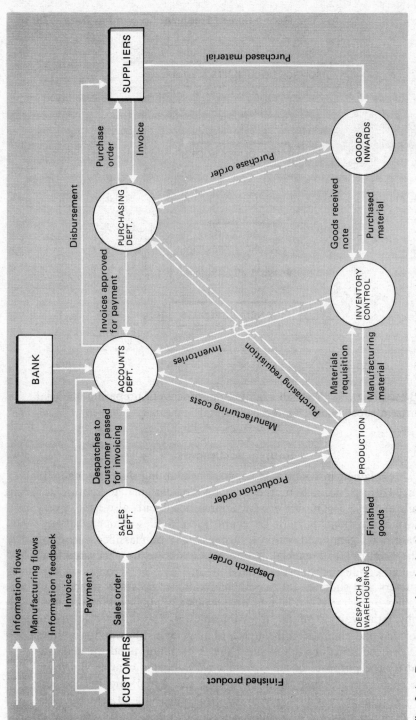

Fig. 2.4 Data sources for the basic business operations of a manufacturing firm. (Adapted from Thierauf, R. F., *Data Processing for Business Management*, John Wiley & Sons, New York, 1973).

the documentation involved in facilitating these flows are illustrated in Fig. 2.4 opposite. Figure 2.4 shows the focal role played by accounting data in relation to the firm's basic operations as well as the nature of the source documents involved in the generation of financial accounting data.

Source documents related to sales

The function of the Sales Department is to encourage the sales of the firm's products. Once a salesman has concluded a sale with a customer, he completes a Sales Order Form. The original copy is sent to the customer as an acknowledgement of the order, and in the case of a credit sale, one copy of the Sales Order Form goes to the Credit Control Department for approval. If the goods are already held in stock, the Credit Control Department will pass the authenticated Sales Order Form to the Inventory Control Department so that the release and despatch of the goods may be effected. An Advice Note is sent to the customer as soon as the goods are despatched advising him of the date of despatch and the mode of transport used. The goods themselves are normally accompanied by a Delivery Note stating the description of the goods and the quantity involved though not the price. The customer acknowledges receipt of the goods by signing the Delivery Note.

Once the goods have been released by the Inventory Control Department for despatch, a further copy of the Sales Order Form stating the date of despatch is sent to the Invoice Section of the Accounts Department, so that the Sales Invoice may be prepared. The Sales Invoice states the nature, quantity and price of the goods ordered and the amount due to the firm from the customer. Customers are normally required to pay within one to three months, depending on the agreed credit terms. Often, however, customers are required to pay on receipt of the invoice, though some firms issue Statements each month showing the number of invoices sent to the customer during the month and the total sum due in respect of the month's orders.

The Sales Invoice is the source document which provides the financial accounting data which will subsequently be recorded in the financial accounting system.

The Sales Order Form is used, therefore, for the following purposes:

(a) As a record and confirmation of a sale. One copy of the Sales Order Form will be kept by the Sales Department.

(b) As a means of initiating a procedure for checking the creditworthiness of a customer prior to proceeding with the completion of the order.

   (c) As a document authorizing the release of the goods from stocks. One copy of the Sales Order will be retained by the Inventory Control Department.

   (d) As a means of checking and despatching the right goods to the right customer by the Despatch Department. One copy of the Sales Order will be kept by this department for this purpose.

   (e) As a means of preparing the Sales Invoice which will state the amount due from the customer. One copy of the Sales Order will be kept by the Accounts Department.

Where goods are not kept in inventory but are manufactured to order, the receipt of an order puts the production process in motion. We examine the Cost Accounting process in Part 3, but for the purposes of this chapter, we may note that a copy of the Production Order will be sent to the Production Manager and one copy to the Accounts Department, which is responsible for collecting all the costs associated with the manufacture of the goods ordered. Figure 2.4 shows that the materials required may be obtained either from existing stocks or by purchase. Where the required materials are held in stock, the issue of a Materials Requisition Form to the Inventory Control Department will procure the release of these materials. One copy of the Materials Requisition Form will be retained by the Inventory Control Department and one copy will be sent to the Accounts Department for costing purposes. Where the required materials have to be purchased, the Production Department will issue a Purchase Requisition Form to the Purchasing Department for the required materials.

Source documents related to purchases

The Purchasing Department is concerned with procuring the raw materials, equipment and supplies needed by the firm. Each request must be made by means of a Requisition Form stating the nature and the quantity required and bearing the signature of the manager having authority to requisition purchases. The Purchasing Department selects a suitable supplier and sends him a Purchase Order Form setting out the description, quantity and required delivery date of the goods, together with instructions as regards despatch and invoicing. The Purchase Order Form will refer to the quoted price of the goods according to the suppliers' catalogue or other statements of the supply price, although quoted prices contained in advertisements for sale are not binding in law on suppliers. In effect, the Purchase Order Form is an Offer to Purchase and once accepted by the supplier constitutes a legal contract between buyer and seller. Copies of the Purchase Order are distributed to the several departments which will be concerned with it, that is, the Receiving Department which will need to know the details and the date of receipt of the order, the Inventory Control Department to advise of the pending arrival of goods and to serve as a check on the Receiving Department, the Accounts Department for checking that the price quoted compares with the price list, and the ordering department, to confirm that the order has been placed.

Source documents related to the receipt of goods

Upon delivery of the goods, the Receiving Department verifies that the goods delivered compare in every detail with its copy of the Purchase Order. Once the Delivery Note is agreed, a Goods Received Note is prepared which details the description of the goods received, their quantity, quality and condition. A copy of the Goods Received Note is sent to the department concerned with the audit of the receipt of goods, which is usually the Purchasing Department. A copy of the Goods Received Note is also sent to the Accounts Department, and the department responsible for the order. The Inventory Control Department is notified of the receipt of the goods as well, since it is responsible for the storage, distribution and control of inventories. The Inventory Control Department keeps records of inventories, and ensures that adequate inventory levels are maintained. As we shall see in Part 3, inventory management relies upon the determination of reorder points in relation to inventory flows and economic order quantities.

In due course, the supplier will send an invoice stating the description, quantity and price of the goods ordered, the date of acceptance of the order, which is usually shown as the date of despatch of the goods, and the amount now owing. The invoice is checked by the Accounts Department against the Goods Received Note, and if there are no queries, the invoice is cleared for payment in due course. Normally, invoices are paid monthly. This permits the workflow in the Accounting Department to be efficiently organized and allows the payment procedure to be properly supervised.

The entry of basic data in the subsidiary books

The accounting record of the events described in the source documents which we have just examined begins with the issue or receipts of invoices. Although legal obligations are created with the acceptance of an order, either by the firm or its suppliers, for practical reasons, accountants do not record these obligations until they are formally stated. Should there be any dispute, however, about the existence of an order, the appropriate source document would provide legal evidence of that order.

The practice of keeping daily records of accounting events in a diary or roughbook dates from the early history of accounting. The practice of keeping a daily journal was recommended by Paciolo in 1494 for the purpose of enabling the businessman to check daily the records kept by his clerk. Once agreed, they could be entered into the Ledger. It became a golden rule in accounting that no entry should appear in the Ledger which has not already passed through the Journal.

At first, the Journal was used to record all commercial transactions. It was entered chronologically and showed the details of these transactions as well as the Ledger Account to which the entry was ultimately posted, as follows:

Date	Journal Description	Folio	(Dr.) £	(Cr.) £
Jan. 5th	Goods Dr. To A. Smith Being 100 shirts bought for resale	L5 L7	100	100
Jan. 5th	B. Jones Dr. To Cash Being wages due to the week ending 5th January	L10	5	5

The basic data entered in the Journal consisted of:

    (a) the date of the transaction
    (b) the name of the purchaser or the asset purchased
    (c) the name of the seller or the asset sold
    (d) the sum involved
    (e) a short narrative describing the transaction.

Periodically, the entries in the Journal were transferred to the main record, described as the Ledger, by a procedure known as posting. The folio references in the Journal indicated the pages in the Ledger to which the postings were made.

As trade expanded and the number of transactions to be entered in the Journal multiplied, it became the practice to group the entries to be made in the Journal into the following classes:

    (a) purchases of trading goods on credit terms
    (b) sales of trading goods on credit terms
    (c) cash payments and receipts
    (d) all other transactions.

This classification not only enabled entries of like nature to be kept together, but facilitated the operation of entering basic data into the books of subsidiary records. It led to the division of the Journal into four parts, which were renamed as follows:

(a) the Purchases Day Book, in which were entered credit purchases;
(b) the Sales Day Book, in which were entered credit sales;
(c) the Cash Book in which were recorded all cash transactions;
(d) the Journal in which were recorded transactions which could not be recorded in the other subsidiary books. To this day, the Journal has retained its particular use as a book of original entry for such transactions.

The Day Books

Since the greatest bulk of source documents relate to the purchase or sale of goods, the function of the Purchases and Sales Day Books is to allow such data to be collected and transferred in a summarized form to the Ledger. Hence, their purpose is to keep the Ledger relatively free from unnecessary data. An example of a Purchases Day Book is given below:

Purchases Day Book

Date	Name	Invoice No.	Folio	£
June 1st	S. Smith	101	L15	50
2nd	W. Wright and Co.	113	L20	35
2nd	J. James	148	L10	140
3rd	T. Tennant	184	L16	20
3rd	Transferred to Purchases Account		L50	245

The posting of the Purchases Day Book to the Ledger is effected by transferring to the account of each supplier the value of the goods supplied in the period, and transferring the total value of all purchases in the period to the Purchases account. The details entered in the Day Books are obtained from the invoices, which are carefully filed and kept for a period of about six years when they may be destroyed.

The Sales Day Book is entered in the same manner as the Purchases Day Book, except that the source document is the duplicate copy of the invoice sent to the customer.

The Cash Book

Only cash transactions are entered in the Cash Book, whose purpose it is to record all payments and receipts of cash. As we shall see later, the Cash Book has a dual role, for in addition to being a book of original entry, it is also part of the Ledger.

As the practice grew of using cheques for the settlement of business debts, so the Cash Book came to reflect this practice, and to record all payments out and into the firm's bank account.

Unlike the Day Books, the Cash Book records receipts and payments side by side, so that concurrent flows in and out are seen together and their impact on the bank balance may be readily seen. At the end of the accounting period, the Cash Book is reconciled with the bank statement by means of a Bank Reconciliation Statement which explains any difference between the balance recorded in the Cash Book and that recorded by the bank. This difference is invariably due to the time lag between the posting of a cheque to a creditor and its clearing through the bank, delays in clearing cheques paid in, bank charges and direct payments into and by the bank.

Where transactions take place in cash as well as by cheques, and trade discounts are given and allowed, the Cash Book is given extra columns, and becomes known as a 'three column Cash Book'. The transfers of cash in and out of the bank account is recorded as well as the receipt and payments by cheques, as follows:

Cash Book

Date	Details	Folio	Dis counts All'd £	Cash £	Bank £	Date	Details	Folio	Dis counts Rec'd £	Cash £	Bank £
Jan. 1	Balance	J1		50	800	Jan. 1	B. Brown	L3	7		103
1	Sales	L15		60		1	Purchases	L14		20	
1	W. White	L9	5		95	1	Cash				20
1	Bank			20							

The explanation of some of these entries is as follows:

Jan. 1st B. Brown—this represents the payment of an account owing to Brown amounting to £110 which was settled by the payment of £103, the balance being in the form of a discount which was received.

Jan. 1 st W. White—this represents the receipt of a cheque for £95 in settlement of an amount owing of £100, a discount of £5 being allowed.

Jan. 1st Bank—this represents a cash cheque drawn on the bank for £20. The corresponding payment of cash by the bank is shown on the other side of the Cash Book.

For security reasons, few firms like to keep large sums in cash about their premises and cash takings are banked daily. Moreover, it is sound practice to use cheques for the settlement of debts, so that there is generally no need to keep cash on hand beyond relatively small sums. All firms, therefore, tend to have a Petty cash box to meet any immediate need for cash, for example, enabling a secretary or porter to take a taxi to deliver a document, or to buy a small article which is urgently required.

The Cashier is usually entrusted with the Petty cash box and any payments must be claimed by means of a Petty Cash Voucher signed by an authorized person, who is usually a head of department. The Cashier is given a Petty cash float which may be say £50 and pays out petty cash only against petty cash vouchers, which he retains. As the petty cash float decreases, so petty cash vouchers of an equivalent value accumulate in the Petty cash box. In due course, the vouchers are checked or audited and the petty cash paid out is refunded to the Cashier, thereby restoring the Petty cash float to its original sum.

The development of data processing systems

Although the system of source documents remains today much as we have described, two important developments have changed the nature of the system of recording financial transactions. The first of these developments is attributable to the mechanization of the record-keeping process, which began gradually with the use of early-generation calculating machines and progressed to the evolution of accounting machines capable of several operations simultaneously, and eventually to increasingly sophisticated electronic data processing systems based on computers. The second of these developments is attributable to the wish to integrate the data generating activities of the various departments of an organization within the scope of formalized management information systems. The availability of computers after the Second World War made such an integration possible, and as a result, a new science emerged which was concerned with the application of computerized information and control systems to the manifold problems of business organizations.

These twin developments acted jointly to produce a number of significant effects. Firstly, they greatly extended the utility of data by its dispersion through the organization, and at the same time, they reduced the duplication of data generation taking place in different departments. Secondly, the efficiency of the data generation process was increased by a progressive reduction in the stages involved, and the increase in the speed with which their operations could be performed. Thirdly, not only did these developments encourage a greater flexibility in the availability and utility of data, but they led to a massive expansion in the data coverage.

The recent history of data processing systems has emphasized the inter-dependency of all sectors of organizational activity, and the inter-dependency of their information needs. For this reason, the term 'integrated data processing' came into vogue in the 1950s to symbolize the nature of modern data systems.

The 'write-it-once' principle

The first development to which we referred is based, conceptually at least, on the 'write-it-once' principle, that is, the simultaneous production of source document and the streamlining of the recording process. Hence, although the source documents which we mentioned earlier remain in common usage, they are no longer always prepared in the step-by-step manner which we described, being either prepared simultaneously or duplicated automatically.

The write-it-once principle is evident in the progressive stages in the development of data processing methods. Three examples of these developments are as follows:

(a) The development of multi-copy stationery involving the use of 'sets' of forms which may be separated once completed. An invoicing set would consist of a top copy, which would be the invoice itself, and beneath would be found the other source documents, that is, a copy of the invoice for accounting records, an advice note, a request to Inventory Control to release the goods for despatch, and a packaging label. These 'flimsy' copies may be distinguished by a system of different colours.

(b) The simultaneous posting of data by means of 'writing boards' to which several records may be pegged and posted in one operation. Thus, once the Sales Invoice has been completed, the details may be posted immediately by pegging on the writing board the customer's monthly statement, his Ledger Account and the Sales Day Book. These sheets are interleaved with carbon paper. The Statement is then returned to the customer's file until further invoices need to be entered, and at the end of the month, it is sent to the customer. The Ledger Account is returned to the permanent file, and the Sales Day Book may remain pegged so that invoices to other customers may be posted. Several writing boards may be in use at the same time. The advantages of this system are that the chances of posting errors are minimized with the reduction in stages in posting data, and documents such as Statements are ready for despatch at the end of each month and do not require further attention, save actual mailing.

(c) The use of 'ledgerless book-keeping' involves the elimination of the traditional posting process mentioned above, thus streamlining the process. Consider for example the Sales Day Book, which is simply an analysis of copy invoices. Its main purpose is to provide a total for posting to the Ledger. It is possible to simplify and streamline the posting process simply by dispensing with the Sales Day Book and rely on the copy invoices, which may be filed in specially made cabinets after they have been recorded in the Ledger.

The process of ledgerless book-keeping may be extended further to provide for a degree of rationalization in the Ledger itself. The Debtors' Ledger, for example, containing all the individual debtors' accounts may also be dispensed with by placing reliance on the record of transactions contained in copy sales invoices. These copy invoices may be filed in an 'unpaid invoices' cabinet. On receipt of payment, the invoice is removed from the 'unpaid invoices' cabinet, a remittance slip is made out, the payment is recorded directly in the Cash Book and the remittance slip is attached to the invoice which is subsequently filed in the 'paid invoices' cabinet.

According to Bower *et al.* (1970), "a ledgerless bookkeeping system is one in which communication media are filed as records rather than being used as source documents from which to post to ledger accounts and other records.... Ledgerless bookkeeping applied to accounts receivable requires that at the time a Sales invoice is prepared, an adequate number of copies of the invoice are made, including at least one accounts receivable copy. The accounts receivable copy is sent to the Accounts Receivable Section where it is filed by customer name. At any given time, the unpaid invoices in the customer file can be totalled to determine the amount which customers owe to the company. When cash is received, the invoice is withdrawn and stamped paid, after which it is filed in a paid invoice file.... There is no more economical system than ledgerless bookkeeping. It is simple and can be effective".

The mechanization of accounting

Clearly, the write-it-once principle made it possible for the accounting process to be mechanized. The first stage in this process was the evolution of accounting machines. Secondly, there followed punched card data processing systems. Thirdly, electronic data processing was made possible by the development of sophisticated digital computers.

Month | Day | Despatch point | Invoice number | Product code | Quantity | Weight | Sales value | Standard cost | Sales area | Customer number | Salesman

ONC 508.

(a) Accounting Machines

In effect, accounting machines are a combination of a typewriter with an adding machine. Accounting machines were an improvement on the writing boards for instead of being handwritten, postings could be typed.

(b) Punched Card Data Systems

Punched card systems rely on the use of cards for recording data. Cards are punched according to a code, and once they have been checked, they may be resorted to almost endlessly for the preparation of records, analyses, reports and statements.

Three basic steps are involved:

   (i) punching the required data on to cards
   (ii) sorting the cards into a desired order
   (iii) tabulating the data recorded on the cards on to printed forms as required.

The most important element in punched card data systems is, of course, the punch card itself, of which an example is shown opposite. The cards may be punched manually by means of a punch. The equipment required consists of a sorter and a tabulator.

As may be seen from Fig. 2.5, it is required to establish a code for the data to be punched on the card. This requires that 'fields' be defined on the card for particular types of data, and that sufficient space be provided for recording the data appropriate to the defined fields. A Sales Card, for example, may be designed to capture data which relates to dates, despatch points, invoice numbers, product groups, weight, sales value, customer, salesman etc. Such cards may be sorted at any time into groups for the purpose of tabulating specific information, such as sales by regions, sales by salesman, product sales analysis etc.

It is evident that punched card data systems are capable of much greater flexibility than conventional accounting systems, which are limited to recording financial transactions. Nevertheless, all typical accounting records and reports may be prepared from punched cards, as may be noted from Fig. 2.6. As may be seen, the data recorded on a Sales Invoice may be punched on to cards, which are tabulated so that the data recorded on them may be entered in the Sales Day Book. Similarly, details of payments made by customers in respect of those Sales Invoices may be punched on other cards and the Cash Book may be completed from the basis of these cards. Both sets of cards may be merged by tabulation with the opening balances on each customer's account in the Ledger, so that monthly Statements may be prepared,

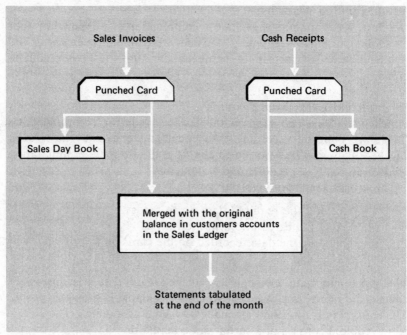

Fig. 2.6   Application of punched card systems to the record of sales.

the Ledger Account may be written up and the new balance on the account may be calculated.

(c) *Electronic Data Processing* (*EDP*)

The main advantages which digital computers enjoy over punched card data systems are as follows:

(i) Computers are much faster than punched card data systems.

(ii) Computers may store data and internalize the operations of data retrieval and analysis.

(iii) Computers may be programmed to make decisions automatically on the basis of the data input, and as we shall see in Part 3 this feature is most important as regards management planning and control.

The steps involved in developing a computer program are as follows:

(a) the problem must be stated in detail with reference to the stages in its solution;

(b) these stages are then stated in the form of a flowchart;

(c) the instruction is coded for the computer in accordance with the flowchart.

Example

Computers may be made to process sales orders relatively easily. Sales orders are fed into the computer, together with information from the Debtors Ledger and up-to-date information on stocks in hand. The computer is programmed to make decisions automatically on the credit status of individual customers and by reference to the inventory level of individual stock items, by the application of predetermined decision rules which are integrated in the program.

Firstly, the computer would decide whether the customer is credit-worthy. Credit limits are established in advance for each customer. The computer adds the value of the order to the balance outstanding on the customer's account in the Debtors' Ledger, and compares the total to the credit limit. If the credit limit has not been reached, the order is cleared for further processing.

Secondly, the computer adjusts the inventory records in respect of the order and calculates a new balance. It compares the new balance with the balance in stock which is required for each particular item. A 're-order point' will have been determined for each item of stock. If the inventory level falls below the re-order point, the computer writes a Purchase Requisition so as to replenish the stock to the designated level.

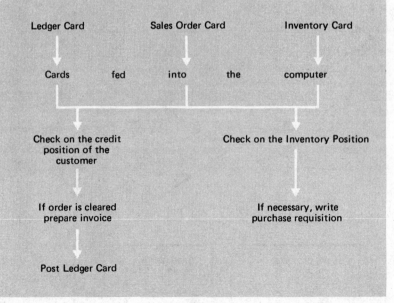

Fig. 2.7

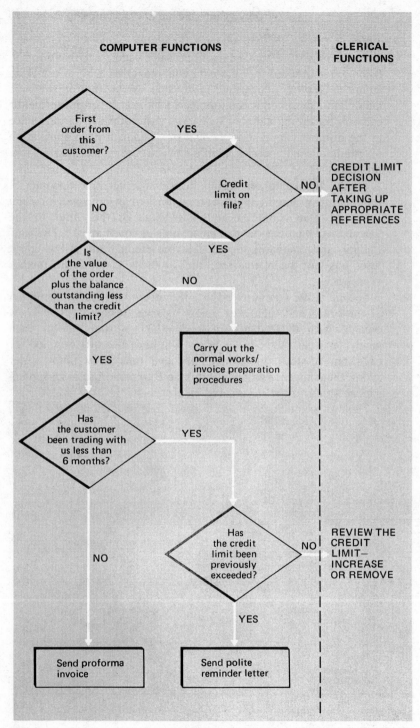

Fig. 2.8   Credit status test. (From Clifton, H. D. & Lucey, T., *Accounting and Computer Systems*, Business Books Ltd, London, 1973).

Thirdly, the computer performs other operations in connection with the order, such as preparing sales invoices and posting the Debtors' Ledger. Figure 2.7 illustrates the simplified procedure mentioned above.

Figure 2.8 explains in detail the manner in which a computer may be programmed to determine the credit status of a customer.

Summary

The generation of financial accounting information is a process involving the following stages:

(a) the generation of data through the preparation of source documents;
(b) the entry of basic data into subsidiary books;
(c) the posting of data from subsidiary books into the Ledger;
(d) the production of financial reports converting financial information data into financial information.

This chapter is concerned principally with stages (a) and (b) above.

Source documents reflect the activities conducted by the firm, so that data flows correspond to activity flows. Two important developments have changed the system of recording financial transactions. The first is the mechanization of the record-keeping process, which has led to increasingly sophisticated electronic data processing systems based on computers. The second is attributable to the integration of data generated by several department.

We examined these twin developments and their effects on the generation and recording of financial accounting data, and noted that, although there have been great advances in data processing methods, the principles underlying these methods have not changed. Indeed, the selection and measurement of data remains subject to the conventions discussed in chapter 1.

Reference

Bower, J. B, Schlosser, R. E. & Zlatkovich, C. T., *Financial Information Systems*, p. 374. Allyn & Bacon Inc. Boston, 1970.

Further readings

Clifton, H. D. & Lucey, T., *Accounting and Computer Systems*, Business Books, London, 1973.

Carruthers, W. M. & Weinwurm, E. H., *Business Information and Accounting Systems*, Charles E. Merrill Inc., New York, 1967.

Gillespie, C., *Accounting Systems*, Prentice Hall, Englewood Cliffs, N.J., 1971.

Heckert, J. B. & Kerrigan, H. D. *Accounting Systems,* Ronald Press Co., New York, 1967.

Sweeney, R. B., *The Use of Computers in Accounting,* Prentice Hall, Englewood Cliffs, N.J., 1971.

Thierauf, R. J., *Data Processing for Business and Management,* John Wiley and Sons, London and New York, 1973.

Macrae, S., *The New Book-Keeping,* Edward Arnold, London, 1965.

3
Data Processing and Double Entry Book-keeping

We saw in the preceding chapter that financial accounting data has its source in original records of financial transactions. We noted two very important aspects of the data generation in accounting. Firstly, in reporting to external users, accounting information is presented in a form which is only concerned with the monetary aspect of a firm's activities. Hence, they ignore data which deals with the type and quantities of resources which the firm utilizes, the nature and the quantity of its products, and the quality and usefulness of those products to society. Equally, accountants are not concerned with the activities of the firm as a social unit consisting of people whose livelihood and happiness depend on its financial success as well as the manner in which their working lives are organized. Nor, indeed, does accounting concern itself with the role and importance of a particular firm as regards society as a whole. In considering the present state of accounting, it should be pointed out that the need for accounting information having a broader socio-economic nature is being recognized, though at the moment the generation of such information is still a matter of conjecture and debate. Secondly, we noted that accounting conventions play a deterministic role as regards the nature and the quality of the data which accountants process.

The purpose of this chapter is to examine the methods of the accountant for recording financial data.

The meaning of book-keeping

The collection and recording of data is known as book-keeping. The practice of recording financial data in 'books' dates from a very long time ago. These books were usually 'bound books'—bound so as to prevent the possibility of fraud either by the insertion or the removal of pages. Nowadays, mechanical and electronic data processing have removed the book-keeper as a person concerned with entering the results of financial transactions into the 'books'. Instead, large firms have computerized the keeping of the 'books', and smaller firms use electronic accounting machines which make use of 'cards' which form part of a 'bank' of cards. The only people nowadays who keep their financial records in bound books or ledgers are those whose businesses are on a very small scale.

The double-entry system of book-keeping remains, however, the basis for record-keeping regardless of whether or not a firm employs advanced electronic data processing techniques (EDP), mechanical or manual methods. It remains, therefore, the logical method for recording financial information, and as such it is the basis of financial accounting practice.

The origin of double-entry book-keeping

Ancient accounting records were usually merely notes kept by scribes of transactions, such as the purchase of goods and assets and the creation of debts. We know that the accounting records kept by Romans were on a single-entry basis, that is, only one entry was employed to record a transaction.

Example

Flavius bought a slave from Atticus for 5 sesterces. In the books of Flavius, the scribe would write:

'Bought from Atticus the slave Lucius for 5 sesterces'.
This entry would be used as evidence of the transaction, and as evidence of Flavius's ownership of the slave Lucius.

The book-keeping methods employed by the Romans had a very limited use. Certainly, the Romans had very great difficulties in calculating 'profit' as a measure of the efficiency of business operations. The Romans themselves were more interested in politics and administration rather than commerce, and the foundations of wealth rested upon military power.

There is a great gap in the history of the Western world between the decline of the Roman Empire and the appearance of our own society which has its important roots in the Renaissance. That gap is usually described as the Dark Ages.

The Renaissance which marks such a great watershed in the history of Western Europe is associated with the economic, social and cultural developments which took place in Italy in the 14th and 15th centuries. One of its most important features was the appearance of a society whose wealth was founded on trade. The accumulation of enormous mercantile wealth and the extension of trade throughout Europe associated with the Renaissance which was centred in Italy in the 14th and 15th centuries, created a need for business methods which would make possible the scientific management of businesses whose ramifications reached the distant areas of Northern and Central Europe. The search by the powerful trading families of the Italian City States of Genoa, Milan, Florence and Venice for a system of record-keeping which would minimize errors, facilitate control, and give at the same time a comprehensive view of the financial state of their businesses culminated in the development of double-entry book-keeping.

The first detailed exposition of this method of book-keeping was given by Luca Paciolo in a treatise included in his *Summa de Arithmetica, Geometrica, Proportioni et Proportionalita*, which was published in Venice in 1494. An excellent English translation of this treatise was made by two Americans in 1963*, and those who care to read it will be surprised to discover how little change there has been in this method of book-keeping in nearly 500 years.

Although the Italians used double-entry book-keeping for the control of commercial and banking empires which stretched across Northern Europe, it was not until the early part of the 19th century that this method was universally adopted by businessmen elsewhere in Europe. The great Tudor merchants, for example, kept their accounting in the single-entry form and in the closing years of the 18th century, Edward Jones, an Englishman, published a treatise advocating a type of single-entry book-keeping, which he called the English Method, and which he argued was superior to the 'so-called Italian Method'. Very soon thereafter, the debate between single-entry and double-entry book-keeping was resolved in favour of double-entry book-keeping. Books on commercial methods began to appear and to popularize this method, and to this day, it has retained its popularity and provides the foundation of financial accounting method.

The nature of double-entry book-keeping

The essential difference between single-entry and double-entry book-keeping is that whereas the former is a simple statement in note form of a transaction, the latter is a more scientific interpretation of a transaction as a flow of money, or of money value having a point of origin and a point of destination. These points of origin and destination are described as accounts, so that a transaction gives rise to a flow of money or money value out of one account into another account.

Example

Harold Smith is a retail trader who keeps his financial records on the double-entry system. He purchases some equipment for £50,

* Gene Brown, R. & Johnston, Kenneth S., *Paciolo on Accounting*, McGraw-Hill, New York, 1963.

for which he pays cash. The transaction would be shown in his books as a flow of money out of the Cash Book in the amount of £50, and a flow of money value amounting to £50 into the Equipment account.

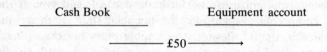

Cash Book	Equipment account
———— £50 ————→	

Business transactions are represented in double-entry book-keeping as flows of money or money value as between the various accounts concerned, but clearly any one transaction involves only one flow, as shown above. In order to identify the direction of any one flow, all accounts are divided into two parts. A flow out of the account is recorded on the right-hand side, and a flow into an account is recorded on the left-hand side. Hence, the transaction shown above would appear as follows:

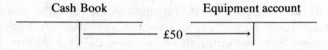

Cash Book	Equipment account
│———— £50 ————→│	

Flows out could conveniently be described by a minus sign, but the accounting convention which dates from the Italian origins of book-keeping utilizes the term *Credit* (Cr.), which means To Give. Likewise flows in could be described by a positive sign, but the accounting appellation is *Debit* (Dr.), which means To Receive. Hence, this additional information may be inserted in the accounts to identify the direction of the flow, and replacing the arrow which we have used up to now.

Cash Book	Equipment account
│ Cr.	Dr. │
│ £50	£50 │

There is now only one additional bit of information which is required to identify the transaction flow, and that is, the point of origin and the point of destination. This, too, is made easy in book-keeping by the simple expedient of describing in the *Credited* account where the flow is going, and by inserting in the *Debited* account the source of the flow.

Cash Book	Equipment account
│ Cr.	Dr. │
│ Equipment A/c £50	Cash A/c £50 │

In practice, accountants know very well that the left-hand side of an account is the debit side, and vice versa for the right-hand side, so that they do not head up the accounts with Dr. or Cr. In the old days, they used to add the work *by* on the narration on *Credit entries*, and *To* on the narration of *Debit entries*—but this too is unnecessary, and many accountants have abandoned this practice. The reader will occasionally find entries recorded as follows:

Cash Book		Equipment account	
	By Equipment A/c £50	To Cash A/c £50	

we shall not, however, use these superfluous terms. Lastly, the date of the transaction must be recorded, and it is done as follows:

Cash Book			Equipment account		
	19X0	£	19X0	£	
	1st May Equipment A/c	50	1st May Cash A/c	50	

In the manner in which transactions are recorded under this method, the reader will have been quick to notice an important feature—the flow has remained constant in value as it has moved from the *credited* account to the *debited* account. As a result, double-entry book-keeping possess a mathematical foundation which has its logic in the simple proposition that as regards any one transaction the *credit* must be equal to the *debit*. At any time, therefore, the arithmetical precision of the book-keeping process may be checked by adding up all the *debit* entries and all the *credit* entries. If the total *debit* entries do not equal, that is *balance* with the *credit* entries, there has been an error in the recording process. As we shall see on page 107, the *Trial Balance* is the means whereby accountants check for arithmetical errors in recording transactions. If the *Trial Balance* shows a difference as little as 1 penny between the *Total Debits* and the *Total Credits*, the error must be found. This is not because accountants are obsessional neurotics, but simply because they know that the result of a great many cumulative errors may boil down to a difference of only 1 penny.

The virtue of double-entry book-keeping is that it is a logical and precise system for recording financial transactions as flows of money or money value. It is easy to operate, and simple to adapt to modern computer methods by using positive and negative electric charges to signal whether an account should be *Debited* or *Credited*.

Double-entry book-keeping as a 'closed' system

We noted in Part 1, that the term 'system' is commonly used to mean any unit which may be identified as an independent whole, having its own objectives and its own internal functions. An 'open' system is one whose behaviour is affected by external factors. The British economy, for example, is an 'open system' because it is affected by its trading relationships with the rest of the world. A 'closed' system is one in which all the functions are internalized in the system, and are not affected by outside factors. Double-entry book-keeping has the characteristics of a closed system in that all the transactions which are recorded take place within the accounts system. By this we mean that all flows resulting from transactions are depicted as having their origin in an account which is found in the system, and they have their destination in another account which is in the system. It is quite impossible from a flow to originate from an account outside the account system. Likewise, it is impossible for a flow of money or of money value to go to an account outside the accounts system.

Example

Let us go back to the example given on page 59 of chapter 1. J. Soap opens up a business under the name of 'J. Soap—Ladies Hairdresser'. He invests £10,000 in cash into the business. The effect of the entity convention is to require J. Soap to open and to keep separate books for the business of J. Soap—Ladies Hairdresser, which is regarded in accounting as a separate entity from J. Soap himself. Double-entry book-keeping gives expression to the entity convention since all the accounts of J. Soap—Ladies Hairdresser relate only the financial transactions of that business. To all intents and purposes, J. Soap himself is an external party as far as the business is concerned.

The question is—how can we depict the flow of £10,000 from J. Soap into the business? Now, we have said that no flow may originate from outside the accounts system. Hence, we must have an account within the accounts system from whence it has originated. That account is the account of J. Soap himself in his capacity as owner of the business, which we described in chapter 1 as the *Capital* account. The source of the flow of £10,000 is therefore found in the *Capital* account, and its destination is the *Cash* account.

Capital account				Cash Book	
19X0	£		19X0		£
1st April Cash A/c	10,000		1st April Capital A/c		10,000

Let us suppose, for a moment, that on the 2nd April, Joe Soap decides that he has put too much money in the business and wishes to take out £3000. In the accounts system, this transaction would be shown as follows:

Capital account

19X0	£	19X0	£
2nd April Cash A/c	3000	1st April Cash A/c	10,000

Cash Book

19X0	£	19X0	£
1st April Capital A/c	10,000	2nd April Capital A/c	3000

The significance of these entries reflects the fact that accounting is not concerned with the destination of the actual sums of money, but simply portraying the full transaction as a *record* of the flow of money. Successive entries are made in accounts which have been opened, and where a transaction involves a new account, then that account is opened. Likewise, if an account is no longer needed, it may be closed.

The implications of these statements as far as book-keeping being a closed system of accounts are:

(1) The book-keeping system of any firm is infinitely elastic in size. As many accounts are opened as are necessary to record in full the transactions which have taken place. It is not surprising, therefore, that large businesses have many thousands of accounts. Prior to the development of accounting machines and computers, these firms needed a very large accounting staff to cope with this work alone. Electronic data processing has had a revolutionary impact on this aspect of the work of the accountant.

(2) All the accounting flows of money or of money value take place between the various accounts found in the system. The accounts system, therefore, consists of a set of 'interlocking accounts'.

(3) The accounts themselves represent 'realities'—whether they are persons or assets involved in transactions.

(4) Firms are continually involved in transactions: this activity is mirrored in the constant flow of money and of money value in the accounts system.

(5) Since all the flows have both their source and their destination in the accounts to be found in the system, the total *debits* and the total *credits* remain equal at all times.

Accounts as descriptions of transactions

We have already noted that the accounts system is used to describe the direction of a flow of money or of money value, as well as the timing of the flow. Business transactions affect a firm in different ways: some are concerned with the acquistion of assets to be used in earning profits, others concern the supply of capital to the firm, either by the owner or by lenders, others relate to goods purchased or sold to persons so that the exchange of goods expressed as money values create rights or liabilities in money terms, and others yet relate to revenues and costs.

If a firm is to make any sense of the large number of accounts which are kept, some grouping of accounts is necessary,so that accounts of the same business nature are kept together. The integration of accounts into groupings enables the accountant to extract the information which he needs with much greater ease. For example, to find out how much is owed to persons by the business, the accountant has merely to go to the accounts of the *Creditors*. This term means that such persons have been the source of a flow of money, or of money value to the firm, and have not been repaid. Likewise, the *Debtors* accounts are referred to find out how much is owing to the business by those people who have received money or money value and have not settled their account.

Transactions frequently involve two different classes of accounts, and indeed may affect more than two accounts.

Example

Midlands Wholesalers Ltd supplies John Brown, a retailer, with goods to the value of £100 on the 1st May, 19X0. In the accounts of Midland Wholesalers Ltd, the transaction will be shown as a flow of money value (goods) from the *Sales* account, which is a Nominal account to the *John Brown* account, which is a Personal account.

Sales account

	19X0	£
	1st May John Brown	100

John Brown account

19X0	£	
1st May Sales	100	

Since John Brown has received money value from Midlands Wholesalers, he is a *debtor* to the amount of £100. At the end of the month, Midlands Wholesalers will send him a statement showing that £100 is now due for payment. John Brown sends his cheque for £100 which will be banked on 1st June. This is shown as another transaction, which is the settlement of a debt, as follows:

John Brown account

19X0	£	19X0	£
1st May Sales	100	1st June Cash	100

Cash Book

19X0	£	
1st June John Brown	100	

Thus, this transaction is one between a *Personal* account and a *Real* account. At this point, we may make two interesting observations:

(a) A 'credit' transaction is treated as a flow of money value to or from a Personal account, and involves the creation of a debt towards the business, or a liability against the business. Hence, the use of the terms *debitor* and *creditor* respectively to denote the nature of such legal rights.
(b) The payment of a debt, or of a liability, involves another accounting transaction which records the flow of money from or to the appropriate Personal account to or from the Cash account. In this connection, the Cash account records all the money flows through the firm's account at its bank.

The mathematical implications of double-entry book-keeping

We have already noted that the arithmetical correctness of the entries made in the accounts may be verified by means of a Trial Balance which involves comparing the total debit flows with the total credit flows.

During any accounting period, there may have been several entries in an individual account, so that several debits and several entries may be shown. A simple calculation may be made to calculate the Net Balance, for the purpose of the Trial Balance itself, and to ascertain the net state of the account.

Example

Let us assume that as regards the previous example, there were several transactions between Midlands Wholesalers Ltd and John Brown during the months of May and June, as follows:

Sales account

		19X0	£
		1st May John Brown	100
		10th May John Brown	50
		17th May John Brown	75
		30th May John Brown	25
		10th June John Brown	50

John Brown account

19X0	£	19X0	£
1st May Sales	100	1st June Cash	100
10th May Sales	50		
17th May Sales	75		
30th May Sales	25		
10th June Sales	50		

Cash Book

19X0	£
1st June John Brown	100

If we wished to extract the *Balance* on John Brown's account, either for the purpose of drawing up a Trial Balance or to find out how much he owes, the procedure for so doing is simply to add up both sides of the account and to calculate the difference. This difference is known as the *Balance*.

John Brown account

19X0	£	19X0	£
1st May Sales	100	1st June Cash	100
10th May Sales	50	10th June Balance	200
17th May Sales	75		
30th May Sales	25		
10th June Sales	50		
	300		300

This balance represents the excess of the debit entries over the credit entries, and it represents also the fact that John Brown is a *debtor* for the amount of £200 at the 10th June. In order to show this fact in the account after it has been balanced, the *Balance* is brought down as a *debit balance*.

John Brown account

19X0	£	19X0	£
1st May Sales	100	1st June Cash	100
10th May Sales	50	10th June Balance	
17th May Sales	75	carried down	200
30th May Sales	25		
10th June Sales	50		
	300		300
11th June Balance			
brought down	200		

Balancing the accounts is the first stage in preparing the Trial Balance. Naturally, some accounts will have *debit* balances and others will have *credit* balances. When we compare the total balances, they should be equal.

The trial balance

The Trial Balance is merely a list of the balances extracted from all the accounts arranged in such a way that the debit balances are listed on one side and the credit balances on the other side.

Example

The following Trial Balance extracted on the 31st December, 19X0 from the books of Samuel Smith, trading as a Jeweller.

Trial Balance as on 31st December, 19X0	Debit Balances £	Credit Balances £
Capital Account on 1st January, 19X0		24,000
Freehold premises	20,000	
Furniture and fittings	1000	
Equipment	200	
Opening inventory on 1st January, 19X0	5000	
Purchases	5000	
Sales		10,000
Trade debtors	1000	
Trade creditors		1500
Light and electricity	120	
Rates	230	
Postages and telephones	150	
General expenses	300	
Cash	2500	
	35,500	35,500

The Trial Balance not only serves to act as a check on the mathematical correctness of the book-keeping process, but it is a summary of the balances of all the accounts, which, as we shall see in the next chapter, serves as a working paper in the course of preparing financial statements. We may note that in the process of summarizing information for the purpose of the Trial Balance, the personal accounts of the debtors and the creditors have been totalled.

The Trial Balance will not reveal the following types of errors:

(a) Errors of omission, where a transaction has been completely overlooked.

(b) Errors of principle, where an amount is correctly recorded but it is placed in the wrong class of account—for example, where the purchase of equipment is shown under Purchases rather than under Equipment.

(c) Errors of commission, where an amount is correctly recorded in the right class of account, but is entered in the wrong account—for example, where a sale of £50 to John Brown is entered in William Brown's account.

(d) Errors of original entry—where the transaction is recorded in the wrong amount—for example, where a sale to John Brown of goods to the value of £50 is recorded as £5.

(e) Errors in recording the direction of the flow—where the correct account is recorded but instead of being shown, for example, as a debit to the Cash Book and a credit to John Brown's account it is shown the other way round.

(f) Compensating errors which cancel each other out will not be revealed. Thus, an error in adding up the Trade Debtors which is cancelled out by a similar error in adding up the Trade Creditors will not be revealed.

Summary

The evolution of double-entry book-keeping in the 14th and 15th century provided accounting with a method of processing data in a systematic manner, and with a means of checking the accuracy of accounting records which was in-built into its processes by virtue of the inter-locking nature of the accounts system. At the end of an accounting period, it is axiomatic that the total debit entries must be equal to the total credit entries.

With the advent of computerized accounting systems, and the widespread use of accounting machines, the usefulness of the double-entry method as a check on the accuracy of record-keeping has largely disappeared. Nevertheless, double-entry book-keeping remains the basis for recording financial transactions as flows of money, or of money value from one account to another, whether or not the accounts system is computerized.

Far more significant, however, as regards the usefulness of the data recorded in the double-entry system are the effects of accounting conventions, which require in particular that the values recorded should be determined by transactions.

Section 2

Periodic Measurement

4

Double-entry Book-keeping and Periodic Measurement

In the previous chapter, we examined the double-entry method as a means of recording financial transactions as flows of money or of money value. We said that firms are continually involved in transactions, and that this activity is mirrored in the double-entry book-keeping process by the constant flow through the accounts system of the money or money values involved in those transactions.

The accounts system is merely a repository of financial data about transactions. To be meaningful, this data must be extracted from the accounts system and organized in such a way that it is useful to those who need information for decision-making. The convention of periodicity which we mentioned in chapter 1 represents the view that, although the activities of a firm continue through time so that the decisions taken at one point of time cannot be separated from their effects whenever they materialize, those activities should be nevertheless regularly assessed. In other words, the financial health of a business should be tested at periodic intervals. The convention of periodicity poses problems in adapting the data recorded in the accounts system so that it will correctly reflect the result of the transactions concluded in the selected period, and the financial health of the firm at the end of that period. The two accounting statements which are employed for this purpose are the Income Statement for the year, and the Balance Sheet as at the end of the year.

The purpose of this chapter is to examine the preliminary stages in the preparation of these statements.

Problems in periodic measurement

The reader will recall that when we discussed the convention of periodicity in chapter 1, we noted that not only should the transactions of a period be identified, but also that the expenses attributable to those transactions should be matched with the revenues derived from them in accordance with the matching convention.

The first major problem, therefore, in adapting the information recorded in the accounts system has a two-fold aspect:

    (a) to identify the revenues attributable to transactions concluded
        during the year;

    (b) to identify the expenses related to those revenues.

The second major problem concerns other adjustments which must be made in order to arrive at a measure of the surplus or deficit of revenues over expenses. These adjustments involve an element of judgement, for example, how much to write off in respect of depreciation and bad debts, and what adjustments to make in respect of expected losses. We are required to make such adjustments because the end-product is intended to be a statement of the income or loss made in the accounting period. We shall consider these problems in the next chapter.

The third major problem, which represents a new departure in accounting practices is to adjust the amounts shown as revenues and expenses so as to eliminate the effect of inflation during the year. One proposal for solving this problem only requires the publication of an additional statement of income or loss adjusted for inflation. This statement is intended to accompany the main statement of income or loss which is not adjusted for inflation. There are a number of difficulties involved in inflation accounting in addition to finding the correct basis for measuring inflation, for example, how to adjust individual items of revenue and expenses in order to eliminate inflation. Clearly, if the rate of inflation during the year in question has been 10% measured as between the first day and the last day of the accounting period, it does not follow that one must automatically adjust all the figures by 10%. The revenues and expenses belonging to the beginning of the period will have suffered more from the effects of inflation than those belonging to the end of the period. Since it is neither possible nor desirable that every single item should be so adjusted, we are required to make some assumptions when adjusting for inflation. Inflation accounting introduces new controversies in accounting measurement, and we shall discuss these new problems in Part 4.

The idea of periodic measurement which underlies financial reporting presents complex problems, and we have devoted much of Part 4 to the analysis of these problems.

Identifying the revenues and expenses of the period

The data recorded in the accounts system provides the basis for identifying the revenues and expenses of an accounting period. Firstly, we need to extract from the accounts system the data recorded in respect of all the transactions concluded in the period. We saw in chapter 3 of this Part that the summary of all the transactions is obtainable by means of a Trial Balance drawn up on the last day of the accounting period.

Example

The following Trial Balance was extracted from the books of John Smith on the 31st December, 19X0, being the end of the first year of trading.

	£ Dr.	£ Cr.
Capital		25,000
Motor vehicles	10,000	
Furniture and fittings	2500	
Purchases	31,000	
Cash at Bank	6000	
Sales		70,000
Sundry debtors	18,000	
Sundry creditors		3500
Rent	4500	
Salaries	22,800	
Insurances	400	
Motor expenses	2000	
Light and heat	1000	
General expenses	300	
	98,500	98,500

The meaning of revenue and expense

The Trial Balance does not make any distinction between flows of income and flows of capital, neither does it make a distinction between expenditure incurred to earn revenue and expenditure on the acquisition of assets. The first problem is to identify the revenues of the year, and this is a matter of definition. By revenue we mean the flows of funds, that is money or rights to money, which have resulted from the trading activities of the business, as distinct from funds (capital) invested by the owner or loans made by creditors and others. In this case, the only revenue item shown on the Trial Balance is the revenue from sales amounting to £70,000. The second problem is to identify the expenses. We define expenses as the costs of running the business during the accounting period. By contrast, capital expenses are the costs incurred in acquiring fixed assets or adding to the income-earning structure of the firm. The calculation of periodic income is by means of a formula which deducts expenses from revenues:

$$\text{Periodic income} = \text{Revenues} - \text{Expenses}.$$

Looking at the Trial Balance, the expenses of the year, as defined, are as follows:

	£
Purchases	31,000
Rent	4500
Salaries	22,800
Insurances	400
Motor expenses	2000
Light and heat	1000
General expenses	300

An alternative way of defining expenses, which is the definition adopted by accountants, is to treat as expenses all those costs the benefit of which has been exhausted during the year. Looking at the expenses which we have identified in the Trial Balance, it is clear that the benefit derived by the firm from expenditure on these items is limited to the accounting period. The only exception is the goods purchased which have not been sold by the end of the year, and we shall discuss this problem in chapter 6.

We have completed, therefore, the first stage in periodic measurement by identifying the revenue and expenses attributable to the 'income-earning' transactions of the firm during the year, which we may list as follows:

	£		£
Purchases	31,000	Sales	70,000
Rent	4500		
Salaries	22,800		
Insurance	400		
Motor expenses	2000		
Light and heat	1000		
General expenses	300		

Periodic measurement and the accrual convention

The next task of the accountant is to verify that the revenues and expenses are attributable to the accounting period. It is the normal practice to record in the expense accounts those amounts actually paid during the period. As a result, at the end of the period, these accounts may be understated or overstated. Likewise, it is possible that there may be some outstanding revenue due to the business, other than sales revenue, which must be brought into the year's income.

The governing principle which affect these adjustments is the accrual convention which we discussed in chapter 1. The accrual convention, it will be recalled, makes a distinction between the receipt of cash and the right to receive cash, and the payment of cash and the legal obligation to pay cash. As there is often no coincidence in time between the creation of legal rights and obligations and the transfer of cash, it follows that the accountant must scrutinize the revenue and expenses accounts to make sure that amounts due and payable are accrued. Similarly, any payments made in advance must be excluded and carried forward to the next accounting period. The adjustments are effected in the accounts themselves.

The accrual of income

At the end of an accounting period, the total sales income for the year will have been recorded already in the accounts system, and the amounts unpaid by customers in respect of these sales will have been included under Sundry Debtors. The outstanding income which may not already have been recorded is limited, therefore, to income other than sales, such as rent receivable, commissions receivable etc. The accountant must adjust his end-of-year figures so as to include all the income to which the business is legally entitled, even though it has not been received.

Example

On the 1st December, 19X0, John Smith had sub-let a portion of his premises, which had never been utilized, for a monthly rent of £60 payable in advance on the 1st of each month. By the 31th December, 19X0, the date of which the Trial Balance was extracted, the rent receivable had not yet been received. To accrue the rent receivable, the accountant must enter the amount accrued in the Rent Receivable account as follows:

Rent Receivable account

	19X0	£
	31st Dec. Accrued	60

This amount is taken to the Income Statement as income for the year 19X0, and at the same time is brought down as a debt due to the business by being shown as a *debit balance*

Rent Receivable account

19X0	£	19X0	£
31st Dec. Income Statement	60	31st Dec. Accrued c/d	60
	60		60

19X1
1st January Accrued b/d 60

Students are often puzzled that rent receivable should be a Credit flow. The reason is that the Rent Receivable account is used to denote the source of a flow of funds so that there is a flow out from the Rent Receivable account into the Cash account. Let us assume that on the 1st January, 19X1, the rent outstanding is paid. The entries would be as follows:

Rent Receivable account

19X1	£	19X1	£
1st Jan. Accrued b/d	60	1st Jan. Cash	60

Cash Book

19X1	£	
1st Jan. Rent Receivable	60	

In adjusting the receipts for the year so that they will correctly show the income of the year, the accountant accrues income not yet received, as we have seen above, but also carries forward to the following year any receipts of the current year which are the income of the following year.

If, however, there had been an omission of income from the accounts of the preceding year, and this income is received in the current year, it would be impossible to go back and adjust the accounts of the previous year. Those accounts will have been closed at the end of that accounting period. The accountant will include last year's income in the current year's income, and indicate that it was an omission from last year, or explain how this income arose. Adjustments of this nature often arise out of the settlement of legal disputes or compensation claims.

The accrual of expenses

The accrual of expenses occurs far more frequently than the accrual of income, for it is the nature of things that businessmen tend to delay the payment of expenses. As a result, nominal accounts such as Rent,

Insurance, Wages, Light and Heat etc., require to be adjusted so as to show the total payments due and payable in respect of the accounting year. Occasionally, however, firms are obliged to pay in advance for services, so that there is a possibility that a portion of the payment relates to the next accounting period.

We may say, therefore, that the accrual of expenses involves two types of adjustments:

(a) an accrual in respect of expenses of the year which have not yet been paid;

(b) an exclusion from the recorded expenses of that part which relates to the next year.

Example

Let us return to the Trial Balance extracted from John Smith's books. We are informed that:

(a) The yearly rent is £6000 payable quarterly. The quarterly rent of £1500 payable on the 1st December had not been paid.

(b) Insurance premiums paid amounting to £400 included a payment of £50 in respect of a new policy taken out on the 31st December 19X0.

It is clear, therefore, that the legal obligation in respect of the rent is understated in the Rent account by £1500. Equally, the insurance premiums applicable to the year ended 31st December, 19X0 amount to £350 and not £400. It is necessary to adjust these accounts as follows:

(a) to increase the rent chargeable as an expense by £1500;

(b) to decrease the insurance chargeable as an expense by £50.

Underpayment of rent

Let us assume that the rent payments were made on due date as follows:

Rent account

19X0		£	
1st Feb.	Cash	1500	
1st May	Cash	1500	
1st Aug.	Cash	1500	

The amount which should be charged against the income for the year ended 31st December, 19X0 is £6000. The rent unpaid at the 31st December, 19X0 may be accrued as follows:

Rent account

19X0		£
1st Feb.	Cash	1500
1st May	Cash	1500
1st Aug.	Cash	1500
31st Dec.	Accrued	1500

Having made this adjustment, the Rent account for the year ended 31st December, 19X0 may be closed by transferring the rent of £6000 to the Income Statement for the year ended 31st December, 19X0. The rent unpaid is, of course, a liability of the firm on the 31st December, 19X0, and this is shown by bringing down the amount accrued as a *credit* balance on the Rent account. The adjusted Rent account will appear as follows:

Rent account

19X0		£	19X0	£
1st Feb.	Cash	1500	31st Dec. Income Statement	6000
1st May	Cash	1500		
1st Aug.	Cash	1500		
31st Dec.	Accrued c/d	1500		
		6000		6000
			19X1	
			1st Jan. Accrued b/d	1500

We note that the rent outstanding at the 31st December 19X0 is £1500, and we have brought this amount down to show:

(a) that there is a *credit* balance outstanding at the 31st December 19X0;

(b) that on the 1st January 19X1 there is an outstanding liability in respect of the previous year, so that the firm will have to pay £7500 during the year ended 31st December, 19X1.

The Trial Balance on the 31st December, 19X0 may now be adjusted as follows:

	£	£
Rent	6000	
Rent accrued		1500

If the firm pays the rent outstanding on the 2nd January, 19X1, and thereafter pays the rent on due date, the Rent account for the year 19X1 will appear as follows:

Rent account

19X1		£	19X1	£
2nd Jan.	Cash	1500	1st Jan. Accrued b/d	1500
1st Feb.	Cash	1500	31st Dec. Income Statement	6000
1st May	Cash	1500		
1st Aug.	Cash	1500		
1st Dec.	Cash	1500		
		7500		7500

Prepayment of Insurance
Let us assume that the insurance premiums were paid in advance as follows:

1st January, 19X0	£350
31st December, 19X0	50
	£400

These transactions will be shown in the Insurance account as under:

Insurance account

19X0		£	
1st Jan.	Cash	350	
31st Dec.	Cash	50	

The premium paid on the 31st December 19X0 is the *Prepayment* of an expense for the year ending 31st December 19X1. Hence, it cannot be shown as an expense for the year ended 31st December, 19X0. Thus the purpose of the adjustment is:

(a) to measure the expense applicable to the year ended 31st December 19X0, and to transfer this amount to the Income Statement for that year;

(b) to carry forward the premium paid in advance to the following year.

The adjusted account will appear as follows:

Insurance account

19X0		£	19X0	£
1st Jan.	Cash	350	31st Dec. Income Statement	350
31st Dec.	Cash	50	31st Dec. Prepaid c/d	50
		400		400

19X1		
1st Jan. Prepaid b/d		50

We may note that the insurance prepaid at the 31st December 19X0 is brought down as a *debit* balance on the 1st January 19X1, and as a result:

(a) there is a *debit* balance in favour of the firm on the 31st December 19X0;

(b) the firm will not have to pay the premium of £50 in the subsequent year, if the yearly premium is only due and payable on the 1st January each year.

The Trial Balance on the 31st December 19X0 may now be adjusted as follows:

	£	£
Insurance	350	
Insurance prepaid	50	

Assuming that the firm pays the insurance premium in the following year on due date, the Insurance account for that year will be as follows:

Insurance account

19X1		£	19X1	£
1st Jan.	Prepaid b/d	50	31st Dec. Income Statement	400
1st Jan.	Cash	350		400
		400		

The reader will have observed how easily the accounts system permits the adjustments made in respect of the accruals of revenue and expenses to be reconciled with the subsequent receipts and payment of cash. Although we have interfered with the recording process in order to adjust the accounts so as to reflect the true picture at the end of the accounting period, the double-entry system continues to record the accounting flows and is not itself affected by the adjustments which have been made.

The results of the accrual adjustments

The reader will recall that the Trial Balance is merely a working paper which the accountant uses to extract the information which he requires from the accounts system, and to check its accuracy. We may alter the original details shown on the first Trial Balance to reflect the adjustments which we have so far made.

Example

The adjusted Trial Balance for John Smith's business as at 31st December, 19X0 may be set out as follows:

	£ Dr.	£ Cr.
Capital		25,000
Motor vehicles	10,000	
Furniture and fittings	2500	
Purchases	31,000	
Cash at Bank	6000	
Sales		70,000
Sundry debtors	18,000	
Sundry creditors		3500
Rent	6000	
Rent accrued		1500
Insurance	350	
Insurance prepaid	50	
Salaries	22,800	
Motor expenses	2000	
Light and heat	1000	
General expenses	300	
Rent receivable		60
Rent receivable	60	
	100,060	100,060

The effect of these adjustments on the revenues and expenses for the year ended 31st December, 19X0 may be summarized as follows:

	£		£
Purchases	31,000	Sales	70,000
Rent	6000	Rent receivable	60
Salaries	22,800		
Insurance	350		
Motor expenses	2000		
Light and Heat	1000		
General expenses	300		

It will be noted also that the adjustments have given rise to the following balances on the accounts:

		£	£
Rent accrued	—Credit balance		1500
Insurance prepaid	—Debit balance	50	
Rent receivable	—Debit balance	60	

As these balances represent sums owing by the business and debts due to the business, they will be shown, as we shall see in chapter

6 (p. 159) as liabilities and assets respectively at the end of the accounting period.

The matching of revenues and expenses

The purpose underlying the accountant's effort to identify and correctly measure the revenues and expenses of an accounting period is to attempt to match them so as to obtain a measure of the 'financial effort' of earning the revenues of that period. The accountant's concern is always with financial efficiency which he equates with income. The matching of expenses and revenues is far more complicated than appears at first sight. So far, we have assumed that by correctly measuring the revenues and expenses attributable to the accounting year they have been correctly matched. In other words, we have made the assumption that the expenses of the accounting period are the expenses related to the revenues of that period. The realization convention permits the accountant to recognize only financial results in the form of sales revenues. It is well-known, of course, that there is a time-lag between buying or manufacturing goods for sale and actually selling those goods. At the end of an accounting period, therefore, there will always be goods awaiting sale and raw materials unused. The expenses attributable to unsold goods and unused materials, usually described as inventories, must be excluded from the expenses of the period and carried forward to the next accounting period, when the goods will have been sold and the materials used. The importance of inventory adjustments to the correct measurement of periodic income is crucial. There are two aspects to this problem:

(a) How to measure the expenses relating to inventories, that is, what is the correct way to 'value' inventories. We shall deal with this problem in Part 4.

(b) How to effect the adjustment in the accounts, this is the problem with which we shall deal now.

Inventory adjustments

By definition, the closing inventory at the end of an accounting period is the residue of the purchases of that period which remains unsold or unused.

Example

John Smith's Purchases account includes all goods purchased during the year ended 31st December 19X0. At the end of the year, the inventory of materials unused is quantified, and its cost price is valued at £3000. The accounting problems relating to this inventory are as follows:

(a) Since the business has to pay for all goods purchased, it would be illogical to reduce the Purchases account by the amount of inventory at the end of the year. Hence, the Purchases account must not be adjusted and the total purchases must be charged as expenses.

(b) By charging all purchases against sales, however, the profit for the year would be overstated by £3000. Means must be found, therefore, to take the closing inventory out of the income calculation. This is effected by opening an Inventory account on the 31st December, 19X0 and posting the inventory to it.

Inventory account

	£	
19X0		
31st Dec.	3000	

As soon as an account is opened for the purpose of recording a flow of value it is necessary to describe the source of the flow and its destination. We know that the Purchases account is not the source of the flow of inventories to the Inventory account, because we have deliberately refused to adjust the Purchases account. We know also that, but for the need to measure income, we would not value inventories at the end of the year. Hence, by a fiction, the accountant states that the inventory adjustment comes from the Income Statement which is employed to measure income. The full accounting entries are, therefore, as follows:

Income Statement for the year
ended 31st December, 19X0

		£
	19X0	
	31st Dec. Inventory	3000

Inventory account

	£	
19X0		
31st Dec. Income Statement	3000	

The effect of these entries is to solve the problem of income measurement, because the *credit* flow from the Income Statement is taken into the calculation of income, as follows:

	£		£
Purchases	31,000	Sales	70,000
		Closing inventories	3000

The debit balance on the Inventory account represents an asset which is carried over to the next year's Income Statement. The Inventory account is an interesting account because it exists only to measure income, and since that is done on the last day of the accounting year, the Inventory account only exists for one day. In fact, the closing inventory on the last day of the year is the opening inventory on the first day of the next accounting year. Hence, on the first day of the next accounting period, the inventory must be posted to the Income Statement of the next period, as follows:

Income Statement for the year
ended 31st December 19X1

19X1	£	
1st Jan. Inventory	3000	

Inventory account

19X0	£	19X1	£
31st Dec. Income Statement	3000	1st Jan. Income Statement	3000

The reader will now observe that the Inventory account has served its purpose and may be closed. This is done by drawing a double line beneath the entries.

Inventory account

19X0	£	19X1	£
31st Dec. Income Statement	3000	1st Jan. Income Statement	3000

In practice, the accountant will not reverse the inventory into the Income Statement of the year 19X1, until the 31st December 19X1 when he prepares that account. As a result, the Trial Balance for the year ended 31st December, 19X1 will include a debit balance in respect of the Inventory account in the amount of £3000. As the Trial Balance is always extracted before the inventory adjustment is made, the opening inventory always appears on the Trial Balance but the closing inventory is never shown.

Summary

In this section of Part 2, we consider the procedural problems involved in periodic measurement. This chapter deals with the problems of adapting the financial accounting data lodged in the data processing system to the objective of measuring periodic income.

The first stages in the measurement of periodic income are:

(a) the identification of the revenues attributable to transactions concluded in the accounting period;

(b) the identification of the expenses related to those revenues.

The accruals convention requires the inclusion of amounts receivable and payable, as well as amounts received and paid, in the measurement of revenues and expenses. We examined the accounting procedures involved in accruing revenue and expenses.

The objective of periodic measurement is the matching of revenues and expenses to establish accounting income. The exclusion of inventories unsold at the end of the accounting period is a further problem in periodic measurement considered in this chapter.

5
Losses in Asset Values and Periodic Measurement

In the previous chapter, we discussed the various adjustments which were needed to the data extracted from the double-entry book-keeping system, so that this data might correctly reflect the revenues and expenses appropriate to the activities conducted during the accounting period in question. The accrual of revenues and expenses involved, as we saw, the exclusion from the data of payments and receipts of other periods.

In this chapter, we shall discuss adjustments which are made in respect of losses in asset values. The first adjustment which we shall examine concerns the depreciation of fixed assets. The second adjustment is the loss in the value of debtors caused by the recognition that a portion of the debtor balances will not be paid and must be recognized as bad debts, and that a further portion may ultimately prove to be bad so that a provision for doubtful debts must also be made.

The treatment of losses in asset values

Unlike gains, losses in asset values do not have to await realization before they may be recognized. The convention of conservatism requires that losses should be recognized as soon as possible, so as to ensure that income and capital values are not overstated in financial accounting reports.

Losses in asset values appear under a variety of guises. Losses of cash and stock by theft, embezzlement or accidental damage are written off immediately against income, insurance recoveries being treated as a separate matter. Losses to fixed assets due to accidental damage, theft or other causes are also written off against income, as are losses arising on the sale of fixed assets which result from a difference between the sale price and the book value of the assets sold. Most fixed assets also diminish in value as their usefulness is exhausted over a period of years. Finally, losses in asset values also result from the exercise of judgement, as in the case of bad debts when accountants have to decide whether a recorded value does exist at all. In this connection, a discretion exists as regards the valuation of such assets as goodwill and organization costs usually described as Fictitious Assets, in that intangible asset values are frequently written off purely as an act of judgement.

Losses in the value of fixed assets

Losses in the value of fixed assets arising through sale, accidental loss or theft present no difficulties from an accounting viewpoint, for such losses are written off immediately against income. By contrast, the diminution in value described as depreciation has been the subject of much controversy. As an accounting concept, depreciation has a complex nature and now occupies an important role in three different areas of the subject. First, it is related to the problem of cost allocation, both as regards the matching of revenues and expenses in the process of income measurement, and as regards product costing in management accounting. Secondly, it is related to the concept of capital maintenance in income theory. Thirdly, as Baxter has shown, it is central to decision-making as regards the life and the replacement of fixed assets (Baxter, 1971). The notion of depreciation has varied and multiplied in such a way that its analysis is not an easy matter. In this chapter, we shall take a limited view of depreciation, and we shall concern ourselves purely with its financial accounting implications.

The nature of depreciation

The term 'depreciation' is susceptible to four different meanings (Goldberg, 1962):

(a) a fall in price
(b) physical deterioration
(c) a fall in value
(d) an allocation of fixed asset costs.

Depreciation as a fall in price

A fall in the price of an asset is one aspect of depreciation, but it is not a reliable guide to a valid accounting concept of depreciation. A fall in price may occur independently of any decrease in the usefulness of an asset, for example, the immediate fall in price occurring on the purchase of a new asset.

Depreciation as physical deterioration

Depreciation in this sense is a physical fact. It means impaired utility arising directly through deterioration or indirectly through obsolescence. It is implied in much of the discussion of this concept of depreciation that an asset is 'used up' through use, so that the 'use' of an asset is the extent to which it has been used up. It is evident that these ideas are represented in the rates of depreciation which are attached to depreciable assets. It should be noted, however, that an asset is not necessarily 'used up' through use, for adequate maintenance may prevent deterioration in some cases. Thus, if irrigation ditches are well-maintained, they will not deteriorate through use.

It is interesting to note that the concept of depreciation as deferred maintenance has not been properly investigated, although it may well be a concept of depreciation which may be more relevant than conventional concepts of depreciation as regards certain types of assets.

Depreciation as a fall in value
There are some problems associated with the use of the term 'value' and the relationship of depreciation to the concept of value. Value may mean 'cost value' 'exchange value', 'use value' (utility), or 'esteem value'. Clearly, 'cost value' is not affected by events occurring after acquisition, so that it is not meaningful to relate depreciation to a fall in cost value. 'Exchange value' changes only twice in the experience of the owner of an asset—at the point of purchase and at the point of sale. In this sense, depreciation may mean only a fall in price between two points, and we have already discussed this concept of depreciation. Depreciation as a decrease in utility is also already covered by the concept of physical deterioration, whilst the notion of the esteem value of an asset is entirely subjective and not amenable to an objective concept of measurement.

If one were to attempt to relate the notion of depreciation to economic income, however, one would have the basis of an accounting concept of particular usefulness for decision-making. The economic value of an asset may be regarded as the discounted value of expected future cash flows associated with that asset in a particular use. Hence, depreciation may be conceptualized and measured as the progressive decrease in the net cash flows yielded by the asset as its economic utility declines through time, for whatever reason. Normally, of course, its income-earning capacity falls due to increasing inefficiency arising from physical deterioration. As regards certain classes of assets, for example computers, falls in economic value have occurred more rapidly from obsolescence. Baxter discusses this concept of depreciation, but rejects it as an operational one for accounting purposes (Baxter, 1971).

Depreciation as cost allocation
The orthodox view among accountants is that depreciation represents that part of the cost of a fixed asset to its owner which is not

recoverable when the asset is finally put out of use by him. Provision against this loss of capital is an integral cost of conducting the business during the effective commercial life of the asset and is not dependent upon the amount of profit earned.

The practice of treating depreciation as an allocation of historic cost is based on two assumptions:

> (a) that the expected benefit to be derived from an asset is proportional to an estimated usage rate;
> (b) that it is possible to measure the benefit.

Hence, the current practice is part of the procedure of matching periodic revenues with the cost of earning those revenues. The essential difference between fixed assets and current operating expenses is that the former are regarded as costs which yield benefits over a period of years, and hence must be allocated as expenses against the revenues of those years, whereas the latter yield all their benefits in the current year, so that they may be treated as the expenses of that year and matched against the revenues which they have created.

The practice of treating depreciation as an allocation of costs presents a number of serious theoretical problems. The known objective facts about an asset are few, and adequate records are not usually kept of the various incidents in the life in use of an asset apart from its purchase price. Repair and maintenance costs, for example, are charged separately as well as running costs. Other unresolved problems concern the selection of appropriate bases for allocating the cost of depreciable assets, for example, should depreciation be calculated by reference to units of actual use rather than simply time use? Finally, should the residual value of an asset be regarded as a windfall gain or should it be set-off against the replacement cost of the asset rather than used as a point of reference for calculating the proportion of the cost of fixed assets which should be allocated as depreciation?

The accounting concept of depreciation

According to the AICPA, depreciation accounting is "a system of accounting which aims to distribute the cost ... of tangible capital assets, less salvage (if any), over the estimated useful life of the unit ... in a systematic and rational manner. It is a process of allocation, not of valuation" (AICPA, 1953).

From the foregoing definition of depreciation accounting, two important points may be made:

> (a) Depreciation accounting is not concerned with attempting to measure the value of an asset at any point of time. One is

trying to measure the value of the benefit the asset has provided during a given accounting period, and that benefit is valued as a portion of the cost of the asset. Hence, the Balance Sheet value of depreciable assets is that portion of the original cost which has not yet been allocated as a periodic expense in the process of income measurement. It does not purport to represent the current value of those assets.

(b) Depreciation accounting does not itself provide funds for the replacement of depreciable assets, but the charging of depreciation ensures the maintenance intact of the original money capital of the entity. Indeed, a provision for depreciation is not identified with cash or any specific asset or assets.

Depreciable and non-depreciable fixed assets

The most common types of fixed assets are:

(a) Land and Buildings
(b) Plant and Machinery
(c) Furniture and Fittings
(d) Motor Vehicles
(e) Tools and Sundry Equipment.

The essential difference in the accounting treatment of fixed assets is to be found in the distinction made between depreciable and non-depreciable assets. Generally, Land and Buildings are not depreciated: on the contrary, they are sometimes revalued from a historical cost basis. Other fixed assets such as Plant and Machinery, Furniture and Fittings, Motor Vehicles, Tools and Sundry Equipment are depreciated, although, exceptionally, Tools and Sundry Equipment are placed on a revaluation basis or a replacement basis as a means of calculating the amount to be charged as a periodic expense. It may be said, therefore, that the distinction between depreciable and non-depreciable fixed assets revolves on the susceptibility of an asset to physical deterioration or obsolescence. Thus, commercial buildings such as shops and offices are not generally depreciated, but industrial buildings are normally depreciated.

Factors in the measurement of depreciation

There are four factors which are important in the process of measuring depreciation from an accounting viewpoint, as follows:

(a) identifying the cost of the asset
(b) ascertaining its useful life

(c) determining the expected residual value
(d) selecting an appropriate method of depreciation which must be systematic and rational.

Identifying the cost of the asset

Depreciation is calculated on historical cost values, which include acquisition costs and all incidental costs involved in bringing an asset into use. In the case of buildings, for example, cost includes any commissions, survey, legal and other charges involved in the purchase, together with all the costs incurred in preparing and modifying buildings for a particular use. In the case of plant and machinery, all freight, insurance and installation costs should be capitalized.

Problems occur where firms manufacture assets, for example, an engineering firm may construct a foundry. In such cases, the cost of labour, materials etc. associated with the activity of construction should be segregated from those associated with the normal income generating activities, and they should be capitalized. There are costing problems involved in the ascertainment of such costs. Moreover, improvements effected to existing assets should also be capitalized. The distinction between a repair and an improvement is not always easy to establish. In some circumstances, the intention may be to repair but the cheaper solution is a replacement. An old boiler, for example, may be replaced more cheaply than repaired. The cost of repairs is chargeable as a current expense: the cost of replacement should be capitalized.

Ascertaining the useful life of an asset

The useful life of an asset may be defined as that period of time during which it is expected to be useful in the income earning operations of the firm. In most cases, the useful life is determined by two factors:

(a) the rate of deterioration
(b) obsolescence.

The rate of deterioration is a function of the type of use to which the asset is put, and the extent of that use. A lorry used by civil engineering contractors may have a shorter life expectancy than a lorry employed by cartage contractors, for the former may operate in rough terrain, whereas the latter will be used on roads. It is not unusual to find that the estimated useful life of a lorry in the first case may be two years or even less, whereas the estimated life in the second case may well be four years. Moreover, an asset which is used more intensively will have a shorter life than an asset which is used for periods of shorter duration. In this respect, assets are built to certain specifications which determine to some extent their durability in use. The useful life in use is determined on the basis of past experience, which is a good indicator of the probable life of a particular asset.

It should be pointed out, however, that the estimated useful life of an asset is also a question of policy and may be determined accordingly. Thus, a car hire firm may decide to renew its fleet each year, and in this case, the useful life of its fleet of cars is one year for the purpose of calculating depreciation.

The problem of taking obsolescence into account in assessing the useful life of an asset is altogether more complex, for obsolescence occurs with the appearance of an asset incorporating the result of technological developments. It is possible to assume in respect of certain assets, such as cars, that each year may see the introduction of an improved model, so that owners of fleets of cars may decide that obsolescence, or assumed obsolescence is a more important factor in the useful life of cars than depreciation. Relying on a pattern of new models or improved versions each year, the owners of fleets of cars may decide to renew the fleet each year. However, it is hard to distinguish the extent to which such decisions are influenced by the need to have the latest product or to avoid excessive repair bills stemming from large mileages. It would seem, therefore, that the problem of obsolescence is one which affects the useful life of existing fixed assets and so accelerates their progress towards the scrapheap. Accordingly, the estimates useful life of an asset should be determined by that length of time which, as a matter of policy, it is wished to employ an asset. That length of time will be a function of a number of factors, but the most important will be the increasing cost of employing that asset due to higher yearly maintenance costs and, possible declining revenues.

From a theoretical point of view, there is a point at which the net cash inflows associated with an asset are equal to the costs of operating that asset. Those costs may be expressed as the opportunity costs represented by revenues foregone as a result of using that asset rather than replacing it, or the opportunity costs represented by alternative returns which may be derived from cash outlays committed to repairs and maintenance. These two measures of opportunity cost need not, of course, necessarily be equivalent. In terms of this analysis, the length of useful life of an asset would be determined as in Fig. 2.9.

Determining the expected residual value

The residual value of an asset must be estimated at the time of acquisition so that the net cost may be allocated to the accounting

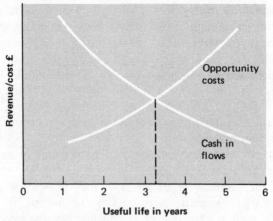

Fig. 2.9

periods during which the asset is usefully employed. The residual value is the expected market value of the asset at the end of its useful life. Hence, the residual value will depend on the manner and on the length of time that the asset is to be used. Where, for example, it is intended to use an asset until it is quite worn out or obsolete, its residual value will be negligible. Where, as in the example of the replacement of fleets of cars, the length of useful life is shortened to one year, the residual value will be high.

Where it is intended to extract the maximum use from an asset, the residual value should be a nominal one: where it is intended to replace the asset when it still has some useful life, its residual value should be estimated on a conservative basis so as to minimize the effects of variations in the price of second-hand assets. The costs to be allocated against the revenues of the accounting periods involved are calculated as follows:

Cost of acquisition (say)	£2000
Residual value (say)	200
Costs to be allocated as depreciation	1800

Selecting the method of depreciation

There are several methods of depreciation but the most common ones are the straight-line method and the decreasing balance method.

The matching convention requires that "the choice of the method of allocating the cost of a long-term asset over its effective working life should depend upon the pattern of expected benefits obtainable in each period from its use" (Barton, 1975).

(*a*) *The straight-line method*

The formula for calculating the annual depreciation under the straight line method is as follows:

$$\text{Annual depreciation} = \frac{\text{Acquisition cost} - \text{Estimated residual value}}{\text{Expected useful life in years}}$$

Example

A lorry is acquired at a cost of £3000. Its estimated useful life is 3 years, and its residual value is estimated at £600.

$$\text{Annual depreciation} = \frac{£3000 - £600}{3 \text{ years}}$$

$$= £800 \text{ per annum}$$

The straight-line method allocates the net cost equally to each year of the useful life of an asset. It is particularly applicable to assets such as patents and leases where time is the important factor in the effluxion of the benefits to be derived from the use of an asset. Whilst it is often used for other assets as well, it suffers from the following disadvantages:

(a) it does not reflect the fact that the greatest loss in the market value of an asset occurs in the first year of its use;

(b) it does not reflect the unevenness of the loss in the market value of an asset over several years;

(c) it does not reflect the diminishing losses in value which occur in later years, as the asset approaches the end of its useful life.

For these reasons, the straight-life method of depreciation does not provide an accurate measure of the cost of the service potential allocated to the respective accounting periods during which an asset is employed.

(*b*) *The decreasing balance method*

To calculate the annual depreciation under this method, a fixed percentage is applied to the balance of the net costs not yet allocated as an expense at the end of the previous accounting period. The balance of the unallocated costs will decrease each year, as a result, and theoretically, the balance of the unallocated costs at the end of the estimated useful life should equal the estimated residual value. The formula which is used to calculate the fixed percentage to be applied to the allocation of net costs as depreciation is as follows:

$$r = 1 - \sqrt[n]{\frac{s}{c}}$$

where n = the expected useful life in years
 s = the residual value (this value must be a significant
   one or the depreciation rate will be nearly one)
 c = the acquisition cost
 r = the rate of depreciation to be applied.

Example

Calculate the rate of depreciation to be applied to a lorry acquired at a cost of £3000, having an expected useful life of three years and an estimated residual value of £600.

$$r = 1 - \sqrt[3]{\frac{£600}{£3000}}$$

$$= 1 - 0.58$$

$$= 0.42 \quad \text{or} \quad 42\%$$

The depreciation calculation for each of the three years would be as follows:

		£
	Cost	3000
Year 1.	Depreciation at 42% of £3000	1260
	Unallocated costs end of year 1	1740
Year 2.	Depreciation at 42% of £1740	731
	Unallocated costs end of year 2	1009
Year 3.	Depreciation at 42% of £1009	424
	Residual value at end of year 3	585

The small difference between the estimated residual value of £600 and the resulting residual value of £585 arises solely from calculating the percentage depreciation to the nearest two decimal places.

In actual practice, the percentage rate of depreciation is not calculated so precisely. A rate is selected which approximates the estimated length of useful life, for example an estimated useful life of three years would imply a $33\frac{1}{3}$ rate of depreciation. This practice is reflected in the depreciation rates applied by the Taxation Authorities for calculating depreciation allowances for tax purposes.

The advantage of the decreasing balance method is that it approximates reality in respect of certain assets, for example motor vehicles, where the depreciation calculated in the first year is greatest thereby reflecting the greater loss in market value at this stage of a vehicle's life.

Depreciation and total asset costs

The total costs associated with the benefits derived from fixed assets consists of depreciation and the cost of repairs and maintenance. It follows, therefore, that the proper application of the matching convention to the allocation of total asset costs requires that depreciation and repairs and maintenance be considered jointly as regards the selection of an appropriate method for allocating total asset costs to the accounting periods benefiting from their use.

The depreciation calculated under the two methods which have been examined may be compared in Figs 2.10 and 2.11.

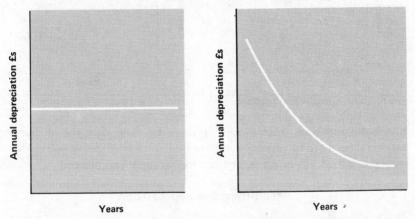

Fig. 2.10   Straight line method.   Fig. 2.11   Decreasing balance method.

The cost of repairs and maintenance may be assumed to increase through time, as the asset deteriorates through use. This is reflected in real-life by the expectancy that the first year in use should be relatively trouble free. The pattern of repair and maintenance cost may be illustrated as in Fig. 2.12.

The total annual asset costs under the straight line and decreasing balance methods of depreciation may be compared as in Figs 2.13 and 2.14.

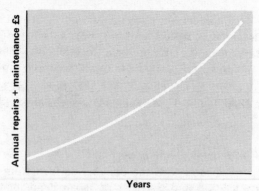

Fig. 2.12　Annual maintenance costs.

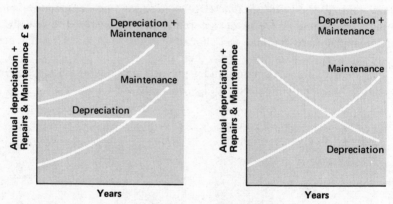

Fig. 2.13 Straight-line method　　　Fig. 2.14 Decreasing method

From the foregoing illustrations, it may be seen that the decreasing balance method provides a better allocation of total asset costs over the useful life of an asset than the straight line method.

Accounting for depreciation

There are several methods for accounting for depreciation. Legislation usually requires that the following information in respect of fixed assets be shown on the Balance Sheet:

(a) the cost or valuation, as the case may be;
(b) the aggregate amount provided or written off since the date of acquisition or valuation, as the case may be, for depreciation or diminution in value.

The method prescribed for arriving at the amount of fixed assets is the difference between (a) and (b) above.

Example

The historical cost of plant and machinery is £100,000. Accumulated depreciation to date is £60,000 and the book value is, therefore, £40,000. This information is disclosed as follows:

Fixed assets	Cost	Accumulated depreciation	Book value
	£	£	£
Plant and Machinery	100,000	60,000	40,000

The accounting procedure required to generate this information is to record the acquisition cost, or valuation as the case may be, in the Asset account, and to accumulate depreciation yearly in a Provision for Depreciation account. The annual provision for depreciation is charged to the Income Statement.

Example

Let us assume that the plant and machinery shown in the previous example was acquired on 1st Jan., 19X0 for £100,000, that its estimated useful life is five years, the expected residual value is nil, and that depreciation is calculated on a straight line basis at the rate of £20,000 a year. The appropriate accounts would record the following data by the end of the year 19X2.

Plant and Machinery account

19X0	£	19X0	£
1st Jan. Cash	100,000	31st Dec. Balance c/d	100,000
	100,000		100,000
19X1		19X1	
1st Jan. Balance b/d	100,000	31st Dec. Balance c/d	100,000
19X2		19X2	
1st Jan. Balance b/d	100,000	31st Dec. Balance c/d	100,000
19X3			
1st Jan. Balance b/d	100,000		

Provision for Depreciation account

19X0	£	19X0	£
31st Dec. Balance c/d	20,000	31st Dec. Income Statement	20,000
	20,000		20,000
19X1		19X1	
		1st Jan. Balance b/d	20,000
31st Dec. Balance c/d	40,000	31st Dec. Income Statement	20,000
	40,000		40,000
		19X2	
		1st Jan. Balance b/d	40,000

Provision for depreciation account (contd.)

19X2		£	19X2	£
			1st Jan. Balance b/d	40,000
31st Dec. Balance c/d		60,000	31st Dec. Income Statement	20,000
		60,000		60,000
			19X3	
			1st Jan. Balance b/d	60,000

Income Statement for the y.e. 31st Dec., 19X0
Provision for Depreciation £20,000

Income Statement for the y.e. 31st Dec., 19X1
Provision for Depreciation £20,000

Income Statement for the y.e. 31st Dec., 19X2
Provision for Depreciation £20,000

Accounting for the sale or disposal of assets

The correct cost of the benefits derived from the use of assets cannot be ascertained until the assets have completed their useful life and have been sold or otherwise disposed of. In the meantime, the annual provision for depreciation is merely an estimate of that actual cost. The practice in accounting for dealing with this problem is to make an adjustment to the income calculated for the year of sale or disposal in respect of any difference between the book value and the realized value of the asset. It is not the practice, therefore, to attempt to re-open previous years to make a correction for the actual depreciation suffered.

The method is to open an Asset Realization account, and to reverse the existing entries in the Asset and the Provision for Depreciation accounts in respect of the asset sold or disposed of, recording directly in the Asset Realization account the sale price, if any, obtained.

Example

On 31st Dec., 19X3, plant and machinery acquired at a cost of £100,000 in 19X0 was sold for £30,000. The accumulated depreciation to date was £60,000. The accounting procedure for dealing with this event is as follows:

	Plant and Machinery account			
19X3		£	19X3	£
1st Jan. Balance b/d		100,000	31st Dec. Asset Realization	100,000
		100,000		100,000

Provision for Depreciation account

19X3	£	19X3	£
31st Dec. Asset Realization	60,000	1st Jan. Balance b/d	60,000
	60,000		60,000

Cash Book

19X3	£
31st Dec. Asset Realization	30,000

Asset Realization account

19X3	£	19X3	£
31st Dec. Plant & Machinery	100,000	31st Dec. Cash	30,000
		31st Dec. Provision for Depreciation	60,000
		31st Dec. Income Statement	10,000
	100,000		100,000

Income Statement for the y.e. 31st December 19X3

	£
Loss on sale of plant & machinery	10,000

Losses through defaulting debtors

The necessity to give credit to customers for the purposes of expanding sales results in the investment of substantial funds in what are in effect short-term loans to customers. There are three important financial aspects as regards debtors which are of interest both to management and investors. Firstly, there is the problem of working capital management in respect of the balance of claims in favour and against the firm, and its implications in respect of liquidity and solvency. Secondly, there is the problem of the overall level of debtors in relation to other assets, and the need for the firm to have sufficient funds to invest in the maintenance and expansion of its income-earning structure. This is a problem which has implications for present and future profitability. Thirdly, there is the problem of risk associated with the recovery of amounts due from debtors. This is a problem of credit control and the prevention of financial losses due to default by debtors.

The valuation of amounts due from debtors at the end of an accounting period presents no difficulty as regards determining debtor balances in an objective manner. Providing that accounting records have been kept properly, the objectivity of the valuation of outstanding debtors is founded in the law of contract and in a claim enforceable at law against the debtors. The recoverability of debts, however, is a question to which the accountant must address himself, since the convention of conservatism requires that losses should be recognized as soon as they arise. The recoverability of debts for financial reporting purposes is a question of law in some cases and judgement in others. Thus, where a debtor has been declared insolvent, the recoverability of the debt is subject to the law of bankruptcy, and where no dividend is likely, the loss must be recognized and the amount written off as a bad debt. Where, however, a debtor cannot be traced or is unable to pay due to personal circumstances and the sum involved does not warrant legal expenses on its recovery, the decision to recognize the loss is a question of judgement. By and large, accountants examine their debtor ledgers at the end of the financial year and identify such debts as are likely to be bad debts by reference to the delay in payment and the attempts made to secure payment. Those debts which are considered to be irrecoverable are written off as bad debts, and if they should be recovered subsequently, the debt is restored in the debtor ledger and the payment recorded.

The failure to deal adequately with the problem of defaulting debtors will distort the measurement of income and asset values in the following respects:

(a) The measurement of income for an accounting period will be overstated to the extent that any credit sales taken into income have created debts which are not recoverable.

(b) The measurement of income for the subsequent accounting period will be understated to the extent that debts created in the previous accounting period are recognized belatedly as bad and written off against the income of the subsequent accounting year.

(c) The Balance Sheet statement of the value of debtors incorporates debts which though legally enforceable are not recoverable. It is not possible, for example, to recover debts from bankrupt persons, or persons who cannot be traced.

It is required, therefore, that:

(a) losses arising from bad debts should be recognized as soon as possible and written off the value of total debtors;

(b) the risk of further possible losses should be anticipated in accordance with the convention of conservatism.

Accounting practice is to deal separately with the problem of debts which are recognized as bad, and the problem of anticipating further losses in the future. In effect, three types of debts are distinguished:

(a) good debts
(b) bad debts
(c) doubtful debts.

The treatment of bad debts

Careful supervision of debtor accounts will minimize the level of bad debts. The enforcement of time limits for the settlement of accounts helps in the prevention of the build-up of arrears of debts and in identifying the possibility of bad debts. Once a debt is recognized as bad, it should be written off immediately to the Bad Debts Account, so that the list of debtor accounts represents only good debts, that is, those which are expected to be honoured.

Example

H. Smith Ltd, a firm of building contractors, had been regular customers of Hervey Building Supplies Ltd and enjoyed a credit limit of £1000. On the 1st January, 19X0, the balance on its account in the books of Hervey totalled £900, and purchases in the month of January 19X0 totalled £150. H. Smith informed Hervey on the 5th February of its inability to make payment in respect of its account. Hervey decided to stop granting further credit to H. Smith until the position was clarified. Shortly thereafter, it was discovered that H. Smith were insolvent, and that it was unlikely that any portion of the outstanding debt of £1050 would be paid. On the 1st March, it was decided to treat the debt as a bad debt.

The accounting entries in the books of Hervey would be as follows:

H. Smith Ltd account

19X0	£	19X0	£
1st Jan. Balance	900	1st March Bad debt	1050
31st Jan. Sales	150		
	1050		1050

Bad Debts account

19X0		
1st March H. Smith Ltd	1050	

At the end of the accounting period, the total on the Bad Debts account is transferred to the Income Statement for the year.

Example

Let us assume that the only bad debt incurred by Hervey Building Supplies Ltd was in respect of H. Smith Ltd in the sum of £1050, as above. The Bad Debts account for the year ended 31st December, 19X0 would be closed as follows:

Bad Debts account

19X0	£	19X0	£
1st March H. Smith Ltd	1050	31st Dec. Income Statement	1050
	1050		1050

Income Statement for the y.e. 31st Dec., 19X0

	£
Bad debts	1050

The treatment of doubtful debts

The question of doubtful debts, as distinct from bad debts, is examined only at the end of each accounting period when the accountant addresses himself to the problem of measuring the income for the year. A final scrutiny of the Debtors account will have eliminated all those accounts which are considered to be bad and the necessary transfers will have been made to the Bad Debts account. Of the remaining debtors, some may ultimately prove to be bad but there may be reasonable grounds for hoping that all remaining debtors will settle their accounts. The convention of conservatism requires that the risk should be discounted of further debts proving to be bad. The normal practice is to create a provision for doubtful debts out of the current year's income, without seeking to identify particular debts as being doubtful of recovery. There are several methods of estimating the level of doubtful debts. The most common method is to allow past experience to establish the percentage of debtors which prove to be bad, and to calculate the provision for doubtful debts by applying this percentage to the debtors outstanding at the end of the accounting period. A more accurate method is to classify debtor balances in terms of their age, and to apply to the several groups of debts the loss rates established by experience.

Example

The debtor balances existing in the books of the Bumpa Trading Company at the end of the accounting year are as follows:

Duration of debts	Balance	Loss Rate %	Provision
	£		£
Less than 1 month	10,000	1	100
1–2 months	3000	3	90
2–3 months	1000	5	50
3–4 months	500	10	50
Over 4 months	100	20	20
	14,600		310

One of the advantages of this method of creating a provision for doubtful debts is that it enables management to understand the relationship between the slow collection of debts and the financial losses caused by defaulting debtors.

The accounting entries would be as follows:

Income Statement for the year ended 31st December, 19X0

£

Provision for doubtful debts   310

Provision for Doubtful Debts account

19X0   £

Income Statement y.e. 31st Dec.   310

The provision for doubtful debts is not identified with any individual debtors. It is carried forward as an estimated liability, and is shown on the Balance Sheet as follows:

Balance Sheet as on 31st December, 19X0

....   £   £

Debtors   14,600

Less: Provision
for Doubtful
Debts   310

14,290

In this manner, the objective of presenting a realistic valuation of trade debtors is achieved.

Summary

This chapter examined two important problems in the measurement of periodic income, namely, depreciation and financial losses resulting from bad debts. Both problems are concerned with the manner in which losses in asset values should be recognized. Depreciation is in itself a difficult problem from a theoretical viewpoint, and its treatment in accounting as an allocation of historical costs is a limited view of this problem. Nevertheless, such treatment is compatible with the matching convention for allocation to cost of acquisition of assets to the revenues derived from their use. Not all assets are depreciable, and depreciation should take into account such factors as all the relevant costs of acquisition as well as the useful life of assets.

Two methods of depreciation were examined, and their implications were discussed. The adjustments required on the sale or disposal of assets were also examined.

Losses through defaulting debtors were analysed and their impact on the measurement of periodic income were discussed. Accounting adopts a two-stage approach to this problem, namely the recognition of losses actually incurred by declaring certain debts as *bad*, and the provision against the risk of loss through creating provisions for doubtful debts.

References

1. AICPA, Accounting Research Bulletin No. 43 (1953).

2. Barton, A. D., *The Anatomy of Accounting*, University of Queensland Press, 1975.

3. Baxter, W. T., *Depreciation*, Sweet and Maxwell, London, 1971.

4. Goldberg, L., Concepts of Depreciation, in *Studies in Accounting Theory* Baxter, W. T. & Davidson, S. (eds), Sweet and Maxwell, London, 1962.

6
Preparing an Income Statement and a Balance Sheet

In chapter 5, we examined the role of the Trial Balance as a working paper which enables the accountant not only to check the arithmetical accuracy of the entries recorded during an accounting period, but which also serves as a basis for considering adjustments to be made for the purpose of measuring periodic income. The extraction of a Trial Balance at the close of the accounting period is the first step, therefore, in the preparation of an Income Statement and a Balance Sheet.

We examined in chapter 4 how the Trial Balance should be adjusted in respect of the accrual into the accounting period of revenues and expenses, and we analysed in chapter 5 the nature of the losses in asset values which have to be taken into consideration in the measurement of periodic income.

The purpose of this chapter is to summarize the various adjustments which must be made to the Trial Balance, and the manner in which these adjustments are incorporated into the process of preparing an Income Statement and a Balance Sheet.

Preparing an Income Statement

The preparation of an Income Statement is a two-stage exercise. The first stage is an informal one and consists of using the Trial Balance as a worksheet for accumulating all the data which incorporate the various adjustments which we referred to earlier. When the adjusted Trial Balance has been certified and confirmed, the adjustments are formally entered in the appropriate accounts, and the Income Statement is formally included in the accounts system. It is important to remember that the Income Statement is an account to which the revenue and expense accounts for the accounting period are transferred as summarized totals, and which exists solely for the purpose of measuring the accounting income for that period. As we shall see in Part IV, the Income Statement also forms part of the process of financial reporting, and many problems in this respect arise from the fact that the Income Statement is an integral element in financial accounting, and is subject to its conventions.

The following example illustrates the nature of the Income Statement.

Example

Let us return to the Trial Balance given on page 114, which showed the following list of balances extracted from the books of John Smith on the 31st December, 19X0, being the end of the first year of trading.

	£ Dr.	£ Cr.
Capital		25,000
Motor vehicles	10,000	
Furniture and fittings	2500	
Purchases	31,000	
Cash at bank	6000	
Sales		70,000
Sundry debtors	18,000	
Sundry creditors		3500
Rent	4500	
Salaries	22,800	
Insurances	400	
Motor expenses	2000	
Light and heat	1000	
General expenses	300	
	98,500	98,500

We noted in chapter 4 that the following adjustments were required:

(1) Rent unpaid at the end of the year was £1500.
(2) Insurance paid in advance amounted to £50.
(3) Rent receivable, but not recorded in the account, amounted to £60.
(4) Closing inventories at the 31st December, 19X0 were valued at £3000.

We are now given the following additional information:

(1) Depreciation is to be charged on the undermentioned assets and is to be calculated on the depreciating balance method. Their estimated residual value is shown in brackets.

| Motor vehicles | 20% | (£1000) |
| Furniture and fittings | 10% | (£250) |

(2) Bad debts to be written off amounted to £180, and a provision for doubtful debts is to be created in the sum of £178.

Adjusting for accruals

We saw in chapter 4 (page 122) that the adjustments for accruals resulted in the following revisions of balances in the Trial Balance:

	Original Balance	Adjustment	New Balance
	£	£	£
(a) Rent	4500	1500	6000
(b) Insurance	400	50	350
(c) Insurance prepaid	—	50	50
(d) Rent receivable	—	60	60
(e) Rent receivable	—	60	60

We explained in chapter 4 that items (a), (b) and (d) represented adjustments to the revenues and expenses of the year and affected the Income Statement. The following resulting balances on the accounts affect the Balance Sheet and we shall see later in this chapter how they are incorporated in that statement:

	£ Dr.	£ Cr.
Rent accrued		1500
Insurance prepaid	50	
Rent receivable	60	

The corrected total revenues and expenses may now be listed on a worksheet used in the preparation of the Income Statement:

Draft Income Statement for the year ended 31st December, 19X0

	£		£
Purchases	31,000	Sales	70,000
Rent	6000	Rent receivable	60
Salaries	22,800		
Insurance	350		
Motor expenses	2000		
Light and heat	1000		
General expenses	300		

Adjusting for inventories

We noted in chapter 4 that periodic measurement involved valuing the inventory of goods unsold at the end of the accounting period. The closing inventory is valued, as we saw in chapter 1, in accordance with the cost convention, and represents the residue of the purchases of the year which have not been sold at the year-end, and which will be sold in the next accounting period. Opening inventories are shown, therefore, as a *debit balance* in the Trial Balance, whereas closing inventories do not appear since they are valued after the close of the accounting period. It is for this reason that the appropriate entries must be made in the Inventory Account to make possible the measurement of periodic income. In the example in question, there is no opening inventory since we are dealing with the first year of trading.

We saw in chapter 2 that the adjustment for closing inventory had a two-fold effect. First, it is effected by means of a credit entry in the Income Statement and a debit entry in the Inventory Account. Second, it results in a debit balance in the Inventory Account which must be incorporated in the Balance Sheet.

The closing inventory adjustment may be entered on the draft Income Statement as follows.

Draft Income Statement for the year ended 31st December, 19X0

	£		£
Purchases	31,000	Sales	70,000
Rent	6000	Rent receivable	60
Salaries	22,800	Closing inventory	
Insurance	350	31st December, 19X0	3000
Motor expenses	2000		
Light and heat	1000		
General expenses	300		

Adjusting for the loss in asset values

We mentioned in chapter 5 the most important losses in asset values which the accountant has to recognize in the measurement of periodic income. We do not propose to deal in this text with the variety of gains and losses in asset values which may occur, since we are concerned only with the analysis of the process of periodic measurement and with an examination of the most significant losses in asset values which enter into this process.

In the example, we are required to deal with depreciation, bad and doubtful debts.

(a) *The calculation of depreciation*

The depreciation to be charged against the income for the year is as follows:

	£	£
(i) *Motor vehicles*		
Cost	10,000	
Estimated residual value	1000	
Net cost for depreciation purposes	9000	
Depreciation for the year 19X0 at 20%	1800	1800
Residual balance for depreciation in following years	7200	
(ii) *Furniture and fittings*		
Cost	2500	
Estimated residual value	250	
Net cost for depreciation purposes	2250	
Depreciation for the year 19X0 at 10%	225	225
Residual balance for depreciation in following years	2025	
Total depreciation for the year		2025

It is the usual practice to detail in the Income Statement the component elements of the provision for depreciation, and as we shall see later Fixed Assets are also described in their categories on the Balance Sheet. The provision for depreciation in respect of the different fixed assets may be reconciled, therefore, with the yearly additional provision for depreciation shown on the Balance Sheet.

(b) *Calculation of the provision for doubtful debts*

Duration of debt	Balance £	Loss Rate %	Provision £
Less than 1 month	15,960	$\frac{1}{2}$	80
1–2 months	1800	5	90
2–3 months	40	10	4
over 3 months	20	25	4
	17,820		178

These adjustments may be included in the draft Income Statement as shown on p. 152.

Calculating the periodic income

The details shown on the draft Income Statement below are sufficient to permit the calculation of the income for the year ended 31st December, 19X0. The Income Statement is set out, however, so as to enable significant information to be immediately apparent. In this respect, a distinction is made between *Gross income* and *Net income*,

Draft Income Statement for the year ended 31st December, 19X0

		£		£
Purchases		31,000	Sales	70,000
Rent		6000	Rent receivable	60
Salaries		22,800	Closing inventory	
Insurance		350	31st December, 19X0	3000
Motor expenses		2000		
Light and heat		1000		
General expenses		300		
Depreciation				
Motor vehicles	1800			
Furniture and Fittings	225	2025		
Bad debts		180		
Provision for doubtful				
debts		178		

the former being the income resulting after the deduction from the gross sales revenue of expenses directly connected with the production or purchase of the goods sold, whilst the latter reflects the deduction of overhead expenses from gross income. Although the Net Income figure is the most important result, dividing the Income Statement into two parts highlights the burden of overhead expenses, as well as focussing attention on important aspects of business activity.

(a) Calculating Gross Income
In the case of a trading business—as is the case in the example quoted—the Gross Income from Trading may be shown as follows:

	£		£
Purchases	31,000	Sales	70,000
Less: Closing inventory at			
31st December, 19X0	3000		
Cost of Sales	28,000		
Gross Trading Income	42,000		
	70,000		70,000

This arrangement shows the following significant points:

(a) Although purchases amounted to £31,000, the cost of goods actually sold amounted to only £28,000. Hence, the gross trading income expressed as a percentage of sales was:

$$\frac{42,000}{70,000} \times 100 = 60\%$$

This percentage is often referred to as the Gross Profit ratio. Expressed as a percentage of cost of sales, the gross trading income was:

$$\frac{42,000}{28,000} \times 100 = 150\%$$

(b) The level of trading activity may also be judged from the average length of time inventory is held. The rate of inventory turnover may be calculated as follows:

$$\frac{\text{Cost of Sales}}{\text{Average Inventory}}$$

The average inventory is obtained by the arithmetic mean of the opening and closing inventory. In the example under consideration, the rate of inventory turnover for the year was as follows:

$$\frac{28,000}{3000} = 9.3 \text{ times}$$

so that inventory was held for approximately 39 days (365 days ÷ 9.3).

The segregation of the Gross Trading Income in the process of calculating periodic income provides useful ratios for the analysis of trading performance, and for indicating areas of trading where efficiency might be improved.

It is the practice for business to seek to identify the gross income. Thus Manufacturing firms show Manufacturing Gross Income, contracting firms show Contracting Gross Income and so on.

The problem of deciding which expenses to include in the calculation of the gross income lies in defining direct as distinct from indirect operating expenses. Direct expenses, such as purchases, freight and other expenses associated with the acquisition of goods for resale, for example, are included in the calculation of gross income.

(b) Calculating the Net Income

The calculation of the Net Income is effected by charging against the Gross Income the indirect expenses which have been accumulated in the Trial Balance, and other expenses such as depreciation, bad debts and provisions for doubtful debts. Using the data given in the example, the Net Income for the year ended 31st December, 19X0 may be calculated as follows.

		£		£
Rent		6000	Gross Trading Income	42,000
Salaries		22,800	Rent receivable	60
Insurance		350		
Motor expenses		2000		
Light and heat		1000		
General expenses		300		
Depreciation				
Motor vehicles	1800			
Furniture and fittings	225			
		2025		
Bad debts		180		
Provision for doubtful debts		178		
		34,833		
Net income		7227		
		42,060		42,060

Miscellaneous income, such as interest, rents and dividends, which form a minor element in the business income are usually shown in the calculation of the net income rather than in the calculation of the gross income.

The segregation of the net income calculation also affords a clearer view of significant ratios. The net income is itself the most significant performance result, and its dimensions may be assessed not only in relation to the gross trading income, but also to gross revenue. The net income as a percentage of Sales indicates the level of activity required to produce one £ of net income, and may be calculated as follows:

$$\frac{\text{Net Income before interest and tax}}{\text{Sales}}$$

Thus, whereas the percentage of gross income to sales was 60% the percentage of net income to sales was only 13%, indicating thereby not only the relative burden of direct and indirect expenses but also the relative efficiency of the business.

The formal presentation of the Income Statement

Although the Income Statement is part of the accounts system, and may be shown in an account form, its formal presentation has been influenced by its use as a financial reporting statement. This influence has encouraged the further classification of indirect expenses into Selling, Administrative and Financial Expenses, and the presentation of the Income Statement in a vertical form as follows:

John Smith, Esq., trading as General Dealer Income Statement for the year ended 31st December, 19X0			
	£	£	£
Sales			70,000
Cost of Sales			
Purchases		31,000	
Less: Closing inventory		3000	
			28,000
Gross Trading Income			42,000
Other Income			
Rent			60
Total Income			42,060
Selling and Distribution Expenses			
Salesmen's salaries	12,000		
Motor expenses	2000		
Depreciation—Motor vehicles	1800	15,800	
Administrative Expenses			
Rent	6000		
Office salaries	10,800		
Insurance	350		
Light and heat	1000		
General expenses	300		
Depreciation—Furniture and fittings	225		
		18,675	
Financial Expenses			
Bad debts	180		
Provision for doubtful debts	178	358	
Total Overhead Expenses			34,833
Net Income			7227

Preparing a Balance Sheet

The preparation of a Balance Sheet is a two-stage exercise, and in this sense, it follows the same pattern as the preparation of an Income Statement, that is, an informal stage based on a worksheet, and a formal stage represented by the Balance Sheet presented as a financial report. There are, however, a number of important differences between an Income Statement and a Balance Sheet. First, from a procedural point of view, the Income Statement is part of the accounts system and as we explained earlier, it is itself an account. By contrast, the Balance Sheet is not an account, but a list showing the balances of the accounts following the preparation of the Income Statement. Second, the Income Statement is the effective instrument of periodic measurement in accounting, whereas the Balance Sheet does not set out to do other than state residual balances. Third, residual debit balances are shown on the Balance Sheet as *Assets*, and there are problems stemming from this description which we discuss in chapter 7. Fourth, by attaching accounting measurements to debit and credit balances described as Assets and Liabilities respectively, the Balance Sheet is often interpreted as indicating the net worth of the business. This is a misconception, and in the case of corporations has led to much controversy. We explore these problems further in Part 4.

Collecting and classifying balances

The preparation of the Balance Sheet need not await the entry of all the adjustments into the individual accounts following the preparation of the Income Statement. It may be prepared in draft form from the Trial Balance and the finalized draft of the Income Statement.

In accounting, debit balances are either assets or expenses. The preparation of the Income Statement involves the removal from the Trial Balance of all expenses in respect of the year, so that any debit balances remaining are treated as assets. These assets, as defined, are classified as follows:

(i) Long-term assets representing an enduring benefit to the enterprise. Long-term assets described as Fixed Assets, for example, plant and machinery, are subject to depreciation. Other long-term assets, such as land and intangible assets may or may not be subject to depreciation or other changes in their book value. We examine these problems in chapter 7.

(ii) Short-term assets, described as Current Assets, are the following:

(a) Closing inventories at the end of the accounting period;
(b) Trade debtors;
(c) Pre-payments on expense accounts, for example, insurance paid in advance;
(d) Cash at bank and cash in hand.

The measurement of closing inventories present particular problems, which we discuss in chapter 7. We have already examined the accounting problems relating to trade debtors which arise from the writing-off of bad debts and the making of provisions for doubtful debts. We shall deal presently with the verification of cash at the bank.

By contrast, credit balances on the Trial Balance are either liabilities, revenues or investments in the firm in the form of capital and long-term loans. The removal of periodic revenues from the Trial Balance means that the remaining credit balances are either liabilities or investments. The Provision for Depreciation is one of a number of exceptions to this rule. These exceptions, as in the case of pre-payments shown as debit balances, arise from accounting procedures. Credit balances are collected and classified as follows:

(i) Capital account, representing the owner's original investment in the firm and accumulated profits;

(ii) Long-term borrowings;

(iii) Short term liabilities, described as Current Liabilities which include such credit balances as Sundry Creditors, Accrued Expenses; Payment Received in Advance, Provisions for Taxation and Bank Overdrafts.

Verifying balances

Accounts are usually subjected to yearly audits, that is, they are checked in detail by a firm of professional auditors, who are themselves accountants. The purpose of the audit is not only to check on the accuracy of the records, but also to ensure that the statements contained in those records are correct. Thus, the existence of assets evidenced in the assets accounts is verified, as well as the existence of liabilities evidence in various creditors's accounts. In the case of corporations, audits are obligatory and auditors are appointed by shareholders to act as watchdogs over their interests. In this connection, they are required to certify that both the Income Statement and the Balance Sheet reflect a true and fair view of the information they are legally required to convey.

Bank Reconciliation Statement

It is unlikely that on the stated day, the balance at the bank as shown in the Cash Book will correspond with the statement of the balance at the bank produced by the Bank itself. This is due not only to the normal delays occurring in the process of clearing cheques, but also to delays in lodging and presenting cheques for payment. Moreover, payments and receipts may be effected directly through the Bank and by-pass the Accountant. For example, dividends and interest receivable may be payable on instruction directly into the Bank Account, and routine payments may be effected by stop-orders and direct debit procedures. The Bank also charges commission, fees and interest directly to the account, and the Bank Statement is used to convey these details to the client.

The Bank Reconciliation Statement is an accounting procedure for reconciling the balance at the bank as per the Bank Statement with the balance at the bank as per the Cash Book, whenever a Bank Statement is received.

When preparing a Balance Sheet, the balance at the bank as shown in the Cash Book must be supported by a Bank Statement stating the balance on the last day of the accounting period, and the Bank Reconciliation Statement explains any differences which have not been already adjusted in the Cash Book. Thus, any charges such as bank commission and interest will be entered in the Cash Book and will be shown as expenses in the Income Statement. In effect, therefore, the Bank Reconciliation Statement explains the nature of the unadjusted differences between the Cash Book and the Bank Statement.

Example

The balance at the bank according to the Cash Book was £6000 on the 31st December, 19X0. According to the Bank Statement the balance was £6500. The difference is explained as follows:

  (i) Cheques received from debtors on 31st December, 19X0 which were not banked until 2nd January, 19X1 amounted to £250.

 (ii) Cheques sent to creditors on 31st December, 19X0 and not presented for payment until after 1st January, 19X1 amounted to £750.

Bank Reconciliation Statement as on 31st December, 19X0	
	£
Balance at bank as per Bank Statement	6500
Add: Cheques received but not lodged	250
	6750
Less: Cheques issued but not presented	750
Balance at bank as per Cash Book	6000

The formal presentation of the Balance Sheet

In the case of corporations, legislation usually provides rules for the presentation of both the Income Statement and the Balance Sheet. As we shall see in chapter 9, these rules apply to published financial reports. The rules reflect the recommendation of the accounting profession, and are designed not only to secure sufficient disclosure, but to permit salient features to be quickly recognized. It is usual, therefore, to classify assets and liabilities in groupings as we mentioned earlier, and also to rank them according to liquidity. Thus, asset groupings are shown from the most fixed to the most liquid, and liabilities from the long-term to the most current.

The importance of the Balance Sheet, together with the Income Statement, for the purpose of financial reporting and investment decision-making, has focussed attention to the arrangement of particular groupings to assist the interpretation and the analysis of results. We shall deal with this analysis in Part 4, but we may mention at this stage that the relationship between long-term finance and long-term investment needs of the firm (long-term capital as defined in finance) and short-term finance and short-term financial needs (working capital) is important to financial analysts. Other areas of interests are, of course, the return on capital employed which is the ratio of net income to equity capital (owner's investment in the firm), liquidity and solvency.

The vertical form of presentation of the Balance Sheet is as follows:

John Smith Esq., trading as General Dealer
Balance Sheet as on 31st December, 19X0

	£	£	£	£
Capital Employed				
Capital account			25,000	
Net income for the year			7227	
				32,227
Represented by				
		Pro-vision for deprecia-		
Fixed assets	*cost*	*tion*	*net*	
	£	£	£	
Motor vehicles	10,000	1800	8200	
Furniture and				
fittings	2500	225	2275	
	12,500	2025	10,475	10,475
Current assets				
Inventories at cost			3000	
Debtors		17,820		
Less: Provision for				
doubtful debts		178	17,642	
Accruals and				
prepayments			110	
Cash at bank			6000	
			26,752	
Less				
Current liabilities				
Creditors		3500		
Accruals		1500	5000	
Net working capital			21,752	
				32,227

Summary

This chapter has been concerned with the accounting procedures for preparing and presenting the two main financial reports, namely, the Income Statement and the Balance Sheet.

The extraction of the Trial Balance at the close of the accounting period marks the first stage in the preparation of these reports. Earlier chapters have examined the adjustments required for the purposes of periodic measurement. These include accruals, depreciation and adjustments in respect of bad and doubtful debts. All these adjustments are effected informally on working sheets, and once they have been verified and confirmed, the final accounts may be drawn up.

The importance of the Income Statement lies not only in the fact that it is the main vehicle of periodic measurement and provides the measurement of periodic income, but also in the fact that it is itself part of the accounts system. The objective purpose underlying the preparation of the Income Statement is the measurement of net income, which is used as a basis for measuring business efficiency. The distinction between gross income and net income facilitates the analysis of the financial results, as does the classification of expenses under various categories.

By contrast, the Balance Sheet is a list of residual balances following the preparation of the Income Statement. It forms not part of the accounts system. The Balance Sheet is used in conjunction with the Income Statement in the analysis of the financial performance of the business, and the treatment and classification of assets and liabilities is important to this analysis. Consequently, particular attention is paid to the manner in which important financial aspects of the business are highlighted in the presentation of the Balance Sheet.

7
The Valuation of Recorded Assets and Liabilities

The purpose of this chapter is to examine further the nature of the various items appearing on the Balance Sheet and to consider the purpose and the reasons for the recorded values. It is necessary to understand the logic and methodology which underlie the recorded values in order to appreciate the nature of financial accounting information. The problem of valuation is particularly important as regards financial reporting and we shall extend our analysis of this problem in Part 4.

We mentioned in chapter 2 that the concept and measurement of value is an element and a process which is central to accounting as a whole, and which, therefore, cannot be restricted to the problem of financial reporting. Nevertheless, the significance of the information communicated to shareholders in financial reports depends entirely on the methods of valuation employed by accountants. Hence, if one is to appreciate the issues involved in current controversies, it is necessary to have a clear understanding of the accounting approach to this problem.

The financial accounting conventions which we examined in chapter 1 of this Part may be said to have their origin in the concept of stewardship accounting. A number of these conventions have a deterministic influence on valuation for financial reporting purposes, and reflect the stewardship concept of financial reporting as regards the manner in which Boards of Directors should communicate information to shareholders about the manner in which their funds have been handled. For example, when a transaction occurs, it is said that both parties to the transaction are agreed as to the exchange value of the asset involved: that value may be verified at that point, that is, it is an objective measure of value for accounting purposes. It follows, therefore, that the cost of acquiring assets has traditionally been thought to provide the best method of valuing assets for financial reporting purposes on the assumption that the objective of financial reporting is to explain to shareholders how their funds have been handled.

Since the stewardship concept of financial reporting has its roots also in the prevention of frauds, it is interesting to note that one of the major arguments in favour of historical cost valuation is the prevention of fraud. Accountants feel that to depart from this basis of valuation would open the way to fraudulent practices since other measures of value are essentially in the nature of opinions.

We shall note that the convention of conservatism leads to a modification of the cost convention in certain cases, and to reporting to shareholders the lowest likely value. If the realizable value of stocks, for example, is lower than its historical cost value, the convention of conservatism requires that the realizable value be adopted.

The convention of consistency requires that once a basis of valuation has been adopted, it should not be changed except for valid reasons.

Finally, it should be noted that Company Law stipulates the manner in which values should be reported. In the United Kingdom, the law generally reflects the conventions of accounting, and in this respect, we may say that in developing legal rules for financial reporting, the law has followed its tradition of codifying conventions existing among practitioners.

The valuation of assets

The key to an understanding of the manner in which the accountant approaches the problem of valuation is to be found in the classification of assets. Fixed assets are long-term assets whose usefulness in the operations of the firm is likely to extend beyond one accounting period. They are not intended for resale, so that their value depends upon the future cash flows which they are intended to generate. By contrast, current assets are those assets which are intended to be exhausted in the income-earning operations of the next accounting period, and this includes their availability for meeting current liabilities.

There are three general rules for valuing fixed assets:

(a) The enterprise should be considered as a going concern, unless the facts indicate to the contrary. This means that the valuation of fixed assets should reflect the continued expectation of their usefulness to the enterprise. For this reason, their realizable value is inappropriate, and their historical cost is regarded as the most objective measure of value. Historical cost includes the original purchase price and, in addition, all other costs incurred in rendering the asset ready for use. In Part 4 we shall see that it may be argued that historical cost does not value a firm as a going concern.

(b) Changes in the market value of fixed assets are generally ignored in the valuation process. In the case of land and buildings, however, it is quite common for revaluations to take place from time to time as their value increases during inflation. The unwillingness of accountants to recognize changes in market values, and the need for information about the market value of certain fixed assets has led to statutory enforcement of the disclosure of material differences between the book and market values in published Balance Sheets in the United Kingdom.

(c) Depreciation in value attributable to wear and tear should always be recognized.

The valuation of fixed assets

The valuation of land

Land is valued at cost despite rises or falls in market value. Cost includes broker's commission, surveying and legal fees and insurance charges. In addition, draining, levelling and landscaping costs and other improvements such as fencing, sewerage and water mains should be included, though it is quite common in the case of farm accounts for these improvements to be shown separately because of the different tax allowances which they occasionally enjoy.

Land is not generally regarded as susceptible to depreciation as understood in accounting, but as indicated earlier, legislation may require material differences between book values and market values to be disclosed.

The definition of assets in accounting reflects its orientation towards the law. In this connection, only assets in the ownership of the business may be classed as assets for accounting purposes. This definition poses a particular problem in the case of land. Strictly speaking, only freehold land lies in the ownership of the business for accounting purposes. Leasehold land enjoyed subject to the payment of rent is not classified as an asset, and the rent-charge appears as an expense in the Income Statement. By contrast, a long lease acquired by the payment of a capital sum is shown as an asset, and the capital payment is usually allocated as expenses over the period of the lease. Leasehold rights extending to 99 and 999 years, for example, are virtually undistinguishable from freehold rights for accounting purposes. Ground-rents are chargeable as yearly expenses.

The valuation of buildings

As in the case of land, buildings are valued on a historical cost basis—whether they have been acquired or constructed. Construction costs include such incidental expenses as architect fees, inspection fees and insurance costs applicable to a construction project. Where an existing building has been purchased, the costs of rendering the building suitable for its intended purpose should be added to the purchase price in arriving at its historic cost value.

The valuation process for buildings differs from that of land in two ways:

(a) A cost of maintenance is involved in the repairs which have to be made from time to time in the upkeep of the building. Such asset maintenance expenses are charged as they are incurred to the Income Statement. Additions and improvements to the building, which are distinguished from repairs, must be capitalized and added to the value of the building on the Balance Sheet.

(b) Buildings depreciate in the course of use and as they become dated. Whereas this may not always be true of residential property, it is invariably true as regards industrial and farm buildings. In such cases, the account value should be shown at cost less the accumulated depreciation to date of the Balance Sheet.

The valuation of plant and machinery and other fixed assets

Plant and machinery, Furniture and fittings, Motor vehicles, Tools and Sundry Equipment are usually valued at historic cost with proper allowance for depreciation. Cost includes purchase price, freight charges, insurance in transit and all installation costs. As we saw in chapter 5, the purpose of depreciation in accounting is to allocate the cost of fixed assets to the several years of their useful life to the firm.

The valuation of natural resources

Natural resources, such as oil, gas, coal and other minerals as well as forests and other plantations are valued at cost—whether they are developed or acquired. Developments cost which must be capitalized include the costs of exploration, such as drilling for oil for example.

The valuation of current assets

Current assets consist of cash and other assets, such as debtors and inventories, which are expected to be converted into cash or to be used in the operations of the enterprise within one year. The most complex problems lie in the valuation of the different types of inventories existing at the end of an accounting period. In Part 3, we shall see that closing inventories consist of three types—raw materials, work-in-progress and finished goods. The production process may be viewed as a process of adding value to successive categories of inventories, that is, from raw material to finished goods. Inventories values, therefore, affect the Income Statement as well as the Balance Sheet. Since they are an important constituent of the expenses chargeable against sales revenue, they occupy a key position in the determination of periodic income.

The valuation of inventories

The general rule is that inventories should be valued at cost. There are, however, many different methods for determining the cost value of inventories, and these methods produce valuations which differ markedly from each other. A simple example serves to illustrate how three different valuation methods lead to divergent values.

Example

A firm has an opening inventory of 100 items valued at £1.00 each. During the accounting period, 100 units were purchased for £1.20 each and a further 100 units were purchased for £1.30 each. There remained 100 units in inventory at the end of the accounting period, that is, after 200 units had been sold.

The firm is considering the effects of the undermentioned three methods of inventory valuation:

    (a) FIFO (first-in-first-out)
    (b) LIFO (last-in-first-out)
    (c) Weighted Average Cost.

The effects of these alternative methods may be seen from the tabulation of inventory data below:

	Unit	Unit Cost	Value
		£	£
Opening inventory	100	1.00	100
First purchase	100	1.20	120
Second purchase	100	1.30	130

(a) The FIFO method assumes that the oldest items in inventory are used first, so that the items in inventory are assumed to be the remnants of more recent purchases. The result of the application of FIFO to the given data is that the cost of goods sold during the year is taken to be £220, and the value of the closing inventory is £130. In effect, during periods of inflation the resultant income measurements tend to be overstated, though closing inventory values are more accurately stated.

(b) The LIFO method assumes that the most recently purchased inventories are used first, so that the items remaining in inventory at the end of the year are assumed to be the remnants of earlier purchases. Under this method, the cost of goods sold during the year is taken to be £250, and the value of the closing inventory is £100. The LIFO method has the reverse effect, therefore, to FIFO on the measurement of income and the valuation of closing inventories.

(c) The Weighted Average Cost method requires the calculation of the unit cost of closing inventory by means of a formula which divides the total cost of all inventory available for sale during the accounting period by the physical units of inventory available for sale.

The weighted average cost of the 300 unit available for sale may be calculated as follows:

$$\frac{\text{Total Cost of Annual Inventory}}{\text{Total Annual Units of Inventory}} = \frac{£350}{300} = £1.167 \text{ per unit}$$

Hence, the cost of goods sold during the year is £233, whilst the value of the closing inventory is £117. The Weighted Average Cost method is a compromise, therefore, between the extreme points established by FIFO and LIFO respectively.

This simple example illustrates that closing inventories may be valued at £130, £100 and £117 depending on the assumptions made about the flow of costs. LIFO is a method of valuation which is commonly used in the United States, but its use in the United Kingdom is prohibited by the Inland Revenue Authorities.

The 'lower of cost or market rule' (LCM)

The valuation of inventories at cost or market value, whichever is lower, is a rule which has long and widely been observed in financial accounting. The rule was originally justified in terms of the convention of conservatism, which as applied to the valuation of inventories meant that there should be no anticipation of profit and that all foreseeable losses should be provided for in the value reported to shareholders. Thus, if the cost value of an inventory item was £1.20 and the market value was £1.00, the end of year inventory valuation should be based on the lower value, and the difference written off against income.

The relation of the LCM rule with the other rules governing cost allocation and income determination in accounting may be questioned. If, for example, periodic income is to be measured by a rigorous process of matching revenues with their related product costs, it would seem inappropriate to charge against current revenues the cost of products which have not yet been sold, thereby relieving the revenues of a future period of a portion of their proper burden. Hence, the rule violates the matching convention, resulting in a distortion of current and future income measurements, thereby affecting their reliability as indicators of business performance. For this reason, some have argued that the rule is 'starkly illogical' and have suggested that it should be abandoned save in the case of obsolete or damaged inventories (van Pelt III, 1962). Others however, have reconciled the rule with the matching convention on the grounds that only 'useful' costs should be carried forward to the next accounting period (May, 1947). Costs which are not useful are those which exceed the market value of the inventory in question. The measure of the loss represented by the difference between cost and market value of such inventories may validly be treated as a cost of conducting business during the currency of the accounting period. According to this interpretation of the LCM rule, the lower of these two values represents the residual useful stock.

Different meanings of 'market value'

Whilst most accountants would agree with the LCM rule, there seems to be little unanimity as to which market value is the most useful. According to one author, the net realizable value interpretation of market value is most commonly accepted in the United Kingdom and Australia; in the United States, market value means replacement or reproduction cost; in Canada and most European countries, net realizable value is used for the valuation of finished goods and replacement cost is applied to the valuation of raw material inventories (Mueller, 1964).

The net realizable value concept is based on the theory that the usefulness of a measurement of inventory value is to be found in its function as an indicator of the recoverable value of the inventory concerned. So long as the expected net realizable value is equal to the costs which have been incurred, there is no possibility of an accounting loss occurring.

The replacement cost concept of market value is based on the idea of the 'utility' of inventory. According to the American Institute of Certified Public Accountants (1953), "as a general guide, utility is indicated primarily by the current cost of replacement of the goods as they would be obtained by purchase or reproduction." Hence, the notion of utility in this context is related to the ability to generate income, for at the time of acquisition, each unit of inventory is regarded as incorporating a gross income potential which is to be realized at the time of sale. The measure of the retained usefulness of inventory held at the end of the accounting period is to be found, therefore, in an assessment of the expenditure which would have to be incurred to produce or to purchase inventory having an equivalent gross profit potential. Where inventory may be replaced at a cost which is lower than the acquisition cost of currently-held inventory, the fall in the replacement cost is regarded as indicating that the expected gross income potential of current inventory has decreased. For this reason, the lower of the cost of current inventories and their replacement cost is used in the United States to measure the residual income potential of inventories on hand, and to determine the amount of their acquisition cost which appropriately should be written off as having lost their usefulness for producing future income. As a result, subsequent revenues are not charged with the cost of acquiring inventories which is higher than current costs, and distortions are not introduced into the measurement of income.

The replacement cost concept of market value assumes that a decrease in the replacement cost will be accompanied by a corresponding decrease in the net realizable value of currently-held inventories. Where there is no evidence to suggest that a fall in selling prices will take place, there is no likelihood of a failure to recover the cost of acquisition of existing inventories. Consequently, no loss of gross income potential is incurred. For this reason, AICPA Research Bulletin No. 43 recommended an upper and a lower limit for replacement cost as a definition of 'market' in the LCM rule. Therefore, no loss should be recognized if the fall in replacement cost does not reflect a similar fall in expected selling price, because a loss should not be recognized in the current accounting period, if it will result in the recognition of abnormal income in a later period.

General criticism of the LCM rule

The LCM rule has long been criticized primarily on the basis of its inherent inconsistency. Thus, if current replacement cost is objective, definite, verifiable and more useful when it is lower than acquisition costs it also possesses these attributes when it is higher than acquisition cost (Sprouse & Moonitz, 1962). The conservatism reflected in the LCM rule for asset valuations in one period results in an overstatement of income in the subsequent period. The consequence of recognizing decreases in value but not increases in value occurring prior to sale is reflected in a shifting effect in periodic income measurement.

The valuation of debtors

The problems associated with the valuation of debtors were discussed in chapter 5.

The valuation of other assets

Investments

In financial accounting, investments are defined as shares and other legal rights acquired by a firm through the investment of its funds. Investments may be long-term or short-term, depending upon the intention of the firm at the time of acquisition. Where investments are intended to be held for a period of more than one year, they are in the nature of fixed assets: where they are held for a shorter period, they are in the nature of current assets. Shares in subsidiary and associated companies are usually not held for resale, and hence would be classified as being of the nature of fixed assets. Short-dated Government stocks, for example, may provide a convenient vehicle for the investment of excess funds not immediately needed. Such short-term holdings would be classified as current assets in the Balance Sheet. It is the practice, however, to show investments separately in the Balance Sheet and not to include them under the heading of Fixed Assets.

Investments are recorded at their cost of acquisition, and whilst substantial decreases in value may be written-off against current income, appreciations in value are not recognized until realized.

Legislation in the United Kingdom requires that a note be appended to the Balance Sheet in respect of both long- and short-term investments, where there is a difference between the book value and the market value. In the case of long-term investments, there is the further requirement of distinguishing investments which are quoted on a Stock Exchange from unquoted investments as follows:

	£	£
Investments		
Quoted securities (market value £57,000)	80,000	
Unquoted securities (Directors' valuation £7000)	15,000	
		95,000
Current assets		
Marketable securities (market value £25,000)	20,000	
		20,000

Intangible assets

Intangible assets are non-physical assets in the form of legal rights, privileges and competitive advantages which are relatively long-lived. They are not intended for sale, but are intended to be used by the firm. The following are examples of intangible assets:

(a) Patents

A patent represents a temporary monopoly which is granted to an inventor and which is protected by law during its duration. It gives the inventor the exclusive right to sell or to use his invention for a fixed period of years. Whilst the cost of registering a patent at the Patent Office is relatively small, firms often pay large sums to inventors for the purchase of patents. The cost of development and registration, or the cost of acquisition, whichever is appropriate, is shown as an asset on the Balance Sheet for it represents a valuable right.

(b) *Trade-Marks*
Firms often market their products under a Trade-Mark, which is a distinguishing mark for their products. 'St. Michael', for example, has become a world-wide trade-mark for the products of Marks and Spencers. Trade-Marks are a form of guarantee that the product is a genuine product of the firm in question. The firm's reputation for quality is associated in the public mind with its trade-marks. Trade-marks are registered and may not be used by another firm. The costs associated with registering Trade-marks are shown as assets on the Balance Sheet.

(c) *Copyrights*
Copyrights are similar to Patents and Trade-Marks, but apply to literary and artistic works. Authors, artists and designers enjoy the exclusive right to use, sell or license their work for a fixed period of years.

Where rights such as patents or copyrights are licensed in favour of another, a royalty is paid to the owner of the right. The export of knowledge in the form of licensing patent and copyrights has become a way of trading, where owing to circumstances a firm has been unable or unwilling to establish a manufacturing base in a foreign country. In such cases, the foreign company manufactures the product under license, and pays a royalty on an agreed basis. Industrial and chemical product and processes are often produced or employed under license.

(d) *Franchises*
A franchise is a monopoly right to trade in a particular area or as regards a particular activity. Franchises are common in the motor trade, for example, where distribution networks are based on accredited dealers who are sole selling agents for particular makes. Another typical franchise is the monopoly right granted by a Government to a corporation to operate a public transport system. The costs of negotiating and acquiring the franchise should be capitalized.

(e) *Organization costs*
The costs involved in setting up a business entity are regarded as constituting intangible assets. They comprise all preliminary expenses

such as the legal costs associated with company formation and registration, and other legal, underwriting and accounting fees. It is the practice to write them off as soon as possible.

(f) *Research and Development costs*
Expenditure incurred on the development of new products and new processes should be capitalized if it is expected to result in future revenues from sales. By carrying forward such costs, they may ultimately be matched against the income which they have generated. On the other hand, non-productive research and development costs should be written off as soon as it is evident that the research is likely to be abortive.

(g) *Advertising expenditure*
It is the practice to write-off advertising expenditure as it is incurred, on the grounds that it supports the current level of sales. Where it is clear, however, that such expenditure is incurred in order to generate future sales, it should be treated as an asset and carried forward until such time as it may be matched with those sales.

(h) *Goodwill*
Goodwill may be described as the sum of those intangible attributes of a business which contribute to its success, such as a favourable location, a good reputation, the ability and skill of its employees and management, its long-standing relationships with creditors, suppliers and customers. The valuation of goodwill is a controversial topic in accounting because of its vague nature and the difficulty of arriving at a valuation which is verifiable. Hence, in view of its lack of accounting objectivity, it is generally excluded from the Balance Sheet. Goodwill only enters the accounting system in connection with a valuation ascribed to it in the acquisition price of a business. In such a case, that portion of the purchase price which exceeds the total value of the assets taken over less the liabilities taken over, represents the amount paid for goodwill. At this point of time, therefore, there is an objective measure of the value of goodwill. Nevertheless, it is the practice of most firms to write-off goodwill.

The valuation of intangible assets creates problems, for although they are often the most important assets, financial accounting conventions inhibit their recognition. The cost and money measurement conventions, for example, inhibit a proper valuation of such assets: the former because the cost of acquisition may be small in comparison with fixed assets, or completely hidden as in the case of goodwill, the latter because of the difficulty of obtaining objective measurements. The convention of conservatism causes such items as research and development and advertising expenditure to be treated as periodic expenses in situations where they should be capitalized. Indeed, it is thought that the presence of large intangible asset values in a Balance Sheet might be interpreted as a sign of financial weakness.

The exclusion of substantial intangible asset values from the Balance Sheet is another aspect of the segregation of the role of the accountant and the role of the investor as regards financial accounting information. The role of the accountant is defined by the framework of conventions which we discussed in chapter 1. The role of the investor is to evaluate the information prepared by the accountant and to form his own judgement about the valuations attached to Balance Sheet assets. In this respect, the investor has to form his own judgement about the value of intangible as well as tangible assets in arriving at a valuation of the business as an investment.

The valuation of liabilities

Liabilities may be defined as currently existing obligations which the firm intends to meet at some time in the future. Such obligations arise from legal or managerial considerations and impose restrictions on the use of assets by the firm for its own purposes.

To be recognized as a liability in accounting, the following tests must be satisfied:

(a) the liability must exist at the present time;
(b) it must involve expenditure in the future;
(c) it must be ascertained with reasonable accuracy;
(d) it must be quantifiable;
(e) its maturity date must be known at least approximately (Barton, 1975).

The capital invested by the owner or shareholders in an enterprise is not regarded as a liability in accounting. We shall deal with the accounting treatment of the owner's or shareholders' equity presently, but we should mention at this stage that shareholders have a right at law to the payment of a dividend once it has been declared. As a result, unpaid or unclaimed dividends are shown as current liabilities. It is the practice to show proposed dividends as current liabilities also, since such proposed dividends are usually final dividends for the year which must be approved at the Annual General Meeting before which the accounts for the year must be laid.

The valuation problem

The valuation of liabilities is part of the process of measuring both capital and income, and is important to such problems as capital maintenance and the ascertainment of a firm's financial position. Hence, "the requirements for an accurate measure of the financial position and financial structure should determine the basis for liability valuation. Their valuation should be consistent with the valuation of assets and expenses" (Barton 1975). The need for consistency arises from the objectives of liability valuation, which are similar to those of asset valuation. Probably the most important of these objectives is the desire to record expenses and financial losses in the process of measuring income. However, the valuation of liabilities should also assist investors and creditors in understanding the financial position of the firm.

In accordance with the manner of valuing assets in economics, liabilities may be valued at their discounted net values; in accordance with accounting conventions, they may be recorded at their historic value, that is, the valuation attached to the contractual basis by which they were created.

Example

A firm acquired a piece of land for £20,000 on the 1st January, 19X0, £10,000 being payable immediately and £10,000 on the 1st January, 19X1. No interest is payable on the outstanding balance. The two different valuations of the outstanding liability at 1st January, 19X0 are as follows:

(a) Discounted net value of £10,000 assuming that the current rate of interest is 10%:

$$£10,000 \times \frac{100\%}{100\% + 10\%}$$

i.e. £10,000 × 0.9091 = £9091.

(b) Historical value of £10,000 by reference to the contract to pay £10,000 on the 1st January, 19X1 is, of course, £10,000.

There is no gap between the two methods of valuation as regards liabilities which are payable immediately, and it is only as the maturity date of liabilities lengthens that the gap appears. Whilst accounting conventions dictates that the valuation of liabilities should be based on the sum which is payable, it is accounting practice to make a distinction between current and long-term liabilities. As regards current liabilities, there is little difference between the discounted net value and the contractual value of liabilities. In this connection, current liabilities are defined as those which will mature during the course of the accounting period. The gap between the two methods of valuation is significant as regards long-term liabilities. Long-term liabilities are valued on the basis of their historical value, that is, by reference to the contract from which they originated, and hence, during periods of inflation or where the interest payable is less than the current market rate of interest, the accounting valuation will certainly be overstated by comparison with the discounted net value. Here again, a true perspective on this problem may be obtained by reference to the separate role of the accounting and the investor which we stated in the introduction to this Part. The accountant records the liability as the sum which will be payable: it is for the investor to value the real cost of that future burden.

Contingent liabilities

Contingent liabilities are those which will arise in the future only on the occurrence of a specified event. Although they are based on past contractual obligations, they are conditional rather than certain liabilities. Thus, guarantees given by the firm are contingent liabilities rather than current liabilites. If a holding company has guaranteed the overdraft of one of its subsidiary companies, the guarantee is payable only in the event of the subsidiary company being unable to repay the overdraft.

Contingent liabilities are not formally recorded in the Accounts system, but appear as footnotes to the Balance Sheet.

Deferred liabilities

The two major types of deferred liabilities are:

(a) Deferred Performance Liabilities
(b) Deferred Tax Liabilities.

Deferred performance liabilities exist under a number of forms, the most common being pre-payments which cannot be taken into the income of the current year and are carried forward to the following year. We examined the adjustments required to deal with pre-payments in chapter 4. Other deferred performance liabilities are created under contracts of sales which provide for post-sale services. Thus, sales of many consumer appliances provide for labour-free servicing of appliances under guarantee. Whilst the realization convention requires the accrual of revenue in the year of sale, provision should be made for the deferred performance liability in the form of an estimate of the after-sale servicing costs. This may be obtained by reference to past experience and expressed as a percentage of total sales for the purpose of calculating the amount which should be shown as a liability.

Deferred tax liabilities arise from the fact that tax is assessed in relation to 'taxable income' and not to 'accounting income'. Hence, whilst the Taxation Authorities use the information contained in the annual accounts for the purposes of computing the taxable income, the tax payable in respect of that income is not finally assessed until the subsequent year or years. For this reason, the accountant will create a provision for the tax likely to be payable and will show it as a deferred tax liability.

The valuation of shareholders' equity

A consideration of the problem of valuing shareholders' equity is beyond the scope of this book and properly belongs to the Theory of Finance. Nevertheless, the shareholders' equity is a significant section of the Balance Sheet for two reasons:

(a) it completes the accounting equation as follows:

$$\text{Assets} - \text{Liabilities} = \text{Shareholders' equity}$$

(b) it links the Balance Sheet and the Income Statement since the Retained profits are absorbed in the Shareholders' equity.

The accounting valuation of the Shareholders' equity is made up of a number of items:

(a) the cash received from shareholders in respect of the shares issued to them;
(b) the premiums, if any, paid by shareholders over and above the nominal value of issued shares;
(c) the accumulated Capital and Revenue Reserves created out of past profits;
(d) undistributed retained profit carried forward for distribution in a subsequent year, in the form of Dividend Equilization Accounts or otherwise.

The accounting valuation of the Shareholders' equity has virtually no significance in relation to the market value of the equity, which may be determined, in the case of quoted companies, by reference to the share price determined by the Stock Exchange. The economic valuation of the Shareholders' equity may be derived from the present value of discounted future net cash flows expected to be earned by the firm.

As regards the valuation of the Shareholders' equity, the accountant is concerned only with recording the historical values associated with its several constituent elements in accordance with accounting conventions. He leaves the problem of valuation to the investor.

Summary

It is necessary to understand the logic and methodology which underlie the recorded values of assets and liabilities in order to appreciate the nature of financial accounting information. A number of conventions surround the problem of valuation of assets and liabilities shown on Income Statements and Balance Sheets.

This chapter examines the accounting approach to the valuation of fixed and current assets, and discusses in particular some of the controversies surrounding the valuation of inventories. The valuation of liabilities is also discussed, although it presents a less difficult problem from an accounting viewpoint. Nevertheless, accounting makes virtually no contribution to the valuation of the shareholders' equity, although this is a central problem for shareholders and investors.

References

1. AICPA, Accounting Research Bulletin No. 43, 1963.

2. Barton, A. D., *The Anatomy of Accounting*, University of Queensland Press, 1975.

3. May, G. O., Inventory Pricing and Contingent Reserves, *Journal of Accountancy*, November, 1947.

4. Mueller, G. G., Valuing inventories at other than historical cost—some international aspects, *Journal of Accounting Research*, Autumn, 1964.

5. van Pelt III, J. V., Inventory valuation lacks accounting standards, *NAA Bulletin*, March, 1962.

6. Sprouse, R. T. & Moonitz, M., A Tentative Set of Broad Accounting Principles for Business Enterprises, Accounting Research Study No. 3, A.I.C.P.A., 1962.

8
Cash-Flow and Funds-Flow Statements

We discussed in chapters 6 and 7 the nature and content of the two main financial statements prepared by accountants from the data lodged in the financial accounting system. The Income Statement and the Balance Sheet are important statements because they are used for the purpose of conveying information about the earnings and the financial postion of a business to management and to shareholders.

Cash-flow and funds-flow statements are addressed to the problems of financial management. Cash-flow statements focus on the cash inflows and cash outflows, whereas funds-flow statements are addressed to the analysis and uses of working capital. Both cash-flow and funds-flow statements converge on the same type of information, but emphasize different aspects of the financial management problem.

As we shall see in Part 3, cash-flow and funds-flow statements are important tools of analysis for management purposes. In recent years, there has been some debate about the usefulness of funds-flow statements for shareholders and investors. We take up this issue in Part 4. It is normal for companies in North America to publish funds-flow statements and the practice is increasing in the United Kingdom.

Cash-flow statements

Cash-flow statements summarize the flow of cash in and out of the firm over a period of time. In this sense, they are really an analysis of the cash account. Cash-flow statements are important for a number of reasons. First, by focussing on cash-flows, they explain the nature of the financial events which have affected the cash inventory. Thus, if a firm had a balance of £x at the beginning of the accounting period and £y at the end of the accounting period, the cash-flow statement will explain the reason for the difference. Second, cash-flow statements are important for financial planning purposes. As we shall see in Part 3 chapter 5, budgeted cash-flow statements are a crucial element in the process of budgetary planning, indicating cash surpluses and shortfalls resulting from budget plans. These surpluses and shortfalls are expressed sequentially over the planning period and require management to deal with the forecasted cash surplus or deficit, the former involving a short-term investment of surplus cash, the latter a short-term borrowing arrangement. Third, cash-flow statements bring into sharp contrast the enterprise's earning capacity with its spending activity. Accounting conventions restrict the Income Statement to matching periodic revenues with the cost of earning those revenues. The cash-flow statement is not restricted in this way: hence, it provides an extended view of the financial inflows and outflows by including both capital and revenue flows. Thus, borrowings and capital injections, as well as proceeds from the realization of assets are incorporated with the cash generated from sales to give a more complete picture of financial inflows: repayments of loans, capital expenditure, dividends and taxation are incorporated with revenue expenses to give a more complete picture of financial outflows.

Our purpose in this chapter is to deal with the historical analysis of cash flows. Planned or budgeted cash flows will be examined in Part 3, chapter 5.

Form and content of Cash-Flow statements

The objective of a cash-flow statement is to reconcile the opening balance with the closing balance of cash at the end of an accounting period. Hence, it begins with the balance at the beginning of the year.

The cash-flow statement is only concerned with cash transactions and makes no distinction as to whether they are of a revenue or of a capital nature. An important distinction between an Income Statement and a Cash-Flow statement is that the former includes adjustments in respect of expenses accrued in the calculation of periodic income, whereas the latter excludes such adjustments. The largest item of difference between them is the allocation of fixed asset costs as depreciation, and it is normal to adjust accounting income in this respect to arrive at a Cash-Flow statement of operating revenues. Other differences between the Income Statement and Cash-Flow statement procedures are reflected in changes in Balance Sheet items. These would include changes in balances of trade debtors and trade creditors stemming from credit as distinct from cash trading.

The form and content of a Cash-Flow statement, and its purpose may be seen from the following example:

Example

The Income Statement for the year ended 31st December, 19X0 showed that Highstreet Stores made a profit of £18,000. Nevertheless, the bank balance had fallen from £10,000 at the beginning of the year to £3000 at the 31st December, 19X0.

Worried by this adverse trend in the cash position in the face of a good profit result, the owner of the business asked his accountant for a full explanation of the fall in the cash balance.

An analysis of the cash receipts and disbursements during the year produced the following summary of cash movements.

	£	£
Cash receipts		
Cash receipts from Sales and Debtors		145,000
Loan raised to extend premises		20,000
		165,000
Cash disbursements		
Purchases of Goods and payments to creditors	109,000	
Payments of wages and salaries	10,000	
Payment of interest and bank charges	1000	
Expenditure on extension of premises	30,000	
Payments in respect of new fittings	5000	
Cash withdrawn by owner	10,000	
Payment of miscellaneous expenses	7000	
		172,000
Excess of cash disbursements over cash receipts during the year		(7000)

From this information, a Cash-Flow Statement for the year may be prepared which will explain the change in the net cash balances at the beginning and end of the accounting period. However, in order to produce a Cash-Flow statement which will provide some insight into the cash position, the analysis of cash receipts and cash disbursements must be re-arranged and classified to show the causes of the cash receipts and the purposes for which cash was expended. It is advisable, therefore, to segregate cash-flows associated with current operations from cash-flows connected with capital items as shown on p. 180.

Financial analysis by cash-flow statement
The explanation of the fall in the bank balance from £10,000 to £3000, despite a profit result of £18,000, is to be found in the extent of the capital expenditure during the year. Total capital expenditure amounting to £35,000 was financed to the extent of £20,000 by loan, and £8000 from the cash-flow generated by current operations. The difference of £7000 had to be found from cash available in the bank account.

Funds-flow statements
According to Jaedicke & Sprouse (1965), there exist three accounting flows, namely income flows, funds-flows and cash-flows. We examined

Cash-flow Statement for the year ended 31st December, 19X0		£
Bank Balance at 1st January, 19X0		10,000
Net cash-flows from current operations		
Cash receipts from sales and debtors		145,000
Less		
Purchase of goods and payments to creditors	109,000	
Payments of wages and salaries	10,000	
Payment of interest and bank charges	1000	
Payment of miscellaneous expenses	7000	
		127,000
		18,000
Less		
Payments from profits to owner		10,000
Cash-flow from current operations available for capital purposes		8000
Net cash-flows on capital items		
Cash obtained by loan		20,000
		28,000
Less		
Expenditure on extension to premises	30,000	
Payments in respect of new fittings	5000	
		35,000
Excess of cash payments over cash receipts during the year		7000
Bank Balance at 31st December, 19X0		3000

income flows in chapter 6, and having discussed cash-flows in this chapter, it remains for us to consider the nature of funds-flows.

There are a number of definitions of the term 'funds' ranging from a narrow definition based on cash to an enlarged one based on the concept of working capital, which is conventionally regarded as being the difference between current assets and current liabilities*. It is our intention to adopt this concept of 'funds' as relating to working capital.

Form and content of funds-flow statements

The funds-flow statement has the same uses as the cash-flow statement, that is, it is concerned with the problems of financial management. It may be used as a supplementary statement to the Income Statement and the Balance Sheet to explain what the firm has done

---

* For a different view of this concept and a criticism of the measurement of working capital as being the difference between current assets and current liabilities see Glautier, M. W. E., Towards a Reformulation of the Theory of Working Capital, *Journal of Business Finance* Vol. 4, No. 2 Summer 1972.

with the additional funds which it has obtained from all sources during the accounting year. The Funds-Flow Statement will show, for example, if the firm has applied its income to increasing its holdings of cash or reducing its liabilities, or a mixture of both. Its only difference, in effect, from a Cash-Flow Statement is that it does not seek to explain changes in cash holdings over the year, but rather states the amount by which working capital has been increased or decreased.

The main sources of funds are as follows:

(1) new capital introduced by the owner
(2) loans to the business
(3) operating income, after adjustment for non-cash expenses
(4) sale of assets or investments.

The main applications of funds are as follows:

(1) withdrawals by the owner
(2) repayments of loans
(3) operating losses, should they occur
(4) purchase of assets or investments
(5) taxation.

In considering Funds-Flow Statements, care must be taken to avoid confusion between two fundamental ways in which changes may be measured. One method is based on identifying the flows of the variables involved, and the second on the inventory of those variables. The mathematical principle is simply that a change may be quantified either: (i) by identifying the sum total of all increases and decreases in funds; or (ii) by measuring the difference between the two total inventories connected by this change. Figure 2.15 illustrates the principle involved. The area $t_0 \times t_1$ represents the change in the inventory of

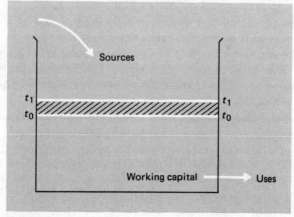

Fig. 2.15

working capital in the time period covered by the Funds-Flow Statement. It may be explained either by: (i) the excess of sources of funds over the uses of funds; or (ii) itemizing the component changes in current assets – current liabilities (CA – CL), that is, as follows:

$$(CA - CL)_{t_1} - (CA - CL)_{t_0}$$

Accordingly, the Funds-flow Statement may be presented as follows:

Funds-flow Statement
For the period from ...... to .....

	Sources	Applications	
Funds at the beginning of period. . .			xxxxxx
Funds changes during the period			
(1) Net funds from operations	xxx		
(2) Funds transactions with owner			
Capital introduced	xxx	xxx	
Withdrawals			
(3) Funds transactions with long-term creditors			
Loans obtained	xxx		
Loans repaid		xxx	
(4) Funds transactions involving plant, and other non current assets			
Acquisitions		xxx	
Disposals	xxx		
Totals			
Net increase (decrease) in funds			xxxxxxx
Funds at the end of the period. . . .			xxxxxxx

Example

The following Balance Sheets relate to Extoll Imports, which is an importing firm owned by Alfred Holfort.

It may be noted that the tax liability existing at 31st December, 19X0 was paid during the year ended 31st December, 19X1, and that the taxation provision of £10,000 existing at 31st December, 19X1 was created out of income. The income for the year amounting to £30,000 represents, therefore, income after provision for taxation.

Note also that premises were sold at cost to Holfort's son during the year.

The analysis of component changes in funds, defined as working capital is as shown on p. 184 (*Note:* The reduction in the balance of creditors has the effect of increasing the level of funds at 31st December, 19X1, where the increase in the taxation liability has the effect of reducing the level of funds, as defined).

Balance Sheets as on 31st December

				19X0			19X1	
				£	£		£	£
Capital employed								
Capital				50,000			60,000	
Income for the year				25,000			30,000	
				75,000			90,000	
Withdrawals				15,000			20,000	
				60,000			70,000	
Long-term loan				20,000			–	
					80,000			70,000

Represented by								
Fixed assets	*Cost*	*Dep.*	*Net*		*Cost*	*Dep.*	*Net*	
	£	£	£		£	£	£	
Premises	30,000	–	30,000		20,000	—	20,000	
Equipment	10,000	2000	8000		15,000	3000	12,000	
	20,000	2000		38,000	35,000	3000	32,000	
Current assets								
Inventories at cost			50,000				46,000	
Debtors			15,000				17,000	
Cash			15,000				8000	
			80,000				71,000	
Less								
Current liabilities								
Creditors	30,000				23,000			
Taxation	8000				10,000			
		38,000				33,000		
Net Working Capital			42,000				38,000	
				80,000				70,000

Funds-flow statement for the year ended 31st December, 19X1

	£	£	£
Funds at 1st January, 19X1 (working capital)			42,000
Net funds from operations			
Income for the year	30,000		
Add: Non-cash expenses			
Depreciation	1000		
	31,000		
Funds transactions with owner			
Withdrawals		20,000	
Funds transactions with long-term creditors			
Loan repayment		20,000	
Funds transactions involving assets			
Sale of premises	10,000		
Purchase of equipment		5000	
	41,000	45,000	
Net decrease in funds			4000
Funds at 31st December, 19X1			38,000

	Increase £	Decrease £
Inventories		4000
Debtors	2000	
Cash		7000
Creditors	7000	
Taxation		2000
	9000	13,000
		9000
Net change		4000

Summary

The Income Statement and the Balance Sheet are important statements because they are used as means of conveying information about the earnings and the financial position of the enterprise. By contrast cash-flow and funds-flow statements are addressed to highlighting the financial management aspect. The cash-flow statement analyses cash inflows and outflows with a view to explaining the difference between cash balances at the beginning and close of the accounting period. The funds-flow statement is addressed to detailing the sources and uses of during the accounting period and working capital.

Cash-Flow and Funds-Flow statements may be used to provide supplementary information to that contained in the Income Statement and Balance Sheet. Funds-flow statements are being increasingly adopted by companies for financial reporting purposes. As we shall see in Part 4, one aspect of the controversy in financial reporting concerns funds accounting as an alternative to income accounting. The argument for Funds-Flow statements in that context is that since a firm's success depends on its ability to maximize its cash flows through time, Cash-Flow and Funds-Flow statements would be more meaningful than conventional Income Statements and Balance Sheets.

Cash-flow and Funds-Flow statements are important for financial planning purposes. In this context, they are associated with budget forecasts. The particular importance of the cash-flow budget is to highlight the financial consequence of budget plans and project the cash surpluses and deficits which will occur periodically through the planning period. This function of Cash-Flow statements will be examined in Part 3.

Reference

Jaedicke, R. K. & Sprouse, R. T. *Accounting Flows: Income, Funds and Cash*, Prentice Hall Foundations of Finance Series, Englewood Cliffs, N.J. 1965.

Section 3

The Application of Financial Accounting Method to Corporate Enterprises

9
Financial Accounting Information for Corporate Enterprises

We mentioned in the Introduction to this Part (p. 54) that the selection for closer analysis of the application of financial accounting procedures to the generation of financial accounting information for corporate enterprises was justified on two grounds:

(a) The industrial and commercial expansion which has occurred in the Western industrialized countries over the last 100 years has been affected to a considerable extent by means of activities organized by companies. Probably the most important factor in this expansion has been the facility afforded by the corporate structure for the mobilization of large supplies of financial capital lodged in the private sector of the economy. Consequently, the study of corporate activity constitutes the most important area of interest to students of accounting and the management sciences generally, many of whom will make their careers as company executives. Applying the criterion of relevance to the selection of teaching material has led us to focus attention on corporate financial accounting as the major application of financial accounting method of interest to students. Therefore we have excluded large areas of conventional material found, for example, in the application of financial accounting method to partnership activities and to such problems as the accounting treatment of royalties and returnable containers.

(b) We have devoted Part 4 to the analysis of financial reporting, which is concerned with the supply of financial accounting information to shareholders and investors. Many financial reporting problems stem directly from the application of financial accounting procedures to the generation of the information content of financial reports. Hence, this Section serves also as a necessary introduction to Part 4. The efficiency of the corporate sector of the economy depends, in the first instance, upon a sufficient flow of investment funds to that sector, and an efficient allocation of available funds among individual companies. The quality of the investment decision-making process depends to a large extent upon the quality and adequacy of financial information available to investors. Herein lies the social importance of the information content of financial report.

The purpose of this chapter is to examine the financial accounting implications of incorporation, and the procedures applied to the financial accounting problems peculiar to public as distinct from private companies. We define public companies as those private sector companies in which the public at large may become shareholders, and private companies as those private sector companies which have a restricted and selected number of individuals as shareholders.

The nature of corporate enterprises

Companies are created and regulated by law. By a legal fiction, the legal personality of a business enterprise established as a company is different from the legal personality of the various individuals having an interest therein, whether as owners, managers or employees. This means, for example, that although a company has no physical life, it may nevertheless own property, enter into contracts, sue and be sued in a court of law and undertake any activity consistent with the objectives envisaged at the time of its creation. It acts through its employees, whether as managers or subordinates, with whom it enters into contracts of employment.

The proprietors of a company are recognized in law as being those persons owning its capital. The capital is divided into shares or stock, and by acquiring shares, investors become *Shareholders*. As evidence of their legal title to the shares they own, shareholders are issued with *Share Certificates*. Shares are transferable property rights, and may be negotiated either privately or through a Stock Exchange. Stock Exchanges have rules for granting permission for the shares of individual companies to be traded on the Stock Exchange, or to be 'quoted on the Stock Exchange', which is the term given to such permission.

Companies are usually established by the formal registration of documents with a Public Registrar charged with enforcing statutory provisions in respect of enterprises operating as companies. In the United Kingdom, for example, individuals wishing to incorporate themselves for the purpose of carrying trade are called *Promoters*, and it is their responsibility to arrange for the process of incorporation. This involves lodging a number of documents with the *Registrar of Companies* and paying the required fees. The two most important documents are the *Memorandum of Association*, which defines the powers and objectives of the companies and the *Articles of Association* which contains the rules for its internal regulation. The name, objectives and the capital clauses are found in the *Memorandum of Association*. For our purposes, the capital clause is the most important for it states the number, classes and value of the shares which the company has power to issue for the purpose of raising capital. The *Authorized Capital* is stated in the capital clause, and it is the maximum capital which the company may raise. The capital clause may be altered, however, by a formal process.

A company obtains capital by the issue of shares. Investors are invited to apply for shares. They usually have to pay a portion of the purchase price on application and the balance when the shares have been formally alloted to them. The capital clause states the value of each share as a nominal figure. Thus, the *Authorized Capital* may be stated to consist of 1 million shares of £1 each, giving the company an *Authorized Capital* of £1 million. When a company offers shares for sale, however, it may set a price which is higher than the *Nominal Value*, and it need not offer for sale all the shares which it is authorized to sell. That portion of the *Authorized Capital* which is sold is called the *Issued Capital*.

Once shares have been issued, they become the property of the individual investors who have acquired them, and these investors are free to sell their shares to anyone. The sale price is negotiated between buyer and seller, and the deal may be effected through a Stock Exchange if the shares are quoted shares. The seller transfers his shares formally to the buyer by notice to the company, and the buyer is registered in the *Register of Shareholders* as the new shareholders. Shares which are transferred in this way are known as *Registered Shares*. An alternative type of shareholding, which is restricted by law in some countries, is known as a *Bearer Share*. A *Bearer Share* is more easily transferred than a *Registered Share* since the *Share Certificate* does not detail the name of the shareholder, and he is not registered in the *Register of Shareholders*. Consequently, *Bearer Shares* are transferable by hand.

A company receives only the issue price of a share. The legal effect of shareholding is to grant ownership rights in respect of the fraction of capital represented by the share, and a right to receive the appropriate portion of corporate net income distributed in the form of *Dividend*. Companies usually retain a portion of net income for re-investment, and distribute the balance as dividends. We shall consider shortly the accounting consequences of the distinction made between *Retained Income* and *Distributable Income*.

The distinction between ownership and management is one of the most distinctive features of corporate activity. As owners, shareholders may be considered as having ultimate control over the activities of the company through their right to appoint *Directors*. The rights of shareholders to exercise control over the affairs of companies is usually defined by legislation. Once appointed, Directors exercise day-to-day control of the company's affairs, and although they are accountable to shareholders, the diffusion of shares among many shareholders usually places Directors in a very strong position *vis-à-vis* shareholders. Although they are treated as stewards of corporate assets on behalf of shareholders, the effective power to make decisions of major importance in respect of those assets lies almost entirely in their hands. We discussed in Part 3 problems of corporate planning and control in terms of managerial responsibility (p. 435).

Social change is affecting the traditional method of regulating corporate enterprises in a number of ways. First, the recognition of the right of employees to share managerial responsibility is an important feature of the democratization of corporate control. Some European countries have already legislated for two-tier Boards of Directors, and this feature has been included in the *Societas Europea SE*, the European Company which is formed by registration in the European Commercial Register kept by the Court of the European Communities in Luxembourg. Employee participation in the management of companies is an explicit admission that the interests of employees are as important as those of shareholders. Second, the concept of social responsibility, which we discuss in Part 5, further broadens the classical notion of stewardship as a definition of the function of Directors to include a responsibility to all sections of society having an interest in the activities of corporate enterprises. Thus, consumers, as well as the local community, are included in the group of those having a vested interest in the nature of corporate activity.

Financial accounting implications of corporate status

Corporate status, as distinct from the simple one-man type of business which we examined in Section 2, implies a distinctive treatment of the Capital Structure and of the allocation of the net income as between dividends and retained income.

The normal procedure for dealing with the financial accounting implications of corporate status is to establish a separation of functions between the Accountant and the Company Secretary. The former is usually concerned with the normal financial accounting procedures directed at recording normal business transactions: the latter usually maintains the Register of Shareholders, including such details as the record of shareholders' names and addresses, class and number of shares held, instructions regarding correspondence and payment of dividends. Much of the routine work of the Secretary's Department in this respect involves recording the transfer of shares and the payment of yearly dividends to shareholders. The specialized nature of share transfer work, as well as its sheer volume in some corporations, often requires a separate department under a Share Transfer Registrar. In such cases, the Share Transfer Registrar is a senior official of the company.

The financial accounting aspects of the Share Capital with which the accountant is concerned consist of the ledger records associated with shareholders, that is, the Share Capital account, the Dividend account, and those accounts retaining income in the form of Capital or Current Reserves. We shall deal with the nature of these accounts shortly. All these accounts are concerned with aggregate figures.

Example

Excel Corporation Limited is a public company having a Share Capital of one million £1 shares held in different proportions by 20,000 individual shareholders. The detailed records of individual shareholding are kept by the Share Transfer Registrar, and the accountant will keep the following ledger record:

Share Capital account

	£
Sundry Shareholders	1,000,000

The capital structure

The capital structure may consist of both share capital and loan capital, and represents the long-term capital available to the company, as distinct from the short-term capital represented by the credit facilities offered by trade creditors and bank overdrafts. Shareholders are regarded at law as owners. The share capital is at risk, and in the event of business failure shareholders may lose all the capital invested since they rank last as claimants on the residual assets of the corporation. By contrast, loan capital is made available by creditors on a long-term basis. Thus, a company may invite the public to supply loan capital for a period of say 5 years at a rate of interest of say 10%. Individuals may offer varying sums, and receive from the company a certificate of indebtedness which is known as a *Debenture Certificate*. Debentures frequently involve the mortgage of specific corporate assets to the body of Debenture-holders represented by a *Trustee for Debenture-holders*, and in the event of the company defaulting in any way on the conditions of the debenture instrument, the specified assets may be seized and sold on behalf of the debenture-holders. The charge on the corporate assets may be fixed, as we have mentioned, or floating, that is, not be specific as regards any particular assets but applying to all corporate assets. Debenture-holders are guaranteed, therefore, both repayment of loan capital and interest as specified in the conditions of issue. It is the duty of the Trustee for the Debenture-holders to act before any loss threatens debenture-holders. Very large and financially strong companies may be able to raise long-term loans without mortgaging their assets to lenders. They issue certificates of indebtness described as *Unsecured Notes*, which also carry an obligation to pay interest and to redeem at the end of the stated period. Holders of unsecured notes rank as ordinary creditors in an insolvency.

Shares, debentures and unsecured notes may all be quoted on a Stock Exchange and transacted between buyers and sellers. Appropriate Registers of Debenture-holders and holders of unsecured notes must be kept by the company.

The Share Capital may consist of different classes of shares, but the two most common classes of shares are Preference shares and Ordinary shares.

Preference shares give preferential rights as regards dividends, and often as regards the repayment of capital on winding-up. Preference shares may be issued as Redeemable Preference shares, that is, they may be redeemed and cancelled by the company. In general, however, the rule is that a company may not acquire its own shares, and a reduction of capital usually has to be approved by the Court. Preference shares may also be issued as Cumulative Preference shares, which means that if the net income of any particular year is insufficient to pay a dividend to Preference shareholders of this class, the right to receive a dividend for that year is carried forward to the following year, and so on, until such time as the accumulated dividend entitlement may be declared and paid out of income. Preference shareholders are usually entitled to a fixed dividend expressed as a percentage of the nominal value of share. Thus, a holder of 100 Preference shares of £1 each carrying a fixed dividend rate of 8% will be entitled to a total yearly dividend of £8. However, Preference shares may also be issued as Participating Preference shares meaning that in addition to the fixed dividend rate entitlement, they participate in the remainder of the net income with Ordinary shareholders. It is common for conditions to be imposed limiting the participating rights of such shares to allow for a minimum level of dividend for Ordinary shareholders. Thus, a Participating Preference share may carry a right to a fixed dividend of 8% and a right to participate in the remaining net income after the Ordinary shareholders have received a dividend of 20%.

Ordinary shares provide the bulk of the Share Capital. In return for bearing the risk involved in financing corporate activities, Ordinary shareholders enjoy the right to the whole of the net income—either as dividends or, if retained, as the increased value of net corporate assets—subject to the rights of Preference shareholders. Some companies do not issue Preference shares, and obtain the whole of the Share Capital in the form of Ordinary shares. The reason for issuing a variety of shares—Preference shares of different classes and Ordinary shares is to tap the funds held by investors with differing investment needs. A young man with money to invest will be looking for growth in the value of his capital and will be attracted to buying Ordinary shares in a company having good prospects of expansion. A retired person will be looking for a safe investment providing a steady income, and will doubtless wish to hold some Preference shares. Institutional buyers, such as Pension Funds and Insurance companies, also have a wish to hold shares of different classes. Where a company has issued Preference shares, the Ordinary shares may be described as Deferred shares. On occasions, however, Deferred shares may be a separate class of shares to both Preference and Ordinary shares, and may be issued in restricted numbers to managers of the company. In such a case, Deferred shares carry an entitlement to dividend only after the Ordinary shareholders have received a specified dividend rate.

Gearing and the capital structure

The nature of the capital structure has important implications for financial management purposes, and in this respect, the gearing is an important consideration.

The gearing expresses the relationship between the proportion of fixed interest (loan capital) and fixed dividend (Preference shares capital) to Ordinary shares. A company with a large proportion of fixed interest and fixed dividend bearing capital to Ordinary capital is said to be highly geared.

Example

Companies Alpha, Beta and Gamma have the same total capital which is issued as follows:

	Alpha £	Beta £	Gamma £
Share Capital			
8% Preference shares of £1 each	40,000	10,000	—
Ordinary shares of £1 each	20,000	80,000	100,000
Loan Capital			
7% Debentures of £1 each	40,000	10,000	—
	100,000	100,000	100,000

The gearing of these three companies may be calculated as follows:

(a) Alpha   (40,000 + 40,000) : 20,000 or   4 : 1
(b) Beta   (10,000 + 10,000) : 80,000 or 0.25 : 1
(c) Gamma   : 100,000 or   ∞

Alpha is, therefore, the most highly geared company.

The importance of the gearing is that fluctuations in net income may have disproportionate effects upon the return accruing to Ordinary shareholders in the case of a highly geared company, and hence on the pricing of Ordinary shares on the Stock Exchange. Directors looking for stability in the price of the company's Ordinary shares will be swayed by this consideration when faced with raising further capital. For taxation reasons, the net cost of debenture interest may be lower than the net cost in dividends of further issues of Ordinary shares. Similarly, fixed dividend Preference shares may also cost less than issuing Ordinary shares. The following example shows the effects of fluctuating net income levels on the return to Ordinary shareholders, assuming that the available net income is wholly distributed.

Example
The consequence of fluctuations in net income on Ordinary shareholders in Alpha Company, Beta Company and Gamma Company geared in the ratios established in the example above may be judged as follows:

	Alpha	*Beta*	*Gamma*
	£	£	£
Assuming net income of £15,000			
Net income	15,000	15,000	15,000
8% Preference shares 3200		800	—
7% Debentures 2800		700	— —
6000		1500	
Available for Ordinary shares	9600	13,500	15,000
Maximum dividend for Ordinary shareholders	$\frac{9000}{20,000} = 45\%$	$\frac{13,500}{80,000} = 16.875\%$	$\frac{15,000}{100,000} = 15\%$

(Continued)

	Alpha		Beta		Gamma
		£		£	£
Assuming net income of £10,000					
Net income		10,000		10,000	10,000
8% Preference shares	3200		800		—
7% Debentures	2800		700		—
		6000		1500	—
Available for Ordinary shares		4000		8500	10,000
Maximum dividend for Ordinary shareholders		$\frac{4000}{20,000} = 20\%$		$\frac{8500}{80,000} = 10.625\%$	$\frac{15,000}{100,000} = 10\%$

Hence in a highly geared company such as Alpha, a fall of $33\frac{1}{3}$ in net income has produced a fall of 56% in the maximum dividend payable to Ordinary shareholders.

Accounting procedures applied to the capital structure
The share capital

We mentioned earlier that a distinction exists between the authorized capital and the issued capital. The former is the maximum limit in the total value of shares of different classes which a company is permitted to issue under the conditions of its registration; the latter is the actual value of shares of different classes which have been issued. The reason why companies do not establish the value of the authorized capital greatly in excess of their anticipated requirement lies in the taxes imposed on the value of the authorized capital, which deter promoters from incurring unnecessary expenses.

The financial accounting procedures applied to the treatment of the share capital may be said to have two main objectives:

(a) recording the issue of shares and the consideration received in respect of such shares;

(b) providing information about the share capital in a Balance Sheet.

We do not propose to deal with the procedures applied to the redemption of redeemable Preference shares, or those applied to the issue of bonus shares, since these procedures are not essential to the thesis of this book. It may be mentioned, however, that bonus shares are commonly issued free of cost to existing shareholders in proportion to their shareholdings by way of distribution of accumulated income.

(a) *Recording the issue of shares*

It has become the practice for companies seeking to make an issue of shares to the public to employ the services of merchant bankers not only to act as advisers but also to deal with the details of the issue, such as issuing the Prospectus advertising the offer of the shares for sale, recording the applications from investors and the monies received with the applications, the allotment of shares to individual share-holders where an offer has been over-subscribed, and arranging for the shares under-subscribed to be taken up by the underwriters who have acted as insurers in respect of the issue of the shares in return for a commission. The detailed accounting procedures for dealing with the issue of shares need not detain us, for they have become part and parcel of a rather specialized aspect of work.

The central financial problems relating to the issue of shares concern the nature of the shares to be issued, that is, whether to issue Preference or Ordinary, how many to issue and the price to be attached to such shares. All these are problems in respect of which a company will seek expert advice. The financial accounting procedures which we shall consider reflect merely the outcome of the decisions taken.

We mentioned earlier that shares may be described in the capital clause of the Memorandum of Association as having a nominal value. This practice applies in the United Kingdom, although in the United States for example, it is the practice for shares not to have a nominal value, and they are issued as 'shares of no par value'. This means that the recorded issue value of the share capital reflects the price deter-mined at the time of issue.

In the United Kingdom, the practice of attaching a nominal value to shares makes it theoretically possible for the following terms to be attached to the issue of shares:

  (i) Shares may be issued at par, that is, a share having a nominal value of £1 is issued at a price of £1.
 (ii) Shares may be issued at a premium, that is, a share having a nominal value of £1 is issued at a price higher than £1.
(iii) Shares may be issued at a discount, that is, a share having a nominal value of £1 may be issued at a price which is less than £1. In practice, legislation attaches very strict conditions to the issue of shares at a discount.

A number of considerations affect the issue of shares, not the least of which is that the issue should be a financial success. This means that the corporation should receive a realistic price for the shares offered and that the issue should be wholly subscribed by the market.

The following examples show the accounting procedures applied to the issue of Ordinary shares at par and at a premium.

The issue of Ordinary shares at par

The Omega Company Ltd has issued 2 million Ordinary shares of £1 each at par. The purchase price has been paid on application and allotment and the corporation's bank account has been credited with the amount received. The entries in the company's accounts are as follows:

Ordinary share Capital Account

	£
Sundry Ordinary shareholders	2,000,000

Sundry Ordinary shareholders

	£		£
Ordinary share Capital	2,000,000	Cash	2,000,000

Cash Account

	£
Sundry Ordinary shareholders	2,000,000

We have already noted that the detailed list of individual shareholdings does not form part of the financial accounting system, but rather of the Register of Shareholders. Hence, the Sundry Ordinary shareholders account does not exist as such: it is represented by the Register of Shareholders. From a financial accounting viewpoint, only the Ordinary share Capital Account and the Cash Book are significant.

The issue of Ordinary shares at a premium

The Onedin Company Ltd has issued 2 million Ordinary shares of £1 each at a premium of 50%, that is, at a price of £1.50 a share. The purchase price has been paid on application and allotment and the company's bank account has been appropriately credited. The practice in the United Kingdom is to separate the par value of the shares from the share premium. Legislation allows a greater flexibility in the application of the share premium account, for example in redeeming Preference shares at a premium.

The accounting entries are as follows:

Ordinary Share Capital account

	£
Sundry Ordinary shareholders	2,000,000

Share Premium account

	£
Sundry Ordinary shareholders	1,000,000

Sundry Ordinary shareholders

	£		£
Ordinary Share Capital	2,000,000	Cash	3,000,000
Share Premium	1,000,000		
	3,000,000		3,000,000

Cash Account

Sundry Ordinary shareholders	3,000,000

As we explained earlier, the Sundry Ordinary shareholders do not exist as a formal account, but are found in the Register of Shareholders. Consequently, the only accounts of significance are the Ordinary share Capital Account, the Share Premium account and the Cash Book.

In the United States and Canada, the practice for the last 50 years has been to issue shares of no par value. These simplify the accounting process, for there is no need to have a share premium account and the share capital account shows the amount actually received from the sale of shares. The case against shares of fixed nominal value is that they bear no relation to any realistic value of the issued shares, and hence the nominal value is virtually meaningless.

The procedures which have been outlined above apply equally to the treatment of other classes of shares, such as Preference shares.

(b) *Providing information about the Share Capital*

Details of the Share Capital are shown on the Balance Sheet, and in this way information is communicated to shareholders and investors about the manner in which the corporation is capitalized. The information which should be disclosed is generally the subject of legislation, and the debate about the nature and extent of information disclosure forms the subject matter of Part 4.

The information which is usually required to be disclosed about the Share Capital is as follows:

(i) The authorized share capital showing in respect of each class of shares the number and the value of the shares authorized to be issued.

(ii) The issued share capital showing in respect of each class of shares the number of the shares issued and the proportion of the share price paid-up. Although it is usual for companies to ask for the whole purchase price to be paid at the time of issue, some ask for the purchase price to be paid upon call. Thus, a portion is payable on application and allotment and the balance remains uncalled until needed. The uncalled capital represents a valuable source of funds to the corporation for once shareholders have agreed to take up shares they are debtors in respect of the agreed purchase price.

(iii) Any calls unpaid on the issued capital are also usually required to be shown.

(iv) Where Redeemable Preference shares are issued, the earliest date of redemption must also be shown.

(v) The Share Premium account, where applicable, must also be shown.

Example

The following information about the Share Capital appears on the Balance Sheet of the Odin Firework Co. Ltd.

Share Capital		£
Authorized: 100,000 8% Redeemable Preference		
shares of £1 each (*see* note 1)		100,000
500,000 Ordinary shares of £1 each		500,000
		600,000
Issued: 100,000 8% Redeemable Preference		
shares of £1 each fully paid		100,000
400,000 Ordinary shares of £1		
each 50 pence paid	200,000	
Less: calls unpaid	500	
		199,500
		299,500
Share Premium Account		5000
Shareholders' Equity		304,500

Note 8%

Redeemable Preference shares. These shares must be redeemed between 1st January, 1990 and 31st December 1992.

Note the following points:

(a) The authorized and the issued capital are both shown, but the authorized capital is ruled off so that it is not included in the calculation of the total shareholders' interest, known as the Shareholders' Equity.

(b) Calls unpaid are deducted from the issued capital.

(c) Notes are usually attached to the Balance Sheet for the purpose of explanation.

(d) In the example, the Share Premium account represents a premium of 5% on the issue of the Preference Shares.

Loan capital

There is very little difference in the accounting treatment of loan and share capital. Registers of Debenture-holders and of holders of Unsecured Notes are kept, and the method of issue is identical to that of shares insofar as the issuing process tends to be conducted on behalf of the company by merchant bankers. Debentures may be issued at par, at a premium or at a discount. Premiums received on the issue of debentures are regarded as capital profits, and are usually transferred to a Capital Reserve account. Discounts allowed on the issue of debentures are treated as capital losses, and legislation in the United Kingdom requires such discounts to be shown separately on the Balance Sheet until they are written off.

Example

Hightrust Investment Company offers for sale 10,000 9% Debentures in units of £100 at a premium of 5%. The Debentures are repayable on 31st December, 1990. The accounting entries are as follows:

9% Debentures 1990 account

		£
	Sundry Debenture-holders	100,000

Capital Reserve account

		£
	Sundry Debenture-holders	5000

Cash Book

	£
Sundry Debenture-holders	105,000

As in the case of the issue of shares, details of individual debenture-holders would be found in the Register of Debenture-holders. There is no such account as a Sundry Debenture-holders account.

The presentation of the Loan Capital on the Balance Sheet is usually as follows:

Loan Capital

		£
10,000 9% Debentures of £100 each		100,000
(see note 5)		

Note 5: These debentures are redeemable at par on 31st December, 1990.

Note the following points:

(a) the Loan Capital appears below the Share Capital on the Balance Sheet;

(b) the Capital Reserve account represents a capital profit belonging to the Shareholders. It would appear, therefore, below the Share Premium account and be incorporated in the calculation of the Shareholders' Equity.

Accounting procedures applied to periodic income

The important difference between a company and an un-incorporated business such as a sole trader lies in the manner in which periodic income is appropriated. In the case of the un-incorporated business, the net income belongs to the owner and is transferred to the Capital account at the end of the accounting period. By contrast, once the net income of a company has been ascertained, the Board of Directors have to decide the proportion which should be paid out to shareholders as dividends and the proportion which should be retained.

In considering the manner in which the net income should be appropriated, the following factors are important:

(a) Adequate provision should be made in respect of corporation tax payable on the net income for the year. In this connection, under- or over-provisions in respect of previous years have to be taken into account.

(b) Adequate provision should be made for anticipated expenditure on the replacement of fixed assets. During periods of inflation, in particular, the cost of replacing fixed assets exceeds amounts provided for in the provision for depreciation.

(c) Adequate provision should be made for capital expenditure which is planned to be financed out of earnings.

(d) Where a company wishes to provide a degree of stability in the level of yearly dividends by means of a Dividend Equalization account, care should be taken that sufficient reserves are accumulated in that account.

(e) The level of retention of income should also be dictated by working capital requirements, and for this purpose, transfer of net income to a General Reserve may be made.

It is quite common for companies to distribute only about half their after-tax income to shareholders. Usually an Interim Dividend is declared during the accounting period in anticipation of a Final Dividend, which is declared after the final results for the year have been ascertained.

Example

Delta Expandite Company made a net income of £5 million for the year ended 31st December, 19X0. Estimated Corporation Tax payable on those profits were calculated at £2 million. The Directors recommended the following appropriations of the distributable net income in the accounts laid before shareholders at the Annual General Meeting:

(a) the Fixed Assets Replacement Reserve should be increased by £200,000;

(b) the Capital Expenditure Reserve should be increased by £500,000;

(c) the Dividend Equalization Reserve should be increases by £300,000;

(d) the General Reserve should be increased by £750,000;

(e) an Interim Dividend of £200,000 having been declared during the year, the Directors proposed a Final Dividend of £1 million to be paid to Ordinary shareholders registered at the close of business on 28th February, 19X1. (Note: there was no other class of share in issue).

The Income Statement laid before shareholders for their approval would show the following appropriations:

	£	£
Net Income for the year before tax		5,000,000
Less: Provision for Corporation tax on the income for the year		2,000,000
Distributable income		3,000,000
Transfers to Reserves:		
Fixed Assets Replacement Reserve	200,000	
Capital Expenditure Reserve	500,000	
Dividend Equalization Reserve	300,000	
General Reserve	750,000	
		1,750,000
Available for distribution		1,250,000
Interim Dividend for the year	200,000	
Proposed Final Dividend for the year	1,000,000	
		1,200,000
Undistributed income carried forward		50,000

Note that it is customary to close the Register of Shareholders for a brief period after the close of the accounting period for the purpose of determining the names of shareholders entitled to the dividend. The reason for this is that share dealings on the Stock Exchange continue, and daily the company is faced with share transfer forms to process as shareholders sell their shares and are replaced by new shareholders. Freezing the Register of Shareholders allows a list of shareholders to be drawn up to whom dividends are paid. If they have already sold their shares, and the buyers have not yet registered the transfer, the conditions of sale apply to the dividend entitlement. Usually, shares are traded on the Stock Exchange *cum dividend* (with dividend) until the formal dividend declaration, when they go *ex dividend*, that is, they are sold without the dividend declared.

Accounting procedures for the payment of dividends

The rule is that shareholders are not entitled to a dividend unless and until a dividend has been declared. Usually, Articles of Association allow Directors to declare an interim dividend, but the declaration of a final dividend is subject to the approval of the body of shareholders convened at the Annual General Meeting, which is held once a year to deal with the business reserved to shareholders. Thus, Directors are not entitled to declare a final dividend, but they propose a final dividend and ask shareholders to approve the proposal. The consequence of these rules are as follows:

(a) the Income Statement laid before shareholders shows the Final dividend as a proposed dividend;
(b) although no liability exists to shareholders for the payment of a final dividend until it is approved by shareholders at the Annual General Meeting, the proposed final dividend is shown on the Balance Sheet as a current liability as follows:

Current Liabilities	£
Sundry Creditors	. . . . . .
Provision for Taxation	. . . . . .
Proposed Dividend	. . . . . .

The responsibility for drawing up the *Dividend List* lies with the Share Transfer Registrar who keep the Register of Shareholders. The Dividend List contains the name, addresses and number of shares held by each individual shareholder. The individual's dividend entitlement is easily calculated, and payment is made either by cheque or direct to a bank account, according to instructions given by the shareholders.

The accountant merely opens a Dividend account to which the

dividend payable is transferred. The exact amount payable in respect of the dividend is transferred to a special dividend account at the bank, so that the dividend warrants issued should tally in total with the credit established at the bank.

Example

The accounting entries in respect of the final dividend of £1 million (Dividend No. 12) proposed by the Directors of the Delta Company would be as follows:

Income Statement for the year ended
31st December, 19X0

£

Dividend No. 12   1,000,000

Dividend No. 12

£

Income Statement
for the year
ended 31st
December, 19X0   1,000,000

Note that it is usual to number the dividends for ease of reference, and to keep the Dividend List for each dividend in company records.

Published financial accounting statements

One of the areas of great controversy in accounting is the extent to which financial information should be disclosed to shareholders. As we shall see in Part 4, it is usual for legislation to be used as a means of compelling companies to disclose information. The central issue revolves around the minimum level of disclosure compatible with the information requirements of shareholders and the protection of business interests.

Until recently, there was little public discussion of the information requirements of shareholders, and it was assumed that their needs were met through the traditional Income Statement and Balance Sheet. In this respect, the information content of these statements is an abridged version of the full financial accounts laid before the Board of Directors. In considering these accounts, the Board of Directors has additional information in the form of detailed cash-flow statements, budget forecasts and analysis of results and may ask for any further information required to enable them to assess the company's financial performance and position much more accurately than is possible from the limited contents of the published financial statements released to shareholders. We consider in Part 4 the manner in which a limited analysis of published financial statements may be made and interpreted by shareholders.

The nature of the information conveyed to shareholders in published reports is depicted in the following example, which conforms with the legal requirements in the United Kingdom, both as to content and as to the additional information which is given in the notes to the accounts.

As may be seen, the corporation is not required to disclose the details of its operating costs, save those listed in the Income Statement. Note 1 explains the accounting policies adopted for treating accounting items, note 4 reveals the distribution of directors' emoluments.

The Balance Sheet emphasizes the make-up of net assets employed in earning income, and the manner in which the corporation is financed. Notes 1, 2 and 3 provide appropriate explanations of items appearing on the Balance Sheet.

The Anglesee and Far-West Corporation (1) Income Statement for the year ended 31st December, 19X5				
			19X5 £	19X4 £
Turnover for year—Net sales			90,000	75,000
Income before taxation			8000	6000
	1975 £	1974 £		
after charging:				
Depreciation of fixed assets (note 1)	1400	1200		
Directors' remuneration as managers	12,000	9000		
Interest on bank and short term loans repayable within 5 years	200	150		
Interest on other loans	450	450		
Cost of hiring plant and machinery	200	250		
Auditors' remuneration	150	150		
and after crediting				
Interest received	70	120		
Taxation (note 3)			3000	2000
Income after taxation for the year			5000	4000
Retained earnings at beginning of year			7000	5000
			12,000	9000
Proposed dividend			4000	2000
Retained earnings at end of year			8000	7000

(2)

The Anglesee and Far-West Corporation
Balance Sheet as at 31st December, 19X5

	19X5 £	19X4 £
Share Capital		
Ordinary Shares of £1 each—Authorized	12,500	6000
Issued and fully paid	12,500	6000
Retained Earnings	8000	7000
	20,500	13,000
Deferred Taxation (note 1)	900	1000
Debenture Stock Secured on the assets of the company:		
£4500 10% Debentures 1985/1987	4500	4500
	25,900	18,500
Represented by		
Fixed assets		
Land, buildings and equipment (note 2)	15,000	14,000
Current Assets		
Inventories (note 1)	16,000	10,000
Accounts receivable and prepaid expenses	13,000	7000
Short-term deposits	1000	2000
Cash and Bank Balance	200	300
Total Current Assets	30,200	19,300
Current Liabilities		
Bank loan and overdraft	2000	1500
Accounts payable and accruals	10,000	8800
Corporation Tax	3300	2500
Proposed dividend	4000	2000
Total Current Liabilities	19,300	14,800
Net Current Assets	10,900	4500
Net Assets employed	25,900	18,500

T. E. Bear, Managing Director
S. N. O. White, Director

(3)

The Anglesee and Far-West Corporation

Notes on the accounts for the year ended 31st December, 19X5

1. Statement of accounting policies:
   Depreciation of fixed assets has been calculated using the straight line method to write off the cost of these assets over their estimated useful lives.
   Inventories are stated at the lower of average cost, and net realizable value. Deferred taxation is computed on the deferral method and arises from timing differences in the recognition of depreciation for accounting and taxation purposes.

2. Land, buildings and equipment comprise:

	Freehold Land and buildings	Plant & Equipment	Total
	£	£	£
Cost at beginning of year	10,000	12,000	22,000
Additions during year	—	4000	4000
Disposals during year	—	(2000)	(2000)
Cost at end of year	10,000	14,000	24,000
Accumulated depreciation	4000	5000	9000
Net book value at end of year	6000	9000	15,000

Government grants have been deducted in arriving at cost.

3. The charge for taxation on the profits for the year under review is computed as follows:

Corporation tax–40%	3200
Deferred taxation	900
	4100
Less: Corporation Tax and Deferred Tax overprovided in previous years	1100
	3000

4. The number of directors in each range of emoluments (excluding pensions contributions) for the year ended 31st December, 1975 was as follows:

Below £2500	2
£2501–£5000	1
£5001–£7500 (Highest paid director: £5500)	1

Auditors' Report to the members of
The Anglesee and Far-West Corporation

In our view, the accounts set out on pages — to — give a true and fair view of the state of the company's affairs at 31st December, 19X5 and of the income for the year ended on that date and comply with the Companies Acts 1948 and 1967.

W. E. Audent & Co.
Anglesee 31st January, 19X6.

Summary

In this chapter, we have examined the nature of corporate enterprise and the financial accounting implications of incorporation. These implications stem from the manner in which they are capitalized and from the manner in which the net income is appropriated. We discussed particular financial problems such as gearing.

The accounting procedures relating to the share capital are concerned principally with recording the issue of share capital, and with providing information about the share capital in financial accounting reports. There is little difference between the accounting treatment of share capital and loan capital.

The accounting procedures application to the periodic income are concerned with the manner in which the income is appropriated to various purposes. The size of the dividend is a problem of financial policy which Directors have to consider in relation to capital requirements, its effect on the share price and the availability of other sources of finance.

We considered also the procedures relating to the payment of dividends, and in this way maintained the focus of the chapter on the financial accounting problems arising directly from corporate status.

Finally, we discussed the extent to which financial accounting information is disclosed to shareholders. We noted the limited extent of this disclosure, and indicated that this is an important controversy in accounting which would be discussed in Part 4.

10
Financial Accounting for Groups of Companies

A major financial feature of the years just before the Second World War and certainly over the last 25 years has been the emergence of large corporate groups, made up of a family of related companies brought together by processes of merger and acquisition. Although a company may not acquire or hold its own shares, it may acquire and hold the shares of another company. Thus, it may become a shareholder of the other company, and by obtaining an effective majority of the shares in issue, it may obtain the control of that company by the power which it acquires with its shareholding to elect and control the Board of Directors. As a result, although both companies are distinct legal persons, the fact that one controls the other links them closely together in the identity of their financial and trading policies.

It is difficult to give one single reason why a Group may consist of 100 companies rather than being just one very large company, but probably the main reason is the degree of specialization permitted by the Group structure. Frequently, different subsidiaries, as the members of the group are known, have different product lines or functions within the Group and enjoy a measure of autonomy, whilst retaining the benefits of management expertise and finance provided within the Group. We discuss in Part 3 chapter 10 the problem of controlling the operations of a Group from an accounting viewpoint.

The parent–subsidiary relationship was originally defensive. If a company had a risky venture in mind, it could form and finance an entirely separate and distinct company, so that if the venture failed, it would insulate itself from the financial repercussion of the failure and only the subsidiary company would be wound up. Nowadays, it is thought unlikely that any major Group would put into liquidation a subsidiary which had got into difficulties, but during the secondary banking crisis which occurred in the United Kingdom in 1974, for example, it became clear that several major financial groups were only willing to provide minimum aid to their subsidiaries.

The Group structure has essentially been used for the purpose of financing and structuring business expansion—either by absorbing

208

competitors or opening up new territories—whilst ensuring the retention of control in the hands of the Group. As a result, financiers and entrepreneurs have succeeded in building up empires with the assistance of funds raised from the public, and they have acquired in this process very great economic and political power. In this respect, the emergence of the multi-national companies presents the spectacle of large and powerful Groups having, in some cases, a larger annual budget than some of the countries in which they operate.

The purpose of this chapter is to consider the nature of the financial accounting information provided to shareholders and investors about Groups of companies.

Legal obligation to disclose financial accounting information

The potential which Groups have to misuse shareholders' funds and the assets of subsidiary companies appears immense. However, whilst major failures, scandals and frauds have involved complicated and confusing corporate structures, there is very little evidence of Groups being deliberately managed in a dishonest manner.

Disclosure of financial accounting information has always been one of the cardinal principles of Company Law, and the view has developed that a Group should report as an economic entity and not as a collection of separate legal entities. In this connection, this view is now firmly established in the United Kingdom, and is likely to be accepted generally in other countries. For this reason, we shall consider the problem of consolidated accounting information in terms of the United Kingdom practice.

At the outset, it should be mentioned that consolidation does not imply that individual companies need not prepare Income Statements and Balance Sheets of their own. Indeed, each individual company in a Group still has to publish its own annual accounts to its shareholders, which, in the case of a wholly-owned subsidiary, will be the parent corporation. These accounts are available for public inspection through the Registrar of Companies. The financial statements of the parent or holding company and those of individual subsidiaries cannot reveal the overall Group financial position, and it is for this reason that Group or Consolidated accounts are required to provide an overall view of the Group.

Although it was left to the Companies Act, 1948 to make the major strides in the development of the law applicable to Consolidated accounts in the United Kingdom, many companies adopted the Group reporting format well in advance of legislation. The previous Companies Act of 1929 had paid scant attention to the problem of consolidation, for the abuses which were subsequently to be perpet-rated were not foreseen. The Act of 1929 required the disclosure in the Balance Sheet of the parent company of holdings of shares in subsidiaries, and also a statement showing how the aggregate income had been dealt with, without requiring the disclosure of the aggregate income involved. Thus, prior to the Companies Act 1948, the disclos-ure of information was left to the discretion of directors in effect. The present position is that companies with subsidiaries must present Group accounts in the form of a Consolidated Income Statement and a Consolidated Balance Sheet.

The definition of a subsidiary company

Consolidated accounts are not required unless a parent–subsidiary relationship exists, as defined in Section 154 of the Companies Act, 1948. A company becomes the subsidiary of another company in any one of the following circumstances:

(1) One company must be a member of the other and control the composition of its board of directors. This is the most common situation and is basically linked with voting power. If a com-pany holds more than half the voting power of a company, usually by becoming the owner of more than half the vote carrying equity shares, the latter company is a subsidiary of the first company. It is quite possible to hold much less than half the total share capital but still have a majority of the voting power, by means of non-voting and restricted voting shares. The Act does not mention voting power because this is only one, albeit the most common one, of controlling the composition of the board. The definition chosen was purposely left wide so that other means of controlling the composition of the board, such as the right to appoint or prevent the appoint-ment of a director might constitute control over the composi-tion of the board.

(2) One company must hold more than half in nominal value of the equity share capital of the other. Equity capital is defined under this section as 'issued share capital excluding any part thereof which, neither as respects dividends nor as respects capital, carries any right to participate beyond a specified amount in a distribution.' Equity capital thus includes the non-voting ordinary share. Under this section a company may become a subsidiary through the medium of another company. If Company A holds 30% of the equity capital of Company C and Company B holds 21% of C's equity capital, then should

B become the wholly owned subsidiary of Company A, this results in C also becoming a subsidiary of Company A.

(3) Where the company is the subsidiary of the holding company's subsidiary. If Company A becomes the parent company of Company B then A automatically takes over as parent any existing subsidiary of Company B.

The Jenkins Committee (1962) proposed the repeal of definition (2) above but it remained unchanged in the 1967 Companies Act. It was pointed out that the present definition may result in a company being considered as a subsidiary of two other companies. For example, through owning most of the non-voting shares, a company could hold more than half the equity shares capital, but another company through holding a majority of the voting shares could control the appointment and removal of directors. Jenkins considered that the entire test of a subsidiary should be based on membership and control of the board, by whatever means this is achieved.

The obligation to disclose information concerning subsidiaries

Following the recommendations of the Jenkins Committee that companies should disclose more information about their subsidiaries, S.3 of the Companies Act 1967 provides that certain information be given in respect of each subsidiary, namely its name, country of incorporation if different from that of the holding company and the identity and proportion of issued shares held of each class of the subsidiary's shares. There is a provision that if there are a large number of subsidiaries, only those whose results principally affect the amount of income need be listed. Schedule 2 of the 1967 Act requires any holding company to disclose separately in its balance sheet the aggregate amounts of:

(a) assets consisting of shares in its subsidiaries;
(b) indebtedness from subsidiaries; and
(c) indebtedness to subsidiaries.

The accounting requirements of Groups are mainly set out in the Companies Act 1948, sections 150–154 and in the Second Schedule to the 1967 Act. The legislation is tortuous in places, being designed to anticipate every situation, but essentially the legislation states that Group accounts are accounts or statements dealing with the state of affairs and the income of the company and its subsidiaries (S. 150) and that Group accounts shall give a true and fair view of the company and the subsidiaries (S. 152), and further that Group accounts shall comprise a consolidated balance sheet and a consolidated profit and loss account (S. 151). Group accounts are required in each case where the company has a subsidiary at the end of its financial year and is not itself the wholly owned subsidiary of another company incorporated in Great Britain (S. 150). Alternative accounting forms to Consolidated accounts are permissible, so long as they give the same or equivalent information and may take the following forms:

(a) Consolidated accounts dealing respectively with the company and one group of subsidaries and other groups of subsidiaries;
(b) separate accounts dealing with each of the subsidiaries;
(c) statements expanding the information about the subsidiaries in the company's own accounts;
(d) any combination of the above. (S. 151)

In certain cases a subsidiary may be omitted from Group accounts but in such a case considerable financial information is required about such a subsidiary (S. 150 and 2 Sch. 1967 Act). Under S. 153 the financial year-ends of holding companies and subsidiaries are required to coincide unless there are good reasons for not doing so. Such reasons must themselves be disclosed.

Consolidated accounts

The purpose of Consolidated accounts is to show in two statements, the Consolidated Income Statement and the Consolidated Balance Sheet, a composite picture of the income and financial position of the several companies which make up the Group. It should be emphasized that each company remains a separate legal entity and a separate accounting entity and that the Group is an economic and reporting entity. The simplest position is that of a parent company with just one subsidiary, and initially this structure will be used to examine the principles behind the construction of Consolidated accounts. The number of subsidiaries and sub-subsidiaries, and the further complications that can be thought up in practice can quickly border on the mind bending, but the majority of these whilst complicating the arithmetic, add nothing to the principles.

In illustrations throughout this chapter the parent company will be called P Ltd, the subsidiary company S Ltd, and the combined Group as G Ltd, rather than as the consolidated accounts of P Ltd and its subsidiary S Ltd. This helps to emphasize an important point—G Ltd does not exist except as an abstract figment of the legislator's imagination. G Ltd is not a real company, it has no books and accounts of its own; it is merely a vehicle for combining the accounts of real underlying companies which by virtue of holding shares in one another are required to report as one economic unit. Thus it is an important first step to realize that although the parent company has a full set of double entry accounting records and so do its various subsidiaries and any other connected companies, G Ltd, not being a legal entity, has no books of its own and its final accounts being the combination of the final accounts of several companies are not prepared from underlying double entry records. In practice Consolidated accounts are prepared by a series of schedules, rather than as the natural end product of a logical accounting system. A moment's thought will show that Consolidated accounts are not just the simple combination of the accounting figures of the underlying companies.

Example 1

P Ltd acquired all the share capital of S Ltd at 1 January after which the two Balance Sheets show the following position.

	P Ltd £m.	S Ltd £m.		P Ltd £m.	S Ltd £m.
Share Capital	100	40	Assets less liabilities	60	40
			Investment—shares in S	40	
	100	40		100	40

The combined balance sheet, G Ltd, is not just £100 m. + £40 m. = £140 m., because one of the main assets of P Ltd is an investment in S Ltd amounting to the entire net assets of S Ltd. The share capital of S Ltd £40 m. must be set against the Investment in S Ltd £40 m. in the books of P Ltd. Although there is nothing at all wrong with either the accounts of P Ltd or S Ltd, the Group position requires that the real position be revealed and that in reality the investment in the books of P Ltd is the various assets less liabilities of S Ltd. The Group balance sheet is as follows.

G Ltd

	£m.		£m.
Share Capital	100	Assets less liabilities	100

To treat the position otherwise would be to count the same item twice—once as an asset and once as a liability—and it is vital that accounts reveal the reality of the situation.

It is evident from the foregoing example that the main work in the preparation of Consolidated accounts consists of cancelling out investments in the shares in subsidiaries held by a parent company against the share capital and reserves of the various subsidiaries, so that the Group accounts reflect the reality of its economic situation.

Problems in the consolidation of Group accounts

Two major problems arise on the consolidation of Group accounts which we avoided in Example 1:

(a) P Ltd bought the investment in S Ltd for exactly the same amount as the net assets involved, £40 m. This is hardly realistic and in most cases the shareholders of S Ltd would demand a premium over the book valuation of the assets before relinquishing control and accepting shares in P Ltd to replace the shares they held in S Ltd. In other words P Ltd would have to pay a premium to persuade them to change management.

(b) Example 1 shows the position immediately after takeover but both companies will still continue to trade independently and make profits. The income of a subsidiary will increase the net assets of that subsidiary and also increase the value of the investment of the parent company in the subsidiary. From the Group point of view, income will increase the net assets of the Group.

Consolidating subsidiaries acquired at a premium
Example 2

Let us assume that P Ltd makes an offer to the shareholders of S Ltd to buy their shares for £2 each.

The Balance Sheet of P Ltd at 1 January is as follows:

	£m.
Ordinary Share capital—shares of £1 each	140
Share premium account	110
General reserve	30
Retained income	20
	300
Fixed and Current Assets less liabilities	300

The Balance Sheet of S Ltd before the takeover on 1 January is as under:

	£m
Ordinary Share capital—shares of £1 each	50
General reserve	20
Retained income	10
	80
Fixed and Current Assets less Liabilities	80

Assuming that the takeover is a complete success, the Balance Sheet of P Ltd will be as follows:

	£m.
Ordinary Share capital—shares of £1 each	140
Share premium account	110
General reserve	30
Retained income	20
	300
Fixed and Current Assets less liabilities	200
Investment—shares in S Ltd at cost	100
	300

The Balance Sheet of S Limited immediately after the takeover bid has gone through will be unchanged. All that has happened from the point of view of S Ltd is that the shares formerly held by various shareholders are now held by one shareholder, P Ltd. The former shareholders in S Ltd have sold their shares to P Ltd for what they have accepted as the market price.

To obtain control, P Ltd has had to pay a premium to ensure that the shareholders in S Ltd would accept the offer. To get control P Ltd has paid £20 m. for an intangible asset usually termed goodwill. Neither of the above balance sheets shows anything for goodwill. P Ltd can legitimately argue that it has bought an investment in shares which cost £100 m. But from the point of view of the Group, the reality is that the acquisition of S Ltd has added net assets of £80 m. and goodwill of £20 m., calculated thus:

		£m.
P Ltd has paid		100
for net assets of S Ltd.		
Share Capital	50	
General reserve	20	
Retained Income	10	80
		20

but more usually shown in accounting form as:

Cost of Control account (G Ltd)

	£m.		£m.
Investment—in S Ltd		Share Capital (S Ltd)	50
	100	General reserve (S Ltd)	20
		Retained Income (S Ltd)	10
		Balance = Group goodwill	20
	100		100
Goodwill b/d	20		

and the Group balance sheet immediately after acquisition:

	£m.
Ordinary Share Capital—shares of £1 each	140
Share premium account	110
General reserve	30
Retained Income	20
	300
Fixed and current assets less liabilities (200+80)	280
Cost of Control/Goodwill	20
	300

It should now be seen that the Investment account in the books of P Ltd has been cancelled against the share capital and reserves of S Ltd so that in the Consolidated Balance Sheet above the underlying assets of S are brought in. The apparent maintenance of the double entry principle in the construction of the Cost of Control account above is illusory. It should be seen for what it is, namely an adjusting schedule where an item in the accounts of P Ltd is cancelled against items in the accounts of S Ltd.

An extension of a principle first brought out in Example 1 can now be examined. In Example 1 the share capital of S Ltd was offset against the investment in the balance sheet of P Ltd, so that neither account appeared in the Consolidated account. In Example 2, not only the share capital of S Ltd but also the reserves at the date of acquisition have been offset against the investment account in the balance sheet of P Ltd. These reserves are regarded from the Group point of view as capitalized at the date of takeover and are not now available for distribution. If the reserves of S Ltd at the date of acquisition were merely added to the reserves of its parent, and it might appear that they are available for distribution, and it is a principle that pre-acquisition reserves are treated as capitalized on the date of takeover. The logic of this practice has been challenged in recent years and there has been some relaxation of this principle and this has led to the pooling of profits as from the date of takeover.

At this stage a definition of Cost of Control, which also appears in published accounts under the name of just 'Goodwill' or 'Goodwill arising on Consolidation' may be attempted. The Cost of Control arising on consolidation is the excess of the purchase price over the book value of the net assets (being capital plus reserves) acquired at the date of acquisition.

At the end of the year, 31 December, the Balance Sheets of the two companies are as follows:

	P Ltd £m.	S Ltd £m.
Ordinary Share Capital—shares of £1	140	50
Share premium account	110	—
General reserve	30	20
Income Statement, 1 January	20	10
Income for the year	12	15
	312	95
Fixed & current assets less liabilities	212	95
Investment—shares in S Ltd at cost	100	—
	312	95

(b) Consolidating Group income

At the end of the year the income of both companies result in a corresponding increase in their net assets. The income of a subsidiary made after acquisition is regarded as distributable from the Group point of view and is combined with the income of the parent to show the Group income on the Consolidated Balance Sheet.

Consolidated Income Statement (G Ltd)

	£m.			£m.
		Balance b.f. at 1 Jan.	(P Ltd)	20
Group Income c.d.	47	Income for year	(P Ltd)	12
		Income for Year	(S Ltd)	15
	47			47
		Balance b.d.		47

and the balance at 31 December is as follows:

Consolidated Balance Sheet—31 December (G Ltd)

	£m.
Ordinary Share Capital—shares of £1 each	140
Share premium account	110
General reserve	30
Retained Income	47
	327
Fixed & current assets less liabilities	307
Cost of Control of subsidiary	20
	327

The income of the subsidiary in future years will also be added along with the income of the parent company and the balance brought forward on the Income Statement, so that a total figure for Group income is carried forward at the end of each year.

The treatment of dividends

Dividends may be paid either by the parent company, or the subsidiary, or by both companies. (The following examples ignore all questions of taxation).

Dividend paid by Parent Ltd

A dividend declared by P Ltd will be paid to the shareholders of P Ltd, and the payment of the dividend will reduce the reserves and the cash resources of P Ltd and of the Group, since the funds will be paid outside the Group. If a dividend of £14 m. is declared the effect on the Group Balance Sheet will be to reduce the balance on the Income Statement to £33 m. (47 m. – 14 m.) and the Group net assets to £293 m. (307 m. – 14 m.) The entries required are those normally required for recording the declaration and payment of a dividend. If the dividend is proposed but will not be paid until after Balance Sheet date, it will appear as a current liability in the Group Balance Sheet.

Dividend paid by Subsidiary Ltd

If S Ltd declares a dividend it will be paid to its sole shareholder—P Ltd. Although S Ltd will pay the dividend and P Ltd will receive it, no funds will pass outside the Group and although it will mean that the Income Statement of S Ltd will be decreased and the Income Statement of P Ltd will be increased by the same amount, there will be no change in the overall Group Income Statement.

Example 3

S Ltd pays a dividend of £10 m. to P Ltd. The Journal entries are as follows:

		Dr. £m.	Cr. £m.
In the books of S Ltd	Income Statement	10	
	Cash or Proposed Dividend account		10
In the books of P Ltd	Cash or Dividend Receivable account	10	
	Income Statement		10

From the point of view of the Group, the total on the Income Statement is still the same, although the distribution between the companies is different:

Consolidated Income Statement (G Ltd)

	£m.		£m.
		Balance b/f at 1 Jan.	
		(P Ltd)	20
		Income for year	
		(P Ltd 12 + 10)	22
Group Income c/d	47	Income for year	
		(S Ltd 15 − 10)	5
	47		47
Proposed dividend			47
(P Ltd)	14	Balance b/d	47
Balance	33		

Thus an inter-company dividend although altering the distribution of income and funds within a Group, does not alter the total income. Only in the case of a dividend which passes outside the Group are the Group income and net assets reduced. Parent companies frequently require subsidiaries to declare and pay dividends to them so that the parent has control over Group financial policy, and may require a profitable subsidiary to make over funds to the parent which the parent itself uses or it may loan the cash to another not so profitable subsidiary. In the above example S Ltd pays a dividend of £10 m. to P Ltd, so that when P Ltd pays a dividend of £14 m. the drain on its cash resources is only a net £4 m. The above covered the situation in which the dividend paid by the subsidiary is declared and paid out of income arising after the date of the acquistion. The dividend received by the parent is regarded as distributable to the shareholders of P Ltd.

Dividends paid out of pre-acquisition income

A dividend paid by a subsidiary to its parent and agreed to be paid out of income existing at the time of takeover (pre-acquisition income) is treated quite differently. Such a dividend is said to be paid out of reserves which have been capitalized for Group accounting purposes and such a dividend amounts to a capital return on the purchase price paid by the parent for the shares it bought in the subsidiary. In effect it amounts to a refund of part of the purchase price and is so treated in the accounts. In practice, it is rare for a dividend to be paid from pre-acquisition income, but where a dividend is paid which is larger than post-acquisition income, a LIFO rule is applied, that is, the most recent income is deemed to have been paid out, and only the excess is assumed to have been paid out of capitalized pre-acquisition income.

Example 4

The Balance Sheets of P Ltd and S Ltd immediately after take-over on 1 January are as follows.

	P Ltd £m.	S Ltd £m.
Ordinary Share capital—shares of £1 each	140	50
Share premium account	110	—
General reserve	30	20
Retained Income	20	10
	300	80
Fixed & current assets less liabilities	200	80
Investment—shares in S Ltd at cost	100	—
	300	80

On 2 January just after the acquisition, S Ltd declares and pays a dividend amounting to £8m. out of its Income Statement which from the Group point of view is out of pre-acquisition income which have been capitalized.

		Dr. £m.	Cr. £m.
In the books of S Ltd	Income Statement	8	
	Cash		8
In the books of P Ltd	Cash	8	
	Investment—shares in S Ltd		8

P Ltd cannot credit the dividend received direct to its Income Statement and the dividend is not regarded as being distributable to the shareholders of P Ltd. From the Group point of view little has changed. The balance on the Cost of Control Account has not changed, and although the detailed figures have changed, the make-up of the goodwill figure is still the same, as shown below:

Cost of Control account (G Ltd)

Investment—cost of shares in S (P Ltd)	£m.	£m.	Share capital (S Ltd)	£m.	£m.
less dividend	100		General reserve (S Ltd)		50
from S	8				20
		92	Retained income less dividend to P Ltd	10 8	2
			Balance being group goodwill		20
		92			92
Balance b/d		20			

The Balance Sheets just after the payment of the dividend would be as follows.

	P Ltd £m.	S Ltd £m.	G Ltd £m.
Ordinary Share Capital—shares of £1	140	50	140
Share premium account	110		110
General reserve	30	20	30
Retained Income	20	2	20
	300	72	300
Fixed and current assets less liabilities	208	72	280
Investment—shares in S Ltd at cost	92		
Cost of control/Goodwill			20
	300	72	300

The Consolidated Balance Sheet is the same as that in Example 2. An intercompany dividend out of pre-acquisition income does transfer cash from the subsidiary to the parent but otherwise has no real effect.

The treatment of minority shareholders

The above examples have assumed that the parent company is able to persuade all the shareholders of the proposed subsidiary to transfer their shares to it, and that the subsidiary becomes a wholly-owned subsidiary. It is not always the case that all the shareholders accept the offer, and a substantial minority may turn down the offer and remain as shareholders in S Ltd. The City Code on Takeovers and Mergers does not allow bids for only part of the share capital of a company, and a takeover bid has to be made for 100% of the shares not already held by the parent. The bidding company in offering to buy 100% of the capital of the proposed subsidiary commonly makes its offer conditional on acceptance by 90% of the outside shareholders, so that it can take advantage of S 209 and compulsorily purchase a small minority of shareholders up to 10% of the outstanding capital. If the bidding company obtains control of more than 50% of the voting share capital, but clearly has no chance of obtaining a 90% acceptance level, because a sizeable minority of shareholders are opposed to the bid, it still may decide to go ahead with the bid and allow a minority of shareholders to retain their shares in what will become a subsidiary company. Most subsidiaries are 100% owned, often having been set up by the parent company itself, but it is not uncommon to find a subsidiary in which a minority of shareholders hold up to 25% of the voting capital. There may well be good reasons for this. Most takeovers are amicably agreed between the parties and are small in size and are often for private companies in family businesses and the former shareholders may wish to retain some small interest in what was their own company, and the parent may be willing to keep the family connection with a view to retaining the goodwill of customers and the management expertise of the former owners.

Such minority shareholders still retain an interest in their original company and are not members of the Group. Their interest, called a Minority Interest, may theoretically extend up to 50% of the net assets but is commonly less than 25%. A minority interest clearly needs to be excluded from the capital and reserves of the Group, because the minority has no claim on the Group. It would be possible to consolidate just (say) the three-quarters of the net assets of the subsidiary company which have been acquired by the Group, but this approach is not adopted. All the assets and liabilities of the subsidiary are included in the Group accounts and the minority interest is shown as a deduction proportional to the interest of the minority shareholders. This is quite proper because although the Group does not own all the net assets of the subsidiary it does have effective control of all of them, including those in which the minority have an interest. A parent company only needs bare voting control which is just a little more than 50% to be in a position to control 100% of the assets. The treatment may be shown diagrammatically:

	S Ltd	
Interest of Group 75%	Fixed and Current Assets less Liabilities 100%	included in Group Accounts 100%
Minority Interest 25%		

Thus the Minority are entitled to their share of the share capital and reserves at the date that the parent company acquires its controlling interest and their share of income made after acquisition. If a subsidiary company which has a minority passes outside the Group, and reduces the total interest of the Minority the proportion paid to the minority passes outside the Group, and reduces the total interest of the Minority by the amount of the dividend as shown in the Group Balance Sheet.

Acquisitions and the creation of minority interests

An example will be worked through in detail to further illustrate the principles and calculations involved.

Example 5

P Ltd acquired a 75% interest in the share capital of S Ltd on 1 April. The draft summarized accounts of the two companies at 31 March next are as follows.

	P Ltd £	S Ltd £
Ordinary Shares of £1 each	100,000	40,000
General reserve	30,000	—
Retained income	11,000	5000
Current liabilities	12,000	8000
Proposed final dividend	5000	6000
Corporation tax	17,000	9000
	175,000	68,000
Freehold property at cost	112,000	30,000
Plant & Machinery at book value	28,000	12,000
Inventory	17,000	10,000
Debtors	14,000	9000
Cash and bank balances	4000	7000
	175,000	68,000

Income Statements

		P Ltd		S Ltd
Income for year		34,000		18,000
less taxation		17,000		9000
		17,000		9000
Balance b/f at 1 April		8000		6000
		25,000		15,000
Dividend paid	9000		4000	
Dividend proposed	5000		6000	
		14,000		10,000
Balance c/f at 31 March		11,000		5000

A Consolidated Balance Sheet of the Group is to be prepared at 31 March taking into account that no entries have been made in the books of P Ltd in respect of the purchase of the shares in S Ltd. These shares were acquired on the basis that five new shares in P Ltd were issued for every six shares in S Ltd, and that each share in S Ltd was agreed to be worth £1·50. The dividend paid by S Ltd was paid shortly after acquisition and is out of pre-acquisition income.

(a) Calculating the purchase price

The first task is to calculate the price P Ltd paid for its 75% interest in S Ltd and to record the transactions in the books of P Ltd which so far have remained unentered. P Ltd buys 75% of the share capital of S Ltd, i.e., 30,000 shares and since each share in S Ltd is agreed to be worth £1·50, the total purchase price is £45,000. The terms of issue are that six shares in S Ltd are to be exchanged for five shares in P Ltd. Thus P Ltd will issue $\frac{5}{6} \times 30,000 = 25,000$ shares and since it is agreed that the total purchase price is £45,000, the 25,000 Ordinary Shares of £1 each are issued at a premium of £20,000. The entries in the books of P Ltd to record the acquisition of the majority interest in S Ltd are:

Journal of P Ltd.	Dr.	Cr.
	£m.	£m.
Investment account—shares in S Ltd at cost	45,000	
Ordinary Share capital account		25,000
Share premium account		20,000

Being purchase of a 75% shareholding
in S Ltd at 1 April at agreed value.

(b) Calculating the cost of control

P Ltd has paid £45,000 to gain a three-quarters holding in S Ltd. The calculation of the Cost of Control is slightly complicated in that shortly after acquisition S Ltd pays a dividend of £4000, agreed to be out of pre-acquisition income and also because a minority of 25% in S Ltd retain their shares in S Ltd.

Cost of Control account at 1 April (G Ltd)

Investment—shares in S (P's books)	45,000	Share capital (S's books)		30,000
less dividend from S (P's books)	3000	Income Statement (S's books)		
	42,000	$\frac{3}{4} \times 6000$	4500	
		less dividend paid	3000	1500
		Balance = Goodwill		10,500
	42,000			42,000
Balance b/d	10,500			

Note that P Ltd acquires three-quarters of the share capital and three-quarters of the Income Statement balance at 1 April. This is three-quarters of the net assets at the date of takeover. The dividend paid by S Ltd will go £3000 to the parent and £1000 to the minority. P Ltd will receive this dividend, debiting cash and crediting the Investment account for the shares in S Ltd. Since no entries for the acquisition have been made in the books of P Ltd, (but they have been recorded for S Ltd) the bank account of P Ltd will be increased by £3000 to £7000.

Journal of P Ltd

	Dr.	Cr.
Cash	3000	
Investment a/c—shares in S Ltd		3000
(Receipt of dividend from S Ltd)		

The Consolidated Income Statement is calculated as:

Consolidated Income Statement (G Ltd)

	£m.		£m.
Cost of Control		Balance b.f. 1 April	
$\frac{3}{4}$ × pre-acquisition		(P Ltd)	8000
income (S Ltd)	4500	Balance b.f. 1 April	
Minority Interest		(S Ltd)	6000
$\frac{1}{4}$ × pre-acquisition			
income (S Ltd)	1500		
		Income for year after	
		tax (P Ltd)	17,000
Minority Interest		Income for year after	
$\frac{1}{4}$ × year's income		tax (S Ltd)	9000
(of £9000)	2250		
Dividend paid (P Ltd)	9000		
Dividend proposed (P Ltd)	5000		
Balance = Consolidated			
income	17750		
	40,000		40,000
		Balance b/d	17,750

The pre-acquisition income is split between the Cost of Control and the Minority Interest. Of the year's income after tax of the subsidiary, one quarter is allocated to the minority, and the dividends of P Ltd, which go to the shareholders of the Group, are deducted in the Group Income Statement. The proposed dividend between the subsidiary and parent does not affect the Group income. When paid it will affect the two companies but not the Group position.

(c) *Recording the Minority Interest*

Minority Interest account (G Ltd)

Dividend paid (S Ltd)		Share Capital	
$\frac{1}{4}$ × £4000	1000	(S Ltd)	10,000
Dividend Proposed		Income Statement	
$\frac{1}{4}$ × £6000	1500	(S Ltd) at 1 April	1500
(current liability)		Income for the year	2250
Balance = Minority			
Interest	11,250		
	13,750		13,750
		Balance b/d	11,250

The interest of the Minority is made up of their share of the capital and reserves at the date of acquisition plus their share of income made since acquisition, less their share of dividends paid and proposed. Clearly their interest is in their one-quarter share of net assets at the balance sheet date, and the minority can be easily cross-checked in this case as:

S Ltd
Ordinary shares   £40,000⎫
Income Statement   5000⎬ at 31 March
          45,000
$\frac{1}{4}$ =   11,250

It is usual to show a proposed dividend due to a minority as part of the Group current liabilities, rather than as part of the Minority Interest because it will be paid shortly after the Balance Sheet date and also is part of the liabilities of the Group, being an amount due to persons external to the Group.

The Consolidated Balance Sheet is as under. The balance sheets of P Ltd and S Ltd are also given.

	P Ltd	S Ltd	G Ltd
Ordinary shares of £1 each	125,000	40,000	125,000
Share premium account	20,000	—	20,000
General reserve	30,000	—	30,000
Retained income	11,000	5000	17,750
Minority interest			11,250
Current liabilities	12,000	8000	20,000
Proposed final dividend	5000	6000	6500
Corporation tax	17,000	9000	26,000
	220,000	68,000	256,500
Cost of Control			10,500
Freehold Property	112,000	30,000	142,000
Plant & Machinery at book value	28,000	12,000	40,000
Inventory	17,000	10,000	27,000
Debtors	14,000	9000	23,000
Cash and bank balances	7000	7000	14,000
Investment—shares in S Ltd at cost	42,000		
	220,000	68,000	256,500

Summary

It has been explained that Group accounts are not the accounts prepared from a set of books kept by a Group, but are an amalgamation of the accounts of the companies making up the Group. Neither are they the straight addition of like items in different Balance Sheets, but a total view of the Group. The accounts of the parent company usually have the biggest influence on the Group accounts and the accounts of the subsidiaries are merged with those of the parent so that the Group reports on the entire income, assets and liabilities under its control. The important adjustments, called primary adjustments, are to bring out the Group figures for Cost of Control, Income and where applicable the Minority Interest.

The Cost of Control (Goodwill) has earlier been defined as the excess of the purchase price over the proportion of net assets acquired in the subsidiary as at the date of acquisition. The income figure for the Group represents the total of the income of the parent plus its share of the profits of the subsidiary made since acquisition, less the dividends of the parent company. Pre-acquisition income is regarded as capitalized and non-distributable. The Minority interest is entitled to its share of net assets of a subsidiary at the date of takeover, plus its share of profits made since acquisition, less its share of any dividends paid or proposed.

Reference

The Jenkins Committee Report, H.M.S.O., 1962.

11
Problems in the Preparation Of Consolidated Financial Statements

In chapter 10, we examined the general principles associated with the practice of consolidating the financial statements of Groups of Companies. The examples which were chosen for this purpose were simplified to avoid many of the complications which arise in practice. This chapter is addressed to an analysis of the financial accounting implications of the most common problems which arise when consolidating financial statements. The list of problems considered in this chapter is not exhaustive, but it may be said, however, that whilst they add to the volume of data to be processed and they increase the arithmetical complexity of consolidation, they do very little to extend the principles which we have already examined. Hence, this chapter serves to test the logic of those principles.

Consolidating the financial statements of multiple subsidiaries

In the examples we examined in chapter 10, it was assumed that the parent company has but one subsidiary. This assumption is unrealistic, and most public companies have several subsidiaries and often a public group will consist of over a hundred companies. Where there is more than one subsidiary company, then in each case, the cost of control, group income statement, and minority interest if applicable, will need to be calculated. The resulting figures will be put together so that in the Group Balance Sheet one total figure will be given for each of the primary adjustments.

The acquisition of a subsidiary at less than book value

Occasionally a subsidiary may be acquired for less than the apparent or given value of its net assets, in which case goodwill will appear as a negative figure. For example, P Ltd acquires for £100,000 a 60%

228

interest in S Ltd, whose Balance Sheet at the date of acquisition shows:

	£
Ordinary shares of £1 each	120,000
Share premium account	60,000
Reserves including retained profits	20,000
	200,000

then the cost of control will be:

Cost of Control account (G Ltd)

	£m.		£m.
		Share capital (S Ltd) 60%	72,000
Investment—S Ltd		Share premium (S Ltd) 60%	36,000
(P Ltd)	100,000	Reserves (S Ltd) 60%	12,000
Balance c.d.	20,000		
	120,000		120,000

The credit balance on the Cost of Control account is usually shown separately as a capital reserve in the Balance Sheet, under a heading such as 'Surplus arising on acquisition of subsidiary'. Less commonly it may be deducted from any goodwill in the Balance Sheet, so that a figure for the net cost of control is shown in the Group accounts.

The treatment of losses made by subsidiaries

Subsidiaries do not always yield income, but may sustain a loss. A parent will have to bear its share of losses made by its subsidiary and a minority interest will also have to bear their proportionate share of any loss.

Example 6

P Ltd acquires 80% of the Ordinary share capital of S Ltd for £70,000, whose Balance Sheet at the date of acquisition shows:

	£
Ordinary Share Capital	100,000
Income Statement (Dr)	(30,000)

During the first year after acquisition S Ltd makes a further loss of £10,000. Then:

Cost of Control account (G Ltd)

Income Statement (S Ltd)		Share Capital (S Ltd)	
80%	24,000	80%	80,000
Investment in S (P Ltd)	70,000	Balance = goodwill	14,000
	94,000		94,000
Balance b/d	14,000		

Minority Interest in S Ltd (G Ltd)

Income Statement (S Ltd)	£	Share capital (S Ltd)	£
20%	6000	80%	20,000
Loss for year 20%	2000		
Balance c/d	12,000		
	20,000		20,000
		Balance b/d	12,000

The parents share of the loss for the year, £8000 will be set against the income of the parent in the Group Income Statement.

Consolidating subsidiaries having complex capital structures

A subsidiary company may have a more complex share capital structure than so far envisaged. Commonly it may be found to have some form of fixed interest share capital, usually Preference shares, with a fixed share of the income and no voting rights. If no offer is made for such shares during the takeover, the Preference shareholders become a minority of the Group and are included in the calculation of the minority interest of that subsidiary.

Example 7

P Ltd acquires 75% of the Ordinary Share capital of S Ltd, but none of the Preference shares, at a time when the net assets of S Ltd are:

		£
Ordinary Share capital		50,000
10% Preference Shares		30,000
Reserves including retained income		40,000
		120,000
The minority interest will consist of		
Ordinary Share capital	25%	12,500
10% Preference shares	100%	30,000
Reserves including retained income	25%	10,000
		52,500

Further, in calculating the proportion of the income of S Ltd due to P Ltd, the dividends paid or due to the minority Preference shareholders must be deducted before calculating the interests of the Ordinary shareholders i.e., P Ltd and the minority holders of Ordinary shares in S Ltd. Suppose that the income is £19,000. It will be apportioned as under:

	£	£
Preference shareholders (fixed dividend)		3000
P Ltd 75%	12,000	
Ordinary Minority in S 25%	4000	16,000
		19,000

A Preference dividend due but not paid will not be included with the minority interest, but will be shown as a proposed dividend under the current liabilities, in just the same way as a dividend due to the Ordinary minority shareholders. Debenture holders are not shareholders and do not form part of a minority interest. They are debt creditors and their position will be considered later.

Subsidiaries acquired during an accounting period

It will be rare in practice for a subsidiary to be taken over on the same day as the first day of the financial year of the parent company so that the two accounting periods coincide. It is a requirement that the financial year-ends coincide after takeover. In the usual case of a subsidiary taken over during its financial year either proper final accounts can be specially prepared at the date of acquisition so that pre- and post-acquisition income can be distinguished or an apportionment can be made on a time or some other rational basis to determine the division of pre- and post-acquisition income. A consolidation may include a subsidiary which is taken over mid-way during the parent's financial year and the income of the subsidiary in that year may have to be split as to 50% prior to acquisition and 50% after acquistion. In fact much of the secret of dealing with problems of Consolidating accounts lies in an appreciation of the significance of the various dates involved. The date of acquisition is important for calculating the goodwill and considering whether any dividends are being paid out of pre-acquisition income, and the date of the final accounts is important for determining the income made since acquisition and the total of the minority interest.

Consolidation and inter-group transactions

As well as Primary adjustments there arise several Secondary adjustments which are commonly needed in Consolidated accounts. These arise mainly because of inter-company trading between a parent and its various subsidiary companies, which if not eliminated during the consolidation process may lead to 'double counting'. For example, P

Ltd may make a loan of (say) £2000 to its subsidiary. P Ltd will include S Ltd in its debtors as a debtor for £2000, and S Ltd will include P Ltd among its creditors for £2000. Just to cross add the debtors and creditors of both companies would lead to an overstatement of the figures for current assets and current liabilities in the Group Balance Sheet. True enough S does owe P £2000, but the Group position is that the £2000 is an internal or inter-company loan and is neither an external asset nor liability of the Group. It must therefore be eliminated by reducing the debtors of P Ltd and also the creditors of S Ltd. viz.

Debtors of P Ltd   £2000   Creditors of S Ltd   £2000

Just the same rules apply for loans made between the various subsidiaries and each other if they are members of the same Group. The same procedure applies for cancelling out in the Group accounts any inter-company current accounts. Where a parent has regular transactions with its subsidiary, probably in the nature of inter-company purchases and sales, each company will maintain a record of its transactions with the other company. At the end of a financial period these two current accounts will be reconciled if they are not in agreement, using the same procedures as for branch accounts.

Example 8

At 31 December the current account of P Ltd with its subsidiary shows a debit balance of £6000 and the current account with P Ltd in the books of S Ltd shows a credit balance of £4500. The difference is due to cash in transit from the subsidiary to its parent which is not received by P Ltd until after the end of the financial year.

Books of P Ltd

Current account with S Ltd

		£			£
Balance b/d		6000	Cash in transit A/c		1500
			Balance c.d.		4500
		6000			6000
Balance b/d		4500			

Cash in Transit Account

Current account—S	1500		

Books of S Ltd

Current account with P Ltd

		Balance b/d	4500

In the Consolidated Balance Sheet the Cash in Transit account will appear as one of the assets and the two current accounts will cancel each other out. Cross holdings of loan capital or debentures between related companies are also cancelled out in the Group accounts. The loan interest paid by one company on loan stock held by another member of the Group must also be cancelled out against the loan interest received by that company.

Where there are mutual dealings—sales and purchases—between the companies in the Group, transfers of goods between the companies may take place at a transfer value which is higher than cost. The point of this is to split the income earned on the completed transaction between the supplying company and the company which eventually sells the product outside the Group. In preparing a Consolidated Income Statement it will be necessary to eliminate such inter-company dealings from the total of Group sales and purchases, so that no double counting occurs. A problem arises where one of the companies is at the financial year-end holding goods in inventory supplied by another company in the Group at a price in excess of original cost. Such inventory will be included in the holder's books and inventory sheets at cost price to the buying company, which is cost price plus a profit margin from the Group viewpoint, and in compiling Group accounts it will be necessary to deal with the unrealized income. If the inventory of S Ltd includes goods received from P Ltd, at a cost of £2200 but the cost to P Ltd was £2000, from the Group point of view, the inventory of S Ltd carries an unrealized income of £200. This would be adjusted on consolidation:

	Dr. £	Cr. £
Consolidated Income Statement	200	
Consolidated Inventory		200

i.e., both the Group income and the Group inventory is reduced by £200. Where the subsidiary is wholly owned by its parent, it is clear that it is proper to remove from the Group accounts the full amount of the unrealized income. If a minority is involved the position is a little more complicated. Where the inventory is held by a partly-owned subsidiary the usual practice is to provide for the whole of the unrealized income, as above, so that inventory appears at its cost price in the Consolidated Balance Sheet. Where the subsidiary is the supplying company and there is a minority shareholding in the subsidiary, the inter-company income has been earned from the point of view of the minority, and the view may be advanced that the minority should not be debited with its proportion of the unrealized income i.e., the minority should be entitled to its proportion of the income for the year before adjustment. But from a Group point of view the income is not yet made and it can be argued that the adjustment should be made in proportion to the shares in the income of the subsidiary company. e.g.,

	Dr.	Cr.
Consolidated Income Statement	150	
Minority Interest	50	
Consolidated Inventory		200

Other treatments are also possible, but in most cases the amounts involved are not material and some variety in practice is permissible.

Much the same sort of situation arises in dealing with inter-Group income arising on a sale or transfer of fixed assets between companies in the same Group. Assume that P Ltd sells an item of plant which stood in its own books at £7000 to its wholly-owned subsidiary for £8000 and that Group policy is for each company to provide depreciation on this type of asset at a rate of 20% per annum. Then the adjusting entries are:

	Dr. £	Cr. £
Consolidated Income Statement	1000	
Consolidated plant account		1000
Being elimination of unrealized income in plant transferred within Group		
Consolidated provision for depreciation	200	
Consolidated Income Statement		200
Being excess depreciation (1600 – 1400) written back		

Consolidated Income Statements

The disclosure requirements of the Companies Acts ensure that a Group publishes a Consolidated Income Statement as part of Group accounts. The parent company has to publish its own Balance Sheet as well as a Consolidated Balance Sheet but the situation with regard to the Income Statement is rather different. Under the provisions of S.149(5) the Income Statement of the parent need not be published if the Consolidated Income Statement "shows how much of the consolidated income for the financial year is dealt with in the accounts of the (parent) company". The information required by this sub-section is usually given as the second part of the Consolidated Income Statement, and the parent's Income Statement is dispensed with.

The major part of the Consolidated Income Statement is constructed by merging the figures given in the separate Income Statements of the separate companies. The full income of each subsidiary is included and the total of the Minority Interest for the year is shown as a deduction. This is consistent with showing the Group position as a whole, and then deducting external claims. Dividends paid between companies will cancel each other out and secondary adjustments for such things as unrealized income in respect of inventory and inter-company loan interest are excluded by the techniques outlined above. The final part consists of a section analysing in which companies income arises and is to comply with S.149. The method of approach will be illustrated by:

Example 9

On 1 July P Ltd which has held 80% of the Ordinary Share Capital of Si Ltd for several years, acquired 90% of the issued Ordinary Share Capital of Sii Ltd. It may be assumed that income occurrs evenly over the year. The share capital and reserves position of the three companies as at 1 January previously were as follows:

	£	P Ltd £	Si Ltd £	£	Sii Ltd £
Ordinary Shares of £1 each		10,000	4000		2000
Income Statement at					
1 January	5000		Dr., 1000	10,000	
less dividends					
(paid in March)	2500	2500		6000	4000

The Income Statements of the three companies for the year to 31 December following were as follows:

	£	P Ltd £	£	Si Ltd £	£	Sii Ltd £
Sales		70,000		40,000		20,000
Cost of sales		40,000		20,000		17,000
Gross income		30,000		20,000		3000
Investment income		1000		400		500
Dividend receivable from						
Si		4000				
		35,000		20,400		3500
Depreciation	3000		2000		1500	
Directors'						
remuneration	7000		3000		500	
Loan interest paid	500		500		—	
Audit fees	500		50		30	
General						
expenditure	1900	12,900	850	6400	2770	4800
		22,100		14,000		(1300)
Corporation tax		9100		7000		
		13,000		7000		(1300)
Dividends						
proposed		6000		5000		—
Net income for the						
year retained		7000		2000		Dr. (1300)

Notes:

(a) During the year P Ltd sold goods totalling £15,000 to Si Ltd, at a price based on cost plus 25%. One third of these goods were still held in inventory by Si Ltd at 31 December.

(b) The loan interest paid by Si Ltd is on a loan stock, half of which is owned by P Ltd.

Working Schedule for Consolidated Income Statement.

	£	£
Sales (130,000 less inter-co. 15,000)		115,000
Cost of Sales (77,000 − 15,000)		62,000
		53,000
Investment Income (1900 less inter-co. 250)		1650
		54,650
Less unrealized income in inventories	1000	
Depreciation	6500	
Directors' remuneration	10,500	
Loan interest paid (1000 − 250)	750	
Audit fees	580	
General expenses	5520	24,850
		29,800

Adjustments for consolidating income

Calculation of Minority Interest

Si 20% × after tax income of £7000	1400	
Sii 10% × loss for year	(130)	1270

Calculation of pre-acquisition loss

Sii 90% × ½ × loss of £1300	585

Calculation of balance on Group Income Statement brought forward

P Balance	2500	
Si 80% × loss brought forward of £1000	(800)	1700

Calculation of analysis of income between companies

P. Profit 7000 + Balance b/f 2500 less		
inventory provision 1000		8500
Si 80% × (income 2000 less		
loss b/f 1000)	800	
Sii 90% × half a year's income 650	(585)	215
Group retained income		8715

Group Income Statement for the year ended 31 December		
	£	£
Group Turnover		115,000
Group trading income		29,800
after taking into account		
Depreciation	6500	
Directors' remuneration	10,500	
Loan interest	750	
Audit fees	580	
and Investment Income	1650	
Taxation		16,100
		13,700
Add pre-acquisition loss of subidiary		
acquired during the year		585
Less Minority Interest		(1270)
		13,015
Add Balance brought forward		1700
		14,715
Proposed dividend		(6000)
Group retained income		8715
Dealt with by the Parent Company		8500
Dealt with by Subsidiaries		215
Group retained income		8715

The sub-subsidiary relationship

A subsidiary company may itself have a subsidiary company which then becomes a sub-subsidiary (Ss Ltd) of the parent company. The principles of consolidation already discussed do not change, but the arithmetic becomes more involved.

Example 10

At the start of year 1, P Ltd acquired a 90% shareholding in S Ltd at a cost of £113 m., when its reserves stood at £10 m.: at the start of year 2 S Ltd acquired a 75% shareholding in Ss Ltd for £65 m. when its reserves amounted to £16 m. At the end of year 2 the separate balance sheets of the three companies making up the group were as follows.

	P Ltd	S Ltd	Ss Ltd
	£m.	£m.	£m.
Ordinary shares of £1 each	300	100	60
Revenue Reserves (at end of year 1)	40	20	16
Income for year 2	15	14	12
	355	134	88
Fixed & Current Assets less Liabilities	242	69	88
Investment—shares in S Ltd at cost	113		
Investment—shares in Ss Ltd at cost		65	
	355	134	88

The cost of control in each company is found as under:

Cost of Control account (G Ltd.)

	£m.		£m.
Investment—shares in S		Share Capital—S Ltd (90%)	90
Ltd at cost	113	Revenue Reserves (90% × £10 m.)	9
		Balance = cost of Control	14
Investment—shares		Share Capital—Ss Ltd (75%)	45
in Ss Ltd	65	Revenue Reserves—(75% × £16 m.)	12
		Balance = Cost of Control	8
	178		178

There are now three claimants to the income of Ss Ltd:

(a) the minority shareholders in Ss Ltd as to 25% of the net income of their company;

(b) the minority shareholders in S Ltd who have a claim to a 10% share in the three quarters of the income of Ss due to S Ltd; and

(c) the shareholders of P Ltd who have a 90% interest in the three-quarters of the income of Ss Ltd which is due to S Ltd.

Thus the post-acquisition income of Ss Ltd is allocated as follows.

	£m.	£m.
Ss Ltd.—Income for year 2		12
(a) minority in Ss—one-quarter		3
due to S Ltd—three-quarters		9
(b) minority in S Ltd—10%	.9	
(c) due to P Ltd—90%	8.1	9

The calculation of the Consolidated Income is:

Consolidated Income Statement (G Ltd)

		P Ltd	
		Balance brought forward	40
		Income for year 2	15
		S Ltd	
		Income for year 1 (90%)	9
Balance = Consolidated		Income for year 2 (90%)	12.6
Income	84.7	*Ss Ltd*	
		Income for year 2	
		(as above)	8.1
	84.7		84.7
		Balance b/d	84.7

The Minority Interest is calculated in the usual way.

Minority Interest account (G Ltd)

	S Ltd	
	Share Capital (10%)	10
	Revenue Reserve (10%)	2
	Income for year (10%)	1.4
	Share of Income of Ss Ltd	.9
		14.3

Balance = Minority
Interest   36.3

	Ss Ltd	
	Share Capital (25%)	15
	Revenue Reserves (25%)	4
	Income for year (25%)	3
		22
36.3		36.3
	Balance b/d	36.3

To prove the accuracy of the Minority Interest in the group, it is necessary to remember that there is an implicit consolidation of Ss Ltd with S Ltd. This notional consolidation would produce the following Balance Sheet:

S Ltd 'Group' Balance Sheet	£m.	£m.
Share Capital		100
Revenue Reserve		20
Retained Income S Ltd	14	
Ss Ltd	9	23
		143
Minority Interest in Ss Ltd (25% × 88)		22
		165
Fixed and Current Assets		
less Liabilities		157
Cost of Control		8
		165

It can now be seen that the one-tenth minority shareholders in S Ltd claim £14.3 m. (i.e., $\frac{1}{10} \times$ £143 m.), and this plus the £22 m. Minority Interest in Ss Ltd. amounts to £36.3 m., which appears in the final Consolidated Balance Sheet.

Consolidated Balance Sheet—end of year 2	£m.
Share Capital—shares of £1 each	300
Consolidated Income account	84.7
Minority Interest	36.3
	421.0
Cost of Control	22
Fixed & Current Assets less Liabilities	399
	421

Merger or acquisition?

In the examples given in chapter 10 the reserves of a newly acquired subsidiary company were treated as capitalized as at the date of acquisition, and it was mentioned at the time that the logic of capitalizing reserves at the point of the takeover which has the effect that such reserves cannot be distributed in the future to shareholders, has been challenged in recent years. Basically it is being suggested that reserves of the parent and those of the subsidiary both before and after acquisition should just be added together and regarded as jointly available for distribution.

It is argued that there are really two types of takeover—the acquisition and the merger—and the difference between the two is really a question of size. (American literature tends to use the terms *purchase* and *pooling* in place of *acquisition* and *merger.*) The takeover of a small company by a large parent company which has the effect that the small company is subsumed as part of a large group is termed a purchase or acquisition. A merger takes place between companies of similar size, and where both businesses are continued side by side. In early 1971 the ASSC issued an Exposure Draft (ED 3) entitled 'Accounting for Acquisitions and Mergers' which recognized these two types of takeovers and that a different accounting treatment for each type could be justified. The main difference between the two methods of accounting is in the treatment of pre-acquisition income, the cost of control and the share premium. The acquisition method has been used in chapter 10 and because the concept underlying it is that of a business purchase, the acquiring company will record the shares acquired at cost price, cost price being the value of the consideration given.

The main concept underlying a merger is that of continuity of the merging businesses. No assets are to be distributed to shareholders and no new capital is being subscribed. The only change that takes place is in the separate ownerships which are considered to have been pooled into one common ownership and re-allocated among the individual owners. It is essential that there should be no gross disparity in size between the amalgamating businesses, otherwise the owners of the smaller business would not have much of a say in the affairs of the combined enterprise. Under the merger method the accumulated profits at the date of the merger are not regarded as pre-acquisition profits and are treated as remaining available for distribution.

Clearly it is not enough to say that in a merger the companies must be of 'roughly similar size' and ED 3 defined the characteristics of a merger under four working rules, all of which must be met:

(a) The substance of the main businesses of the constituent companies continues in the amalgamated undertaking. Thus the takeover of a subsidiary company following which most of the fixed assets were sold off or where the nature of the business was changed would not be a merger.

(b) The equity voting rights of the amalgamated undertaking to be held by the shareholders of any one of the constituent companies is not more than three times the equity voting rights to be held by the shareholders of any of the other constituent companies. Thus if three companies A, B and C Ltd, agree to merge and the former shareholders of A Limited receive 50% of the shares in the combined undertaking, 30% of the shares going to the former shareholders of B Ltd, and 20% to C Ltd, the combination could be classed as a merger as the largest constituent company A Ltd (with 50% of the shares) is not more than three times the size of the smallest company, C Ltd (with 20% of the shares). But if the figures were A Ltd 50%, B Ltd 35%, and C Ltd 15%, company C would not be regarded as a party to the merger since the former shareholders of A Ltd would receive more than three times the number of shares allotted to the former shareholders of C Ltd. B Ltd could be regarded as a merger with A Ltd, but C is an acquisition.

(c) At least 90% in value of the offer is in equity voting capital identical to the original equity capital.

(d) The offer is accepted by shareholders representing at least 90% of the total equity capital (voting and non-voting).

If all the four conditions are met it is considered that the companies have in effect become partners and there is a genuine pooling of profits. The suggested three to one rule in (b) above is arbitrary, but offers a working guide as to whether an individual company is being merged or purchased. The 90% criteria in rules (c) and (d) are also arbitrary but intended to demonstrate that the ownership has continued much as before.

The ASSC recommended the following accounting method for mergers. The shares transferred to the holding company as part of a merger should be recorded in the books of the holding company at the nominal value of the shares issued in exchange. No share premium is recognized or necessary on the new shares issued by the holding company. As a consequence of using the nominal value the only difference to be dealt with on consolidation will be the difference between the nominal value of the shares issued as consideration by the holding company and the nominal value of the shares transferred by the shareholders of the new subsidiary company to the holding company. Where the nominal value of the shares issued is less than that of the shares transferred the difference should be treated as a reserve (non-distributable) arising on consolidation. If the nominal value of the shares issued is greater than that of the shares received in exchange, the difference is the extent to which the reserves of the subsidiary have in effect been capitalized consequent on the merger, and this difference should therefore be treated on consolidation primarily as a reduction of the existing reserves; it should be applied firstly against any unrealized surplus and secondly against revenue income or realized surpluses. Essentially this indicates that to the extent that reserves are regarded as capitalized, non-distributable reserves are capitalized before distributable reserves.

Where there is some additional consideration in some form other than equity shares, for example cash or loan stock, the value of such additional consideration should be included by adding it to the nominal value of the shares issued by the holding company, so as to arrive at the total consideration paid for the shares in the merged subsidiary, and this total of the consideration would be debited to the investment in subsidiary account. By following these procedures the reserves in the Consolidated accounts will thus be either:

(a) the total of the reserves of the constituent companies increased by any reserve arising on consolidation; or
(b) the total of the reserves of the constituent companies reduced by any part of the reserves of subsidiaries which have been in effect capitalized as a result of the merger.

Example 11

In this example the reserves of the constituent companies are increased by a reserve arising on consolidation.

P Ltd has just increased its share capital by issuing 70,000 Ordinary shares of £1 each plus a cash payment of £10,000 to gain 90% control of the issued share capital of S Ltd. The separate Balance Sheets of the two companies immediately after the merger are as follows.

	P Ltd £	S Ltd £
Ordinary shares of £1 each	270,000	100,000
Capital reserves		20,000
Revenue reserves	50,000	30,000
	320,000	150,000
Fixed & Current Assets less Liabilities	240,000	150,000
Investment—shares in S Ltd	80,000	
	320,000	150,000

Note that the cost of the shares in S Ltd is recorded in the books of P Ltd at the nominal value of the shares issued in exchange (£70,000) plus the value of any additional consideration (£10,000 in cash). The 70,000 Ordinary shares of £1 each will have been issued at a premium (they must have been to comply with condition (c) above that 90% in *value* of the offer is in equity voting capital) but such premium is not recognized when using the merger or pooling of interest method. In preparing the Consolidated Balance Sheet the investment account in P's books is set against the nominal value of the shares purchased in S Ltd, thus,

		£
Nominal value of shares in S Ltd pooled by P Ltd		90,000
Cost of investment in S Ltd:		
Shares at nominal value	70,000	
Cash	10,000	
		70,000
Capital reserve arising on consolidation		10,000

and the full Consolidated Balance Sheet appears as under:

Consolidated Balance Sheet after Merger—G Ltd	
	£
Ordinary Shares of £1 each	270,000
Capital reserve arising on consolidation	10,000
Capital reserves (90% × 20,000)	18,000
Revenue reserves (50,000 + 90% × 30,000)	77,000
Minority Interest (90% × 150,000)	15,000
	390,000
Fixed & Current Assets less Liabilities	390,000

The Minority interest is calculated in the same manner in a merger as in an acquisition.

Example 12

Illustrates the situation where the nominal value of the shares issued by P Ltd exceed the nominal value of the shares purchased in S Ltd, and the excess is treated as a capitalization of reserves of the subsidiary. The facts are as in the previous example but P Ltd issues 110,000 £1 Ordinary shares plus cash of £10,000 to gain control of a 90% shareholding in S Ltd. In this case the separate balance sheets of the two companies immediately after the merger are as follows.

	P Ltd £	S Ltd £
Ordinary shares of £1 each	310,000	100,000
Capital reserve		20,000
Revenue reserves	50,000	30,000
	360,000	150,000
Fixed & Current Assets less Liabilities	240,000	150,000
Investment—shares in S Ltd	120,000	
	360,000	150,000

The cost of the shares in S Ltd as recorded in the books of P Ltd is 110,000 shares of £1 each plus £10,000 in cash, a total of £100,000. Offset against this is the proportion of share capital and reserves acquired in S Ltd up to a total of £120,000, viz.

Cost of investment in S Ltd		120,000
Share Capital of S Ltd (90% × 100,000)	90,000	
Capital reserve (90% × 20,000)	18,000	
Revenue reserves (90% × 30,000 is 27,000 but only 12,000 needs to be capitalized, the remainder can be pooled)	12,000	120,000

The Consolidated Balance Sheet will be as follows:

Consolidated Balance Sheet after Merger—G Ltd	
	£
Ordinary shares of £1 each	310,000
(Capital reserves—nil)	
Revenue reserves (50,000 + 27,000 − 12,000)	65,000
Minority Interest	15,000
	390,000
Fixed & Current Assets less Liabilities	390,000

The main difference between the merger method and the more commonly used acquisition method lies in the treatment of the reserves of the subsidiary at the date of acquisition. The acquisition (purchase) approach regards these as capitalized at the date of the takeover against the purchase price. The purchase price is based on a realistic assessment of the current values of the shares issued by the parent company. So where the purchase price exceeds the value placed on the proportion of the net assets acquired in the subsidiary, a difference or figure for goodwill will arise. The merger or pooling method regards the situation as being one where previously independent companies have merged as voluntary partners and that consolidation should be the mere amalgamation of balance sheets. Taking the valuation of the shares exchanged at face or par value is a mere book-keeping device to cancel out the shares issued by P Ltd against those of S Ltd on consolidation, with any resulting difference being treated as an increase in reserves (Example 11 above) or as a capitalization of existing reserves (Example 12 above).

On acquisition the assets of the newly purchased subsidiary are usually revalued so that a realistic figure may be attached to goodwill. In a merger of companies, a revaluation may not take place, so that similar assets but with very different book values may be added together because, for instance, different depreciation policies have been followed in the two companies. This has become one of the objections to the merger method but a revaluation of net assets at the time of merger with consequent adjustment to reserves would remove these objections. Generally there has been little enthusiasm for adoption of the merger method, and although Exposure Draft 3 was issued in early 1971, it has not appeared as an accounting standard.

Summary

This chapter has examined some of the complications in consolidating accounts. Some of the complications discussed have been of minor significance but the sections on Consolidated Income Statements and the Merger system of accounting are of great importance. The reader will now be aware of some of the conceptual difficulties which arise when consolidating the accounts of a group of companies, and of some of the practical solutions put forward to deal with these difficulties. The standards of reporting for groups of companies has advanced considerably since 1948 but it still remains one of the more difficult areas in which to attempt to standardize financial accounting.

Part 3

Planning and Control

Part 3   PLANNING AND CONTROL

Introduction   255

Section 1   **A Framework for Planning and Control**

1 The Meaning of Planning and Control   260
The processes of management   260
   Planning   260
   Organizing   262
   Control   264
   Communication   266
   Motivation   268
Information and decision-making   268
Extended meanings of 'control'   271
Summary   272
Reference   273
Further readings   273

2 The Cost Accounting Framework   274
Introduction   274
The elements of cost   275
   Manufacturing costs   275
   Non-manufacturing costs   276
   Total product costs   277
The problem of overhead costs   278
   The allotment of factory overhead costs to production
      cost centres   278
   The allotment of production cost centre costs to
      products   281
   The selection of an appropriate level of activity   286
   The allotment of non-manufacturing costs to products
      288
   Limitations of total cost calculations   289
The cost of joint-products and by-products   290
   Joint-products   290
   By-products   291
Actual and planned costs   291
Appendix: Historical cost accounting systems   293
Cost accounting systems   294
Job order costing   294
   Accounting for cost flows   296
   The measurement of periodic profit   298
Process costing   300
   Accounting for cost flows 301
   The problem of calculating actual output   302
Summary   303
Further readings   304

Section 2 **Planning**

   3 Long-Range Planning   306
      The determination of long-range objectives   306
         The importance of cash flows   306
         Objectives and goals   307
         Organizational objectives   307
         Organizational goals   308
      The position audit   309
         The external audit   309
         The internal audit   309
      The formulation of strategy   310
         Gap analysis and the profit goal   310
         Long-range planning and gap analysis   311
      The preparation and implementation of the plan   312
      The continuous review and up-dating of the plan   313
      The importance of the long-range profit goal   313
         Setting profit targets   316
         Divisional profit targets   316
      Financial planning   317
         The long-range financial plan   318
      Long-range profit planning and other long-range objectives   321
      Summary   321
      References   322
      Further readings   322

   4 Planning Capital Expenditure   324
      Capital investment decisions   324
      Types of capital investment decisions   325
      The analysis of capital investment proposals   325
      The relevant cash flows   326
      Methods of appraising capital investments   327
         The pay-back period   327
         The accounting rate of return   329
         Discounted cash flows   330
         The net present value   332
         The internal rate of return   333
         Net present value and internal rate of return compared   334
         Taxation and other factors   336
         The cost of capital   336
         Gearing and the cost of capital   337
      Summary   338
      Further readings   339

   5 Budgetary Planning   340
      The nature of budgetary planning   340
      Budgetary control   341
      The need for flexibility   341
      Responsibility accounting   342

The organization of budgeting   342
Steps in budgeting   342
Forecasting sales   344
An illustration of the budgeting process   346
Evaluating the budget proposals   358
Summary   359
Further readings   359

6 Risk Analysis   360
Uncertainty and information   360
Adjusting the discount rate for risk   361
Sensitivity analysis and the measurement of risk   361
Risk analysis and sensitivity analysis   363
The certainty equivalent method of risk appraisal   365
Decision trees   368
Application of decision tree analysis   370
Large-scale simulation   373
Utility theory and risk aversion   375
Summary   379
Reference   379
Further readings   379

7 Cost-Volume-Profit Analysis   381
Applications of cost-volume-profit (c-v-p) analysis   381
Cost analysis and profit planning   382
Break-even analysis   384
Calculating the break-even point   384
    The equation method   384
    The contribution margin method   385
    The graph method   386
The profit-volume chart   389
Profit planning through change   391
    Changes in fixed costs   391
    Changes in variable costs   391
    Changes in selling price   393
The sales mix   395
Cost-volume-profit analysis: some limitations   397
Summary   398
Further readings   399

8 Pricing   400
The nature of the pricing problem   401
The nature of pricing theories   402
Pricing theory in economics   402
Cost-based pricing theories   404
Full-cost pricing   405
    Indirect costs and full-cost pricing   406
    Fixed costs and volume changes   407
    Full-cost pricing and the mark-up percentage   408
Conversion cost pricing   408
Return on investment pricing   410

Variable cost pricing   411
Going-rate pricing   412
Summary   413
Further readings   413

9 Short-run Tactical Decisions   414
The nature of relevant costs   414
The importance of the contribution margin   415
Opportunity costs   418
Dropping a product line   419
Selling or further processing   421
Operate or lease   421
Make a buy   422
Decision-making in the face of limiting factors   423
Linear programming and decision-making   425
Summary   431
Further readings   432

Section 3 Control

10 Organizing for Control   434
The integration of planning and control   434
Responsibility accounting   435
    Expense centres   437
    Profit centres   440
    Investment centres   446
Summary   451
Further readings   451

11 Standard Costs and Variance Analysis   453
Standard costs and budgeted costs   453
Applications of standard costing   454
Setting cost standards   455
    Standard costs for raw materials   455
    Standard costs for direct labour   456
Variance analysis   456
    Direct material variances   456
    Direct labour variances   458
The accounting disposition of variances   459
The control of overheads   461
Flexible budgeting   462
The advantage of flexible budgets over fixed budgets for control
    464
The analysis of overhead variances   465
    Variable overhead variance analysis   466
    Fixed overhead variance analysis   468
Sales variance analysis and the control of revenue   468
    Sales price variance   469
    Sales volume variance   470
    Sales mix variance   470
Responsibility for variances   472

The investigation of variances   472
Opportunity cost variances   474
Summary   475
References   476
Further readings   476

12 The Control of Managed Costs   477
The control of administrative costs   477
The control of research and development costs   478
The control of marketing costs   479
  Determining the profitability of sales territories   480
  Determining the profitability of products   480
  Controlling marketing costs   481
Summary   483
Further readings   484

13 Inventory and Project Control   485
Inventory control   485
The control of manufacturing inventories   486
Determining the economic order quantity (E.O.Q.)   487
The determination of inventory safety level   490
The determination of the re-order point   490
Programme evaluation and review technique (P.E.R.T.)   490
Summary   495
Further readings   495

14 Behavioural Aspects of Performance Evaluation   497
The objectives of performance evaluation   497
Leadership styles and the problem of control   498
  Theory X   498
  Theory Y   499
The effects of budgets on people   500
  Reactions to pressure   500
  Over-emphasis on the short-run   500
  Poor quality decision-making by top management   501
  Poor communication   501
  Departmental self-centredness   502
  The stifling of initiative   502
The need for several measures of performance   503
The importance of participation   503
Management by objectives   504
Organization theory   507
Approaches to organization theory   507
Summary   509
References   509
Further readings   510

Section 4 **The Design of Management Information Systems**

15 The Design of Management Information Systems   512
The 'systems approach' to the design of information systems
  512

The stages in the design of a management information
    system   514
        The specification of objectives   514
        The determination of 'critical success factors'   515
        Devising the organizational structure   516
        The determination of information needs   516
        Designing channels of information   519
Design criteria   519
        Relevance   520
        Timeliness   520
        Cost effectiveness   520
        Accuracy   520
        Flexibility   520
Behavioural aspects of systems design   520
        The formulation of objectives   521
        The search procedure   521
        The avoidance of uncertainty   521
        Organizational learning   521
The influence of the computer on the design of information
    systems   522
Accountants and the design of information systems   524
Summary   525
References   526
Further readings   526

Introduction

Part 2 was concerned with an examination of accounting method applied to the selection and processing of data and its emergence as financial accounting information communicated to users of financial accounting reports. We noted that these reports are historic by nature, and although they are of interest and importance to management, the information they contain is not directly relevant to the decisions which it is the function of management to make. Financial accounting reports are more relevant to the stewardship function of management which is concerned with disclosing information to shareholders and investors about the management of the firm in the period reported upon.

In this Part, we address ourselves to an analysis of the organizational decision-making process from an accounting viewpoint and the function of accounting information in that process. Decision-making is concerned with future events. The first observation which may be made, therefore, is that the information which is needed for decision-making should be information about the future rather than the past. This rules out much of the accounting information which is stored in the financial accounting system. Indeed, as we shall see, the role of financial information in the management context is to provide feedback on the results of decisions. In this way, of course, such information is useful to management when making decisions which are to alter the direction of previous plans.

The need for management to have information relevant to decision-making has compelled accountants to look beyond the information recorded in the financial accounting system. We shall note, therefore, how much of the accounting information used in decision-making is free from the constraints of the accounting conventions which we examined in Part 2. In this connection, the money measurement convention and the effects of inflation on the money standard of measurement pose serious problems in management decision-making. Thus, all aspects of planning must take into account likely changes in price levels. This is particularly true as regards long-range planning, capital budgeting and pricing. In this Part, we shall assume that the effects of expected price level changes have been taken into account when making forecasts, so that we are left free to consider the central problems in planning and control. We shall discuss the implications of price level changes on accounting measurements in detail in Part 4.

Our objective is to provide our readers with a coherent and intelligible framework in which to integrate the subject matter of organizational planning and control, and in which to appreciate the relevance of accounting information in this area. It is evident that in seeking to present a global view, we may only hope to provide a broad outline of what is a large area of knowledge. We believe that the contents of this Part are adequate to the needs of first-year students. We would warn our readers, however, that many of the topics which we introduce have become themselves major subject-areas, for example, long-range planning and capital budgeting. Readers requiring a more thorough analysis should refer to the more advanced literature which explores the complex problems which abound in this field.

Our scheme of work is as follows.

Section1: A framework for planning and control

In this section, we examine the concepts of planning and control as they are applied to business organizations. We shall see that central to this analysis is the selection of the goals towards which the activities of such organizations are to be directed. These goals, therefore, provide the focus to the decision-making process.

We examine the management process in some detail so as to establish the role of information in this context. From an accounting viewpoint, the emphasis in planning and control lies in the management of costs. Hence, we discuss the importance of cost accounting. Having established the nature of the cost accounting framework and discussed the cost concepts involved, we have a point of reference to which we shall return whenever appropriate as we proceed with the examination of the various topics which are studied in this Part.

Section 2: Planning

This section is concerned with a relatively detailed analysis of the planning process. It begins with a discussion of long-range planning as a means of attaining the organization's long-term goals. We proceed with an examination of the stages by which these goals may be realized. This involves, on the one hand, providing the assets which will enable the firm to operate and involves capital expenditure, and on the other hand, realizing long-range plans in annual stages by means of the activities envisaged in the annual budget.

Planning decisions are made in the face of uncertainty. We devote a chapter, therefore, to the analysis of risk and the means by which this problem may be reduced to some extent.

Our discussion of the nature and importance of the annual budget leads us to such problems as the relationship between costs, volume of output and profit, and pricing. Lastly, we examine those types of decisions which tend to be made on a 'once-and-for-all' basis and do not form part of the long-range planning process, for example, such decisions as the acceptance of special offers, dropping product lines, and making or buying decisions.

Section 3: Control

We begin this section by relating control to planning by establishing that the purpose of control is to ensure that the firm's activities conform with its plans. We relate the concept of control also to an organizational framework which is aimed at securing the performance of the tasks involved in implementing plans. This enables us to introduce the idea of responsibility accounting.

The importance attached in accounting to the control of costs, which we mentioned earlier, and the use of costs in the control of performance is considered in a chapter on standard costing and associated techniques such as flexible budgeting. Throughout this section, we stress the importance of information feedback as a means of ensuring that actual performance conforms with planned and required performance. We devote a concluding chapter to performance appraisal, in which it will be noted that we recognize the importance of the behavioural factors associated with the human element in organizations.

Section 4: The design of management information systems

This section is intended to provide a conclusion to this Part, and it represents our belief that the problems associated with the provision of information for planning and control compel the accountant to respond to the need of management for a broader view of its information needs, and in particular the integration of accounting and non-accounting information in a coherent manner. We argue that the accountant should accept a larger role in the design of management information systems. In a sense, this section provides a synthesis for much of the discussion of earlier problems.

A Framework for Planning and Control

1

The Meaning of Planning and Control

There are two conflicting schools of thought regarding the extent to which the firm is in charge of its own destiny. Market theory postulates that the firm is solely at the whim of prevailing economic and social forces, so that successful management depends upon the ability to 'read' the environment. By contrast, planning and control theory asserts that management has control over the firm's future and believes that the firm's destiny may be manipulated and hence planned and controlled. In this view, the quality of managerial planning and control decisions is the key factor for success.

In reality, business organizations normally operate somewhere in between these two extreme views: many elements, such as raw material prices, are completely outside their control; on the other hand some elements, such as the selling price of its product, are determined by the organization itself. One may make a distinction, therefore, between controllable and non-controllable items. It is the function of management to manipulate the controllable items to the firm's best advantage, and to ensure that it is prepared to meet changes in the non-controllable ones, so as to take full advantage of favourable changes and minimize the impact of unfavourable ones. Planning is essential for all the factors which affect the organization, irrespective of whether or not they are controllable or non-controllable. We may infer from this fact that in the degree that a firm's management reflects the views of control theorists the greater are its chances of success.

The processes of management

Although there are different schools of thought as to what may be understood by the term 'management' and how it should be practised, it is generally accepted that management has five main functions: planning, organizing, controlling, communicating and motivating.

Planning

Planning is the most basic of all management functions, and the skill with which this function is performed determines the success of all operations. Planning may be defined as the thinking process that precedes action and is directed towards making decisions now with the future in mind. Theoretically, the function of planning is to improve the quality of decision-making by a careful consideration of all the relevant factors before a decision is made, and ensuring that decisions conform with a rational strategy by which the firm's future is to be shaped. Planning may be seen as consisting of five stages:

(a) Setting organizational objectives.

(b) Assessing the environment in which the organization will be operating, by reference to the external factors which are likely to affect its operations. For this purpose, forecasts have to be made which attempt to predict what will happen in the future, with and without policy changes on the part of the planning organization.

(c) Assessing existing resources, for management is concerned with making the most efficient use of those scarce resources, often called the four M's: men, machines, materials and money. This aspect of the planning function involves both making an estimate of external resources which are accessible, and resources already held which are either idle or which might be more efficiently utilized.

(d) Determining the strategy for achieving stated objectives by means of an overall plan which specifies strategic goals. Strategic decisions are concerned with establishing the relationship between the firm and its environment.

(e) Designing a programme of action to achieve selected strategic goals by means of both long-range programmes and short-range programmes, the latter covering a period of a year or less and containing sets of instructions of the type found in annual budgets.

Thus, decisions are essential at every stage of the planning process, and the key areas may be stated as deciding 'what should be done, when it should be done, how it should be done and who should do it'.

The importance of environmental factors to the planning process is obvious; and it is equally clear that environmental information should not be subjected to a less disciplined treatment than the internal or analytical information, which an organization itself provides. There may sometimes be important areas in which one may criticize the quality of analytical information as being inadequate for the purpose of efficient decision-making. Deficiencies in the nature and quality of analytical information will be examined in much greater detail elsewhere in this book. However, there is a need for a continuous flow of information on the environment, for the most important determinant of a firm's potential for growth and improved efficiency is the ability of its management to learn about this aspect. Information systems are now moving away from a heavy emphasis on internal or analytical information and incorporating much more environmental data. As surveys in the United States have shown, the scan of environmental data in which management is interested ranges from market potential of new and existing product lines, to new processes and technology, the actions of competitors, sales regulations, resources and supplies available to government actions and policies.

We may distinguish three kinds of planning activities:

(1) Strategic planning which is concerned with a period from three to ten years ahead and which is usually called long-range planning. This forms the subject of chapter 3.

(2) Project planning is an activity which follows the long-range plan, and involves developing plans for the capital expenditures necessary to meet long-term objectives. This forms the subject of chapter 4.

(3) Budgetary planning which converts the firm's long-range plan to the needs of the immediate future. This is usually described as budgeting, and is generally carried out on a one year basis. The annual budget is then broken down into months, and in some cases into weeks, to chart the path the firm should take in the immediate future. This forms the basis of chapter 5.

Organizing

Organizing involves setting up the administrative structure for implementing strategic decisions. The administrative design area is therefore concerned with establishing the structure and the shape of the firm or organization, and defining responsibilities and lines of authority. It involves a definition of the tasks necessary to achieve strategic goals, determining who is to perform these tasks and assigning responsibility for their performance. The function of organizing is to co-ordinate these tasks in such a way that the organization is able to work efficiently in fulfilling its objectives. The process of organizing is achieved through departmentalization, by which different specialisms are hived off into separate departments. These departments are linked in a hierarchy, a formal communication structure that enables instructions to be passed downwards and information to be passed upwards to senior management. Figure 3.1 shows a partial organization structure for a firm which is concerned with two main activities—furniture and floor covering.

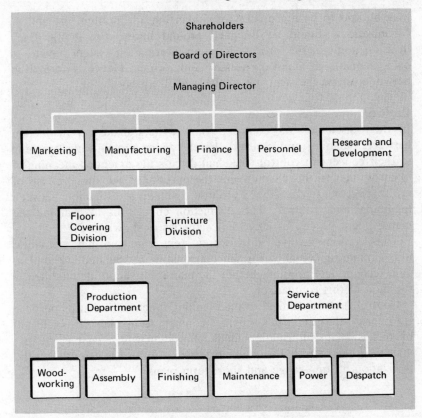

Fig. 3.1

A manager may be allotted the task of managing the activities in each of these boxes, which then represent executive positions; the lines represent the formal channels of communication between them. The top five boxes represent the five major functions of this firm—marketing, manufacturing, finance, personnel and research and development. For administrative purposes, the firm is organized according to its product categories; therefore, two divisions—furniture and floor covering—are established.

At the bottom of the pyramid in the figure are the basic organizational units, known as departments; this illustrates the six departments belonging to the Furniture Division. Departments form an occupational classification—in this case they are divided into Production and Service Departments.

A major purpose of any organizational structure is to facilitate the flow of information to and from decision-makers. Since management may be said to be the process of converting information into action, organizations should be designed around information flows. Each decision point in this process is a sub-information system having its own elements as input, processor and output. Hence, information networks shape the structure of the organization.

Control

In their discussion of 'control', some writers make no distinction between 'planning' and 'control', thereby giving a much wider meaning to their concept of control. We shall discuss the extended meaning of 'control' later in this chapter. For the purpose of our own analysis of the management process, we propose to make a distinction between 'planning' and 'control'. This distinction enables us to examine the management process as a cycle of activities as shown in Fig. 3.2.

The decisions involved in this area stem from two main activities, first, comparing actual performance against that stipulated in the plan, and, second, determining whether the plan itself should be modified in the light of this comparison.

Control is closely linked to the planning function in that its purpose is to ensure that the firm's activities conform to its plans. It is effected by means of an information feedback system which enables performance to be compared to planned targets. Control is essential to the realization of long-range and short-term plans.

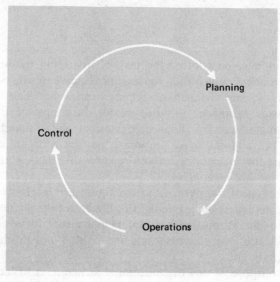

Fig. 3.2

In long-range planning, information feedback enables management to assess what progress has been made towards the realization of the long-range objectives specified in the long-range plan. Additionally, it allows management to review long-range objectives in the light of new circumstances which may have rendered those objectives unrealistic.

In practice, by far the greatest emphasis is attached to the control of operations so as to meet the objectives contained in the annual budget which, as we noted earlier, should be seen as part of the long-range plan. Information feedback is an integral part of budgetary control procedures which are intended to be highly sensitive to operational variations on a day-to-day basis. Their aim is to highlight deviations from the budget plan as soon as possible so that remedial action may be taken immediately.

A pre-requisite to the successful performance of the control function is an efficient information system which will reveal the need for corrective action at an appropriate time, enabling managers to judge whether their targets are still appropriate as the environment changes month by month and year by year. The control function is closely linked to the planning function by means of a feedback system which provides information on the results of past decisions. Such a system is necessary to the assessment of the quality of the decision-making process and to its improvement, and is illustrated in Fig. 3.3.

The feedback system provides the great bulk of analytical information used in the planning process. It provides a means also of evaluating planned objectives. Should, for example, the economic climate change, the efficiency of the organization's operations will depend on the swiftness of its reaction to this change by way of alterations to the planned objectives. The feedback system is also instrumental to the making of control decisions for it provides a means of continuously

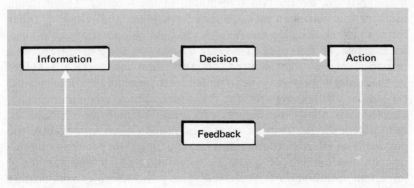

Fig. 3.3

assessing current performance against the strategic plan. Decision-making in this sense thus involves making day-to-day adjustments to changing conditions in order to map out the most appropriate course of action needed to implement strategic decisions. Thus, information is the life-blood of any system, and the responsibility for the design of adequate information systems is of paramount concern to management.

Communication

Communication is an exchange of facts, ideas and opinions by two or more persons. The exchange is successful only when actual understanding results. Merely saying is not enough; a receiver of information must understand the message which the sender is trying to communicate. Communication occurs when the former understands what the latter means to convey.

Communication involves linking all the management functions by transmitting information and instructions within the organization. Additionally, the communication process relates the organization to its environment by linking it to suppliers of resources, and to the consumers for whom its products are intended.

In any organization, the specialization of tasks and the consequent division of labour creates a situation in which an unrestricted flow of ideas and fact is necessary if it is to function efficiently. A high degree of communication binds the various members of the organization together, uniting them in the pursuit of organizational goals. Hence, an organization may be viewed not only as a decision-making system, but also as a communication system as well.

The major components in the communication system are the sender, the message and the receiver. The *sender* may be an individual or a computer or other device which is capable of sending a message. The *message* is the information transmitted to the receiver. The medium used for transmitting a message may be written, oral, visual or other forms of communicating meaning. A red light on operating equipment, for example, is often used to indicate a breakdown or a danger. From a management viewpoint, written communication has special advantages in that information may be planned and incorporated into formal procedures, forms, reports etc. by which means communication is effected. Essentially, procedures which are designed to communicate information should focus on what is important, so as to maximize the possibility of effective communication occurring. This requires a limitation on the number of messages communicated so that the really important information is perceived. The principle of communicating only 'exceptional' information, that is, information about a variance from a predetermined plan which requires immediate attention is a feature of successful communication systems. Moreover, the frequency of communication should be considered in the light of the needs of the receiver, having regard to the effective action which may result from the communication.

Occasionally, the context or situation surrounding communication may affect its transmission or reception. This occurs when interference, such as static on a radio message, prevents the message from being transmitted or distorts the manner in which it is received. The 'gap'/ 'noise' is the result of factors causing distortions or loss of meaning, and one of the tasks of the designers of information systems is to minimize 'noise' and preventing 'noise' from being accepted as true information.

Lastly, the *receiver* must recognize the context in which the message is sent and received in order that he may interpret the message correctly. The last stage in the communication process involves a human factor, in that the reception of information should produce the correct response. Behavioural factors which impede the required response may render the entire process of communication futile.

The detailed analysis of the design requirements of information systems will form the subject matter of a separate chapter (see page 512), but at this stage, the way in which information is communicated and related to planning and control may be illustrated as in Fig. 3.4.

Figure 3.4 shows how environmental and analytical information is

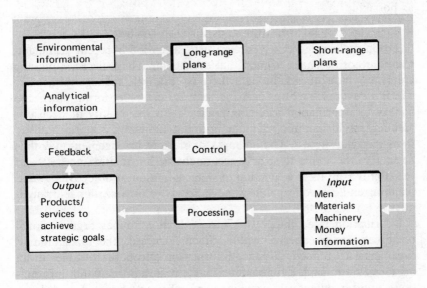

Fig. 3.4

combined in the plans which are designed to meet the organization's objectives. These plans are implemented as resources become inputs which are converted into products and services. The feedback and control systems should function as to ensure the effectiveness of the plans.

Motivation

This involves getting all the members of the organization to pull their full weight, and finding ways in which individual performance may be improved. When we study motivation, we are studying the influences on a human being and what affects his behaviour. For example, when we ask someone to perform a certain task which we know to be within his capability and experience and it is not done satisfactorily, this failure may well be the result of poor motivation rather than lack of ability.

Some motivating factors are basically biological or physiological and may be looked upon as natural or inherent such as the need for air, water, food, sleep, clothing and housing. Some motivating factors are learned, for example, the combination of needs associated with the individual's ego and a correct evaluation of himself.

Other motivating factors are related to social needs, and these are influenced by the organization of the work situation. Many studies have examined the effects of these needs, and they illustrate how the size, cohesiveness and motives of the group act as controls on the members' own motives. Hence, the organization should create a situation in which group and individual goals coincide to as great a degree as possible.

Information and decision-making

Decision-making has received increasing attention in recent years, and some authorities have argued that management and decision-making are synonymous terms. Indeed, there is very little managerial activity which does not involve decision-making in some form. Since the quality of information available is crucial to the quality of decision-making, an efficient and adequate information system is a pre-requisite to managerial success. The hallmark of efficient management may thus be seen in the ability to specify accurately the information needed, and this ability is in itself a function of clear definition of objectives, sound planning and control capability and satisfactory organizational arrangements.

Information is an integrating force which combines organizational resources into a cohesive whole directed towards the realization of organizational objectives. Since information affects the fortunes of an organization in such a fundamental way, it is important that information should be effectively organized and efficiently handled, and this is achieved through what has become known as a management information system. A management information system provides individual managers with the information required for making decisions within their own particular areas of responsibility. It may be likened to the central nervous system of an organization in that it consists of a network of information flows to which each decision may be related.

Within this information network decision points may be identified at three levels—strategic planning, management control and operational control (Anthony, 1965).

Strategic planning involves the determination of corporate objectives and goals, as well as the development of broad policies and strategies by which they may be achieved. This activity relies heavily on information about the environment, and has an irregular pattern. Management control is a lower level activity which is concerned with the implementation of the strategic plan and assures that the necessary resources have been obtained, and assures additionally that they are being used effectively and efficiently. This activity is rhythmic, and follows a weekly, monthly, or quarterly pattern. Operational control is the process of ensuring that specific tasks are being carried out effectively and efficiently. It is an activity which focuses on individuals' jobs and transactions, and its tempo is 'real time' (that is, data reported as events occur). Operational control is thus exercised over operating systems, and these include stock records, personnel records, data handling, and maintenance records. Examples of the relationship between these levels of activity are illustrated as follows:

Strategic planning	Management control	Operational control
Setting marketing policies	Formulating advertising programmes	Controlling the placement of advertisements
Setting personnel policies	Planning staff levels	Hiring and controlling staff

The relationship between these three levels of activities and the information flows is shown in Fig. 3.5 (overleaf).

Strategic planning decisions are based upon data derived both from outside and within the system in the form of environmental and analytical information; the latter identifies the organization's strengths and weaknesses, and the former enables it to formulate its strategy.

The constraints imposed upon management control decisions emanate from the strategic decisions incorporated in the strategic plan, and for the purposes of management control decisions these constraints are contained in long- and short-term plans. These plans themselves are broken down into detailed programmes for the various operational

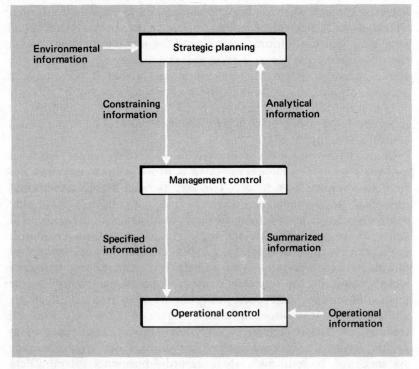

Fig. 3.5

sub-systems, and into specified information for the purposes of operational control. Hence, management control decisions are based on summarized information which compares the actual performance of cost and profit centres against their planned performance. In order that management should not be inundated with irrelevant information, reports to management should be in the form of statements of variances from the budget plan, and the reasons why these variances have occurred. Management control which is exercised in this way is known as management by exception. Management control decisions are thus concerned with investigating variances, and issuing instructions to operating managers on how to deal with them. Alternatively, management may recognize that the variances are inevitable and uncontrollable, and therefore recommend that the strategic plan should be altered to take account of this fact. In such a case, the decision will take the form of a recommendation of an adjustment to the strategic plan.

Operational control decisions are made at the meeting point between specified and operating information associated with the various sub-systems. Specified information sets up standards of performance in terms of volume and costs of production and allocated time. Operating information discloses the results in the form of items produced, and production performance in terms of costs and time actually taken. Operational control decisions, unlike management control decisions, are concerned with day to day variances occurring in detailed operations, such as the time taken to perform individual tasks.

Extended meanings of 'control'

The term control has acquired a variety of uses in our daily language. We speak, for example, of traffic control, arms control and pest control. It is evident, however, that in applying the term control to different situations, we are thinking of different kinds of actions. Thus, when we speak of traffic control, we are really thinking of traffic regulation; when we speak of arms control, we have in mind arms limitation; and when we are speaking of pest control, we mean pest eradication. A similar flexibility of use in the term control is to be observed in the manner in which it is employed in the context of business affairs. Control is used to describe key functions, such as production control, quality control and budgetary control. These functions, however, represent quite different types of activities; production control refers to the production process and the need to regulate that process; quality control implies the rejection of sub-standard work; and budgetary control is concerned with keeping expenditure within a firm in line with a budget plan.

The term control also may be given both a narrow and a broad definition. A narrow definition of control is associated often with the maintenance of standards and the imposition of penalties. The broad concept of control which is to be found in the literature of management science treats the term control as synonymous with management itself. In this sense, control embraces the various processes by which management determines its objectives, draws up plans to attain those objectives, organizes and supervises the operations necessary for the implementation of plans and appraises performance. Control also implies the investigation of deviations from planned objectives, so that performance levels may be brought into line with planned levels. Where necessary, plans and objectives may be changed to meet new circumstances.

Moreover, management may be said to be concerned with a control problem having two aspects, that of 'control-in-the-large' and 'control-in-the-small'. These terms signify two dimensions to the control problem facing management, namely, that of controlling the firm's relationship with its environment (control-in-the-large) and controlling its internal operations (control-in-the-small).

One may subject the concept of control to a more complex theoretical analysis which suggests that both normative and descriptive theories of control may be developed. In either context, the crux of control is in measurement. Measurements are required in setting objectives as targets for plans, and since plans are directed towards the future, such measurements are based upon predictions. Prediction is an integral part of control, which in this sense contemplates a future course of action. A normative theory of control recognizes that numerous possible courses of action may exist, each requiring its own control procedure if a system is not to get out of control. Control theory in this sense is based upon what is known as the *law of requisite variety* which states that there must be at least as many variations in the controls to be applied as there are ways for a system to fall out of control. The following example illustrates this principle.

Example

A firm is experiencing a decline in sales and hence has cut-back its level of production. Stocks of raw materials, however, are increasing because the purchasing function uses decision rules which are appropriate only for normal conditions, and is not scaling down its levels of purchases. Hence, the control system operating within the firm may be said not to be flexible enough to take into account abnormal circumstances, that is, it has not enough variety to cope with the range of situations with which the system is faced. To remedy this defect, two alternative steps are open to management; either new decision rules must be formulated for the purchasing function which take into account abnormal situations, or the purchasing function must be free to generate its own response to changing circumstances.

The law of requisite variety has important implications for the design of information systems. It implies that decision rules should be devised for making routine decisions. As we saw in Part 1, such decisions may be programmed, and as a result, they may be automated. On the other hand, where decisions involve judgement and experience, the law of requisite variety requires that enough information be provided so that the decision-maker himself may generate appropriate responses.

Summary

Planning occurs at all management levels, and the success of other management functions depend upon the quality of planning.

Planning is concerned with both controllable and uncontrollable factors which affect the organization. Controllable factors should be manipulated to the organization's advantage, and the effects of uncontrollable factors should be minimized.

Management is also concerned with such functions as organization, control, communication and motivation. Since decision-making is a key characteristic of all management functions, decision-making has become synonymous with management.

Information is necessary for decision-making, and the quality of information will affect the quality of decisions. Hence, an adequate and efficient information system is a pre-requisite for managerial success.

Decision-making may be classified according to the following areas:

(a) strategic planning—which involves the determination of corporate objectives and goals as well as the broad policies and strategies by which they may be achieved;

(b) management control—which is concerned with implementing the strategic plans;

(c) operational control—which is the process of ensuring that specific tasks are carried out effectively and efficiently.

In this part, we shall consider the role of accounting as the most important element of a management information system, and we shall also examine the manner in which accounting information assists management in its various functions.

Reference

Anthony, R. N., *Planning and Control Systems: A Framework for Analysis*, p. 24 Harvard Business School, Boston, 1965.

Further readings

Drucker, P., *The Practice of Management*, Heinemann, London, 1955.

Gray, Jack & Johnston, Kenneth S., *Accounting and Management Action*. McGraw-Hill, New York, 1973.

Kast, Fremont E., & Rosenweig, James E., *Organization and Management, A Systems Approach*. McGraw-Hill, New York, 1970.

Mills, Arthur E., *Management Control Systems*, Business Publications. London, 1967.

Miner, John Burtram, *The Management Process, Theory Research and Practice*, Macmillan, New York, 1973.

Murdick, R. G. & Ross, J. E., *Information Systems for Modern Management*, Prentice Hall, Englewood Cliffs, N.J., 1971.

2
The Cost Accounting Framework

Introduction

Costs are essentially money measurements of the sacrifices which an organization has to make in order to achieve its objectives. Consequently, costs play a very important role in management decision-making, and it is not surprising that accountants are very involved with the collection and the analysis of cost information.

Cost information is collected and analysed for three major purposes:

(a) To assist in planning decisions, such as the determination of which products to manufacture, the quantities which should be produced and the selling prices. Since planning is addressed to the future, we are interested in future costs for this purpose. Historical costs are useful only insofar as they are reliable indicators of future costs.

(b) To assist in the control of operations by maintaining and improving the efficiency with which resources are employed. Control involves comparing the actual costs of current operations against their planned costs. It follows that since actual costs are monetary surrogates of the resources which have been exhausted in current operations, we should be interested in replacing those resources. Hence, for this purpose, we require replacement costs. The control process assists in keeping current costs in line with planned costs by highlighting inefficiencies. It may also lead to a revision of planned costs.

(c) To assist in the measurement of reported profits, that is, income measurement as understood in accounting. As we shall explain in Part 4, profit calculations based upon historical costs fulfill a legal rather than a decision-making role. Moreover, for the purpose of performance evaluation and for profit forecasts, adjustments should also be made for changes in the value of money.

As we explained in the Introduction to this Part, planning, control and performance evaluation are integral parts of the management control process. Cost information which relates to these activities is indispensible to management. It is appropriate, therefore, that before we begin our examination of the various aspects of management control, we should understand how cost information is accumulated.

Costs are accumulated in two forms: in terms of their relationship to a person (responsibility accounting) and in terms of product. Responsibility accounting, which uses costs accumulated in the first form, is directed at the control of costs by associating them with individuals in the management hierarchy. This form of accounting plays a central role in the control of operations and we shall deal with it in chapter 11 of this Part.

Here we deal with the accumulation of costs in order to calculate full product costs, that is, all the manufacturing costs incurred in bringing the product to a marketable state. One application of full product costs is computing inventory values. Sometimes, non-manufacturing costs such as administrative and marketing costs are added to the full product costs for the purpose of determing the profitability of products and for establishing pricing policies. These product costs are also used in Government contracts which seek to established a 'fair price' by basing the price on total costs.

The actual routine involved in recording costs should not detract from an analysis of the problems of computing product costs, and their usefulness in decision-making. For this reason, we are treating the routine of cost recording separately in an appendix to this chapter.

Before we proceed with our analysis of full product costs, we should note that different costs are used for different purposes. A cost which is provided by the accountant is useful only if it relates to the problem on hand. For this reason, the term 'cost' is qualified, and we have, for example, opportunity cost, sunk cost, fixed cost, variable cost, differential cost and so on. We shall explain the technical meaning of these terms as we proceed.

The elements of cost

The costs of transforming raw materials into finished products are classified into two major categories—manufacturing and non-manufacturing costs.

Manufacturing costs

These costs comprise three elements:

    (a) direct materials costs
    (b) direct labour costs
    (c) factory overhead costs.

The term 'direct' cost is applied only to those costs which can be readily identified with the product. Therefore, direct material costs include only those costs which can be directly associated with the finished product. Similarly, if an employee performs a task connected with the making of the product, his wage is considered as a direct labour cost. Direct material and direct labour costs are referred to as 'prime costs'.

In deciding which costs to treat as direct costs, the accountant has to take into consideration the materiality of the item. It will be recalled that we discussed the convention of materiality in Part 2. Producing cost information is expensive, and the expense of determining that some item is a direct cost rather than regarding it as a factory overhead cost may outweigh any benefit attached to such information. Thus, the expense of recording as direct costs such small items as washers, nuts and bolts far outweigh any benefit which may be derived from this exercise.

Factory overhead costs include all the remaining production costs, after direct costs have been determined. They include indirect material costs such as lubricants, and supplies of materials for repairs and maintenance. They also include indirect labour costs such as the salaries and wages of inspectors, timekeepers and workmen who do not work on specific products. Factory overhead costs also include other indirect costs such as heat, light, power and the depreciation of factory buildings, plant and equipment.

Another term which is used in cost accounting is 'conversion cost', which refers to the cost of converting raw materials into the finished product. Conversion costs, therefore, consist of direct labour and factory overhead costs.

The manufacturing cost is the total of all direct and indirect costs, that is, both prime and factory overhead costs. It is the cost of manufacture which is recorded as the stock value of the finished product while it is awaiting sale. Upon sale, the manufacturing cost forms part of the cost of sale for the purpose of calculating the trading profit.

We may summarize the terminology of manufacturing costs as follows:

$$
\left.
\begin{array}{l}
\text{Prime cost}\;\left\{\;
\begin{array}{l}
\text{Direct material costs} \\[6pt]
\text{Direct labour costs}
\end{array}
\right. \\[10pt]
\text{Conversion cost}\;\left\{
\begin{array}{l}
\text{Factory overhead costs}
\end{array}
\right.
\end{array}
\right\}\text{Manufacturing cost}
$$

Non-manufacturing costs

These costs are not included in the cost of manufacturing the product, and they are not included, therefore, in the cost of sales. Hence, they are assumed not to attach to the product costs for income measurement purposes. Non-manufacturing costs are 'period' rather than 'product' costs, and they are associated with accounting periods rather than with output. Non-manufacturing costs include administrative and marketing costs. Administrative costs are defined as the costs incurred on executive salaries, head office staff expenses including all clerical and secretarial staff, legal expenses, and depreciation on office equipment, furniture etc. Marketing costs includes the activities associated with obtaining orders, such as advertising and selling costs, and activities concerned with fulfilling orders, such as warehousing, packing, and delivery.

Total product costs

The elements of cost involved in the calculation of total product costs for a unit of a product may be summarized by the following ascertained unit costs:

	£
Direct material costs	4
Direct labour costs	6
Prime cost per unit	10
Factory overhead costs	8
Manufacturing cost per unit (Full-product cost)	18
Administrative costs	5
Marketing costs	4
Total product cost per unit	27

From the foregoing, we may observe that the only difference between total product costs and the expenses (expired costs) allocated to an accounting period for the purpose of calculating the net profit (see Part 2) is that total product costs are unit costs, whereas expenses are the aggregated costs of producing all the units of the product which are sold in that accounting period.

In calculating total product costs, the accounting problem is to find means of attributing to units of products their appropriate costs for the various decisions which management have to make. The task of calculating the direct material and direct labour costs attributable to individual products is relatively easy. The direct material costs are calculated by ascertaining the quantities of materials used in the product, making due allowance for normal waste, and multiplying the quantity by the raw material purchase price. Similarly, the direct labour costs are obtained by specifying the operations involved in production and the time taken, and multiplying the time factor so derived by the appropriate labour rates. It is in the calculation of total overhead costs per unit that the major accounting problem of cost determination lies.

The problem of overhead costs

The problem of ascertaining the overhead costs applicable to a unit of a product is first and foremost a function of the number of different products which the firm manufactures. Where the firm manufactures only one product, the problem is relatively simple. If, for example, the firm produces 1000 units of the product, and the overhead costs total £2000, the total overhead costs per unit is £2.

Where the firm manufactures more than one product, however, many problems arise in computing unit overhead costs of production. We shall discuss these problems in terms of the undermentioned stages in the ascertainment of full-product costs:

(1) The allotment of factory overhead costs to production cost centres.
(2) The allotment in turn of the costs of production cost centres to individual products.
(3) The selection of an appropriate level of activity for calculating unit product costs. This is necessary because unit costs vary with activity levels, and a choice has to be made as to the activity level which is applicable to future output.
(4) The allotment of non-manufacturing costs to the products.

The allotment of factory overhead costs to production cost centres

Cost centres are locations with which costs may conveniently be associated for the purpose of product costing.

Basically, there are two types of cost centres for which costs are accumulated—production and service cost centres. Production cost centres are those actually involved in production, such as machining and assembling departments. Service cost centres are those which exist to facilitate production, for example, maintenance, stores and canteen.

The first stage in the allotment of factory overhead costs to production cost centres is to collect and classify factory overhead costs as between indirect material, indirect labour or other identifiable cost heading. The next stage is to allocate these costs, where possible, to production and service cost centres. The term 'cost allocation' has a special meaning, being used to refer to the allotment of whole items of cost to cost centres. For example, the salaries of foremen in charge of individual cost centres may be allocated to those cost centres. Items of costs which cannot be allocated to cost centres must be apportioned. The term 'cost apportionment' means the allotment of proportions only of items of cost to cost centres. For example, the cost of rates cannot be alloted to any particular cost centre and must be apportioned between cost centres.

The third stage is to apportion the costs of the service cost centres to the production cost centres. If we assume that a firm has three service cost centres and two production cost centres, as in Fig. 3.6, the apportionment of the service cost centre costs involves selecting appropriate methods for apportioning these costs to the production cost centres:

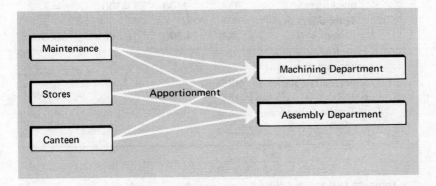

Fig. 3.6

When the apportionment is completed, the major production cost centres will have accumulated both prime costs and factory overhead costs.

Example

The production process of Simplex Limited is based on a Machining Department and an Assembly Department, which are supported by one service department which is a Maintenance Department. Consider the cost information shown on p. 280.

From this information, we may observe that the first stage in the treatment of overhead factory costs has been completed, since those factory overhead costs which may be directly associated with cost centres have already been allotted. In this connection, it should be mentioned that the direct overhead factory costs are said to be direct to the cost centres concerned, but they remain indirect to the units of the product.

The next stage, therefore, is to apportion the indirect overhead factory costs as between the three cost centres. It will be recalled that

Departmental Cost Data

Direct (or allocated overheads)	Total £	Machining £	Assembly £	Maintenance £
Indirect materials	15,000	8000	5000	2000
Indirect labour	6000	4000	1000	1000
Depreciation of machinery	7000	2500	4500	—
Total direct over- head costs	28,000	14,500	10,500	3000
Indirect (or un- allocated overheads				
Supervisory salaries	6000			
Rates	10,000			
Total overhead factory costs	44,000			

indirect factory overhead costs are those which cannot be directly associated with any particular cost centres, but are attached to the factory as a whole. Bases are needed, therefore, to apportion them to the three cost centres in question. These bases should reflect the benefits received by the three departments from these costs. For example, since rates are related to the area occupied by the factory, the area occupied by each cost centre may serve as a basis for apportioning rate charges.

Simplex Limited has adopted the undermentioned bases for the apportionment of indirect factory overhead costs:

Basis of apportionment	Total	Machining	Assembly	Maintenance
Number of employees	60	30	20	10
Square feet of floor space	100,000	50,000	40,000	10,000
Maintenance man hours	2500	1500	1000	—
Direct labour man hours	10,000	5000	5000	—

Applying these bases to the apportionment of indirect factory overhead costs to the three cost centres, the following distributions are obtained:

Apportionment of factory overhead costs

Overhead costs	Basis	Total £	Machining £	Assembly £	Maintenance £
Indirect materials	Direct	15,000	8000	5000	2000
Indirect labour	Direct	6000	4000	1000	1000
Depreciation of machinery	Direct	7000	2500	4500	—
Supervisory salaries	No. of employees	6000	3000	2000	1000
Rates	Floor space	10,000	5000	4000	1000
		44,000	22,500	16,500	5000
Apportionment of Maintenance Cost Centre Overheads	Maintenance man hours	—	3000	2000	(5000)
		44,000	25,500	18,500	—

We may note from the foregoing example that the final stage in apportioning factory overhead costs to production cost centres was the apportionment of the service cost centre overhead costs. The basis used was the number of maintenance man hours expended in each of the production cost centres. Among other methods commonly used in respect of other service cost centres are the following examples:

Service Cost Centres	Basis of apportionment
Purchasing	Cost of materials purchased or number of orders placed
Stores	Cost of materials used, or the number of stores requisitions
Personnel Canteen	Number of employees
Building maintenance	Space occupied

The allotment of production cost centre costs to products

This stage is the second major step in the ascertainment of full-product costs. As we mentioned earlier, difficulties arise where production cost centres produce more than one product, which is usually the case. It is necessary in such cases to establish a method for attributing to each product an equitable proportion of the production cost centre's overhead costs. The method to 'recover' or 'absorb' these costs relies on the calculation of an 'overhead rate', which is usually linked to one of three factors:

(a) direct labour costs
(b) direct labour hours
(c) machine hours.

A pre-requisite for the calculation of an 'overhead rate' is the selection of an appropriate base for this purpose.

Example

Having completed the apportionment of factory overhead costs to the two production cost centres—Machining and Assembly—the next problem facing Simplex Ltd is to select an appropriate overhead base for apportioning overhead costs to the products manufactured in these two centres. The following information relates to the Machining cost centre:

Direct labour costs	£5000
Direct labour hours	10,000
Machine hours	15,000

On the basis of this information, we are able to calculate three different 'overhead rates' for absorbing overhead costs into the full-product costs of each unit of the different products manufactured by Simplex Ltd. The calculations are as follows:

(a) Overhead rate based on direct labour costs

$$\frac{\text{Cost centre overhead costs}}{\text{Cost centre direct labour costs}} \times 100$$

$$\frac{£25,500}{£5000} \times 100$$

$$= \underline{510\%}$$

Thus, for each £1 of direct labour cost which each unit of a product has incurred in the Machining cost centre, that unit will also attract £5.1 of the cost centre's overhead costs. Given that the prime costs incurred by Product A in the Machining cost centre are:

	£
Direct labour costs per unit	1.00
Direct material costs per unit	2.00

The full-product costs per unit of Product A at the end of processing through the Machining Department would be:

	£
Prime costs as above	3.00
Factory overhead costs	5.10
	8.10

(b) *Overhead rate based on direct labour hours*

$$\frac{\text{Cost centre overhead costs}}{\text{Cost centre direct labour hours}}$$

$$\frac{£25,500}{10,000}$$

$$= £2.55 \text{ per direct labour hour}$$

Thus, for every hour of direct labour spent on making a unit of a particular product in the Machining Department, that unit will attract £2.55 of that cost centre's overhead costs. Hence, if Product A needs $2\frac{1}{2}$ direct labour hours, the overhead costs apportioned would be £6.375 per unit.

(c) *Overhead rate based on machine hours*

$$\frac{\text{Cost centre overhead costs}}{\text{Cost centre machine hours}}$$

$$\frac{£25,500}{15,000}$$

$$= £1.70 \text{ per machine hour}$$

Thus, for every hour which is spent on machining a unit of a product in the Machining Department, that unit will attract £1.70 of that cost centre's overhead costs. Hence, if product A needs $3\frac{1}{2}$ hours of machining, the overhead costs apportioned would be £5.95 per unit.

The choice of one particular overhead rate as against the others may substantially affect the amount of overhead costs apportioned to a unit of product. Consequently, variations in full-product costs may result simply from the manner in which the overhead rate is selected. The 'best' rate to use depends on the particular circumstances facing the firm. The 'direct labour cost' base is easy to use since the necessary information is usually readily available. There may be no relationship, however, between direct labour costs and overhead costs: indeed, most factory overhead costs are incurred on a time basis and are not related to the labour payroll. A further problem resulting from the use of this overhead base is that there will be distortions in the absorption of overhead cost by different products if the rate of pay for similar work is not comparable. The 'direct labour hour' base is usually found to be a better method because most factory overhead costs are more related to time than any other factor. Where, however, there is a greater reliance on machinery rather than on labour, the 'machine hour' base may be the most suitable overhead base for absorbing overhead costs into full-product costs.

Plant-wide versus department overhead rates of recovery

In our discussion so far, we have examined methods of calculating overhead rates which were related to departmental overhead bases. We took the information for the Machining Department, for example, as a means of calculating overhead rates for the absorption of its own factory overhead costs into the costs of various products processed in that department. It may be felt that an easier and less extravagant method would be to select an overhead base for use by every department, rather than having different overhead bases used by different departments. The argument in favour of departmental overhead rates is that different departments do not incur the same amount of factory overhead costs, as we have already seen, and do not necessarily use the same number of labour or machine hours, nor do they have the same labour costs. It follows, therefore, that the use of a plant-wide overhead rate will not produce an accurate measure of the departmental costs associated with each unit of product. Departmental overhead rates, by contrast, lead to more accurate measurement, as may be seen from the following example.

Example

Eastlands Carburrettors Limited manufactures two types of carburrettors, Type X and Type Y, both of which are processed in two departments—Department A and Department B. The following cost information is available:

	Type X	Type Y
	£	£
Prime factory costs per unit	8	8
Direct labour hours		
Department A	4 hours	1 hour
Department B	1 hour	4 hours
Total hours	5 hours	5 hours

Overhead rates based on direct labour hours are given as follows:

Overhead rates	Per direct labour hour
	£
Departmental basis	
Department A	6
Department B	1
Plantwide basis	
Department A	3
Department B	3

This information enables us to compare the costs per unit which would result from the use of a plant-wide overhead rate as against departmental overhead rates.

Unit costs using a plant-wide overhead rate

	Type X	Type Y
	£	£
Prime factory costs per unit	8	8
Add: Overhead charge per unit		
(5 hours at £3.00)	15	15
Manufacturing costs per unit	23	23

Unit costs using departmental overhead rates

	Type X	Type Y
	£	£
Prime factory costs per unit	8	8
Add: Overhead charge per unit		
Department A (at £6 per hour)	24	6
Department B (at £1 per hour)	1	4
Manufacturing costs per unit	33	18

It is noteworthy that:

(a) Product X, which spends more processing time in Department A which has the higher overhead rate, is undercosted by £10 when a plant-wide overhead rate is used.

(b) Product Y, however, which spends more processing time in Department B, which has the lower overhead rate, is overcosted by £5 when a plant-wide overhead rate is used.

These wide differences highlight the dangers of using cost measurements which do not lead to accurate statements of unit costs. The absorption of factory overhead costs by means of departmental overhead rates rather than a plant-wide overhead rate yields a more accurate measurement of the costs incurred in manufacturing products. Management decisions which require accurate cost measurements for such purposes as pricing policies and production-mix decisions would be made incorrectly where a plant-wide rather than departmental rates is employed.

The selection of an appropriate level of activity

So far we have classified costs into two categories—prime costs and overhead costs. This classification is helpful in understanding how costs are related to products for the purposes of measuring unit costs of production. We mentioned earlier in this chapter that different cost concepts perform different functions. In order to understand the manner in which costs are affected by different levels of activity, we use another classification. This classification requires that costs be categorized into fixed and variable costs, and its purpose is to define how particular items of costs are affected by changes in activity levels.

Fixed costs are those costs which do not vary with changing levels of activity, for example, factory rent, insurance, and rates. Variable costs are those costs which do change directly with changes in the level of activity, for example, raw material costs and direct labour costs. There are costs, however, which are partly fixed and partly variable, for example, maintenance and repairs of machinery and plant equipment, heat, light and power. These are called mixed costs.

Prime costs are variable costs, since in total they vary with changes in the level of activity.* However, such costs are constant as regards unit costs of production. Overhead costs, however, contain both fixed and semi-variable cost elements. In order to examine how changes in levels of activity affect the apportionment of overhead costs to units of output, accountants classify all factory overhead costs as between fixed and variable costs so as to calculate two types of overhead rates—a fixed overhead rate and a variable overhead rate. This means that they must attempt to analyse semi-variable costs into their fixed and variable elements.

The level of activity, therefore, is an economic factor which affects the calculation of the unit cost of output produced. Since fixed and overhead costs remain constant as output fluctuates, the greater the output, the lower will be the fixed overhead cost per unit. For example, if fixed overhead costs for the period are £10,000, the fixed overhead cost per unit will depend upon the total number of units produced. If 10,000 units are produced, the fixed overhead cost per unit will be £1; if 5000 units are produced the fixed overhead cost per unit will be £2. This problem does not affect the variable overhead rate, for as we have already noted, variable costs per unit of output remain constant at all

---

* Labour regulations have led to an increasing tendency for firms to regard direct labour costs as fixed rather than variable costs.

levels of activity, assuming always that prices remain stable. For management decision-making based on full unit costs, however, the level of activity is an important ingredient which must be taken into account when providing relevant information for such decisions.

From the foregoing discussion, we must examine the usefulness of the actual—that is current—volume of output as a level of activity upon which to base calculations of full unit costs. Current unit costs will fluctuate according to the actual level of activity, here costs are of little use for decisions regarding the future. Thus, pricing decisions require a more stable view of full costs than that provided as a result of fluctuating levels of output. Moreover, cost control implies that full unit costs incurred in one period are compared with those of other periods. Comparisons based on actual levels of output are unreliable because fixed costs per unit will be different where the output levels are different. Even for inventory valuation purposes, which, as we mentioned, was central to profit measurement, calculations based on actual volume will introduce distortions. Finally, since the calculation of unit costs based on actual volume can only be effected at the end of an accounting period, such a calculation is not readily available. relevant to its decision problems is more concerned with future than with past costs. We discuss this particular problem later in this chapter.

Since actual volume is not a satisfactory basis for calculating a fixed overhead rate which will be useful for the purposes which we have mentioned, the following alternative bases may be considered:

(a) theoretical capacity, which is the capacity of a particular department to maintain output at a 100% level without interruption;
(b) practical capacity, which is the result of making allowances against the theoretical capacity in respect of unavoidable interruptions to output such as time lost for repairs and holidays;
(c) expected capacity as a short-run view of capacity, which is determined by immediate expectations of output levels;
(d) normal capacity, which is an estimate of output capacity based on a period of time long enough to level out peaks and troughs of cyclical fluctuations.

Normal capacity, as defined above, is the most useful level of activity for the purpose of determining a fixed overhead rate which will be relatively stable over a number of years. It will be appreciated that there is an element of subjectivity in the assessment of normal capacity, and it will lead invariably to some under- or over-absorption of fixed factory overhead costs depending on whether the actual level of activity is under or over the normal level. We shall deal with this problem in chapter 11. Normal capacity often does provide, however, the most reliable and stable basis for calculating full-product costs for decision-making purposes.

The allotment of non-manufacturing costs to products

For income measurement purposes, non-manufacturing costs such as administrative and marketing costs are treated differently by different firms. Some firms, for example, made a distinction between factory administration costs and those incurred by head office administration. Factory administration costs are apportioned to cost centres and charged to product costs by means of overhead rates. Head office administration costs are not charged to the product, but are treated as 'period' costs for the purpose of measuring periodic income. Other firms, by contrast, charge all administrative costs to the product by means of appropriate bases which apportion them to the various cost centres. Marketing costs conventionally are not taken into the product, but are treated as 'period' costs by the great majority of firms for income measurement purposes.

Regardless of the manner in which firms may treat non-manufacturing costs in the measurement of income, total unit cost measures are useful for certain decision problems, such as those stemming from the profitability of products and the determination of selling prices. Suitable measurements of total product costs are required for these purposes, and these may vary from firm to firm. Methods of alloting non-manufacturing to product costs include the following:

(a) administrative costs may be alloted to product costs on the basis of the ratio of sales of the product to total sales expressed in terms of revenue from sales, or the cost of sales or the gross profit on sales;

(b) delivery costs may be alloted to product costs on the basis of weight, cubic capacity or distances involved in delivering the products;

(c) warehousing and storage costs may be alloted on the basis
of the goods received and issued by the warehouse of stores
as measured by the number of items, weight or cubic capacity.

Limitations of total cost calculations

It is clear from the foregoing examination of the problems associated
with overhead costs that full-product costs cannot be measured with
complete accuracy. To some extent, all methods used for apportioning
overhead costs are arbitrary, and are based upon assumptions, which
are subjective to a degree. We stated that the 'benefit received' should
be the main criterion for apportioning factory overhead costs to cost
centres. It is difficult, however, to find bases which are suitable for this
purpose. For example, the cost of the Factory Personnel Department
may be apportioned to cost centres on the basis of the relative number
of their employees, but this base assumes that all employees will
benefit equally from the services of this department. This example is,
of course, a gross simplification of the general problem of apportioning
overhead costs. Labour turnover and the difference in skills between
different classes of employees will influence the time and the effort
expended by the Personnel Department.

We have referred already to the element of subjectivity which enters
into the selection of the methods of apportioning overhead costs. This
is excacerbated by the degree of subjectivity which may be attached to
the selection of the level of activity selected from recovering overhead
costs. Indeed, two equally competent accountants may arrive at very
different product costs simply because their view of what constitutes a
'normal level' of activity may differ. This problem applies similarly to
the allotment of administrative costs. The bases for alloting these costs
which we mentioned may be rationalized but may not be defended as
being adequate cost accounting procedures. The cost of operating the
Purchasing Department cannot be related, for example to any of the
bases which we mentioned.

It is apparent that the main difficulty in computing full and total
product costs stems from the presence of fixed overhead costs. The
allotment of these costs to product costs on bases which are arbitrary
renders the end result of doubtful accuracy. As we shall see elsewhere
in this book, incorrect decisions may arise from the inclusion of fixed
costs in product costs. For the purpose of external financial reporting,
for example, we argue in Part 4 chapter 8 that more useful information
may be provided if fixed overhead costs are not absorbed in output,
but are treated as period costs. Moreover, their inclusion in product
costs may give a misleading view of profit results. It is often claimed

that for the purpose of long-range planning, product cost information should reflect total costs. However, as we shall see in chapter 8, there is a case for directing attention away from a narrowly conceived view of price determination based on mark-up percentages on costs to the broader implications of cost-volume-profit relationships. As we shall also see, because of the behaviour of fixed and variable costs over different volumes of output, product cost information based on full costs is irrelevant to the problem of control. A distinction has to be made, therefore, between fixed and variable cost information for control purposes.

It follows that the limitations inherent in full-cost computations should be appreciated by all those using such information for decision-making. From an accountant's point of view, specific instruction from management should be awaited for the calculation of product costs inclusive of fixed costs. Even then, a clear distinction should be made between fixed and variable cost components.

The costs of joint-products and by-products

The previous sections in this chapter have dealt with the problem of applying overhead to units of output. The problem is aggravated when products are produced jointly i.e. they emerge from a common process. In such situations the problems of apportioning costs becomes extremely arbitrary.

Joint products

A key characteristic of joint products is that production is of either both (or all) products or none at all. One is not able to produce A and not B. The distillation of petroleum oil, for example, results in the production of a number of joint-products in the form of various grades of petrol, paraffin, fuel oil and lubricants. There is a split-off point at various stages of the distillation process at which products are separated and subjected to further independent processing. The problem of costing joint products is to find some reasonable basis for allocating to each of the joint products the costs incurred to the split-off point. Thereafter, of course, the further separate processing costs can be readily ascertained and allocated to the separate products.

Essentially, the costing of joint products raises problems akin to those involved in apportioning indirect overhead costs to cost centres: we need measures of the benefits received by each joint product from the joint costs incurred. The selection of suitable measures of these benefits is very difficult, and the following methods of apportioning joint costs illustrate the problem of finding satisfactory surrogates.

(a) Market value at the split-off point

If, for example, Product A and Product B are jointly produced and are saleable at the split-off point for £300 and £200 per ton respectively, the joint costs up to the split-off point may be apportioned in the ratio of 3:2, so that they show the same percentage of profit or loss. The apportionment does not reflect the benefit which each product receives from the joint costs but depends rather upon their market value. Hence, in situations where the relative price changes, so will the proportion of joint costs charged against the products change.

(b) Physical measurement at the split-off point

If, for example, Product A and Product B are jointly produced in the ratio of 40 tons to 20 tons, the joint costs up to the split-off point may be apportioned in the ratio 2:1. This method may be unsatisfactory where the market value of the two product differs widely. It assumes, for example, that in the case of petroleum distillation that the value of a gallon of petrol is equal to that of a gallon of paraffin.

The apportionment of joint costs is necessary in order to calculate stock values so as to arrive at a measure of periodic profit. The product costs derived are not useful to management for decision-making; where joint costs exist, total rather than unit product costs and revenues are relevant.

By-products

By-products are a special kind of joint product, being of comparatively trivial value in relation to the major product at the split-off point. Very often, socially useful by-products are wasted because there is no readily available technology to recover them and to market them. Numerous examples may be given: gas burnt-off at oil wells and refineries, hot water produced in the cooling process at electricity generating stations. Many by-products are recoverable, however, and the net revenue derived from their sale is commonly deducted from total joint costs in calculating the profit attributable to producing the major product.

Actual and planned costs

At the beginning of this chapter, we stated that cost information is required for the undermentioned three major purposes:

(a) to assist in planning decisions;
(b) to assist in the control of operations;
(c) to assist in the measurement of reported profits.

Obviously, the measurement of reported profit requires information of the actual costs of production during the accounting period in question. Such costs are collected in the manner which we have discussed, and, as we have already indicated, illustrations of the recording process will be found in the appendix to this chapter.

For the purposes of planning and control decisions, however, information is required not only of historical costs but also of future costs. As planning decisions are directed towards future events, historical cost information is useful only as a guide to future costs. General and specific price changes render historical costs unreliable for decision-making, and consequently, it is necessary for accountants to provide estimates of future costs on which planning decisions may be based.

Planning and control decisions are often made on the basis of special types of unit costs which are called standard costs. A standard cost is a pre-determined cost which is established in relation to specific operating conditions, and takes into consideration all the factors and circumstances which are likely to influence production costs. They are applied to both prime and overhead costs, and their objective is to establish standards both for the rate of usage of resources and their input price. Whereas cost standards may be established comparatively easily in respect of prime costs, cost standards for overhead costs require the use of pre-determined overhead rates for the purpose of alloting them to product costs. As we mentioned earlier, the need to use a 'normal' level of activity for determining a fixed overhead rate for the recovery of fixed overhead costs means that under- or over-absorption of overhead costs will occur where actual levels of activity fail to conform with planned levels. We shall discuss this problem more fully in chapter 11.

Actual costs serve two very useful roles for planning and control purposes. As regards planning decisions, they act as feedback information which either validates those decisions, or assists in improving the planning process by examining the reasons for previous errors. For control purposes, actual costs are compared with planned costs as a means of checking that actual performance is conforming with planned performance. Variance analysis, as we shall see in chapter 12 is a central aspect of the control process.

Appendix: Historical cost accounting systems

Where a standard cost accounting system has been installed, only the established standard costs are recorded in the cost accounts. Information concerning actual costs emerges from the financial accounting records which we discussed in Part 2. From a cost control point of view, the significance of actual costs lies in the fact that when compared to the established standard costs, they highlight variances, which are differences between planned and actual performance. In this appendix we shall examine historical cost accounting for two reasons:

(i) to enable us better to understand the process of income measurement which we discussed in Part 2;

(ii) to enable us to acquire a better knowledge of the structure of a cost accounting system, thereby facilitating our transition to standard costing.

From an accounting viewpoint, the manufacturing process may be analysed as a progressive transformation of raw materials into finished products through three categories of inventory—raw materials, work-in-progress and finished goods. The recording of actual costs of production is effected in the Manufacturing account. Manufacturing costs are attached to these categories of inventory as they enter the factory as raw materials and proceed to that ultimate point where they leave the factory as finished goods.

As far as the measurement of income is concerned, the problem facing accountants lies in the manner in which inventory values should be calculated. As we have seen in our discussion of full-product costing, the conventional accounting method of valuing inventory is to include all manufacturing costs into full-product cost calculations. The matching convention which applies to the measurement of accounting income, requires that until goods are sold, they should appear on the Income Statement only as inventory values. The factory fixed overhead cost element of full-product costs could be charged quite properly against periodic income rather than being incorporated in inventory values. We have mentioned already that different firms adopt different attitudes to this matter, and needless to say, differences in inventory valuation methods could affect the size of reported incomes.

Thus, recording the flow of costs is a matter of keeping records for each cost centre, and subsequently aggregating the recorded costs in order to calculate periodic income. In this Appendix, we shall concern ourselves with the aggregated records of cost flows, but we ask the reader to bear in mind that they are based on cost data collected for cost centres. The relationship between the various flows of costs which we shall examine may be depicted diagramatically as in Fig. 3.7.

Cost accounting systems

There are two basic methods of recording cost flows in a given accounting period—job order costing and process costing. These cost systems may be integrated with the firm's financial accounting system, or they may exist as separate systems. Most firms favour the advantages which arise from the integration of cost accounting and financial accounting systems, so that for the purpose of this discussion, we shall assume that they are integrated.

Job order costing

Job Order Costing is suitable for firms engaged in the manufacture of products to order or contract. The productive process is non-repetitive, and the products are more or less distinctive since they are made usually to the customer's specification. Where the products are similar in quality, the quantities contracted for differ from customer to customer.

The cost accumulation procedure centres on a Job Order Cost Sheet, which is identified either by the customer order number, or by identifiable batches of product. In effect, therefore, the cost of direct materials, direct labour and direct expenses applicable to each order or batch is made the subject of a separate accounting record. The total accumulated costs for each order or batch is divided by the number of units of finished product in order to calculate the average unit cost of production.

Example

An order is received from W. Williams and Co. for 100 flanges. The order is immediately given a reference number—no. 1010, and as costs are incurred, so they are entered on the Job Order Cost Sheet, as shown on page 296.

At the same time as the cost information is recorded on the Job Order Cost Sheet, entries are also made in the Work-in-Progress account. Thus, the Job Order Cost Sheets contain the detailed information which supports the entries appearing in the Work-in-Progress account. Equally, when a job has been completed, the Job Order Cost Sheet provides the data needed to transfer the cost of goods completed from the Work-in-Progress account to the Finished Goods account.

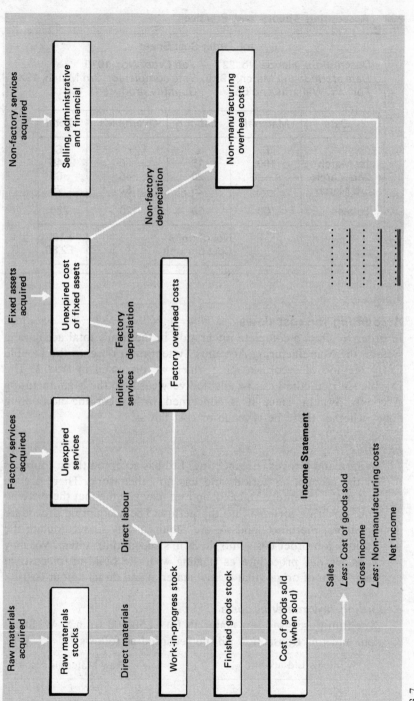

Fig. 3.7

```
┌─────────────────────────────────────────────────────────────────┐
│                        Job Order Cost Sheet                        │
│  Description: Flange No. 22      Job Order No: 1010                 │
│  Date started: 1st March, 19X0  Date completed: 3rd March, 19X0    │
│  For: W. Williams and Co.       Quantity produced: 100             │
└─────────────────────────────────────────────────────────────────┘
```

Date	Material	Labour	Overheads	Total
	£	£	£	£
1st March	100	15	30	145
2nd March	—	20	40	60
3rd March	—	25	50	75
Totals	100	60	120	280
	No. of units			÷100
	Cost per unit			£2.80

Accounting for cost flows

In order to effect a complete integration in the firm's total accounting system, the Manufacturing Accounts System must observe the Double Entry method of record-keeping which we discussed in Part 2. The Double Entry method can be adapted very easily to the Manufacturing Accounts System, since it is concerned with recording accounting flows, whether these be revenue or cost flows.

Example

Wilson and Groves (Engineering) Ltd has accepted three contracts in the accounting period, and has no other work. There are no materials' inventory on hand, and we may assume that there are no costs to bring forward into the period. The accounting procedure is simple, therefore, and we are required only to accumulate the various job order costs into the firm's accounting system. We may consider this procedure as starting with the build-up of costs at their point of origin, that is, raw material and direct labour costs.

Recording raw material costs

The firm purchased raw materials for £250,000 from S. W. Steels Ltd and this transaction will be recorded as follows:

S. W. Steels Ltd account		Raw Materials account	
	£		£
Raw Materials 250,000		S. W. Steels Ltd 250,000	

Materials issued to the jobs during the period amounted to £150,000, of which £130,000 were classified as direct materials costs, and the remaining £20,000 were materials used generally in the factory and could not be traced to any particular job. This material was classified, therefore, as part of Factory Overhead Costs. The accounting entries to record these issues are:

Raw Materials account

	£		£
S. W. Steels Ltd	250,000	Work-in-Progress	130,000
		Factory Overhead Costs	20,000
		Balance c/d	100,000
	250,000		250,000
Balance b/d	100,000		

Work-in-Progress account

	£	
Raw Materials	130,000	

Factory Overhead Costs account

	£	
Raw Materials	20,000	

Recording labour costs

Wage costs for the period amounted to £200,000, of which £150,000 were identified as direct labour costs, and the remainder as indirect labour costs. The accounting entries are:

Wages account

	£		£
Cash	200,000	Work-in-Progress	150,000
		Factory Overhead Cost	50,000

Work-in-Progress account

	£	
Raw Materials	130,000	
Wages	150,000	

Factory Overhead Cost account

	£	
Raw Materials	20,000	
Wages	50,000	

Recording factory overhead costs

In addition to the indirect materials and indirect wages which have already been recorded, other factory overheads were incurred in

respect of power and light £60,000, rates £10,000, and depreciation £160,000. The accounting entries are:

Factory Overhead Cost account

	£	
Raw Materials	20,000	
Wages	50,000	
Power and Light	60,000	
Rates	10,000	
Depreciation	160,000	

These various accounts will have been debited with these sums
initially, so that by their transfer to the Factory Overhead Cost
A/C they may ultimately be associated with the individual jobs.

The measurement of periodic profit

The convention of periodicity, which as we saw in Part 2 requires that
financial results be calculated periodically, affects the treatment of the
flow of manufacturing costs. At the end of an accounting period, those
jobs which are uncompleted must be shown as work-in-progress in the
Balance Sheet and carried forward as inventory to the next accounting
period. Those jobs which will have been completed will be transferred
as costs of sales in order to measure periodic profit. The measurement
of periodic profit presents, therefore, an inventory valuation problem
which has two aspects:

(a) the calculation of the cost value of work-in-progress,
(b) the calculation of the cost value of completed jobs.

Thus, in the process of building-up costs from their point of origin,
the Work-in-Progress account has played a focal role. Prime costs will
have been transferred to this account, whilst indirect material and
indirect labour costs will have been accumulated in the Factory Overhead Cost account, where other overhead costs will also have been
transferred.

At the end of an accounting period, the Factory Overhead Cost
account is closed by the transfer of the balance to two accounts: the
Cost of Sales account and the Work-in-Progress account. As there is
no problem in ascertaining the prime costs attributable to particular
contracts, the main problem is apportioning overhead costs to particular contracts. We have already examined the various methods of

apportioning overhead costs. Let us assume that in the example given on page 296, the apportionment of factory overhead costs is made on the basis of the direct labour costs attributable to each job. This apportionment, it will be recalled, will have been made on the basis of a pre-determined direct labour rate. As a result, the Job Order Cost Sheet for the three jobs in the example will show the undermentioned details:

Job No.	Direct Materials	Direct Labour	Factory Overheads	Total
	£	£	£	£
1	60,000	100,000	200,000	360,000
2	30,000	20,000	40,000	90,000
3	40,000	30,000	60,000	130,000
	130,000	150,000	300,000	580,000

The cost of work-in-progress at the end of the accounting period may be easily ascertained, for it is necessary only to extract from the Job Order Cost Sheets the cost of finished work, and to use this information to transfer the cost value of finished work to the Finished Goods account. Let us assume that Job Nos 1 and 2 were completed by the end of the accounting period. The accounting entries would be as follows:

Work-in-Progress account

	£		£
Raw Materials	130,000	Finished Goods	450,000
Wages	150,000	Balance c/d	130,000
Factory Overhead costs	300,000		
	580,000		580,000
Balance b/d	130,000		

Finished Goods account

	£	
Work-in-progress	450,000	

The flow oɪ cost is completed when the finished jobs are accepted by the contractor. If we assume that in the example given above only Job No. 1 has been accepted by the contractor at the end of the accounting period, we may transfer its cost to the Cost of Sales Account, as follows:

Finished Goods account

	£		£
Work-in-progress	450,000	Cost of sales	360,000
		Balance c/d	90,000
	450,000		450,000
Balance b/d	90,000		

Cost of Sales account

	£	
Finished Goods	360,000	

The measurement of periodic profit results, therefore, in the calculation of three different inventory valuations—Raw Material, Work-in-Progress, and Finished Goods Inventories. These inventory values will appear on the Balance Sheet, and periodic profit will be shown on the Income Statement drawn up in the manner explained in Part 2.

In this example, we have applied all the overhead to the jobs completed. In practice, the use of predetermined overhead rates implies that overheads at the end of a period will be under- or over-absorbed. Transfers of costs will be made from Factory Overhead account to jobs before the overhead costs are actually incurred. Therefore, a balance will exist in the Factory Overhead account at the end of any period and this may arise from several factors:

(1) The prices of indirect services may be different from those on which the overhead rate is based.
(2) The amounts of indirect services used may be greater or smaller than the production warrants.
(3) The production volume achieved may differ from budgeted activity. This variance relates to fixed costs.

The problems which arise from the difference between predetermined overhead rates and those actually incurred are examined in chapter 11.

Process costing

Process cost accounting systems are usually installed in industries which produce large quantities of homogeneous products on a continuous basis. Steel, cement, flour and chemicals are examples of products which lend themselves to process costing.

Accounting for cost flows

In process costing, costs are accumulated by process departments, which are the cost centres directly engaged in processing the product. Indirect overhead costs are allocated to these process departments, so that all factory costs are charged to the process departments. The number of units produced in each department, however measured, is applied to the department's costs incurred by each department. The costs so calculated for each processing department form the basis of the process costing records.

Example

Summerdrinks Ltd operates a soft drink bottling plant which has three processes—Mixing (A), Bottling (B) and Packing (C). The following data were collected for the month of January 19X0:

			£
Materials used:	Process	A	10,000
		B	5000
		C	2000
Direct labour:		A	5000
		B	2000
		C	1000
Factory overheads—direct		A	500
		B	1000
		C	500
indirect (apportioned to process)		A	400
		B	200
		C	100

During the month of January, 100,000 gallons were produced and bottled. There were no opening or closing inventories of work in process. The process cost accounts will appear as follows:

Process A

	£		£
Materials	10,000	Transferred to Process	15,900
Direct labour	5000	B (100,000 units at	
Direct overheads	500	£0.159)	
Indirect overheads	400		
	15,900		15,900

Process B

	£		£
Transferred from Process A (100,000 units at £0.159)	15,900	Transferred to Process C (100,000 units at £0.241)	24,100
Materials	5000		
Direct labour	2000		
Direct overheads	1000		
Indirect overheads	200		
	24,100		24,100

Process C

	£		£
Transferred from Process B (100,000 units at £0.241)	24,100	Transferred to Finished Goods Stock (100,000 units at £0.277)	27,700
Materials	2000		
Direct labour	1000		
Direct overheads	500		
Indirect overheads	100		
	27,700		27,700

From the foregoing example, we may see not only how aggregate costs are built up through the consecutive processing departments, but also how the full-unit costs are accumulated.

The problem of calculating actual output

The task of calculating the total number of units produced in an accounting period is complicated by two factors:

(a) the presence of work-in-progress started in the prior accounting period and completed in the current period;

(b) the presence of work-in-progress at the end of the current accounting period which will be carried forward for completion in the subsequent accounting period.

This problem is overcome by using the notion of 'equivalent completed units' which converts all units of production in a department to a common base.

Example

Let us assume that the undermentioned data relates to the output of Process A of Summerdrinks Ltd in the current accounting period:

20,000 units were one-quarter completed at the beginning of the period.

80,000 units were completed during the period.

40,000 units were half-completed at the end of the period.

The equivalent completed units of output for the current accounting period may be calculated as follows:

Completed units	80,000
Add: Half completed units $(40,000 \times \frac{1}{2})$	20,000
	100,000
Less: Opening inventory of work in	
progress $(20,000 \times \frac{1}{4})$	5000
Equivalent units of output	95,000

Given that the total departmental costs for the period amount to £15,900, the cost of each equivalent unit of output may be calculated as follows:

$$\frac{\text{Total department costs}}{\text{Total equivalent units of output}} = \frac{£15,900}{95,000}$$

$$= £0.167$$

Summary

Cost information is required for three main purposes:

(a) for planning decisions;
(b) for control decisions;
(c) for the measurement of reported income.

The type of cost information required may be different in each of these cases. We shall analyse the nature and the use of various cost measurements in this Part.

This chapter has been concerned with the accounting problems involved in the measurement of unit costs of production. In this connection, a distinction has been made between two measurements of unit costs:

(a) full-product costs consisting of direct costs and factory overhead costs; and
(b) total product costs which consist of all costs, inclusive of administrative and marketing costs.

The major difficulty in the measurement of full-product costs lies in the calculation and assignment of factory overhead costs. The process of assigning factory overhead costs to units of product occurs in the following stages:

(a) alloting factory overhead costs to production cost centres and finding appropriate levels of activity for this purpose;
(b) alloting the costs of production cost centres to units of product and finding appropriate methods for this purpose.

The problem of measuring total product costs, which are needed for determining profitability and considering pricing policies, may involve finding suitable methods for apportioning non-manufacturing costs to units of product.

The appendix to this chapter was concerned with two basic methods for recording cost flows—job order costing and process costing. The selection of the appropriate method of recording costs depends on the nature of the manufacturing activity.

Further readings

1. Backer, Martin & Jacobsen, Lyle E., *Cost Accounting*, McGraw-Hill, New York, 1964.

2. Benston, George J., *Contemporary Cost Accounting and Control*, Dickenson Publishing Company, Belmont California, 1970.

3 Bierman, Harold Jr. & Dyckman, Thomas R., *Managerial Cost Accounting*, Macmillan, New York, 1971.

4. Dearden, John, *Cost Accounting and Financial Control Systems*, Addison-Wesley, New York, 1973.

5. Horngren, Charles T., *Cost Accounting: A Managerial Emphasis*, 3rd editions, Prentice Hall, Englewood Cliffs, N.J., 1972.

6. Ijiri, Yuji, *Management Goals and Accounting for Control*, Rand McNally & Company, Chicago, 1965.

7. Lynch, Richard M. & Williamson, R., *Accounting for Management*, McGraw-Hill, New York, 1967.

8. Matz, Adolph & Curry, O. J. *Cost Accounting*, South-Western Publishing Company, Cincinnati, 1972.

9. Shillinglaw, G., *Cost Accounting*, Richard Irwin, Homewood, Illinois, 1972.

Section 2

Planning

3
Long-Range Planning

Long-range planning is not a single technique, nor is it just one area of management responsibility. It is a systematic attempt to plan the entire behaviour of the organization in the long-run, and in the case of profit-making organizations, it attempts to increase the rate of profitable growth (Perrin, 1968). In this chapter, we shall examine the stages involved in long-range planning, and we shall discuss the accountant's role in that process.

Long-range planning is concerned with:

(1) the determination of long-range objectives;
(2) the preparation of the position audit;
(3) the formulation of strategy;
(4) the preparation and implementation of the plan;
(5) the continuous review and up-dating of the plan.

The determination of long-range objectives

The importance of cash-flows

In the final analysis, cash flows into and out of a business enterprise are the most fundamental events upon which accounting measurements are based. Management and investors, in particular, are very concerned with the cash-flows generated by corporate assets. These cash-flows are not only central to the problem of corporate survival, but they are essential to the attainment of corporate objectives. In this Part, we are concerned with the management of corporate assets with the view to generating cash-flows. The size and timing of future cash flows are critical aspects of this analysis. In Part 4, we shall argue that the purpose of income measurement is to enable investors and shareholders to predict future cash-flows. The adequacy and timing of these cash-flows are important not only as regards liquidity and solvency, but also for dividend purposes.

The recognition of the importance of future cash-flows has led many writers to define *the* objective of business corporations in terms of maximizing corporate wealth, defined as the present value of the future stream of net cash-flows to be earned by corporate assets. This objective is also expressed as the maximization of shareholders' wealth, since they are deemed in law to be the owners of the enterprise.

In Part 1, we explained that the distinctive feature of the modern business corporation as an 'entrepreneurial unit' is the separation of ownership from management. The power of shareholders to control management is limited to a number of issues, which is the business reserved by law to the Annual General Meeting of Shareholders. This business includes the election of directors, the appointment of auditors, the approval of annual financial reports and of dividend recommendations. In the process of adjusting to social pressures both external and internal to the firm, management has tended to utilize its relative freedom from ownership control to re-define the concept of managerial responsibility. Responsibilities to employees, consumers and to society at large may conflict with responsibilities to shareholders. Nevertheless, the sufficiency of profit to maintain and expand operations is and remains a necessary condition for business success. Hence, profit-making—which symbolizes the generation of cash-flows—is still the basic aim of management.

Objectives and goals
We may identify two basic types of organizational objectives:

(1) Broad corporate objectives which are general statements of policy which represent the ideals of the organization.
(2) Goals which are derived from these objectives and which establish specific targets for the organization. They include also lesser goals such as targets for sub-units, such as departments, and performance standards for managers and employees.

It follows, therefore, that there exists a hierarchy of goals applicable to every level of the organization, which are subordinated to the main goals and which interpret those goals. The management problem is not simply setting goals, but securing the attainment of those goals. We shall examine the behavioural aspects of the latter problem in chapter 14, where we discuss the manner in which the style of management known as 'management by objective' attempts to create a high degree of goal congruence between the personal objectives and organizational goals. For the moment, we shall concern ourselves with the analysis of organizational objectives and organizational goals.

Organizational objectives
These objectives serve as guidelines for establishing goals.

Example

Hygrade Cutlery Limited has the following objectives:

(1) Profit objective—to achieve a profit level sufficient to re-
    ward shareholders adequately and to protect the interests of
    creditors.
(2) Financial objectives—to secure adequate financial resources
    and to report to management on the utilization of these
    resources.
(3) Market objective—to build public confidence and to create
    goodwill for products bearing the company's name, thereby
    increasing customers' preference for the company's goods.
(4) Production objective—to increase the efficiency of produc-
    tion of high-quality products.
(5) Employee objective—to provide good jobs, wages and
    working conditions, work satisfaction, stability of employ-
    ment and opportunity for advancement, in return for
    loyalty, skills, initiative, effort and teamwork.
(6) Innovation objective—to develop new and better products.

Organizational goals

Goals are objectives which have been quantified and set as targets.
Whereas objectives may sound rather vague or obvious, goals are targets
which are intended to apply to the time-span of the planning period.

Example

The goals established by Hygrade Cutlery Limited for the next
five years are as follows:

(1) Profit goals—to attain a profit level of 20% before tax on
    the market value of the shareholders' equity by the end of
    the fifth year; to attain a profit level of 16% on total assets
    by the end of the fifth year; to achieve a profit before
    tax/sales ratio of 12% for each year; to increase after tax
    earnings per share by at least 10% per year.
(2) Financial goals—to improve the present cash position; to
    reduce debtors by 5%; to secure a return of 14% after tax
    on new capital expenditure.
(3) Market goals—to increase total sales of stainless steel cut-
    lery over the period by 30%; to increase marketing facilities
    abroad so that the number of customers served by the
    company will be 20% higher in five years' time.
(4) Production goal—to increase output per employee by 15%
    over the next five years.

(5) Employee goals—to reduce labour turnover by 15%; to improve the current management development scheme; to introduce management by objectives within two years.

(6) Innovation goal—to introduce a new range of stainless steel family-size teasets within one year.

The position audit

In estimating future cash-flows which are intended to result from a planned course of action, managers are able to draw on a great deal of inside information which is at their disposal. Top managers are placed in a unique position to assess a wide range of opportunities open to the firm, and to relate its present or potential technological, production and financial resources to these opportunities in the process of selecting the best strategy for attaining corporate objectives. This process of assessment is conducted by means of a position audit, which has an external and an internal aspect.

The external audit

The external audit is concerned with the environment in which the firm exists. It is also concerned with identifying opportunities and dangers facing the organization, and in particular in assessing changes in the economic, political, social, technological and industrial environment. If management is able to forecast significant changes in these various aspects of the firm's environment, it will be in a better position to deal with the opportunities and the problems which these changes present.

Forecasting plays a crucial role in the external audit. Two techniques are useful in this respect—economic forecasting and technological forecasting. Economic forecasting is concerned with predicting economic conditions which may have important implications for the firm. Technological forecasting is concerned with predicting changes in technology, so as to anticipate the nature of technological innovation to the advantage of the firm.

The usefulness of forecasts is realized only when they influence decisions, that is, when predictions are assumed to be part of the firm's environment in formulating objectives and goals, and preparing a strategy for attaining them.

The internal audit

The internal audit is focused on the organization's own strengths and weaknesses. It involves an appraisal of every aspect of the organization, including management, labour, products, markets, distribution channels, finance, assets and research and development. The purpose of this appraisal is to discover the reasons for present successes and failures, and to identify key success factors for the future. In conducting the internal audit, management will have much to learn from the experience of its competitors, and in identifying key success factors it will seek to compare its own strengths and weaknesses with those of its competitors.

The main purpose of both external and internal audits is to relate the organization's prospects with the prospects of the industry in which it is operating. The outlook for the industry affects the demand for the products or services of the industry; the supply of products or services is affected not only by productive capacity in the industry, but by labour and material costs peculiar to the industry. The firm's prospects within the industry are a function of its own position in the industry, the degree of competition existing in the industry and the firm's own cost structure. The position audit is, therefore, a learning exercise for the firm.

The formulation of strategy

The position audit outlines the array of factors which should be considered when formulating a strategy for attaining organizational objectives and goals. The role of strategy, therefore, is to select the best way of getting from the present position to the goals which have been derived from the organization's objectives. The first stage in the formulation of a strategy is an analysis of the gap between the present position and the desired position, which takes into account the forecasts which will have been made. Gap analysis involves the following questions:

(1) What will happen if nothing is done?
(2) What will happen if we pursue present policies?
(3) What should be done to attain organizational goals?

Gap analysis and the profit goal

The effects of alternative policies on profits is a very good example of gap analysis. Once the profit goal has been determined, it may be compared with the level of earnings for the business as it is presently operated. If no changes were made, present earnings would probably begin to decline after a period of time. This is because, as technology changes, as market demand and tastes change, as competitors improve performance etc., existing products are likely to become less profitable.

Previous long-range planning exercises, however, will have built into the operations of the firm's tactics to counter the fall-off in performance which would have occurred due to the causes mentioned. The

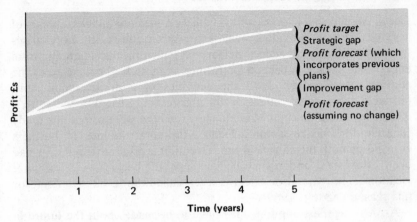

Fig. 3.8

difference between these two forecasts may be called the 'improvement gap'. It illustrates the value to the firm of former plans. The difference between the profit improvement figure and the profit goal is called the strategic gap. This represents the profit which the firm is required to make to meet the shortfall in its profit goal, and may be illustrated as in Fig. 3.8.

Long-range planning and gap analysis

The essence of long-range planning is really one of gap analysis. The problem involved in this analysis is the evaluation of alternative strategies for closing the strategic gap and selecting that strategy which is seen as the best one. Future cash flows, and consequently profits, are highly constrained by past and present capital expenditure decisions. Therefore, a pre-requisite to gap analysis is a *search* process to discover suitable projects in which the firm should invest. Throughout the search process, the firm is concerned typically with the following questions:

Can present operations be extended to meet organizational goals? If so, what does this mean in terms of greater penetration of existing markets, the exploration of new markets, the need for finance, assets, manpower etc.?

If present operations cannot be extended, how should the firm proceed? Should less profitable activities be abandoned and resources redeployed in new activities?

The search process is costly and time-consuming. An influential factor in determining the scope of search is the affinity between search areas and the present activities of the organization. Areas of search should be chosen which will complement current areas of activity, thereby providing synergistic opportunities. Synergy arises when two activities or actions performed jointly produce a greater total effect than if they had been performed separately. For example, the addition of a restaurant to the activities of a departmental store produces a synergistic effect in that the restaurant makes the store a more convenient place in which to shop, and the store provides a ready clientele for the restaurant. Hence, the total volume of business enjoyed by both the store and the restaurant is greater than if they had been established and maintained as separate businesses in different locations. The synergistic effect is often called the '2 + 2 = 5 effect' for this reason (Ansoff, 1969).

At this stage, assumptions may have to be made about the future in order that realistic plans may be prepared. Clearly, the possibility of making grave and expensive errors exists as a result of making such assumptions. In this connection, one has only to think of the many expensive defence projects undertaken by governments since the Second World War which ultimately have had to be abandoned. Unlike a government, a business enterprise is much more exposed to penalties for errors of large magnitude. Risk analysis has an important role to play in planning. It is a technique which, as we shall see in a subsequent chapter, involves assigning a 'probability factor' to assumptions. Obviously, there is a great difference between a plan which has only a 50% chance of success, and one for which the chances of success are thought to be as high as 95%. This notion is central to risk analysis.

The preparation and implementation of the plan

The selected strategy for the long-run will concentrate on the key factors for success and on the major decisions required. In particular, it will be concerned with basic issues such as the selection of the kinds of products or services which should be produced, their markets, the production process and its location, and the asset structure required.

Once the strategy has been selected, it has to be expressed in more detailed plans which then become the basis for action. Responsibility for implementing the plan will fall upon the management personnel in the various divisions and departments of the organization. In this chapter, we shall examine briefly a small aspect of the planning process, namely financial planning. The reader should bear in mind that long-range planning covers every spectrum of the firm's activities, and detailed plans for all these activities will be drafted.

The continuous review and up-dating of the plan

Corporate planning is a continuous process which responds to feed-back information. Up-dating may occur both on a continuous and on an annual basis. Corporate planning departments will be continually accumulating information and interpreting the significance of that information to the plan. The time-period envisaged by different firms for long-range planning purposes does vary, but it is quite normal to review the plan at the end of each year, and to incorporate those changes which are deemed to be necessary. This allows changes of every kind to be recognized and so introduces a degree of flexibility into the corporate planning process. At the end of each year, the plan must be extended for a further year so that the roll-over maintains a view of a constant time-period associated with long-range planning. The relationship between the long-range plan and the annual budget plan is very significant, and we shall consider this problem in chapter 5.

The importance of the long-range profit goal

We stated at the beginning of this chapter that the firm's success depends on its ability to generate a sufficiency of cash flows, symbolized by profit. The selection of a profit target for long-range planning purposes is not just a matter of fixing an arbitrary figure such as £5 million. A profit target of itself has little meaning: its significance appears when it is related to some other measurement, such as total assets employed, when it becomes a meaningful measure of performance. Thus, the Return on Capital Employed (R.O.C.E.) which relates profits to assets employed provides an assessment of the significance of a profit target by means of the following formula:

$$\text{R.O.C.E.} = \frac{\text{Planned Net Profit}}{\text{Planned Total Assets}}$$

There is general agreement that the R.O.C.E. is the most important performance measurement for long-range planning and for setting long-range profit targets. It is a common practice to compute the R.O.C.E. for each year covered by the long-range plan in order to show whether planned increases in annual profits will keep pace with annual increases in assets. This analysis also indicates the effectiveness with which management will be required to use corporate assets.

In recent years, the usefulness of R.O.C.E. measures has been questioned. We shall discuss the controversies involved in the use of R.O.C.E. in chapter 10 of this Part. Further difficulties are caused by the manner in which profits and assets might be defined and measured. These difficulties are considered in Part 4.

According to Drucker (1961), there are eight areas of activity to which the firm should direct its attention when formulating its objectives—market standing, innovation, productivity, physical and financial resources, profitability, manager performance and development, worker performance and attitude, and public responsibility. It is in these areas of activity that the several parties having a stake in the firm—shareholders, management, employees, Government, customers and suppliers, and the local community—have vested interests. Of the eight areas listed above, profitability is the most important because it provides a means of achieving objectives in the other seven areas. Unless a firm achieves a satisfactory profit goal, it may not survive in the long term.

The accountant's task is not to attempt the impossible by deciding what should be the maximum possible long-range profit on the basis of assumed long-range resources for planning purposes: his job is to quantify the size of the profit which is required as the profit objective. The required profit as a planning goal is never a theoretical ideal, such as 'the maximum long-term profit' or 'the maximum long-term return to shareholders', but represents rather the outcome of discussion as to what is a possible and desirable target for the time-span considered.

The longer the time-span envisaged as a planning period, the less reliable is the profit target selected as a planning objective. It is for this very important reason that we suggested earlier that the 'maximum long-term profit' is never a planning goal, for it falls beyond a planner's vision. Instead a firm aims to earn a 'satisfactory' profit over the planning period.

As a guide to selecting the profit target, one of the most influential factors is the minimum rate of return expected by investors and creditors. A satisfactory profit ensures that debt and dividend payments may be made thereby reducing the risks attached to investing in the firm.

If the profit target is set too low to provide a fair dividend for shareholders and sufficient retained profit to finance future expansion, the Stock Exchange's dissatisfaction with performance will be reflected in the company's share price, which in turn will impede the firm's ability to raise fresh capital and undermine its financial standing with creditors. It is, therefore, desirable that the share price should reflect a satisfactory profit target for the value of a company is represented by the market price of its shares. It is through capital gains, as these shares appreciate in value, that shareholders receive much of their return. The amount of takeover activity in recent years has drawn attention to the fact that management should be aware of the importance of the behaviour of share prices.

Another important factor in long-range profit planning arises from the need of firms to generate capital to finance expansion. Capital generated in this way represents a substantial portion of the capital required by established companies, and profit retentions for this purpose often amount to 50% of net profit.

The firm is faced, therefore, with the unavoidable problem of selecting a long-range profit target which will be satisfactory as regards the various points which we have just discussed. This is a minimum requirement, and unless an attempt is made to attain this profit objective in the long-range plan, the plan itself cannot be regarded as satisfactory.

Before we can calculate a target return on capital employed we must first estimate the returns which shareholders are likely to expect over the planning period. The following factors will affect these returns:

  (i) The rate of return which shareholders have had in recent years.

 (ii) The rate of return which they could earn elsewhere. If a better rate of return is obtainable from similar companies, there will be a pressure from management to increase the profit target.

(iii) The impact of inflation on the rate of return. The rate of return may have to be increased to compensate shareholders for the falling value of money.

 (iv) The effects of changes in Government policy with regard to taxation. For example, the introduction of capital gains tax, and the restrictions which Governments have imposed on dividends in recent years have had serious repercussions on shareholders.

  (v) The effects of changes in gearing. It may be possible to increase the return on shareholders' funds by altering the capital structure.

 (vi) The character of the firm's dividend policy. There are two methods by which the risk borne by ordinary shareholders may be rewarded. The first method emphasizes a high annual rate of dividend, and the second stresses the capital gain which accrues as a result of the increased value of the shares where a company retains and re-invests a high proportion of its profit. There are some who argue that the interests of investors and of the community would best be served by the total distribution of profit as dividends, and that individual companies should go to the market for any capital which is needed for expansion. In practice many companies attempt to strike a balance, distributing approximately half their profits as dividends and retaining an re-investing the balance in their capital expansion plans. As a result, most ordinary shareholders receive a return which is a mixture of annual dividend and capital gain.

Setting profit targets

Once having agreed the returns to shareholders, the next step is to incorporate the results of these calculations in a return on capital employed. This takes into account the amount to be retained in the business and the tax liability.

Consider the position of a firm for which it is calculated that a necessary return to shareholders of £30,000 has been calculated; whilst it is estimated that £20,000 should be retained in the business.

From the figures listed below it is apparent that an earnings figure of £100,000 is required in order to provide for these estimates.

		£
Returns to shareholders		30,000
Retained in business		20,000
Tax (50%)		50,000
	Earnings required	100,000

If the firm's total assets are forecasted at £500,000, then a return of 20% on capital employed is required, viz:

$$\frac{\text{Earnings required}}{\text{Total assets}} = \frac{£100,000}{£500,000} \times 100 = \underline{\underline{20\%}}$$

Divisional profit targets

Once the company's overall long-range profit target has been agreed, the next task is to apportion it across the separate parts of the enterprise, whether these be divisions or subsidiary companies. It is not necessary, nor indeed desirable that the overall profit target be evenly spread across the enterprise, for different growth rates and different profit targets are perfectly compatible with sound strategic planning. Thus, it is possible to select a distribution showing an expected rate of return on investments of 30% in respect of one division as against a 10% rate for another division. The reasons for a diversity among planned divisional profit targets may lie in the type of market in which the divisions operate: fast growing markets may offer higher return prospects than mature and established markets. Equally, varying rates of return may reflect the different degrees of risks attached to the different types of activities in which the several divisions may be engaged.

In the discussions leading to the formulation of the overall profit target, the various divisions will have submitted their estimates of the possible profit targets. If there should have existed a gap between the aggregated divisional profit recommendations and the overall target which top management sought to attain, it may have been necessary to revise the corporate strategy and re-examine both the company and divisional profit targets.

Financial planning

We have seen how the main objectives of the firm are expressed in financial form. Detailed financial analysis is necessary to support these financial targets. Since this type of analysis is dealt with throughout this book, this chapter is not detailed in this respect. Indeed, the purpose of this chapter is to emphasize the necessity of setting long-run objectives and of relating short-term decisions to these objectives.

In the field of long-range planning, the accountant's role is to contribute to the management team. The importance of this role should be apparent from our discussions earlier in this chapter of the way profit targets are set.

The accountant's role in this regard has been defined as embracing the following activities:

(i) Providing background information which serves as a prelude to planning. A valuable contribution which the accountant may make in this respect is the preparation of preliminary studies in the form of reviews of past performance, product-mix studies, surveys of physical facilities, and estimates of capital expenditure requirements. Moreover, he has special skills in the analyses of cost-volume profit relationships, profit margins by product lines, cash flows and so on.

(ii) Assisting in the evaluation of alternative courses of action which are being considered, and assessing the financial feasibility of the proposed course of action. This requires the accountant to decide what data is relevant, prior to its analysis and expression in financial terms, so that the data base of the long-range plan shall be reliable.

(iii) Assembling, integrating and co-ordinating detailed plans into a corporate master plan. In this respect, the accountant has a traditional skill in aggregating data which is particularly relevant.

(iv) Translating plans into overall schedules of costs, profit and financial conditions. These schedules may subsequently be used to prepare detailed operating budgets.

(v) Presenting the anticipated results of future operations in financial terms.

(vi) Assisting in the critical appraisal and, where necessary, the revision of long-range plans to ensure that they do constitute a realistic basis for directing and controlling future operations.

(vii) Establishing and administering the network of operational controls that are necessary to the attainment of the planned objectives. This vital phase of the planning process requires the integration of long and shortrun profit plans, the monitoring of current performance against that planned for the long-term and reporting to management on the realization of the long-term plan.

The long-range financial plan

Long-range financial planning is concerned with ensuring the continuing soundness of the financial structure of the firm, maintaining adequate working capital, and providing additional capital for expansion from earnings, borrowings or by the issue of new shares.

The essential components of the long-range financial plan are a projected income statement, a projected cash-flow statement, a capital expenditure forecast, a financing plan and a projection of the capital structure. We shall briefly examine each of these components of the financial plan.

(a) The projected income statement

The projected income forecast for the long-range planning period will be set out in the traditional manner, as follows:

Projected Income Statement

	Years				
	1	2	3	4	5
Sales					
Cost of Goods Sold					
Selling and Administrative Expenses					
Depreciation					
Interest Charges					
Income before Tax					
Tax					
Income after Tax					

(b) *The projected cash-flow*

The accountant will be particularly concerned with ensuring that the company remains solvent, that it has no liquidity problems and that financial resources for growth are provided. He will be required to estimate the financial needs of the long-range plan and advise on the financing arrangements which may be made to meet these needs.

An estimate of the cash-flow pattern broken down over the long-range plan will show when shortages and surpluses of cash are likely to occur, and hence will enable plans to be drawn up to arrange the firm's finances to best advantage.

Long-range cash flow

	Years				
Source	1	2	3	4	5
Net cash inflow from operations					
Other receipts					
Total cash available					
Use					
Taxation					
Dividends					
Loan repayment					
Capital expenditure					
Investments					
Total requirement					
Surplus/Shortfall					
Financed by					
New share issues					
Debentures					
Bank balances					

As may be seen from the example on the previous page, the long-range cash flow profile is a very useful tool of analysis in a number of ways. Firstly, it indicates whether or not fresh injections of cash will be necessary to finance the long-range plan, or whether future capital expenditure and the planned expansion of operations can be financed from retained income after taking into account anticipated tax liabilities and dividend payments. Secondly, the long-range cash flow will point out when deficits and surpluses will occur, and so assist in the formulation of a financial strategy over time. Thirdly, the cash-flow plan will establish the relative duration of deficits and surpluses, and this information will likewise be most useful from a financing point of view.

(c) *The capital expenditure forecast*

We devote chapter 4 to an examination of the problem of planning capital expenditure. The capital expenditure forecast will be simply the annual financial requirement to support this expenditure.

(d) *The financing plan*

The financing plan is concerned with ensuring that the necessary finance will be available to support the long-range plan. If, as a result of the planned activities for the period, a deficit is forecast and it is likely to be of short duration, it may be financed from a number of different sources, for example, by means of a bank overdraft or a temporary run-down of stocks. If, however, the deficit is likely to exist for a longer period, it may be necessary to raise new capital. The financing plan considers the manner in which a financial deficit is to be covered. This may be formulated as follows:

Financing Plan

	Years				
	1	2	3	4	5
Finance required					
Financed by:					
New Share issue					
Debenture issue					
Short-term borrowing					
Total Finance provided					

(e) *The capital structure projection*

It is clear from the foregoing that the financial plan which is devised to support the long-range plan may have important implications for the capital structure of the firm in a number of ways.

First, the company will have to form a view as to the merits or otherwise of altering the gearing of the company. As we saw in Part 2, the gearing represents the ratio of fixed interest stock as against equity capital, and the reader will recall (see page 194) that if a company is highly geared and profit fluctuates over time, the rate of return payable to Ordinary shareholders will fluctuate to a proportionately greater extent with consequential effects on the value of the Ordinary shares on the market.

Secondly, the management of working capital will be a critical success factor, particularly should the economic climate change during the period, with adverse effects on liquidity and credit facilities. Working capital is defined as the excess of current assets over current liabilities, and is regarded as being available for supporting current operations as distinct from the financing of capital expenditure.

Thirdly, a decision to finance capital expenditure by means of new share or debenture issues will also affect share prices unless dividend rates can be maintained through increased profits. The outcome, in any event, will largely depend upon management's previous record and the firm's standing in the market. The capital structure projection may be formulated as follows:

Year-end Capital Structure Projection

	Years				
	1	2	3	4	5
Shareholders' equity					
Long-term debt					
Total capital					
Debt ratio					

Long-range profit planning and other long-range objectives

In this chapter, we have discussed long-range planning almost exclusively in terms of long-range profit planning and its financial implications. This is because it is one of the most important company objectives, and one of special interest to accountants. It should not be forgotten, however, that long-range planning requires that careful attention should similarly be given to the attainment of other objectives of great importance to the company, for example, those relating to employees, consumers and the local community. Unless a firm gives attention to developing realistic objectives in these other areas the firm will find its ability to make profits very restricted. These other objectives form the basis of Part 5.

It is evident from the nature of the accountant's skills, and the range of activities in which he may be involved, that he has a central role to play in long-range planning. The result of his involvement in long-range planning is to bring him into contact with functions beyond his direct control such as marketing, research and development and production to a much greater extent than is possible in short-term planning.

Summary

The purpose of this chapter has been to emphasize the necessity of setting long-run objectives and of relating short-term decisions to these objectives. Long-range planning has received increasing attention in recent years due to rapidly changing business conditions, which have persuaded management to take a longer view of the firm's activities than has hitherto been thought necessary. It is becoming widely recognized that effective long-range planning should result in a firm being always in the best position with products, resources and processes deployed in such a way as to take advantage of all the opportunities which present themselves. Long-range planning is seen as providing a systematic way of running a company so that not only can it anticipate change, but may actually profit from change. The absence of long-range planning may be detrimental to a firm in a number of ways: for example, current profitability may induce so much complacency that danger signals may be ignored, and in due course, valuable opportunities may not be seized. Equally, an excessive concern with short-term planning may encourage actions in the short-term which are detrimental to the long-term interests of the firm.

A long-range plan may be damaging, however, if it is badly implemented. Thus, a rigid long-range plan may turn out to be inappropriate for new circumstances. It is necessary, therefore, that long-range planning should have a degree of flexibility, so as to allow for adjustments to changing circumstances. Long-range planning should include a continuous scanning process aimed at discovering opportunities defining contraints and assessing risks.

The accountant has an important role to play in long-range planning, particularly in long-range financial planning.

References

1. Ansoff, H. I., Towards a Strategic Theory of the Firm, reprinted in *Business Strategy*, pp. 21, 22 Ansoff, H. I. (ed.), Penguin Books, London, 1969.

2. Drucker, P. F., *The Practice of Management*, p. 52 Heinemann, London, 1963.

3. N. A. A. Research Report No, 42; Long-Range Profit Planning, National Association of Accountants, 1964.

4. Perrin, R., Long-range planning; the concept and the need, *Long-Range Planning*, September, 1968.

Further readings

Ansoff, H. I., *Corporate Strategy*, Penguin Books, London, 1968.

Aguila, F. J., *Scanning the Business Environment*, Macmillan, New York, 1967.

Denning, Basil W., (ed.), *Corporate Planning, Selected Concepts*, McGraw-Hill, London, 1971.

Ewing, David W., (ed.), *Long-Range Planning for Management*, Harper and Row, New York, 1972.

Sadler, Philip & Robson, Alan, (eds), *Corporate Planning and the Role of the Management Accountant*, I.C.M.A. and the Society for Long-Range Planning, 1973.

Scott, Brian W., *Long-Range Planning in American Industry*, American Management Association, 1965.

Steiner, G. A., (ed.), *Managerial Long-Range Planning*, McGraw-Hill, New York, 1963.

Steiner & Cannon, W. M., *Multinational Corporate Planning*, Macmillan, New York, 1966.

4
Planning Capital Expenditure

The level of a firm's profits depends upon the success with which it is able to employ all its assets—human and non-human. The firm's future profitability depends on two factors, firstly, maintaining and enlarging its asset structure, and secondly, devising a successful strategy for that asset structure. The previous chapter drew attention to the fact that preparing the capital expenditure plan is part of the long-range planning process. The activity of investing in new assets, often termed *capital budgeting*, involves planning capital expenditure and arranging the financing of this expenditure. It is an area of management decision-making which has attracted a great deal of interest among accountants and economists in recent years, and much research has been devoted towards evolving methods for improving the quality of these decisions.

In this chapter, we can only hope to touch upon the main issues. We shall deal mainly with capital expenditure decisions, and we shall examine the relevant factors and the methods which are currently employed for making capital investment decisions. Financing capital expenditure, which is the other aspect of capital budgeting, belongs to a sophisticated area of study known as the Theory of Finance. We shall make only brief reference to this aspect of capital budgeting, and must refer the reader to the literature of the Theory of Finance for a proper treatment of this subject.

Capital investment decisions

Probably the most significant factors affecting the level of profitability in a business is the quality of managerial decisions affecting the commitment of the firm's resources to new investments within the firm. The reasons which render such strategic decisions so important may be listed as follows:

(a) they involve the commitment of substantial sums of money;
(b) this commitment is made for a long period of time, and the element of uncertainty is therefore much greater than in the case of decisions whose effects are limited to a short period of time;

(c) once made, capital investment decisions are almost impossible to reverse should they appear subsequently to have been wrongly made;

(d) occasionally, the success or the failure of a firm may depend upon a single decision. In all cases, the future profitability of the firm will be affected by the decision;

(e) not only is capital expenditure policy of major importance to a firm, but it is of great significance to an industry as well as to the national economy.

Types of capital investment decisions

A capital investment may be defined as an investment which yields returns during several future time periods, and may be contrasted with other types of investments which yield all their return in the current time period. Capital investment decisions may concern the following:

(a) the acquisition or replacement of long-lived assets, such as buildings and plant;

(b) the investment of funds into another firm from which revenues will flow;

(c) a special project which will affect the firm's future earning capacity, such as a research project or an advertising campaign;

(d) the extension of the range of activities of the firm involving a capital outlay, such as a new production line or indeed a new product.

Most of these decisions concern a firm's non-human capital, but as we shall see in Part 5, businessmen are now realizing that a firm's human capital is as important as its non-human capital and this new view is encouraging the development of human asset accounting as a means of assisting management in deciding how best to invest in and use human resources.

Capital investment decisions encompass two aspects of long-range profitability: first, estimating the future net increases in cash inflows or net savings in cash outlays which will result from the investment; and second, calculating the total cash outlays required to effect the investment.

The analysis of capital investment proposals

In the analysis of capital investment proposals, many of the important facts are uncertain, so that the first problem is to reduce the area of uncertainty before a decision is made. As we shall see in chapter 6, risk analysis offers methods for handling the problem of uncertainty. The second problem is to ensure that all known facts are correctly assessed and quantified. Both known and uncertain facts are estimated in cash terms, and the methods of capital investment appraisal focus on cash flows.

The selection of investment projects is always a question of considering which of several competing alternatives is the best from the firm's point of view. By quantifying the cash inflows and the cash outlays which are involved in the various alternatives, a decision may be made by selecting that alternative which is preferred by the firm.

Example

Wall Street Finance Ltd is offered the opportunity of selecting two investments each of which will yield £500,000 yearly. Investment A requires a total cash outlay of £5,000,000—hence it promises a rate of return of 10%. Investment B requires a total cash outlay of £50,000,000—and therefore offers a rate of return of 1% per annum. The firm would prefer investment A. However, if the firm has a minimum acceptable rate of return of 15%, neither project would be acceptable.

We may conclude, therefore, that there are three major factors affecting capital investment decisions:

(a) The net amount of the investment required, expressed as the total cash outlay needed to support the project during its entire life.

(b) The net returns on the investment, expressed as the future expected net cash inflows. These may be actual cash flows, or cash savings.

(c) The rate of return on investment, expressed as a percentage. The determination of the lowest acceptable rate of return on investment will be influenced by a number of factors, among which are the firm's rate of return on its other investment opportunities and the cost of capital to the firm.

The relevant cash flows

Before we proceed to examining the methods of selecting investment projects, let us briefly define the meaning of the terms which we shall be employing.

(a) *Net investment outlays*

These consist of initial investment outlays required to established the project, and the subsequent investment outlays which are envisaged at the outset, and are distinguishable from operating cash outlays. Thus, initial investment outlays may comprise expenditure on equipment, installation costs, manpower training, working capital etc. Subsequent investment outlays may include 'second stage' developments, plant extensions etc. The analysis of capital project is in terms of net cash costs to the firm, so that where tax credits are allowable, these credits must be deducted from the total cash costs to obtain the relevant cash outlay.

(b) *Net cash inflows*

These are the operating cash flows associated with the investment over the period of its useful life. They are calculated after deducting operating cash expenditure and taxation. Since there may be year to year variation in the profile of these net cash flows, and since their periodic pattern is largely guesswork, they are the most difficult cash flows to quantify.

All cash flow calculations are made on the basis of the estimated useful life of the investment, which is defined as the time interval that is expected to elapse between the time of acquisition or commencement and the time at which the combined forces of obsolescence and deterioration will justify the retirement of the asset or project. The useful life of the investment may be shortened by market changes which will diminish its earnings.

Methods of appraising capital investments

The more commonly used methods of evaluating capital investment proposals are:

(a) the pay-back period;
(b) the accounting rate of return;
(c) the discounted cash flow techniques, of which there are two main forms:
  (i) the net present value method (NPV)
  (ii) the internal rate of return (IRR).

The pay-back period

This method attempts to forecast how long it will take for the expected net cash inflows to *pay back* the net investment outlays. The pay-back period is calculated as follows:

$$\text{Pay-back period (years)} = \frac{\text{Net investment outlays}}{\text{Average net cash inflows}}$$

Example

Northend Engineering Co. Ltd, is considering the acquisition of machinery which will considerably reduce labour costs. The following are the relevant facts:

Net investment outlays	£200,000
Estimated annual cash savings (after tax)	60,000
Estimated useful life	5 years
Salvage value	Nil

The pay-back period is as follows:

$$\frac{£200,000}{60,000} \text{ i.e. } 3\tfrac{1}{3} \text{ years}$$

The pay-back method has the advantage of simplicity. By advocating the selection of projects by reference only to the speed with which investment outlays are recovered, it recommends the acceptance of only the safest projects. It is a method which emphasizes liquidity rather than profitability, and its limitations may be stated to be:

(a) It lays stress on the pay-back period rather than the useful life of the investment, and ignores the cash flows beyond the pay-back period. Hence, it focusses on breakeven rather than on profitability.

(b) It ignores the time profile of the net cash inflows, and any time pattern in the net investment outlays. Any salvage value would also be ignored. This method, therefore, treats all cash flows through time as having the same value, so that in the example given, the value of £200,000 invested now is equated with £200,000 of net cash inflows over $3\tfrac{1}{3}$ years.

These problems may be illustrated as follows.

Example

Multiplexed Ltd is considering four different investment projects each costing £20,000. The undermentioned information relates to these projects.

Project No.	1	2	3	4
	£	£	£	£
Initial Investment Outlay	20,000	20,000	20,000	20,000
Cash Inflows				
Year 1	9000	11,000	3000	10,000
Year 2	11,000	9000	6000	6000
Year 3	—	—	8000	4000
Year 4	—	—	10,000	4000
Year 5	—	—	10,000	3000
Pay-back period (years)	2	2	$3\frac{1}{3}$	3

A crude application of the pay-back method would select projects 1 or 2 but would be unable to decide between these two projects.

The accounting rate of return

The accounting rate of return method seeks to express the average estimated yearly net inflows as a percentage of the net investment outlays. As, however, it is possible to recover depreciation from the yearly net inflows, the formula is expressed as follows:

$$R = \frac{C - D}{I}$$

where R = the accounting rate of return
C = average yearly net inflows
D = depreciation
I = net investment outlays

Substituting the figures given in our example on p. 328, the accounting rate of return would be calculated as follows:

$$R = \frac{£60,000 - £40,000}{£200,000} \times 100\%$$

$$= 10\%$$

It may be argued, however, that the recovery of depreciation over the useful life of the investment reduces the value of the net investment outlays through time. Assuming an average recovery through depreciation at the rate of £40,000 per year, the average net investment over the estimated useful life of 5 years is £100,000, calculated by using the arithmetic mean method as follows:

$$\text{Average lifetime investment} = \frac{£200,000}{2}$$

$$= £100,000$$

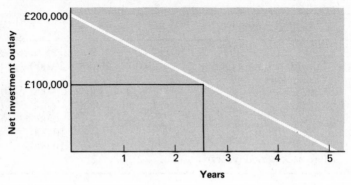

Fig. 3.9

The average lifetime investment may be calculated graphically in Fig. 3.9.

In the light of this argument, the accounting rate of return on investment should express the annual net cash inflows as a percentage of the average annual net investment outlays, so that, substituting the values given in our example, the average return on investment is:

$$R = \frac{£60,000 - £40,000}{£100,000} \times 100\%$$

$$= 20\%$$

This method of evaluating investment projects overcomes the disadvantage of the pay-back method in that it attempts to calculate the profitability of the various projects under study. Its main disadvantage is that it fails to consider the changing value of money through time, and treats the value of £1 in the future as equal to £1 invested today. Moreover, it ignores also the differences which may occur through time in the rate of net cash inflows. In both these senses, it suffers from the same defects as the pay-back method.

Discounted cash flows
The methods of investment appraisal which we have just examined are generally regarded as producing misleading results. Discounted cash flow has gained widespread acceptance for it recognizes that the value of money is subject to a time-preference, that is, that £1 today is preferred to £1 in the future unless the delay in receiving £1 in the future is compensated by an interest factor. This interest factor is expressed as a discount rate.

In simple terms, the DCF method attempts to evaluate an investment proposal by comparing the net cash flows accruing over the life of the investment at their present-day value with the value of funds presently to be invested. Thus, by comparing like with like it is possible to calculate the rate of return on the investment in a realistic manner.

To find the present equivalent value of £1 receivable one year hence, one applies the rate of interest to discount that £1 to its present day value. This is the same thing as asking "what sum of money invested today at the rate of interest would increase in value to £1 a year hence?".

Example

Given that the rate of interest is 10% per annum the following calculations may be made:

£1 invested now at 10% will amount to £1.10 in a year. Conversely, the value of £1.10 a year's hence is worth £1 now if the rate of interest is 10%.

Using this principle, discount tables may be constructed for the value of £1 over several time periods ahead by compounding the interest rate through time, i.e., £1.00 invested for 1 year at 10% will be worth £1.10 at the year end, £1.10 then reinvested for another year at 10% will be worth £1.10 + 0.11 = £1.21 at the end of the second year.

Example

The value of £1 at the end of 1 year at 10% is £1 + .10 = £1.1

£1	2 years	$(£1.1)^2 = £1.21$
£1	3	$(£1.1)^3 = £1.331$
£1	4	$(£1.1)^4 = £1.464$
£1	5	$(£1.1)^5 = £1.611$

Conversely, the present value of £1 receivable at a future date is:

£1 receivable in 1 years' time is $\dfrac{£1}{1.1} = £0.9091$

£1	2	$\dfrac{£1}{1.21} = £0.8264$
£1	3	$\dfrac{£1}{1.331} = £0.7513$
£1	4	$\dfrac{£1}{1.464} = £0.6831$
£1	5	$\dfrac{£1}{1.611} = £0.6208$

The value of money is, therefore, directly affected by time and the rate of interest is the method which is used to express the time value of money. Compound interest tables and discount tables are available which show the value of money at different interest rates over a number of years, so that in actual practice, it is a simple matter to apply the DCF method to the evaluation of an investment.

(i) *The net present value*

This method is based on an assumed minimum rate of return. Ideally, this rate should be the average cost of capital to the firm (see p. 336) and it is this rate which would be used to discount the net cash inflows to their present value. The net investment outlays are subtracted from the present value of the net cash inflows leaving a residual figure, which is the net present value. A decision is made in favour of a project if the NPV is zero or a positive amount. This method may likewise be applied to the comparison of one project with another when considering mutually exclusive investments.

The rule may be stated as follows:

Accept the project if:

$$\frac{a_1}{(1+i)^1}+\frac{a_2}{(1+i)^2}+\cdots+\frac{a_n}{(1+i)^n}\geq A$$

where A is the initial project cost
a are the net annual cash inflows

Example

Corween Ltd is considering a project which has a life of 5 years and which will produce an annual inflow of £1000. The investment outlay is £3000 and the required rate of return is 10%.

Year	Inflow	Discount Factor (at 10%)	Present Value of Inflow
1	£1000	0.9091	£909.1
2	£1000	0.8264	£826.4
3	£1000	0.7513	£751.3
4	£1000	0.6831	£683.1
5	£1000	0.6208	£620.8
Present value of net inflows			£3790.7
Cost of investment outlay			£3000.0
Net present value of the project			£790.7

Since the net present value of the cash inflows (a) is greater than the present value of the cash outlay (A), the project should be accepted.

(ii) *The internal rate of return*

This method requires us to calculate that rate of interest which used in discounting will reduce the net present value of a project to zero. This enables us to compare the Internal Rate of Return (IRR) with the required rate.

The rule may be stated as follows:

Accept the project if:

$$A = \frac{a_1}{(1+r)} + \frac{a_2}{(1+r)^2} + \cdots + \frac{a_n}{(1+r)^n}$$

and $r > i$

where A is the initial project cost

a are the net annual cash inflows

r is the solution discount rate

i is the required rate of return

Example

Let us return to the example given above and assume that Corween Ltd applies the Internal Rate of Return analysis to the project under consideration. The analysis would be as follows.

Year	Inflow	Discount Factor at 19%	Present Value at 19%	Discount Factor at 20%	Present Value at 20%
	£		£		£
1	1000	0.8403	840.3	0.8333	833.3
2	1000	0.7062	706.2	0.6944	694.4
3	1000	0.5934	593.4	0.5787	578.7
4	1000	0.4987	498.7	0.4823	482.3
5	1000	0.4190	419.0	0.4019	401.9
Present value of net inflow			3057.6		2990.6
Cost of investment outlay			3000.0		3000.0
Net present value of the project			+57.6		−9.4

We can see that the IRR is almost 20%. (It is often possible to approximate the true rate more closely by assuming a linear relationship and interpolating between the two nearest points.) The ascertainment of the IRR at 20% enables us to compare the IRR with the required rate of return on investment by the company.

Net present value and internal rate of return compared

When dealing with simple investment appraisal projects, that is, those involving a once and for all investment outlay followed by a stream of cash inflows, both the NPV and the IRR methods produce the same YES or NO decisions.

But the advantage of the NPV method is the simplicity with which the results are stated. Our example shows that with the NPV method, the expected results are expressed in terms of £s which directly reflect the increased wealth position. The Internal Rate of Return, on the other hand, produces a result which is shown as a percentage, and this result has to be compared with a minimum required rate of return before a decision may be made.

Example

Norwell Industries Ltd is studying two projects, each of which requires a net investment outlay of £3000. Both have a useful life of 5 years, and the estimated profile of the net cash inflows are:

End of Year	Project A £	Project B £
1	500	2000
2	1000	1500
3	1500	1500
4	2000	1000
5	2000	500
	£7000	£6500

The desired minimum rate of return is 10%.

Analysis—Net present value

The present value of the two projects may be calculated by using the desired minimum rate of return as a discount factor.

End of Year	Discount Factor 10%	Project A £	Present Value £	Project B £	Present Value £
1	0.9091	500	454.6	2000	1818.2
2	0.8264	1000	826.4	1500	1239.6
3	0.7153	1500	1073.0	1500	1073.0
4	0.6831	2000	1366.2	1000	683.1
5	0.6208	2000	1241.6	500	310.4
Present value of total cash inflows			£4961.8		£5124.3
Less: net investment outlay			£3000.0		£3000.0
Net present value			£1961.8		£2124.3

Both projects are acceptable to the firm, and if a choice has to be made between them, Project B would be selected since it produces the highest net present value of the two. The time profile of the net cash inflows is seen to be a deterministic influence on the result, for although the total cash inflows before discounting are higher with Project A, the cash flows associated with Project B are concentrated in the earlier years and, when discounted, have a higher net present value than A's.

Analysis—The internal rate of return

Taking the net cash inflows estimated for Project A, the rate which will discount the net cash inflows to £3000 is found once again by trial and error. Using discount tables, we establish in this way that the discount rate is between 28% and 29%, as follows:

Cash Inflows	Discount Factor at 29%	Present Value at 29%	Discount Factor at 28%	Present Value at 28%
£		£		£
500	0.7752	387.7	0.7813	390.7
1000	0.6009	600.9	0.6104	610.4
1500	0.4658	698.7	0.4768	715.2
2000	0.3611	722.2	0.3725	745.0
2000	0.2799	559.8	0.2910	582.0
		£2969.2		£3043.3
Original investment outlay		£3000.0		£3000.0
		−30.8		+43.3

Using the same approach, the IRR from Project B may be calculated as 39%.

The crucial test upon which the final acceptance of a project depends is whether or not the IRR compares favourably with the required rate of return. If the required rate of return is 20% both projects qualify.

One of the problems of comparing rates of return on projects is that direct comparisons between two percentages are meaningless unless referred to the initial outlays, so that their true dimensions may be perceived. This problem should never be lost sight of when using IRR percentages.

With more complicated investment problems, for example those which require that cash surpluses be set aside to meet an obligation arising at the end of the project's life, both methods assume that those cash surpluses are re-invested at the appropriate rate of return. Thus, where a loan has been raised to finance the project*, the IRR method envisages that the cash surpluses will be re-invested at the IRR discounting rate, whereas the NPV method envisages that they will be re-invested at the minimum acceptable rate of return used in that method. Thus, the advantage of the NPV method is that it makes more realistic assumptions about re-investment opportunities.

More complex problems arise when applying the IRR method to investment projects which do not have the simple pattern of cash flows of the above examples, but we regard these problems as beyond the scope of this text.

Taxation and other factors

In order that DCF calculations should lead to correct results, it is important that all factors affecting the calculations of cash flows should be taken into account. The most important of these factors is, of course, taxation. Indeed, we have assumed from the outset that the cash flow figures were net after tax. Apart from the direct effects of taxation, we should also adjust our figures for indirect aspects of taxation, such as investment grants, and the reader will recall that in calculating the net investment outlay, any recoveries in the form of investment incentives must be deducted from the amount brought into the DCF calculation. It is important to note that taxation is not neutral as between projects.

The cost of capital

The evaluation of an investment project by DCF analysis requires a firm to calculate its cost of capital. This is true in selecting the discount rate for appraisal by means of the Net Present Value method, or for establishing the acceptability of the internal rate of return.

A full discussion of the concept of the 'cost of capital' is beyond the scope of this book; indeed, the subject is perhaps the most difficult and controversial topic in the Theory of Finance. Our discussion will be a very elementary one so as to provide the reader with some understanding of investment planning.

The first problem in discussing the cost of capital lies in different meanings which the term has acquired. From a lender's point of view, the cost of capital represents the cost to him of lending money which may be equated to the return which he could have obtained by

---

* The simplifying assumption which we are making for the purpose of illustrating the point is that the firm's finances are linked to specific investment projects, which in reality is not perhaps the case.

investing in a similar project having similar risks. This concept of the cost of capital is founded on its 'opportunity cost'. The 'opportunity cost' approach to the assessment of the cost of capital is one which a firm must always consider when considering an investment project. A firm may find, for example, that investing funds outside the firm may produce higher returns than an internal project. The main obstacle to a more widespread use of the opportunity cost concept is that of identifying investment of equal risks and hence measuring the opportunity cost.

Another concept in use is the actual cost incurred by a firm in borrowing money. A firm may obtain funds in a variety of ways: and each way has a different cost attached to it. Thus, a firm may issue shares and will pay a dividend on those shares, which must represent the cost of raising funds in that way. It may also borrow money, either by the issue of debentures or bank and other methods of borrowing, and in these cases interest is payable. The fact that the firm may have raised its finance in several different ways makes it more realistic to use the 'average cost of capital' which is based on an analysis of its capital structure.

Example

The Keystone Corp. Ltd, has a capital structure distributed as to 80% Share capital and 20% Loan capital. The dividend rate is 10% and the interest payable on the Loan capital is 8%. Calculate the average cost of capital.

Source of Funds	Proportion of Total Funds %	Cost of Capital %	Product
Share Capital	80	10	800
Loan Capital	20	8	160
	100		960

The weighted average cost of capital is: $\dfrac{960}{100} = 9.6\%$

The average cost of capital so calculated would in the case of this firm represent the minimum acceptable rate of return.

Gearing and the cost of capital

It will be recalled from Part 2 that the distribution of a firm's capital structure as between share capital (equity capital) and fixed interest stock (Preference shares and debentures) is known as the gearing. A firm which is highly geared has a higher ratio of fixed interest stock to equity capital. By changing its gearing, a firm may alter its average cost of capital.

Example

The firm in the above-mentioned example increases its gearing by raising the proportion of loan capital to share capital from 20% to 40%. Its average cost of capital, as a result, is reduced to 9.2%:

Source of Funds	Proportion of Total Funds %	Cost of Capital %	Product
Share capital	60	10	600
Loan capital	40	8	320
	100		920

The average cost of capital is: $\dfrac{920}{100} = 9.2\%$

It should be noted that financial theorists have argued that it is due only to the influence of a corporation tax system which allows loan interest as a tax deductible expense that gearing is of any significance.

Financial planning requires a firm to give very serious consideration to its capital structure and to its gearing. Very complex issues are involved in planning an appropriate capital structure. Circumstances may make it advantageous to attempt to increase the proportion of loan capital, that is, increase the gearing, such as the tax deductibility of loan interest which we have already mentioned. There is an upper limit to debt finance, however, for not only are there obvious dangers in the presence of large fixed interest charges against corporate income, but there are practical limits to the amount of funds which may be borrowed for long-term purposes.

Summary

Preparing the capital expenditure plan is part of the long-range planning process. The quality of managerial decisions committing the firm's resources to new investments is probably the most significant factor affecting the level of future profitability.

Capital investment decisions encompass two aspects of the long-range profit plan—first, estimating the future net increases in cash inflows or net savings in cash outlays which will result from an investment; second, calculating the total cash outlays required to carry out an investment.

There are three well-known techniques for appraising investment proposals from a financial viewpoint:

  (a) the pay-back method, which emphasizes the length of time required to recoup the investment outlay;

  (b) the accounting rate of return, which seeks to express the average estimated yearly net inflows as a percentage of the net investment outlays for the purpose of assessing the profitability of a proposed investment;

  (c) discounted cash flow methods, which attempt to evaluate an investment proposal by comparing the present value of the net cash inflows accruing over the life of the investment with the present value of the funds to be invested.

Discounted cash flow techniques provide the most useful procedures for evaluating capital investment proposals. They comprise two methods—the Net Present Value and the Internal Rate of Return. Both methods take into account the time value of money, unlike the other methods mentioned which ignore this factor.

In many situations it is difficult to forecast the time profile of future cash flows with any degree of certainty. The next chapter considers risk analysis as a means of handling the problem of uncertainty.

Further readings

1. Bierman, Harold J. & Smidt, Seymour, *The Capital Budgeting Decision*, 2nd edn, Macmillan, New York, 1966.

2. Merrett, A. & Sykes, A., *The Finance and Analysis of Capital Projects*, Longmans, London, 1973.

3. Quirin, G. D., *The Capital Expenditure Decision*, Richard D. Irwin, Homewood, Illinois, 1967.

4. Robicheck, Alexander A. & Myers, S. C., *Optimal Financing Decisions*, Prentice Hall, Englewood Cliffs, N.J., 1965.

5. Van Horne, J. C., *Financial Management and Policy*, Prentice Hall, Englewood Cliffs, N.J., 1975.

6. Weston, J. F. & Brigham, Eugene F., *Managerial Finance*, Holt Dryden, New York, 1975.

5
Budgetary Planning

The process of budgeting focuses on the short-term, normally one year, and provides an expression of the steps which management must take in the current period if it is to fulfil organizational objectives. As we explained in chapter 1, it is useful to distinguish between the two functions—planning and control. Applying a similar distinction to budgeting, we may examine in turn the functions of budgetary planning and budgetary control. This chapter deals with the planning aspect of budgeting. The control aspects are dealt with later in Section 3 of this Part.

The nature of budgetary planning

In chapter 2 we found that long-range planning involved the determination of corporate objectives and the determination of a suitable plan for attaining these objectives. The budget represents the expression of this plan in financial terms in the light of current conditions. Therefore, the long-range plan is the guide for preparing the annual budgets and defines actions that need to be taken now in order to move towards long-term objectives. Indeed, the budget represents the first one year span of the long-range budget.

The reader will recall that one important feature of planning is the co-ordination of the various activities of an enterprise, and of its departments, so that they are harmonized in the overall task of realizing corporate objectives. For example if the marketing function were to increase sales massively over a short period of time, the manufacturing function would have to increase output substantially—probably through the use of costly overtime labour, or by buying goods from an outside supplier at high prices. Conversely, excessive production may force the marketing function to sell at unrealistically low prices in order to avoid excessive investment in stock. The function of budgetary planning is to co-ordinate the various activities of an organization in order to achieve company rather than divisional or departmental objectives. Therefore it is necessary to establish objectives for each section of the organization which are in harmony with the organization as a whole.

Budgetary control

Planning alone does not necessarily affect the realization of plans. It is also necessary to have control. This process necessitates the establishment of standards of performance which will act as day-to-day guidelines for the successful realization of the budget plan. In effect, the annual budget is subdivided into shorter periods for control purposes—into months and weeks. For these periods, the budget is compared with actual, the reasons for deviations are established, and corrective action is taken if necessary.

As with budgetary planning, budgetary control is geared to the long-range plan. The continuous review of current progress indicates the extent to which the organization is moving towards the long-range plan.

The need for flexibility

Because business conditions are always changing, it is necessary to view the budgeting process as a guide to future action, rather than a rigid plan which must be followed irrespective of changing circumstances. The latter approach may place the manager in a straitjacket in which he is forced to take decisions which are not in accordance with company objectives. For example, a departmental manager may find, due to changing conditions, that he has not spent all of his budget on a particular item. In order to spend all his budget allowance, so as to prevent the possibility of a cut in his allowance next year, he may squander funds which could have been put to better use in other sections of the organization.

Some firms relate their planning budgets to changing conditions by means of a rolling budget which is prepared every quarter, but for one year ahead. At the end of each quarter the plans for the next three quarters are revised, if this is necessary, and a fourth quarter is added. By this process the budgets are kept continually up to date.

Flexibility is also required if budgetary control is to be effective Indeed the type of budget which may be suitable for planning may be inappropriate for control purposes. Therefore, budgets should be established for control purposes which reflect operating conditions which may be different from those envisaged in the planning stages. This is essential if individual managers are to be held responsible only for those deviations over which they have control. Such a requirement is called for by the use of a responsibility accounting system.

Responsibility accounting

If a plan is to be fulfilled, the responsibility for doing so must be assigned to the people responsible, i.e., the managers and foremen of the organization. As we pointed out in chapter 1, the responsibilities for decision-making must be distributed throughout all but the smallest firms. Those who are going to make the decisions will be more highly motivated if they have taken part in the planning stage. Hence, each manager must feel that the budget for his section is relevant, realistic and not imposed upon him by some higher authority.

In planning activities leading towards his section's budget, each manager is concerned only with those items which he and his subordinates can influence. The key to this statement is in the concept of controllability. There is little sense in assigning, planning and operating responsibility to an individual if he cannot take the management action necessary to develop or achieve the plan. This aspect of budgeting will be developed in chapter 11.

The organization of budgeting

The budgeting process itself requires careful organization. In large firms, this process is often in the hands of a Budget Committee which acts through the Budget Officer whose function it is to co-ordinate and control the budgeting process for the whole organization. Departmental budget estimates are requested from divisional managers, who in their turn collate this information from estimates submitted to them by their own departmental managers. Hence, budget estimates are based on information which flows upwards through the organization to the Budget Committee. The Budget Committee is responsible for co-ordinating this information, and resolving any differences in consultations with the managers involved. The final budget proposal is presented to the Board of Directors, for its final approval.

Steps in budgeting

The first stage of a budgeting exercise is the determination of the 'key' factors or constraints which impose overall limits to the budget plan. Among these factors are the productive capacity of the plant, the finances available to the firm, and, of course, the market conditions which impose a total limit on the output which the firm is able to sell.

Normally from a management point of view, the critical question is "what is the firm able to sell in the budget period?", and this question summarizes all the limits to the budget plan. It is for this reason that the sales budget is at once the starting point and the fulcrum of the budgeting process.

Figure 3.10 illustrates how the various resources and activities of an enterprise are co-ordinated.

The arrows indicate the flow of relevant information. Once the level of sales is established, selling and distribution costs may be ascertained.

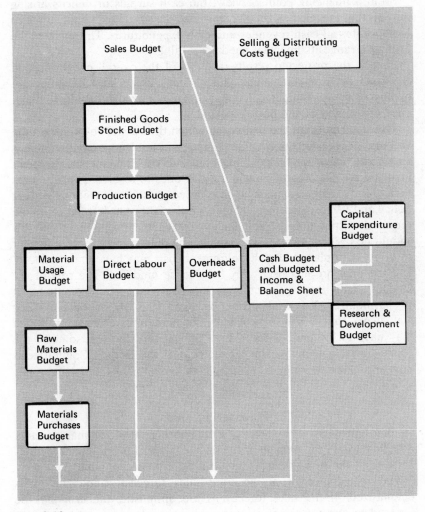

Fig. 3.10

The production budget itself is determined by the sales forecast, the desired level of inventory of finished goods and plant capacity. From the production budget may be estimated the production costs, and the cost schedules for materials, labour and overheads.

In addition, the budgeting process for capital expenditure reflects decisions taken in developing the long-range plan. The capital expenditure budget is concerned with expenditure during the budget period on the maintenance and improvement of the existing productive capacity. Associated with this budget are research and development costs for improving methods of production and product improvement as well.

From a financing point of view, the cash surplus or deficits arising out of the overall budget are revealed by the Cash budget which incorporates all cash revenues and cash expenditures. This enables the firm to arrange its financial needs accordingly.

Finally, the projected results in terms of the overall net profit, and the changes in the structure of the firm's assets and liabilities are expressed in the Budgeted Income Statement and the Budgeted Balance at the end of the budget period.

This description of the manner in which the budget co-ordinates the various activities of the firm is a simplified one. Budgetary planning is an activity which is of critical importance to the firm, and the problems involved are often complex and difficult ones to resolve. A firm's sales policy, for example, cannot be considered in isolation from its pricing policy and its cost structure. The firm's planned costs in relation to the required output may be too high to reach the profit target. If this should be the case, pricing and advertising policies may require further scrutiny, both planned and development costs may have to be reduced, and the final product itself may have to be modified. The role of the Budget Committee is, therefore, a very important one: not only has it to harmonize all the divisional budgets into an overall planning framework, but it has to deal with the numerous adjustments which may have to be made if the overall budget fails to meet some of the firm's stated objectives. Hence, the role of the Budget Committee is not only important in a practical sense: it affects important and sensitive areas of policy-making and management.

Forecasting sales

A major problem in budgeting is forecasting sales, for many factors affecting sales are outside the firm's control, for example, the behaviour of the firm's competitors and the future economic climate.

The importance of an accurate sales forecast cannot be over-emphasized. If the sales forecast is too optimistic, the firm may be induced to expand its capital expenditure programme and incur costs which may not be recoverable at a later date. In the meantime, the production target may be set too high, resulting in the pile-up of inventory of finished goods, which in itself has important financial consequences. Moreover, an optimistic sales forecast may disguise a deteriorating sales position, so that the necessary economies are not made which would produce a satisfactory profit. If, on the other hand, the sales forecast is pessimistic, the firm will miss the opportunity of larger current profit and may be misled as to its future prospects. The firm may, as a result, not undertake the necessary capital expenditure which would place it in a good position to exploit the market.

The sales forecast is the initial step in preparing the sales budget. It consists not only of analysing the market for the firm's products, but includes forecasting the levels of sales at different prices. Hence, the study of the firm's pricing policy is an integral aspect of sales forecasting. Once the sales forecast is completed, the sales budget may be derived from the target sales established both as regards price and sales volume.

There are various methods of forecasting sales, for example:

(a) The sales force composite method. This method places responsibility upon individual salesmen for developing their own sales forecast. The advantage of this method is that if participative budgeting is to be encouraged, the sales staff should assist in the preparation of the sales forecast.

(b) The analysis of market and industry factors. This method recognizes the importance of factors not within the knowledge of the sales force, such as forecasts of the gross national product, personal incomes, employment and price levels etc. The salesmen's estimates are modified by the information so obtained.

(c) Statistical analysis of fluctuations through time. Sales are generally affected by four basic factors: growth trends, business cycle fluctuations, seasonal fluctuations and irregular variations in demand. A time series analysis of sales is a statistical method of separating and analysing the historical evidence of the behaviour of sales to identify these several effects and their impact on sales. The results of this analysis are applied to the sales forecast, and are means of testing the quality of the forecast.

(d) Mathematical techniques for sales forecasting. Of recent years, mathematical techniques have been applied to the study of the relationship between economic trends and a firm's sales pattern through time, to arrive at a projection of future sales.

These techniques usually involve the use of computers. One such technique is known as exponential smoothing, which is really a prediction of future sales based on current and historical sales data, weighted so as to give a greater importance to the latest incoming information.

An illustration of the budgeting process

Once the sales forecast is known, a firm may begin to prepare the budget. We believe that the reader will obtain a better understanding of budgeting if we work through a simple example.

The Edco Manufacturing Co., Ltd.,
Forecast results for the year ending 31st December, 19X0
Income Statement

	£	£	£
Sales		135,000	
Cost of goods sold		80,000	
Gross margin		55,000	
Selling and Administrative expenses		25,000	
Income before tax		30,000	
Tax at 40%		12,000	
Income after tax		18,000	

Balance Sheet

	£	£	£
Shareholders' equity			
Ordinary share capital		210,000	
Retained earnings		26,000	
			236,000
Represented by			
Fixed Assets			
Plant and Machinery		250,000	
Less: accumulated depreciation		30,000	220,000
Current Assets			
Inventories			
Finished goods		6025	
Raw materials		1650	
		7675	
Debtors		20,000	
Cash		5325	
		33,000	
Less: Current Liabilities			
Sundry creditors	5000		
Tax	12,000	17,000	
Net working capital			16,000
			236,000

Example

The Edco Manufacturing Company manufactures two products, A and B.

A formal planning system had been introduced some time ago as a means of steering the company into more profitable levels of operation. Considerable progress had already been made in streamlining production and reducing costs. The budgeting process normally began in October, prior to the end of the accounting year on 31st December.

The expected results for the current year ending on the 31st December 19X0 were as shown on the page opposite.

From these forecast results, the expected performance for the current year may be calculated as follows:

$$\text{Return on shareholders' equity: } \frac{£18,000}{£236,000} = 7.6\%$$

$$\text{Return on capital employed: } \frac{£18,000}{£253,000} = 7.1\%$$

The following additional information was obtained for the purpose of preparing the budget for the year ending 31st December, 19X1.

(i) *The Sales Forecast*

	Product A	Product B
Expected selling price per unit	£11	£14
Sales volume forecast		
1st quarter	1500 units	2000 units
2nd	1000	2000
3rd	1000	2000
4th	1500	2000
Total for the year	5000	8000

(ii) *Factory costs forecast*

Two departments are concerned with production: the Preparation Department and the Machining Department. The following analysis relates to the production of these departments:

(a) Direct Costs

	Direct labour required per unit of product (in labour hours)		Departmental wage rate (£)	Direct labour cost per unit of output (£)	
	A	B		A	B
Preparation Department	1/5	1/2	£2 per hour	£0.40	£1.00
Machining Department	1/2	1/2	£2 per hour	£1.00	£1.00
				£1.40	£2.00

(b) Raw material requirement forecast

The standard quantities of the two raw materials, X and Y, which should be used in the manufacture of the two products, and the prices of these raw materials have been estimated as follows:

Standard quantities
Raw material X—2 units for each unit of product A
Raw material Y—3 units for each unit of product B

Estimated costs
Raw material X—£0.50 for each unit of X
Raw material Y—£0.30 for each unit of Y

(c) Overhead Costs

Factory overheads are classified into fixed and variable costs. The fixed overhead costs are deemed to be incurred in equal amounts quarterly for the purpose of allocation, whereas the variable overheads vary according to the level of production. The following estimates are available:

Fixed overheads

Depreciation	£10,000 per annum
Rates and insurances	4000
Supervisory salaries	6000
	£20,000

Variable overheads

	Cost per unit of output	
	A	B
	£	£
Indirect labour ⎫ Indirect material ⎪ Repairs and ⎬ maintenance ⎪ Power ⎭	£0.50	£1.00

(iii) *Stock forecasts*

Finished goods
Product A—estimated opening inventory: 750 units
Product B—   : 1000 units

It was planned that the closing stock level at the end of each quarter should be maintained at a level equal to half the expected sales for the next quarter for both products.

For the purposes of calculating the expected profit, the closing inventory is to be valued on a variable costing basis, as follows:

	A	B
Raw materials	£1.00	£0.90
Direct labour	1.40	2.00
Variable overheads	0.50	1.00
Total variable costs per unit	£2.90	£3.90

Raw materials
Raw material X—estimated opening inventory: 1500 units
Raw material Y: 3000 units

(iv) *Administrative and selling costs forecast*

(a) *Administrative costs*

Office salaries	£18,000	
Stationery	1000	
Other	1000	
		£20,000

(b) *Selling costs*

Salaries	15,000	
Advertising	5000	
		20,000
Total		£40,000

(v) *Cash-flow forecast*

(a) *Sales receipts*

50% of sales received in cash during month of sales
50% of sales received in cash in the following month

(b) *Cash expenditure*

Production costs
Direct labour, direct materials and variable overheads paid in the month in which incurred
Fixed overheads paid in equal amounts quarterly
Administrative and selling costs
Paid in equal amounts quarterly

Other costs

Tax outstanding amounting to £12,000 will be paid off in equal instalments quarterly over the year

Capital expenditure

Expenditure on the acquisition of fixed assets is planned as follows:

1st quarter	£10,000
2nd	15,000
3rd	8000
4th	20,000
	£53,000

(vi) Sundry creditors balance

The amount outstanding to Sundry Creditors will remain at a constant amount of £5000 throughout the year.

Preparing the budget for the year ending 31st December, 19X1

The task of preparing the overall budget involves a sequence of steps:

Step 1. The Sales Budget
    2. The Production Budget
    3. The Direct Materials Usage Budget
    4. The Materials Purchases Budget
    5. The Budgeted Direct Labour Costs
    6. The Overhead Costs Budget
    7. The Closing Inventory Budget
    8. The Selling and Administrative Costs Budget
    9. The Capital Expenditure Budget
    10. The Cost of Goods Sold Budget
    11. The Cash Budget
    12. The Budgeted Income Statement
    13. The Budgeted Balance Sheet

Step 1. The Sales Budget

The Sales Budget is prepared from the Sales forecast as follows:

	1st quarter	2nd quarter	3rd quarter	4th quarter	Total
Units					
Product A	1500	1000	1000	1500	5000
Product B	2000	2000	2000	2000	8000
Value					
Product A(£11)	£16,500	£11,000	£11,000	£16,500	£55,000
Product B(£14)	28,000	28,000	28,000	28,000	112,000
	£44,500	£39,000	£39,000	£44,500	£167,000

Step 2. The Production Budget

The Production Budget is designed to plan the resources required to produce the output envisaged by the Sales forecast. A pre-condition to an agreement as to the size of the Sales Budget is the adequacy of the productive capacity of the plant to provide the required output. If existing capacity is inadequate, decisions will have to be made as to the advisability of introducing overtime working, of sub-contracting production, or of hiring or purchasing additional plant and equipment. If, on the other hand, the Sales forecast falls short of productive capacity, sales promotion schemes may be considered as a means of closing or reducing the gap. With the tendency of businessmen to use inventory levels as buffers to insulate an efficient rate of production from variations in sales, the production budget is also dependent upon the planned levels of closing inventory.

Using the information given in our example, the following Production Budget may be prepared:

	1st quarter	2nd quarter	3rd quarter	4th quarter	Year
Product A			(UNITS)		
Desired closing inventory (units)	500	500	750	750	750
Add: Sales	1500	1000	1000	1500	5000
Total required	2000	1500	1750	2250	5750
Less: Opening inventory	750	500	500	750	750
Production required	1250	1000	1250	1500	5000
Product B					
Desired closing inventory (units)	1000	1000	1000	1000	1000
Add: Sales	2000	2000	2000	2000	8000
Total required	3000	3000	3000	3000	9000
Less: Opening inventory	1000	1000	1000	1000	1000
Production required	2000	2000	2000	2000	8000

Step 3. The Direct Materials Usage Budget

The rate of usage of raw materials is known, so that the Direct Materials Usage may be budgeted by multiplying the usage rate by the production required.

	1st quarter	2nd quarter	3rd quarter	4th quarter	Year
Material X (2 units for A)	2500	2000	2500	3000	10,000
Material Y (3 units for B)	6000	6000	6000	6000	24,000

Step 4. The Direct Materials Purchase Budget

The purpose of this budget is to determine both the quantities and the values of raw material purchases which are necessary to meet the production levels stipulated in the Production Budget. The information required for this budget is found in the Direct Materials Usage Budget, inventory forecasts and raw materials purchase prices.

	1st quarter	2nd quarter	3rd quarter	4th quarter	Year
Raw Material X					
Desired closing inventory	1000	1000	1500	1500	1500
Add: material usage (step 3)	2500	2000	2500	3000	10,000
Total required	3500	3000	4000	4500	11,500
Less: Opening inventory	1500	1000	1000	1500	1500
Purchases required (units)	2000	2000	3000	3000	10,000
Price per unit	£0.50	£0.50	£0.50	£0.50	£0.50
Total purchases (value)	£1000	£1000	£1500	£1500	£5000
Raw Material Y					
Desired closing inventory	3000	3000	3000	3000	3000
Add: Material usage (step 3)	6000	6000	6000	6000	24,000
Total required	9000	9000	9000	9000	27,000
Less: Opening inventory	3000	3000	3000	3000	3000
Purchases required (units)	6000	6000	6000	6000	24,000
Price per unit	£0.30	£0.30	£0.30	£0.30	£0.30
Total purchases (value)	£1800	£1800	£1800	£1800	£7200
Total purchases (value)	£2800	£2800	£3300	£3300	£12,200

Step 5. Budgeted Direct Labour Costs

This budget is based upon calculations of the manpower requirements necessary to produce the planned output. The direct labour costs are computed by multiplying the manpower requirements by the forecast of wage rates payable during the budget period.

	1st quarter	2nd quarter	3rd quarter	4th quarter	Year
Production (Step 2—units)					
Product A	1250	1000	1250	1500	5000
Product B	2000	2000	2000	2000	8000
Labour hours					
Preparation Department					
Product A (1/5)	250	200	250	300	1000
Product B (1/2)	1000	1000	1000	1000	4000
Total	1250	1200	1250	1300	5000
Machining Department					
Product A (1/2)	625	500	625	750	2500
Product B (1/2)	1000	1000	1000	1000	4000
Total	1625	1500	1625	1750	6500
Direct labour costs					
Preparation department					
Labour hours	1250	1200	1250	1300	5000
Wage rate/hour	£2	£2	£2	£2	£2
Direct labour cost	£2500	£2400	£2500	£2600	£10,000
Maching department					
Labour hours	1625	1500	1625	1750	6500
Wage rate/hour	£2	£2	£2	£2	£2
Direct labour cost	£3250	£3000	£3250	£3500	£13,000
Total direct labour cost	£5750	£5400	£5750	£6100	£23,000

Step 6. The Overhead Costs Budget

Having disposed of the direct costs of production in the form of materials and direct labour, we now come to the preparation of the estimates of the overhead costs of production. These costs are divided into the two categories mentioned earlier. We are told that the fixed overheads are incurred in equal amounts quarterly, and we may calculate the total variable costs per quarter by multiplying the expected variable costs per unit by the planned quarterly output.

	1st quarter	2nd quarter	3rd quarter	4th quarter	Year
Production (Step 2)					
Product A (units)	1250	1000	1250	1500	5000
Product B (units)	2000	2000	2000	2000	8000
Variable costs					
Product A					
(£0.50 per unit)	£625	£500	£625	£750	£2500
Product B					
(£1.00 per unit)	2000	2000	2000	2000	8000
Total	2625	2500	2625	2750	10,500
Fixed costs					
Depreciation	2500	2500	2500	2500	10,000
Rates & Insurance	1000	1000	1000	1000	4000
Supervisory					
Salaries	1500	1500	1500	1500	6000
Total	5000	5000	5000	5000	20,000
Total overhead costs	£7625	£7500	£7625	£7750	£30,500

Step 7. The Closing Inventory Budget

The Closing inventory Budget consists of an estimate of the value of planned closing inventory of raw materials and planned stocks of finished goods. It is arrived at by calculating the budgeted unit cost of stock and multiplying the result by the planned inventory level.

(a) *Budgeted Closing Raw Material Inventory*

Raw Material	X	Y
Closing inventory (units)	1500	3000
Cost per unit	£0.50	£0.30
Value of closing inventory	£750	£900
Total		£1650

(b) *Budgeted Finished Goods Inventory*

We are told that the accountant values the inventory of finished goods on a variable costing basis, and that the unit cost of Products A and B has been calculated to be £2.90 and £3.90 respectively. These values are applied to the budgeted closing inventory figures as follows:

Product	A	B
Closing inventory (units)	750	1000
Cost per unit	£2.90	£3.90
Value of closing inventory	2175	3900
Total		£6075

Step 8. The Selling and Administrative Expenses Budget

Selling Expenses		
Salaries	£15,000	
Advertising	5000	£20,000
Administrative Expenses		
Office salaries	18,000	
Stationery	1000	
Other expenses	1000	20,000
Total		£40,000

Step 9. The Capital Expenditure Budget

We devoted chapter 4 to a discussion of capital budgeting as an aspect of Long-range Planning. The Annual Capital Expenditure Budget must be seen, therefore, as a one-year slice of the Long-term Capital Budget. The purpose of the Annual Capital Expenditure is to make provision in the current budget for the planned capital expenditure in the current year. This information has been provided as follows:

Capital Expenditure	
1st quarter	£10,000
2nd	15,000
3rd	8000
4th	20,000
Total for the year	£53,000

Step 10. The Cost of Goods Sold Budget

The reader will recall that all the previous budgets mentioned have dealt with the various aspects of the production process, in unit and value terms, including the expenses associated with selling and administration and the valuation of closing inventory. The purpose of this budget is to bring all these items together to arrive at an estimate of the cost of the goods sold. This estimate will be used in the budgeted income statement. It is compiled as follows:

Opening raw materials inventory (Balance Sheet 31/12/19X0)	£1650
Add: Materials Purchases (Step 4)	12,200
Raw materials available for production	13,850
Less: Planned closing inventory of raw materials (Step 7)	1650
Cost of raw materials to be used in production	12,200
Cost of direct labour (Step 5)	23,000
Factory overhead costs (Step 6)	30,500
Cost of goods to be manufactured	65,700
Add: Opening inventory of finished goods (Balance Sheet 31/12/19X0)	6025
	71,725
Less: Planned closing inventory of finished goods	6075
Budgeted Cost of Goods Sold	£65,650

Step 11. The Cash Budget

The Cash Budget consists of the estimates of cash receipts and cash payments arising from the planned levels of activities and use of resources which are considered in the various budgets we have examined. The Cash Budget is a complete survey of the financial implications of expenditure plans both of a current and a capital nature during the year. Moreover, by comparing the anticipated outflows of cash with the expected inflows, the Cash Budget enables management to anticipate any deficits so that the necessary financing arrangements may be made, and to decide upon a policy for placing any cash surpluses.

As its name implies, the Cash Budget deals only with 'cash' flows—it excludes expenses of a non-cash nature, such as depreciation. The Cash Budget is one of the last budgets to be prepared because it depends upon the other budgets which form part of the budgeting process.

	1st quarter	2nd quarter	3rd quarter	4th quarter	Total
	£	£	£	£	£
Opening cash balance	5325	10,900	11,450	15,275	5325
Receipts:					
Debtors (Balance Sheet)	20,000	—	—	—	20,000
50% of current sales (Step 1)	22,250	19,500	19,500	22,250	83,500
50% of previous quarter (Step 1)	—	22,250	19,500	19,500	61,250
Total receipts	42,250	41,750	39,000	41,750	164,750
Total cash available	47,575	52,650	50,450	57,025	170,075
Payments:					
Purchases (Step 4)	2800	2800	3300	3300	12,200
Direct labour (Step 5)	5750	5400	5750	6100	23,000
Factory overheads (Step 6) (excluding depreciation)	5125	5000	5125	5250	20,500
Selling and administrative expenses (Step 8)	10,000	10,000	10,000	10,000	40,000
Capital expenditure (Step 9)	10,000	15,000	8000	20,000	53,000
Tax (Balance Sheet)	3000	3000	3000	3000	12,000
Total payments	36,675	41,200	35,175	47,650	160,700
Closing cash balances	10,900	11,450	15,275	9375	9375

The Cash Budget, it will be noted, is planned through time: for the time profile of cash receipts and cash payments is critical to the analysis of a firm's cash needs at any given point of time.

In practice, determining the level of cash which is required at any point in time may not be an easy matter. The dilemma of cash management lies in the conflict of liquidity with profitability. If a firm holds too little cash in relation to its financial obligations, a liquidity crisis may occur and may lead to the collapse of the business. On the other hand, if a firm holds too much cash it is losing the opportunity to employ that cash profitably in its activities. Idle cash balances usually earn very little profit for the firm. A reasonable balance must be found, therefore, between the financial objectives of maintaining a degree of liquidity and of minimizing the level of unproductive assets. The problem of ascertaining optimal balances of physical stocks has for long attracted the attention of operational researchers, and certain of the ideas which they have developed may have applicability as regards the holding of optimal cash balances. Essentially these ideas relate the cost of holding cash with the cost of obtaining cash: total costs are minimized when the two are equated.

Step 12. The Budgeted Income Statement

The purpose of the Budgeted Income Statement is to summarize and integrate all the operating budgets so as to measure the end result on the firm's income.

Sales (Step 1)	£167,000
Cost of goods sold (Step 10)	65,650
Gross margin	101,350
Selling and Administrative Expenses (Step 8)	40,000
Net income before tax	61,350
Tax (40%)	24,540
Net income after tax	£36,810

Step 13. The Budgeted Balance Sheet

The final stage is the projection of the budgeted results on the firm's financial position at the end of the year. The following Balance Sheet reflects the changes in the composition of assets and liabilities as a result of the planned activities:

Capital employed		£	£
Ordinary Share Capital		210,000	
Retained Income		62,810	
			272,810

Represented by				
Fixed Assets	*Cost* £	*Provision for Depreciation* £		
Plant & Machinery	303,000	40,000		
			263,000	
Current Assets				
Inventories		£		
Raw materials		1650		
Finished goods		6075		
Debtors		22,250		
Cash		9375		
		39,350		
Less: Current Liabilities				
Sundry creditors	5000			
Tax outstanding	24,540			
		29,540		
Net Working Capital			9810	
				272,810

Evaluating the budget proposals

As a means of comparing the planned performance for the coming year with the results of the current year, the planned performance may be interpreted as follows:

Return on shareholders' equity: £36,810 ÷ £272,810

$$= 13.5\% \text{ (previous } 7.6\%)$$

Return on capital employed: £36,810 ÷ £302,350

$$= 12.2\% \text{ (previous } 7.1\%)$$

It is evident, therefore, that the firm is expected to make considerable improvements in the forthcoming period. If the budgeted results are considered to be satisfactory the final stage is a recommendation that the budget proposal be accepted by the Board of Directors as its policy, and as conforming with its view of the future.

Summary

Budgetary planning is an activity which should be seen as being concerned with the implementation of a yearly segment of the long-range plan. The budget expresses this plan in financial terms in the light of current conditions.

Successful budgetary planning depends on a number of other factors, for example, a sound formal organizational structure which designates clearly areas of authority and responsibility, as well as an accounting information system which allows effective financial control.

A major problem in budgetary planning is the forecasting of sales. The budget plan itself consists of some 13 stages as follows:

(1) The sales budget
(2) The production budget
(3) The direct materials usage budget
(4) The materials purchases budget
(5) The budgeted direct labour costs
(6) The overhead costs budget
(7) The closing inventory budget
(8) The selling and administrative costs budget
(9) The capital expenditure budget
(10) The cost of goods sold budget
(11) The cash budget
(12) The budgeted income statement
(13) The budgeted balance sheet

Budget plans may be evaluated by means of financial ratios such as the return on shareholders' equity and the return on capital employed.

Further readings

1. American Management Association, *Materials and Methods of Sales Forecasting*, Special Report No. 27, New York, American Management Association, Inc., 1957.

2. Anton, Hector H. & Firmin, Peter A., *Contemporary Issues in Cost Accounting*, 2nd edn, Houghton Miflin, Boston, 1972.

3. Heckert, J. Brooks & Willson, James, D., *Business Budgeting and Control*, Ronald Press Co., New York, 1967.

4. Knight, W. D. & Weinwurm, E. H., *Managerial Budgeting*, Macmillan, New York, 1964.

5. Welsch, G. A., *Budgeting: Profit Planning and Control*, Prentice Hall, Englewood Cliffs, N.J., 1971.

6
Risk Analysis

The process of rational decision-making in organizations requires the harnessing of all the relevant facts so that the likely outcome of the different alternatives open for selection may be correctly measured. As we have seen many times so far in this book, if one were able to predict the future with complete accuracy, the problems of decision-making would be largely eliminated. In a world which is characterized by change, the decision-maker cannot rely entirely on the forecasts prepared for him of the likely outcome of different alternatives no matter how carefully these forecasts are prepared. By the very nature of things, predictions of future events are tentative and uncertain.

The process of decision-making is fraught with risk and uncertainty. Strictly speaking, a decision problem under conditions of 'risk' is one where one knows the risk or probability attached to the outcome of the different alternatives being considered, whereas a decision problem under 'uncertainty' is one where the risk or probability attached to the outcomes is not known. The distinction between the terms risk and uncertainty is becoming quite blurred, and we shall use them interchangeably.

The purpose of this chapter is to examine the methods currently available for evaluating the risk element in business decisions.

Uncertainty and information

Uncertainty may be regarded as a deficiency of information. Under conditions of certainty, complete knowledge about the future would be available, and profit as a reward for risk-bearing would not be a business phenomenon. Profits and losses occur as a result of uncertainty. The purpose of information, therefore, is to increase and improve knowledge so as to reduce uncertainty as much as possible. The greater the degree of uncertainty affecting a particular decision, the more valuable is the benefit to be derived from additional information.

The problem of the uncertainty involved in capital budgeting decisions has received much attention of recent years. Such decisions are not easily reversible, if at all, and the hazard of making wrong decisions may be minimized to a considerable extent by improving the quality and extent of the information coverage. The methods for dealing with uncertainty in capital budgeting decisions may also be applied to other types of decisions, and it is our purpose to examine these methods in this chapter.

Adjusting the discount rate for risk

In chapter 4, we examined the usefulness of discounted cash flow techniques for making capital investment decisions. One method of allowing for uncertainty is to adjust the discount rate to take account of the expected degree of risk. Thus, whereas a discount rate of 10% might be used to discount future cash flows under conditions of certainty, an organization might impose a decision rule that a higher discount rate would have to be employed for projects which face conditions of uncertainty. In calculating the internal rate of return for a project, the required rate of return, that is the 'hurdle rate', may be increased to allow for the degree of uncertainty involved in the project.

In adjusting the discount rate or increasing the hurdle rate, we are assuming a knowledge of the risk involved in the project. But the main difficulty about using a risk-adjusted discount rate lies in the problem of measuring different degrees of risk. The question really is "how does one measure the difference between a project with a high degree of risk and one with a low degree of risk?" Furthermore, since those who are concerned with preparing the relevant information and those who will make the investment decisions are rarely the same people, means must be found of quantifying the degree of uncertainty present in the forecast of outcomes.

All in all, the risk-adjusted discount rate method of dealing with the problem of uncertainty presents a difficult measurement problem for although it recognizes the existence of uncertainty, it does not accurately evaluate it.

Sensitivity analysis and the measurement of risk

One of the ways of assessing the effects of uncertainty attached to any decision is to improve the quality of the relevant information. Sensitivity analysis is such a method. It is really a critical analysis of the factors which determine the forecasted results. Its purpose is to indicate which factors are more crucial to the predicted outcome and to provide insights into what would happen to the predicted outcome if there were subsequently any deviation from the predicted values of the key factors. For example, the estimates of the net inflows and outflows associated with a capital investment decision are based on forecasts of such factors as sales volume, selling prices, raw material costs, operating expenses, the useful life of the project and capital costs. Sensitivity analysis is directed to such questions as "what would be the effect if capital costs turned out to be 10% higher than estimated?" or "what would be the effect if the cash inflows were 5% lower than planned?" By asking such questions, it is possible to identify those factors which are likely to have proportionately a much greater impact on the planned rate of return should there be a relatively small change in their estimated value.

Sensitivity analysis is particularly useful in the study of capital investment decisions where considerable uncertainty exists or where large amounts of capital are involved, for it provides information which places management in a better position to decide whether the risks surrounding the project are too large to permit its acceptance.

Example

Spectrum Engineering Ltd, is considering a capital investment project and assumes that a 15% rate of return will be earned. It has undertaken a detailed sensitivity study of the effect of possible changes in the key factors on the expected rate of return as follows:

Estimated Maximum Possible Change in the Factors Involved	Internal Rate of Return			
	Expected	Adjusted for Possible Change	Difference	Effect of Change on the Expected Rate of Return
	%	%	%	%
10% decrease in sales volume	15	13.0	2.0	13.4
10% decrease in sales price	15	7.3	7.7	51.4
10% decrease in project life	15	14.0	1.0	6.7
10% increase in raw material costs	15	9.1	5.9	39.3
10% increase in operating costs	15	14.5	0.5	3.3
10% increase in capital investment costs	15	14.0	1.0	6.7

This table reveals that the expected rate of return is most sensitive to possible changes in selling price and raw material costs, so that it is in respect of these estimates that errors in their forecasts are likely to be most damaging. Hence, management will be encouraged to a further investigation of the circumstances affecting the two factors in question so as to validate their estimate of their behaviour before a final decision is made.

Sensitivity analysis is subject to important limitations, which are similar in nature to those we noted in respect of the risk-adjusted rate of return method for dealing with uncertainty. First, sensitivity analysis depends on a knowledge of the chances of any deviations in the key factors from their predicted behaviour in the future. Second, sensitivity analysis also requires the effects of changes in each key factor to be isolated, whereas management is interested too in the combined effect of changes in two or more key factors and the probability of such combined changes occurring.

Risk analysis and sensitivity analysis

In order to use sensitivity analysis to full advantage, it is necessary to combine it with risk analysis which uses probability theory in the measurement of variability. Increasingly, in every aspect of accounting one sees a growing emphasis on mathematical techniques in the solution of measurement problems, and nowhere is this truer than in risk analysis.

The mathematical propositions of probability theory are relatively simple. We ascribe the number 1 to the certainty that an event will occur, and the number 0 to the certainty that it will not occur. Clearly, the chance that an event will occur depends upon the number of events which could occur. Let us take, for example, the measurement of the probability attached to the outcome of the tossing of a coin. Since there are only two events which could occur and each is equally likely, that is heads or tails, the probability of either event occurring is 1/2 or 0.5. Similarly, if throwing dice, the probability of turning up any of the numbers is 1/6 or 0.1667.

The same reasoning may be used to measure the likelihood of financial estimates and predictions turning out to be true. Since capital investment decisions require quite a long view of the future, and as uncertainty increases as the time spans covered by a decision problem lengthens it is not surprising that risk analysis has a particular importance to such decisions.

Example

The Hydra International Corporation is faced with selecting one of two investment projects, both of which would require an investment of £10,000 and each of which is expected to yield £5000 annually for 5 years.

Using the investment appraisal methods described in chapter 4 there would be no way of preferring either of the projects against the other. The firm, in effect, would have to toss a coin to decide which project to select.

If, however, it is discovered that the probabilities attached to estimated cash inflows are different, then it is clear that the two projects may be distinguished. Let us assume, therefore, that the probabilities of receiving the total net cash inflows from the two projects are as depicted in Fig. 3.11.

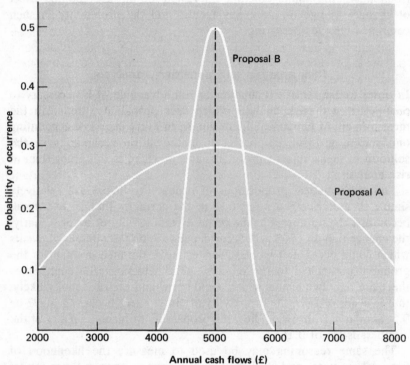

Fig. 3.11

In terms of the risks involved, the two projects are quite different. The chances of receiving a yearly cash inflow of £5000 are much higher for Project B than they are for Project A, there being a 0.5 chance attached to the probability of receiving £5000 in Project B, whereas there is only a 0.3 chance of receiving £5000 in Project A. By contrast, the probability of receiving sums below £4600 are much higher in Project A than in Project B. The table shows, for example, that the chance of receiving less than £4000 in Project B is zero, whereas there are chances of receiving smaller sums in Project A. On the other hand, Project A offers chances of larger returns than Project B—there is no chance whatsoever of returns higher than £6000 in Project B, but there are probabilities of returns in excess of that sum in Project A. Consequently, a conservative management would prefer Project B, and would reject Project A.

The certainty equivalent method of risk appraisal

We may consider the aforementioned example in terms of the distribution of the probabilities around the mean $(\bar{x})$ so that the standard deviation (σ) may be used to represent the entire probability distribution. Students of statistics will appreciate that the standard deviation represents a measure of dispersion round the mean. Figure 3.11 shows that the dispersion around the mean is much smaller for Project B than it is for Project A. The mean return is defined for this purpose as the expected return, that is £5000 for both projects. The standard deviation indicates the degree of risk attached to receiving the expected return, so that the higher the standard deviation the greater the risk.

We may observe that the distribution of probabilities for both projects assumes the shape of a normal curve, that is, a symmetrical curve with the shape of a bell. The normal curve is an important statistical concept, and the implications of the normal curve are well-known to students of elementary statistics. From these curves we may read off the following possibilities:

Project A		Project B	
Cash Flows £	Probability	Cash Flows £	Probability
2000	0.10	4250	0.05
3500	0.25	4500	0.20
5000	0.30	5000	0.50
6500	0.25	5500	0.20
8000	0.10	5750	0.05
	1.00		1.00

The standard deviation as a measure of the risk attached to obtaining the expected return, that is £5000, is obtained by a formula which concentrates on the deviations from the expected return which are represented in the total sample taken into the probability calculations.

The formula for calculating the standard deviation is as follows:

$$\sigma = \sqrt{\frac{fd^2}{n}}$$

where σ is the standard deviation
f is the frequency with which a value occurs (in this
case the probability attached to receiving a sum)
d is the deviation of the value of a sum from the mean $\bar{X}$
n is the size of the sample (in this case the total
probabilities represented by the number 1)

Hence, we may calculate the standard deviation for Projects A and
B as follows:

Project A

Cash Flow X	Probability f	fX	$\bar{X}$	(d) $X-\bar{X}$	(d^2) $(X-\bar{X})^2$	(fd^2)
£2000	0.10	200	£5000	−£3000	9,000,000	900,000
3500	0.25	875	5000	−1500	2,250,000	562,500
5000	0.30	1500	5000	—	—	—
6500	0.25	1625	5000	1500	2,250,000	562,500
8000	0.10	800	5000	3000	9,000,000	900,000
	1.00	5000			22,500,000	2,925,000

$$\text{Standard deviation} = \sqrt{\frac{2,925,000}{1}}$$
$$= 1710.265$$

Project B

Cash Flow X	Probability f	fX	$\bar{X}$	(d) $X-\bar{X}$	(d^2) $(X-\bar{X})^2$	(fd^2)
£4250	0.05	212	£5000	−£750	562,500	28,125
4500	0.20	900	5000	−500	250,000	50,000
5000	0.50	2500	5000	—	—	—
5500	0.20	1100	5000	500	250,000	50,000
5750	0.05	288	5000	750	562,500	28,125
	1.00	5000			1,625,000	156,250

$$\text{Standard deviation} = \sqrt{\frac{156,250}{1}}$$
$$= 395.28$$

The significance of finding the value of the standard deviation lies in
the fact that we can now estimate the degree of risk involved in a
project. In a normal curve it is known that 68.27% of all possible
outcomes will be within plus or minus one standard deviation from the

mean. Furthermore, 95.45% of all possible outcomes will be within plus or minus two standard deviations from the mean, and 99.73% will fall within plus or minus three standard deviations from the mean.

We can see from our calculations of one standard deviation that as regards Project A, we can be approximately 68% certain that the cash flows will be within the range £3290–£6710 (that is £5000±£1710). As regards Project B, we can be 68% certain that the value of the expected cash flows will fall within the range £4605–£5395 (that is £5000±£395). Clearly, we are more certain of receiving £5000 or a sum close to it from Project B than from Project A, as seen from Fig. 3.12.

Project B may be preferred to Project A, therefore, because of the degree of risk of receiving a sum which deviates from the expected return of £5000 is less in Project B than it is in Project A. The reason

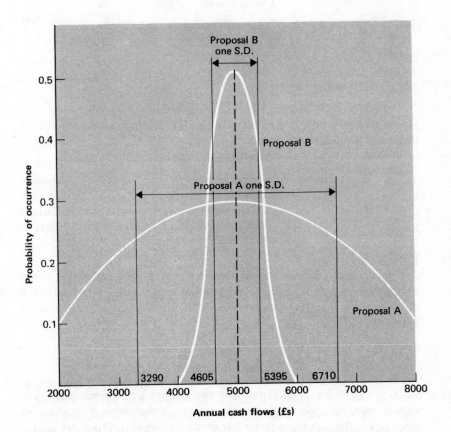

for this preference arises if we assume that decision-makers are 'risk-averse', and that they will prefer smaller but more certain returns than larger and more uncertain returns. Given this assumption, we are able to relate the standard deviations and the means to give a risk percentage which may be measured as follows:

$$\text{Risk percentage} = \frac{\text{Standard deviation}}{X} \times \frac{100}{1}$$

The risk percentage for Project A would be as follows:

$$\frac{1710.25}{5000.00} \times 100 = 34\%$$

so that the certainty equivalent may be expressed as

$$100\% - 34\% = 66\%$$

Hence, the risk adjusted expected value of cash flows associated with Project A would be:

$$£5000 \times 66\% = £3300$$

The risk percentage for Project B would be as follows:

$$\frac{395.28}{5000.00} \times 100 = 8\%$$

and the certainty equivalent:

$$100\% - 8\% = 92\%$$

Hence, the risk adjusted expected value of cash flows associated with Project B would be:

$$£5000 \times 92\% = £4600$$

Thus, the procedure involved in using the certainty equivalent approach is to adjust the expected cash flows for risk. The adjusted cash flows may then be discounted to their present value. In the foregoing example, the certainty equivalent is higher for Project B than for Project A and reflects the higher degree of risk attached to Project A.

The certainty equivalent approach to the measurement of risk solves the problem which we noted earlier in our analysis of the risk-adjusted discount rate, that is, the problem of determining the risk existing between projects.

Decision trees

So far we have been concerned with the problems of assessing projects with a view to making simple accept-reject decisions. However, in most cases, the values of some variables are dependent on the values of others. A decision tree illustrates this dependence by following a chain of events to some final outcome.

A decision tree consists of a series of rods and branches. Each alternative course of action under consideration is represented by a main branch which, in turn, may have subsidiary branches for related chance events that appear in chronological order. In other words, the tree diagram charts the paths that lead to possible consequences.

Let us take as a simple example the decision to launch a new product. It is very likely that sales of a new product in the second year will be influenced by the level of sales in the first year. We assume that management estimates that sales in the first year have a .6 probability of being excellent, let us say 7000 units, and .4 probability of being good, let us say 5000 units. The probability distribution of sales in the second year will vary depending on whether the first year achieved excellent or good results. Assuming that we can estimate these probabilities for either excellent or good first year sales, we may draw a decision tree as follows:

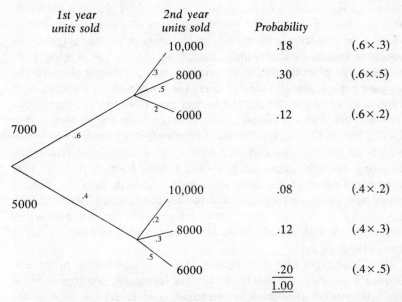

1st year units sold	2nd year units sold	Probability	
	10,000	.18	(.6 × .3)
	8000	.30	(.6 × .5)
	6000	.12	(.6 × .2)
7000			
5000			
	10,000	.08	(.4 × .2)
	8000	.12	(.4 × .3)
	6000	.20	(.4 × .5)
		1.00	

From this diagram it can be observed that the sum of the probabilities of each event is still the sum of the separate probabilities, but the probabilities of each of the six possible outcomes is the product of their individual probabilities. For example, if we chart the path on the top most branch we get .6 × .3 = .18.

To avoid having to show each sales probability separately which is a laborious task when the number of chance events is larger and to avoid a possible confusing array of numbers, a frequency distribution may be prepared as follows:

Units sold	Probability
10,000	.26 i.e. (.18+.08)
8000	.42 i.e. (.30+.12)
6000	.32 i.e. (.12+.20)
	1.00

Application of decision tree analysis

Decision tree analysis has a number of important applications to the solution of management problems. It has an important role to play in the study of investment projects which depend upon a series of events occurring in the right order, and which depend also upon the factors involved behaving according to forecast.

We shall take as our specific example the application of decision tree analysis to the problem of budgeting. In all budget planning exercises, there is a strong element of probability forecasting. It is possible to examine the probable outcome of the elements of the budget, and this process is known as *Probabilistic Budgeting*. As we saw in chapter 5, the objective of budgeting is to produce an operational plan for the planning period, and if a change occurs in an important variable, such as the price of raw materials, the budget may have to be revised. Such a revision involves a laborious effort to reconstruct the budget, and in practice because of the time element required, it is normal to construct budgets on the basis of a limited number of assumptions. Traditional budgeting, therefore, does not provide a flexible instrument which may be adjusted to meet changing conditions. At best, they are flexible merely as regards varying sales and production levels. Moreover, such budgets are determined after considering only a limited number of alternative possibilities, which are aimed at attaining satisfactory rather than optimal targets.

With the advent of the computer, it is now possible to prepare in advance a number of budgets to meet all forseeable contingencies, so that if they occur it is possible immediately to select the appropriate course of action to take.

Example

Let us assume that the budget of a firm is based upon forecasts of the behaviour of three crucial elements—sales volume, material prices and operating costs. Let us assume that there is a 0.6 chance of sales volume being 90% of productive capacity, and a 0.2 chance of it being 100% and 80% of capacity respectively. The chances of raw material costs and operating costs rising rapidly are estimated at 0.1 and 0.3 respectively. Negligible rises in these costs were also 0.1 and 0.3 with the chances of moderate rises being much higher at 0.8 and 0.4 respectively. We may tabulate these probabilities as follows:

Forecast	Sales Volume	Raw Material Costs	Operating Costs
High	0.2	0.1	0.3
Average	0.6	0.8	0.4
Low	0.2	0.1	0.3
	1.0	1.0	1.0

We may observe from these probabilities that the chances of moderate increases in raw material prices are much higher than for moderate increases in operating costs. It is possible to combine the effects of these combinations so as to produce 27 possible budgets by means of a decision tree analysis (Fig. 3.13 on p. 372).

Having worked out a total possible number of budgets, it would be too time-wasting in practice to go to the length of envisaging all the probable combinations of events which might occur and to plan budgets accordingly. It is advisable, therefore, to establish a cut-off point below which contingencies are not planned for, and in our example, we might select the probability of .024 as the cut-off point. Let us consider the effect of imposing such a cut-off point by reference to the frequency distribution of the probabilities.

Probability	Frequency	Pf
.006	8	.048
.008	4	.032
.018	4	.072
.024	2	.048
.056	18	.200
.048	4	.192
.064	2	.128
.144	2	.288
.192	1	.192
.438	9	.800
Total	27	1.000

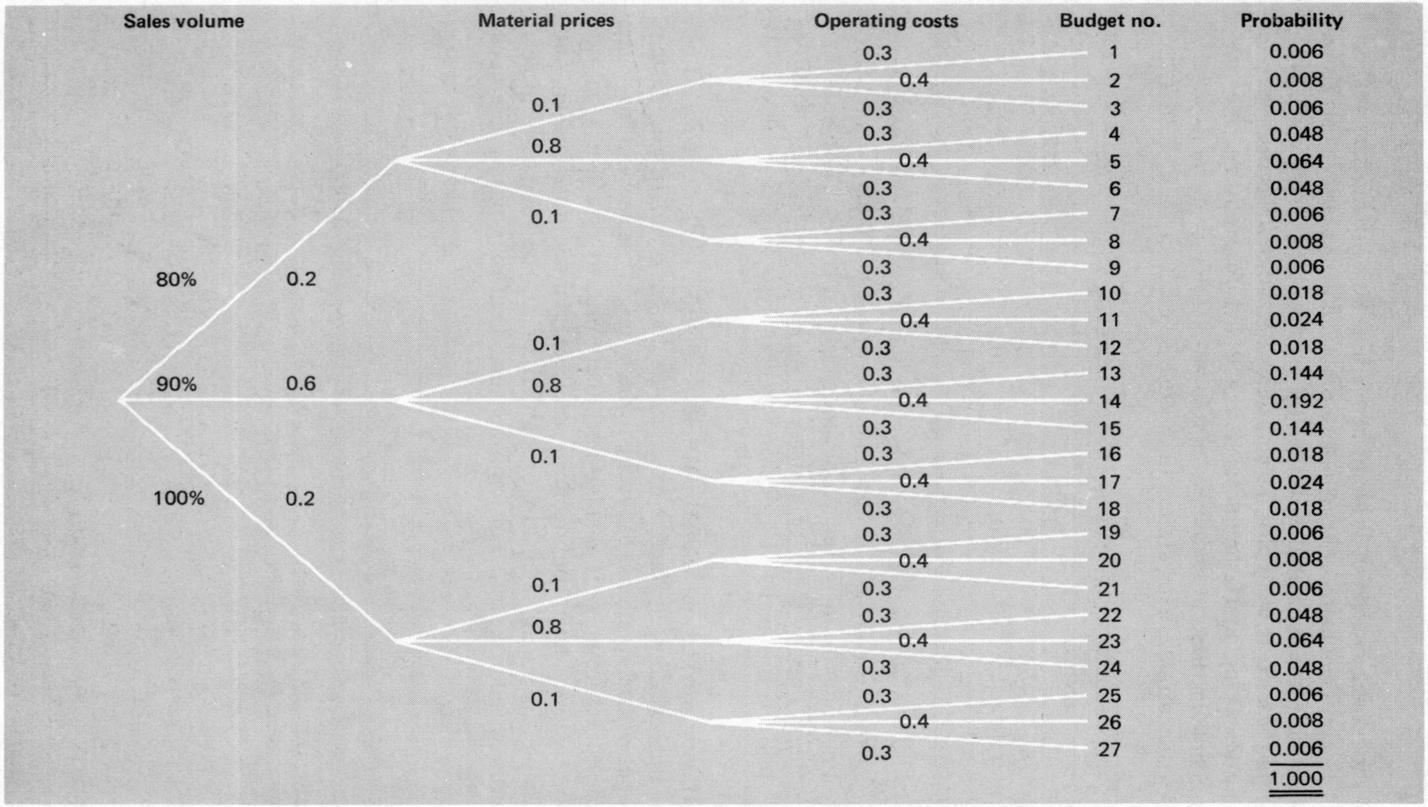

Fig. 3.13

As a result of selecting the cut-off point at the probability of .024, we can omit 18 budgets from the reckoning with a loss of coverage of only .2 of the total budgets which may be needed to meet all eventualities. As the table above shows, there is a probability of .8, or 4 chances out of 5, that the nine budgets included in part of the frequency distribution above the cut-off point will occur. Management may concentrate, therefore on the preparation of these nine budgets only.

Probabilistic budgeting increases dramatically the effectiveness of budgetary control systems, for as circumstances change the firm is ready to meet these changes. As we have noted above, probabilistic budgeting is concerned with planning for contingencies well in advance of their occurrence, so that the firm may alter its plan should these contingencies materialize. As a result, the firm is in a better position to make the best use of its resources; its plans include the possibility of shifts in resource allocations should circumstances change. Equally important is the manner in which probabilistic budgeting enables management to understand the manner in which changes affect the firm and alters the inter-relationship of its various elements.

Large-scale simulation

Our analysis of the effects of risk on decision-making has been based so far on three assumptions:

(a) that the distribution of probabilities of events occurring has the characteristic of a normal curve;
(b) that the variables with which we are concerned are limited in number; and
(c) that these variables have a limited range of values: high, average and low.

Modern computers have greatly extended the range of probabilities which may be considered in planning and decision-making, and the application to such problems of simulation techniques which are more representative of real-life situations. It is as though the computer acts as a laboratory in which a plan may be tested and exposed to the circumstances which may probably occur in real-life.

The application of mathematical techniques to management problems and the use of computers afford a means of improving budgetary planning by means of a budget model which incorporates a large number of variables. Using a computer to simulate the result of alternative budget strategies enables management to evaluate alternative courses of action by reference to all the relevant factors which may determine their outcome. A budget simulation model defines the relationship between the various elements of an organization's financial structure in terms of a series of mathematical equations. This set of mathematical statements is a financial model of the organization, and the manipulation of the various elements simulates alternative courses of action, which when run through the computer indicate the probable outcome of alternative strategies. Hence, budget planning by means of simulation models makes possible a better allocation of resources than traditional methods. Furthermore by processing more up-to-date information, a simulation model reflects current events more correctly than the traditional budget, which is usually out-of-date soon after it has been drawn up.

There are numerous applications of large scale simulation, and it is evident that as the scale of a problem increases, so this technique becomes more useful. Thus, simulation of a proposed budget for a large company is an immensely valuable method of testing out the budget proposal and discovering any weak spots, which may be remedied before the budget is finally agreed.

One of the major contributions of simulation techniques to management science is in improving our understanding of the way in which organizations work, and therefore in improving the efficiency with which decisions are made. By contrast, traditional budgeting methods fail to recognize adequately that any business is an inter-related organism of many inter-dependent functions. As a result, undue bias may be attached to specific functions because their relationship to other parts of the organization is not considered. Computer based simulation models enable management to analyse the inter-relationships existing between the various organizational functions in a comprehensive manner.

Large scale simulation not only helps with the difficulties created by the number of variables existing in a decision-problem, but it also is useful in handling a much wider range of values attached to these variables. The analysis of investment proposals may be carried out through simulation in order to test the probabilities attached to receiving the expected return and the nature of the dispersion which surrounds these probabilities. The method for calculating the dispersion is derived from what is known as the Monte Carlo technique, which, as its name implies, is concerned with the study of chance.

The assumptions underlying the Monte Carlo technique are reasonable enough, for example, if one were playing roulette one would expect that over a long sequence of games each number should come up the same number of times. Therefore, if we were to take a large enough sample of a very large number of games, the sample should represent, that is simulate, the results of all the games. This principle forms the basis of the Monte Carlo technique. The appraisal of capital investment programme by means of the Monte Carlo method involves four stages, as follows:

(1) The determination of the factors which are important in evaluating an investment proposal. Hertz (1964), for example, considers the following factors to be relevant: market size, market growth rate, share of market, selling prices, investment required, the residual value of the investment, operating costs, fixed costs, and the useful life of the investment.

(2) The determination of a frequency distribution for each of these factors showing the probability of any particular value of that factor occurring.

(3) The selection at random from each of these several distributions of a particular value which are combined so as to compute the rate of return which would result.

(4) Stage three is repeated a large number of times to ascertain the probability attaching to each possible rate of return. Although the selection made from the values of the factors on each occasion is made on a random basis, it must be remembered that the chances of any particular value for a factor being selected depends entirely on the forecast made of the probability distribution for that factor. This probability distribution will have been worked out during stage 2. The frequency distribution so obtained enables an evaluation to be made of the expected return and the degree of dispersion about the expected return. By comparing the probability distributions of one proposal with those of another, management is able to evaluate the respective merits of risky investments.

The large scale simulation technique as a method of forecasting and eliminating risk is one of the most significant steps forward in the application of mathematical techniques to the solution of traditional accounting problems.

Utility theory and risk aversion

We have assumed in this chapter that investors are risk-averse. This statement contains an implicit assumption about the utility or satisfaction derived from money (either income or wealth), namely, that the marginal utility of money declines as the level of income or wealth rises. Thus, the utility to be derived from an additional £100 if one has

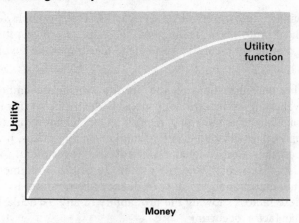

Fig. 3.14   The utility function of money.

only £1 is considerably greater than if one has £100,000. The utility
function of money may be shown as in Fig. 3.14.

It is possible to derive the utility function of money for different
individuals. Moreover, it may be postulated that the utility function of
money will be different between individuals according to their degree
of risk-aversion. Thus, Fig. 3.14 may be associated with a risk-averse
investor, whose utility function declines as his level of income or
wealth increases. Figure 3.15 below shows the utility function of
money for an investor who is 'risk neutral', that is, who regards each
additional £100 as having the same value regardless of his level of
income or wealth. Figure 3.16 below shows the utility function of a

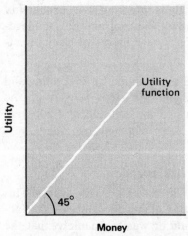

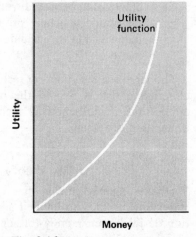

Fig. 3.15   Differing utility function   Fig. 3.16
of money with Fig. 3.16.

risk-loving investor, that is, an investor whose utility function increases as his level of income or wealth rises. Thus, he derives less satisfaction from £100 when his income or wealth is low than when his income or wealth is high.

The assumption that risk-aversion represents rational investor behaviour may be validated by the following example:

Example

An investor is faced with the following alternative returns:

(a) £1,000,000 to which is attached a probability of 1
(b) £3,000,000 to which is attached a probability of 0.5 and a 0.5 probability of £0.

The expected returns may be stated as follows:

(a) £1,000,000
(b) £1,500,000
. i.e. $3,000,000 \times 0.5$

Confronted with this choice, it may safely be assumed that the investor would prefer the certainty of receiving £1,000,000 than the gamble involved in the prospect of receiving £1,500,000.

In gambling situations, different individuals may react differently when faced with the prospect of gaining large sums to which different odds are attached. Thus, faced with a certainty of receiving £1,000,000 or sums of £1,500,000, or more to which different odds are attached, many will still prefer the certain return of £1,000,000 though others may be tempted to take a chance. Utility theory applied to the problem of risk aversion assists in understanding individual behaviour under conditions of risk. It proposes that individuals attempt to optimize the expected value of something which is defined as utility, and assumes that for each individual a relationship may be established between utility and money. Utility may be expressed in utiles* and the certainty equivalent is needed to determine the individual utility function.

Example

An individual owns a lottery ticket which offers him a 0.5 chance of winning £1 million and a 0.5 chance of winning £0. He is asked what he would accept in cash to sell the lottery ticket. If he

---

* The 'utile' has long featured in the literature of economics as a measure which would prove useful to the expression of utility. It is, however, purely a theoretical measure. A practical expression of a utile does not appear possible, and it has been stated that "the search for a utile is bound to be futile".

answers £400,000, we may attach a utile value of 0.5 to £400,000, for we have determined the certainty equivalent at which he is indifferent between £400,000 and the chance of gaining the lottery prize.

The foregoing analysis may be applied to an investment decision requiring a choice between two projects, both of which involved the same initial and certain cash outlay and the same expected cash inflow, save that the cash inflow has a different dispersion for each project.

Project A

Cash Inflow	Probability	Utility	Cash Inflow × Probability		Utility × Probability
£			£		
−2000	0.3	−2.8	−600		−0.84
0	0.3	0	0		0
1000	0.1	0.10	100		0.01
5000	0.1	0.36	500		0.036
25,000	0.2	0.54	5000		0.108
		Expected income	5000	Expected utility	0.07

Project B

Cash Inflow	Probability	Utility	Cash Inflow × Probability		Utility × Probability
£			£		
3000	0.1	0.25	300		0.025
4000	0.2	0.31	800		0.062
5000	0.4	0.36	2000		0.144
6000	0.2	0.40	1200		0.080
7000	0.1	0.43	700		0.043
		Expected income	5000	Expected utility	0.354

The discovery of the utility function attached to each possible outcome in both projects enables us to understand that the maximization of utility is relevant to risk analysis. In the foregoing example, Project B would be selected because it has a higher utility than Project A. We may deduce, therefore, that Project B would have been preferred even had it yielded a smaller expected income than Project A.

Despite its appeal, it is unlikely that such an application of utility theory to the appraisal of risk will become operational, since it is virtually impossible to specify a reliable utility for this purpose. Attitudes towards risk are affected, moreover, by particular circumstances affecting a firm. It is doubtful also if one can talk meaningfully about the utility function of a large organization for the purpose of risk appraisal. Thus, this analysis has little usefulness other than throwing light on the nature of risk.

Summary

A proper understanding of decision-making is impossible unless the problem of risk is taken into account. As regards capital expenditure decisions, for example, risk implies the possibility that the actual outcome may be different from the expected outcome.

Uncertainty may be regarded as a deficiency of information, and the objective of an information system should be seen as reducing this deficiency where possible. In this respect, opportunities exist for the accountant to apply probability analysis to the problem of risk. Several approaches were considered—adjusting the discount rate for uncertainty, sensitivity analysis and the certainty equivalent method.

Methods of risk analysis have a wide-ranging usefulness. In addition to providing means of appraising investment projects, these methods offer solutions to other management problems. Decision tree analysis, for example, extends probability analysis to the study of activities which consist of a chain of dependent events. In this connection, probabilistic budgeting increases the effectiveness of budgetary control systems. The advent of computers has made possible the study of the effects of risk through simulation techniques.

Risk analysis rests on the assumption that decision makers are risk-averse. Despite its limitations in practice, utility theory is useful for providing an understanding of decision-making under risk.

Reference

Hertz D. B., Risk Analysis in Capital Investments, *Harvard Business Review*, 42, pp. 95–106, Jan-Feb. 1964.

Further Readings

Hespos, R. & Strassman, P., Stochastic Decision Trees for the Analysis of Investment Decisions, *Management Science*, August, 1965.

House, William C. Jr., *Sensitivity Analysis in Making Capital Investment Decisions*, N.A.A. Research Monograph No. 3, New York, National Association of Accountants, 1968.

Lowes, Bryan, Budgeting to Meet Problem of Uncertainty, *Management Accounting*, January, 1973.

Magee, J., How to Use Decision Trees in Capital Investment, *Harvard Business Review*, September-October, 1964.

Van Horne, J. C., *Financial Management and Policy*, Prentice Hall, Englewood Cliffs N.J., 1975.

Weston, J. Fred & Brigham, Eugene F., *Managerial Finance*, Holt Dryden, New York, 1975.

7
Cost-Volume-Profit Analysis

Much of the discussion in the previous three chapters was concerned with the importance of the distinction between the long-term and the short-term for decision-making, and consequently of the nature of the accounting problem of providing relevant information for decisions affecting different time periods.

The essential qualitative difference between the long-term and the short-term is that the long-term may be defined as planning for change, whereas the short-term implies adapting to change. In this sense, the firm's resources may be planned in the long-term to take advantage of changing opportunities in such a way that not only its structure may be altered but its objectives as well. In the short-term, however, the firm's output capacity is fixed, so that the firm's freedom of action is limited.

Short-term planning, which is the subject of this chapter, considers the most desirable course of action to take to achieve a planned profit given that the firm's output range is relatively fixed. Cost-volume-profit analysis is an important tool in short-term planning for it explores the inter-relationship which exists between the four principal variables—cost, revenue, volume of output and profit. In planning its short-term strategy management will require to know what will be the effect of changing one or more of these variables, and the effect of this change on profit.

Applications of cost-volume-profit (c-v-p) analysis

Cost-volume-profit analysis lies at the centre of short-term profit planning because it has a wider application to a whole series of decision problems. In view of the relationship between costs and volume of output, c-v-p is helpful in establishing a pricing strategy. C-v-p is also relevant to the selection of the best sales mix, where a firm produces several different products. In such a case, it is essential to select the most profitable combination of the different products having regard to their costs of production and the prices which are obtainable. A decision to produce a sales mix which is less profitable may be made, for example in order to penetrate a market or to establish a stronger position in a particular market from a sales point of view, and in such a case c-v-p will enable management to assess the cost of that strategy in terms of lost profit. Other applications include the study of product alternatives, the acceptance of special orders, selecting channels of distribution, the strategy for entering a foreign market and changing plant lay-out.

C-v-p analysis lays emphasis on cost behaviour patterns through different volumes of output as a guide to the selection of profit targets and the adoption of an appropriate pricing policy. By uniting the behaviour of all four variables together in one short-term model, c-v-p analysis provides management with a sweeping overview of the planning process.

Cost analysis and profit planning

The response of costs to a variety of influences is invaluable to management decision-making. As we saw in chapter 2, some costs are constant, or fixed, in a given time-span, whereas other costs vary. Cost-volume-profit analysis focuses on the distinction between 'fixed' and 'variable' costs: the former being defined for this purpose as the costs which do not change over a range of output, and the latter being those which change directly with output.

C-v-p analysis requires that the fixed and variable elements be segregated and calculated so that all costs may be divided into simply fixed and variable costs.

One of the most important uses of the distinction between fixed and variable cost lies in the analysis of these costs through different levels of production.

Example

Unit sales	40,000 Total	40,000 Unit	50,000 Total	50,000 Unit
		£		£
Revenue	400,000	10.0	500,000	10.0
Variable costs	160,000	4.0	200,000	4.0
Contribution margin	240,000	6.0	300,000	6.0
Fixed costs	150,000	3.8	150,000	3.0
Net profit	90,000	2.2	150,000	3.0

Duofold Ltd produces an article which it sells for £10. Fixed costs of production are £150,000 per year, and variable costs are £4 per unit. The present yearly volume of output is 40,000 units, but could be increased to 50,000.

Problem: What will be the effect on total costs of the projected increase in output, and the impact of profit?

The analysis shows that total variable costs increase proportionally with output for unit variable costs are constant. Total fixed costs, however, remain constant at both levels of output so that unit fixed costs fall as output rises and vice versa. It is because unit fixed costs are falling that total unit costs are less for an output of 50,000 units than for one of 40,000 units.

If we assume that selling prices remain unaltered, costs savings themselves will lead to increased profitability. The contribution margin is an important concept in cost-profit analysis. As may be seen from the example above, the contribution margin is calculated by deducting the variable costs from revenue. It is the first stage in calculating the net profit and measures the profit which is available to cover fixed costs. Since fixed costs are incurred irrespective of sales, a firm will make a loss if the contribution margin is insufficient to cover fixed costs. At low levels of output the firm will make a loss because fixed costs are greater than the contribution margin. As output increases, so does the contribution margin which will ultimately equal and then exceed fixed costs. The relationship between fixed costs and the contribution margin may be illustrated as in Fig. 3.17. The critical point at which the contribution margin is equal to fixed costs is known as the break-even point which indicates that level of output (OA) at which the firm makes zero profits, that is, where total costs are equal to total revenues.

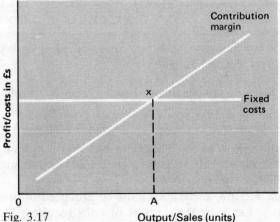

Fig. 3.17

Break-even analysis

Break-even analysis focuses on the measurement of the break-even point. Before we attempt any calculations, it is necessary to make certain assumptions about the behaviour of costs and revenues. Thus, we assume that costs and revenue patterns have been reliably determined and that they are linear over the range of output which is being analysed. These assumptions also imply that costs may be resolved without difficulty into fixed and variable costs; that fixed costs will remain constant, that variable costs will vary proportionally with volume of output; and that all other factors will remain constant, that is, that selling prices will remain unchanged, that the methods and the efficiency of production will not be altered and that volume is the only factor affecting costs. It is because these assumptions are difficult to maintain in a 'real life' situation that break-even analysis cannot pretend to be anything but a rough-guide. Its real value to management lies in the fact that it highlights the inter-relationships between the factors affecting profits, allowing management to make certain assumptions about these factors and seeing the likely effects of changes in these assumptions. Hence, break-even analysis is useful as a management decision model.

Calculating the break-even point

There are three methods commonly employed in solving break-even problems:

  (i) the equation method
  (ii) the contribution margin method
  (iii) the graph method.

The equation method

The relationship between sales, variable and fixed costs and profits may be expressed as an equation:

$$\text{Sales} = \text{Variable Costs} + \text{Fixed Costs} + \text{Net Profit}$$

Example

Take the values given in the previous example, that is, that the unit sale price is £10, variable costs are £4 per unit and fixed costs £150,000 per year.

Problem 1: How many units must be produced to break-even?

Analysis: Let x be the number of units required. Our equation

will be:
$$£10x = £4x + £150,000 + £0$$
$$\text{and } £10x - £4x = £150,000 + £0$$
$$\text{so that} \quad x = \frac{£150,000}{6}$$
$$= 25,000 \text{ } units$$

Problem 2: Alternatively, the problem may be calculating the sales revenue required to break-even.

Analysis: Since net profit is zero, our formula remains:

$$\text{Sales} = \text{Variable Costs} + \text{Fixed Costs}$$

Let the unknown level of sales revenue be x, and knowing that variable costs are $\frac{4}{10}$th of x, we can substitute:

$$x = \tfrac{4}{10}x + £150,000$$
$$\text{and } x - \tfrac{4}{10}x = £150,000$$
$$\tfrac{6}{10}x = £150,000$$
$$x = £250,000$$

The break-even sales revenue can be equally derived from the break-even volume of sales (25,000 units at £10 = £250,000), but the calculations are intended to show that the results can be calculated independently.

The contribution margin method

This method makes use of the variable profit or contribution margin per unit of output which is required to cover fixed costs.

Problem 1: On the basis that the unit sale price is £10, that the variable costs are £4 per unit and that fixed costs total £150,000 a year, calculate the break-even volume of sales.

Analysis: Let x be the number of units required. We know that the unit contribution margin is the difference between unit sale price and unit variable costs. Our formula is:

$$x = \frac{\text{Fixed Costs} + \text{Net Profit}}{\text{Unit Contribution Margin}}$$
$$x = \frac{£150,000 + 0}{(£10 - £4)}$$
$$= \frac{150,000}{6}$$
$$= 25,000 \text{ units}$$

Problem 2: Using the same values calculate the break-even sales revenue.

Analysis: In this case, we make use of the contribution margin ratio to calculate the sales revenue required to cover fixed costs. The margin contribution ratio is:

$$\frac{\text{Unit Contribution Margin}}{\text{Revenue per unit}}\%$$

Our formula may be expressed as follows:

$$x = \frac{\text{Fixed Costs} + \text{Net Profit}}{\text{Contribution Margin Ratio}}$$

Substituting the given values we have:

$$x = \frac{150,000 + 0}{60\%}$$

$$= \underline{\underline{£250,000}}$$

Alternatively, the break-even revenue may be found from the following formula:

$$x = \frac{\text{Fixed Costs} + \text{Net Profit}}{1 - \dfrac{\text{Total Variable Costs}}{\text{Total Sales Revenue}}}$$

$$= \frac{150,000}{1 - \dfrac{160,000}{400,000}}$$

$$= \underline{\underline{£250,000}}$$

It is clear that both the equation method and the contribution margin method can be applied to profit planning by the substitution of the net profit figure, which for the purpose of our analysis of the break-even point we have taken to be zero.

The graph method

This method involves using what is usually called a break-even chart. This description is not very satisfactory because it gives undue emphasis to the break-even point whereas other points on the graph are just as important.

A break-even chart is easy to compile, but the accuracy of the readings will depend on the accuracy with which the data is plotted. The output or sales in units may be drawn on the horizontal axis, and the vertical axis is used to depict money values.

Method: Using the values given for the previous examples, the stages in compiling the break-even chart are as follows:

   (i) Using suitable graph paper, draw a horizontal axis to measure total output in units (50,000 units). Draw a vertical axis representing this output at its selling price of £10 per unit (£500,000).

  (ii) Draw the variable cost curve as a straight line from zero to £200,000 at 50,000 units of output (50,000 @ £4).

 (iii) Draw the fixed cost curve parallel to the variable cost curve but £150,000 higher, so that total costs including variable costs will be represented by the area below this curve.

 (iv) Insert the total revenue curve from zero to £500,000 at 50,000 units.

Figure 3.18 vividly depicts the relationship between costs, revenues, volume of output and resultant profit. The area between the revenue

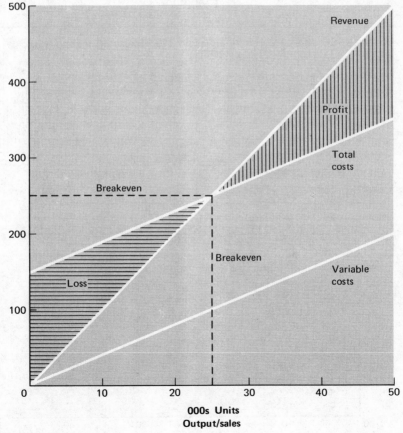

Fig. 3.18   Breakeven chart.

curve and the variable cost curve represents the contribution to fixed costs and profit at each level of output. The point at which the revenue curve crosses the total cost curve is the break-even point. As output expands from zero, fixed costs are gradually recovered until the break-even point, and thereafter each unit of output contributes to profit.

The excess by which actual sales exceed break-even sales amounts to £250,000, so that sales could be reduced by £250,000 before losses start to be incurred. This excess is known as the margin of safety. The margin of safety ratio is the percentage by which sales revenue may fall before a loss is incurred and is expressed as follows:

$$\text{Margin of Safety Ratio} = \frac{\text{Margin of Safety Revenue}}{\text{Actual Sales}}$$

Hence, in the example given, the margin of safety ratio is

$$\frac{£250,000}{£500,000} \text{ i.e. } 50\%$$

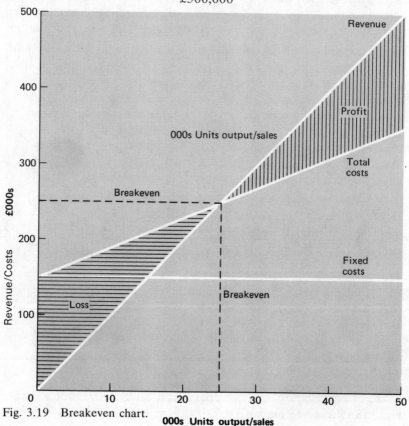

Fig. 3.19 Breakeven chart.

000s Units output/sales

Clearly, the higher the margin of safety ratio, the safer the firm's position.

An alternative way of constructing the break-even chart is as in Fig. 3.19. The disadvantage of this form of presentation is that unlike Fig. 3.18, it does not emphasize the importance of the contribution margin to fixed costs.

The profit-volume chart

The profit-volume-chart is a special type of break-even chart. It is concerned with analysing profit and loss at different levels of activity. As in the break-even chart, the horizontal axis is used to measure the volume of output or sales in units, but the vertical axis is employed to measure the profit or loss at any given level of output or sales.

Using the same information as above, Fig. 3.20 below shows the profit-volume-chart. Only three items are needed to plot this chart— the fixed costs DC, which are £150,000 and which must be recovered before a profit is made, the break-even point E, which represents sales of £250,000 necessary to cover fixed costs, and the profit at an assumed level of activity (which in this case is 50,000 units yielding a profit of £150,000).

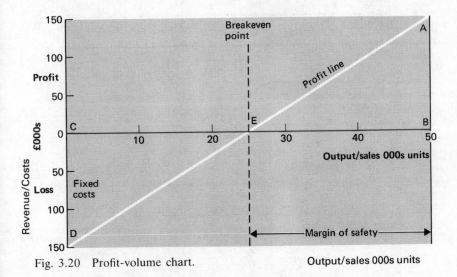

Fig. 3.20   Profit-volume chart.

The profit-volume chart (Fig. 3.20) is simply the conventional break-even chart re-arranged to show changes in profit or loss which occur through volume changes either of sales or output. It is less detailed since it does not show separate curves for costs and revenues, but its virtue lies in the fact that it reduces any changes down to two key elements—volume and profit. For this reason, the volume-profit chart is useful for illustrating the results of different management decisions.

Insofar as the volume-profit chart focuses simply on the relationship between volume and profit, it allows for an extended analysis of this relationship. Thus, the slope of the curve DA indicates the contribution margin ratio, which may be measured by AB/BE or DC/CE—either calculation giving the same results in this case (60%).

The slope of the curve DA also indicates the rate at which changes in volume assist in the recovery of fixed costs and affect profit: the greater the slope the greater will be the effect of changes in volume on profits. Equally, the steeper the slope of the profit curve the quicker will the margin of safety be eroded and the break-even point reached as the volume of output or sales falls, as may be seen from the 3 cases in Fig. 3.21.

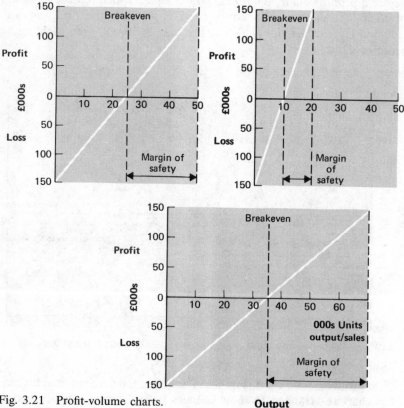

Fig. 3.21   Profit-volume charts.

Profit planning through change

Profit planning is related to a consideration of four factors—fixed costs, variable costs, selling price, and sales volume. Any change in one or several of these factors will affect planned profit. Cost-volume-profit analysis enables management to consider the effects of these changes.

Changes in fixed costs

Assuming that all other factors remain unchanged, a change in fixed costs will affect only the break-even point.

Example

The consequential effect of an increase of £15,000 in head office costs on the break-even level is as follows:

	Original	After increase in fixed costs
	£	£
Sales	500,000	500,000
Variable costs	200,000	200,000
Contribution margin	300,000	300,000
Fixed costs	150,000	165,000
Net profit	150,000	135,000
Contribution margin ratio	60%	60%

The new break-even point is:

$$\frac{\text{Fixed Costs}}{\text{Unit contribution margin}} = \frac{165,000}{£6} = 27,500 \text{ units}$$

Hence, a 10% increase in fixed costs has resulted in a 10% increase in the sales volume (and sales revenue) required to break-even from 25,000 units (£250,000) to 27,500 units (£275,000). Thus, additional sales of 2500 units at £10 a unit are required to cover an increase of £15,000 in fixed costs. It should be noted that as the contribution margin ratio has remained constant, the change in fixed costs is the only factor affecting profit. The change may be illustrated as in Fig. 3.22 on p. 392.

Changes in variable costs

A change in variable costs will have the immediate effect of changing the contribution margin ratio, and consequently the break-even point.

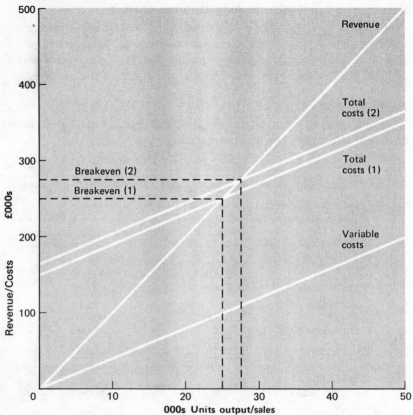

Fig. 3.22   Changes in fixed costs.

Example

It is decided to improve the quality a product by incorporating more expensive materials. As a result, variable costs are increased by 10%, and the consequential effects on the break-even level are as follows:

	Original	After increase in variable costs
	£	£
Sales	500,000	500,000
Variable costs	200,000	220,000
Contribution margin	300,000	280,000
Fixed costs	150,000	150,000
Net profit	150,000	130,000
Contribution margin ratio	60%	56%

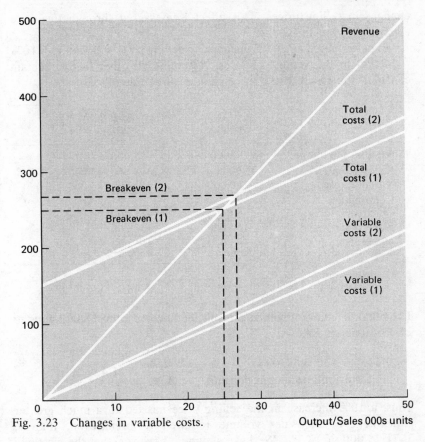

Fig. 3.23 Changes in variable costs.

The new break-even point will be:

$$\frac{\text{Fixed costs}}{\text{Contribution margin per unit}} = \frac{£150,000}{5.6} = 26,786 \text{ units}$$

Note that whereas a 10% increase in fixed costs led to a 10% increase in the sale volume (and sales revenue) required to break-even in this instance, a 10% increase in variable costs has led to a proportionately smaller increase in the sales volume required to break-even, that is, 1786 units or 7.14%. We may illustrate the change as in Fig. 3.23.

Changes in selling price

Successful profit planning through changes in selling prices depends upon management knowing how the market will react to these price changes. If the price is reduced will customers buy greater quantities of the product so as to increase the total revenue derived from sales? In other words it is important to know the effect upon total revenue of changes in selling prices. This effect is measured through the price elasticity of demand.

Let us assume that a 10% increase in selling price will lead to a 10% reduction in the volume of sales. Assuming all other factors remain constant, the result of the price change will be as follows:

	Original	After increase in selling price
Sales in unit	50,000	45,000
Sales revenue	£500,000	£495,000 (45,000 @ £11)
Variable costs	200,000	180,000 (45,000 @ £4)
Contribution margin	300,000	315,000
Fixed costs	150,000	150,000
Net profit	150,000	165,000
Contribution margin ratio	60%	63.6%

The break-even point will, as a result, be lowered from 25,000 units to 21,429 units as follows:

$$\frac{\text{Fixed costs}}{\text{Contribution margin per unit}} = \frac{£150,000}{£7} = 21,429 \text{ units}$$

Thus, a 10% increase in the selling price has led to a much greater adjustment in the sales volume required to break-even, that is, 3571/25,000 or 14.3%. We have assumed, however, that the elasticity of demand for the product was unity, that is, that a percentage alteration in the price would lead to the same proportionate alteration in the volume of sales. In most situations this would be an unreal assumption to make, so that it becomes crucial to management to know the slope of the demand curve for the commodity, that is, the elasticity of demand if their analysis of the impact of a price change on the net profit is to be valid. We may compare the three different results that would be obtained by the same price change under three different demand conditions for the commodity as follows:

(1) Where demand is *elastic*, i.e., elasticity is greater than unity. In this case we assume that a 10% increase in selling price will lead to a 20% reduction in sales.

(2) Where the elasticy of demand is unity. In this case we assume, as in the example above that a 10% increase in selling price will lead to a 10% reduction in sales.

(3) Where demand is inelastic. We assume a 10% increase in selling price will lead to a 5% reduction in sales.

	Elastic	Unity	Inelastic
Sales units	40,000	45,000	47,500
Sales revenue (£11)	£440,000	£495,000	£522,500
Variable costs (£4)	160,000	180,000	190,000
Contribution margin	280,000	315,000	332,500
Fixed costs	150,000	150,000	150,000
Net profit	£130,000	£165,000	£182,500

This example illustrates the importance to management of knowing the nature of the demand for their products. In the example, where demand is elastic, we witness a sharp fall in net profit from the original £150,000 to £130,000. On the other hand, a unitary or inelastic demand schedule results in an increase in net profit.

The sales mix

We mentioned at the beginning of this chapter that c-v-p was important to short-term profit planning, and that it was helpful also to the solution of other types of managerial problems. One such problem is that of selecting the best sales-mix. So far in our discussion, we have assumed that the firm had only one product so that profit planning involved a consideration of only four factors, that is, fixed and variable costs, selling price and sales volume. Most firms, however, either produce or sell more than one product and management has to decide in what combination these products ought to be made or sold. It may be possible, for example, that by altering the existing sales mix by selling proportionately more of the product which has the highest contribution margin, the overall contribution margin and the break-even point may be improved.

Example

Assume that Maximix Ltd has data concerning the three products which it markets as follows:

Product	A	B	C	Total
	£	£	£	£
Sales	100,000	100,000	50,000	250,000
Variable costs	50,000	30,000	20,000	100,000
Contribution margin	50,000	70,000	30,000	150,000
Fixed costs				150,000
Net profit				Nil
Contribution margin ratio	50%	70%	60%	60%

If the firm could switch its sales so as to sell more of product B which has a higher contribution margin ratio than the other two, it will succeed in improving its profitability. At the present moment, the firm is just breaking even. Let us assume that it maintains the present total sales of £250,000, but that the sales mix is altered as shown below:

Product	A	B	C	Total
	£	£	£	£
Sales	50,000	175,000	25,000	250,000
Variable costs	25,000	52,500	10,000	87,500
Contribution	25,000	122,500	15,000	162,500
Fixed costs				150,000
Net profit				12,500
Contribution margin ratio	50%	70%	60%	65%

Hence the new product mix has raised the contribution margin ratio by 5% leading to a profit of £12,500 and a lowering of the break-even point from £250,000 to £230,769 as follows:

$$\frac{\text{Fixed costs}}{\text{Contribution margin ratio}} = \frac{£150,000}{65\%} = £230,769$$

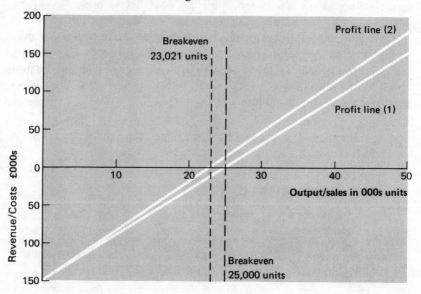

Fig. 3.24   Change in sales-mix.   Output/Sales

The effect of the change in the product mix may be depicted graphically as in Fig. 3.24.

Cost-volume-profit analysis: some limitations

C-v-p analysis, though it is a very useful tool for decision-making, is based upon certain assumptions which can rarely be completely realized in practice. Hence the fragility of these assumptions places limits on the reliability of c-v-p analysis as a tool in decision-making. For example, it is assumed that fixed costs are constant, and that both the variable cost and the revenue curves are linear over the relevant volume of output. It is also assumed that volume is the only factor affecting costs, and that both the price of cost factors and of the product produced or sold remains unaffected by changes in the volume of output.

All these assumptions may be challenged. Fixed costs may not remain constant over the entire output range considered in the analysis, that being particularly true if the volume range considered is fairly extensive. Fixed costs may indeed be constant over a band of output, but then will rise sharply and remain constant for another stage, as indicated in Fig. 3.25.

Equally doubtful is the assumption that the variable cost curve is linear so that variable costs change in direct proportion to changes in volume. As demand for input factors increase so will their price, with the effect that the variable cost curve is likely to increase proportionately faster as volume of output expand.

To overcome these limitations, and to retain the usefulness of c-v-p analysis it is necessary to limit the volume range to be examined so that the behaviour of both fixed and variable costs may be more accurately determined. The basic assumption that the cost-volume relationship is a linear relationship is realistic only over narrow ranges of output which is called the relevant range.

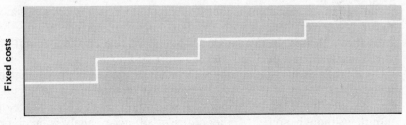

Volume

Fig. 3.25

As regards the revenue curve, to increase sales it may be necessary to reduce price, so that a straight line is not an accurate portrayal of the behaviour of sales. Therefore, computations are often needed at several price levels—several total revenue curves are needed instead of just one.

Finally, the break-even chart presents an extremely simplified picture of cost-revenue-volume relationships. Each of these three is subject to outside influences as well as to the influence of the other two. Above all, the break-even analysis should be viewed as a guide to decision-making, not a substitute for judgement and common sense.

Despite its limitations, the real usefulness of c-v-p is that it enriches the understanding of the relationship between costs, volume and prices as factors affecting profit, enabling management to make assumptions which will assist the decision-making process in the short-run planning period.

Summary

In the short-run, the firm's output is fixed, so that its freedom of action is limited in this respect. Given this condition, short-range planning considers the most desirable action to take to achieve a planned profit. Cost-volume-profit analysis (c-v-p) has an important role to play in short-run planning by providing an insight into the relationships between costs, volume of output, revenue and profit. In particular, c-v-p analysis highlights the significance of the distinction between fixed and variable costs and the behaviour of these two types of costs through changes in the volume of output.

C-v-p analysis makes an important contribution to short-run profit planning by providing an understanding of the conditions required to break-even. It does not assist in the discovery of the conditions required to maximize profits, in sharp contrast to economic theory which pays particular attention to this aspect of profit planning. Its advantage to management is that it is a method which is operationally useful. Moreover, it deals with the most important consideration—the avoidance of losses. In this sense, c-v-p analysis reflects the assumption of risk analysis that decision-makers are risk-averse.

C-v-p analysis has limitations as a result of the assumptions that it incorporates. Many of these assumptions may be challenged, for example, the linearity of the behaviour of costs and revenues over a range of output. Although some of the criticism of c-v-p analysis may be partially refuted, its real usefulness lies in the manner in which it enriches the understanding of the relationship between cost, volume of output and revenue for profit planning purposes in the short-run, thereby assisting management in the making of short-run profit planning decisions.

Further readings

1. Bierman, H. Jr. & Dyckman, T. R., *Managerial Cost Accounting*, Macmillan, New York, 1971.

2. Charnes, A, Cooper, W. W. & Ijiri, Y, Breakeven Budgeting and Programming to Goals, *Journal of Accounting Research*, Spring, 1963.

3. Jaedicke, R. K. & Robichek, A., Cost-Volume-Profit Analysis Under Conditions of Uncertainty, *The Accounting Review*, October, 1964.

4. National Association of Accountants, *The Analysis of Cost-Volume-Profit Relationships*, New York, 1950.

5. Tse, J., *Profit Planning Through Volume-Cost Analysis*, Macmillan, New York, 1960.

6. Welsch, G., *Budgeting: Profit Planning and Control*, Prentice Hall, Englewood Cliffs, N.J., 1971.

8
Pricing

It is evident from the foregoing chapters that there are many factors which are critical to the success of the firm's long-term and short-term plans. For the purpose of discussion, we have been obliged to focus upon these factors independently of each other, so as to examine their salient features more closely. As a result, the reader may have been tempted to forget that the most important point about these factors is not their independence but their inter-dependence. Indeed, successful management control is the activity of harmonizing all the elements operating within the firm.

Managers and accountants attach a great deal of importance to cost control because costs are more susceptible to control than other factors such as sales volume and profits. As we saw in chapter 7, cost-volume-profit analysis lies at the centre of short-term planning, but we did say that given the firm's cost structure, price changes could affect both the sales volume and the profit level. How successfully management may be able to improve profits through price changes depends on its knowledge of how the market will react to such changes. Hence, management needs to formulate a pricing policy or strategy which takes into account the likely effects of price changes on the market's demand for the firm's product, so as to plan a level of operation which, given the firms cost structure, will produce the required profit.

We may say, therefore, that in the study of pricing we see the problem of management in the two-fold aspect mentioned in chapter 1, that is, the problem of control-in-the-large and that of control-in-the-small. By means of its pricing policy, the firm is able to control to a degree its relationship with its environment (control-in-the-large), and at the same time, it is controlling its internal operations accordingly (control-in-the-small).

There is also a further dimension to the problem of pricing which the reader will readily appreciate. If the firm formulates a pricing policy which affects its relationship with the market, such a policy has long-term as well as short-term implications. Any alteration in the volume of demand for the firm's products which results directly from its own pricing policy will affect its capital budgeting programme; hence, we may say that the firm's long-range plan should reflect its long-term pricing policy. Thus, short-term changes in that policy should be effected solely for the purpose of providing that degree of flexibility which is essential to effective long-range planning and control.

The nature of the pricing problem

By and large, it may be said that the firm's long-term survival depends on its ability to obtain prices for its products which will cover all its costs, which for this purpose may be regarded as including a reasonable rate of return to investors. Therefore, it may appear that the pricing problem is relatively easy to solve, in that the accountant may calculate unit costs of production and add a percentage for profit. Indeed, it is this type of approach which, as we shall see later, has been highly influential in the past.

The truth is that the pricing problem is much more complex than simply estimating total costs per unit. The firm's cost structure in the short-term will determine whether a given price will produce a profit or a loss on each unit sold, but the total profit may equally well be affected by changes in consumer demand and the firm's environment. Indeed, competition and economic policies which affect the level of aggregate demand are frequently more significant to the pricing decision than the firm's total unit costs. Moreover, since there are different cost concepts and measures of costs which are relevant to different decision-problems, there is a variety of circumstances which call for different pricing policies.

It should be remembered, however, that pricing is only one of the ways in which the firm can influence the demand for its product. If the firm wishes to expand sales, it may do so in a number of ways, for example, by advertising, expanding its sales force, improving its selling style, improving product presentation as well as by lowering the price. Indeed, altering its pricing policy may not necessarily be the best way of expanding sales and improving total profits. Conversely, a fall in demand for the product may be remedied by improvements in selling methods rather than increasing its price competitiveness. We may say, therefore, that in analysing the pricing problem, we are concentrating on only one of the factors which may influence the level of sales.

The nature of pricing theories

Two distinct influences are seen at play on the various pricing theories which we propose to discuss. Firstly, there is the influence of classical economic theory which has been concerned to lay down guidelines for finding the best or optimum price. This school of thought does not regard the problem of pricing in isolation from other economic problems. Indeed, the pricing theory advocated by classical economists is consistent with their ideas on the manner in which resources may best be allocated throughout the economy. We do not propose to dwell on this point as most of our readers will have a knowledge of economic theory. The second influence on pricing theories stems from business traditions of conservatism or sound management which look to costs as setting a minimum point for a price. Inevitably, this school of thought focuses on the discovery of the appropriate costs for pricing decisions, Some members of this school believe that full-cost is the best basis for determining the selling price: other members insists that variable costs provide better guidelines for the pricing decision both in the long-run and the short-run. In sharp contrast to the views of classical economists, businessmen and accountants have been less concerned with finding the best price than with establishing a price which covers an agreed measure of costs and provides a sufficient profit. Hence, to the latter, pricing is an integral part of the activity of long-range and budgetary planning.

Pricing theory in economics

Classical theorists hold that the firm should seek to discover the best or optimum price, which they argue is that price which will maximize the firm's profits. From their point of view, the price which maximizes profits implies the most efficient use of the economic resources held by the firm. Furthermore, such a pricing policy is necessary if capitalist enterprise is to reflect correctly the tenets of classical philosophy of Capitalism, that is, that the objective of the firm is to maximize the returns accruing to the owner of its capital. The efficient allocation of resources through the economy is secured by the assumption that every owner of capital has the behavioural characteristics of that celebrated fiction, the '*homo economicus*'—which was invented specially to give validity to classical theory. Since such persons will seek to maximize the return on invested capital, scarce economic resources will be distributed between competing ends in a manner which will produce the greatest national wealth.

The complete confidence which rests in the validity of these assumptions by those who still share a commitment to classical theory under other guises, is reflected in the exuberance with which the method for establishing the optimum price is taught. The price which maximizes profits is found at that level of sales where the addition to total revenue resulting from the sale of the last unit (the marginal revenue) is equal to the addition to total costs resulting from the production of that last unit (marginal cost).

It is clear that economic theory imposes very exacting conditions on the analysis of the optimum price, and in particular makes demands for information which are extremely difficult to meet. Classical theorists argue, nevertheless, that this principle is a useful guide to profit maximization.

Example

Let us assume that a firm producing Widgets in large numbers has sufficient knowledge of the revenue and cost schedules at different volume levels associated with different selling prices. The accountant is able to produce the undermentioned data:

Selling Price per unit	No. of units which may be sold	Total Sales Revenue	Total Variable Costs	Fixed Costs	Profit (loss)
£		£	£	£	£
30	100,000	3,000,000	1,800,000	800,000	400,000
32	90,000	2,880,000	1,620,000	800,000	460,000
34	80,000	2,720,000	1,440,000	800,000	480,000
36	70,000	2,520,000	1,260,000	800,000	460,000
38	60,000	2,280,000	1,080,000	800,000	400,000
40	50,000	2,000,000	900,000	800,000	300,000

It is clear that the price of £34 a unit yields the maximum profit, and that this is the price which the firm should establish. At this price, marginal revenue equals marginal costs.

The limitations of the classical theorists' approach arises from the failure to appreciate the many practical problems with which managers are faced. In particular, it is extremely difficult to estimate the exact shape of the demand curve, that is, how much will be sold at any particular price.

There are further reasons for doubting the assumptions of classical theory. It is not only myopic in ignoring the information problem completely, but it assumes that the volume of sales is solely a function of price. As we mentioned earlier, expenditure on sales promotion may well affect the demand curve without the need to adjust the price of the product.

There is little doubt that businessmen are not as a general rule profit-maximizers. Not only are there too many social pressures acting against excessive profit-seeking, but their behavioural instincts do not correspond with those of the '*homo economicus*'. Indeed, the business-man is a human being, whose decisions are influenced by moral, social, political as well as by financial considerations. As we saw in chapter 3, the required profit as a planning goal is never a theoretical ideal such as the maximum long-term profit but represents what is thought to be a possible and desirable target for the time span considered.

Economic theory makes an important contribution to pricing theory, despite the criticisms which we have just mentioned, because it draws attention to the factors which are relevant to the pricing decision, in particular the importance of the interaction of revenue and cost information for deciding upon a 'good' price, and draws attention to those cost elements which are relevant to such a price. It has most certainly encouraged the idea of variable or marginal cost pricing, and the formulation of flexible pricing strategies.

Cost-based pricing theories

Businessmen have for long been aware that pricing a product is one of the most important and complicated problems which they have to face. In attempting to resolve this problem, and in trying to find some general guidelines by which to establish a sound pricing policy, they are in agreement that cost is one of the factors which must be taken in to account. Consistently selling below full costs will lead to bankruptcy, whilst if the firm is to survive it must try to sell at prices which will not only cover costs but yield a sufficient profit. No hard and fast rules may be laid down since each firm's product and market situation have features which themselves may be unique.

The influence of costs on pricing decisions varies according to circumstances. Where firms are under contract to supply on a cost-plus basis, their costs are all important in deciding the contract price. In other situations, for example a liquidation sale, costs are irrelevant because the price at which the goods are sold are not related to their costs. Normally, the importance of the firm's costs lies somewhere between these two extremes.

The relevance of costs to pricing decisions is influenced also by the firm's drive to meet certain objectives, for example, earning a specified rate of return, increasing its share of the market or penetrating a new market. Moreover, the firm's relative marketing strength in a particular market may be a more dominant influence on pricing than its costs. Thus, a firm may be so strong as to be a price-maker, so that it is able to fix a price which other producers will have to follow. Conversely, a firm may be a price-taker, that is, its position in the market is so weak that it cannot influence the price.

In general, cost-based pricing theories are concerned with two elements of price. The first is the relevant costs which should be included in the price, and the second is the profit margin which must be added to reach the price. The profit margin will reflect a degree of caution about the likely reactions of customers or the nearness of a substitute if the firm is contemplating improving its profitability. Its relationship with near competitors may affect the firm's views on the size of its profit margin. Price cutting through the reduction of profit margins may lead to a price war, and profit margins may be safeguarded and increased by means of trading agreements. Some of these agreements in restraint of trade, which were really agreements in restraint of competition, are now illegal.

Cost-based pricing theories have a moral quality which economic theory does not evince. In the sense that cost-based pricing reflects the notion that a cost-plus formula is 'fair', it reflects that medieval notion of a 'just price' which was such an important part of the teaching of such men as St Thomas Aquinas, and which still dominates our own conception of fair trading. It is incorrect to suggest, as does economic theory, that business theories and the actions of businessmen may be divorced from the rules of morality by which their behaviour as individuals is affected. It is evident that businessmen are concerned with finding a 'fair' price, and that this 'fair price' is one, which on the one hand will cover their own costs, and on the other will contain that measure of reward which the buyer will regard as reasonable. In this sense, cost-based pricing theories do reflect the interaction of demand and supply, but unlike economic theory, do so in a way which reflects behavioural realities.

Full-cost pricing

This theory requires that all the costs both fixed and variable of bringing the product to the market be included in the selling price. Once the full-costs have been established, it suffices to add the agreed profit margin.

Example

High Speeds Castings Ltd produces two castings, Type A and Type B. The total unit costs are as follows:

	Type A £	Type B £
Direct Materials	4	12
Direct Labour	6	4
Factory overheads: Variable	6	3
Fixed	4	1
Total Manufacturing Costs	20	20
Marketing and Administrative Costs:		
Variable	2	3
Fixed	4	3
Full-Costs per unit	26	26

To calculate the selling price under this method, we simply add the required profit margin, as follows:

	£	£
Full-costs per unit	26	26
Add: Mark-up (50% on costs)	13	13
Selling price	39	39

Full-cost pricing appears on the surface to be an easy method. By ignoring demand considerations completely and concentrating on costs, it avoids one of the major problem-areas of pricing. Nevertheless, there are problems in calculating full-costs which are not easy to resolve. By and large, one may assume that the calculation of unit variable costs present no serious measurement difficulties. By contrast, the assignment of fixed costs to units of output is an extremely complex matter.

Indirect costs and full-cost pricing

Many factory, administrative and marketing costs cannot be identified clearly with a particular cost centre. Furthermore, there is the problem of selecting an appropriate basis for assigning them to individual products. Under full-cost pricing, this problem is critical to the determination of the selling price.

Consider the previous example of High Speed Castings Ltd and let us assume that the demand for Product B is buoyant whereas the demand for Product A is slack. In these circumstances, it may be a good idea to transfer a higher proportion of fixed costs to Product B, and so enabling the price of Product A to be lowered to encourage more sales. By introducing such considerations to the problem of the allocation of fixed costs in multi-product firms, one is introducing a new principle to full-cost pricing, that is, the ability of the market to accept costs. Consequently, one is moving away from the essence of full-cost pricing.

Fixed costs and volume changes

The impact of changes in the sales volume upon unit fixed costs leads a circular discussion, because price changes affect the volume of sales which in turn affect unit fixed costs which finally open up the possibility of further price changes. Since full-cost pricing implies flexible pricing in this sense, it is difficult to see its usefulness to those businessmen who instead of wanting a 'safe' price are looking for an aggressive price which will encourage the expansion of sales. Hence, they will tend to select a price which will be below full-costs and look to the expanded volume of sales to cover total costs ultimately. It is in the nature of things that until such men are satisfied with their market position, price will always be below full-costs. This is explainable in terms of the wish of businessmen to achieve market as well as profit objectives.

The following table shows the relationship of fixed costs and volume changes. Given that the percentage mark-up remains constant, there is a range of selling prices which will cover costs at a particular volume of sales.

Table 1

No of units (thousands)	100	200	300	400	500
Variable cost per unit	£4.00	£4.00	£4.00	£4.00	£4.00
Fixed cost per unit	2.00	1.00	0.67	0.50	0.40
Full cost per unit	6.00	5.00	4.67	4.50	4.40
10% mark-up	0.60	0.50	0.47	0.45	0.44
Selling price	6.60	5.50	5.14	4.95	4.84

It is also interesting to note the resulting aggregate profits which these different prices produce.

Table 2

No. of units (thousands)	100	200	300	400	500
Selling price	£6.60	£5.50	£5.14	£4.95	£4.84
Profit per unit (at 10%)	0.60	0.50	0.47	0.45	0.44
Aggregate profit (£000s)	60.00	100.00	141.00	180.00	220.00

Clearly, faced with these production possibilities, management would wish to pursue an aggressive pricing policy which would place the highest aggregate profits within the firm's reach. As explained above, full-cost pricing would stand in the way of such a pricing policy because of the decreasing nature of fixed costs per unit as output expands. A stage will be reached, of course, when the firm has reached the limit of production under existing capacity. In other words, a point exists where the firm must stabilize production or incur further capital expenditure on the expansion of productive capacity. This would involve the firm in a capital investment decision and a complete reconsideration of its pricing policy.

The price which the firm would wish to establish under full-cost pricing, therefore, is that price which will not only be the best price from a profit point of view, but one which is related to the best output capacity which the firm can maintain. It is for this reason that a 'normal volume' of output must be established so that the firm may decide the appropriate full-costs which are to form the basis of the price. This is a most important consideration for customers do not like frequent price changes.

Full-cost pricing and the mark-up percentage

Having gone through the complicated process of ascertaining the full-cost per unit, one moves to the final problem of determining the mark-up percentage which, when added to full-costs, will yield the price.

We have already mentioned that there are a number of influences which bear upon the size of the percentage mark-up. First, there is the notion of the 'fair price', and businessmen will argue strongly that such-and-such a percentage is a 'fair profit' for a given trade. There is a connection between the rate of turnover and the mark-up percentage, for example, it is quite normal to expect jewellers to impose a higher mark-up percentage on their goods than butchers. Second, the mark-up is influenced by the elasticity of demand for the product, and market conditions generally. Third, as we have already mentioned the mark-up is influenced by the nature of the firm's long-term strategy. Fourth, although businessmen argue that they seek a reasonable profit, it is evident that they mean the highest profit which they can 'reasonably' make. Finally, there is evidence also in the pricing policies of large firms, and particularly State Corporations, that the need to generate capital to finance expensive capital projects influences the profit mark-up, and hence the price.

Conversion cost pricing

Unlike full-cost pricing, conversion cost pricing takes into account only the costs incurred by the firm in converting raw materials and semi-finished goods into finished products. One of the limitations of full-cost pricing is that where the firm is selling two products which require different degrees of effort to convert to a marketable state, no distinction is drawn between them.

Conversion cost pricing, therefore, exclude direct materials and may be calculated easily from the example given on page 406 which is repeated below.

	Product A £	£	Product B £	£
Direct materials		4		12
Conversion costs				
Direct labour	6		4	
Factory overheads	10		4	
		16		8
Total factory costs		20		20

Under full-cost pricing, both products were priced as £39 as follows:

	Product A £	Product B £
Total factory costs	20	20
Selling and administrative costs	6	6
Full costs	26	26
Mark-up at 50%	13	13
Selling price	39	39

The objective of conversion cost pricing is to provide a pricing policy which will relate the cost or effort required by the firm to convert raw material into a marketable product to the selling price of the product. From the foregoing example, it is evident that Product A takes twice the effort to produce (£16) than Product B (£8). Hence, the firm should wish to formulate a pricing policy which will encourage the expansion of Product B, two units of which may be produced for the same production effort as Product A. This may be achieved by conversion cost pricing which will establish a lower price for Product B than for Product A. Under conversion cost pricing, the mark-up is calculated on the conversion costs, as shown on following page.

It will be recalled from chapter 7 that in selecting an appropriate sales mix from a profit planning point of view, the firm is attempting to plan production in such a way as to have that mix of product which will produce the best aggregate profit situation. Conversion cost pricing will assist the firm which is faced with such a problem. If the demand for

	Product A £	Product B £
Conversion costs		
Direct labour	6	4
Factory overheads	10	4
	16	8
Mark-up at 100%	16	8
	32	16
Other costs		
Direct materials	4	12
Selling and administrative costs	6	6
Selling price	42	34

Product B were such that the firm could switch entirely to that product, the firm would simply cease manufacturing Product A. It is the fact that the firm is compelled to produce both products because demand is limited that the sales-mix problem arises. It is equally for this reason that conversion cost pricing is useful in such situations.

Return on investment pricing

The cost-based pricing theories which we have examined so far focus on costs of production. Although such costs will include depreciation, they exclude any consideration of the capital employed by the firm. The firm has profit expectations, of course, and these are stated in terms of a percentage mark-up on costs of production. Return on investment pricing attempts to link the mark-up to the capital employed, and so set a price which includes a return on capital employed. The formula used is as follows:

$$\text{Selling price} = \frac{\text{Total costs} + (\text{Desired \% Return on capital} \times \text{Capital employed})}{\text{Volume of output}}$$

Example

Let us assume that High Speeds Castings Ltd, which produces the two products Type A and Type B, has a 'normal' output of Product A amounting to 20,000 units a year. Let us assume, also, that the capital employed by the firm is £1½ million of which £1 million is employed in the production of Product A. The desired rate of return which the firm has imposed on all its capital investment decisions is 20%. Accordingly, the firm seeks a profit mark-up which reflects this objective. The selling price may be calculated as follows:

	Product A £
Total costs of production (20,000 × £26)	520,000
Desired return on capital employed (20% of £1 m.)	200,000
Expected sales revenue	720,000
Selling price per unit (£720,000 ÷ 20,000)	£36

The attraction of this method of establishing a mark-up to costs is that it relates the problem of pricing to financial objectives and criteria, and integrates pricing decisions with the firm's overall planning objectives. It is clearly superior from a rational point of view than simply deciding upon a percentage mark-up in the basis of what is considered to be 'fair'. At the same time, return on investment pricing has all the tendencies to rigidity which are the features of full-cost pricing policies.

Variable cost pricing

Sometimes referred to as the contribution method of pricing or marginal pricing, this method of pricing is related to the ideas which we discussed in chapter 8. No one seriously disputes that in the long-term a firm's pricing policy must cover full-costs, whether these are interpreted as full-production costs or the replacement of the capital invested, as well as providing an acceptable margin of profit. As we saw earlier, this is the main argument put forward by the supporters of full-cost pricing. For short-term decisions, however, no one can doubt the usefulness of variable cost pricing.

There are many situations in which a price which covers variable costs but not full-costs will nevertheless make a contribution to profits. Thus, if a firm has spare capacity and has covered its fixed costs in the price set for its regular customers, and no further sales can be made to this market, the firm may attempt to reach another market by selling the article at a lower price with a slight alteration to the product presentation. Price discrimination, as this practice is known, enables the firm to sell the same product in different markets at different prices. The firm's total profits will be much greater as a result. This aspect of imperfect competition is commonly treated in economic textbooks. Similarly, where the firm is facing a fall in demand for its product due to a temporary market recession with the result that it is operating at a loss, any sales at a price which is above variable costs will contribute to the recovery of fixed costs.

Variable cost pricing enables the firm to pursue special marketing policies, such as the penetration of a new market, or the development of an export market, by imposing upon the home market a price which recovers fixed costs so as to permit sales at variable costs in the new market. Some call this practice 'dumping', and it was successfully carried out in Germany, notably, in the 1930s. Variable cost pricing is useful, therefore, because it indicates the lowest limit for a price decision. For example, the variable costs of the two products of High Speed Castings Ltd, are as follows:

	Product A	Product B
	£	£
Direct materials	4	12
Direct labour	6	4
Variable factory overheads	6	3
Variable selling and administrative overheads	2	3
Minimum price—Variable costs	18	22

Although variable cost pricing is useful for dealing with temporary market difficulties or for exploiting new marketing strategies, there may be a danger that variable cost pricing becomes the established method of pricing. The firm should therefore try to evolve both long-term and short-term pricing strategies, and return to a long-term pricing strategy once the short-term situation has been cleared.

In this section we have discussed the advantages of variable cost pricing for short-term situations. It has also advantages for the long-term. Full-cost pricing, as we have already suggested, may inhibit the firm from developing sales and production strategies which management considers to be desirable from a profit planning point of view. Variable cost pricing takes account of the relationship between price, volume and costs, and in this sense it enables better profit planning decisions to be made.

Going-rate pricing

Where the price for a product is determined by the market, so that the firm is faced with a 'going rate', the major problem for the firm is how much to produce. In such situations, the volume produced is determined by the firm's costs and its profit planned accordingly. The classic examples where firms are faced with the going rate are the various commodity markets. Producers try to solve the price uncertainty by selling in the 'futures markets', that is, contracting now to supply say in three months time at an agreed price.

Summary

Pricing decisions form an integral part of the firm's planning process, and are related directly to its objectives. The nature of the firm's product, the market situation, and the firm's short-term and long-term objectives are all factors which are relevant to pricing decisions.

Pricing policies must be examined in terms of the particular objectives which they seek to achieve, and we have already said that occasions may arise where a short-term objective requires a policy which would be unacceptable in the long-term. Numerous examples may be given of business objectives which require their own tailor-made pricing policies. The introduction of a new product may require a 'skimming price policy', that is, setting a high price initially and lowering the price as the product gains acceptance and popularity and permits the firm to expand the scale of production, so reducing its costs. Ball-point pens, nylons, television sets have all undergone this process. 'Penetration price policies' on the other hand have been a popular way of entering a foreign market and call for low prices to encourage rapid acceptance of the product.

For all these reasons, the only general rule that can be laid down is that unit variable costs provide a means of determining the lowest limit of an acceptable short-term price, whilst in the long-term the price should cover all costs and provide the margin of profit required by management.

Further readings

Dean, J., *Managerial Economics*, Prentice Hall, Englewood Cliffs, N.J., 1951.

Hague, D. C., *Pricing in Business*, Allen and Unwin, London, 1971.

Taylor, B. & Wills, G. (eds) *Pricing Strategy*, Staples Press, London, 1967.

Tucker, S. A., *Pricing for Higher Profit*, McGraw-Hill, New York, 1966.

9
Short-Run Tactical Decisions

We discussed in chapters 7 and 8 the importance of the relationship between cost and volume of output for profit planning purposes. Cost behaviour is a crucial element in profit planning, but a knowledge of the behaviour of future costs is equally important for a whole range of other decisions which management has to make.

We may divide the accountant's task of providing information as to costs for decision-making into two parts. First, when planning the volume of output in the short-term, the accountant has to provide information as to the behaviour of fixed and variable costs over the planned range of output. Second, for a number of 'special decisions' relating to alternative courses of action, such as the acceptance or rejection of a special order, he has to provide cost information which will guide management towards making the best, that is, the most profitable decisions.

The nature of relevant costs

The nature of the costs which are relevant for short-run tactical decisions will depend on the type of decision problem for which they are required. We shall examine several different types of decision problems, and in this way ascertain the type of cost information which ought to be supplied by the accountant. In general, however, the relevant costs have two important characteristics:

(a) They are future costs, that is, they are costs which are not yet incurred. This is a most important point, for it is easy to fall into the error of believing that costs which have already been incurred must be recovered. Past cost, that is, sunk costs are irrelevant costs: their only usefulness is the extent to which they may help the accountant to estimate the trend of future costs.

Example

Excelsior Ltd has spent £5000 on developing a new process. A revised estimate of further expenditure required to complete the development work shows an increase of 20% on the original total estimate of £10,000. The cost which is relevant to the decision to continue with the development work is £7000, that is, the future cost which will be incurred, and not the new estimate of total costs of £12,000. Hence, the costs already incurred are irrelevant to the decision to be made concerning the completion of the development work.

(b) Relevant costs are differential costs. Not all future costs are relevant costs: differential costs will be different under the alternative courses of action under examination.

Example

John Brown has decided to go to the cinema, and he is considering whether to go by bus or by car. The price of the cinema ticket is not a relevant cost, for it is not affected by the manner in which he travels to the cinema. Likewise, since cars tend to depreciate over time, the additional mileage on the car is also not a relevant cost. Although Brown's decision on his mode of travel will be influenced by his individual preference, the relevant cost is the cost difference between the cost of using the car, that is, petrol and parking, and going by bus. This cost difference is the differential cost.

From the foregoing examples, it might appear that only variable costs will be relevant costs, and that fixed costs cannot be relevant costs, since by definition they are not susceptible to change. The examples show that not all variable costs are relevant costs, for this depends on whether in the circumstances under review they are also differential costs.

In the long-term, of course, fixed costs do become variable costs, so that in decisions affecting the long-term, fixed costs may be differential costs and so will become relevant costs.

For short-run tactical decisions, however, it is possible, as we shall see for fixed costs to be relevant costs. Thus, if a decision affects the short-run activity level, requiring further capital expenditure, the extra fixed costs so incurred will be relevant costs as regards that decision.

The importance of the contribution margin

Usually, short-run tactical decisions are aimed at making the best use of existing facilities. The contribution margin is an important concept in this analysis. It is defined as the excess of the revenue of any activity over its relevant costs, which is available as a contribution towards fixed costs and profits. Profits, of course, will not be made until all fixed costs have been covered, but under certain circumstances the expectation of a contribution margin will be sufficient to justify a particular decision.

One decision problem with which a businessman is frequently faced is the acceptance of a special order, which may be a large order at a price below the usual selling price, and sometimes below total manufacturing costs.

Example

Minnies Kurt Ltd manufactures a garment which is sold under the trade name of Withitog. Its total productive capacity is 100,000 units in the current period, and actual production is running at 80% of productive capacity. The product sells at £1.00 per unit, and the firm's costs of production are as follows:

Fixed costs	£25,000
Variable costs	£0.50 per unit

The firm receives a special order for 10,000 Withitog from a mail order firm, subject to the firm agreeing to sell the product at £0.60 per unit. The Managing Director is reluctant to accept the order because the selling price is well below the manufacturing costs, which he has calculated as follows:

Fixed costs per unit (allocated over 90,000 units)

$$\frac{£25,000}{90,000} \qquad £0.28$$

Variable costs per unit	0.50
Total manufacturing costs per unit	£0.78

The contribution margin approach to the solution of this decision problem leads to a different conclusion. The revenue per unit is £0.60, and the relevant costs associated with the decision are the variable costs of production only, that is, £0.50, per unit. Hence, there is a unit contribution margin of £0.10 per unit, and on that basis, the firm should accept the special order. The fixed costs are not relevant costs for two reasons, firstly, they are sunk costs, that is they are not future costs and secondly, they are not affected by the decision to accept the special order, that is they are not differential costs.

The result of accepting the special order on the firm's total profit may be seen as follows:

		Without the special order		With the special order	Contribution margin
		(80,000 units)		(90,000 units)	—
Sales revenue		£		£	£
80,000 units @ £1.00		80,000		80,000	
10,000 units £0.60		—		6000	
		80,000		86,000	6000
Manufacturing costs					
Fixed costs	25,000		25,000		—
Variable costs @ £0.50 per unit	40,000		45,000		
		65,000		70,000	5000
Net profit		£15,000		£16,000	£1000

It is clear, therefore, that it is advantageous to the firm to accept the special order, since overall profits will be improved by £1000, which is the amount of the contribution margin resulting from the acceptance of that order.

It is evident, too, that the widespread belief that all costs should be covered may influence businessmen in considering special offers. Absorption costing is useful in determining the full costs of production, but leads to erroneous conclusions if indiscriminately applied.

Example

Speedo Engineering Limited manufactures an electrical component widely used in the motor industry. It is currently producing 5000 units selling at £10 a unit. Its total productive capacity is 8000 units, and budgeted costs at different levels of output have been estimated as follows:

Output (units)	5000	6000	7000	8000
Variable costs	£30,000	£36,000	£42,000	£48,000
Fixed costs	10,000	10,000	10,000	10,000
Total costs	£40,000	£46,000	£52,000	£58,000
Total costs per unit	£8.00	£7.67	£7.43	£7.25

The firm receives three offers for three lots of 1000 units at selling prices of £8, £7 and £6.50 per unit respectively. Should these offers be accepted or rejected?

The unit costs of production under the absorption costing method may be calculated and compared with the respective offers, as shown below:

Output (units)	6000	7000	8000
Total costs per unit	£7.67	£7.43	£7.25
Selling price per unit	8.00	7.00	6.50
Profit (loss) per unit	£0.33	£(0.43)	£(0.75)

From these calculations one might deduce that the firm should accept the order at £8 per unit, which will produce a profit of £0.33 per unit, but should reject the other two offers of £7 and £6.50 since they would result in losses.

An examination of the relevant costs leads to a different conclusion. The fixed costs are not relevant costs, since they will be incurred irrespective of the level of output. By comparing the relevant costs with the three offers, we may calculate the differential profits as under:

Output (units)	6000	7000	8000
Differential units	1000	1000	1000
Differential selling price	£8.00	£7.00	£6.50
Differential unit cost	6.00	6.00	6.00
Differential profit per unit	2.00	1.00	0.50
Differential total profit	£2000	£1000	£500

These figures illustrate the misleading effect of using absorption costing methods for decision making, and the necessity for using the relevant cost analysis. Using this latter method, it is clear that all three offers should be accepted, for in each case they provide a contribution margin towards fixed costs and profits.

Opportunity costs

Opportunity costs are not recorded in the accounting process, and although they are favoured by economists as appropriate costs for decision-making, they are difficult to identify and to measure in practice. Hence, accountants prefer to record and use more objective measures of costs, such as past costs or budgeted future costs as guidelines for decision-making. There are a number of decision problems, however, in which the only relevant cost is the opportunity cost. The opportunity cost may be defined as the value of the next best opportunity foregone, or of the net cash inflow lost as a result of preferring one alternative rather than the next best one. In cases where it is clear that only the opportunity cost will assist in making the decision, the accountant is often able to attempt its measurement.

Example

The Nationwide Investment Corporation Ltd, seeks to invest £1 million. It has selected two investment projects for consideration: Project A which is estimated to produce an annual return of 15%, and Project B which is expected to yield 20% annually.

On the basis of these facts, it is clear that the Corporation will select Project B. The additional gain resulting from that decision may only be measured in terms of the opportunity costs of sacrificing Project A, as follows:

Estimated annual return from Project B	£200,000
Less: Opportunity Cost (the sacrifice of the estimated annual returns from Project B)	150,000
Advantage of Project B	£50,000

The opportunity cost is always a relevant cost concept when the problem facing the firm is a problem of choice: the measure of the cost of the decision is the loss sustained by losing the opportunity of the second best alternative. It is the opportunity cost which must be taken into account in calculating the advantage of choosing one alternative rather than the other.

The use of the opportunity cost concept is illustrated in the following situations:

(a) dropping a product line
(b) selling or further processing a semi-manufactured product
(c) operate or lease
(d) make or buy a product.

Dropping a product line

Invariably the reason for wishing to drop a product line is that it is unprofitable, or it is less profitable than another product line to which the firm could switch resources.

Example

Mechanical Toys Ltd, manufactures three products, whose contributions to total profits for the year just ended are as under:

	Products A	B	C	Total
	£	£	£	£
Sales	200,000	100,000	150,000	450,000
Variable costs	100,000	70,000	80,000	250,000
Contribution	100,000 (50%)	30,000 (30%)	70,000 (47%)	200,000 (44%)
Fixed costs	60,000	40,000	50,000	150,000
Net profit (loss)	40,000	(10,000)	20,000	50,000

The company is considering dropping product B as it is showing a loss. By dropping product B, fixed costs could be reduced by £10,000, though the remaining balance of fixed costs of £30,000 being overhead fixed costs allocated to the produce would have to be re-allocated to products A and C.

The only choice facing the company is to continue or to cease making product B, and the financial consequences of that choice may be shown as follows:

	Keep Product B £	Drop Product B £
Sales	450,000	350,000
Variable costs	250,000	180,000
Contribution	200,000	170,000
Fixed costs	150,000	140,000
Net profit	50,000	30,000

It is clear that although an overall loss appears to result from producing product B, the contribution which product B makes to the firm's fixed costs would be lost if the decision were made to drop product B. The net cost of dropping product B would be £20,000, that is, the contribution margin less the fixed costs of £10,000 incurred solely as a consequence of its production.

Expressed in terms of opportunity cost analysis, the company has the choice between a profit of £50,000 associated with a decision to keep product B, and a profit of £30,000 associated with a decision to drop product B. Clearly, it cannot have both: hence the cost of selecting the profit of £50,000 is the sacrifice of the opportunity of the alternative profit of £30,000. Hence, the opportunity cost of the decision to keep product B is £30,000, and the advantage of this decision over the alternative of dropping product B is £20,000.

There may be other alternatives open to the firm, of course, besides the two alternatives which we have discussed, such as replacing product B by a more profitable product. In such a case, all the available alternatives must be examined and their outcomes accurately estimated if the best decision is to be made.

Selling or further processing

On occasions, it is possible for a firm to bring a product to its semi-finished state and then to sell it, rather than proceed to complete the production process and sell the finished article.

Example

Product A, which cost £4.8 per unit to produce, is sold as a refined petroleum product at £8 a unit. It could be put through a further processing stage after which it may be sold for £12 a unit. The costs associated with the further processing stage are estimated at £2 per unit.

The outcome of the two alternatives facing the firm, to sell or to further process the product may be stated in the following terms:

	To sell	To process further
Revenues associated with the decision	£8	£4
Costs associated with the decision	4.8	2
Differential profit per unit	£3.2	£2

It is clear that if the firm decides to sell rather than to process further, it will lose the additional profit of £2 per unit. Hence, the opportunity cost of the decision to sell is £2 and the advantage of selling over further processing is £1.2.

Operate or lease

The decision as to whether to operate or lease assets is another example of the importance of opportunity costs for decision-making.

Example

Betashoes Ltd, owns a desirable freehold in Puddingford High Street, which it uses as a selling outlet. The Managing Director receives an offer to lease the property to a local company willing to pay an annual rent of £30,000. The net contribution of the selling outlet in Puddingford to the group profits of Betashoes Ltd, is £40,000, after deducting the expenses attributable to it. The information which is relevant to the decision to continue to use the selling outlet may be set out as under:

Contribution to group profits	£40,000
Opportunity cost (rent)	£30,000
Net advantage of operating	£10,000

In the absence of other factors which may induce Betashoes to sell the site, the offer to lease the premises should be rejected and Betashoes should continue to use them as a selling outlet.

Make or buy

It is quite common for firms to subcontract the making of components to specialist firms. This practice does increase their dependence on outside suppliers and reduce to some extent their control on the quality of the components. The opportunity cost approach to this type of decision enables the firm to consider the advantages which could be obtained from alternative uses of the productive capacity released as the result of subcontracting the making of components.

Example

Highperformance Motors Ltd, specializes in the manufacture of sports cars, making some of the components which are required and buying others. Alparts Ltd, offers to supply a part currently made by Highperformance Motors Ltd, at a price of £7. The costs incurred by Highperformance Motors in making the part are as follows:

Variable costs	£4
Traceable fixed costs	2
Allocated fixed costs	3
Total Unit Costs	£9

Let us assume for the moment that the productive capacity released as a result of accepting the offer will remain idle. On the basis of a monthly production of 5000 units a month, the relevant monthly costs, that is, those which would be affected by the decision to buy the units, are as follows:

Variable costs	£20,000
Traceable fixed costs	10,000
Relevant costs	30,000
Cost of buying	35,000
Advantage in making	5000

The allocated fixed costs are irrelevant to the decision since they are not affected, and will continue to be incurred by Highperformance Motors irrespective of whether the parts are made or bought. Since the relevant costs of making are less than the costs of buying, the firm should reject the offer and continue to make the parts.

Let us now consider the possibility that if the firm accepted the offer, the productive capacity released as a result will not remain idle, and will be used to extend the production line of motor cars. It is calculated that an additional four cars a month could be produced, leading to an increase in profits of £10,000. The opportunity costs of not accepting the offer, therefore, amount to £10,000. Hence, the information which is now relevant to the decision as to making or buying the part is as under:

Cost of making	
Relevant manufacturing costs	£30,000
Opportunity cost	10,000
	40,000
Cost of buying	35,000
Advantage of buying	£5000

The introduction of the opportunity cost of not accepting the offer has altered the nature of the decision completely, and reversed the previous conclusion that it was advantageous to make the part.

Decision-making in the face of limiting factors

In the examples which we have examined so far, the selection of alternative courses of action has been made on the basis of seeking the most profitable result. Business enterprises are limited in the pursuit of profit by the fact that they have limited resources at their disposal, so that quite apart from the limitation on the quantities of any product which the market will buy at a given price, the firm has its own constraints on the volume of output. Hence at a given price, which may be well above costs of production, the firm may be unable to increase its overall profit simply due to its inability to increase its output.

The limiting factors which affect the level of production may arise out of shortages of labour, material, equipment, and factory space to mention but a few obvious examples. Faced with limiting factors of whatever nature, the firm will wish to obtain the maximum profit from the use of the resources available, and in making decisions about the allocation of its resources between competing alternatives, management will be guided by the relative contribution margins which they offer. Since the firm will be faced with limiting factors, however, the contribution margins must be calculated not in terms of units of product sold which fail to reflect constraints on the total volume of output, but should be related to the unit of quantity of the most limited factor. A simple example will serve to explain this point.

Example

Multiproduct Ltd, manufactures three products about which is derived the following data:

Product	Machine Hours Required Per Unit of Product	Contribution Margin Per Unit	Contribution Margin Per Machine Hour
A	3 hours	£9	£3.0
B	2 hours	£7	£3.5
C	1 hour	£5	£5.0

The three products can be made by the same machine, and on the basis of this information, it is evident that product C is the most profitable product yielding a contribution of £5 per machine hour, as against product A, which shows the smallest contribution per machine hour. Hence, in deciding how to use the limiting factor the firm should concentrate on the production of product C, rather than products A and B. If there were no limits to the market demand for product C, there would be no problem in deciding which product to produce—it would be product C alone.

Firms undertake the manufacture of different products because the market demand for any one product is limited, so that firms seek to find that product-mix which will be the most profitable. Let us assume that the maximum weekly demand for the three products and the total machine capacity necessary to meet this demand is as follows:

demand is as follows:

Product	Maximum Demand in Units	Machine Hours Equivalents
A	100	300
B	100	200
C	100	100
		600

Machine capacity is limited to 450 hours per week, so that the most profitable product-mix is a function of both machine capacity and market demand. The following product-mix would maximize profits:

Product	Output Units	Machine Hours	Contribution Per Machine Hour	Total Contribution
C	100	100	£5.0	£500
B	100	200	£3.5	£700
A	50	150	£3.0	£450
		450		£1650

This product-mix reflects the order of priority in allocating machine use to the products with the highest contribution margin per hour. Product C receives the highest priority, then Product B, and lastly Product A. If machine hours were further limited to 300 hours, the firm would cease to make Product A.

Linear programming and decision-making

Linear programming is a mathematical technique which seeks to make the best use of a firm's limited resources to meet chosen objectives, which in accounting terms may take the form of the maximization of profits or the minimization of costs. In those situations, for example, where a manufacturer has a limited plant capacity, the level and cost of output will be determined by such capacity.

Example

Blackamoor Steels Ltd, manufacture two high quality steel products in respect of which the following information is available:

	Product A £	Product B £
Selling price per unit	30	20
Variable costs per unit	15	10
Contribution margin	£15	£10

Milling and grinding machines are used in the manufacturing process, and the total machine hours necessary to produce one unit of each product are:

	Product A	Product B
Milling	5 hours	$1\frac{1}{2}$ hours
Grinding	2	2
	7	$3\frac{1}{2}$

Both products are in great demand, and the only constraint on expanding output is machine capacity. The total machine hours available per month are:

Milling (3 machines at 200 hours a month)	600 hours
Grinding (2 machines at 200 hours a month)	400 hours.

On the basis of the facts given above, the problem facing management is to ascertain that combination of output of products A and B which will maximize the total contribution margin to overheads and profits. This problem is similar to the example discussed in the previous section (see page 425). At first glance, it would appear that the firm should maximize the production of product A since that product yields the highest unit contribution margin. Analysed in terms of the machine capacity limit, the total number of units of *either* product A *or* product B which could be manufactured as follows:

Product A	600 hours ÷ 5 hours = 120 units
Product B	400 hours ÷ 2 hours = 200 units

These output limits are derived in the case of product A by the fact that output is limited to the capacity of the milling machines for product A requires 5 hours of milling as against only 2 hours of grinding. Product B, however, is limited in output by the capacity of the grinding machines of which it requires 2 hours per unit, as against $1\frac{1}{2}$ hours of milling time.

By relating the calculation of the contribution margin to the machine capacity limits, the total contribution to overhead costs and profits which will be obtained by the production of *either* A *or* B is as follows:

Product A: 120 units × £15 = £1800
Product B: 200 units × £10 = £2000

It follows, therefore, that given the option of making either product A or product B the firm should concentrate on the making of product B.

The approach to the solution of this problem under linear programming consists, firstly, of formulating the problem in simple algebraic terms. There are two aspects to the problem, the first being the wish to maximize profits and the second being the need to recognize the production limits. The two aspects may be stated algebraically as follows:

(a) The objective is to maximize the contribution to fixed overheads and profit. This objective is called the objective function, and may be expressed thus:

$$\text{Maximize } C = 15A + 10B$$

where C is the total contribution and A and B being the total number of units of the two products which must be manufactured to maximize the total contribution. This equation is subject to the limits that:

$$A \geqslant 0$$

$$B \geqslant 0$$

for it is not possible to produce negative quantities of either A or B.

(b) The constraints on production arising from the machine capacity limits of the Milling Department (600 hours) and of the Grinding Department (400 hours) may also be expressed in algebraic terms as follows:

$$5A + 1\tfrac{1}{2}B \leqslant 600$$

$$2A + 2B \leqslant 400$$

the first inequality states that the total number of hours used on milling must be equal to or less than 600 hours; the second inequality states that the total hours used on grinding machines must be equal to or less than 400 hours.

The problem may now be summarized in the form:

$$\text{Maximize } C = 15A + 10B$$

subject to the constraints:

$$5A + 1\tfrac{1}{2}B \leqslant 600$$
$$2A + 2B \leqslant 400$$
$$A \geqslant 0$$
$$B \geqslant 0$$

It is possible to solve the problem by means of a graph (Fig. 3.26) showing the manufacturing possibilities for the two departments, viz:

Milling Department

Product A	$600 \div 5 = 120$ units
or Product B	$600 \div 1\frac{1}{2} = 400$ units

Grinding Department

Product A	$400 \div 2 = 200$ units
or Product B	$400 \div 2 = 200$ units

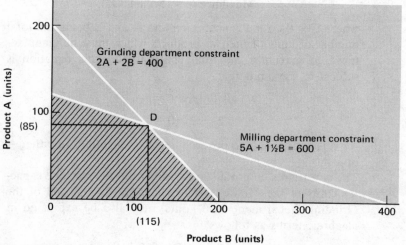

Fig. 3.26

The shaded region contains all the combinations of products A and B which are feasible solutions to the problem, hence its name—the feasibility region. The optimal solution, that is, the product combination of A and B which is the best of all the feasible solutions lies at the intersection of the lines at point D, and may be read off as 85 units of A and 115 of B. It will be observed that the optimal solution lies on a tangent which is the furthest away from the point of origin. The graphical method of solving the problem is susceptible to error unless carefully plotted, and a more reliable answer may be obtained by solving the problem mathematically.

The optimal combination of products A and B may be found by solving the simultaneous equation given above, that is,

$$(1) \quad 5A + 1\frac{1}{2}B = 600$$

$$(2) \quad 2A + 2B = 400$$

The solution is obtained by multiplying (1) by 4 and (2) by 3 to give us the value of A, as follows:

$$20A + 6B = 2400$$
$$-6A + 6B = 1200$$

$$14A \quad\ = 1200$$
$$A \quad\ =\ 85\tfrac{5}{7}\text{ths}$$

Since we are concerned only with completed units of A, the optimal production of product A is 85 units. The optimal number of units of B may be calculated by inserting the known value of A into the equation, as follows:

$$6 \times 85 + 6B = 1200$$
$$\text{i.e.,}\quad 510\ + 6B = 1200$$
$$6B = 1200 - 510$$
$$B = 115.$$

Hence, the optimal combination of products A and B is 85 units and 115 units respectively, in terms of the limited machine capacity which will be utilized as follows:

	Milling Department (hours)	Grinding Department (hours)
Product A—85 units	425 (85×5)	170 (85×2)
Product B—115 units	172.5 (115×1½)	230 (115×2)
Total hours used	597.5	400
Total hours available	600	400

The optimal combination will produce a total contribution to overheads and profits of £2425 as follows:

Product A:	85 units at £15 =	1275
Product B:	115 units at £10 =	1150
		£2425

We may verify that this combination of products is the optimal one in terms of profits and available machine capacity, as follows:

(a) Altering the product combination from 85 units of A and 115 units of B to 84 units of A and 116 units of B, which would affect machine use as follows:

	Milling Department (hours)	Grinding Department (hours)
Product A—84 units	420 (84×5)	168 (84×2)
Product B—116 units	174 (116×1½)	232 (116×2)
Total hours used	594	400
Total hours available	600	400

Hence, this combination is as efficient in the utilization of the grinding department but less efficient in the utilization of the milling machines. It is less profitable also yielding a contribution of only £2420 as against £2425 as follows:

Product A:	84 units at £15 =	1260
Product B:	116 units at £10 =	1160
		£2420

(b) Altering the product combination from 85 units of A and 115 units of B to 86 units of A and 113 units of B, which would affect machine use as under:

	Milling Department (hours)	Grinding Department (hours)
Product A—86 units	430 (86×5)	172 (86×2)
Product B—113 units	169½ (113×1½)	226 (113×2)
Total hours used	599½	398
Total hours available	600	400

Hence, whereas this combination is more efficient in the use of the milling machines than the optimal combination, it is less efficient in the use of the grinding machinery. Moreover, to keep within the capacity limits of the milling department we have had to forgo the production of 2 units of product B to expand the manufacture of product A by one unit. The consequential contribution to profits is also only £2420 as against the optimal contribution of £2425, which may be calculated as follows:

Product A:	86 units at £15 =	1290
Product B:	113 units at £10 =	1130
		£2420

It is noteworthy, also, that the linear programming approach to the best product combination mix gives a solution which is more profitable than the one which relates the contribution margin to the machine capacity limits, which we discussed on page 426, and which suggested that only product B should be made so that 200 units of B would be manufactured to yield a contribution of £2000.

We have so far only discussed simple cases involving at the maximum only two resource constraints. In real life, a firm may be faced with more than two constraints, but mathematical techniques exist for coping with larger numbers of limits. The Simplex Method, for example, which is based on matrix algebra may be employed in such cases and it is ideally suited for solutions using a computer.

Summary

In addition to providing information for short-run profit planning purposes, the accountant also often has to provide information for a number of short-run tactical decisions such as dropping a product line or choosing between selling or further processing a semi-manufactured product. As in other areas of accounting, cost information plays an important role in short-run tactical decisions. The costs which are relevant for such decisions are future differential costs.

As in the case of c-v-p, short-run tactical decisions are aimed at making the best use of existing facilities. Particular use is made of the contribution margin, which is the excess of the expected revenue resulting from a decision over the expected relevant costs of that decision which is available as a contribution towards fixed costs and profits.

Although opportunity costs are not recorded in the accounting process, there are a number of decision problems where opportunity costs are the only relevant costs. Opportunity costs may be defined as the value of the next best opportunity foregone, or of the net cash inflow lost as a result of preferring one alternative rather than the next best one. Opportunity costs are useful and relevant costs for the following decisions:

(a) dropping a product line,
(b) selling or further processing a semi-manufactured product,
(c) operating or lease assets,
(d) making or buying a product.

Limits placed on resources have to be recognized in decision-making. Product-mix decisions illustrate the nature of this problem and the manner in which the best use of limited resources may be made. In this connection, linear programming affords a useful technique for maximizing profits or minimizing costs in the face of constraints on resources.

Further readings

1. Backer, Martin & Jacobsen, Lyle E., *Cost Accounting*, McGraw-Hill, New York, 1964.

2. Bierman, Harold Jr. & Dyckman, Thomas R., *Managerial Cost Accounting*, Macmillan, New York, 1971.

3. Dopuch, N., Birnberg, J. D. & Demski, J., *Cost Accounting Data for Management's Decisions*, Harcourt Brace and World Inc., New York, 1974.

4. Horngren, Charles T., *Cost Accounting: A Managerial Emphasis*, Prentice Hall, Englewood Cliffs, N.J., 1972.

5. Lynch, Richard M., *Accounting for Management*, McGraw-Hill, New York, 1974.

6. Shillinglaw G., *Cost Accounting*, Richard Irwin, Homewood, Illinois, 1972.

7. Terrill, William A. & Patrick, Albert W., *Cost Accounting for Management*, Holt, Rinehart & Winston, New York, 1965.

Section 3

Control

10
Organizing for Control

The integration of planning and control

We mentioned in the introduction to Part 3, that control may be related to planning by defining the purpose of control as being to ensure that the organization's activities conform with its plans. Control is itself an activity, therefore, and it should and does affect every aspect of the organization. We may depict the control cycle in the form of a generalized model as shown in Fig. 3.27 opposite.

The control cycle illustrated thereon shows that the origin of control is in the objectives of the organization from which plans are developed. These plans, as we saw in Section 2, consist of both long-range and annual plans. It is evident from the model depicted above that the control cycle integrates both the long-range and the annual plan. Information feedback enables actual performance to be compared with the planned performance required by the annual plan, thus enabling management to control operations and the resources allocated to those operations. At the end of the year, the results may be compared with those envisaged in terms of the long-range plans, thereby providing information feedback for the purposes of reviewing the long-range plan. Finally, the control process allows achievements to be compared with the organization's desired objectives, thereby enabling new goals and new objectives to be formulated.

The control model illustrates the multi-dimensional nature of the control process, and the coincidence of the control process with the planning process. It is this coincidence which allows the planning and the control process to be integrated into one model which is focused on organizational objectives and the goals derived from those objectives. Overall control is concerned with measuring progress towards the realization of organizational objectives and the strategic goals defined in the strategic plan. This aspect of control is exercised by top management. Using the terminology adopted in chapter 1, management control is a subordinate activity concerned with the efficient use of resources committed to the realization of organizational goals. Finally, operational control is concerned with ensuring that the tasks defined in the operational plan are carried out effectively. Specific

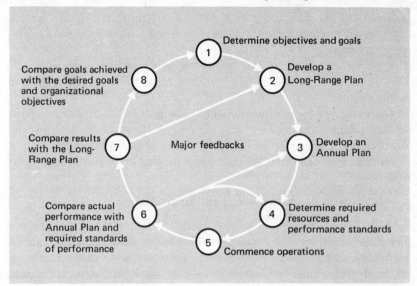

Fig. 3.27

performance standards are attached to these tasks, and information feedback allows actual performance to be compared with the required performance.

From the foregoing, it follows that control standards are designed in the planning process. They are used as indices by which the effectiveness and the result of organizational activities are to be assessed, for they provide the basis by which actual and planned performance are to be compared. Moreover, since organizational activities emanate from the planning process, plans themselves also constitute performance standards.

There remains, however, a perceptible distinction between planning and control in the sense in which we consider these terms in this text. A plan reflects the expectations and the means of achieving stipulated goals during a specified period. If such a plan is to be useful for control purposes as well, it should reflect adequately the extent to which those expectations and those means are subject to organizational control. Hence, it should provide the basis for the system of responsibility accounting which requires a clear definition of the controllable elements at every level of responsibility.

Responsibility accounting

Control depends on the existence of an organizational framework which will define the responsibility for securing the performance of individual tasks. This is achieved by establishing responsibility centres throughout the organization, and defining the responsibilities of managers accordingly.

A responsibility centre may be defined as a segment of the organization where an individual manager is held responsible for the segment's performance.

The nature of the organizational framework and the kinds of responsibility centres established will depend partly on the size of the organization and partly on the style of management adopted.

As organizations grow, top management faces two continuing problems:

(a) how to divide activities and responsibilities
(b) how to co-ordinate sub-units.

Inevitably, authority for decision-making has to be allocated to various managers, and as soon as this occurs, the result is the decentralization of the decision-making process. In essence, therefore, decentralization is the process of granting the freedom to make decisions to subordinate managers. In theory, there are two extreme states: total decentralization meaning a minimum of constraint or control on managers and a maximum of the freedom to make decisions even at the lowest level of the management hierarchy and total centralization implying the maximum of constraint or control on managers and the minimum freedom to make independent decisions. In practice, total centralization and total decentralization rarely occur. Total centralization is not feasible because it is impossible for top management to attend to all the decisions which are required to be made. Equally, total decentralization is rarely found because the degree of freedom which it implies would result in an organizational structure consisting of a collection of completely separate units all aiming at their own individual goals. The extent to which an organization will be decentralized depends upon the philosophy of its top management, and the benefits and costs associated with decentralization.

Having decided to decentralize to a greater or lesser extent, the problem of control nevertheless remains. It may be resolved by establishing new responsibility centres called 'divisions'. These divisions may take the form of profit or investment centres. We shall consider these responsibility centres later in this chapter.

The problem of controlling divisional operations is more complex than that of controlling a single activity within an organization. Where decision making is centralized, for example, it is possible to establish expense centres and to control their activities by means of budgetary control. Some of these expense centres may be cost centres, which are smaller segments of activity or areas of responsibility in respect of which costs are accumulated. Control may be exercised, therefore, by means of information feedback about the level of costs arising from the activities of these responsibility centres. Indeed, cost control has been the traditional means of securing the control of operations, though as we shall see later, the failure to recognize behavioural factors affecting performance has implications for the effectiveness of cost control. Where decision-making is decentralized, however, the control of divisional performance is made more difficult for a number of reasons. The range of decisions over which divisional managers have authority is much more extensive. Thus, they may have authority over the determination of the pricing of products, make or buy decisions and some investment decisions. The problem goes beyond the control of costs, therefore, to the control of profits and to ensuring that there is a high degree of goal congruence between the various divisions and the organization's top management.

Our analysis of the problem of control through responsibility accounting should recognize the problems created by the degree of centralization and decentralization of authority. The first category of responsibility centre which we shall examine, namely expense centres, are appropriate to highly centralized organizations or units. The second and third categories of responsibility centres, namely profit and investment centres, are appropriate to those organizations where the authority for decision-making has been decentralized to some extent, and where the problem of control is necessarily more complex. We shall deal with the behavioural aspects of control which such a degree of decentralization creates in chapter 14. For the time being, we shall focus attention on the accounting problems stemming from the establishment of these various types of responsibility centres.

Expense centres

An expense centre may be defined as a responsibility centre in which the manager has no control over revenue but is able to control expenditure. It will be recalled that in chapter 2, we drew a distinction between the accumulation of costs for product costing purposes and for control purposes. In product costing, we noted that costs are first allocated and apportioned to service departments and production departments; next, that service department costs are apportioned to the production departments; finally, overhead recovery rates are computed to enable overhead costs to be absorbed into product costs. Since the production departments are the focal points on which the process of cost accumulation converges, these departments are known as 'cost centres'.

From the foregoing, we may distinguish an expense centre from a cost centre. An expense centre is a department which incurs expenditure. A cost centre is a production department in which product costs are accumulated.

As we stated earlier, a prerequisite for an effective responsibility accounting system is the establishment of an organizational framework which will define the formal relationships which link the different executive roles in the organization. Levels of responsibility may be delineated for foremen, departmental managers, works managers and upwards to director level. Figure 3.28 is an organizational chart applied to a centralized organization and shows that the three foremen are responsible to the manager of Department B, who in turn reports to the works manager. The works manager is responsible to the Board.

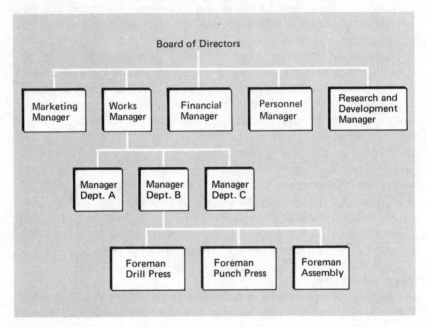

Fig. 3.28

An important facet of a comprehensive planning and control programme is a system of performance reports incorporating comparisons of actual performance against planned performance for individual responsibility centres throughout the enterprise. These reports provide a means of instituting responsibility accounting, which is a method of cost control in which the costs of responsibility centres are identified with individual managers who are given authority over such costs and responsibility for them. The nature of the relationship existing between

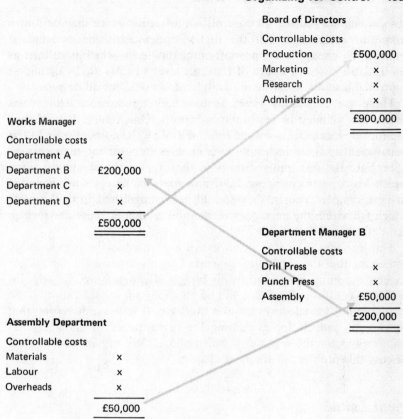

Fig. 3.29 Levels of responsibility reporting.

various levels of management and the flow of information between these levels may be illustrated as in Fig. 3.29.

Responsibility budgets deal only with the costs for which each manager is to be held responsible, and their performance as managers is evaluated by reference to the success with which they have managed their own area of responsibility. It is important, therefore, to make a distinction between those costs which are under the control of a particular manager and those for which other managers are responsible. For example, the foreman of the Assembly Department may be responsible for the amount of direct labour used, but he will certainly not be responsible for the wage rate which is paid to these workers. This is determined by collective bargaining and is outside his sphere of influence. In assessing managerial performance under systems of responsibility accounting, a manager should not be held responsible for costs which are outside his control. An inference which may be drawn from our diagram is that the higher one ascends the pyramid of control, the greater is the proportion of total costs which is defined as controllable costs: at Board of Director level all costs are by definition controllable as the Board is ultimately responsible for all costs.

There are conflicting views as to whether non-controllable costs should be included in performance reports. One view is that, if they are included, managers will be informed of all the costs affecting their departments. Their inclusion also enables department managers to appreciate the size and the costs of the organizational support upon which his department depends. If non-controllable costs are included in performance reports, they should be distinguished from the costs which fall within the manager's responsibility, that is, those costs which are defined as controllable.

The manager in charge of an expense centre has the responsibility for seeing that the expenditure incurred by his department should not exceed the limits contained in his budgeted expenditure. Clearly, his ability to control expenditure will be an important consideration in the evaluation of his effectiveness as a manager. It follows, therefore, that the use of budgets for evaluating the performance of managers has implications for the manner in which budgets are organized. We shall discuss this problem in the next chapter.

Profit centres

In recent years, there has been a tendency for organizations to grow in size, and the problem of control which this growth has created has encouraged the devolution of authority in large organizations by the creation of organizational structures based upon the concept of 'divisions'. The rationale underlying this process of decentralization is founded on the belief that divisionalization enhances overall corporate profitability. Several reasons are adduced for this belief. Firstly, the responsibility for decision-making is transferred to executives who are 'on the spot', and who are directly concerned with the particular problems of manufacturing and marketing divisional products. Hence, they are able to devote all their energies to these problems, whereas under systems of centralized control, top management is able to devote less time to the problems of individual divisions. Secondly, it is considered that the greater degree of freedom enjoyed by divisional executives increases their motivation towards the attainment of organizational goals, and in particular the profit goal. Thirdly, the opportunity which divisionalization affords of using accounting information to measure the contribution of each division towards the profit goal, also reveals areas of weakness and may suggest possibilities for profit improvement. Finally, the decentralization of the decision-making process provides a training ground for managers as they progress successively through the organization to higher levels of responsibility.

Conventional accounting measurements of performance, such as the return on capital employed, may serve a useful purpose in evaluating the financial performance of individual divisions, where they are completely independent of each other. Where, however, the activities of individual divisions are inter-related, so that the output of one division provides a substantial part of the input of another division, the usefulness of conventional accounting measurements of financial performance is less clear. Under these circumstances, there is a need to establish a price for transferring these so-called intermediate products between the divisions, and this price will clearly affect their profits.

Transfer pricing

From the foregoing, the use of profit centres for the control of divisional performance may give rise to the problem of determining the price at which the product of one profit centre should be transferred to another profit centre. The transfer price is critically important to the profit of both centres, being at once revenue to the selling centre and cost to the buying centre. The evaluation of managerial performance based on the size of the divisional profit requires that the transfer price should be so calculated as to reflect accurately the value-added to the product by the selling centre. If it is set too high, it will reflect too favourably upon the selling centre and too unfavourably upon the buying centre, and vice-versa. Hence, financial results may be heavily biased by the prices adopted for the transfer of intermediate goods. Defects in the transfer price mechanism may frequently invalidate the conclusions which divisional profit figures might seem to suggest. In such cases, these figures may not merely fail to produce the right decisions, they may actively promote wrong ones.

In chapter 8, we examined pricing as a means of regulating the exchange of the firm's products with the outside world. In this chapter, we shall examine transfer pricing as a method of controlling the activities of profit centres within the firm. Hence, we shall see that the distinction between pricing and transfer pricing lies in their different purposes.

Transfer prices should satisfy the following three criteria:

(a) They should promote goal congruence within the organization by harmonizing the interest of individual divisions with the interest of the organization as a whole, by preventing divisional managers from optimizing divisional profits by policies which are harmful to the rest of the organization.

(b) They should make possible reliable assessments of divisional performance for the following purposes:
  (i) making predictions for decision-making purposes
  (ii) appraising managerial performance
  (iii) evaluating the divisional contribution to corporate profits.

(c) They should ensure that the autonomy of the individual divisions is respected, and that their profits are not dependent upon the actions of other divisions.

Transfer pricing methods

There are three main methods for establishing transfer prices:

(a) market-based transfer pricing
(b) cost-based transfer pricing
(c) negotiated pricing.

Market-based transfer pricing

Where external markets do exist for the selling centre's products, it is preferable to use market prices rather than cost-based prices. This is because a market price is a better guide to the value-added to products than a cost-based price which incorporates a profit element. If the external market is competitive and divisional inter-dependence is minimal, the market price generally leads to optimal decisions within the organization, that is, decisions which satisfy the three criteria stipulated above. Where market prices can be used with a large measure of success, the divisions are effectively separate business entities.

When using market prices, it is essential that the transfer price should be no higher than the buying centre would have to pay on the market. Otherwise, it is evident that an imbalance will be created between the interests of the selling and the buying centres. The existence of an independent market price imposes an upper limit to the transfer price, for given that the selling centre is able to sell at that price, the buying centre should be compelled to buy internally rather than to purchase from external suppliers.

A number of problems arise from the use of the market price as the basis for the transfer price. Thus, changes in supply may lead to large price changes, and the recognition of these changes will cause large variations in the transfer price. As a result, a degree of instability will be introduced in the control mechanism. Further problems are associated with the weight which should be attached to different market prices ruling during the transfer period, and to such other factors affecting market prices, such as, quantity discounts, area and trade channel differentials, transportation and delivery allowances and service factors. The market price also reflects the result of a bargain, and a reconciliation between what one has to accept to effect a sale, and what one has to pay to effect a purchase. The effects of relative bargaining positions on the market price has implications for the transfer price selected—should it favour the selling or the buying division?

Hence the determination of a fair market price for establishing a viable transfer pricing system which will satisfy the three criteria which have been stipulated, calls for a solution to the various problems mentioned above. In many cases, the solution may be arrived at only by an independent arbitrator. This process immediately undermines the third criterion—the preservation of the autonomy of individual divisions—and results in the establishment of a negotiated price.

Cost-based transfer pricing

In many cases, the transfer of products between profit centres involves intermediate goods in respect of which an external market does not exist. In such cases, it is necessary to use cost-based transfer prices.

A common problem which may arise in employing cost-based transfer prices is that they may conceal inefficiencies in the activities of the selling centre. It is essential, therefore, that the transfer price should be based on standard costs rather than actual costs. As we shall see in the following chapter, the standard cost represents what an item should cost to produce rather than what it does cost, that is, it excludes inefficiencies which have arisen in production. Hence, the use of standard costs prevents inefficiencies which have occurred in one profit centre from being transferred to another profit centre.

As we mentioned in chapter 8, there are different kinds of cost-based prices. Two commonly used cost-related prices are full-cost and variable (or marginal) cost prices.

Full-cost transfer pricing

The major disadvantage of using full-cost, or rather full-cost plus a profit percentage, as a transfer price is that this method may encourage managers to make decisions which are not in the interest of the firm as a whole.

Example

The following data relates to profit centre A which sells to profit centre B at full-cost plus a profit percentage:

Profit centre	A £	B £ £
Variable costs	10	30+10
Fixed Costs	10	10
Mark-up (50%)	<u>10</u>	<u>25</u>
Total unit cost	<u>30</u>	<u>75</u>

Profit centre B treats the input of £30 from profit centre A as a variable cost. Hence, before Profit Centre B is able to have a contribution margin (defined, it will be remembered, as the excess of sales revenue over variable costs which contributes to fixed costs and profits) it must be able to sell its own output at £40 a unit. It is clear, however, that as far as the firm as a whole is concerned, total variable costs per unit are only £20. Given that both profit centres have spare capacity, it is in the firm's interest that Profit Centre B should produce and sell if it can obtain a price of £20 or over per unit for its output. If it regards £40 as its minimum acceptable price, the firm will lose the benefit of a contribution margin which otherwise it would have had.

In addition to the limitations of full-cost transfer pricing illustrated by the previous example, the use of full-costs as a basis for transfer pricing may import a rigidity in an organization which contradicts the rationale for establishing profit centres. Managers should be able to control all the determinants of profits (selling price, volume, fixed and variable costs) if they are to be held responsible for profits. Thus, in the example given above, the manager of Profit Centre A may feel that his output is constrained by the obligation to sell to Profit Centre B at a transfer price of £30 a unit. Furthermore, his production is also dependent upon the sales volume attained by Profit Centre B. This volume may be too low to enable Profit Centre A to achieve a satisfactory profit, and the manager of that profit centre may well wish to sell his output outside the firm, if he is able to, at varying prices.

Therefore, the rigidity imposed on a firm by virtue of the inflexibility of an agreed full-cost transfer pricing system does not provide a sound basis for the delegation of decisions to profit centres.

Variable-cost transfer pricing

Transfer prices based upon variable costs are designed to overcome some of the problems stemming from the use of full-cost measurement. Thus, in the aforementioned example, Profit Centre A would have transferred to Profit Centre B at a unit price of £10. In the short-run, when both profit centres have surplus capacity, this would enable Centre B to adopt a more realistic pricing policy to the benefit of the organization as a whole. Such a decision, however, applies only in special circumstances. In the long-run, transfer prices based upon variable costs are of little value for the purpose of performance evaluation, for they result in a loss to the selling division, and would impair the degree of motivation which is one of the reasons for decentralizing.

As we saw in chapter 8, pricing policies should be based on differential costs and revenues of the company as a whole in order that better profit planning decisions may be made. This implies that decisions about the output volume of divisions cannot be determined independently, thereby undermining the autonomy of individual divisions.

Negotiated pricing

Whatever method the firm adopts for determining transfer prices, it is evident that some form of negotiated price must be agreed between the managers of profit centres if the transfer pricing system is to operate satisfactorily. It is assumed that independent negotiations between managers will produce results which are beneficial to the firm as a whole, and that the resolution of conflicts of interests will not reflect any bias in favour of any particular groups. These assumptions are probably questionable for a number of reasons. First, transfer price negotiations are very consuming, and may lead to a diversion of managerial interest from their own work as they get more involved in the negotiations. Second, conflicts which undoubtedly will occur may lead to recriminations and the involvement of top management as arbitrators may be required.

The advantages of transfer pricing

The various transfer pricing systems which we have examined seem fraught with problems and drawbacks. Nevertheless, these difficulties should be weighed against the advantages which may be derived from setting up profit centres. Equally, these difficulties do not amount to a substantial case for abandoning the practice of assigning transfer prices to inter-divisional products. Some value must be found and attached to each element of input and output for the purpose of effective organizational control. Without some form of transfer pricing, the whole structure of intra-departmental analysis and control would collapse.

Very few aids for planning and control are perfect. This is certainly true of transfer pricing. It should be recognized that no available transfer pricing system is likely to serve all the purposes for which it is needed. The limitations found present in any transfer pricing system should be recognized, and any results obtained should be interpreted in the full knowledge of those limitations.

Investment centres

Investment centres represent the ultimate stage in the decentralization of the decision-making process. Divisional managers are made responsible not only for cost goals (expense centres), profit contribution goals (profit centres), but also for elements of the capital invested in the division.

Investment centres extend the principles underlying profit centres by associating divisional profits with the capital invested in the divisions. The criterion most commonly employed for assessing the financial performance of investment centres is the Return on Capital Employed (R.O.C.E.). It is a comprehensive measure of financial performance which enables comparisons to be made between companies and divisions for the purpose of evaluating the efficiency with which assets are utilized. The R.O.C.E. is calculated as follows:

$$\text{R.O.C.E.} = \frac{\text{Net Profit before interest and tax}}{\text{Average Capital Invested}} \times 100$$

This formula may be extended so as to incorporate the ratio of net profit to sales, and the ratio of sales to capital employed (the rate of asset turnover),

$$\text{R.O.C.E.} = \frac{\text{NP PBIT}}{\text{Sales}} \times \frac{\text{Sales}}{\text{Average Capital Invested}} \times 100$$

The expanded formula is useful for focusing attention on the important elements which affect the R.O.C.E. It implies that profitability may be improved in the following ways:

(a) by increasing the volume of sales
(b) by reducing total assets
(c) by reducing costs
(d) by improving the profit mark-up, for example by raising selling prices or improving the product mix.

The asset turnover will be improved by (a) and (b), and the profit margin by (c) and (d).

Example

The following table compares the sales, profit and capital employed for three divisions of a large organization. Their profit contribution is £50,000 in each case.

	Division A	Division B	Division C
Sales	£500,000	£500,000	£1,000,000
Net Profit PBIT	£50,000	£50,000	£50,000
Capital Employed	£250,000	£500,000	£500,000
Return on Sales	10%	10%	5%
Asset Turnover	2	1	2
R.O.C.E.	20%	10%	10%

It is clear that Division A has the most effective financial performance since its R.O.C.E. of 20% is higher than the R.O.C.E. of the other two divisions. Division B's return on sales, that is its profit margin, is equal to that of Division A, but its asset turnover is half as high as A's, implying that it employs twice as much capital as A to earn the same profit. This position indicates that either sales could be improved or that excessive capital is being carried by Division B, and that an investigation of asset use may reveal that plant and stocks could perhaps be reduced. Division C has the same R.O.C.E. as Division B. Its profit margin on sales, however, is inferior to that of both other divisions, thereby indicating that selling prices may be too low or that operating costs may be too high.

The foregoing example shows that a R.O.C.E. analysis may isolate factors requiring investigation. These factors are illustrated in Fig. 3.29 overleaf.

Problems associated with R.O.C.E. measurements of performance
Three major problems arise as a result of employing R.O.C.E. measures for assessing divisional performance. They stem from the following factors:

(a) the measurement of profit and capital employed
(b) the appropriation of costs and assets as between divisions
(c) the limitations inherent in R.O.C.E.

The measurement of profit and capital employed
The use of R.O.C.E. measures of performance for comparing the performance of similar divisions requires measurements of profit and capital employed which are free from any accounting bias. Thus,

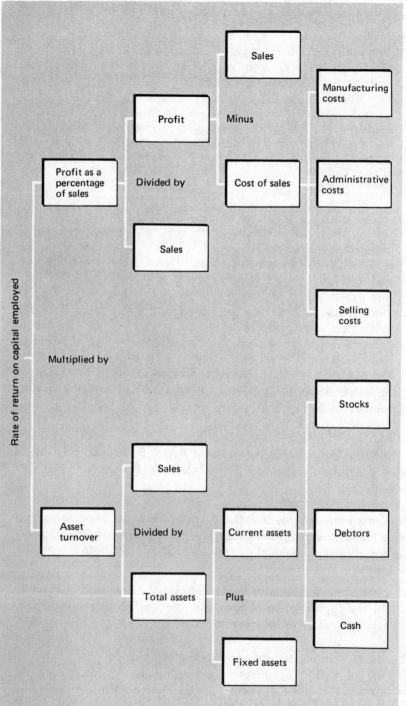

Fig. 3.30 Relationship of factors influencing the rate of return on capital employed.

uniform accounting procedures should be established for valuing inventory, and charging against profit such costs as depreciation, research and development and advertising costs. If comparisons are to be meaningful, the effect of price level changes should also be eliminated from accounting measurments. Moreover, profit and capital employed as measured by conventional accounting methods tend to reflect a much better rate of return than is the case. The valuation of assets on a historic cost basis means that the assets forming the capital investment base is a composite of assets of different monetary dimensions. It follows that the same problem applies to the measurement of costs applied to current revenues for profit calculation.

In order to overcome these problems, therefore, current operating revenues should be associated with the current costs of earning them, and the current value of the assets comprising the capital employed in current operations.

The appropriation of costs and assets as between divisions
In circumstances where factory buildings, production facilities, office, canteen and other facilities are shared by more than one division, the problem arises of apportioning the costs of these facilities and the value of the investment which they represent. In any event, certain facilities will invariably be conducted by the organization on behalf of all the divisions, and apportionments may have to be made in respect of such items as Head Office costs, Management and Technical Services, etc.

The problem of finding suitable bases for apportioning such costs and assets as between several divisions bears a strong resemblance to that of apportioning factory overheads to product costs, which we examined in chapter 2. As we saw, such apportionments tend to be arbitrary, and seldom are the methods selected entirely immune from criticism.

There is a strong case for avoiding apportionments, whether of costs or assets for the purpose of R.O.C.E. calculations. In accordance with our definition of responsibility accounting, the evaluation of performance should recognize only those elements which are under the Divisional Manager's control. The incorporation of non-controllable items with controllable ones in performance reports is admissible for information purposes, so long as they are distinguished from each other, and the fundamental principles enshrined in responsibility accounting are maintained.

Limitations inherent in R.O.C.E.
The main disadvantage of R.O.C.E. measures of performance is that they contain a conceptual weakness. This stems from the fact that

different investment centres will have different R.O.C.E. measurements. Thus, the R.O.C.E. for the whole organization may be 10%, whereas the various investment centres may have R.O.C.E.'s ranging from under 10% to over 10%. The manager of an investment centre enjoying a R.O.C.E. of 15% will be unwilling to consider any project offering a rate of return on investment of less than 15%, even though it offers a rate of return of over 10%. This is because the evaluation of his own performance will be made in terms of the current R.O.C.E. for his own investment centre. Hence, the use of R.O.C.E. for the evaluation of divisional performance may well motivate divisional managers to act in a way which is inconsistent with the financial objectives of the organization as a whole.

It was to deal with this difficulty that the General Electric Company introduced the Residual Income method of performance appraisal in the 1950s. Under this method, the performance of investment centres is evaluated by the residual profit after charging an appropriate amount calculated by reference to the rate of return on investment being earned by different types of assets. Because the residual income is an absolute figure and not a ratio, a division which is trying to improve its residual income figure will undertake investment programmes even where the expected rate of return is less that the current R.O.C.E.

Example

The net assets (total assets − current liabilities) of a division are valued at £1000. The company has decided that a return of 10% on these net assets is an appropriate target. The division's income statement for the current year is given below:

Revenue	£1000
Less costs	700
	300
less taxes	150
Income after taxes	150
Capital charge (10%)	100
Residual income	£50

If the manager of this division were evaluated on the R.O.C.E. basis, he would not invest in a project which produced a return of below 15% $\left(\text{i.e.} \dfrac{£150}{£1000} \times 100 \right)$. However, if he were evaluated on residual income he will invest in a project which gives a return above 10% because this will increase residual income. This action will be beneficial to the company.

Summary

Control and planning are integrated processes which affect every aspect of organizational activity, including the determination of objectives and the development of long-range and short-range plans. The comparison of actual performance with the goals stipulated in these plans discloses the extent to which they have been attained.

Responsibility accounting underpins the control process, and requires the establishment of responsibility centres throughout an organization. A responsibility centre is a segment of an organization where an individual manager is held responsible for the segment's performance.

Responsibility centres may take three forms:

(i) expense centre in which the manager has no control over revenue but is able to control expenditure;
(ii) profit centres where the manager has control over both revenue and costs;
(iii) investment centres where the manager has responsibility not only for revenues and costs but also for the capital invested.

The control problem is made more complex by the size of business organizations and the occurrence of transactions between various divisions of such organizations. In order that divisional performance should be accurately assessed for control purposes, transfer prices should be established which will be useful in this respect. If transfer pricing systems are to operate satisfactorily, some form of negotiated pricing must be agreed by divisional managers. Investment centres pose additional problems as regards the assessment of financial performance. The R.O.C.E. is a comprehensive measure of performance, but its limitations should be understood.

Further readings

1. Beyer, Robert, *Profitability Accounting for Planning and Control*, Ronald Press Co., New York, 1963.

2. Beyer, Robert & Trawick, D. J., *Profitability Accounting*, Ronald Press, New York, 1972.

3. Claydon, Roger, A New Way to Measure and Control Divisional Performance, *Management Services*, September–October, 1970.

4. Dearden, J., The Case Against ROI Control, *Harvard Business Review*, May–June, 1969.

4. Ferrara, William L., *Responsibility Accounting: A Basic Concept*, N.A.A. Bulletin, September, 1964.

5. Mauriel, J. & Anthony, R., Misevaluation of Investment Centre Performance, *Harvard Business Review*, April, 1965.

6. O'Connell, Neil F., Responsibility Accounting and Reports, *Journal of Accounting*, September, 1968.

7. Solomons, D., *Divisional Performance: Measurements and Control*, New York, Financial Executive Research Foundation, 1965.

11

Standard Costs and Variance Analysis

We turn now to a consideration of an important method of establishing standards of performance by the use of standard costs. The difficulty about using data recorded in the financial accounting system for planning purposes is that it relates to the past and although managers are interested in the results of previous decisions, they are primarily concerned with decisions which will affect the future.

For control purposes, historical costs are of little use. Particularly in times of inflation, past experience will not inform management whether an operation, a job or a department costs too much. Indeed, what management wishes to know is not what costs were in the past but what they ought to be, in the present. Once it has been determined what these costs ought to be, actual costs can be compared with them, and any difference may be analysed.

Standard costing has been evolved as a method to meet this need. It relies upon predetermined costs which are agreed as representing acceptable costs under specified operating conditions.

Standard costs and budgeted costs

The principal differences between standard costs and budgeted costs lie in their scope. Whilst both are concerned with laying down cost limits for control purposes, budget costs impose total limits to costs for the firm as a whole, for departments or for functions for the budget period, whereas standard costs are attached to products and to individual manufacturing operations or processes. For example, the production department's budget for the period ahead may envisage a total production of 100,000 units at a cost of £10 a unit, so that the production department will be allocated an expenditure ceiling of £1 million. The unit cost of £10 will have been based upon the established standard costs relating to material usage and price, labour usage and labour costs as well as allocated overhead costs. Moreover, standard costs are only revised when it is clear that they have ceased to be realistic in terms of current costs, and these revisions do not necessarily coincide with budget periods.

The relationship between budgeted costs and standard costs is clear: the setting of standard costs as performance standards for control purposes implies that they must be used as a basis for drawing up budget statements and calculating budget costs, for otherwise there can be no confidence in their use as a basis against which actual performance may be measured.

Applications of standard costing

Standard costing is a useful method of control in a number of ways. First, the process of evaluating performance by determining how efficiently current operations are being carried out may be facilitated by the process of management by exception. Very often the problem facing management is the time lost in sifting large masses of feedback information and in deciding what information is significant and relevant to the control problem. Management by exception overcomes this problem by highlighting only the important control information, that is the variances between the standard set and the actual result. This process allows management to focus attention on important problems so that maximum energy may be devoted to correcting situations which are falling out of control.

Second, a standard costing system may lead to cost reductions. The installation of such a system demands a re-appraisal of current production methods as it necessitates the standardization of practices. This examination often leads to an improvement in the methods employed which is reflected in a reduction of the costs of the product. One example of cost reductions through increased efficiency may be seen in the simplication of the clerical procedures relating to inventory control. All similar items of inventory may be recorded in the accounts at a uniform price; this eliminates the need which arises under historical costing for re-calculating a new unit price whenever a purchase of inventory is made at a different price.

Third, standard costs are used as a basis for determining selling prices. Standard costs represent what the product should cost, and are a much better guide for pricing decisions than historical costs which may contain purchasing and production inefficiencies which cannot be recouped in competitive markets.

Finally, perhaps the most important benefit which may be derived from a standard costing system is the atmosphere of cost consciousness which is fostered among executives and foremen. Each individual is aware that the costs and output for which he is responsible are being measured, and that he will be called on to take whatever action is necessary should large variances occur. As we concluded earlier in this chapter, if the philosophy of top management is positive and supportive, standard costing may act as an incentive to individuals to act in the best interest of the firm. Moreover, a standard costing system which allows subordinates to participate in setting the standards fosters a knowledge of costing down to shop floor level, and assists in decision-making at all levels. Thus, if there should occur spoilt work necessitating a decision from the foreman in charge on whether to scrap or rectify the part involved, a knowledge of costs will enable him to make the best decision.

Setting cost standards

The setting of cost standards is no easy task. If they are set too high, for example, large variances will appear and in the degree that production managers consider them to be unrealistic so they will tend to ignore them. If standards are set too low, however, they will not act as incentives to efficiency and production efficiency may fall. The best standards are those which are set at levels which though high are nevertheless attainable, so that they will encourage efficient performance.

The process of setting cost standards requires the standardization of all the elements affecting a product so that specific standards for these elements may be established prior to its actual production. There are two component parts of this process: the determination of a physical standard and the selection of an appropriate value to be attached to the physical standard. This problem may be examined in the context of establishing standard costs for raw materials and labour, which are the two of the major direct costs of production.

Standard costs for raw materials

Most companies rely on engineering studies for calculations of the quantities of raw materials required for each unit of the product. If different types of raw materials are required, a Bill of Materials is drawn up which itemizes the standard quantities of each type of raw material required for a specific unit of the product. The computation of the quantities required should include an allowance for inevitable (i.e., normal) wastage in production, for example, those which arise due to machining, evaporation or expected breakages.

The purchasing manager should bear the responsibility for providing information regarding the prices of raw materials. These prices are not the historical prices which have been recorded as costs in the books: they are forecasts of expected prices during the period for which the standard costs are to apply, and they are essentially predetermined prices.

Standard costs for direct labour

Standard labour costs also consist of two components—quantity and price. Firstly, standard labour grades are established which take into account the various skills required to perform the operations involved in production. Time and motion studies are employed to set labour standards which reflect the labour hours which should be spent by each grade of labour in each department to manufacture the finished product. If there are several types of product, these calculations must be made for each product.

Secondly, wages rates must be applied to the labour hours in order to calculate a unit cost of labour for each unit of product. Once again, these wages rates are not the current or past wage rates but the forecast of the expected wage rates which will prevail during the period when the standard costs are to be valid.

Variance analysis

As we mentioned earlier in this chapter, the use of standard costs simplifies the control of performance for if standard costs are correctly set one needs only to be concerned with the differences or variances between actual costs and standard costs. We mentioned in this connection the method of management by exception as the appropriate means of controlling operations by variance analysis. In a general sense, the aim of variance analysis is to investigate variances to ascertain whether they are justified or unjustified. If they are justified either because estimates of quantities of input resources or input prices are wrong, clearly the standard costs must be adjusted. If, however, they are unjustified, the causes for these variances must be investigated and corrective action taken.

It is the accountant's function to assist in the evaluation of performance where a standard costing system is in operation, and he will calculate the variances by comparing actual costs of production with their standard costs. As the standard costs are made up of two components—quantity and price, so too does variance analysis seek to ascertain whether the variances are due to quantity differences or price differences. Let us consider in turn the calculation of direct material and direct labour variances.

Direct material variances

Example

A firm manufactures decorative plates from aluminium. The standard costs for raw materials in respect of each plate were estimated as follows:

quantity	3 lbs
price	£0.50 per lb

During the period under review, 4000 plates were produced, and the following information was obtained:

quantity used	11,000 lbs
quantity purchased	15,000 lbs
purchase price	£0.55 per lb

The following points are immediately brought to our attention:

(a) *Price.* The purchase price turned out to be 5 pence per lb higher than estimated.

(b) *Quantity.* An output of 4000 plates should have required a consumption of 12,000 lbs of aluminium, according to the standard usage on which the standard cost of £1.50 per plate was estimated. As only 11,000 lbs were actually used, a saving in material usage of 1000 lbs was realized.

The accounting analysis of these differences are made in terms of a material price variance and a material usage variance, as follows.

Material price variance

This variance shows the difference between the actual cost of materials and their standard cost, and is best calculated when raw materials are purchased and before they are committed to production. In this way, the variance is highlighted at the earliest possible stage so that action may be taken immediately to deal with future purchases should it turn out to be necessary. For example, the buyer may have purchased at a high price, while alternative sources may be available at the old price. A further advantage of this method is that it enables inventory to be valued in the accounts at standard cost, thereby reducing the clerical effort which is necessary if inventory is valued at actual cost. The material price variance results, therefore, from a comparison of the price of raw materials purchased with an estimate of what these purchases should have cost. The material price variance is calculated as follows:

Actual quantity of material purchased × price variance per lb.

i.e., $15,000 \text{ lbs} \times £(0.55 - 0.50)$

$$= £750$$

Since material purchase costs were greater than estimated by the standard, the variance is an unfavourable one.

Material usage variance

This variance expresses the difference between the actual quantities used to manufacture the actual output and the standard quantities envisaged for that output. For the reasons stated above, price variances are normally calculated first and this eliminates the influence of price variations from the calculation of the material usage variance. The variance is calculated after production has occurred when the difference between the amount of material used, and what should have been used in manufacturing the output produced is known. The material usage variance is expressed as follows:

$$\text{Variance in quantity used} \times \text{standard price per lb}$$
$$\text{i.e., } 1000 \text{ lbs.} \times £0.50$$
$$= £500.$$

Since the material usage is less than anticipated it is a favourable usage variance.

Direct labour variances

Example

The standard costs for labour in respect of each plate were determined as follows:

Standard time per plate	0.25 hour
Standard rate for labour	£1.00 per hour

The actual output of 4000 plates was conducted under the following conditions:

Labour hours worked	900 hours
Actual rate	£1.10 per hour

Analysis. As in the calculation of direct material variances, this analysis is concerned with a price variance and a usage variance. The wage rate variance expresses the difference between standard wage set and the actual wage paid. The labour usage variance relates to the amount of labour required to produce the output as against the standard, and it is called the labour efficiency variance. The following differences appear immediately:

(a) The actual rate of pay turned out to be higher than the standard rate to the extent of 10 pence per hour.

(b) The standard labour costs were based on a standard time of 0.25 hour per plate, so that the output of 4000 plates should have taken 1000 hours. As only 900 hours were taken, there has been a more efficiency use of labour.

We may calculate the wage rate and labour efficiency variances as follows.

Wage rate variance

This variance shows the impact of an increase in the wage rate over the rate which should have been incurred in relation to the output. We note, therefore, a similarity between the material price variance and the wage rate variance in that both are concerned with the net impact of price changes. In this instance, we are concerned with calculating the effect of the higher wage rate on the number of labour hours actually used.

$$\text{Actual labour hours} \times \text{Wage rate variance per hour}$$
$$\text{i.e., } 900 \times £(1.10 - 1.00)$$
$$= £90$$

The wage rate variance is an unfavourable one in the sense that had the output been obtainable at the standard wage, the total wage cost would have been £90 less.

Labour efficiency variance

The labour efficiency variance is calculated by finding the difference between the actual number of hours worked and that estimated by the standard, and multiplying this difference by the standard wage rate. The formula is as follows:

$$\text{Labour variance} \times \text{Standard wage rate per hour}$$
$$\text{i.e., } 100 \text{ hours} \times £1.00 \text{ per hour}$$
$$= £100$$

This variance is a favourable one, since it took less hours to produce the output.

The accounting disposition of variances

The accounting records for the entries relating to the direct material and direct labour costs charged to production, and the adjustment to be made in respect of the variances which have been ascertained would appear as under:

Creditors

		Stores	£7500
		Material price variance	750

Stores

Creditors	£7500	Work in progress	£6000
Material usage variance	500		

Wages

Direct wages	£990	Work in progress control	£1000
Labour efficiency variance	100	Wage rate variance	90

Work in progress

Stores	£6000	
Wages control	1000	

Material price variance

Creditors control	£750	

Material usage variance

	Inventory control	£500

Labour efficiency

	Wage control	£100

Wage rate variance

Wages control	£90	

These records emphasize the fact that all records of inventories—from stores to work in progress to finished goods—should be valued at standard price. For example, the closing stores inventory is £2000 which represents 4000 lbs at the standard price of £0.5 per lb. The fact that work in progress is valued at standard cost enables the variances to be calculated in order to highlight the responsibility of the centre concerned. For example, if work in progress is transferred between two departments A and B, B will receive the unfinished inventory at standard cost, so that any variances which occur in Department A will be highlighted while work is being done on the inventory in that department, and will not be confused with the responsibilities of Department B. Most accountants believe that it is desirable to show activity at standard cost and to transfer earnings to the Income Statement. In our example the variance accounts will be closed by transfer to the income statement, viz.

	£
Net sales	1000
Standard cost of sales	400
Standard gross margin	600

	£	
Less: variances from standard		
material price variance	(750)	
material usage variance	500	
Labour efficiency variance	100	
Wage rate variance	(90)	240
Actual gross margin		£360

The control of overheads

We have so far examined the control problem in two different senses. Firstly, we have looked at the annual budget as laying down the targets of performance in the short-term in respect of the activities of departments and functions. In providing a short-term planning framework, budget plans place limits upon the expenditure which the different departments may undertake or in other words the costs which they may incur. The objective of budgetary control systems is to control these costs. Secondly, we examined standard costing as a means of controlling the unit costs of production. We stressed, however, that because budget plans are based upon these standard costs, adherence to standards is necessary if budgeted plans are to be realized.

In chapter 5, we drew a distinction between budgetary planning and budgetary control. We stressed that the two management processes of planning and control demanded the construction of different types of budgets, because the type of budget which may be suitable for planning may be inappropriate for control purposes. Earlier in the present chapter, we noticed that the higher one ascends the hierarchy of management, the greater the proportion of total costs which is defined as controllable cost. Therefore, at the Board level it is possible to use a planning budget as a control device, because at this level all costs are controllable. Below this level, management will be interested in only those deviations over which they have control. It is necessary that a measure of flexibility is built into control budgets which will reflect operating conditions which may be different from those envisaged in the planning stages.

In this section we analyse the control problem created by changes in the planned volume of production during the budget period. In chapter 7, we classified all costs as falling into two categories—fixed costs and variable costs. The characteristics of these costs are such that changes in the total volume of production affect them, but affect them in a different way. Thus, variable costs vary with the volume of output, and if the volume of production should rise or fall so will variable costs. Therefore, we may say that changes in the volume of output will affect budgeted costs in the sense that the total budgeted variable costs will be affected by volume changes. The control problem regarding fixed costs is the reverse. In the short-term, we assume that fixed costs will remain constant: this implies that budgeted fixed costs will not vary irrespective of variations in the volume of output which may not, of course, exceed the productive capacity.

For these various reasons, the control of overheads requires a method of control which takes into account the possibility of changes in the volume of production during the planning period. It is very rare that actual output equals budgeted output, and ideally one would wish to devise a system which, taking into account changes in the volume of production, will enable a comparison to be made between the actual overhead costs of production at that level of output and the budgeted costs which have been allowed for the level of output attained. The accounting method for dealing with this problem is flexible budgeting.

Flexible budgeting

As a means of controlling costs at fluctuating levels of output, the aim of flexible budgeting is to answer the question we posed for calculating direct material and direct labour variances "what should this output have cost to produce?". The determination of this amount enables appropriate variances to be calculated by comparing this cost with the actual cost incurred.

Example

An Assembly Department produced 5000 units of output during a period, and the budgeted factory overhead costs at that level of output were as follows:

Indirect material	£5000
Indirect labour	2500
Repair and maintenance	5000
Insurance	1500
Rates	3000
Depreciation	3000
	£20,000

The overhead costs per unit are:

$$£20,000 \div 5000 = £4$$

These costs added to the direct material standard costs and the direct labour standard costs would indicate what costs of production should be incurred in a situation where the actual volume of production is the same as the planned volume of production.

If it were possible to contemplate in the budget plan different levels of output so as to meet possible changes in market demand during the planning period, we could not say that the departmental overhead costs per unit would remain at £4. We could not assume that departmental overheads costs would be as follows:

6000 units	£24,000
7000 units	28,000
8000 units	32,000

Overhead costs of production do not behave in this way, for they consist of fixed elements as well as variable elements; in the above computations we have assumed that all the costs are variable.

Therefore, an analysis is needed of the fixed and variable elements. We will assume that this revealed the following:

	Fixed Costs	Variable Costs Per Unit
Indirect materials		£1.0
Indirect labour		0.5
Repairs and maintenance	£2000	0.6
Insurance	500	0.2
Rates	3000	
Depreciation	3000	
	£8500	£2.3

This analysis enables us to calculate the total overhead costs which should be incurred at different levels of output, by means of a Budget Allowance the formula for which is:

Budget Allowance = Total Fixed Costs + (Unit Variable Costs ×
Units Produced)

Hence, for an output of 4000 units, the cost control budget would be calculated as follows:

	Total Variable Costs	Fixed Costs	Total Budget Allowance
Indirect materials	£4000		£4000
Indirect labour	2000		2000
Repairs and maintenance	2400	£2000	4400
Insurance	800	500	1300
Rates		3000	3000
Depreciation		3000	3000
	£9200	£8500	£17,700

It follows that it may be possible to establish budget allowances for a range of output, assuming that the same fixed and variable cost information is valid for that range of output, as follows:

Output (units)	3000	4000	5000	6000
Indirect material	£3000	£4000	£5000	£6000
Indirect labour	1500	2000	2500	3000
Repairs and maintenance	3800	4400	5000	5600
Insurance	1100	1300	1500	1700
Rates	3000	3000	3000	3000
Depreciation	3000	3000	3000	3000
	£15,400	£17,700	£20,000	£22,300
Overhead costs per unit	£5.1	£4.4	£4.0	£3.7

These calculations illustrate the nature of overhead cost behaviour over a range of output: variable overhead costs increase as output increases but fixed costs remain constant. As a result, total overhead costs per unit fall as output expands.

The advantage of flexible budgets over fixed budgets for control

In circumstances where changes in the volume of output are likely to occur, a fixed budget will be irrelevant to a solution of the control problem. The failure to recognize and provide for the different behaviour of fixed and variable overhead costs would be reflected in faulty comparisons being employed.

Consider the case where the planning budget called for the production of 5000 units, but that only 4500 units were produced during the period. Actual costs of production are those shown in column 1 in the table below. If we use a fixed budget for control purposes, we would compare the original budget (column 3) with the actual costs of production (column 1). This is shown in column 4, where an overall gain of £850 is disclosed. One might conclude from these computations that the control of costs had been better than planned.

Our previous discussion would lead us to compare the actual costs with the budget allowance for the level of output attained. The allowance is shown in column 2, and the comparison between the budget allowance and the costs of production shows that what appeared to be a gain of £850 is in fact a loss of £300. The use of fixed budgets therefore for control purposes, conceal changes in cost due to volume changes.

	(1) Actual Cost of Production	(2) Total Budget Allowance	(3) Original Budget	(4) Variation From Original Budget	(5) Variation From Budget Allowance
Units produced	4500	4500	5000	(1−3)	(1−2)
Indirect materials	£4700	£4500	£5000	£300F	£200U
Indirect labour	2400	2250	2500	100F	150U
Repairs and maintenance	4600	4700	5000	400F	100F
Insurance	1450	1400	1500	50F	50U
Rates	3000	3000	3000	—	—
Depreciation	3000	3000	3000	—	—
	£19,150	£18,850	£20,000	£850F	£300U

The analysis of overhead variances

An important conclusion which emerges from the previous section is that the flexible budget alone does not supply all the answers which are necessary for evaluating performance. For example, does the unfavourable variance for indirect labour represent higher wage rates or an inefficient use of labour? If realistic responsibilities for variances are to be established it is necessary to analyse overhead variances in greater detail. The use of overhead variances enables us to extend the analysis of variations from the budget.

In chapter 2, we considered the problem of choosing a suitable volume base for recovering overheads. So far in this chapter we have conducted our analysis in terms of units of output. However, most concerns manufacture several products and this creates difficulties with regard to the recovery of overheads. As we noted in the earlier chapter, if products are different a uniform overhead charge such as the unit of production method may result in incorrect costing. This problem may be overcome by the use of standard hours. A standard hour is a unit of output which measures the amount of work which should be performed in one hour. Therefore, the output of many products is reduced to a common denominator, and from now on we will consider output in standard hours rather than units.

Variable overhead variance analysis

In chapter 2, we noted that two overhead rates are usually established—a variable overhead rate and a fixed overhead rate. This distinction is important with regard to variance analysis, and makes the analysis of overhead variances somewhat more complicated.

Example

Let us assume that the Assembly Department is budgeted for an output of 5000 standard hours. Actual hours worked were 4800 and the variable costs incurred were as follows:

Indirect materials	£5200
Indirect labour	2400
Repairs and maintenance	3200
Insurance	800
Total variable costs	£11,600

There are two variances for variable overheads which must be ascertained, firstly the difference between the budget allowance based upon the actual hours worked and the actual expenses incurred, which is called the spending variance. Secondly, an efficiency variance must be calculated to show the difference between the standard hours allowed and the actual hours worked, multiplied by the standard overhead rate.

The formulae for these variances are as follows:

Spending Variance: (Actual hours at actual cost) − (Actual hours at the standard cost)

Efficiency Variance: (Standard hours at the standard cost) − (Actual hours at the standard cost)

Example

We may calculate these variances for the Assembly Department given that the variable costs per standard hour is £2.3 at a budgeted output of 5000 standard hours, as follows:

Spending variance:
  (4800 hours at £11,600) − (4800 hours at £2.3 per hour)
     = £11,600 − £11,040
     = £560

As overhead costs were higher than the budget allowance, the variance is an unfavourable one.

Efficiency variance:
(5000 hours at £2.3 per hour) − (4800 hours at £2.3 per hour)
     = £11,500 − £11,040
     = £460

As the number of hours worked was less than the standard hours allowed, the efficiency variance is a favourable one.

It is possible to extend this analysis to the breakdown of all the individual items of overhead costs represented in the total overhead costs analysed above. The variances for the individual items may be calculated as follows:

	(1) Actual Costs	(2) Actual Hours at Standard Cost	(3) Standard Hours at Standard	(4) Spending Variance (1−2)	(5) Efficiency Variance (3−2)
Indirect materials	£5200	£4800	£5000	£400 U	£200 F
Indirect labour	2400	2400	2500	—	100 F
Repairs & Maintenance	3200	2880	3000	320 U	120 F
Insurance	800	960	1000	160 F	40 F
	£11,600	£11,040	£11,500	£560 U	£460 F

The breakdown of the total spending variance over the individual elements of overhead variable costs discloses how much expenditure on these elements have varied from the budgeted amounts. For some items, the variance may include both usage and price elements.

The efficiency variance, on the other hand, does not represent efficiency in the use of overhead costs. Instead, it measures efficiency in the use of the factor used to recover overhead, in this case direct labour.

Fixed overhead variance analysis

Our discussion of flexible budgeting illustrated that it is the variable cost element which necessitates the computation of allowances over various ranges of output; and that fixed costs remain constant over a relevant range.

The difference between budgeted fixed costs and actual fixed costs gives the fixed overhead budget variance (also called spending variance). Using again the example of our Assembly Department, and assuming that actual fixed costs incurred are those shown in the table on p. 463, we may prepare a variance report as follows:

	Actual	Budget	Variance
Repairs & Maintenance	£2100	£2000	£100 U
Insurance	600	500	100 U
Rates	3200	3000	200 U
Depreciation	3000	3000	
	£8900	£8500	£400 U

Another fixed overhead variance occurs when absorption costing methods are employed. As we discussed in chapter 2, the use of an absorption costing system necessitates the recovery of fixed overheads by a predetermined rate. In that chapter we examined also the problem of choosing an activity level to enable the recovery of fixed overheads to be made. In our present example the normal (or standard) level of activity is 5000 hours and the standard rate for recovering fixed overheads is £1.7 per standard hour (£8500 ÷ 5000). If in a period, the standard hours allowed for the output were 4800, the fixed overhead for the period would be under-absorbed by 200 standard hours multiplied by the standard rate, viz.

$$200 \times £1.7 = 340$$

This is an unfavourable volume variance.

Sales variance analysis and the control of revenue

In general terms, the procedures appropriate for the control of revenue are similar to those applied to the control of costs, and may be summarized as follows:

(a) The establishment of a sales plan.
(b) The prompt determination and reporting of variances between actual and planned performance.
(c) The investigation and analysis of variances so as to ascertain their causes and those responsible for them.
(d) The implementation of appropriate corrective action.

The determination of the sales plan has both long-range and budgetary aspects. Long-range planning will be concerned with establishing revenue objectives and goals, from which may be derived specific sales targets and prices for the budget planning period. Since the level of demand for most products exhibits a seasonal pattern, the annual sales plan should be divided into smaller periods so as to make possible a system of responsibility accounting based on a meaningful comparison of actual and planned performance.

So far, we have discussed the control of revenue in terms of analysing the difference between actual and planned sales. It should be apparent, however, that management is not really so much concerned about sales themselves as the profit from sales. It is for this reason that sales variance analysis has been developed to measure the effects on profits of variances between actual sales and planned sales, and not the effect of such variances merely on revenue.

Three different variances are commonly applied to the analysis of sales:

(a) Sales price variance
(b) Sales volume variance
(c) Sales mix variance.

Sales price variance

It is quite common for actual selling prices to differ from the planned selling price. Numerous factors may be responsible for sales price variances, such as the need to adjust prices to meet competition, or to provide a new marketing strategy. By far the largest factor is the discretion allowed to individual sales managers to adjust prices to meet particular circumstances, such as price reductions for slightly spoiled goods or to secure the goodwill of a client.

The sales price variance is an ordinary price variance of the type which we have already discussed. It may be calculated from the following formula:

Sales price variance = Units sold × (Actual contribution per unit less the standard contribution)

It indicates, therefore, the total effect on profit of differences between set prices and the prices at which goods were actually sold.

Sales volume variance

This variance discloses the effect on profits of differences between the planned sales volume and the actual volume of sales. It is calculated as follows:

Sales volume variance = standard contribution per unit
                        × (actual number of units sold − budgeted units of sales)

Sales mix variance

As we saw in chapter 7, a change in the product mix may change the profitability of the total mix if the contribution margin of the different products is different. In these circumstances, changes in the product mix will lead to a variance between planned and actual profits. The dimension of this variance may be computed as follows:

Sales mix variance = Standard contribution per unit of each product ×
                     (actual quantities of units sold − actual total
                     sales of units in budgeted mix proportions)

Example of all 3 variances

The following data relates to Products X and Y sold by Biproducts Limited during the quarter ended 31st December, 19X0

Budgeted sales: X 5000 units at £10 (standard contribution margin £4)

Y 5000 units at £5 (standard contribution margin £2)

Actual sales: X 4000 units for £44,000 (i.e. £11 per unit)
              Y 8000 units for £32,000 (i.e. £4 per unit)

These data may be tabulated as follows:

	(a)	(b)	(c)	(d)	(e)	(f)	(g)	(h)
	Actual Con-tribution	Actual Quantity	Standard Con-tribution Margin	(b)×(c) Value	Actual Quantity in Standard Proportions	Standard Con-tribution Margin	(e)×(f) Value	Budgeted Margin
	£	Units	£	£	Units	£	£	£
X	20,000	4000	4	16,000	6000	4	24,000	20,000
Y	8000	8000	2	16,000	6000	2	12,000	10,000
	28,000	12,000		32,000	12,000		36,000	30,000

Notes
1. Column (a) is derived from the following formula:
   Actual Contribution
   = Actual Sales less (Actual Units × Standard Cost)

$$= £44,000 - (4000 × £6)$$
$$= £20,000$$

2. Column (e) is derived by taking total actual sales of 12,000 units and applying the budgeted mix proportions. According to the budget, 50% of X and 50% of Y should be sold. Total sales were 12,000 units, which expressed in budgeted mix proportions amount to 6000 units of X and 6000 units of Y.

The variances which may be extracted from these data are as follows:

(a) *Sales price variance*
x = Units sold × (Actual contribution per unit less standard contribution)
= Column (a) − column (d)
= £28,000 − £32,000
= £4000 U

The sales price variance is unfavourable to the extent of £4000 because 3000 units of Y were sold at a price which was £1 lower than the standard, whilst only 1000 units of X were sold at a price which was £1 higher than the standard price.

(b) *Sales volume variance*
X = Standard contribution per unit × (actual number of units sold less budgeted units of sales)
= Column (g) − column (h)
= £36,000 − £30,000
= £6000 F

This variance reflects the fact that 12,000 units were actually sold as against a budgeted volume of only 10,000 units. Its value is the contribution which the extra 2000 units would have brought if they were at standard price and mix.

(c) *Sales mix variance*
= (Standard contribution per unit of each product × the actual quantities of units sold) − (standard contribution per unit of each product × actual total sales in budgeted mix proportions)
= Column (d) − column (g)
= £32,000 − £36,000
= £4000 U

This variance discloses the reduction in budgeted profits caused by selling a greater proportion of units having a lower contribution margin than the standard.

Responsibility for variances

We have stressed that under responsibility accounting only those costs incurred by a responsibility centre over which it can exercise control may be used as a basis for revaluation. Therefore, in variance analysis it is necessary that the precise cause of a variance be determined and that the cause be traced to the individual responsible. It is the function of the individual in charge of each responsibility centre to act promptly upon reports of variances which are within his control. Therefore, variances are not ends in themselves. Rather, they raise the questions why did the variance occur? What must be done to eliminate them? Obviously the importance of these questions depends on the significance of the deviations. We shall see how the significance of a variance is determined in the next section.

The material usage and labour efficiency variances respectively reveal that the quantities of material and labour used in production are either more or less than planned, depending on whether the variances are unfavourable or favourable. If more material is being used than planned, the cause may lie elsewhere than in the production department, for example in the purchase of inferior materials by the purchasing department. The fault, however, may lie in the production department and may be found to be attributable to careless supervision, or the use of untrained staff, or faulty machines. An unfavourable labour efficiency variance may be due to poor control by the foreman, bad labour relations, health factors, production delays, inferior tools and badly trained staff. Again the responsibility for the variance should be located. For example, if due to badly trained staff this may be caused by inefficiency on the part of the personnel department; but if, on the other hand the variance is caused by the economic conditions prevailing at the time which had produced a shortage of specialized labour, the variance is considered to be uncontrollable.

Price and wage rate variances may not be controllable by the firm, and this is particularly true of raw material prices and wages agreed nationally with Trade Unions. On the other hand variances may occur in the negotiation of contracts for materials which are the responsibility of the Purchasing Department. Purchasing Department controls prices by getting several quotations, taking advantage of economic lots and securing cash discounts. Inefficiency in these areas will reveal unfavourable variances for which that department should be held responsible.

With regard to overhead variances, spending variances are usually the responsibility of the departmental head, because they are usually controllable by him. The volume variance is not normally controllable by the departmental manager; it is usually the responsibility of the sales department or production control.

The investigation of variances

Managerial time is too valuable to be wasted on the unnecessary checking of performance. When standard costs are properly established, they provide an automatic means of highlighting performance variances upon which management may concentrate their attention. Thus, the investigation of variances is concerned only with exceptional variances and not those which are minor deviations from the established standards.

The investigation of a variance is a three stage process consisting of:

(a) an investigation to determine whether the variance is significant;

(b) if it proves to be significant, its causes are investigated;

(c) if the variance can be corrected, action is taken to ensure that it will not occur in the future.

The determination of the significance of a variance in itself may be problematic. If its definition is left to managerial judgement and experience, inconsistencies may arise in the treatment of different variances solely by reason of behavioural factors affecting a manager's judgement of a situation. Thus, pressure of work in itself may lead him to perceive the significance of a variance as less important than it really is. Moreover, there is unlikely to be complete agreement between different managers about the investigation of borderline cases.

It is necessary, also, to distinguish 'chance' or 'random' variances from significant variances requiring investigation. By viewing the standard as an arithmetical mean about which fluctuations will occur, it is possible to eliminate random variances from significant variances. Experience of the investigation of variances shows that random variances are inherent in standard costing systems. Such variances assume the shape of a 'normal distribution' about the standard, and they are not controllable. It follows that a statistical control chart may be utilized to enable a manager to determine whether a variance is significant or not. It will define the limits within which random or normal variances occur, so that those variances which fall outside these limits may be assumed to be abnormal and, therefore, significant variances.

Statistical control charts have been used for many years for the purpose of quality control, but it is only recently that this technique has been applied to the control of standard cost variances. Statistical control charts permit the elimination of random variances whilst providing a high probability that non-random variances will be revealed.

The use of statistical control charts requires that upper and lower limits of random variance tolerance be laid down with precision. Setting these limits requires an analysis of the pattern of sample variances, and the standard deviation of the sample may be used to determine the acceptable limits of tolerance. These limits are illustrated in Fig. 3.31.

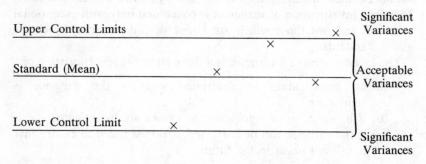

Fig. 3.31

Opportunity cost variances

Developments in management science, in particular mathematical programming and computer science, have presented accountants with a considerable potential for extending the scope of standard costing by means of 'opportunity cost variances'. In this context, the opportunity cost variance is the variance which results from the failure to optimize profit by taking into consideration post-budget environmental changes. For example, if the price of a material used in the production process increases, the original plan may become sub-optimal, and losses may be incurred by adhering to the old (and no longer optimal plan). As Demski (1968) points out "because of its emphasis on comparison between actual and planned results, and consequent disregard of changes in these planned results, the traditional accounting model does not act as an opportunity cost system".

Linear programming affords a method for dealing with the opportunity cost problem, as defined above, but it does require changes in the traditional accounting information systems so that relevant information is made available. Thus, the detection of opportunity cost variances requires not only information about actual transactions, but also transactions which could have been made but were not made. Salkin & Kombluth (1973) have stated this problem as follows:

> "The standard costing system fails to account for opportunity losses because it is constructed without reference to the best possible plan or its alternative. . . . If we want to devise a system that recognizes opportunity losses in its control process, we must use an economic costing and control system, of which the linear programming model is a good example."

The discussion of such a system is beyond the scope of this book, but interested readers should refer to the literature described in the bibliography.

Summary

Standard costing underlies most business activities. The cost of a product must be ascertained prior to production for pricing and control purposes. Standard costing may also lead to cost reductions. Perhaps the most important benefit which results from a standard costing system is the atmosphere of cost consciousness which is fostered among managers.

Standard cost data are compared with actual cost data for the purpose of ascertaining variances. Such variances are normally broken down into two basic components—quantity variances and price variances. The control of overhead costs as distinct from direct costs requires a method which takes into account the possibility of changes in the level of production during the planning period. Flexible budgeting affords such a method, and provides for each department a series of budget allowance schedules for various volume levels within the normal range of operations.

The ascertainment of variances is only the first stage in assessing results. Variances should be analysed in depth in order to establish whether they are significant, whether they are controllable and if so where responsibility lies. At the same time, the analysis of variances enables established standards to be validated and methods for establishing standards in the future to be improved.

Standard costing not only provides a means of controlling costs but also monitoring revenue through the analysis of sales variances. Linear programming may allow the control process to be improved, providing that future developments in accounting information systems allow opportunity costs to be recorded.

References

1. Demski, J. S., Variance Analysis using a Constrained Linear Model, in *Studies in Cost Analysis* David Solomons (ed.), Sweet and Maxwell, London, 2nd edn, 1968.

2. Salkin, G. & Kornbluth, J., *Linear Programming in Financial Planning*, Accountancy Age Books, 1973.

Further Readings

Bierman, J. Jr. & Dyckman, T. T., *Managerial Cost Accounting*, Macmillan, New York, 1971.

Dopuch, N., Birnberg, J. G. & Demski, J., *Cost Accounting: Accounting Data for Management's Decisions*, Harcourt, Brace and World Inc., New York, 1969.

Dyckman, T. R., The Investigation of Cost Variances, *Journal of Accounting Research*, Fall, 1969.

Horngren, C. T., *Cost Accounting: A Managerial Emphasis*, 3rd edn, Prentice Hall, Englewood Cliffs, 1972.

12
The Control of Managed Costs

Traditionally, cost accountants have been concerned with the control of manufacturing costs. In recent years, the rising proportion of non-manufacturing costs as a percentage of total costs has led to an increasing interest in the control of such costs. Non-manufacturing costs may be divided into three categories—administrative, marketing, and research and development costs. Because such costs are incurred at the discretion of management, they are often referred to as 'managed' or 'discretionary' costs.

As we saw in chapter 12, it is possible to apply standards to estimates of manufacturing costs as a means of controlling them. In the case of direct labour costs, for example, engineering time studies determine the amount of labour time required for each operation, and the application of appropriate wage rates to labour time results in a monetary value for labour costs at a given level of output. Consequently, it is possible to establish a clear relationship between output levels and direct labour costs.

By contrast, the problem of controlling managed costs is made difficult by the absence of a method for determining appropriate cost levels since the benefits associated with these costs cannot always be measured in financial terms. Research and development costs, for example, may ultimately lead to the development of better products or production processes, but there is little if any direct connection between the costs incurred in any one year and the financial benefits attributable to such costs in that year. Similarly, advertising costs incurred in any one year are difficult to relate to any financial benefits directly attributable to such costs in that year.

This chapter is devoted to the consideration of the problem of controlling managed costs.

The control of administrative costs

We examined the nature of administrative costs in chapter 2 of this Part, and we noted that such costs are relatively fixed in the short-run irrespective of short-term changes in the level of business activity.

As yet, the stricter costing procedures applied to manufacturing activities have not been applied generally to administrative activities. Management would certainly argue that administrative functions are not susceptible to work study methods. Nevertheless, certain tasks such as clerical ones are susceptible to work study, and some organizations have attempted to establish standards of efficiency by which to determine staff requirements. Examples of some of the control factors which have been employed are:

Activity	Control Factors
Purchasing	No. of orders placed
Typing	No. of letters typed
Receipting cheques	No. of cheques received

Generally, however, administrative services are rendered indirectly to many different departments, and it is practically impossible to establish input-output relationships which would enable over-all evaluations to be made. Hence, the control of administrative costs is one of the most difficult areas of management control.

To some extent, budgets can assist in exercising control over administrative costs. The budgetary control of such costs requires that accounting responsibility be clearly identified with particular managers. Financial requirements must be submitted as budget requests by individual managers, and should be scrutinized, modified as necessary and should be incorporated subsequently into an overall administrative budget. The administrative budget becomes the standard against which expenditure is to be assessed.

The difficulty in using this method of controlling administrative costs lies in determining whether the initial budget is reasonable for the proposed level of activity, for there is no way of establishing an acceptable standard of administrative expenditure in relation to particular activity levels. Hence, decisions regarding administrative cost budgets must be based largely on executive judgement and experience.

The control of research and development costs

There are two main reasons why research and development costs are difficult to control. First, since there is little connection between research costs and their benefits, research spending is no indicator of the effectiveness of a research department, or indeed, of a research project. Secondly, there is a long lead time between costs incurred and benefits received.

We noted in chapter 3 that research and development is an activity directly related to long-range planning. The effectiveness of research and development expenditure may be assessed only in relation to the attainment of goals specified in the long-range plan. These goals should be selected by top management as crucial areas to which major research effort should be directed. In this connection, research expenditure should be concentrated on specific projects which form part of the research effort in a particular area. The control of such expenditure may be exercised by reference to the progress made towards the completion of such projects. As we shall explain in chapter 13, P.E.R.T. offers a useful means for controlling these projects.

The control of marketing costs

Marketing costs have become significant elements in total costs, due to the rising burden of such costs as advertising and market development. It follows that attention should be directed towards developing the most efficient cost control methods in this area, so as to provide marketing managers with information which will enable them to make the best decisions from the firm's point of view.

Marketing costs cover a wide range of activities, including obtaining sales orders, warehousing and distribution, handling returns and after-sales service. They may be analysed on three different bases—the nature of the cost, the function performed and the appropriate sector of the firm's business, as follows:

(a) *Classification as to costs*
   Salesmens' salaries and commission
   Travelling
   Advertising

(b) *Classification as to function*
   Selling
   Advertising
   Transportation
   Credit collection
   Warehousing
   Invoicing

(c) *Classification as to business sector*
   Territory
   Product
   Marketing channels
   Operating divisions
   Customers

The analysis of marketing costs is helpful in providing information which is useful for a number of purposes, such as:

Determining the profitability of sales territories
Evaluating the profitability of product lines
Setting selling prices
Selecting from among alternative channels of distribution
Evaluating salesmens' performance
Determining the importance of individual customers
Analysing order size profitability.

It is evident from the description of the range of decisions for which information is required that the analysis of marketing costs is concerned essentially with profitability, which is a function both of revenue control and cost control.

Determining the profitability of sales territories

Most marketing activities are organized on a territorial basis. As a first stage in the analysis of territorial profitability, it is necessary to distinguish direct and indirect marketing costs. Direct costs are those incurred in respect of a territory: indirect costs are those incurred for all the various sales territories. Direct costs will be controllable by territorial sales managers: indirect costs are beyond their control. Nevertheless, we have mentioned already that despite difficulties in effecting accurate apportionments of indirect costs, such apportionments serve the useful purpose of providing regional managers with information of the back-up services which support their own activities and should be made, provided that they are distinguished from controllable items on reports.

Table 1 should how the analysis of the profitability of sales territories may be made. Its purpose is to locate territories where weaknesses and problems exist. Once they have been located, prompt and intelligent managerial action is required, which may include such decisions as an increase in the number of salesmen operating in the area, or an improvement of the services provided. The contribution margin analysis which is applied in this context has already been discussed in chapter 9, and it will be recalled that the existence of a contribution margin warrants the continuance of operations in the short-run even though conventional calculations indicate a loss.

Determining the profitability of products

The analysis of the profitability of different products is useful to management in a number of ways. Not only does it indicate the

Table 1. *Income analysis by territories*

Sales	Terri- tory 1 £500,000	Terri- tory 2 £300,000	Terri- tory 3 £100,000	Total £900,000
Direct costs by territories:				
Cost of goods sold	250,000	160,000	40,000	450,000
Transport & outside ware- housing	30,000	20,000	10,000	60,000
Regional office expenses	50,000	30,000	20,000	100,000
Salesmens' expenses	25,000	15,000	6000	46,000
Other regional expenses	15,000	10,000	5000	30,000
Total direct cost by territories	370,000	235,000	81,000	686,000
Contribution to headquarter's overheads and profit	130,000	65,000	19,000	214,000
Indirect costs:				
Central administration	50,000	22,000	8000	80,000
Central warehousing	20,000	8000	2000	30,000
Advertising	30,000	15,000	5000	50,000
Total indirect costs	100,000	45,000	15,000	160,000
Net profit	30,000	20,000	4000	54,000
Percentage of net profit	56%	37%	7%	100%
Percentage of sales	56%	33%	11%	100%
Contribution/sales %	26%	22%	19%	23%

relative profitability of different products, but also areas of strength and weakness which should be noted in the development of corporate strategy. The application of techniques such as contribution margin analysis may assist in deciding whether or not to drop a product line. Pricing decisions may also be based on profitability analysis.

As we explained in chapter 2 of this Part, the selection of appropriate bases for determining profitability is problematical, as it is for other management purposes which require the apportionment of indirect costs.

Table 2 below shows how the analysis may be conducted. It indicates that Product C is the least profitable product in the product range, for although it makes a contribution of £78,000 to fixed expenses and profit, a net loss of £28,000 is associated with its manufacture. Hence, the analysis implies that action should be taken to improve its profitability in the future.

Controlling marketing costs

Marketing costs may be classified into order-getting and order-filling costs. The former are associated with such activities as advertising, sales promotion and other selling functions: the latter are incurred after the order has been obtained, and cover such costs as packing, delivering, invoicing and warehousing finished products.

Table 2. *Income analysis by products*

	Products			
Sales	*A*	*B*	*C*	*Total*
Sales	£350,000	£300,000	£250,000	£900,000
Variable cost of goods sold	90,000	85,000	125,000	300,000
Gross contribution	260,000	215,000	125,000	600,000
Variable marketing costs:				
Transport and warehousing	15,000	12,000	12,000	40,000
Office expenses	30,000	30,000	20,000	80,000
Salesmen's salaries	20,000	15,000	10,000	45,000
Other expenses	6000	5000	4000	15,000
Total variable marketing costs	71,000	62,000	47,000	180,000
Contribution to fixed expenses and profit	189,000	153,000	78,000	420,000
Fixed expenses:				
Manufacturing	55,000	50,000	45,000	150,000
Administration	30,000	25,000	25,000	80,000
Marketing	50,000	50,000	36,000	136,000
Total fixed costs	135,00	125,000	106,000	366,000
Net profit (loss)	£54,000	£28,000	£(28,000)	£54,000
Contribution/Sales %	51%	51%	31%	47%

(a) *Order-getting costs*

The effectiveness of such costs may only be satisfactorily assessed by relating them to sales revenue. Many factors which affect sales, however, are outside the control of the Sales Department, and for this reason, it is difficult to establish standards of performance which are relevant to the problem of maintaining and increasing the effectiveness of order-getting activities. Budgetary control may be used to determine the limits of expenditure but it is not possible to use such budgetary control methods as flexible budgeting in respect of some items, particularly advertising. Flexible budgeting is designed to control expenditure through changing levels of activity: advertising is incurred in order to increase the level of activity. It would be nonsense, therefore, to attempt to apply flexible budgeting to the control of advertising expenditure.

The search for suitable methods of controlling order-getting costs continues. Objective measures may be too limited in their scope to be useful. Firms are using such objective measures of selling cost per order, selling costs per call, or calls per day to control selling costs. These measures should be used with care, for they do not necessarily reflect difficulties in selling to different markets at different times.

Advertising costs, in particular, involve such a large financial commitment that it is necessary that the effectiveness of such costs should be assessed. Market research departments are better equipped than accountants to assess the effectiveness of advertising, since its effects go beyond the expansion of immediate sales.

(b) Order-filling costs

It is comparatively easier to control order-filling costs than order-getting costs, since order-filling costs are associated with internal procedures. These procedures are of a standard form and of a repetitive nature making them susceptible to standard control methods: the costs of invoicing, packaging and despatching can be reference to such objective standards as number of invoices dealt with, number and size of packages etc. Moreover, unlike order-getting costs, flexible budgeting may be applied to the control of order-filling costs.

Example

Bloxwich Limited has a sales budget which envisages the sales of 100,000 units of its product in the current year. Budgeted delivery costs are based on standard delivery costs of £1 per unit. If only 80,000 units were sold and delivered by the end of the year at a cost of £90,000, it would be evident that the unfavourable delivery costs variance of £10,000 would require investigation.

Summary

There are two main costs classification—manufacturing and non-manufacturing costs. Non-manufacturing costs may be sub-divided into three categories—administrative, research and development, and marketing costs. These costs are frequently referred to as 'managed' or 'discretionary costs' since they are incurred at the discretion of management.

The difficulty of controlling managed costs is created by the absence of a method for determining appropriate cost levels since it is not possible to relate accurately and in financial terms the benefits associated with such costs. Moreover, it is not possible to determine whether a change in managed costs represents an improvement in performance. For example, providing product specifications are maintained, a reduction in manufacturing costs represents an improvement in performance. No such inference may be drawn from a reduction in managed costs.

In view of the rising proportion of managed costs as a percentage of total costs, the analysis and control of such costs is important and means should be found of overcoming the problems caused by the inability to establish rigorous standards.

Further Readings

1. Braithwaite, M. E., Management Control of Research Expenditure, *Accountancy*, April, 1967.

2. Jones, R. L. & Trentin, H. J., *Budgeting General and Administrative Expenses: A Planning and Control System*, Management Bulletin 74, New York, American Management Association, 1966.

3. Kelty T. C., The Marketing–Accounting Partnership in Business, *Journal of Marketing*, July, 1966.

4. King, W. R., Performance Evaluation in Marketing Systems, *Management Science*, July, 1964.

5. Martin V. P., Marketing looks at the Accountant, *The Australian Accountant*, April, 1970.

13
Inventory and Project Control

The reader will recall that we discussed in Part 1 the increasing use of quantitative methods in decision-making. Two areas of application of direct importance to the accountant are inventory and project control.

The Inventory Model is an example of a decision model which can be programmed to become an integral part of the information system. Decisions of a routine and repetitive nature, for example, those relating to the control of raw material inventories and the routine purchase of replenishment inventories may be entirely automated, that is, programmed on a computer. An inventory control model may be built which will take into account such factors as the expected level of production and the time needed to obtain new deliveries, so that the re-ordering of inventories may be scheduled by reference to a designated critical inventory level. From this inventory control model, a definite procedure may be established which will virtually automate inventory purchase decisions.

Sometimes, budgetary planning and control procedures have a project orientation, that is, they are applied to a series of events culminating in a completed project. The cost of each activity leading to each event, and the time for completing each event is the focus of budgeting. Each event is laid out in a sequence and tied together by a network of activities. They form the basis of the Programme Evaluation and Review Technique (P.E.R.T.) which is a popular technique for planning and controlling the work on projects.

The purpose of this chapter, therefore, is to examine the techniques of inventory control and P.E.R.T. in the context of the problem of control.

Inventory control

Inventory control is concerned with establishing and maintaining optimum inventory levels. Inventories represent an investment of financial resources, and the opportunity cost may be measured by reference to the next best use of the funds so invested. Thus, if inventory levels were reduced to a minimum level, the funds released could be applied in income-generating operations or in reducing a bank overdraft. Firms hold inventories, however, because of the benefits attached to the availability of supplies. In the case of raw material inventories, for example, minimum inventory levels are required to prevent dislocation in the production process and a consequential loss of income. In the case of inventories of finished goods, minimum levels are required to meet the needs of customers and retaining their goodwill. It is the value of these benefits which induces organizations to ensure that minimum inventory levels are maintained. In a theoretical sense, we may say that the minimum inventory level should be determined at that point where the perceived benefits attached to holding inventories is equal to the opportunity cost of the financial resources thereby committed. Clearly, the cost-benefit analysis involved presents considerable problems since it is very difficult to measure the benefits associated with inventory holdings in financial terms. Nevertheless, it is possible to arrive at a partial solution of the problem of establishing an optimal inventory policy, as will be seen in the following examination of the control of manufacturing inventories.

The control of manufacturing inventories

Manufacturing organizations hold three kinds of inventories—raw materials, work-in-progress and finished goods. Raw material inventories are required, as we mentioned above, to avoid interruptions in the production process. They may also be held for speculative reasons, especially at times of price instability. Inventories of work-in-progress arise because of different production flows between operations. If such inventories did not exist, each production process would be entirely dependent on the time schedule of the preceding process. Hence, they provide that degree of flexibility in the production process which ensures the smooth flow of operations. Inventories of finished goods are held to meet the requirements of customers, and to ensure, particularly, that no shortages of supply occur which might lead to the loss of customer goodwill. Moreover, inventories of finished goods act as buffers between the production and the selling processes, so that there is a degree of flexibility between them.

There is a close correlation between the inventory levels of the three types of manufacturing inventories, because of the manner in which they are linked by the rate of inflow of external supplies of raw materials, the rate of demand for the firm's products and functioning of the internal production processes. The costs associated with these inventory holdings should be brought into the calculus of the minima of inventory holdings when formulating an inventory policy which is financially efficient.

Determining the Economic Order Quantity (E.O.Q.)

One of the main problems associated with inventory control is the determination of the 'economic order quantity'. Inventory management is concerned with relating the costs of holding inventories with the costs of replacements. Costs of holding inventories include warehousing costs, handling and insurance costs. Costs of ordering tend to be relatively fixed, and may be ascertained by reference to the buyer's time and expenses and the costs associated with the operations of the Purchasing Department.

Assuming that there is a constant demand for goods held as inventories and that inventory replacement orders are obtainable immediately, it is possible to plot the movement of inventories as in Fig. 3.32. OQ indicates the size of each inventory purchase order and

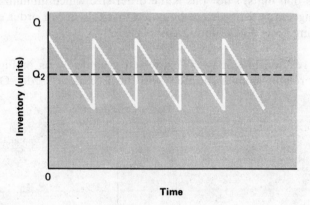

Fig. 3.32

OQ_2 is the average level of inventory held in the given period.

It is possible to relate the costs of holding and the costs of ordering inventory by expressing these costs in average unit cost terms and to examine the movement of these average costs over a given period of time.

Example

Engineering Suppliers Ltd operates a business concerned with the supply of specialist parts to the engineering industry. The annual sales of parts to the industry amount to 5400 units, and the costs associated with holding and ordering the parts for the various possible number of units ordered are given below:

No. of order per year	Order size (units)	Average Inventory (Order size ÷ 2)	Annual order Costs (£20 per order)	Annual Holding Costs (£0.6 per unit)	Annual Total Costs
			£	£	£
6	900	450	120	270	390
7	780	390	140	234	374
8	675	338	160	203	363
9	600	300	180	180	360
10	540	270	200	162	362
11	491	246	220	148	368
12	450	225	240	135	375

From this table, we may calculate the Economic Order Quantity to be 600 units, since this is the order size which minimizes total average costs. It is also to be noted that this size of order equates holding costs and ordering costs.

These relationships may be expressed graphically as in Fig. 3.33. The cost relationships associated with the Economic Order Quantity

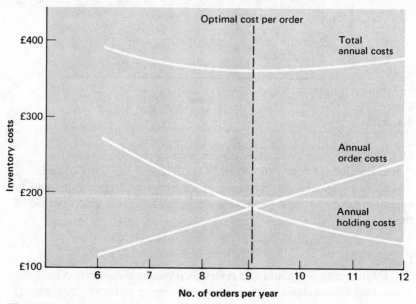

Fig. 3.33

are as follows:

Let T = Total cost

       D = Annual Demand in units

       C = Cost of placing an order

        i = Average unit cost of holding stock during the year

The annual costs of *ordering* inventories associated with the Economic Order Quantity may be stated as:

$$\frac{CD}{\text{E.O.Q.}}$$

Substituting the figures given in the example, we have

$$\frac{£20 \times 5400}{600}$$

$$= £180$$

The annual costs of *holding* inventories associated with the Economic Order Quantity may be stated as:

$$\frac{i \times \text{E.O.Q.}}{2}$$

Substituting the figures given in the example, we have

$$\frac{£0.6 \times 600}{2}$$

$$= £180$$

The total costs associated with the Economic Order Quantity may be expressed as follows:

$$T = \frac{CD}{\text{E.O.Q.}} + \frac{(i \times \text{E.O.Q.})}{2} = £360$$

The Economic Order Quantity itself may be derived from the following formula

$$\text{E.O.Q.} = \sqrt{\frac{2DC}{i}}$$

Substituting the figures given in the example, we have

$$\text{E.O.Q.} = \sqrt{\frac{2 \times 5400 \times £20}{£0.6}}$$

$$= 600$$

The determination of inventory safety level

In our discussion so far, we have assumed that the demand for goods held in inventory was constant through time, and that no delays occur in the fulfilment of replacement orders. In practice, demand is not constant and the lead time between the placing of an order and its fulfilment is subject to fluctuations. Therefore, unless provision is made for these factors in the shape of buffer or safety inventories, delays may occur in meeting customers' orders or disruptions may occur in the production process.

In deciding upon the dimensions of safety inventories, the additional costs associated with holding such costs must be weighed against the benefits to be derived from the maintenance of regularity in the production process or in meeting customers' orders. We do not propose to go into the details of the methods employed to establish safety levels, but we would mention that this problem may be solved by applying a statistical analysis to the lead time and the rate of inventory usage so that the probabilities attached to them may be ascertained. These probabilities open the way for the application of risk analysis to the question of inventory levels.

The determination of the re-order point

In addition to knowing the economic order quantity to order on each occasion, the analysis of inventory levels requires the determination of the point in time when inventory orders should be placed. The re-order point is determined by multiplying usage (number of units per day) by the lead time (in days). The lead time is the time required from the despatch of an order to the receipt of the goods.

Example

The Better Products Company makes washing machines. The average daily output is 100 units. The company buys the electrical motors which are installed in the washing machines. The average lead time in respect of normal purchases is 10 days. The re-order point for the electrical motors is 1000 units as follows:

$$\text{Re-order point} = \text{Usage} \times \text{lead time}$$
$$= 100 \times 10$$
$$= \underline{1000 \text{ units}}$$

Hence, a new order for electrical motors should be placed whenever the inventory level falls to 1000 units. However, for the reasons given in the preceding section, the company dare not risk such a tight schedule, and requires a margin of safety. Assuming that the margin of safety has been estimated at 200 units, the re-order point is determined according to the following formula:

Re-order point = Average daily usage × lead time in days
+ margin of safety

$$= 100 \times 10 + 200$$

1200 units

Programme evaluation and review technique (P.E.R.T.)

The application of such techniques as network analysis and critical path analysis to the study of management planning has led to the demand for information which is useful and relevant to such problems as measuring the progress being made towards the realization of plans, forecasting future changes likely to affect planning, and predicting future costs.

P.E.R.T. has been designed as a technique for planning and controlling a variety of programmes such as construction, research and development projects, and budgeting and auditing procedures. P.E.R.T. employs a network analysis of the events and activities which are required to be accomplished in order that the programme goals may be realized. The network is a pictorial model of the programme or project in which activities are designated as project tasks and are represented by arrows. The junction points to which these activities converge are designated as events and are represented by circles. Hence, events may represent the ending or the beginning of activities. Activities may be related in two different ways: they may be sequential, when one activity must be completed before another may be commenced, or they may be parallel, when two or more activities may be conducted simultaneously.

Example

The network analysis of a construction project reveals the relationships in Fig. 3.34 between activities and events (see p. 492). The expected time periods associated with these various activities are as follows:

A–B	3 days	C–D	5 days
A–C	5 days	D–F	7 days
B–D	5 days	E–F	3 days
D–E	3 days		

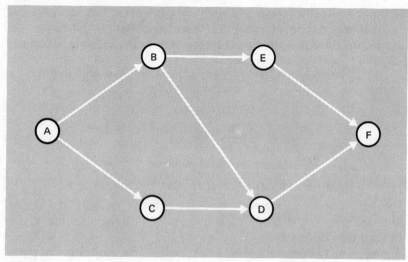

Fig. 3.34

Hence, the time completion for the sequences of activities and events depicted in the network analysis are as follows:

Path 1	A–B–E–F	$3+3+3=$ 9 days
Path 2	A–B–D–F	$3+5+7=15$ days
Path 3	A–C–D–F	$5+5+7=17$ days

These time schedules are the expected completion times, which we may denote as te. We may insert them into the network analysis as in Fig. 3.35.

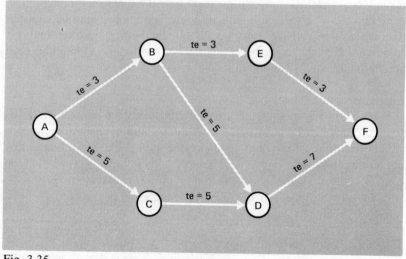

Fig. 3.35

The critical path denotes that sequence of activities and events which has the longest completion time. It is the critical path which determines the completion time for the entire project. It follows that if the time taken on the project is to be reduced, such reduction may only be achieved by a time reduction in the critical path. In our example, the critical path is Path 3, which takes 17 days to complete. Since the other paths will be shorter, by definition, there will be some slack between the time required to complete them and the time required for the critical path. The 'slack' associated with Paths 1, 2 and 3 is 8, 2 and 0 days respectively.

The analysis of P.E.R.T./Cost is an expansion of P.E.R.T. in that it brings into network analysis the budgeted costs of activities. From an accounting point of view, it is clearly important that as a project is progressing towards completion, there should be a careful control of both expected time and expected costs. For this reason, information feedback in the form of actual time and actual costs for each completed activity will provide a means of exercising control over the progress of projects by the analysis of both time and cost variances.

Example

The costs associated with the activities in the previous example are budgeted as follows:

A–B	£100	C–D	£180
A–C	140	D–F	300
B–D	250	E–F	150
B–E	130		

Let us assume that activities A–B, and A–C have been completed and that the results are as follows:

	Actual Time (ta)	Actual Costs (ca)
A–B	4 days	£140
A–C	5 days	£130

We may represent these budgeted time and costs and actual time and costs in the network chart as in Fig. 3.36.

The unfavourable time variance in activity A–B is not significant because it has occurred in a path where time slack exists. It has, however, reduced the time slack for Path 2 to one day, so that any

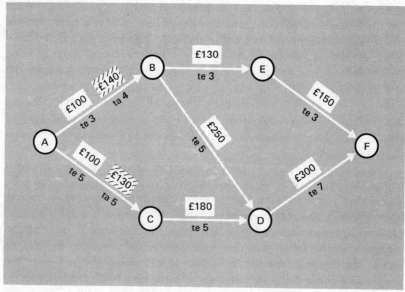

Fig. 3.36

further time losses in the activities connected with that Path may become significant. The unfavourable cost variances in both activities A–B and A–C will require investigation.

So far we have assumed that the expected time and expected costs associated with network activities are normal. It is frequently necessary to calculate the 'crash time', which is the minimum time required to complete an activity. Similarly, the 'crash cost' is the minimum cost of completing an activity. Crash time and crash costs associated with the project in the previous example are given below:

| Activity | Normal | | Crash | | Cost slope |
	Time (days)	Cost	Time (days)	Cost	
A–B	3	£100	2	£200	£100
A–C	5	140	3	440	150
B–D	5	250	3	410	80
B–E	3	130	3	130	—
C–D	5	180	2	300	40
D–F	7	300	4	900	200
E–F	3	150	3	150	—

The importance of the cost slope is that it indicates the relationship between the reduction in normal time which may be achieved and the increase in costs necessary to obtain that reduction in time. For activity

A–C, for example, a reduction of 2 days is obtainable at an increased cost of £300: hence, the cost slope is £300/2 or £150 per day.

The analysis of the cost slope of the different activities in the network is useful for indicating where reductions in time may be achieved at the least cost. From the table above, it is evident that activity C–D is ranked first in this respect.

Example

Let us assume that time is the most important constraint in the project which we have been discussing. A reduction in the overall time needed to complete the project is requested. The analysis of expected time indicates the possibility of reducing the critical path time by two days. Clearly, the most efficient way of securing this time saving is by reducing the time taken by that activity which has the lowest cost slope in the critical path. Activity C–D can be reduced by two days at an increased cost of £80. Should the project manager be asked to reduce time still further, Path 2 will become a critical path as well as Path 3, for both would require 15 days for completion. Hence, time reductions in both Paths would have to be sought.

From the foregoing discussion, it is clear that PERT/Cost is a management technique which extends the budgeting process and presents a challenge to the accountant to provide an extended information service for the activities of planning and control.

Summary

The purpose of this chapter has been to consider the role of two techniques of control of particular interest to accountants—inventory control and P.E.R.T.

As applied to the control of manufacturing inventories, the former shows how it is possible to arrive at a partial solution of the problem of establishing an optimal inventory policy by considering the Economic Order Quantity, the inventory safety level and the determination of the re-order point. P.E.R.T. is concerned with such problems as measuring the progress being made towards the realization of plans, forecasting future changes likely to affect planning and predicting future costs. Hence, it is relevant to understanding how the development of quantitative decision models have increased the efficiency of the management planning and control processes.

Further readings

1. Buchan, Joseph & Koenigsberg, Ernest, *Scientific Investment Management,* Prentice Hall, Englewood Cliffs, N.J., 1963.

2. Buffa, E., *Production Inventory Systems: Planning and Control*, Richard Irwin, Homewood, Illinois 1968.

3. Decoster, P. T., Pert/Cost—The Challenge, *Management Services*, May–June, 1969.

4. Hanssman, Fred, *Operations Research in Production and Inventory Control*, John Wiley, New York, 1962.

5. Levin, R. I. & Kirkpatrick C. A., *Planning and Control with PERT/CPM*, McGraw-Hill, New York, 1966.

6. Miller, D. & Starr, M., *Executive Decisions and Operations Research*, Prentice Hall, Englewood Cliffs, N.J., 1969.

7. Paige, H. W., How Pert/Cost Helps the Managers, *Harvard Business Review*, November–December, 1963.

8. Starr, M. & Miller, D., *Inventory Control: Theory and Practice*, Prentice Hall, Englewood Cliffs, N.J., 1962.

9. Wagner Harvey, M., *Principles of Operations Research*, Prentice Hall, Englewood Cliffs, N.J., 1972.

14

Behavioural Aspects of Performance Evaluation

In recent years, the behavioural aspects of decision-making has assumed an increasing importance in management literature. Traditionally, accountants have followed economists in assuming the main organizational problem to be the maximization of profit and allocation of resources necessary to this end. Consequently, accountants have tended to regard organizations from a technical viewpoint, treating men as adjuncts to or as substitutes for machines, to be hired and employed for the purpose of maximizing productivity and profits. The growing realization that the importance of accounting is related to decision-making has highlighted the need to understand human behaviour in organizations. This development was well summarized by a committee of the American Accounting Association which reported:

> "To state the matter concisely, the principal purpose of accounting reports is to influence action, that is, behavior. Additionally, it can be hypothesised that the very process of accumulating information, as well as the behavior of those who do the accumulating, will affect the behavior of others. In short, by its very nature, accounting is a behavioral process." (Accounting Review Supplement, 1971)

Therefore, accountants should have an understanding of human behaviour and a knowledge of the work of behavioural scientists in this connection. This chapter is concerned, therefore, with the behavioural aspects of performance evaluation.

The objectives of performance evaluation

The objectives of performance evaluation may be stated as follows:

(a) to assess how effectively the responsibilities assigned to managers have been carried out;
(b) to identify areas where corrective actions should be taken;
(c) to ensure that managers are motivated towards organizational goals;

  (d) to enable comparisons to be made between the performance of different sectors of an organization, to discover areas where improvements may be made.

In our analysis of the process of control, we have so far discussed two important prerequisites for performance evaluation. In chapter 10, we discussed the problem of identifying areas of responsibility over which individual managers exercise control (responsibility accounting), and in chapter 11, we discussed the setting of standards of performance to be used as yardsticks for the evaluation of performance. In this chapter, we address ourselves to some of the behavioural problems of budgets as measures for evaluating performance.

Leadership styles and the problem of control

There is a tendency for firms to expect desired results merely from the use of appropriate techniques, thereby failing to recognize that success in organizational control depends upon the actions of responsible individuals and their appreciation of the importance of sound interpersonal relationships. The manner in which the budgeting process is viewed depends on the leadership style adopted by management. McGregor has characterized the two extremes of management styles as 'Theory X' and 'Theory Y' (McGregor, 1960). According to McGregor, these extreme views are conditioned by the manager's view of man.

Theory X

The Theory X view of man, as summarized below, is supportive of an authoritarian leadership style:

  (1) Management is responsible for organizing the elements of productive enterprise—money, materials, equipment and people—in activities directed to economic ends.

  (2) As regards people, management is concerned with directing their efforts, motivating and controlling their actions, and modifying their behaviour to fit the needs of the organization.

  (3) Without this active intervention by management, people would be passive—and even resistant—to organizational needs. Therefore, they must be persuaded, rewarded, punished, controlled. In short, their activities must be directed, and therein lies the function of management. This view is often summed up by the assertion that management consists of getting things done through other people.

Theory Y

By contrast, Theory Y is supportive of a more democratic and participative leadership style:

(1) Management is responsible for organizing the elements of productive enterprise—money, materials, equipment and people—in activities directed to economic ends.

(2) People are not by nature passive or resistant to organizational needs. They appear to have become so as a result of negative experiences of organizational needs.

(3) The motivation, the potential for development, the capacity for assuming responsibility, the readiness to direct behaviour towards organizational goals are all present in people. Management does not put these qualities in people. It is the responsibility of management to make it possible for people to recognize and develop these human characteristics.

(4) The essential task of management is to arrange organizational conditions and methods of operation so that people can achieve their own goals best by directing their efforts towards organizational objectives.

There is evidence that the Theory X leadership style is widely prevalent and is clearly operational. Those who prefer the assumptions of Theory Y claim that the Theory X leadership style has a human cost in the frustration and the lack of personal development which results from its application to people. The trend in behavioural research suggests that benefits may be derived from leadership and organizations based on the assumptions of Theory Y. These assumptions recognize, in particular, that the basic motivating forces affecting people at work include biological, egoistic and social factors.

As a person, the employee at whatever organizational level, has certain needs which condition his own objectives. He is seeking *compensation* for his efforts to enable him to provide some desired standard of life for himself and his family. He needs outlets for his physical and intellectual energies which provide both *stimulation* and *satisfaction*. He seeks *self-realization* in a sense of his own worth and usefulness. He is pursuing further *growth* and greater *personal effectiveness*. He seeks the *recognition* of his fellows, whether his organizational equals, superiors or subordinates. He appreciates his *identification* with a worthwhile and successful undertaking.

In order to maximize the employee's contribution to organizational activities, it follows that these personal needs and goals should be capable of realization in the task in which he is employed. An awareness of the nature of personal needs, therefore, is an important aspect of control.

The effects of budgets on people

Research suggests that there is a great deal of mistrust of the entire budgetary process at the supervisory level (Argyris, 1953). There is a tendency for traditional budgets to provide the following responses.

Reactions to pressure

The evaluation of a manager's performance in terms of his departmental budget is one of the few elements in performance appraisal which is based on concrete standards. There is little room for manipulation or escape if results are not going to turn out as expected in the budget. If budget pressure becomes too great, it may lead to mistrust, hostility and eventually to poorer performance levels as reaction sets in against budgetary control.

The problem of distinguishing between controllable and non-controllable costs is an important cause of tension among managers. The task of the manager of a department or expense centre, for example, is to attain his goals with the minimum cost. One of the initial difficulties which arises in evaluating his performance applies to all levels of management, namely, the treatment of factors beyond his control. This problem is aggravated when the responsibility for an activity is shared by two or more individuals or functions. Labour inefficiency, for example, may be due to excessive machine break-downs (maintenance function), inferior materials (purchasing function), defective materials (inspection function), or poor calibre personnel (personnel function). Establishing standards of performance in itself is not an easy task. It demands the clear definition of goals and responsibilities, the delegation of authority, the use of satisfactory surrogates for the activities concerned, effective communication of information and an understanding of the psychology of human motivation.

Over-emphasis on the short-run

One of the dangers facing organizations which evaluate the effectiveness of managers in profit terms is that too much emphasis is given to achieving short-term profitability, and measures taken to improve short-term profitability may be detrimental to the organization's long-term prospects. Short-term increases in profits gained at the expense of reductions in research and development and the failure to maintain adequate standards of maintenance are two examples of short-term cost savings which are detrimental to the firm in the long-term.

Poor quality decision-making by top management

Excessive reliance on the profit performance of divisions may also affect the quality of decisions made by top management. If the managerial competence of divisional managers is assessed solely on the basis of the profit performance of their respective divisions, serious errors of judgement may result. Moreover, if profit results are used as part of an early warning system, action may be taken by top management which may not be warranted. Therefore, although profit budgets are indispensible for planning purposes, great care should be taken in utilizing them for control purposes. The attainment of profit targets is dependent on many factors, some of which are entirely outside the control of a divisional manager. The uncertainty attached to profit forecasts, in particular, limits the usefulness of profit targets for the evaluation of the performance of a divisional manager. The process of formulating the divisional profit forecast also introduces bias in the evaluation of performance. Divisional profit targets are usually based on the divisional manager's forecast of future events. Therefore, it is his ability to forecast the future successfully rather than his ability to manage successfully, which form the basis on which his performance is evaluated. This consideration also affects the validity of comparisons between the performance of different divisions. For example, it is easier to determine an attainable profit goal for a division whose major constraint is productive capacity, where sales are limited only by output, than for a division which sells in a highly competitive market.

Another problem arising from the use of profit budgets in evaluating divisional performance stems from the fact that an annual budget covers too short a period in which to obtain a realistic picture of managerial performance. The effects of decisions in some instances may take several years before being reflected in profit performance. Thus, the decision to introduce a new product is one of several decisions whose impact on divisional profits take some years before they are fully realized. The more complex and innovative the division the longer will be the time period necessary for the evaluation of performance. In the light of these considerations, the use of an annual profit result may give a completely inaccurate view of divisional performance.

Poor communication

Where a Theory X style of management exists, negative attitudes may be generated against organizational goals which may lead to faked budget results and the unwillingness to transmit information. Managers will feel that their own survival justifies these tactics.

The prevalence of negative behaviour in an organization which practices management by domination may be aggravated by the response of top management, when it is realized that information which is needed for decision-making is not transmitted. Their immediate reaction may be to impose even tighter controls, which will reinforce the negative attitudes held by subordinate managers leading to the transmission of even less accurate and useful information. The progressive tightening of the managerial reins may well result, therefore, in a progressive deterioration of the information flow.

The communication of information is of central importance to the processes of planning and control, as it provides the link between various levels of management and the various decision points. Any reluctance on the part of subordinate managers to communicate information is a serious impediment to the efficiency with which planning and control decisions are made. It is not a sufficient condition for success that an organization should have accounting control systems and that it should have stipulated standards of performance. These control methods will not operate successfully and standards of performance will not be attained if the style of management adopted fails to secure a high degree of motivation and goal congruence within the organization.

Departmental self-centredness

The budget process which involves defining areas of responsibility, measuring and comparing performance accordingly, concentrates the manager's entire attention on his own department. The tendency to departmental self-centredness which is thus encouraged obscures the important relationships between departments, so that inter-departmental dependencies may be ignored or overlooked in the quest for optimizing departmental results. Consequently, economies which would result from greater inter-departmental collaboration may be lost to the organization.

The stifling of initiative

The planning and control aspects of budgeting may be over-emphasized within an organization with the result that opportunities for the exercise of personal initiative may be excluded. Budgets which appear to be strait-jackets discourage managers from deviating from budget stipulations even when circumstances indicate that individual action should be taken. It has been noted, for example, that employees who were subject to audit procedures conformed closely to company policy even when more efficient alternatives were available (Churchill, Cooper & Sainsbury, 1964).

The need for several measures of performance

Whilst the use of standard costs and variable budgets play an important role in the control of activities and in the evaluation of performance, undue attention to cost control tends to diminish the importance of other goals. For example, a Factory Manager is expected to maintain a high level of productive efficiency, to maintain the quality of the product, to meet production schedules on time, to minimize expenses and to maintain satisfactory relations with employees.

The evaluation of performance, therefore, requires both quantitative and qualitative measures of performance. It is evident that some organizational and departmental goals may conflict, such as for example the need to minimize costs and to maintain product quality. Emphasis on specific goals, therefore, will mean that other goals may not be attained. The objectives of performance evaluation, which we have stipulated, require a balanced view of performance covering the various areas of managerial responsibility. In this connection, as we shall see in Part 5, there has developed in recent years an increased recognition of the potential of human resource accounting. If management uses only conventional measurements of revenues, expenses, profit, cost variances and output, it is possible that short-run economic gains may be achieved at the expense of long-run goals. The failure to appreciate the impact of control techniques on individuals responsible for organizational activities may adversely affect employee morale, loyalty, trust and motivation.

The importance of participation

The active participation by managers in the planning process not only enhances their personal sense of involvement in the organization, but improves the efficiency of the planning process. Moreover, such participation establishes a common understanding of purpose, and promotes the acceptance of organizational objectives and goals at all levels. Likewise, the control process is aided by the active participation of managers in the investigation of variances, the evaluation and selection of appropriate solutions, and the development of related policies.

The degree of effort expended by members of an organization in attempting to achieve designated goals is particularly dependent upon their personal aspiration level. The aspiration level may be defined as that level of future performance in a familiar task, which an individual explicitly undertakes knowing his past performance level (Stedry, 1960). For example, a manager's aspiration level as regards costs is the spending level which he accepts as realistic and with which he will strive to comply. Hence, we may identify three potential levels of cost performance (Welsch, 1971):

(a) the budgeted level
(b) the aspiration level
(c) the actual level.

Since the aspiration level is the real inner goal acceptable to the manager, the purpose of participation is to bring the aspiration level in harmony with the budgeted level (or vice-versa). Clearly, a budgeted level which is significantly at variance with the aspiration level will have a negative effect on managerial behaviour.

It follows that managers should be motivated and not pressurized into achieving their budgetary goals. This may be achieved by recognizing the importance of aspiration levels in the planning stage and the timely communication of results as a basis for improving performance, where necessary. The purpose of participation in the control process, therefore, is to motivate managers and to generate in each participant the desire to accomplish or even improve his level of performance.

Management by objectives

From the foregoing discussion of the problem of controlling the activities of an organization and evaluating managerial performance, it follows that several conditions must be satisfied if the accounting function is to play a useful role.

(a) Divisional and departmental goals must be clearly identified and defined, and appropriate measurements selected by which to express them and evaluate managerial performance. Where objectives are too vague or too ambiguous to be susceptible to clear definition in conventional terms, surrogates should be sought which will enable them to be defined and measured.

(b) There should be participation by all levels of management in the control process, thereby ensuring good communication between supervisor and subordinate.

(c) A style of management is required which pays particular attention to the human element in organizations, and in so doing, provides an environment conducive to the employment of all resources.

The aim of management by objectives is to provide a framework for administering a control system which embraces the abovementioned three conditions. By translating organizational objectives and goals in such a way that they become the personal objectives and goals of all management personnel, whether they be divisional or departmental managers, management by objectives seeks to create a high degree of goal congruence within an organization. The unity of personal and organizational objectives encourages managers to take actions which are in the best interest of the organization.

Some organizational goals are too remote from individual managers, and therefore, have little significance for them, for example, goals relating to the return on capital employed or overall growth targets envisaged in the long-range plan. Management by objectives seeks to establish personal targets at all levels as a means of overcoming this problem. By relating personal goals to departmental and divisional goals and thence to organizational goals, an integration is achieved between them which may be depicted as follows:

Personal Goals ⟶ Divisional Goals ⟶ Organizational Goals

In chapter 1 of this Part, we examined the meaning of control in an administrative context. Management by objectives gives rather a different slant to the meaning of control which is discussed by Drucker in the following terms:

"Control' is an ambiguous word. It means the ability to direct oneself and one's work. It can also mean domination of one person by another. (Management) objectives are the basis of 'control' in the first sense; but they must never become the basis of 'control' in the second, for this would defeat their purpose. Indeed, one of the major contributions of management by objectives is that it enables us to substitute management by self-control for management by objectives' (Drucker, 1954).

It would seem that most of the problems which researchers have discovered in relation to the budgeting process have arisen where a Theory X view of man has been reflected in management by domination as a method of control. Man has always rebelled against coercion and domination. By contrast, his most significant achievements have been attained when he has acted as a free agent, exercising self-control in his ability to direct himself and his work.

Management by objectives involves the following processes:

(1) The review of long-term and short-term organizational objectives and goals.

(2) The revision, if necessary, of the organizational structure. An organizational chart is required to illustrate the titles, duties and the relationships between managers.

(3) Standards of performance necessary to fulfill key tasks are set by the job-holder himself in agreement with his immediate

supervisor. Unless the job-holder participates in setting performance standards, he will not feel committed to them. The standards of performance which result from systems of management by objectives are not 'ideal', nor are they minimum acceptable levels of performance. They indicate what are agreed to be 'satisfactory' levels of performance. As far as possible, they should be expressed in quantitative terms.

Management controls are operated so that supervisors do not act as watchdogs but rather as sources of help and guidance to their subordinates. A divisional profit goal in this sense is not only a target for the divisional manager, for it may also act as a means whereby top management may help to solve divisional problems should they become apparent through the failure to reach a stipulated figure.

(4) Results are measured against goals. An important aspect of this stage is the use of periodic performance appraisal interviews, in which supervisor and subordinate jointly discuss results and consider their implications for the future. The performance appraisal interview is essentially a discussion between manager and subordinate about objectives and their achievement. It is an integral part of the process of managing by results by which both parties to the interview assess their efficiency as managers. The manager himself assesses his role as tutor to the subordinate; the subordinate considers his role in supporting the manager.

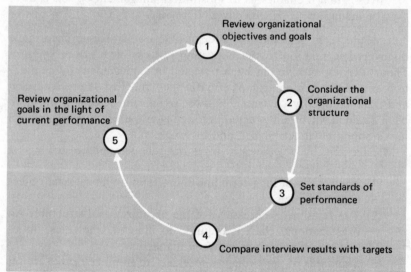

Fig. 3.37

(5) Long and short-term organizational goals are reviewed in the light of current performance.

These stages in management by objectives are illustrated in Fig. 3.37.

Organization theory

Some of the assumptions upon which we have so far relied have been necessary for the purpose of facilitating the examination of the basic aspects of accounting for planning and control. If an accounting system is to be effective in providing information for planning and control purposes, it should be capable of adapting to organizational and environmental factors peculiar to individual enterprises. Different enterprises may require different methods of control depending on the internal and external influences affecting their own activities. Hence, some of our assumptions may be more applicable to some organizations than to others. In this respect, organization theory attempts to provide a framework for understanding the influences which bear upon organizations and is important, therefore, for clarifying issues of importance to the accountant.

Approaches to organization theory

By regarding the organization as a logical and rational process, the Classical Approach focusses in some detail on the organizing function of management. Hence, the Classical Theory is concerned with the structure of organizations and the determination of the tasks necessary to attain organizational objectives. By contrast, the Human Relations Approach stresses people rather than structures, their motives and behaviour rather than the activities which need to be harnessed for achieving organizational goals. This approach originated in the Hawthorne experiments of the 1920s which revealed that social and human factors in work situations were often more important than physical factors in affecting productivity. The Human Relations Theory asserts that since the most important factors are individual needs and wants, the structure of organizations should be geared to individuals rather than the individual being geared to the structure.

Finally, there has developed the Contingency Approach which starts with the premise that there is no single organizational design that is best in all situations. According to Sketty & Carlisle (1972), there are four factors or forces of particular significance in the design of an organizational structure, namely: (1) forces in the manager; (2) forces in the environment; (3) forces in the task; (4) forces in the subordinates.

(1) Forces in the manager. This refers to factors relating to the personalities of managers and their influence on the design of the organizational structure. Managers tend to perceive organizational problems in a unique way, which is a function of background, knowledge, experience and values. These factors shape organizational decisions in such areas as strategy, organizational structure and style of management. Accordingly, organizations do not have objectives—only people have objectives. In this analysis, these objectives will differ from manager to manager.

(2) Forces in the environment. Some studies suggest that the most effective pattern of organizational structure is that which enables the organization to adjust to the requirements of its environment (Burns & Stalker, 1961). These studies indicate that organizations with less formal structures are best able to cope with uncertain and heterogeneous environmental conditions. Conversely, highly structured organizations will be more effective in stable environmental conditions. Hence, bureaucratic structures as implied in Classical Theory are more appropriate to stable conditions, whereas more democratic structures are required to enable organizations to adapt to a changing environment.

(3) Forces in the task. Empirical studies indicate that technology has an important impact on the design of an organizational structure. For example, Woodward (1965) has found that organizational structures varied according to the technology involved. According to Woodward fewer managers are required under systems of unit production than under systems of mass production. The technology associated with unit production systems may also require relatively higher levels of operative skill, and there is evidence to suggest that skilled workers feel more involved in their jobs and are more anxious for an opportunity to participate in decision-making relating to their jobs than unskilled workers. This makes it possible to delegate more authority to lower levels in an organization and has important implications for devising schemes based on 'management by objectives'.

(4) Forces in the subordinates. This refers to the psychological needs such as the subordinate's desire for a measure of independence, for the acquisition of skills and the motivation for assuming responsibility. The desire to participate in decision-making is not uniform among employees, and as implied earlier it is much stronger among skilled workers and employees with a professional background than it is among unskilled workers. Hence, organizations employing relatively more skilled than unskilled employees will be faced with a greater desire for a democratic structure.

Summary

The budget process alone is not sufficient to maintain adequate management control. Too often, organizations tend to expect results from budgetary control and fail to recognize its behavioural implications. As a result, pressures are created leading to mistrust, hostility and actions detrimental to the long term prospects of an organization. It follows that accountants should work more closely with behavioural scientists and that they should learn more about the behavioural implications of organizational control.

Participation schemes should be introduced into organizations with due consideration for the psychological problems entailed. One such scheme is management by objectives. Management by objectives differs from the conventional budgetary control theory in that it enables the precepts of Theory Y to be put into practice by creating an environment which allows employees to develop as individuals and to exercise responsibility through self-control. Self-control is found to induce stronger work motivation, for by giving individual managers greater freedom of action, it affords them in greater measure the satisfaction and pleasure which a sense of accomplishment confers.

Being concerned with the provision of information for planning and control, the accountant should find a knowledge of organization theory particularly useful in understanding the internal and external influences which affect the nature of organizational activities and the environment in which decisions are made. These influences have implications for the design of control systems, and the significance of contingency theory lies in the identification of their sources.

References

1. Argyris, C., Human Problems with Budgets, *Harvard Business Review*, January–February, 1953.

2. Drucker, P. F., *The Practice of Management*, p. 131, Heinemann, London, 1963.

3. Churchill, N. C., Cooper, W. E. & Sainsbury, T., Laboratory and Field Studies of the Behavioral Effects of Audits, in *Management Controls*, Bonini, E. C., Jaedicke, R. K., & Wagner (eds) McGraw-Hill, New York, 1964.

4. McGregor, D. M., *The Human Side of the Enterprise*, McGraw-Hill, New York, 1960.

5. Report of the Committee on the Behavioral Science Context of the Accounting Curriculum, *Accounting Review* Supplement to Vol. XLVI 1971.

6. Stedry, A. C. *Budget Control and Cost Behavior* Prentice Hall, Englewood Cliffs, N.J., 1960.

7. Welsch, G. A., Some Behavioral Implications in Profit Planning and Control, *Management Adviser*, July–August, 1971.

8. Burns, T. & Stalker, G. M., *The Management of Innovation*, Tavistock Publications Ltd., London, 1961.

9. Sketty, Y. K. & Carlisle, H. M., A Contingency Model of Organization Design, *California Management Review* Vol. 15 No. 1, 1972.

10. Woodward J., *Industrial Organization: Theory and Practice*, Oxford University Press, 1965.

Further Readings

1. Caplan, E. H., *Management Accounting and Behavioral Science*, Addison Wesley, New York, 1971.

2. Hofstede, G. H., *The Game of Budget Control*, Tavistock, London, 1968.

3. Hopwood, A., *Accounting and Human Behaviour*, Accountancy Age Books, London, 1974.

4. Humble, J. W., *Management by Objectives in Action*, McGraw-Hill, New York, 1970.

5. Odiorne, G. S., *Management by Objectives*, Pitman Publishing, London, 1965.

6. Schiff, M. & Lewin, A. Y., *Behavioral Aspects of Accounting*, Prentice Hall, Englewood Cliffs, N.J., 1974.

7. Williams, M. R., *Performance Appraisal in Management*, Heineman, London, 1972.

Section 4

The Design of Management Information Systems

15
The Design of Management Information Systems

As we have stressed previously in this book, the management accounting system is the most important element of an organization's management information system (MIS)—the total complex in which data are generated, processed and refined to produce the information needed at all levels of the organization. The management information system may be viewed as a federation of subsystems based on functions performed within an organization. In Part 1, we saw that the accounting system is the most important information system and links together other information systems such as personnel, research and development and production information. Figure 3.38 illustrates the focal role which accounting plays in an organization's information network.

According to Limberg (1970):

> "The purpose of an MIS is to determine and provide, as efficiently, effectively, and economically as possible, what management needs to know. It should facilitate the accomplishment of objectives, prevent failures to reach objectives, and correct conditions which hamper the fulfillment of objectives."

In this chapter, some of the various threads from previous chapters are drawn together to provide a fuller understanding of the concepts underlying the design of a MIS and the expanded opportunities which have arisen for accountants in this area in recent years.

The 'systems approach' to the design of information systems

As we mentioned in Part 1, chapter 3, the systems approach is a method of analysing an organization as a whole within its environmental setting, and of studying the relationships existing between its various parts. This approach focuses on the overall objectives of the organization, and on the means by which they may be most effectively realized. In like manner, the systems approach may be applied to the design of a management information system by focusing attention firstly on management information needs as the overall objective of a management information system, and then on the means by which

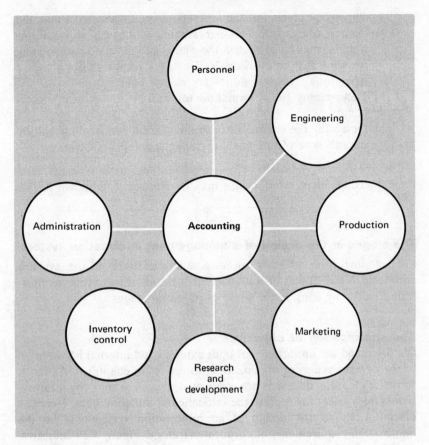

Fig. 3.38

these needs may be satisfied. Hence, such an approach requires that a management information system be designed around the decisions which must be made if the organization is to achieve its overall objectives, and must highlight the tasks involved in implementing those decisions.

Accordingly, the steps to be taken in designing a management information system may be identified as follows:

(1) Specifying the objectives of the organization and evaluating the various strategies available for attaining these objectives.
(2) Selecting the best strategy, and identifying its critical decisions and operations. These decisions and operations are called 'critical success factors'.

(3) Preparing plans for the operations necessary to attain the desired objectives. This necessitates setting up an organizational structure to realize the plans, and in so doing assigning responsibility to individuals. Thus, the responsibility attached to various tasks and duties are clearly defined.

(4) Determining the information relevant to the critical success factors.

(5) Designing the channels of communication which will allow the smooth flow of information throughout the organization.

The major determinants of management information design, and their interdependent relationships may be illustrated as shown in Fig. 3.39.

The stages in the design of a management information system

Let us now proceed to a more detailed analysis of the systems approach to the design of a management information system as illustrated below by considering some of its major stages.

The specification of objectives

We discussed the importance of both external and internal information to the determination of organization objectives in chapter 3. As far as strategic planning decisions are concerned, it is clear that any information system must incorporate the critical environmental data. Hence, a crucial factor in the design of an information system will be the information requirements of corporate strategy. Figure 3.39 indicates, therefore, that corporate strategy is a product of the organization's environment and of its resources. It will be recalled, of course, that the term corporate strategy refers to the fundamental long-term goals of an organization, and the policy adopted to attain these long-term goals.

The formulation of a successful strategy hinges upon the extent of knowledge on two key points, that is, the opportunities open to the enterprise and the resources available; it depends, therefore, on the amount and quality of information emanating from both internal and external sources. As we explained in chapter 3, environmental information is necessary to assess the opportunities open to the organization and internal or analytical information enables it to assess its resources and the effectiveness with which they are employed. Naturally, the strategy may call for the acquisition of new resources, which together with the existing resources, will be critical success factors to the strategy.

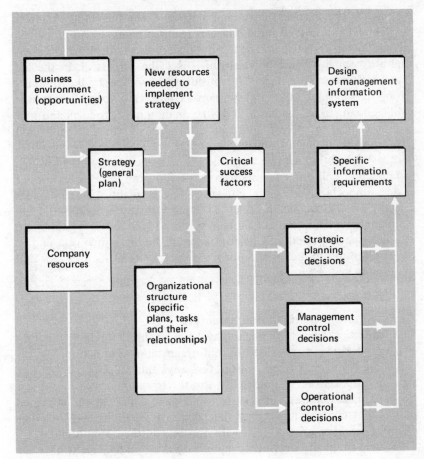

Fig. 3.39

The determination of 'critical success factors'

The 'critical success factors' were defined earlier as those decisions and operations which have to be accomplished efficiently in order that the organization might be successful in attaining its objectives. The business environment, the availability of resources, the strategy selected, and the organizational structure devised are all areas in which critical success factors exist. It is easy to appreciate why the availability of resources and their effective use should be a critical success factor, and similarly the importance of the correct strategy and of a good organization structure to the success factors existing in the business environment may, on the other hand, be peculiar to the industry in which the firm operates, and knowledge of them assists in establishing certain priorities when setting up a management information system.

As regards the making of strategic decisions, the following examples may be given of critical success factors in the business environment. In the car industry, styling and dealer outlets are two critical success areas where a company must be strong if it is to be successful: in the life assurance industry, a successful business cannot be built without a strong agency and sales organization as well as a sound investment management: in the chemical industry, finding new products and new uses is critical to success and puts a high premium on research and development: in manufacturing consumer products such as cigarettes and soft drinks, persuasive advertising and sufficient outlets outweigh in importance all other factors to a successful firm. Other examples of critical importance in some industries is the quality of spare parts service, or high quality product, or rapid delivery schedules.

Once the critical success factors have been identified, it is possible to evaluate the organization's performance of the tasks involved, and to direct attention to means of improving the quality of its decisions and operations in the future.

Devising the organizational structure

The framework in which plans may be formalized for implementing strategic decisions is provided by the organizational structure, and all tasks must be performed within the environment created by this structure. Once the responsibility for these various tasks has been assigned, individual executives are required to supervise the activities under their control, making all the necessary decisions and fostering effective working relationships with and among their subordinates.

As we saw in the previous chapter, styles of management have an important bearing on the performance of tasks. An organizational structure based on the principles of Theory Y places the responsibility for decision-making not on a few top executives, but on those managers and personnel who are thought to be in the best position to make sound decisions and to take prompt action at the appropriate level. The decentralization of responsibility leads to the formulation of goals for each department which are more personal to its members than to organizational goals. Therefore it makes these goals more meaningful in the degree to which departmental personnel and managers see themselves as playing an important role in the organizational structure.

The determination of information needs

Once individual responsibilities have been established within the organizational framework, departmental managers are able to define the information relevant to their needs, and specify the information requirements of a management information system.

The technological revolution brought about by electronic data processing and computerized systems has gone hand in hand with the increasing use of mathematical models for the study of business problems, and the application of mathematical techniques to their solution. From an accounting point of view, the consequences of the revolution in data processing and analysis are most clearly seen in the changing design of information systems, which are becoming increasingly computer based. Hence, the designer of information systems should automate as far as possible the wide range of decisions which rely on data stored in the computer. This means that he should seek to maximize programmed decisions, that is those which may be made automatically by the computer, and to eliminate as far as possible the need to make non-programmed decisions, that is those requiring a conscious management intervention. The designer therefore, is directly concerned with improving the efficiency of the decision-making process.

(a) Programmed decision models

Decisions which may be automated rely on mathematical decision models built into a computer's own programme. Such decisions are of a routine and repetitive nature, for example in controlling raw material inventories a routine decision is 'how much to buy?'. By taking into account such factors as the expected level of production and the time needed to obtain new deliveries, a decision rule can be formulated for the re-order of supplies when inventories fall below a certain level. Decision rules may, therefore, be devised which will enable routine decisions to be made economically by means of mathematical models programmed into computers.

The procedure for programming decisions for computer applications involves four stages:

(a) determining the decision to be made
(b) devising the best rule for making the decision
(c) programming the decision rule for the computer
(d) designing computer inputs and outputs so that the decision may be made by the computer.

Numerous writers in recent years have taken the view that computerized management information systems will, in future, provide purely programmed decisions—a 'total systems' concept which would be the theoretical goal of information system design. If the ultimate goal is to eliminate non-programmed decisions, an important part of the work of the accountant in the future will be to devise methods for increasing the number of programmed decisions.

(b) *Non-programmed decision models*

These decision models lie outside the control of the designer. The main problem in programming decisions is to establish appropriate decision rules, and it is not possible to programme such rules for situations calling upon managerial experience, judgement and intuition. In such situations, the function of the designer is to devise a system which will provide management with information for making non-programmed decisions. The output of the information system then becomes the inputs to the decision models, whereas, of course, in the case of programmed decisions the models are built into the information system.

As Fig. 3.39 indicates, decision-making in any organization falls into the three areas which we have analysed in earlier chapters, namely, strategic, management control and operational control decisions. Each of these decision levels require their own specific kinds of information. An operational control decision, for example, seldom if ever, requires information concerning the extent of foreign competition in the home market, or the distribution of the national income as between income-earning groups, yet this type of information is highly relevant to the making of strategic decisions. On the other hand, the type of information pertinent to operational control decisions concerns such matters as machine set-up time, machine breakdown preventative maintenance schedules, defects of quality and so on. Many decisions of such a nature are capable of being programmed on a computer, whereas strategic planning decisions are made irregularly and the problem is indeed often a question of deciding when a decision has to be made.

The first stage in the analysis of the design requirements of a management information system is to determine the information needs of the three decision areas. Initially, therefore, one should ask the following questions—what decisions need to be made? What factors are important in making those decisions? How and when should the decisions be made? What information is necessary in making the decisions?

At all three levels of decision-making, the critical success factors assist in indentifying the decisions which need to be made. Sometimes these factors are referred to as the 'key tasks' which are those parts of a manager's job which are of central importance to departmental and organizational objectives. The precepts of Theory Y stress how essential it is that individual managers should participate fully in the definition of these key tasks. It is imperative that performance standards be established to act as guidelines to managers as to how well they are expected to perform key tasks and this implies that the information system should provide feedback information on the performance of these tasks.

We have already analysed some of the critical success factors, or key tasks involved in strategic planning decisions. There are likewise critical success factors in management control decision areas, but they are more susceptible to control than are some of the success factors in the strategic planning area, and it is much easier to quantify performance standards. A production manager, for example, may have performance standards for labour, machines, stock levels and material usage, all of which are readily quantifiable.

In conclusion, the information which is more vital to management is that which relates to key tasks. Indeed, the evidence of research into key tasks indicates that although the performance of key tasks accounts for only 15–20% of a manager's time, 75–90% of the value of his services to the organization is derived from his performance of those tasks.

Designing channels of information

It seems almost trite to say that information is only useful if it is communicated, but nevertheless to assert that an information system is also a system of information communication serves to underline that the design of an information communication network is as important as the relevance of information itself to an effective management information system.

As illustrated in chapter 1, the decision points within an organization structure are inter-connected by means of a network of information channels, so that, in effect, one may consider the decision-process itself to be an extension of the information-communication process. An information system, therefore integrates all the various management functions within an organization as it acts as a link between all the decision points. Hence, the design of an information network is a central feature in the design of an organizational structure.

Design criteria

Design criteria are rules which are utilized to evaluate designs as to their acceptability. Given a number of different designs, which one is the best? Cohen (1971) lists five basic criteria for designing successful systems.

Relevance

The first, and paramount, criterion is that the system must be relevant to the specified business requirements. It is necessary to articulate clearly the objectives of the system, to specify who will use it, how the users will relate to it, and to describe the manner in which the system will satisfy the stipulated objectives.

Timeliness

It is important to define the response-time criterion in advance of the system's implementation. If the lapse between a useful time frame and the actual time frame is excessive, it may be better not to proceed with the system design.

Cost effectiveness

The effectiveness of the system, both in respect of tangible and other benefits should be related to the cost of installing and operating the system in order to determine its feasibility.

Accuracy

Basic controls, checks or balances should be applied to data sources and system components to ensure that the system is not only efficient, but that its output is correct and usable.

Flexibility

A system should be flexible to handle (i) normal activity growth for a foreseeable period ahead; and (ii) inevitable changes in the planning process or the operations of the organization.

Behavioural aspects of systems design

The growing awareness of the importance of the behavioural sciences for management in recent years, which we discussed in chapter 14, has important implications also for the designer of MIS.

One of the most elaborate theories of business behaviour put forward by Cyert & March (1963) has its focus on the organizational decision-making process, and throws useful light on the behavioural considerations which affect the design of MIS. The four following major areas covered by Cyert & March in the process of analysing organizational decision-making illustrate these behavioural considerations:

(1) formulation of objectives
(2) search procedure
(3) avoidance of uncertainty
(4) organizational learning

The formulation of objectives

An organization represents a coalition of members having different objectives and different power to influence organizational objectives. Objectives are best conceived of as contraints on business behaviour being established through a bargaining process among coalition members. Organizational objectives change over time as new coalition members enter and old members leave the organization. Cyert & March isolated five major objectives—profit, market share, sales, production, and inventory—which shifted with changes in aspiration levels. Most importantly, they asserted that satisficing rather than maximizing objectives were adopted, thereby reflecting the will of the coalition that objectives should be attainable.

The search procedure

Decisions made in organizations depend upon the expectations formed by their members, and upon the information available to them. According to Cyert & March, search activity will tend to be standardized locally, either close to the symptom or close to the solution. If this type of routine search activity fails to produce satisfactory solutions which satisfy organizational constraints and obtain the support of the coalition, the search procedure will proceed at a higher, and more intensive level. No effort is made, however, to secure perfect information, decisions are based on relatively few alternatives, and only a few anticipated consequences of these decisions are examined.

The avoidance of uncertainty

According to behavioural theories of organizational decision-making, risk will be avoided at the expense of expected revenue. In general, a reduction in the expected value of an outcome will be exchanged for an increase in the certainty of the outcome. Thus, an alternative offering a 90% chance of yielding £10 is more likely to be acceptable than one offering only a 15% of yielding £100. We examined the behavioural aspects of decision-making under risk in chapter 6.

According to Cyert & March, the organization seeks to avoid uncertainty by following regular procedures and a policy of reacting to feedback information rather than attempting to forecast the environment.

Organizational learning

Organizations display adaptive behaviour over time. They change their objectives and goals and revise their procedures for search on the basis of experience. The aspiration levels are assumed to change in response to the results obtained. In the steady state, aspiration levels are a little above achievement: in the face of improving results, aspiration levels lag behind achievements; and in the face of declining performance, aspiration levels decrease but remain above the achievement level.

Behavioural theories of the firm have important implications for the design of information systems. Thus, the designer of MIS should be aware of the practical behavioural problems of optimizing models which assume consistent organizational objectives, whereas behavioural theories emphasize the existence of inconsistent organizational objectives. Moreover, he should ensure the provision of adequate search information to assist and improve the decision-making process by making it possible to expand the search process. The wish for rationality in systems design should be modified by a behavioural tendency to avoid uncertainty. Finally, he should be aware of the changing nature of objectives and aspiration levels.

Behavioural theories recognize that even when managers are given all the information they need for making a decision, a wrong decision may nevertheless be made. One solution which has been suggested to mitigate this problem lies in a better understanding of the attitudes and the thought-processes of the manager as a person. The designer of a management information system should recognize the peculiar characteristics of the management personnel, in addition to providing feedback information and in assisting in the formulation of decision rules which will enable them to identify and to learn from their mistakes.

The influence of the computer on the design of information systems

We have already mentioned that the evolution of the computer is one of the most significant factors in the changes which have revolutionized the accounting environment. As a result, those involved in operating information systems of whatever nature tend to concentrate their efforts on developing computer based systems. However, an effective information system must be devised before it may be computerized, and the use of a computer does not of itself guarantee a more efficient management information system. One authority cites the example of a large company which had made an extensive use of computer applications in its accounting and production control areas and yet had an ineffective management information system. "In the accounting field, for example, it was found to have a well-integrated computer system for payroll, general accounting, invoicing, paying creditors and cost accounting. In short, it had made good use of computers. Yet, that company had no formal system for long-range planning; it had no budgets of any kind; its cost accounting system was archaic, and, consequently, seriously inaccurate. In other words, it had a totally inadequate management information system, and its profit performance reflected that situation" (Dearden, 1965).

In many cases, the failure to make the best use of computers lies in an excessive concern with hardware, so that computerization is in essence the conversion of a mechanical procedure into another one. The success of a management information system depends primarily not on the relative efficiency with which information is processed, but on whether the system provides the information needed by decision-makers. Once an effective management information system has been devised, the advantages to be gained by the use of a computer are, as we have noted, two-fold: firstly, the computer is a very flexible instrument for handling masses of data, and secondly, its processing operations are very rapid. When a management information system is computerized, its control tends to be delegated to computer specialists, who are really highly skilled technicians in computer hardware and computer methods. The accountant may not be involved in the control of such a system, and the delegation of his information control function to computer technicians may have disastrous consequences. By concentrating attention on the computer's technical possibilities rather than the information needs of decision-makers, for example, there is no guarantee that the information required will be available. Moreover, technicians have limited skills and do not have the background which would enable them to identify the information needs of decision models. We have argued earlier that those responsible for the design and control of management information systems should be broadly educated in all the cognate disciplines which are brought together in the corpus of modern management science. To place the control of computerized management information systems in the hands of computer specialists is clearly a reversal to a less desirable state of affairs.

It is not surprising, therefore, that when the design and control of management information systems have been placed in the hands of computer technicians, they have been successful, on occasions, in forcing through their own creations against all odds. Research has shown for example, that the active participation of management in the selection of computer projects, their manning and the responsibility for their development was a crucial factor in distinguishing those companies which used computers effectively, and those which did not. One must conclude, therefore, that computer applications are successful only when well managed.

Accountants and the design of information systems

Traditionally, accountants have not only been responsible for the provision of accounting information, but also for the design of accounting information systems. They have been answerable for the completeness and accuracy of the information so provided. Organizations have had also additional sources of information systems providing information of a non-financial type, for example, stock levels in physical terms, names and addresses of shareholders and so on. Developments in computer technology and operations research methods now provide the impetus compelling organizations towards unified information systems, in which accounting information systems are being merged with other information networks. Figure 3.40 below illustrates the integration of accounting and other management information systems. The financial and non-financial information systems have become increasingly integrated in recent years, and the shaded area reflecting this integration has become larger.

The changing environment which has re-defined the accountant's role as providing information for decision-making, equally compels him to re-think his attitude towards the nature of the information systems which he has traditionally operated as a means of providing accounting information. Clearly, if he is to retain his control over the provision of accounting information, he will have to seek a controlling interest in the design and operations of unified information systems. In every sense, therefore, the accountant must become an information specialist. Indeed, some have gone so far as to assert that the key to the survival of the accountant lies in a complete re-thinking of his internal control functions reshaping them around the data processing centre where information converges. Hence, they argue that the accountant must project himself into information systems design if there

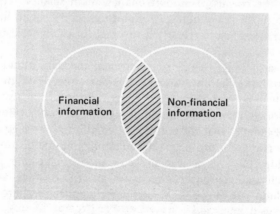

Fig. 3.40

is to be any measure of integrity associated with those systems and their outputs.

In fact, most accountants who have been involved in the design of management accounting systems would no doubt regard the concept of a management information system as merely an extension of management accounting systems. In the sense that the accountant has always been engaged in the process of gathering, measuring, analysing and disseminating information, it would be the most logical step for him to extend his sphere of influence and authority to the non-financial type of information, and so be responsible for the design and operation of integrated information systems. In effect, the accountant should apply the expertise he has acquired in the design and operation of accounting systems to broadening his services to management in the design and use of information systems in general.

Several reasons may be advanced in support of the accountant's claim to executive control over management information services. Firstly, a person steeped in management accounting has normally acquired a broad knowledge of all aspects of business activity. Secondly, he has gained a wide experience in gathering, interpreting and presenting both financial and non-financial information to management. Thirdly, he will already have exercised responsibility over the operation of the most highly developed information system in the organization, namely the accounting information system. Indeed, the management accounting function with its emphasis on cost behaviour, cost and performance standards and economic analysis has really provided much of the foundation on which the structure of modern information systems is erected. Fourthly, he is familiar with computers, and even though his technical knowledge of them may be limited, he does have a degree of understanding of the methods, capabilities and problems associated with computer technology.

Summary

Management information systems should be designed to meet the information needs of decision-makers. For this purpose, objectives and goals must be established, the information needed to evaluate performance must be determined, and an effective mechanism must be developed and installed. The adequacy of the information output of the system for organizational decision-making should be reviewed and appraised continually.

The distinction between programmed and non-programmed decisions is important for the designer of a management information system. Decision-making is an expensive process in terms of scarce resources—managerial time and energy. Programmed decisions are an efficient means of conserving these scarce resources, and enhancing managerial productivity. Such is the nature of non-programmed decisions that no general model can be developed for programming them. The ultimate aims of the designer should be to eliminate non-programmed decisions by programming them as far as possible.

The behavioural aspects of decision-making are particularly important. Behavioural theory emphasizes the following characteristics of organization behaviour:

(1) the prevalence of satisficing rather than maximizing objectives and goals;
(2) the existence of inconsistent objectives reflecting the compromise sought by current coalition members;
(3) the existence of local search procedures;
(4) the wish to avoid uncertainty;
(5) the adaptive nature of organizational behaviour.

Finally, the computerization and integration of information systems afford the accountant an expanded opportunity for playing a more important role in the design of information systems. We have argued in previous chapters that he is well qualified for this role, and we have examined the nature of this claim in the context of the importance of accounting information for planning and control. This chapter, therefore, brings together the many different threads of this Part of the book.

References

1. Cohen, J. B., *Cost Effectiveness Systems*, pp. 13–16, American Management Association, 1971.

2. Cyert, R. M. & March, J. G., *A Behavioral Theory of the Firm*, Prentice Hall, Englewood Cliffs, N.J., 1963.

3. Dearden, J., Management Information Systems and the Computer, in *Management and Control Systems* pp. 519–23, Anthony R. N., Dearden J. & Vancil, R. F. (eds) Richard Irwin, Homewood, Illinois, 1965.

4. Limberg, H., How to Meet Management's Information Needs, in *Management Information Systems* the Association for Systems Management, p. 39, 1970.

Further Readings

Argyris, C., Management Information Systems: the Challenge to Rationality and Emotionality, *Management Science*, February, 1971.

American Accounting Association Report of the Committee on Accounting and Information Systems, *Accounting Review*, 1971.

Bower, J. B. & Welke, W. R. (eds), *Financial Information Systems*, Houghton Miflin, Boston, 1968.

Coleman, R. J. & Riley, M. J. (eds), *MIS: Management Dimensions*, Holden Day, New York, 1973.

Crandall, R. H., The Future Role of the Managerial Accountant, *Canadian Chartered Accountant*, August, 1970.

Davies, G. B., *Management Information Systems: Conceptual Foundations, Structure and Development*, McGraw-Hill, New York, 1974.

Holmes, R. W., Twelve Areas to Investigate for Better Management Information Systems *Financial Executive*, July, 1970.

Murdick, R. G. & Ross, J. E., *Information Systems for Modern Management*, Prentice Hall, 1971.

Robinson, L. A. & Alexander, M. J., The Accountant as Designer of Management Information Systems, *N.A.A. Management Accounting*, November, 1971.

Zani, W. M., Blueprint for Management Information Systems, *Harvard Business Review* November–December, 1970.

Part **4**

Financial Reporting

Part 4   FINANCIAL REPORTING

          Introduction   533

Section 1   Conceptual Considerations in Financial Reporting

          1 Objectives of Financial Reporting   538
          Concepts of financial reporting   539
              The stewardship concept of financial reporting   540
              The decision-making concept of financial reporting   542
              The general user concept of financial reporting   543
          Developing a normative theory of financial reporting to
              investors   544
          Summary   545
          References   546

          2 Developing a Financial Reporting Framework   547
          The need for financial reporting standards   547
          The purpose of a financial reporting framework   548
              The Trueblood Report   548
              Characteristics of corporate reports   551
          The decision model approach   552
          Financial reporting and the scientific method   553
          Summary   554
          References   555

Section 2   Value and Income Measurement

          3 Capital, Value, Income   558
          Capital   558
          Value   560
              What is 'value'?   560
              Value and exchange   561
              Value and decision-making   562
          Capital valuation   563
          Income   564
          The objectives of income measurement   565
              Income as a measure of efficiency   565
              Income as a guide to future investment   566
              Income as an indicator of managerial effectiveness   566
              Income as a tax base   566
              Income as a guide to creditworthiness   567
              Income as a guide to socio-economic decisions   567
              Income as a guide to dividend policy   567
          Criteria for the selection of income measurements   567
          Summary   568
          References   569

          4 Accounting and Economic Concepts of Income and
          Value   570
          Accounting concepts   570
              The effects of the cost convention   570
              The effects of the realization convention   571

Economic concepts   572
   Estimation of ex-ante income   574
   Estimation of ex-post income   575
   The subjective nature of economic income   576
Summary   577
References   578

5 Accounting for Price-level Changes   579
Partial adjustments for price-level changes   579
Adjustments for general price-level changes   581
   Monetary and non-monetary items   582
   An appraisal of C.P.P. accounting   587
Summary   589
References   590

6 Current Value Accounting   591
Introduction   591
Replacement cost accounting   592
   Components of replacement cost income (RCI)   592
   Income measurement by historic cost and replace-
     ment cost compared   594
   Historic cost and Replacement cost Balance Sheets
     compared   596
   The treatment of holding gains   597
   An evaluation of replacement cost accounting   598
Realizable value accounting   599
   The case for realizable value accounting   599
   Components of realizable income   600
   Limitations of exit values   601
'Value to the business' as a criterion   602
Current cost accounting v. C.P.P. accounting   604
   Monetary items   605
   Non-monetary items   607
Summary   608
References   609

Section 3   **Comparability and the Interpretation of
Financial Reports**

7 Increasing the Comparability of Financial Reports   612
Alternative information sources   612
Arguments against uniformity   613
The role of judgement in financial reporting   614
The influence of management on financial reports   615
Accounting standards   616
   The statutory enforcement of standards   618
Summary   618
References   619

8 The Valuation of Inventories   620
The importance of inventory valuation   620
Classification of inventories   621

Institute recommendations on inventory valuation   622
Current practices   623
   Limitations of current practices   624
   Research findings on current practices   625
   Recommendations for reducing diversity   625
Appendix: The case for variable costing for inventory
   valuation   628
   Different methods of matching   628
   The treatment of overheads   629
   Absorption and variable costing compared   630
   Results where sales fluctuate but production is con-
      stant   632
   Results where sales are constant but production fluc-
      tuates   633
   Variable and absorption costing: their impact on
      income summarized   635
   The variable costing controversy   635
   The need for a definition of assets   636
Summary   637
References   637

9 Interpreting and Comparing Financial Reports   638
The nature of ratio analysis   639
The analysis of solvency   640
   Short-term solvency   641
   Long-term solvency   645
The analysis of financial performance   646
   The analysis of efficiency as earning power   647
   The analysis of the efficiency of investment decisions   649
Summary   651
References   651

Section 4   **Increasing Financial Information**

10 Increasing Financial Information   654
Events accounting   654
Multiple value reports   655
Disclosure of budgets   656
Cash-flow accounting   658
   Contents of cash-flow reports   659
   The case for cash-flow reporting   663
   Advantages of cash-flow reports   664
   Disadvantages of cash-flow forecasting   665
Summary   666
References   666
Selected further readings   667

Introduction

We mentioned in Part 1 that the provision of information to meet the needs of users of accounting information should determine the objectives of an accounting information system. Therefore, the criterion by which the effectiveness of an accounting information system should be judged is the usefulness of its information output for the various purposes to which it is applied. Hence, if we were able to identify the nature of the decision-problems facing the several groups of persons with vested interests in organizations, we should be able to develop normative theories of accounting which would enable us to construct models for communicating information to these groups.

The reader will recall that in Part 1, we identified the following groups as having vested interests in business organizations, namely, management, shareholders and investors, employees, Government, creditors, the local community and customers. In Part 3, we examined the manner in which the information needs of management were met, and for the purpose of our analysis we defined the management decision-problem as being concerned with organizational planning and control. In this Part, we shall address ourselves to an analysis of the problems associated with the disclosure of information to shareholders and investors. We shall note that some of the information disclosed to shareholders and investors is also relevant to the needs of Government and creditors, as well as employees. It is not our purpose, however, to address ourselves to the information needs of these latter groups in this Part.

A distinction is often made between what is described as internal reporting and external reporting. Internal reporting is associated with the provision of information for management purposes. External reporting is used to describe the process by which information is made available to groups other than management. Within this classification, it may be said that external reporting appears to be developing in three directions. Firstly, the needs of shareholders and investors traditionally have been recognized by law in most countries in the form of obligations imposed on companies to publish to their shareholders annual reports and accounts, the form and content of which are specified by statute. Financial reporting, as this form of external reporting is known, has been in the forefront of interest since the appearance of

Joint Stock companies. It is for this reason that we shall devote this Part to the problems of financial reporting. Governments and creditors also use financial statements, the former for taxation purposes and the latter frequently for the purpose of evaluating creditworthiness. Both, however, usually require additional information to that contained in published financial statements, though creditors, unlike Governments, often have to rely on sources other than the company itself. The financial well-being of the private sector is of such importance to the economy that interest in the financial statements published by companies extends beyond the groups which we have already mentioned. There is a general concern with the profitability of public companies from a national and a local point of view, and their capacity to provide employment. These considerations are of particular interest to such other groups as employees and the local community.

Secondly, the growing awareness of the social effects of organizational activities has led to an entirely new concept of external reporting which has found its expression in the 'social audit', that is, the publication of information revealing how a firm has observed its social obligations in the course of conducting its business. This new concept has not yet been clearly defined in terms of reporting standards, and there is much debate on this issue. Some countries, notably France, are already moving towards legislation for the disclosure of social accounting information. Clearly, the Government, the local community, employees, customers as well as shareholders and investors have an interest in the manner in which management conducts its operations, though individually these various groups would wish to emphasize different aspects of that conduct. We shall discuss the problem of social responsibility accounting in Part 5.

Thirdly, the changing social framework which is producing a call for greater employee participation in management decision-making has also increased interest in the provision of information to employees and their organization. In this area of reporting, it becomes less easy to make a distinction between what may be called external as distinct from internal reporting. Many countries have, or are in the process of legislating for employee participation in the management of organizations. The nature and extent of required disclosure have not yet been agreed, but we shall touch on this problem in Part 5. This Part is divided into four sections, as follows:

Section 1. Conceptual considerations in financial reporting
This section examines the objectives of financial reporting and the approaches which have been taken to the formulation of financial reporting theory (chapters 1 and 2).

Section 2. Value and income measurement
This section discusses the various concepts of value and income measurement which have been developed (chapters 3 to 6).

Section 3. Comparability and the interpretation of financial reports
This section examines attempts to increase the comparability of financial reports, and discusses the problems of interpreting these reports (chapters 7 to 9).

Section 4. Increasing financial information
This section discusses suggestions which have been advanced in recent years for increasing the supply of data to users of financial reports (chapter 10).

Section 1

Conceptual Considerations in Financial Reporting

1

Section

Objectives of Financial Reporting

As we saw in Part 1, financial reporting has its roots in the problems created by the grant of Joint Stock company status to business firms, and the separation of the ownership and management of such companies which resulted. Having its roots in law, the early objectives of financial reporting were concerned with the prevention of fraud by the promoters and managers of Joint Stock companies, and giving some protection to creditors and shareholders against the possibility of malpractices by company managers. Although 19th century legislators were not very precise in the manner in which they apprehended this problem, they did see that the publication of accounting information provided one important means whereby their aims might be realized. In a sense, therefore, the objectives of financial reporting may be discerned through the historical process in which various countries enacted successive laws in the 19th and 20th centuries for the disclosure of financial information by companies.

A common thread which may be seen as uniting various countries in this area was the recognition that shareholders, as owners of the capital of such companies, were the persons to whom information should be disclosed. Thus, the legal principle enshrined in the concept of financial reporting reiterated the stewardship function which the accounting process had served from time immemorial. Although the respective rights and obligations of shareholders and directors are delineated by statute, their position *vis-à-vis* each other is in no significant way altered by the act of incorporation. In effect, therefore, directors are answerable to shareholders for their stewardship of the company, and to no other persons; and directors may be removed from office by shareholders in whom ultimate control vests.

We may say, therefore, that financial reporting has been traditionally concerned with the production and communication of information to shareholders. This information is extracted from the accounting system, which we examined in Part 2, and is presented to shareholders by means of annual Income Statements and Balance Sheets. Additionally, these Financial Statements are accompanied by other reports, such as the Chairman's report, the report of the Board of Directors and the

Auditors' Report. Although the Auditors' Report is confined to the financial accounts, the Directors' Report covers a wider area of interest, and in the United Kingdom, for example, includes both financial and non-financial information. The contents of the Financial Statements, the Directors' and Auditors' Reports are determined by law. There is nothing to prevent more extensive disclosure of information for the purpose of law has been to compel minimum levels of information disclosure. Many firms have ventured beyond these minimum legal requirements, and published more information about their activities to shareholders. Additionally, the Chairmen of public companies often issue quite extensive statements to accompany the financial reports, and the Annual General Meeting provides an opportunity for shareholders to request further information or explanations regarding the activities of the company. The socio-political environment existing in different countries has affected the nature, extent and development of financial reporting practices in these countries. Some countries, therefore, require more extensive disclosures than others—the USA, for example, has legislated for the disclosure of funds statements, whereas the United Kingdom has not done so. All countries, however, have found it necessary to use coercive legal powers to compel companies to disclose financial information to shareholders. In this respect, therefore, legislatures have recognized the conflict of interests between shareholders and management and have sought to intervene in the former's behalf.

Although financial reports are published for the benefit of shareholders, the information they contain may be used by other groups, as we have mentioned, notably, investors, lenders and creditors who have, or intend to have financial relations with the company. If we are to understand the nature of financial reporting, however, we should always bear in mind that financial reports are primarily addressed to the supposed needs of shareholders, since by law it is to them that they are addressed.

Concepts of financial reporting

Financial reporting practices have been the subject of controversy of recent years. Essentially, the root cause of the criticisms which have been levelled at existing practices appears to stem from a growing gap between what some are perceiving to be the objectives of financial reports and the traditionalist view which is established by law.

The definition of the objectives of financial reporting is a crucial stage in the development of a theory of financial reporting and the construction of a financial reporting model. Evidently, some unanimity is required for these aims to be realized. There have developed three different schools which emphasize different viewpoints of the financial reporting function:

(a) The traditional view of financial reporting based on the concept of stewardship accounting.
(b) The view which extends the stewardship function to include the recognition that shareholders and investors are decision-makers who require information for that purpose.
(c) The more modern view that companies should report to a larger class of general users rather than merely to shareholders and investors.

The stewardship concept of financial reporting

This concept represents the view that financial reports should be essentially statements in the nature of an account rendered by management to shareholders of their stewardship of the resources with which they have been entrusted. The concept of stewardship accounting may be said to have a number of characteristic features. Firstly, it has always been concerned with safeguarding assets. Secondly, it has also always been concerned with ensuring that assets have been well-managed. Thirdly, throughout its history, the concept of stewardship has recognized the delegation of authority to the steward and his accountability for his actions. Hence, it has laid particular emphasis on the importance of 'feedback information', that is, ex-post information. The major concern of the stewardship theory of financial reporting has been with the problem of selecting the type of information which should be revealed to shareholders and the extent of the disclosure of information. Indeed, if one looks back upon the development of company law in this respect one may see quite clearly the manner in which this approach has led progressively to an enlarged view of the needed level of information disclosure.

Although financial reporting is associated with the development of Joint Stock companies, the concept of stewardship accounting goes back to the origin of accounting as a method by which the owners of wealth made their stewards accountable for the assets entrusted to their care.

The United Kingdom has a longer history in the area of financial reporting than other nations, since this country had a lead in the various developments associated with the Industrial Revolution. The Joint Stock Company was an important development in this context since it permitted the mobilization of capital for the large-scale industrial commercial operations which the Industrial Revolution inspired. The development of financial reporting took a rather tortuous path, however, for the concept of stewardship as traditionally understood and associated with the ownership of wealth was not faithfully adopted by the legislature. Indeed, it is noteworthy that although Parliament gave ultimate control of Joint Stock companies to their shareholders, such control could only be exercised by vote at company meetings. Stewardship accounting in its traditional meaning would have required the disclosure by management of all the information necessary for shareholders, as owners, to be properly informed of the activities of the company and its servants. Financial reporting practices did not develop out of regard for the needs of shareholders to have information that would permit such a degree of control. Rather, the legislature was intent on giving the power of management into the hands of full-time managers or directors as a body, and at the same time affording shareholders and creditors a measure of protection against their excesses. Indeed, if one examines the development of financial reporting, the disclosure of information to shareholders has been consistently limited to a view of what was desirable for these purposes. The Companies Registration and Regulation Act 1844, for example, merely required that a full and fair Balance Sheet should be prepared annually and approved by the directors of companies before delivery to the auditors. Subsequently, the Limited Liability Act 1855 made these requirements optional by including them in a model set of Articles of Association which could be adopted at the discretion of company promoters. The Companies Act 1900 restored the requirement to publish Balance Sheets and the auditors were required to state whether these documents exhibited a true and fair view of the state of the company's affairs as shown by the books of accounts. The extension of disclosure requirements by successive statutes, and the current demand for social audits are based on the same view of right of management to manage which was implicit in the early legislation. The development of financial reporting followed similar patterns in other European countries and in the United States.

The concern with the prevention of abuse by management is reflected by the emphasis attached to the terms 'true and fair view' which were required to be appended to Balance Sheets and Income Statements. Truth and fairness have been terms which have been the subject of much debate. According to Chambers (1965), "the early company laws appear to have assumed that the practice of accounting followed well-defined rules which were directed towards the discovery of the 'true' state of affairs. But in fact the profession had given little if any thought to the matter. Understandably so. Reporting for the protection of investors and creditors was in a sense a novel responsibility, thrust upon accountants whose methods were either habitual or *ad hoc.* They saw their duty as serving the demands of businessmen, a situation they were accustomed to and against which they had no grounds for complaint". This attitude undoubtedly mitigated against the interests of shareholders, for accountants saw themselves as answerable to management and not to shareholders.

A further factor which did not assist the establishment of a proper concept of stewardship reporting were the conventions associated with the manner in which financial reports were compiled. Addressing the Cohen Committee on Company Law Reform in 1945, for example, the Institute of Chartered Accountants in England and Wales maintained that "a balance sheet does not as a general rule purport to show the net worth of an undertaking at any particular date or the present realizable value of such items as goodwill, land, buildings, plant and machinery, nor except in cases where the realizable value is less than cost, does it normally show the realizable value of stock in trade".

From the foregoing, it is clear that the stewardship concept of financial reporting applied by Parliament to legislation for the disclosure of information did not envisage that this information should be used by shareholders and investors for the purpose of investment decision-making.

The decision-making concept of financial reporting

The second school of thought considers the purpose of financial reporting as being the provision of information for decision-making, by shareholders and potential shareholders. This school recognizes that the predominant interest which shareholders have in companies is the return which they are able to obtain on their invested capital in the form of dividends and increased share values. Since shareholders are essentially concerned with the optimal allocation of their capital as between the competing investment opportunities offered by different companies, the adherents of this school argue that financial reports ought to be relevant for this purpose. This implies that they are more interested in information about future prospects than about the past: hence, they are concerned about the predictive ability of financial information.

In Part 1, we stated that prediction is an integral part of the process of decision-making. Indeed, it is a prior condition to a decision. The predictive-ability criterion allows alternative accounting measurements to be evaluated in terms of their ability to predict events of interest to decision-makers. The measure which has the greatest predictive ability in respect of a given event is judged to be the 'best' measure for that particular event.

The efficiency with which management employs the company's resources is crucial for profitability, and likewise the manner in which it maintains and expands those resources is crucial for future profitability. For this reason, there are some who would argue that there is fundamentally no distinction between the two schools of thought. In making his original investment decision, the shareholder decides which 'stewards' should be entrusted with his funds. He uses financial reports to compare the firm's results with his expectations. If the results have not met his original expectations, he may decide to look for an alternative investment for his funds. Hence, the feedback information contained in financial reports is an integral aspect of the investment decision process for it reveals whether or not the objectives of the investment decision have been attained.

The general user concept of financial reporting

The third school of thought considers that all parties who have an interest in an organization have a right to information about the organization's activities. One study (ASSC, 1975) identified the following groups as having a reasonable right to information which should be recognized in corporate reports:

(a) *The equity investor group* including existing and potential shareholders and holders of convertible securities, options or warrants.

(b) *The loan creditor group* including existing and potential holders of debentures and loan stock, and providers of short-term secured and unsecured loans and finance.

(c) *The employee group* including existing, potential and past employees.

(d) *The analyst–adviser group* including financial analysts and journalists, economists, statisticians, researchers, trade unions, stockbrokers and other providers of advisory services such as credit rating agencies.

(e) *The business contact group* including trade creditors and suppliers and in a different sense competitors, business rivals, and those interested in mergers, amalgamations and takeovers.

(f) *The Government* including tax authorities, departments and agencies concerned with the supervision of commerce and industry and local authorities.

(g) *The public* including taxpayers, ratepayers, consumers and other community and special interest groups such as political parties, consumer and environmental protection societies and regional pressure groups.

The special information needs of two of these groups (employee and the public) are considered further in Part 5.

Developing a normative theory of financial reporting to investors

If we wished to develop a normative theory of financial reporting for investment decision-making, our first problem would be to define the decision-problems facing investors. If we were able to identify the general nature of these problems, we should be able to construct a normative theory to help us in the analysis of current financial reporting practices.

It is clear that the interest which shareholders have in a company stems from the fact that they have made an investment of their capital into its shares. Hence, we may say that the decisions which they make revolve on a consideration of two issues. Firstly, shareholders are concerned with the value of their investment, and any likely change in that value. In this connection, they are looking for an increase in the value of shares, or at least in the maintenance of their value, so that any contradictory evidence will cause them to consider whether to continue to hold the shares or to realize them and place their capital elsewhere. Obviously, such decisions contain a risk element which accounting information may help to reduce but not to eliminate entirely. Secondly, shareholders are concerned with the income which they derive and expect to derive from their capital. This income may be expressed as a percentage rate of return, and is indicative of the efficiency of the resource allocation decisions which they have made. If they are dissatisfied with their income, shareholders may wish to sell their shares and buy shares in other companies with better income performance and prospects.

We may deduce, therefore, that the critical determinants in the decisions which shareholders and investors make are value and income. Hence, we may say that a normative theory of financial reporting should be based upon concepts of value and income which will meet the needs of shareholders and investors in making decisions based on future changes in value, that is to say, future income. As we shall see in chapter 4, the present value of future cash flows provides a possible solution to this problem. Indeed, under conditions of certainty, it offers the ideal basis of valuation and income determination for the purposes of financial reporting. Many of the controversies and difficulties in these areas are caused by uncertainty and changes in the value of money. Nevertheless, an analysis of value and income based on the present value of future cash flows provides useful insights into the real nature of these concepts, and enables us to construct models which may serve as yardsticks by which to judge other concepts of value and income.

Creditors in respect of loan capital also have information needs which are very similar to those of shareholders. Basically, loan creditors are interested in the following two aspects:

(a) the ability of the firm to pay interest on the loan with regularity;
(b) the security of the investment.

As regards the second aspect, attention will be focussed initially on the asset structure for some basis on which the value of future cash flows may be estimated, as well as on the current financial position. At a later date, as the loan reaches maturity, they will be concerned with the ability of the firm to repay the loan.

Usually, loan creditors are debenture holders whose rights are secured by either a fixed or a floating charge over the assets of the company. Unsecured debenture holders, however, are no better off than ordinary creditors in the case of an insolvency.

Loan creditors are concerned with the problem of capital maintenance and income. In this respect, the difference between them and shareholders is one of degree rather than one of kind. Hence, our comments in this Part will apply to loan creditors as well as to shareholders.

Summary

Traditionally, financial accounting reports have been based on the stewardship concept of accounting, which is concerned with safeguarding assets and ensuring that they have been honestly managed. Legislation has reiterated the stewardship concept, and has been applied to compelling minimum levels of information disclosure.

In recent years, a view has developed which extends the traditional stewardship concept of financial reporting to include meeting investors information needs for the purpose of decision-making. Because prediction is an integral part of decision-making, users of financial reports are concerned about the ability of financial reports to predict future events which may affect their own decisions. More recently, the view has been expounded that all users who have an interest in an organization have a right to information about that organization's activities.

Shareholders and investors, as the main users of financial reports, may be assumed to have two main objectives:

(a) an increase in the value of the shares they hold or intend to acquire, or at least the maintenance of that value;
(b) a return in the form of dividends.

It is important to bear these objectives in mind when developing a theory of financial reporting.

References

1. Accounting Standards Steering Committee, *The Corporate Report*, London, 1975.

2. Chambers, R. J., Financial Information and the Securities Market, *ABACUS*, Vol. 1, 1965.

3. *Report of the Committee on Company Law Amendment*, para. 98, London, HMSO, 1945.

2
Developing a Financial Reporting Framework

Shareholders do not have access to the range and quality of information available to management. Although they are also interested in the timing and size of future cash flows, the information which management makes available to shareholders is contained, by and large, in financial reports which are published annually. These reports deal with the results of business activities conducted in the past accounting period, and are measured in terms of accounting profit. Hence, financial reports are historic documents, and in no way do they address themselves to the future. Accounting conventions require that users of financial reports should be reasonably assured that the information they contain is not speculative: hence, these conventions stress the objectivity and verifiability of such information as defined by accounting practices. We may say, therefore, that accounting conventions play a deterministic role in discriminating between the interests of management and the interests of investors for information about future cash flows, and in preventing the latter from having access to the type of information which is most relevant to the value of their investment and their future income.

The need for financial reporting standards

This problem is exacerbated by conflicts of opinion among accountants, which have been revealed in recent years in a number of cases which have attracted a certain notoriety in the financial press. As a result of these cases, the accounting profession has been criticized on the grounds that given the same data, two accountants could well produce two different sets of financial figures, both being equally conforming with generally accepted accounting standards.

The loss of public confidence engendered by these criticisms was countered in the United Kingdom by the establishment of the Accounting Standards Steering Committee (ASSC) whose terms of reference was to lay down 'standards' which would produce greater uniformity in financial accounting practices. Similarly, in the United States the accounting profession established the Financial Accounting Standards Board (FASB) and by agreement with the accounting profession in many countries, there has been set up the International Accounting Standards Committee (IASB).

The purpose of a financial reporting framework

The awareness of the limitations of external financial reports has provided an impetus for the discussion of a financial reporting framework. It has also encouraged a wish to eliminate unjustifiable variances in financial reporting practices and so increase the comparability between the financial reports of different companies.

The accounting profession has struggled for a long time to develop a theoretical framework for all the activities involved in financial reporting. As mentioned in Part 1 the traditional approach to the formulation of accounting theory has been to select what is considered to be good practice, and to express the product of this process as being 'accounting theory'. One of the consequences of this approach to the formulation of accounting theory is a denial of its most important role, namely the provision of criteria based on stated objectives by which to judge the selection of appropriate practices. As we saw from our discussion of financial accounting conventions (Part 2, chapter 1), what passes for accounting theory allows the existence of rules which may conflict, and hence of practices which lead to different results. Where alternative rules or procedures exist which lead to significantly divergent reported results, we would hold that it is the function of theory to provide guidelines to enable accountants to select the best practices. At the moment, the absence of a sound theoretical framework means that accountants are expected to rely on professional judgement and intuition.

In Part 1 we noted that the process of reasoning from the particular to the general is known as the inductive method of reasoning; that of reasoning to the particular from the general is the deductive approach. The accounting profession has not used the inductive approach exclusively, but it has been influential in developing the hazy outlines of whatever theoretical framework exists today. In recent years the deductive approach has received much attention and this chapter is concerned basically with this method of approach.

The Trueblood Report

In 1971 the American Institute of Certified Public Accountants established the Study Group on the Objectives of Financial Statements, which after two years deliberations produced the Trueblood Report (1975).

The opening paragraphs of the report summary (p. 61) states that:

'In the development of objectives of financial statements, the Study Group has attempted to identify and evaluate the desirable goals of the financial accounting process.

Accounting is not an end in itself. As an information system, the justification for accounting can be found only in how well accounting information serves those who use it. 'Thus, the Study Group agrees with the conclusion drawn by many others that:

(1) 'The basic objective of financial statements is to provide information useful for making economic decisions.'

   This the report sees as the prime objective and then goes on to list the following additional objectives (pp. 61–66).

(2) '... to serve primarily those users who have limited authority, ability, or resources to obtain information and who rely on financial statements as their principal source of information about an enterprise's economic activities.'

(3) '... to provide information useful to investors and creditors for predicting, comparing and evaluating potential cash flows to them in terms of amount, timing, and related uncertainty.'

(4) '... to provide users with information for predicting, comparing, and evaluating enterprise earning power.'

(5) '... to supply information useful in judging management's ability to utilise enterprise resources effectively in achieving the primary enterprise goal.'

(6) '... to provide factual and interpretive information about transactions and other events which is useful for predicting, comparing and evaluating enterprise earning power. Basic underlying assumptions with respect to matters subject to interpretation, evaluation, prediction, or estimation should be disclosed.'

(7) '... to provide a statement of financial position useful for predicting, comparing, and evaluating enterprise earning power. This statement should provide information concerning enterprise transactions and other events that are part of incomplete earning cycles. Current values should also be reported when they differ significantly from historical cost. Assets and liabilities should be grouped or segregated by the relative uncertainty of the amount and timing of prospective realisation or liquidation.'

(8) '... to provide a statement of periodic earnings useful for

predicting, comparing, and evaluating enterprise earning power. The net result of completed earnings cycles and enterprise activities resulting in recognisable progress toward completion of incomplete cycles should be reported. Changes in the values reflected in successive statements of financial position should also be reported, but separately, since they differ in terms of their certainty of realisation.'

(9) '. . . to provide a statement of financial activities useful for predicting, comparing, and evaluating enterprise earning power. This statement should report mainly on factual aspects of enterprise transactions having or expected to have significant cash consequences. This statement should report data that requires minimal judgement and interpretation by the preparer.'

(10) '. . . to provide information useful for the predictive process. Financial forecasts should be provided when they will enhance the reliability of users' predictions.'

(11) '. . . for governmental and not-for-profit organisations an objective is to provide information useful for evaluating the effectiveness of the management of resources in achieving the organizations goals. Performance measures should be quantified in terms of identified goals.'

(12) '. . . to report on those activities of the enterprise affecting society which can be determined and described or measured and which are important to the role of the enterprise in its social environment.'

Finally the Study Group concludes:

'. . . the objectives developed in this report can be looked upon as attainable in stages within a reasonable time. Selecting the appropriate course of action for gaining acceptance of these objectives is not within the purview of the Study Group. However, the Study Group urges that its conclusions be considered as an initial step in developing objectives important for the ongoing refinement and improvement of accounting standards and practices.'

We have set out the objectives in full in order to show the comprehensive nature of the Report. This Report supports the thesis adopted in this book that prediction is an integral part of the decision making process. A report of this nature is bound to bring in its wake a lot of discussion and criticism and the Study Group themselves expressed the desire that this should be so. Sorter & Gans (1974) have argued that the Report "can have profound implications for the development of accounting standards and the resolution of the accounting problem."

They believe that accounting standards will no longer be laid down by fiat, but that new standards will be established by a process of logic and reasoning. However, in view of the reactions to earlier studies, the reactions to the Trueblood Report of the majority of commentators were reasonably predictable. These reactions may be summed up in the criticism that 'the report is disappointing because it fails to show how improved accounting standards and practices will flow logically from the objectives established.' (Stamp, 1973).

The Report must be judged in terms of the brief given to the Study Group by the AICPA (1973). This was to refine the objectives of financial statements and to consider the following questions:

Who needs financial statements?
What information do they need?
How much of the needed information can be provided by the accounting framework?
What framework is required to provide the needed information?

Clearly the objectives which the report provides are intended to answer these questions. The Study Group promised (pp. 10–11) that the actual implementation of these objectives will appear in Volume II of the Report, which is not yet published.

Characteristics of corporate reports

The Trueblood Report sets out characteristics which information contained in corporate reports should possess. These characteristics are more comprehensively dealt with in *the Corporate Report* (1975) which states that reports should be: (a) Relevant (b) Understandable (c) Reliable (d) Complete (e) Objective (f) Timely (g) Comparable.

(a) 'Relevance is the characteristic which embodies the fundamental notion that corporate reports should seek to satisfy, as far as possible, users' information needs.'

(b) 'Understandability does not necessarily mean simplicity, or that information must be presented in elementary terms, for that may not be consistent with the proper description of complex economic activities. It does mean that judgement needs to be applied in holding the balance between the need to ensure that all material matters are disclosed and the need to avoid confusing users by the provision of too much detail.'

(c) 'The information presented should be reliable in that users should be able to assess what degree of confidence may be reposed in it. The credibility of the information contained in corporate reports is enhanced if it is independently verified although in certain circumstances it may be useful for an entity to supply information which is not verifiable in this way.'

(d) 'The information presented should be complete in that it provides users, as far as possible, with a rounded picture of the economic activities of the reporting entity. Since this is likely to be complex it follows that corporate reports as we define them are likely to be complex rather than simple documents.'

(e) 'The information presented should be objective or unbiased in that it should meet all proper user needs and neutral in that the perception of the measurer should not be biased towards the interest of any one user group. This implies the need for reporting standards which are themselves neutral as between competing interests.'

(f) 'The information presented should be timely in the sense that the date of its publication should be reasonably soon after the end of the period to which it relates.'

(g) 'The information should be expressed in terms which enable the user to compare the entity's results over time and with other similar entities.'

The Corporate Report (p. 30) considered the question of size of companies and concluded that their recommendations for providing new information should not apply equally to all. The smaller entities should be allowed a lesser degree of disclosure for three reasons. First, the economic and social impact of the entity will normally be generally smaller, the smaller its size. Secondly, the proprietors or managers of small entities tend to be more easily accessible to employees, customers and the public than is the case with larger entities. Thirdly, there is the practical consideration that the time and money cost to small entities of disclosing new information is disproportionate and very likely to outweigh the possible benefits to report users.

The decision model approach

The approach we have discussed so far in this chapter assumes that financial statements are prepared for a set of general users with multiple objectives. The objectives then focus on providing relevant information necessary for the making of decisions by people or organizations outside the reporting entity. A second approach is to set as an objective the provision of information relevant to specific user decision models. This approach is based on the predictive-ability criterion of accounting data. Since the validity of predictions depends upon their subsequent confirmation by events, the determination of the predictive-ability of an accounting measure is inherently an empirical question

(Carsberg, Hope & Scapens, 1974). If we assume that shareholders wish to maximize the present value of future cash flows, the appropriate measure for financial reporting purposes is that which has the best predictive-ability of future cash flows to shareholders. Using the scientific method discussed in Part 1, financial reporting models may be formulated for predicting future dividends. These are based on records of past transactions and used various combinations of measurements for example, historical income, price-level-adjusted income, income based on replacement cost calculations. These models would be tested, and if a particular model led to better shareholders' decisions, that is a more efficient allocation of investment funds evidenced by superior returns, the measurement upon which the model is based should be adopted for financial reporting purposes (Arnold & Hope, 1975).

Financial reporting and the scientific method

In the past two decades, the application of the scientific method to the solution of managerial problems has had widespread implications for the management accountant. As regards financial reporting, however, the scientific method has had less of an impact. In this respect, two significant points may be made:

(1) In terms of its ultimate objectives and standards, financial accounting is as vigorous as any other discipline.
(2) In terms of its ability to develop and apply empirically verified theories, it is far from being a vigorous subject, although it is striving in this direction.

It is evident from the literature of accounting that there is agreement on one important issue, that is, that the current state of financial reporting is unsatisfactory. But theories of financial reporting which are generally acceptable have not yet been developed to provide a framework for improving accounting practices. Both the general user and the decision model approaches to financial accounting theory construction face complex problems. The general user approach has failed so far to produce rules from broad objectives which would be acceptable in practice. The decision model approach seeks to establish such rules from the results of empirical analysis.

From our discussion in Part 1 of the applicability of the scientific method to accounting, it is evident that empiricism is a desirable feature in the formulation of theories. The absence of this feature renders the formulation of a theory entirely subjective and allows the acceptance of arguable premises. The problems which are present as regards the formulation of theories of financial reporting founded in empiricism stem not only from the difficulty of identifying the decision models of external users of financial reports, but also from the difficulty of measuring the various components of these models. Many of these components are capable of being measured in different ways, and uncertainty exists as to the ability of different measures meeting users' needs. As we shall see in chapter 3, there are at least three different concepts of income having quite different measurements. Hence, there remains considerable controversy about the usefulness of different measurements in given situations. Owing to these difficulties, Sterling (1972), an advocate of the decision model approach states:

> 'Although many of my critics agree in principle with the decision model approach, they throw up their hands in despair at the prospects of trying to apply it.'

As a consequence, the task of developing normative theories of financial reporting which are based on empiricism, and are not subjective, is a very difficult one. Nevertheless, a normative theory often provides a useful means of examining a problem, especially when knowledge about its underlying environment is limited and empirical tests are not feasible. Under such conditions, moreover, a normative theory provides a useful starting point for the development of what may subsequently prove to be a testable hypothesis.

Ultimately, research in the financial reporting area should reduce existing controversies. For the moment, it is necessary to make assumptions when discussing the relevance of a particular accounting measurement. The research which has been undertaken so far into financial reporting problems is inadequate. Rarely does it develop enough evidence to warrant making useful and significant generalizations. One reason is obviously the limited resources which have been devoted to accounting research. According to Anthony (1966), 'More is probably spent for research on a single weapon than has been spent from 1492 to date for research on accounting systems. Although we do the best we can with what we have, I think it unlikely that we will be even reasonably well satisfied with the adequacy of our work unless it is expanded many fold.'

Summary

The interest in financial accounting theory has arisen from a growing dissatisfaction with the state of financial reporting practices, especially the lack of comparability between the financial reports of different companies. One obstacle to the development of a theory of financial reporting has been the lack of knowledge of users' decision models. There has been much controversy on this point. In the short-term, one solution to this problem is to expand the flow of data to users so that they may use it as input into their own decision models. Suggestions for expanding the flow of data in this way are discussed in Section 4.

References

1. Accounting Standards Steering Committee, *The Corporate Report*, pp. 28–29, London, 1975.

2. American Institute of Certified Public Accountants Study Group on the Objectives of Financial Statements, *Objectives of Financial Statements*, New York, 1973.

3. Anthony, R. N., *Research in Accounting Measurement*, p. 266, Yaedicke, R. K., Ijiri, Y. & Nielsen, O., (eds), American Accounting Association, 1966.

3a. Arnold, J. & Hope, A., Reporting Business Performance, *Accounting and Business Research*, Vol. 18, Spring 1975.

4. Carsberg, B., Hope, A. & Scapens, R. W., The Objectives of Published Accounting Reports, *Accounting and Business Research*, Summer, 1974.

5. Sorter, G. H. & Gans, M. A., Opportunities and Implications of the Report on Objectives of Financial Statements, *Journal of Accounting Research*, Supplement to Vol. 12, 1974.

6. Stamp, E., The Trueblood Report: A Curate's Egg?, *Canadian Chartered Accountant*, December, 1973.

7. Sterling, R. R., Decision-Oriented Financial Accounting, *Accounting and Business Research*, Summer, 1972.

Value and Income Measurement

3

Capital, Value, Income

We stated in the previous chapter that the objectives of financial reporting to investors should be found in the decisions which investors have to make about their investment in companies. Hence, we argued, financial reporting should be concerned with the provision of such information as is required for making those decisions. We assumed, also, that investors were principally concerned with the worth of their investments in two senses. Firstly, they are concerned with maintaining and increasing the value of their capital. Secondly, they are concerned with maintaining and increasing the income which is derived from that capital. Financial reporting ought to be concerned, therefore, with the valuation of shareholders' capital and income. In accordance with the stewardship concept of financial reporting, feedback information is required in order that investors may ascertain the present value of share capital and income. The decision-making concept of financial reporting asserts that financial reports should contain information which is useful in assisting investors to predict future changes in capital and income.

Three concepts are involved in financial reporting—capital, value and income. Together they provide the focus for this Part. The purpose of this chapter is to introduce and explain the nature of these three concepts.

Capital

To the economist, the term 'capital' relates to those assets which are used in the production of goods and services. The capital of the firm is represented by the firm's inventory of assets, and investment by the firm occurs when that inventory is increased. From the point of view of society, the term 'capital' is restricted similarly to those assets which produce goods and services. Capital includes, therefore, physical assets in the form of buildings, plant and machinery, housing, hospital, schools as well as intangible assets such as technology, human skills (human capital) etc.

In accounting theory, a person's capital is increased by that portion of his periodic income which he has not consumed. Financial accounting procedure effects this transfer by crediting the net income to the capital account, and if his level of consumption, or drawings, is less than that income, the capital is increased by the difference. In the case of companies, dividends are analogous to drawings, and retained income is added to the total of the shareholders' equity. One of the important implications of income measurement in the case of companies lies in calculating what may safely be distributed as dividends.

Early writers on book-keeping recommended, as a first step in the record-keeping process, the preparation of an inventory or statement of capital showing all the personal and real property, as well as debts due and owing on the first day of business. Paciolo in 1494 advised the businessman to prepare his inventory in the following way:

> 'First of all, he must write on a sheet of paper or in a separate book all his worldly belongings, that is, his personal or real property. He should always begin with the things that are more valuable and easier to lose ... He must then record all other things in proper order in the Inventory' (Gene Brown & Johnson, 1963).

It is evident that at this stage of development, accounting made no distinction between personal capital and business capital. In the course of subsequent developments, however, a distinction emerged between total wealth and wealth committed to business activities. Whereas in Paciolo's time, capital was taken to mean the entire amount of what was owned, the capital account became ultimately a device which described and quantified that portion of private wealth invested in a business enterprise.

The development of the entity theory of accounting, as distinct from the proprietory theory, which culminated in the appearance of the Joint Stock company, gave expression to two important notions. First, as we saw in Part 2, an enterprise could be separated from its owner by a legal fiction and used by him as a vehicle for conducting business. Second, the fictional life granted to the enterprise by accounting practice, and additionally in the case of corporations by law was to serve limited purposes. The capital account was to remain the umbilical cord linking the enterprise to its owner or owners. In line with this view, the enterprise continued to be regarded as an asset and this view has important implications for the valuation of capital and income.

From the foregoing, it is evident that there are some fundamental differences between economists and accountants in the manner in which the notion of capital is conceptualized. As Littleton (1961) points out, the Balance Sheet presentation of 'capital' emphasizes its legal rather than its economic aspect, for capital is shown as a liability, whereas in economics, capital refers to assets. The assets held by a business and actively employed by it are usually greater in value than the so-called 'capital'. In the light of modern interests, we may say that the terminology of financial reports in this respect is misleading. However, supposing that the total assets employed by an enterprise were to be re-defined as its 'capital', there remains a number of problems:

(a) the valuation of business capital;
(b) the valuation of investors' financial interests, that is, personal capital;
(c) the methods selected for these valuations;
(d) the manner in which these valuations are to be communicated.

From our previous discussion of the objectives of financial reporting, we may say that investors are interested primarily in the valuation of their shareholding and this valuation is dependent on the valuation of business capital.

Value

The concept of value and the problems attached to the process of valuation feature extensively in the literature of accounting and economic theory. Value is a central concept in decisions concerning the allocation and use of economic resources, and has been placed at the centre of a framework of ideas designed to base such decisions on methods which will produce an optimal allocation and use of economic resources. Value, therefore, is not simply an abstract theoretical concept designed to give meaning to the set of notions which it attempts to define: it is very much related to the practical need to evaluate alternative ways of allocating and using economic resources so that the best or optimal one is chosen. It is, therefore, a very important tool of analysis in economic theory.

Value and its measurement is also a central problem in accounting, for if we accept—and we have argued this point from the outset—that accounting is concerned with providing information for decision-making, then much of that information will be in the form of valuations. The measurement of value poses enormous problems, and the definition of these problems must be found before we may proceed to the process of measurement.

What is 'value'?

Value relates to the benefits to be derived from objects, abilities or ideas. It is often very difficult, however, to find a satisfactory measure of such future benefits. To the economist, for example, value may be defined very simply as the utility, that is, the satisfaction of an economic resource to the person contemplating or enjoying its use. A concept of value based on utility poses problems in that things of great use or utility do not necessarily have value in the conventional monetary sense in which the term value is commonly employed. Indeed, value is a term popularly used to indicate the worth of an economic resource, and that worth is established as a money equivalent. One has to have recourse, therefore, to using a monetary surrogate to give significance to a concept which is really founded in utility. As a result, a concept which is essentially a subjective one, that is to say, refers to the usefulness of an economic resource to an individual, has to be expressed by another concept—money—which has a different purpose.

A conflict is created, therefore, between value and price, because price is usefulness for the purpose of exchange, whereas value is concerned with keeping an object and using it. If value is expressed as price, therefore, the measurement of value involves the comparison of the utility which others attach to an object and the strength of this utility is measured in their desire to exchange one commodity which they hold, that is money, for the other commodity whose utility is considered greater. Generally, therefore, value is indicated by a measurement which results from the process of exchange, whether assets or asset services are exchanged.

Thus, we may say that the concept of value is attached to the description of economic resources, and if we are to ask the question what is the value of any particular economic resource, we should probably say that it is its worth. Worth and value are equated in people's minds because they prefer to measure value on the possibility of an exchange between the utility which is enjoyed from an economic resource as against that which would be derived from money. It is clear, therefore, from this discussion that value is an absolutely basic element in decision-making about the allocation and use of every kind of economic resource.

Value and exchange

Accounting is concerned with the process of exchange in many ways. Financial accounting, as we have noted, is concerned with recording the result of transactions. The result of the transactions for an accounting period form the substantial basis for calculating the accounting profit, which is one of the fundamental purposes of financial reporting.

In a larger sense, the concept of value is central to the process of exchange if we define exchange as a question of choice. In this sense, the decision to hold an asset and utilize its services rather than to sell is, in effect, the exchange of something now for something in the future. The decision to hold an asset rather than sell it is likewise based on measurements of the value or worth of the two alternatives. It is a question of the comparative efficiency of use. The result or financial effects of such a choice is as important to investors as the results of transactions, and therefore we may say that information about such decisions is also one of the fundamental purposes of financial reporting.

Moreover, the process of exchange is also one of preferring different uses of economic resources. Thus, the decision to hold an asset and enjoy its value, so that in the course of using the asset its value is progressively exhausted, is also a form of exchange between the value which may be realized through a sale and the value which may be realized through its use. It follows equally that the financial effects of such a preference is equally important to investors as the other forms of exchange which we have discussed.

We may say, therefore, that all decisions affecting the allocation and use of economic resources held by business organizations are concerned with the process of exchange, and that in the process the concept of value and the measurement of value are the key elements.

Value and decision-making

If we accept that business organizations should be concerned primarily with profit maximization, we are making a normative statement which bears decisively on the manner in which we interpret the concept of value and the manner in which value should be measured. We mentioned earlier the problem of confusing utility based on a subjective view of value, and value measured in monetary terms which derives from a general consensus of the utility which others as well as oneself attach to the assets in question.

Income measurement implies that the concept of value should be expressed, not in terms of subjective utility, but in terms of money. In effect, as a normative statement related to making decisions regarding the exchange of resources in the different forms which we have stated, the appropriate concept of value used in such decisions should be based on an external or objective assessment of the money worth of the subject of the exchange. This means, for example, that the only valid reason for preferring to use an asset rather than selling it, is that the monetary value which is expected to be derived from its use in the future is greater than the monetary value which could be derived from a present sale. To make the comparison of these two valuations possible, it follows that means must be found to reduce the expected future value derived from continued use to its present money value. This is effected, as we saw in Part 3 by the discounted cash flow method.

If we were to relax the profit maximization hypothesis, and we were to assume that a firm has wider objectives, we do undermine the validity of decisions based on monetary interpretation of value. Thus, if we suggest that the decision to acquire and use an asset is not for profit but for the welfare of employees or the welfare of the community, it follows that it is with the utility of the asset that we are concerned and not its monetary value based on the possibility of its exchange. Hence, we have preferred a benefit to a profit. Of course, in making such a decision, the cost of gaining that benefit is important. We discuss in Part 5 the relevance of cost-benefit analysis to organizational decision-making.

Moreover, if we accept that firms do not necessarily have the objective of maximizing income but of attaining a mix of objectives, subject to making the required level of income to achieve this end, then it follows that decision-making is not based in every instance on the maximization of value in terms of money.

A further problem which arises from the use of value measurements stated in money terms for the purpose of decision-making, stems from the instability of the money measurement through time due to inflation. To achieve a measure of comparability between an exchange of future value as against a present value, some accuracy in the prediction of future money values is required. Equally, variations in the money value of specific assets through time also mitigate against accuracy of measurement. The instability of the money measurement creates difficulties in decision-making about values found in monetary exchanges, as well as reporting to shareholders and investors the consequences of financial decisions. We devote chapter 5 of this Part to a consideration of some of the problems of inflation accounting, as this phenomenon has become known.

Capital valuation

Four different methods of valuation may be applied to the valuation of assets:

(a) historical cost,
(b) present value,
(c) replacement cost,
(d) net realizable value.

(a) *Historical cost*
As we mentioned in Part 2, the conventional method for valuing assets in accounting is the historical cost method. According to this method, the value of an asset to its owner is the exchange transaction price.

(b) *Present value*
The present value is related to the decision to hold an asset and to derive utility from its use. It is defined as the present value of the sum of the future expected net cash flows associated with the use of the asset.

(c) *Replacement cost*
The replacement cost of an asset is the current cost of acquiring another asset which will be put to the same use by the firm. Therefore, current market price data is employed to generate reports on business results.

(d) *Net realizable value*
This represents the amount at which assets are offered for sale less any direct expenses of disposal.

These four methods of valuation result in different income measurements. We discuss the relevance of these different asset valuations and income measurements for decision-making in subsequent chapters.

Income
The concepts of capital and income are closely related. Irving Fisher (1919) expressed their relationship as follows:

> "A stock of wealth existing at a given instant of time is called capital; a flow of benefit from wealth through a given period of time is called income".

An analogy may be found in the relationship between a tree and its fruit—it is the tree which produces the fruit, and it is the fruit which may be consumed. Destroy the tree, and there will be no more fruit: tender the tree with care and feed its roots and it will yield more fruit in the future.

Once the concept of value is introduced into the relationship between capital and income, however, the exact nature of this relationship becomes clearer. According to Irving Fisher (1969):

> 'It would seem ... that income must be derived from capital; and, in a sense, this is true. Income is derived from capital goods, but the value of the income is not derived from the value of capital

goods. On the contrary, the value of the capital is derived from the value of the income . . . . Not until we know how much income an item will probably bring us can we set any valuation on that capital at all. It is true that the wheat crop depends on the land which yields it. But the value of the crop does not depend on the land. On the contrary, the value of the land depends on its crop.'

Economic and accounting theory are both concerned with the relationship between capital and income and in the implications of this relationship. There is agreement between accountants and economists on a number of aspects of the relationship and considerable disagreement as regards the valuation of capital and income. There is agreement, for example, that only income should be available for consumption, and that in arriving at a measure of income, it is necessary to maintain the value of capital intact. Since the ultimate aim of economic activity is the satisfaction of wants, it follows that income is identified as a surplus which is available for consumption. The valuation of income in this analysis is subject to a fairly conservative criterion which Hicks expressed as follows:

'The purpose of income calculations in practical affairs is to give people an indication of the amount which they can consume without impoverishing themselves. (Hicks, 1946).

Income plays a central role in many business and personal decisions since it is based essentially on the notion of spending capacity. As Hicks pointed out, income should be an operational concept providing guidelines to spending. As applied to business corporations, Hicks' definition of income has been interpreted to define the income of a corporation in any one year as the "amount the corporation can distribute to the owners of the equity in the corporation and be as well off at the end of the year as at the beginning" (Alexander, 1962). It is evident, however, that income is used for other purposes as well. For this reason, we should examine the objectives of income measurements before proceeding to the analysis and selection of appropriate concepts.

The objectives of income measurement

Income as a measure of efficiency
Income is used as a measure of efficiency in two senses. First, the overall efficiency of a business is assessed in terms of the income generated. Hence, income tends to provide the basic standard by which

success is measured. There are clearly problems in focusing upon financial efficiency to the detriment of other concepts of business efficiency—such as its effectiveness as a social unit and its efficiency in developing and using new ideas and processes. Nevertheless, those who support the use of income as a measure of business efficiency argue that in the last analysis, all other aspects of efficiency converge on income. Second, shareholders assess the efficiency of their investments by reference to reported income. Hence, the allocation of investment funds, the selection of portfolios and the operations of the financial system depend upon income as a standard by which decisions are taken.

Income as a guide to future investment

As we saw in Part 3, the selection of investment projects is made on the basis of estimates of future cash flows. These estimates are self-fulfilling to the extent that risk and uncertainty have been sufficiently discounted in the decision-making process. In a more general way, however, current income acts to influence expectations about the future. This is particularly so as regards investors who have to rely on financial reports and whose willingness to hold and to subscribe for further shares will be affected by reported income.

Income as an indicator of managerial effectiveness

Management is particulary sensitive about the income which is reported to shareholders since its effectiveness both as decision-makers and as stewards of resources is judged by reference to reported income. It is in this respect that auditors play a key role in ensuring that the statements placed before shareholders reflect a 'true and fair' view of the financial results. What is 'true and fair' may be a contentious problem among accountants. Nevertheless, what is evidently neither true nor fair rarely avoids comment.

Income as a tax base

The tendency of most governments to require a substantial share of corporate income in the form of taxation means that the manner in which corporate tax is assessed is critically important to shareholders and management. Although taxation legislation does not define 'income', it does specify what is taxable and what is deductible in arriving at a measure of taxable of income. Much litigation in this area has revolved around the meaning of words, but the taxation authorities accept accounting income as the base from which to work out taxable income.

Income as a guide to creditworthiness
A firm's ability to obtain credit finance depends on its financial status and its current and future income prospects. For this reason, credit institutions and banks require assurances of a firm's ability to repay loans out of future income and look upon current income levels as a guide in this respect.

Income as a guide to socio-economic decisions
A wide range of decisions take into account the levels of corporate income. Thus, price increases tend increasingly to be justified in terms of income levels and wage bargaining procedures usually involve appeals by both sides to their effects on corporate income. Government economic policies are guided by levels of corporate income as one of the key social indicators.

Income as a guide to dividend policy
The distinction between capital and income is central to the problem of deciding how much may be distributed to shareholders as dividends. A series of important cases have been concerned with the concept of capital maintenance, and rules have been established for the measurement of distributable income with a view to protecting the interests of creditors. Thus, there is a rule which provides that losses in the value of current assets should be made good, whereas in arriving at the measure of distributable income, there is no need to make good losses in the value of fixed assets.

Nowadays, however, dividend policy is much more directed towards establishing the proportion of current income which should be retained and the proportion which should be distributed. This is because companies expect to finance their investment needs from retained income.

Criteria for the selection of income measurements
We noted earlier that different methods of valuations may be applied to the valuation of assets. The different income measurements which result from these methods of valuation are:

(a) the traditional accounting concept of income based on historical revenues and costs;

(b) the economic concept of income based on the present value of capital measured between two intervals of time (see chapter 4);

(c) the replacement cost concept of income which is based on current replacement costs and revenues (see chapter 6);

(d) realizable income which is based on selling prices (see chapter 6).

Before alternative income measurement may be appraised, there has to be some agreement on the criteria by which their acceptability is to be judged. We noted in chapter 2 that the Corporate Report concluded that relevance was the most important characteristic for judging the acceptability of accounting reports. We may likewise accept this criterion for income measurement purposes. All the other criteria which make a method of measurement acceptable for practical purposes may be regarded as being included in the second criterion, namely, feasibility. These include objectivity, low cost of implementation, ease of understanding by those users for whom intended. If a measurement fails to meet these criteria, it has to be rejected. Unfortunately, these criteria do not result in a simple set of accept/reject decision rules for the various income measurements mentioned above. To some extent, each measure meets both major criteria postulated—relevance and feasibility—but each gives a different mix of qualities. For example, accounting income provides a high degree of feasibility but little relevance, whereas economic income has a high degree of relevance but little feasibility. Our search will be, therefore, for a measure of income which will provide the best mix of these qualities.

Summary

The capital of a firm is represented by its inventory of assets, and investment occurs when that inventory is increased. The valuation of a shareholder's capital is dependent on the valuation of business capital.

Value relates to benefits to be derived from assets, abilities or ideas. The problem which accountants face is that of measuring such benefits, for they have their foundation in the concept of utility which is subjective. Accountants use a monetary surrogate to give significance to the concept of value. Four methods of valuing capital discussed in the literature of accounting are: historical cost, present value, replacement cost and net realizable value.

Income is closely related to the concept of capital. Indeed, it is the value of income which determines the value of capital. For example, the value of land depends on the income which the land is capable of yielding.

The concept of income is of central importance to financial reporting for a number of reasons. First, it provides a key to understanding the manner in which capital should be valued. Second, it has as objectives the provision of guidelines for a range of important decisions, for example, dividend policy, investment decisions and the determination of tax liability. Third, it provides a framework for assessing business efficiency and managerial effectiveness.

Four concepts of income arise from the use of the four methods of measurement mentioned in this chapter—traditional accounting income, economic income, replacement cost income and realizable income. Two criteria considered appropriate for deciding which income concept to use are—relevance and feasibility. Unfortunately, these criteria do not provide a base for a simple accept/reject decision. Each concept of income will satisfy both criteria to some extent though each will give a different mix of qualities.

References

1. Alexander, S. S. revised Solomons, D. Income Measurement in a Dynamic Economy, in *Studies in Accounting Theory*, p. 139, Baxter, W. T. & Davidson, S. (eds) Sweet and Maxwell, London, 1962.

2. Fisher, I., *Elementary Principles of Economics* p. 38, (New York, 1919).

3. Fisher, I., Income and Capital, in *Readings in the Concept and Measurement of Income*, p. 40, Parker, R. H. & Harcourt, G. C. (eds), Cambridge University Press, 1969.

4. Gene Brown, R. & Johnston, K. S., *Paciolo on Accounting*, p. 27, McGraw-Hill, New York, 1963.

5. Hicks, J. R., *Value and Capital* 2nd edn, p. 172, Oxford University Press, 1946.

6. Littleton, A. C. *Essays on Accounting*, p. 244, University of Illinois Press, 1961.

4
Accounting and Economic Concepts of Income and Value

Accounting concepts

Accounting concepts of income and value have been influenced mainly by two conventions—the cost and the realization convention. These conventions have received much criticism in recent years because they restrict the usefulness of financial accounting reports for decision-making purposes.

The effects of the cost convention

The basis of valuation in financial accounting is historical cost. This convention clearly conflicts with the going concern convention of valuation when the value of money itself is changing. In effect, historical cost income is based on a venture rather than a going-concern view of the firm.

Under the venture concept, each asset purchased is regarded as a separate venture, so that income is determined for each venture. Thus, net income is measured by setting off against revenues the cost of the assets ventured in earning those revenues. The replacement of those assets is treated as a distinct second venture, for which funds should be raised independently.

By contrast, the going-concern concept which is supported by most businessmen and economists holds that the business enterprise should be considered as a unified continuing concern rather than a series of separate individual ventures.

The historical cost method of valuation seriously distorts the measurement of income, when the value of money is changing. This distortion results from the difference between the historical cost and the current cost which, as we shall see later, is a function of the time gap between the acquisition and the utilization of assets committed to earning periodic revenues. For items such as wages and other current expenses, this difference may be very small, but for such assets as inventories and fixed assets, there may be a substantial difference between the acquisition cost and the current cost when those assets are charged against revenue under the matching rule. Under conditions of rising prices, the historical cost may bear no resemblance to the current cost of assets, with the result that income is overstated. Conservative asset values on the Balance Sheet are contrasted by over-optimistic income measurements in the Income Statement.

The main advantage which is claimed for historical cost valuation is that it is verifiable. The stewardship approach to financial reporting theory is the major factor which supports this method of valuation. It may be argued, however, that if it is objectivity which the accountant is seeking, he should restrict himself purely to counting cash, since this asset is virtually the only one in respect of which complete objectivity is possible. As soon as the accountant moves away from cash, he is dealing with subjective factors. For example, there are many alternative measures available for valuing inventories, calculating depreciation, allocating overheads and providing for bad debts. Consequently, a 'true' measure of objectivity under historical cost valuation is not possible. Moreover, the historical cost method of valuation creates a particular 'problem in periods of inflation in that money units of different values are brought together in the accounting process as though they were of the same value.

The effects of the realization convention

In accordance with the realization convention, the accountant does not recognize changes in value until they have crystallized following a transaction. Until a right enforceable at law comes into existence, gains in book values are ignored for the purpose of income measurement.

It has been suggested that there are two principal reasons which favour the practice of measuring income on realization rather than on accrual. The first is that a sale affords an objective measure of a change in value, and the second is that "the sale is generally considered to be the most decisive and significant event in the chain of transactions and conditions making up the stream of business activity" (Paton, 1962).

By focusing on realized gains and ignoring unrealized gains, the realization convention can lead to absurd results.

Example

Two investors each have £1000 to invest. They both invest £1000 in the shares of Texton Ltd. The shares of Texton Ltd double in value by the end of the accounting period. On the last day of the accounting period, the first investor sells his shares for £2000 and places this sum in the Homestead Building Society. Hence, one investor has £2000 in the building society and the other holds shares in Texton valued at £2000. They are both equally well-off, yet under the realization convention, the investor who has sold his shares is seen as having realized income of £1000, whereas the investor who has held on to his shares is shown as having no income from this source.

Economic concepts

The process of valuation is central to all aspects of decision-making. As we saw in Part 3, capital budgeting decisions require forecasts to be made about the present value of streams of future net cash receipts associated with investment projects. Similarly, investors may also be regarded as exchanging current assets, namely cash or cash equivalents, for a stream of future dividends in the form of cash dividends or increments in the value of their shares.

In this analysis, capital is valued on the basis of discounted future net receipts. Therefore, it is directly relevant to the information needs of shareholders and investors. The value of the firm to the shareholder is computed in such a way as to facilitate the investment decision, which is to seek that investment which will yield the highest value.

In economics, the value of capital is derived from the value of income. The economic concept of income relies on Hick's definition of income as "the amount which a man can consume during a period and still remain as well off at the end of the period as he was at the beginning." (Hicks, 1946) This concept of income was adopted by Alexander to define the income of a company as the amount the company can distribute to shareholders and be as well off at the end of the year as it was at the beginning (Alexander, 1946).

In contrast with accounting valuations based on money values, economic income is measured in real terms, that is, by eliminating the influence of variations in the value of money. Moreover, it results from changes in the value of assets rather than from the matching of revenues and expenses. It is, therefore, what Hendriksen (1972) has termed a 'capital maintenance concept of income', since 'well-offness' may be interpreted as maintaining capital intact. It is measured by comparing the value of the company at two points in time in terms of the present value of expected future net receipts at each of those two points.

The economic concept of income treats assets of all kinds as representing future receipts expected to flow from them to the firm. The main measurement problem lies in comparing the capitalized value of these future net receipts expected both at the beginning and at the end of the accounting period, for the difference represents income, that is, what may be consumed under the Hicksian criterion. Hicks himself recognized the problems of measurement involved in his criterion in the following terms:

> 'At the beginning of the week the individual possesses a stock of consumption goods, and expects a stream of receipts which will enable him to acquire in the future other consumption goods, .. Call this Prospect I. At the end of the week he knows that one week out of that prospect will have disappeared; the new prospect which he expects to emerge will have a new first week which is the old second week... Call this Prospect II. Now if Prospect I were available on the first Monday, we may assume that the individual would know whether he preferred I to II at that date; similarly, if Prospect I were available on the second Monday, he would know if he preferred I to II then. But to enquire whether I on the first Monday is preferred to II on the second Monday is a nonsense question; the choice between them could never be actual at all; the terms of comparison are not in pari materia' (Hicks, 1946).

Hicks was making a very crucial point regarding the measurement problem of his criterion, for comparative states of well-offness at Prospect I and Prospect II must be established in order to know how much may be spent. Neither points or prospects are comparable in reality for they exist at different times.

The economic concept of income based on Hicks' criterion is an estimate, since in deciding how much may be spent, Prospect II must be estimated from the standpoint of Prospect I. In view of this problem, two concepts of economic income have evolved. The first concept is called ex-ante income, and compares Prospect II to Prospect I from the time perspective of Prospect I. The second concept is called ex-post income, and compares Prospect II to Prospect I from the time perspective of Prospect II. Neither concept overcomes the fundamental difficulty which Hicks pointed out, that is, that one cannot compare alternatives which are not available together at the same time in making decisions requiring a concept of income. Despite this difficulty, income ex-ante and income ex-post have become established as central concepts in the theory of economic income.

It is important always to remember that both income ex-ante and income ex-post are based on estimates of future expected net receipts both at Prospect I and Prospect II. The valuation of income is inseparable, therefore, from the valuation of assets, since assets are valued in terms of the present value of the sum of future expected net receipts associated with the use by the firm. The valuation of income and capital in economics is based, therefore, on predictions.

Estimation of ex-ante income

The nature of ex-ante income may be seen from the following example.

Example

Seeking to maximize the return on its funds, Excel Ltd plans to invest those funds in the purchase of assets, which at the 1st January, 19X0 are expected to produce the following future net receipts:

Year	Amount
	£
19X0	10,000
19X1	10,000
19X2	10,000
19X3	10,000

This stream of expected future net receipts represent a return on investment of 10%, which may be assumed to be the best return obtainable by Excel Ltd. Accordingly, the present value of those future net receipts discounted at 10% may be calculated as follows:

Year	Expected Net Receipts at end of year	Present Value on 1st January, 19X0
	£	£
19X0	10,000	$10,000/1.10 = 9091$
19X1	10,000	$10,000/(1.10)^2 = 8264$
19X2	10,000	$10,000/(1.10)^3 = 7513$
19X3	10,000	$10,000/(1.10)^4 = \underline{6831}$

Present value of expected future net receipts at

1st January, 19X0   31,699

Since the present value of expected future net receipts associated with the purchase of those assets is £31,699, Excel Ltd would be unwilling to pay more than this sum for those assets. Hence, we may say that economic value of those assets is £31,699 at the 1st January, 19X0.

The present value of the expected future net receipts on the 1st January, 19X1 may be calculated as follows.

	£
Cash received at end of year 19X0	10,000
Present value of future new receipts	
end of year 19X1	9091
end of year 19X2	8264
end of year 19X3	7513
Present value of the assets in terms of actual and	
future expected net receipts on 1st January, 19X1	34,868

These two valuations of the present value of the assets enable us to calculate ex-ante income as follows:

	£
Present value of assets at 1st January, 19X1	34,868
19X0	31,699
Ex-ante Income for the year 19X0	3169

Note that since the income of £3169 represents the expected increase in the value of the assets during the year, given an expected rate of return on investment of 10%, it also represents 10% of the initial value of those assets estimated at £31,699 on 1st January, 19X0.

Estimation of ex-post income

In the foregoing example, the income for the year 19X0 has been calculated on the basis that the expected future net receipts at the end of the year 19X0 remained the same as those at the beginning of the year. Under such conditions, ex-ante and ex-post income would be the same.

If, however, the present value of expected future net receipts at the end of the year 19X0 are different from the present value of those expected receipts at the beginning of the year, we may say that the ex-post income is different from the ex-ante income. The ex-ante income refers, therefore, to the estimated income derived from the time perspective of the beginning of the year, and the ex-post income refers to the estimated income derived from the time perspective at the end of the year.

Example

Let it be assumed that the revised estimates of the present value of future net receipts on the 1st January, 19X1 is as follows: (the estimates at 1st January, 19X0 are in brackets)

Year	Expected Net Receipts at end of year as at 1st January, 19X1		Present Value of expected receipts as at 1st January, 19X1		
	£	£	£	£	£
19X0	10,000	(10,000)	10,000		(9091)
19X1	9000	(10,000)	8182 (9000/1.10)		(8264)
19X2	9000	(10,000)	7438 $(9000/(1.10)^2$		(7513)
19X3	9000	(10,000)	6762 $(9000/(1.10)^3$		(6831)
Present value of expected future net receipts on 1st January, 19X1			32,382		(31,699)

Ex-post income for the year 19X0, based on the revised estimates established on 1st January, 19X1 is as follows:

	£
Estimated present value on 1st January, 19X1	32,382
19X0	31,699
Ex-post income for 19X0	683

The ex-post income for the year 19X0 is made up of the following components:

	£
Ex-ante income	3169
Ex-post adjustment	2486
Ex-post income	683

The subjective nature of economic income

The net present value method of valuation presents measurement problems in a number of ways. Accuracy of measurement depends upon the degree of certainty under which the forecasts of expected future cash flows are made. Ideally, the size of the net future cash flows should be estimated with reasonable accuracy as should the time-profile of these future cash flows. This is because a sum of money in two years' time is worth more than the same sum of money in three years'. The reader will recall that we discussed these problems in chapter 4 of Part 3 when we examined capital budgeting decisions.

The net present value concept also requires that the discount rate selected for reducing the future cash flows to their present value should reflect accurately the time-value of money. If interest rates are going to fluctuate during the time period considered for using the asset, it follows that the correct present value of the asset will be distorted simply because the correct discount rate has not been applied.

Because the future cash flows and discount rate cannot be determined with certainty, Edwards & Bell (1961) call economic income 'subjective income', and dismiss the concept on the grounds that it cannot be satisfactorily applied on an operational basis. They echo, therefore, Hicks' own dissatisfaction with the concept, which we mentioned earlier in this chapter.

We mentioned in Part 2, that because of uncertainty surrounding the valuation of a firm, it is not the accountant's function to value the firm for the shareholder or investor. On the contrary, it is for the investor to establish the firm's value as an investment and to bear the risk implied in such a valuation. The role of the accountant is to furnish information which is useful for this purpose. The usefulness and relevance of the information provided in financial reports lies in its effectiveness with which it allows the investor to formulate valuations with some degree of accuracy. In the face of uncertainty, accuracy can never be guaranteed, but information about past and current performance may be used as a basis of developing projection and estimates of likely future trends. The adequacy of the accountant's presentation of information for this purpose, the clarity and sufficiency of disclosure are the central problem, therefore, facing the accounting profession in this area. The investor should use the information provided to make his own estimates of future net receipts, and taking into account his assessment of the degree of uncertainty involved in those estimates, he should discount those estimated net receipts by an appropriate discount rate to arrive at his valuation of the firm. This valuation will retain, of course, a high degree of subjectivity. For all these reasons, the concept of economic income has little applicability to the problem of financial reporting.

Summary

Conventional accounting concepts of income and value possess a limited usefulness for decision-making, because of the limitations inherent in the conventions of historical cost and realization which govern the measurement of accounting income. Under conditions of inflation, conservative asset values on the Balance Sheet contrast with over-optimistic income measurement in the Income Statement. Changes in value are not reported as they occur. Changing money values also undermine the stability of the unit of measurement in accounting.

Under conditions of certainty, economic income provides an ideal concept for financial reporting purposes. The value of the firm's future net receipts may be capitalized, thereby providing the investor with a basis for decision-making.

The presence of uncertainty, which is the general rule, precludes the use of economic income because of its essentially subjective nature. Future cash-flows and discount rates cannot be estimated with certainty. For this reason, the accountant does not attempt to value the firm. Instead, financial reports are concerned with past performance, and the investor is required to make his own valuations from the information made available to him.

Despite these practical limitations, the importance of economic concepts of income and value lies in the emphasis they place on the importance of value and value changes rather than on historic costs. Moreover, they stress the limitations of accounting conventions such as the realization convention for financial reporting purposes, and emphasize the importance of the concept of capital maintenance to income measurement.

References

1. Alexander, S. S., Income Measurement in a Dynamic Economy, in *Studies in Accounting theory*, Baxter, W. T. & Davidson, S. (eds), Sweet and Maxwell, London, 1962.

2. Hendriksen E. S., *Accounting Theory*, Richard Irwin, Homewood, Illinois, 1972.

2a. Edwards, E. O. & Bell, P. W., *The Theory and Measurement of Business Income*, University of California Press, 1961.

3. Paton, W. A., *Accountants Handbook* 3rd edn quoted in Alexander, S. S. Income Measurement in a Dynamic Economy in *Studies in Accounting Theory* Baxter, W. T. & Davidson S. (eds), Sweet and Maxwell, London, 1962.

5
Accounting for Price-level Changes

Accounting measurements are based on a monetary standard which hitherto has been assumed to be stable. However, experience of recent history has proved this assumption to be unrealistic with the result that the measurement of corporate income during periods of changing price levels has become a controversial issue.

Price changes may be seen as having general and specific effects. General price changes reflect increases or decreases in the value of the monetary unit. In this case, all individual prices are assumed to change in the same direction, so that the value of a currency in relation to goods and services is different through time. For example, if £15 can only buy today what £10 would have bought on an earlier date, we may say that the price level has increased, the purchasing power of money has fallen, and the economy is in a period of inflation.

By contrast, specific price changes occur for several reasons. Changes in consumer tastes, technological improvements, speculation by buyers are all reasons found at the root of specific price changes. Thus, increased demand for houses in the face of a limited supply will force up the price of houses, even if the general price level is constant. It is common, however, for people to hedge against inflation by investing in property and this factor may also influence property prices. Hence, we may say that whilst specific price changes may occur independently of changes in the general price level, changes in the price level may induce disproportionate changes in the price level of specific goods.

Adjusting for the effects of price changes may take the following forms:

(a) partial adjustments,
(b) general adjustments,
(c) specific adjustments based on current replacement costs (see chapter 6).

Partial adjustments for price-level changes

The impact of price-level changes is more pronounced on those assets which have a fairly long life in use, and where a time-lag exists

579

between acquisition and the apportionment of acquisition costs to the income earning process. The two major classes of assets in this group are depreciable fixed assets and inventories. Many companies have begun the practice of revaluing fixed assets as a counter to inflation. In the United States, the Last-In-First-Out (LIFO) method of valuing inventories has become increasingly important in recent years. We discuss these adjustments in this section.

(a) *The revaluation of fixed assets*

The growing practice of revaluing fixed assets in the United Kingdom contrasts with the position in the United States, where companies are not permitted to revalue Balance Sheet values but must retain historical cost valuations.

The practice of revaluing assets was recognized by legislation in the United Kingdom in 1948, when the Companies Act of that year stipulated that fixed assets should be shown at cost, or, if it stands in the company's books at a valuation, the amount of the valuation. No guidance was given, however, by the Act as to when a valuation should be made, except in the case of property where a 'substantial difference' between book and market value should be indicated in the Balance Sheet. Surveys carried out by the Institute of Chartered Accountants and by the Sandilands Committee, established by the British Government to consider the problem of inflation accounting, revealed that many companies were departing from the historical cost principle in their financial reports, though revaluations of property were much more common than revaluations of other fixed assets, whilst most companies were retaining the historical cost method of calculating depreciation. The Sandilands Report (1975) concluded that "the piecemeal way in which revaluations have been carried out has created considerable confusion and difficulty. Few companies have revalued all their assets, few revalue their assets on a regular annual basis, and few disclose the exact basis of the revaluation. The result is that present-day Balance Sheets in this country consist of a mixture of entries at historic cost and valuations prepared on different bases."

(b) *The LIFO method of inventory valuation*

According to an American Accounting Association Committee (1964), the ideal situation from the standpoint of the determination of accounting income is that in which the cost of identified assets are matched against the revenues resulting from their sale. This Committee concluded that ideally the measurement of accounting income involves the matching precisely of identified costs of specific units of products with the sales revenues derived therefrom.

As we noted in Part 2 chapter 5, the valuation of inventories requires assumptions to be made about the flow of inventory, that is, the manner in which finished products enter into inventory and are sold from inventory. We concluded that under conditions of inflation, the First-In-First-Out (FIFO) method of inventory valuation had the effect of understating the cost value of goods sold because earlier rather than recent values are utilized in the measurement process. By contrast, the Last-In-First-Out (LIFO) method of inventory valuation assumes that the latest items to go into inventory are the first to come out, so that the items remaining in inventory at the end of the accounting period are assumed to represent earlier items produced or purchased. It has become a very popular method of inventory valuation in the United States, for under conditions of inflation, it permits a more realistic calculation of income by taking into account the most recent cost price.

Though LIFO approximates the replacement cost basis of valuation as regards the input of resources to the income earning process, it does not necessarily correspond with replacement cost valuation. LIFO reflects the latest cost price of the specific commodity, which may or may not be the actual replacement cost. In the case of seasonal buying, for example, the cost of the last purchase may not be equivalent to the current replacement cost. As a result, LIFO eliminates only an indeterminate part of the effects of specific price changes. Indeed, when sales exceed purchases, that is, when inventories are being depleted, the gap between replacement cost and LIFO may become very great. A classic example of this situation arose in the United States during the Korean War, which resulted in inventory reduction on such a scale that Congressional approval was given for Next-In-First-Out inventory valuation as a relief for taxpayers who were on the LIFO basis! (Fremgen, 1962).

A further disadvantage of the LIFO method of inventory valuation is that it leads to distortions in Balance Sheet valuations. This is defended on the grounds that the Income Statement is the more important document since income measurement is the major point of interest among shareholders. According to Moonitz (1953), however, "this leaves unanswered the important query as to how it is possible to have reasonably accurate statements of income accompanied by admittedly inaccurate balance sheets. Where is the difference buried and what is its significance?"

Adjustments for general price-level changes

In 1974, the professional accounting bodies in the United Kingdom recommended that a supplementary statement should be attached to the financial reports of companies showing the conversion of the figures in the financial reports in terms of their current purchasing power (C.P.P.) at the closing day of the accounting period. They recommended that the Retail Price Index (R.P.I.) should be used to effect the conversion of historic cost values into current purchasing power equivalents (S.S.A.P 7, 1974).

C.P.P. adjustments are limited to dealing with changes in the general purchasing power of money which occurs during periods of inflation or deflation. Accordingly, the view is taken that the purpose of price level adjustments is to express each item in the financial report in terms of a common monetary unit, that is, in terms of £s of the same purchasing power. The Retail Price Index is assumed to reflect the general movement in price of all goods and services. Thus, the doubling of the Retail Price Index from 100 to 200 between two points in time would mean that the purchasing power of money had fallen by half during that time interval.

Historical cost accounting is based essentially on the money capital maintenance concept. Such a concept asserts that all funds available to the firm in excess of the original contribution of funds by shareholders make the firm better off. High levels of inflation experienced in recent years has undermined the validity of this assertion. C.P.P. accounting attempts to deal with this problem by adjusting historical cost measurements for the effects of inflation. As a result, the purchasing power held by the firm is maintained. The income which results from C.P.P. adjustments may be defined as those gains arising during the accounting period which may be distributed to shareholders so that the purchasing power of the shareholders' interest in the company is the same at the end of the year as it was at the beginning. However, as we shall see in this chapter, the adjustment of historic cost for the effects of inflation of itself cannot ensure the maintenance of the productive capacity of the assets held by the company. The price level correction alone ignores the fact that capital may be dispersed through changes in individual prices if those relevant to the individual firm rise at a rate slower than the rate of change in the price level. Also the real capital will increase if the relationship is reversed.

Monetary and non-monetary items

For the purpose of C.P.P. accounting it is necessary to distinguish two classes of items—monetary and non-monetary items.

Monetary items may be defined as those fixed by contract or by their nature and are expressed in £s regardless of changes in the price level. They include monetary assets such as cash, debtors and loans, and exist as money or as claims to specified sums of money. Holders of monetary assets suffer a loss in the general purchasing power of their assets during periods of inflation. Thus, if one holds money in the form of a bank deposit and the yearly rate of inflation is 25%, the loss in the purchasing power of that money by the end of the period will be 25%.

Monetary items include monetary liabilities such as creditors, bank overdrafts and long-term loans. As the value of money falls during a period of inflation, it follows that the value of such liabilities in current £s will fall similarly, and this fall represents a purchasing power gain to the debtor. Consequently, those who incur monetary liabilities gain at the expense of creditors during periods of inflation, since they will settle these liabilities with £s possessing less purchasing power than those they have previously received—directly or indirectly at the time the liabilities were incurred.

Non-monetary items are assets and liabilities such as fixed assets, inventories and shareholders' equity which are assumed neither to gain nor to lose in value by reason of inflation (and vice versa in the case of deflation). This is because price changes for these items will tend to compensate for changes in the value of money. For example, if one had inventories on hand at the beginning of the year which remained unsold at the end of the year, there would be no purchasing power loss since one may assume that when sold, the sale price would be adjusted upwards to take account of the fall in the value of money.

For example, assume that £100,000 were spent on the purchase of land on a date when the Retail Price Index stood at 100, and that the Index now stands at 150. The assumption underlying this movement in prices is that £150,000 in today's £s have the same purchasing power as £100,000 when the Retail Price Index stood at 100. Hence, to report on the purchasing power invested in the land, its acquisition cost should be stated as £150,000. This value does not say anything about the present market value of that particular piece of land. Property values may have increased more or less than the general movement in prices indicated by the Retail Price Index. The particular piece of land mentioned in this example may now be worth £300,000 or only £90,000. Hence, the figure of £150,000 represents only the historic cost of acquisition adjusted for the decrease in the general value of the £.

Nevertheless, the acceptance of the need to adjust accounting measurements for inflation is a recognition of a fundamental proposition in income theory, namely, that provision should be made for maintaining the value of capital intact. Hence, there can be no recognition of income for a period unless it has been established that the purchasing power of the capital employed in a firm is the same at the end of the accounting period as it was in the beginning.

A simple example serves to explain the nature of adjustments which
are required to financial reports based on historical cost measurements
in order to remove the effects of general price level changes.

Example

Bangored Supplies Ltd was formed on 1st January, 19X0, with a
Share Capital of £75,000 which was fully subscribed in cash on
that date. On the same day, equipment was purchased for
£45,000, of which £20,000 was paid immediately, the balance of
£25,000 being payable 2 years hence. The price level index was
100 on the 1st January, 19X0.

Goods were purchased in two instalments prior to actually
commencing business as follows:

1st purchase in the sum of £44,000, when the price level index
was 110

2nd purchase in the sum of £45,000, when the price level index
was 120

All sales were made when the price level index was 130, and
expenses of £16,000 were also incurred at the same index level.
Inventories were valued on the FIFO methods, and the closing
inventory was valued at £29,000. The price level index at the 31st
December, 19X0 was 130.

The Income Statement and Balance Sheet in respect of this year,
prepared on a historical cost basis were as follows:

Balance Sheet as at 31st December, 19X0			
	£	£	£
Share capital		75,000	
Retained income		19,500	
Long term loan		25,000	
		119,500	
Represented by			
Fixed assets		45,000	
Less: Accumulated Depreciation		4500	
		40,500	
Current assets			
Inventories	29,000		
Debtors	19,000		
Cash	39,500		
	87,500		
Less:			
Current liabilities	8500		
Net working capital		79,000	
			119,500

Income Statement for the year ended 31st December, 19X0	£	£
Sales		100,000
Cost of goods sold		60,000
Gross operating income		40,000
Expenses	16,000	
Depreciation (10% of £45,000)	4500	
		20,500
Net operating income		19,500

We are required:

(a) To calculate the purchasing power gain or loss on the monetary items.
(b) To prepare an inflation adjusted Income Statement for the year ended 31st December, 19X0.
(c) To prepare an inflation adjusted Balance Sheet as at 31st December, 19X0 when the price level index was 130.

(a) *Calculation of purchasing power gain or loss on monetary items during the year ended 31st December, 19X0*

	Unadjusted Monetary Items	Conversion Factor	Adjusted Monetary Items
	£		£
Net Current Monetary Items on 1st January, 19X0 (cash invested)	75,000	130/100	97,500
Add: Sales	100,000	130/130	100,000
	175,000		197,500
Less:			
Purchases of equipment	20,000	130/100	26,000
Purchase of goods			
(i) index at 110	44,000	130/110	52,000
(ii) index at 120	45,000	130/120	48,750
Expenses	16,000	130/130	16,000
	125,000		142,750
Net Current Monetary Items on 31st December, 19X0	50,000		54,750
Unadjusted net current monetary items on 31st December, 19X0			50,000
Purchasing power loss for the year ended 31st December, 19X0			4750

(b) *Preparation of inflation adjusted Income Statement for the year ended 31st December, 19X0*

	Unadjusted	Conversion Factor	Adjusted
	£		£
Sales	100,000	130/130	100,000
Cost of goods sold			
At index 110	44,000	130/110	52,000
At index 120	16,000	130/120	17,333
Expenses	16,000	130/130	16,000
Depreciation	4500	130/100	5850
	80,500		91,183
Net income	19,500		8817

(c) *Preparation of inflation adjusted Balance Sheet as at 31st December, 19X0*

	Unadjusted	Conversion Factor	Adjusted
	£		£
Share capital	75,000	130/100	97,500
Retained income	19,500	—	8817
Accumulated purchasing power gain			2750
	94,500		109,067
Represented by			
Fixed assets	45,000	130/100	58,500
Less: Accumulated Depreciation	4500	130/100	5850
	40,500		52,650
Current assets			
Inventories	29,000	130/120	31,417
Debtors	19,000	130/130	19,000
Cash	39,500	130/130	39,500
	87,500		89,917
Less: Current liabilities	33,500	130/130	33,500
Net working capital	54,000		56,417
Total assets	94,500		109,067

Calculation of accumulated purchasing power gain
Gain on unpaid balance of purchase price of equipment

Adjusted balance (£25,000 × 130/100)	32,500
Unadjusted balance	25,000
	7500
Less: Loss as computed on monetary items	4750
Net accumulated purchasing power gain	2750

An appraisal of C.P.P. accounting

C.P.P. accounting restates historical cost in terms of current purchasing power. It is an attempt to remove the major objection to historical cost valuations, which we discussed in the previous chapter, namely that the unit of measurement changes when price levels change. The intention is that this objection should be removed by an adjustment which results in units of the 'same purchasing power' being added together in the measurement process.

As we stated earlier, S.S.A.P. 7 recommended that companies should continue to publish accounts on an historical cost basis, but that in addition, a supplementary statement should be presented showing the effect of converting conventional accounts into £s of current purchasing power. The Sandilands Report ruled out C.P.P. accounting because it did not like the idea of two sets of accounts, nor the use of different measurement units. According to the Sandilands Report, users of financial reports would be confused. This view was expressed as follows:

> "Our description of the application of the C.P.P. method. . . shows that it is complicated, and we believe that many users of accounts are likely to misunderstand the information presented in C.P.P. statements unless it is carefully interpreted by the company. We consider that C.P.P. accounting is conceptually the most difficult method of inflation accounting suggested to us in evidence. The main reason for this is the use of a unit of measurement other than the monetary unit on which to base the published accounts of companies. We believe that it is not widely understood that C.P.P. supplementary statements are drawn up in different units of measurement from the basic accounts to which they relate." (Sandilands Report, 1975 p. 121).

Another objection to C.P.P. accounting is raised by some authorities who believe that there is no such thing as generalized purchasing power (Gynther, 1974). Organizations and people do not see themselves as holding general purchasing power when they hold money; rather, they see themselves as holding specific purchasing power in respect of those relatively few items which they wish to purchase. Hence, the purchasing power of money should be related to those items on which money is intended to be spent. A unit of measurement which relies for its validity on the purchasing power of money assessed by reference to a set of goods and services will not be equally useful to all individuals and entities.

Moreover, the concept of income on which these adjustments are based is not one which maintains the service potential of capital. A general price index, particularly a consumer's price index, is a weighted average of the price change occurring in a wide variety of goods and services available in the economy. Therefore, adjusting financial data for the effects of inflation is not the same as reporting current values. Price-adjusted data still represents costs, or funds, committed to non-monetary items: these costs are merely translated into the equivalent costs in terms of today's £s.

General price indices assume that the movement in the price of all goods correspond with each other. However, only by coincidence will a change in the general price index correspond with the change in the price of any particular good or service during the same period. Indeed, there is no reason why they may not move in opposite directions. For example, the price of colour television sets was falling in the 1960s in the UK at a time when the general price index was rising. Hence, if the general price index has increased, many specific price changes will be running at a lower level than the general index, whilst many others will be running at a higher level, and there may be some specific price decreases. Furthermore, the discrepancies between specific price and general price changes are likely to be even more pronounced when the general price index is based on consumer goods, and the specific price index relates to producer goods, such as those represented by the assets of a typical business enterprise. Thus, a general price index will not be relevant to any business entity which needs to make adjustments to asset valuations in order to maintain the value of its capital in the long-term.

Controversy surrounds the treatment of gains and losses arising on monetary items. General price level accounting includes such gains and losses in the periodic income. Hence, a company's pre-tax income will be dramatically different, according to the nature of its financial structure, before and after these adjustments have been made. Property companies, whose largest Balance Sheet item is often their liabilities to banks, finance houses and other credit institutions, find their adjusted Income Statement showing exceptionally good results. But the 'gains' resulting from these adjustments do not increase sums available for distribution as dividends to shareholders, since they are purely accounting adjustments. They could only be distributed by drawing on existing cash resources or by borrowing. Hence, if the net 'gains' on monetary items are regarded as available for distribution, the users of adjusted financial reports could be seriously misled.

The Sandilands Committee summarized its view of C.P.P. accounting as follows:

"In summary, we do not think the concept of profit adopted by C.P.P. supplementary statements, when appended to historic cost accounts, is useful to shareholders. It fails to show the company's 'operating profit', it is potentially misleading in including net gains on monetary items which exist only in terms of current purchasing power units and not in terms of monetary units, and it shows how far the 'purchasing power' of a shareholder's investment has been maintained in a sense which is not useful to him for any practical purpose. If C.P.P. does not provide useful information for shareholders, from whose point of view it is conceived, it is unlikely to provide useful information for other users of accounts." (Sandilands Report, 1975 pp. 131–132).

Summary

If the value of money is changing, it is clear that the money standard of measurement ceases to be efficient. Financial reports should be adjusted, therefore, for the effects of changes in the value of money for the following reasons:

(a) to provide a more accurate basis for assessing the value of a shareholder's investment in a company;

(b) to enable more meaningful comparisons to be made between the reported results of successive years;

(c) to enable more meaningful inter-company comparisons to be effected.

The unsatisfactory nature of historical cost as a basis for financial reporting is reflected in the fact that companies have been increasingly incorporating partial adjustments for inflation in their reported values. The revaluation of fixed assets by firms in the United Kingdom, and the adoption of LIFO by companies in the United States are examples of this phenomenon.

C.P.P. accounting allows adjusted historical costs to be matched against current revenues. It computes losses arising through holding monetary items during periods of inflation.

C.P.P. accounting has serious limitations. It may be argued, for example, that the concept of generalized purchasing power does not exist; that individuals hold specific purchasing power for the assets they wish to buy. Price level accounting, moreover, does not necessarily maintain the productive capital of the firm: it merely maintains the general purchasing power of the firm. Also, the distribution of monetary 'gains' could seriously affect the firm's liquidity.

References

1. American Accounting Association Report of the Committee on Concepts and Standards Underlying Corporate Financial Statements and Inventory Pricing, Supplementary Statement No. 6, 1964.

2. Fremgen, J. M., Involuntary liquidation of LIFO inventories, *Journal of Accounting*, December, 1962.

3. Gynther, R. S., Why use general purchasing power?, *Accounting and Business Research*, Spring 1974.

4. Moonitz, M., The Case against LIFO, *Journal of Accountancy*, June, 1953.

5. *Report of the Inflation Accounting Committee*, p. 100, HMSO Cmmd paper 6225, 1975.

6. S.S.A.P. No. 7, *Accounting for Changes in the Purchasing Power of Money* London, 1974.

6
Current Value Accounting

Introduction

The debate concerning the appropriateness of adjustments for price level changes has highlighted the problems associated with historic cost measures. As we noted in chapter 5, neither partial nor general adjustments to historic cost measures deals satisfactorily with the problem of price level changes.

Current value accounting is a radical alternative to the proposals we discussed in chapter 5. It represents an attempt to combine desirable aspects of economic theory with the conventional accounting method based on historic costs. Current value income models use current market prices which are incorporated in the traditional accounting format.

For reporting purposes, concepts of income are required which satisfy the criteria of relevance and feasibility. We noted in chapter 3 (page 567) that concepts of income which were relevant were not necessarily feasible and vice versa. Whereas economic income is more relevant to decision-making than accounting income, it does not satisfy the criteria of feasibility. By contrast, accounting income fails to satisfy the criteria of relevance, though it does meet the criteria of feasibility.

Current value accounting attempts to bridge the gap between accounting and economic income by providing measurements which are both relevant and feasible. Current values are applied to the measurement of income and capital for the purpose of financial reporting, thereby providing more relevant information to investors than the information based on historical cost records found in the financial accounting system. Objectivity is maintained in an accounting sense by retaining the realization convention for timing value changes.

The result is that the financial accounting system recording historical cost data retains its usefulness for establishing the legal rights and obligations created as a result of transactions, whereas the financial reports which are directed at given investors information concerning the value of income and capital are based on the current value of the items appearing in those reports.

Current Value Accounting takes two forms:

(a) Replacement Cost Accounting—which is based on the current acquisition value of assets, so that in effect, they are valued at their current entry price.

(b) Realizable Value Accounting—which is based on the current realizable value of assets, that is, at their current exit price.

Replacement cost accounting

The basic concept underlying replacement cost accounting is that the firm is a going-concern, which is continuously replacing its assets, so that the cost of consuming these assets in the generation of income should be equivalent to the cost of replacing them. It is addressed to the problem of capital maintenance from the viewpoint of the firm, and involves:

(a) calculating current operating income by matching current revenues with the current cost of resources exhausted in earning those revenues;

(b) calculating holding gains and losses;

(c) presenting the Balance Sheet in current value terms.

Components of replacement cost income (RCI)

According to Edwards & Bell (1961), the purpose of accounting income is:

(a) To provide useful information for evaluating past business decisions.

(b) To provide data which will allow a sound and equitable basis for the assessment of tax.

They assert that two components of income which are relevant to their analysis of the function of accounting are not identified in the conventional statement of accounting income, namely:

(a) Current operating income, which results from operating activities and which may be calculated by matching current revenues with the current cost of resources exhausted in these activities.

(b) Holding gains, which result from holding activities. These gains are also referred to as cost savings.

The importance of the distinction between operating and holding gains has received considerable attention from many quarters. One committee of the American Accounting Association stated that:

"Typically revenue may be related to at least two efforts of management. One of these is the effort to operate effectively in carrying out the production/and or service functions of the business. The other is the effort to occupy an advantageous position in the market.... This would help interested parties to evaluate the effectiveness of management insofar as its buying efforts were concerned; but more importantly, it would remove from the data pertaining directly to operations those amounts realised simply as a result of market fluctuations." (A.A.A. Committee, 1965).

In contrast to accounting income, replacement cost income recognizes holding gains as well as operating gains. In identifying holding gains as they arise, thereby distinguishing these gains from gains occurring on realization, the pattern of income recognition differs under replacement cost accounting from that associated with conventional accounting income, as may be seen from the following example:

Example

During the year ended 31st December, 19X0, an asset was acquired at a cost of £40. By the 31st December, 19X0 its replacement cost had risen to £60. It was sold during the year ended 31st December, 19X1 for £100, and at the time of sale, its replacement cost was £65.

For the purpose of measuring accounting income, the income arising from the sale of the asset (assuming no depreciation) would accrue in the year ended 31st December, 19X1 and would be calculated as follows:

$$\text{Accounting Income} = \text{Revenue} - \text{historical cost}$$
$$= £100 - £40$$
$$= £60$$

For the purpose of measuring replacement cost income, three distinct gains are recognized which occur as follows:

(i) A holding gain in the year ended 31st December, 19X0 measured as the difference between the replacement cost at 31st December, 19X0 and the acquisition cost during the year, that is, £60 − £40 = £20.

(ii) A holding gain in the year ended 31st December, 19X1 measured as the difference between the replacement cost at 31st December, 19X0 and the replacement cost on the date of sale, that is, £65 − £60 = £5.

(iii) An operating gain resulting directly from the activity of selling measured as the difference between the realized sale price and the replacement cost at the date of sale, that is, £100 − £65 = £35.

These differing timings of income recognition may be compared as follows:

Year ended 31st December	19X0	19X1
	£	£
Accounting income	—	60
Replacement Cost Income		
Holding gains	20	5
Current operating gain	—	35

It is clear from this example that the replacement cost income concept provides more detailed information than the accounting income concept for the purpose of evaluating the results of activities. Moreover, replacement cost income indicates whether the sales proceeds are sufficient to cover the cost of the resources sold, that is, whether the activity of selling itself is efficient. Where the goods sold are manufactured by the firm, current operating income indicates whether the manufacturing process is profitable, for the input factors of production are valued at their current replacement cost. Hence, from a long-term point of view, it affords a means of evaluating the firm as a going-concern.

Income measurement by historic cost and replacement cost compared

The extent of the differences between these two concepts of income are revealed by a more comprehensive example.

Example

The financial position of Preifat Ltd, as revealed by the Balance Sheet as at 31st December, 19X0 using historical cost measurements, is as follows:

	£		£
Share Capital	1400	Fixed Asset	1000
		Inventory	400
	1400		1400

The fixed asset shown on the Balance Sheet was acquired on the 31st December, 19X0 and has an estimate life of 5 years, with no scrap value.

Data recorded in respect of the year ended 31st December, 19X1 is as follows:

	£
Sales	2000
Purchases at historical cost	700
Closing inventory at historical cost	200
at replacement cost	250
Cost of goods sold at replacement cost	1000

It was also estimated that the replacement cost of the fixed asset had risen to £1200 by the 31st December, 19X1.

On the basis of this information, the accounting income for the year 19X1 may be computed as follows:

Accounting Income for the year ended 31st December, 19X1

	£	£
Sales		2000
Cost of Goods sold:		
Opening inventory	400	
Purchases	700	
	1100	
Closing inventory	200	
		900
		1100
Depreciation (£1000 ÷ 5)		200
Accounting Income		900

By contrast, the calculation of the components of replacement cost income gives a more comprehensive analysis of the nature of operating and holding gains, as follows:

Replacement Cost Income for the year ended 31st December, 19X1

	£	£
Sales		2000
Cost of Goods sold (at replacement cost)		1000
		1000
Depreciation (£1200 ÷ 5)		240
(i) *Current Operating Income*		760
(ii) *Holding gains*		
(a) Realized through use during the year:		
Fixed Assets	40	
Inventory	100	
	140	
(b) Unrealized at the end of the year		
Fixed Assets	160	
Inventory	50	
	210	
Total holding gains		350
Current operating income plus holding gains		1110

Note:

(a) Depreciation is calculated on the replacement cost of the fixed assets (£1200) rather than on the historical acquisition cost (£1000). By this means, the depreciation provision is more realistic in relation to the current cost of resource utilization.

(b) Inventories are charged against sales at their current replacement cost at the time of sale.

(c) Holding gains are of two kinds:

    (i) Realized holding gains which result from the application of replacement cost values to the input of resources to the income generation process. In the example, depreciation charged under replacement cost accounting is £40 greater than that charged under historic cost accounting. Similarly, the cost of goods sold under replacement cost is £100 greater than that charged under historic cost accounting. Both amounts represent holding gains realized by reason of the use or the sale of assets.

    (ii) Unrealized holding gains which result from the increased value of assets held by the firm and remaining unused or unsold at the end of the accounting period. In the example, the unrealized holding gains are calculated as follows:

        (a) Fixed Assets: unallocated value at the end of the accounting period:

under replacement cost: £1200 − 240 =	£960
under historic cost: £1000 − 200 =	800
unrealized holding gain	160

        (b) Inventories: inventories unsold at the end of the accounting period:

under replacement cost:	£250
under historic cost:	200
unrealized holding gain	50

Historic cost and Replacement cost Balance Sheets compared

The effect of applying historic and replacement cost valuations to Balance Sheets is seen in the following Balance Sheet drawn from data given in the example.

As may be observed, the application of replacement cost values attempts to reflect economic reality by maintaining the value of asset

Balance Sheet as at 31st December, 19X1
(assuming that all sales and purchases were paid in cash)

	Historic Cost £	Replacement Cost £
Share Capital	1400	1400
Retained income		
Accounting income	900	
Current operating income		760
Revaluation Reserve		350
	2300	2510
Represented by:		
Fixed Assets	1000	1200
Less: Accumulated depreciation	200	240
	800	960
Current Assets		
Inventories	200	250
Cash	1300	1300
	2300	2510

Note. Cash balance is calculated as follows:

Sales £2000 – Purchases £700 = £1300 cash balance

balances in line with changes in the value of money and changes in the specific value of the assets concerned.

The treatment of holding gains

One of the controversial issues in the debate about replacement cost accounting is whether holding gains constitute income. There is little doubt that current operating income satisfies the accounting convention relating to realization, and at the same time is directed to the maintenance of capital, which is a basic principle in the measurement of economic income.

From a theoretical viewpoint, there is strong support for the argument that holding gains should not be treated as income, that is, they should not be regarded as available for distribution. Assuming that the firm is a going-concern, the holding gain resulting from the increase in the current replacement cost of specific assets should be retained for the purpose of replacing those assets, for one of the objectives of replacement cost accounting is to ensure the maintenance of capital through the replacement of the values exhausted in earning income. The distinction between realized and unrealized holding gains, which is important in this respect may be preserved in the appropriate account, which is the Asset Revaluation Reserve account.

An evaluation of replacement cost accounting

As a method of financial reporting, the objective of replacement cost accounting is to provide a concept of income which will satisfy the criteria of relevance and feasibility which were discussed earlier.

Replacement cost income is more relevant to investors than accounting income for the purpose of decision-making. First, it provides for the maintenance of the service potential of capital by charging against revenue the cost of replacing the assets exhausted in earning revenue. Second, an important distinction is made between operating income and holding gains, thereby allowing investors to appraise the firm as a going-concern. Third, it recognizes changes in the value of assets, since they are related to current market prices. For these reasons, investors are provided with information which is more relevant than accounting income for evaluating the business, and they are placed in a better position to predict the future. By providing more accurate valuations of assets in use, replacement cost accounting is likely to lead to a more efficient allocation of financial resources than that afforded by conventional accounting method. A further argument in favour of replacement cost accounting lies in the diversity of values found in conventional accounting due to the employment of a variety of valuation methods, such as LIFO, FIFO, Average Cost. With replacement cost accounting, however, values are uniformly derived from the current replacement cost of specific assets, so that comparisons are much more meaningful.

As regards the criterion of feasibility, Dickerson (1965) has shown that replacement cost accounting is not too time-consuming and costly for practical implementation. Applying himself to the problem of converting data from historical cost to replacement cost for a small producer of moulded plastic articles, he reported that 95 hours of work were involved in that translation, of which 40 hours were spent on familiarizing himself with the data.

Criticisms are sometimes advanced against replacement cost accounting on the ground that the measurements involved are subjective. There exist, however, Government Indices which relate to fixed assets of various kinds which may be employed for the purpose of calculating the replacement cost of specific fixed assets. The Sandilands Committee recommended that the Government Statistical Service should publish as soon as possible a new series of price indices specific to particular industries for capital expenditure on plant and machinery. Such a series of indices should be designed to provide a 'standard reference basis' for making reasonable approximations of current replacement costs. The derivation of replacement costs for inventories could present problems. However, when the various different methods of valuing inventories at the present time are considered, it appears that replacement cost provides a more objective measure. Another criticism made by Sterling (1970) is that replacement cost measurements imply the substitution of specific asset values for money measurements, thereby abandoning a common unit of measurement.

A major problem arises, however, during periods of rapid technological change. Most authorities argue that since a measure of the profitability of existing operations is required, current replacement costs should be measured in terms of the market prices prevailing for the actual fixed assets which are exhausted in producing income. Some authorities are opposed to this view since it seemingly ignores the effect of technological change. They argue that the replacement cost of new generation assets should be used, because "the primary interest is in the long-run prospects of the firm, and there seems to be no particular reason why these long-run prospects would be indicated by the prospects of the present mode of production, when becoming obsolete". Accordingly, if the firm is using a second generation computer made obsolete by the development of third generation computers, they argue that the current replacement cost should be based on the current market price of third generation rather than second generation computers.

Realizable value accounting

Both historical cost and replacement cost accounting employ entry values, that is, they are based on the acquisition cost of assets. By contrast, realizable value accounting employs exit values, that is, it is based on the realizable price of assets.

The distinction between entry and exit values leads to two different concepts of income—realized and realizable income. Realized income arises only upon sale, so that unsold assets are valued at cost. By contrast, realizable income is based on the current selling price of the assets, thereby indicating the revenue which could be obtained should the assets be sold. As a result, unsold assets are valued not at cost, but at realizable value.

The case for realizable value accounting

The Realizable Value model is based on the concept of opportunity cost, that is, value is expressed in terms of the benefit lost in holding assets in their present form rather than in the next best alternative form. For example, as regards closing inventories, the next best alternative to holding inventories is selling them, so that on an opportunity cost basis, the value of closing inventories is what they would realize if sold.

Chambers and Sterling have argued in favour of realizable value accounting. According to Chambers, for example, the most important characteristic of the firm is its capacity to adapt to a changing environment, and in this way, to ensure its survival. The survival of the firm depends, therefore, on its ability to acquire goods and services, which is related to the realizable value of its existing assets. Chambers coined the term 'current cash equivalent' to indicate the realizable value of the firm's currently-held assets, that is, the cash represented by those assets and available, if sold, for investing in market alternatives and consequently redeploying its resources.

By contrast, replacement cost accounting reflects a relatively static situation, and does not inform investors about the economic sacrifice made in holding resources in their current form.

Another argument in favour of realizable value accounting is that realizable value income is an acceptable surrogate for economic income, for it indicates future cash flows which may result from the realization of currently-held assets. As we argued in chapter 4, the present value of future cash flows associated with the holding of assets is the most relevant concept of value from the point of view of investors. Backward looking concepts, such as historical cost and replacement cost values, are poor surrogates as predictors of future cash flows.

Finally, a further argument in favour of realizable value lies in its relevance to the needs of creditors for information about the market value of the assets held by a company to which they have extended credit facilities, particularly if the security for loans and other forms of credit is represented by liens or mortgages over such assets.

Components of realizable income

Realizable income reflects the periodic change in the value of enterprise capital measured in terms of resale price. It consists of two components:

(a) Realized gains resulting from the sale of assets during the accounting period, which are measured as the difference between the actual realized revenue from sale and the realizable value estimated at the beginning of the period.

(b) Unrealized gains resulting from changes in the realizable value of assets which have remained unsold at the end of the accounting period.

Example

During the year ended 31st December, 19X0 an asset was acquired for £40. At the 31st December, 19X0, its estimated realizable value was £85, and it was sold during the year ended 31st December, 19X1 for £100. The realizable income for the years ended 31st December, 19X0 and 19X1 is as follows:

	19X0	19X1
Realizable income		
Unrealized gain	£85 − 40 = £45	
Realized gain		£100 − 85 = £15

We noted in our earlier discussion of holding gains arising under replacement cost accounting that such gains could not be treated as part of replacement income. The reason for this view is to be found in the capital maintenance criterion to which replacement cost income is directed. By contrast, the realizable value concept of income is directed towards measuring the firm's ability to adapt to a changing environment, and for this purpose, income is required to measure changes in the firm's command over goods and services. This may be measured by reference to both realized gains, and unrealized gains which result, as we mentioned earlier, from changes in the realizable value of assets during the year. Hence, under realizable value income, no distinction is maintained between current operating income and holding gains. Assets are shown on the Balance Sheet at their realizable value.

Limitations of exit values

Exit values imply a short-run approach to the analysis of business operations because they entail disposition and liquidation values being shown on the Balance Sheet. Hence, business operations resulting in realizable income only indicate that it is worth staying in business in the short-run, not that it is worth replacing assets and staying in business in the long-term. Realizable value accounting values all assets at exit prices even though many assets are not held for resale.

It has been argued that the crucial test of the usefulness of exit values in financial reports lies in the treatment of highly specific assets, which may have very little value for anyone except the present owner for whom they were constructed (Solomons, 1971). The most extreme example of such assets are mineshafts—which being large holes in the ground have no exit value. Such assets may be presumed to have been worth as much to the firm as their acquisition or construction costs. Otherwise, it is clear that they would not have been acquired or constructed. The question is—what would be the sense of writing such assets down to their current realizable value?

Another limitation of exit values lies in their anticipation of operating income, before the critical event giving rise to revenue has occurred. It has been argued, for example, that "if profit is to be recognized at a moment of time, we must select that moment. The economist gives a clue in the formulation of entrepreneurship as the function of directing a business, bearing the risks and reaping the rewards of the business. This suggests that profit is earned at the moment of making the most crucial decision or of performing the most difficult task in the cycle of a complete transaction." (Myers, 1973). Where production is the critical event and sale presents no problem, the valuation of inventory at net realizable value gives a better indication of managerial performance than does replacement cost. Where selling is the main difficulty, the sale is the critical event which must occur before managerial performance may be correctly evaluated, for without a contract of sale or an active quoted market for the product, the accountant has little evidence of managerial accomplishment. The accountant must assume, in these circumstances, that the product will be sold for at least the break-even price, so that replacement cost is the most suitable measurement of value in these circumstances.

'Value to the business' as a criterion

The concept of 'value to the business' should determine whether exit or entry values should be used in the valuation process. One way of determining 'value to the business' is to reverse the opportunity cost concept, and to define opportunity value as the least costly sacrifice avoided by owning the asset. This approach to the valuation of an asset to the business has been adopted by a number of economists. Bonbright (1937), for example, defined opportunity value in the following terms:

> "The value of a property to its owner is identical in amount with the adverse value of the entire loss, direct and indirect, that the owner might expect to suffer if he were deprived of the property."

In no sense may historical cost be measured as the value of an asset to the business because it is not related to the amount which would have to be paid for the asset, the amount that might be gained from disposing of it, or the amount to be gained by holding it. It remains to consider therefore, the other three bases of valuation which were listed in chapter 3:

(a) the current purchase price (replacement cost) of the asset (RC);
(b) the net realizable value of the asset (NRV);
(c) the present value of expected future earnings from the asset (PV).

It has been argued (Parker & Harcourt, 1969) that six hypothetical relationships exist between these three values:

		Correct Valuation Basis
(1)	NRV > PV > RC	RC
(2)	NRV > RC > PV	RC
(3)	PV > RC > NRV	RC
(4)	PV > NRV > RC	RC
(5)	RC > PV > NRV	PV
(6)	RC > NRV > PV	NRV

In (1) and (2) above, NRV is greater than PV. Hence, the firm would be better off selling rather than using the asset. The sale of the asset necessitates its replacement, if the NRV is to be restored. We may say, therefore, that the maximum loss which the firm would suffer by being deprived of the asset is RC.

In (3) and (4) above, PV is greater than NRV, so that the firm would be better off using the asset rather than selling it. The firm must replace the asset in order to maintain PV, so that the maximum loss which the firm would suffer by being deprived of the asset is again RC.

The general statement which may be made, therefore, in respect of the first four cases (1) to (4) is that, where either NRV or PV, or both, are higher than RC, RC is the appropriate value of the asset to the business. As regards a current asset, such as inventories, RC will be the current purchase price (entry value). In the case of a fixed asset, RC will be the written down current purchase price (replacement cost), since the value of such an asset will be the cost of replacing it in its existing condition, having regards to wear and tear.

As regards cases (5) and (6), RC does not represent the value of the asset to the business, for if the firm were to be deprived of the asset, the loss incurred would be less than RC. Case (5) is most likely to arise in industries where assets are highly specific, where NRV tends to zero and where RC is greater than PV, so that it would not be worth replacing the asset if it were destroyed, but it is worth using it rather than attempting to dispose of it. The conclusion which may be reached as regards fixed assets, is that except in the rare occurrence of case (5), fixed assets which are held for use should be valued at RC if such assets are to represent their value to the business.

Case (6) applies to assets held for resale, that is, where NRV must be greater than PV. If RC should prove to be greater than NRV, such assets would not be replaced. Hence, it implies that they should be valued at NRV or RC whichever is the lower. This recommendation, despite its superficial resemblance to the lower of cost or market value which we argued to be illogical in Part 2, is not a concession to the convention of conservatism, but represents an attempt to measure the value of assets to the business. If RC exceeds NRV, inventories will not be replaced so that NRV represents their value to the firm. Conversely, where NRV exceeds RC, inventories are worth replacing, so that their value to the firm is determined by RC.

Current cost accounting v C.P.P. accounting

The 'value to the business' criterion was supported by the Sandilands Committee which recommended that an accounting system known as *current cost accounting* (C.C.A.) should become the basis of financial reporting. The principal features of C.C.A. are:

(a) Financial reports should continue to be drawn up in terms of monetary units.
(b) Financial reports should show the 'value to the business' of the company's assets at the Balance Sheet date.
(c) Income for the year should consist of the company's operating gains and should exclude all holding gains. Extraordinary gains may be shown as income, but they should be distinguished from operating gains.
(d) Financial reports drawn up in this way should become the basic published financial reports of companies. In addition to the net book value of assets and depreciation for the year on a historic cost basis should be shown in note to the financial report.

The Sandilands Committee did not recommend that C.P.P. statements should be attached to C.C.A. reports for the reason that "little useful additional information would be presented to a user of accounts by such a procedure and the effect would be to confuse him and to make the annual statements too complex." (Sandilands Report, 1975 p. 165).

As we mentioned in chapter 5, the Sandilands Report rejected the profession's proposals for C.P.P. accounting. This action was bound to provoke heated discussion about the relative merits of the two systems. The Consultative Committee of the Accountancy Bodies in the United Kingdom and Ireland (C.C.A.B.) found the Sandilands Report unacceptable on the grounds that C.C.A. did not take account of all aspects of inflation. Therefore, they did not agree with the statement made in the Sandilands Report that "C.C.A. is a fully comprehensive method of accounting for inflation." (Sandilands Report, 1975 p. 4). In a memorandum the C.C.A.B. put its case in the following terms:

"The aspects of inflation which the C.C.A. system does not deal with at all, or does not deal with adequately are:

(a) the decrease in value of monetary assets;
(b) the decrease in value of obligations represented by monetary liabilities;
(c) the whole effect of inflation on the value of the proprietor's interest in the company or other organization concerned, irrespective of whether that interest is represented by non-monetary or monetary assets;
(d) the description of the incremental difference between an asset's original cost and its value to the business as a 'holding gain' is potentially misleading as the whole or part of the 'gain' will be the result not of a real gain in wealth, but of a decrease in the value of money;
(e) the problems of making valid comparisons over a period of time when the unit of measurement (the £ sterling) is unstable."

(*Accountant's Weekly*, 7th November, 1975 "What the C.C.A.B. has finally told the Government.")

Monetary items

In the C.C.A.B. memorandum a simple example was given of the problems which would be created by the Sandilands Report proposal in the case of monetary items

Example

A company has £100 in the bank at the beginning of the year. During that year, no transactions were conducted and the closing balance at the bank at the end of the year remains £100.

The application of the proposals of the Sandilands Report would result in the firm showing neither a profit nor a loss. Given that the rate of inflation is 20% a year, however, it is true of course that the £100 at the bank is worth less at the end of the year than it was at the beginning. As a result, the business has lost 20% of the value of its asset and the proprietors have lost 20% of the value of their investment.

The decrease in the value of obligations represented by monetary liabilities is the converse. Thus, if a business has an overdraft of £100 at the beginning of the year, conducted no transactions and had an overdraft of £100 at the end of the year, inflation at the rate of 20% per annum would be reflected in a corresponding decrease of the real burden of the obligation of the business, even though the monetary obligation to the bank remains at £100.

The question is—how should such gains and losses be treated? Where a monetary loss has been sustained, as in the case of bank balances, it is suggested that a debit entry should be made in the Income Statement, thereby reducing the Income for the year, and that a corresponding credit entry should be made in a "Diminished Purchasing Power of Money Reserve". As regards monetary gains, as in the case of bank overdrafts, the converse accounting entries could be made.

However, the problem with such treatment of monetary gains and losses is that it implies that the greater the borrowings the greater are the monetary gains. Property companies are a particular case in point. The largest monetary items on their Balance Sheet are liabilities to banks, finance houses and other credit institutions. Since inflation makes a virtue of indebtedness, the Income Statements of such companies would be painted in glowing terms.

A study conducted by London stockbrokers Phillips and Drew (see *Accountants' Weekly* 31st October, 1975 "C.C.A. could badly hit company profits") illustrated the massive size of monetary gains involved in reported corporate income under conditions of inflation, and the effects of alternative accounting methods.

Phillips and Drew took as their figures total United Kingdom corporate income for 1974—excluding banks and oil companies—and worked out the following figures:

    (a) under historical cost accounting, total corporate income in 1974 amounted to £3.9 billion;

    (b) under C.C.A., total corporate income in 1974 would have been £1.6 billion, that is, 60% less than under historical cost accounting;

    (c) under C.C.A. plus the recognition of gains on monetary items as discussed above, which would have amounted to £1.7 billion, total corporate income in 1974 would have been £3.3 billion, that is, 15% less than under historical cost accounting.

The implications for companies, shareholders, investors and the Government of these figures need hardly be explained. They affect the size of reported income as regards retained income and dividends and the real burden of corporate taxation. Hence, because of the dangers of making accounting entries in respect of gains or losses on monetary items, there is a case for showing them separately in a supplementary statement rather than adding them to operating gains.

Non-monetary items

The proposals put forward by the Sandilands Committee show the change in the value of proprietorship interest in a company, but fail to show how that change in value is to be compared to the general rate of inflation. The C.C.A.B. illustrated this point in its memorandum by the following example: (see *Accountants' Weekly* 7th November, 1975 "What the C.C.A.B. has finally told the Government").

Example

At the 1st January, 19X0, the capital invested in a business was £200, represented by non-monetary (fixed assets) valued at £100 and monetary assets (cash at bank) amounting to £100.

At the 31st December, 19X0, the business held the same fixed assets, but on the basis of C.C.A. these had been revalued at £115. The business still held £100 at the bank.

The general price level increased by 25% during the year 19X0.

Ignoring the results of trading operations and the effect of taxation, the effect of C.C.A. would be as follows:

(a) there would be a holding gain of £15 on non-monetary assets calculated by reference either to the Index of Asset Values proposed by Sandilands or their realizable value;

(b) there would be no gain or loss in respect of monetary assets;

(c) there would be an increase in the value of capital invested from £200 to £215.

However, given that the general price level increased by 25% during the year, the value of the capital invested should have risen to £250 in order that its value be maintained at the end of the year to its level at the beginning of the year. In fact, under C.C.A., it is only £215, which is £35 less than its value under C.P.P. This difference of £35 consists of:

	£
(a) a loss on monetary assets (reflecting the whole of the fall in the value of money)	25
(b) a loss on non-monetary assets (because the money value of these assets has not increased at the same rate as the general increase in the price level)	<u>10</u>
	<u><u>35</u></u>

This example highlights that the holding gain of £15 measured under C.C.A. does not reflect the decrease in the purchasing power of the capital invested in the business (£50). Accordingly, the C.C.A.B.

argued that "the full extent of the fall in the purchasing power of the capital invested should be recognized in accounts which purport to show the effects of inflation." (*Accountants' Weekly* 7th November, 1975 *op. cit.*)

The foregoing example does not discredit C.C.A. in those cases where the replacement cost of non-monetary assets is higher than its value under C.P.P. In such a case, C.P.P. accounting will not maintain the firm's operating structure. As we have mentioned in the previous chapter, the concept of capital maintenance is more relevant to the operations of a business enterprise than the general purchasing power concept. Therefore, if a choice has to be made between C.C.A. and C.P.P., C.C.A. should be adopted. If the proprietors wish to know the impact of general inflation on the company's assets and income, it is better that such information be disclosed in supplementary statements than be incorporated in the basis financial reports.

Summary

Current Value Accounting combines the best characteristics of economic and accounting income, by associating values and changes in values with transactions. Current Value Accounting takes two forms: Replacement Cost Accounting and Realizable Value Accounting.

Replacement Cost Accounting involves:

(a) calculating current operating income by matching current revenues with the current cost of resources exhausted in earning those revenues;

(b) calculating holding gains and losses;

(c) presenting the Balance Sheet in current value terms.

It provides a long-run income concept, which is associated with existing production processes, thereby maintaining the service potential of capital employed. It provides more useful and more detailed information for decision-making than traditional accounting concepts, while not impairing their 'objectivity'.

Realizable Value Accounting is a short-run concept of income, because it implies liquidation values. Hence, it is not a feasible method of accounting for general use.

The concept of 'value to the business' should be applied to the selection of 'entry' or 'exit' values. The value to the business of an asset is the maximum loss which the firm would suffer if it were deprived of that asset. In the vast majority of cases, the maximum loss is the replacement cost of the asset.

The Sandilands Report supported the 'value to the business' criterion in its recommendation regarding C.C.A. The professional accounting bodies criticized the Sandilands Report on the grounds that it did little to recognize the effect of inflation on monetary assets and liabilities. They suggested a compromise which would combine C.C.A. and C.P.P.

References

1. A.A.A. Committee on the Matching Concept, *Accounting Review*, April, 1965.

2. Bonbright, J. C., *The Valuation of Property*, p. 71, McGraw-Hill, New York, 1937.

3. Dickerson, P. J., *Business Income—A Critical Analysis*, Institute of Business and Economic Research, Berkeley, University of California Press, 1965.

4. Edwards, E. O. & Bell, P. W., *The Theory and Measurement of Business Income*, Berkeley, University of California Press, 1961.

5. Lemke, K. W., Asset Valuation and Income Measurement, *Accounting Review*, January, 1966.

6. Myers, J. H., The Critical Event and Recognition of Net Profit, in *Financial Accounting Theory*, p. 159, Zeff, S. A. & Keller, T. F. (eds) McGraw-Hill, New York, 1973.

7. Parker, R. H. & Harcourt, G. C., *Readings in the Concept and Measurement of Income*, p. 17, Cambridge University Press, 1969.

8. Solomons. D., Asset Valuation and Income Determination: Appraising the Alternatives, in *Asset Valuation and Income Determination*, p. 110, Sterling, R. R. (ed) Scholars Book Co., New York, 1971.

9. Sterling, R. R., *Theory and Measurement of Enterprise Income*, University of Kansas Press, 1970.

Section 3

Comparability and the Interpretation of Financial Reports

7
Increasing the Comparability of Financial Reports

In the previous section, we discussed the inevitable compromise between meaningful reporting on changes in economic value and verifiable reporting which can be audited and tested. In this section, we focus on another important issue which faces the accounting profession that of comparability.

The relevance and usefulness of financial reports to investors requires that the financial reports of different companies should be comparable. This criterion recognizes that decisions which involve the allocation of resources among different companies require an assessment of their relative economic situations. The current concern with the standardization of accounting practice so as to create a greater degree of uniformity in financial reports reflects an awareness by the accounting profession that financial reports should be influential as regards the decisions which investors make.

This does not imply that a uniform accounting treatment should be imposed in every circumstance. There is a necessary trade-off between comparability and information which reflects reality in each particular circumstance. For example, capitalizing product development costs might provide a realistic and accurate picture in one situation but not in another. Therefore, the standardization of accounting practice must allow firms to reflect differing economic circumstances in their financial statements.

Alternative information sources

Some writers have questioned the objective of narrowing areas of difference in accounting practice which is the purpose of the policy of standardization which many countries are now pursuing. Hageman *et al.* (1973), for example, carried out research studies into the influence of financial statements on the manner in which investment decisions were made. Under laboratory conditions, investors presented with financial reports based on alternative accounting methods, and having access to no other information, were unable to distinguish between the different accounting interpretations of the same economic event. Under real-life conditions, the possession of information about the events underlying the financial reports enabled investors to adjust the decisions which they would have made otherwise, and these adjustments compensated for the effects of differences in accounting interpretations. The conclusion of these research studies were that if investors have alternative sources of information available to them, such as reports in the financial press and security analyses, which provide them with a clear understanding of events underlying financial reports, the search for the best financial reporting procedures is unnecessary. Hopwood (1974) appears to have reached the same conclusion. He distinguished two alternative information contexts. Firstly, in the absence of competing sources of information, or where there are difficulties in using sources of information other than published financial reports, in other words in what Hopwood described as a 'monopolistic information context', the accounting interpretation of events is not subject to validation by alternative sources of information, and constitutes the major part of the relevant information available to investors. Secondly, in a 'competitive information context', not only it is possible to validate the accounting interpretation of events, but the role of accounting information becomes relatively less important. The availability of many competing or often more timely sources of information enables the investor to gauge more readily the accuracy or the bias of accounting information and to ignore its conclusions wherever appropriate.

Although we would agree that information derived from sources other than financial reports is often very important and indeed more important to investors, the accounting profession has a responsibility to improve the quality of financial reports. Until recently, it has tended to shrug off its responsibility for the contents of financial reports by attributing this responsibility, firstly, to the law which restricts the area for choice and judgement, and secondly, to Boards of Directors in whom the law has vested the power to exercise choice and judgement in areas where a discretion exists.

Arguments against uniformity

In arguing against greater uniformity, some writers appear to confuse the concept of comparability with basic identity. Basic identicalness is unlikely to be found between any two companies. Even if every company followed precisely the same accounting principles, they would differ in actual practice, for example, in such matters as the level of expenditure on maintenance, research and development and advertising. Other writers have implied that comparability cannot be achieved because of the absence of basic identity. Kemp (1963), for example, has stated that "the idea that financial statements of two companies should be comparable is based on the assumption that the companies themselves are comparable, which might or might not be true." But comparability does not require the existence of identical operating conditions. The existence of differences in operating conditions does require, however, that careful attention should be given to the identification of dissimilar circumstances. Thus, the objective of financial reporting in this sense should be to reflect similarities as similarities and differences as differences (Simmons, 1967). Hence, the fact that basic identity does not exist among companies enhances the importance of achieving comparability in financial reporting.

Some writers have objected to greater uniformity on the grounds that it would act as a bar to progress. According to Pelouket (1961), "it is far more important to allow for change and improvements than to endeavour to enforce a Byzantine rigidity merely for the sake of uniformity". Obviously, the adoption of a code of standards does place a limit on the permissible level of variability, but as we stated earlier, such standards should not place accounting in a strait-jacket. They should allow for different treatment where appropriate if differing economic circumstances are to be reflected in financial reports.

The role of judgement in financial reporting

The role of judgement in financial reporting is excluded from those areas where there exists uniformity of method. The financial accounting procedures upon which financial reports are based exhibit a high degree of uniformity in such areas as the double entry recording system, data classification and methods of revenue and cost allocation. Judgement comes into play in such areas as the interpretation and evaluation of economic events and the data which is relevant for the purpose of recording and assigning such data to accounts and extracting information relevant to accounting periods. From a conceptual point of view, the role of judgement is to be concerned with complex problems such as 'proper allocation', 'matching', 'current performance' and 'income determination' rather than with uniformly agreed concepts such as 'debit', 'credit' and 'posting'. Hence, judgement comes into play when something is either not self evident or obvious.

The process of income determination with which financial reporting is concerned affords a great deal of scope for subjective judgements. Thus, the creation of provisions for bad and doubtful debts, the depreciation of fixed assets, the writing-off of damaged or obsolete inventories, the treatment of research and development expenditure, are all subject to the process of judgement.

One argument against greater uniformity in financial reporting is that it will make judgement unnecessary, resulting in the removal of professional judgement in accounting and the reduction of the accountant to the role of a technician (Tempelaar, 1975). However, the proper role of the accountant is to deal with problems which properly require the exercise of judgement. Hence, rather than narrowing the scope for professional judgement, adherence to standards would allow the accountant to use his talents to best advantage. We may compare the accountant's role under these conditions to that of the lawyer who has to work within a framework of rules, which do in fact require the use of judgement.

Judgement retains an important role in financial reporting. But in attempting to control the applicability of judgement to situations, accounting reflects the influence of the scientific method in reducing areas over which doubt exists. The fact that the accounting profession is seeking to improve guidelines for the exercise of judgement has led to the claim that accounting is becoming more rigorous.

The influence of management on financial reports

One aspect of the diversity of methods in accounting has been to give management an important influence on financial reports. With regard, for example, to the statutory requirement that the Balance Sheet shall give a 'true and fair' view of the state of affairs of the company, and that the Income Statement shall give a 'true and fair' view of the income of the company for any given year, the words 'true and fair' can, within flexible limits, mean very much what the directors and auditors wish them to mean.

The root of the problem lies in the relationship between the auditor and the management, for although auditors are formally appointed by shareholders at a general meeting, the effective choice of auditors lies with the directors. The theory underlying the appointment of the auditor by the shareholders is that he should act as an umpire, and render an opinion on the fairness and consistency of the financial reports submitted to them by the directors, and prepared in accordance with the principles which the latter are free to select. In actual practice, the initiative for proposing the name of auditors to shareholders usually comes from the directors, and the power of the directors to choose an auditor in this way means that if one auditor's decisions do not please, another may be appointed ultimately who can rationalize an alternative kind of measurement. Hence, auditors may not be independent agents for their fees are paid by the very people they may wish to criticize. The conclusion which may be drawn from the relationship between auditors and management is that management's influence over financial reports is deterministic, because where alternative measurements are available, it is management which in reality makes the choice.

The failure of the accounting profession to establish a code of accounting principles has been detrimental to the independence of auditors, for unless it is clearly laid down what is right and what is wrong practice, the auditor is not able to appeal to 'ethical' principles in any discussion with management as to the treatment of data for the purpose of financial reporting.

Accounting standards

The search for uniformity in financial accounting practices has induced the accounting profession, both in the United States and in the United Kingdom, to establish study groups to consider the need for accounting standards. In 1958, the Accounting Principles Board (APB) was established in the United States. It incurred criticism because instead of seeking to establish standardized practices, it devoted itself to a search for the best practice. It was replaced in 1971 by the Financial Accounting Standards Board (FASB) which was composed of a more representative body of interests than the APB, for it consisted of bankers and Government agencies in addition to professional accountants. In the United Kingdom, the Accounting Standards Steering Committee (ASSC) was set up following the publication of a Statement of Intent on Accounting Standards in 1969. The terms of reference of the ASSC was to consider 20 topics in a period of five years. Its procedure was to issue, in respect of each topic, an 'exposure draft' for discussion by accountants and the public, and then to take comments into consideration when issuing the formal Statement of Standard Accounting Practice in respect of that topic. Following the adoption of the formalized standard practice by the profession, any material departure by a company from the standard practice was to be revealed in the financial report.

Similar developments were also taking place in Europe under the aegis of the Union Européenne des Experts Comptables, Economiques et Financiers, but perhaps the most significant development was the establishement of the International Accounting Standards Committee (IASC) in 1973, whose objectives are to formulate and publish in the public interest basic standards to be observed in the presentation of audited accounts and financial statements and to promote their worldwide acceptance and observance.

The problems associated with the formulation of accounting standards may be judged from the British experience. The aim of the

ASSC appears to have been the establishment of 'uniform and improved' standards, as stated in the programme of the Statement of Intent. According to Bird (1973), uniformity should be the dominant motive until a clearer view has developed of the purposes of financial reports, since the impetus for a rapid standardization came from dissatisfaction with the diversity of accounting practices. Moreover, Bird argues, no criteria have yet been developed by which to judge whether any particular practice is 'better' than another.

Nevertheless, it is recognized that the urgent need for uniformity will be influenced towards a consideration of the need for standards themselves to improve as the results of research reveal the directions to take, and as the business environment itself changes. This flexible approach has been explained in the following terms:

> "accounting standards are not intended to be a comprehensive code of rigid rules. It would be impracticable to establish a code sufficiently elaborate to cater for all business situations and circumstances and every exceptional or marginal case. Nor could any code of rules provide in advance for innovations in business and financial practice." (ASSC, 1971)

Standardization in itself is an improvement, according to Bird and since "it makes accounts into more effective instruments for communication of information, the only criterion for success for a Statement of Standard Accounting Practice is whether it prescribes only one practice for each clearly defined situation within its terms of reference." Applying this criterion, the ASSC has succeeded very well for there has resulted an increasing commitment to the elimination of alternatives and imprecisions. For example, Exposure Draft 3, 1971, clearly defined 'mergers' and 'acquisitions', so that the accounting method used for one cannot be used as an alternative for the other. SSAP 'Accounting for the results of Associated Companies' also issued in 1971 provides another example of this clear approach:

> "A company (not being a subsidiary of the investing group or company) is an associated company of the investing group or company if:
>
> (a) the investing group or company's interest in the associated company is effectively that of a partner in a joint venture or consortium; or
>
> (b) the investing group or company's interest in the associated company is for the long term and is substantial (that is not less than 20% of the equity voting rights) and, having regard to the disposition of the other shareholdings, the investing group or

company is in a position to exercise a significant influence over the associated company.

In both cases, it is essential that the investing group or company participates (usually through representation on the board) in commercial and financial policy decisions of the associated company, including the distribution of profits".

It may be noted that this SSAP has become controversial and has been ignored by some enterprises.

Other statements issued by the ASSC also seek to reduce the alternative accounting methods available. Exposure Draft 15 Accounting for Depreciation and SSAP No. 9 Stock and Work in Progress are exceptional cases. ED 15 Accounting for Depreciation provides only the basic elements to be considered—asset cost, length of life and residual value. Although SSAP 9 limits the valuation of inventory and work-in-progress to the "lower of cost and net realizable value", only partial guidance is given as to how cost should be calculated.

From the foregoing examination of the work of the ASSC, the statements on accounting standards so far produced aim for uniformity. Unfortunately, although uniformity will assist the users of financial reports, the standards are still based on accounting conventions, such as 'going concern', 'accruals', 'consistency' and 'conservatism'. As we have already stated, these conventions themselves act as obstacles to progress in providing information which is relevant to economic decisions. Uniformity will not of itself achieve this end under existing conventions, though of course financial reports will be made more comparable.

The statutory enforcement of standards

The ASSC has no authority to impose standards on companies, and the accounting profession is in a weak position when it comes to disciplining accountants, who in their capacity as directors, do not support their profession's views. For this reason, it has been argued that accounting standards should have the force of law, since only statutory enforcement would ensure their observance. In this view, the accounting profession ought to establish accounting standards, and the Government should enforce these standards by legislation. This view has been rejected by the ASSC itself, though it is evident that this problem has not yet been resolved.

Summary

Financial reports in isolation do not necessarily provide the best type of information for investment decisions. A knowledge of their underlying economic events may be needed for this purpose. In a competitive information context, financial reports may be less successful than other sources for investors.

Improvements are needed to narrow the areas of difference and to eliminate undesirable alternative practices in financial reporting. These improvements will render financial reports more comparable. In the United Kingdom and in the United States, committees have been established for the purpose of formulating accounting standards which will ensure a higher degree of uniformity. Judgement will not be entirely removed, however, from this area since judgement is a necessary and inevitable aspect of financial reporting.

References

1. Accounting Standards Steering Committee, *Statement of Accounting Practice*, para. 8, 1971.

2. Bird, P., *Accountability: Standards in Financial Reporting*, p. 68, Accountancy Age Books, London, 1973.

3. Hageman, R. L., Keller, T. F. & Petersen, R. S., Accounting Research and Accounting Principles, *Journal of Accountancy*, March, 1973.

4. Hopwood, A., *Accounting and Human Behaviour*, Accountancy Age Books, London, 1974.

5. Kemp, P. S., Controversies in the Construction of Financial Statements, *Accounting Review*, January, 1963.

6. Pelouket, M. E., Is Further Uniformity Desirable or Possible?, *Journal of Accountancy*, April, 1961.

7. Simmons, J. K., A Concept of Comparability in Financial Reporting, *Accounting Review*, October, 1967.

8. Tempelaar, A. F., Standards have their Dangers, *The Accountant*, May, 1975.

8

The Valuation of Inventories

In the previous chapters, we examined the problems relating to establishing financial reporting objectives, those created by changes in the value of money, and the problem of ensuring greater uniformity in the information content of financial reports as a means of providing better guidelines for comparing the performance of different companies. In this chapter, we bring together these various problems in an analysis of the valuation of inventories. The purpose of this chapter, therefore, is to provide a topic on which to focus the substance of our earlier discussion thereby rendering this discussion more tangible and significant.

One of the weakest links in the process of income measurement is the valuation of inventories. Indeed, it has been described as the accountant's Achilles heel (Johnson, 1954). This situation arises from the large number of alternative methods which are available for valuing inventories. In this chapter, we consider the importance of inventory valuation to financial reporting and the various recommendations which have been put forward by professional accountants for valuing inventories. We examine the case for variable costing as a means of reducing the diversity in inventory valuation existing at the moment.

We conclude that the basic factor which has hindered the development of realistic principles by which to value inventory has been the failure to recognize the need for a theoretical framework based on the definition of financial reporting objectives by which to evolve such principles. In our view, there is little point in developing accounting standards as guides to accounting practice, unless these standards are developed from a realistic framework of objectives.

The importance of inventory valuation

Surveys in the United States, Canada and the United Kingdom have shown that inventories generally constitute, after fixed assets, the largest Balance Sheet item in the financial reports of manufacturing firms. Expressed as a percentage of total assets after depreciation, a small sample (Accountants International Study Group, 1968) of such firms revealed the size of such inventories to be as follows:

United States	24%
Canada	25%
United Kingdom	29%

(Accounts International Study Group, 1968)

Although this sample was taken in the late 1960s, and given that the size of inventories is influenced by economic conditions, the percentage of inventories to total assets is generally significant. Hence, since the ratio of inventories to pre-tax income is generally high (for the United Kingdom companies in the sample, it was 2.5 to 1), relatively small changes in inventory valuation can have a disproportionate effect on reported income. Assuming that the inventory levels and price levels relating to the sample companies remained constant, variations of ±5% in inventory valuations as between one year and the next would affect pre-tax income by ±12.5% approximately.

The effect of inaccuracy in measurement is greater in inventory valuation than for fixed assets, for though both classes of assets are turned over by firms in the income-generating process, they are turned over at a widely differing rate. In most cases, inventories are completely replaced within one accounting period. Whereas the effects of inventory valuations exercise an immediate influence on profitability, errors in estimating depreciation may take some years to work themselves out, so that their effect is not as pronounced.

Classification of inventories

Inventories are commonly classified as follows:

(a) Merchandise inventories, which are goods on hand purchased by a trading firm for resale. The physical form of the goods is not altered prior to resale.

(b) Manufacturing inventories consist of:

  (i) raw material inventories;
  (ii) work-in-progress, which are goods partly processed and requiring further processing before sale;
  (iii) finished good inventories, which are ready for sale;
  (iv) manufacturing supplies, which consist of goods required in the manufacturing process, such as lubricants, and supply items which may comprise product components, such as speedometers in motor vehicles;
  (v) miscellaneous inventories, such as office supplies and display materials.

A basic cause of many inventory valuation problems stems from the fact that there is no exact correspondence between goods bought or manufactured during an accounting period and goods sold in the same period. Increases or decreases in physical inventories necessitate corresponding allocations of costs as between goods sold or used, and those which have remained in inventory. ————

Institute recommendations on inventory valuation

In the United Kingdom, the profession has issued recommendations on inventory valuations. The "Recommendations on Accounting Principles" issued by the Institute of Chartered Accountants in England and Wales (Statement No. 22, 1960), for example, contains the following guidance:

The elements making up the cost of inventories are:

(a) direct expenditure on the purchase of goods bought for resale and of materials and components used in the manufacture of finished goods;

(b) other direct expenditure which can be identified specifically as having been incurred in acquiring the inventory or bringing it to its existing condition and location, for example, direct labour, transport, processing and packaging expenses;

(c) such part, if any, of the overhead expenditure as is properly carried forward in the circumstances of the business, instead of being charged against the revenue of the period in which it was incurred.

Overhead expenses may be divided into production expenses, other administrative expenses, selling expenses and financial charges. Opinions differ on the extent to which overhead expenses should be included in computing the cost of inventories, though it is generally agreed that it cannot properly include selling, financial and other expenses which do not relate to bringing inventories to their existing condition and location. Examples of practices which reflect the divergence of views on this problem are as follows:

(a) In some firms, only the variable costs are included in the cost of closing inventories, all other expenses, including depreciation, are dealt with as periodic expenses and charged as such against the income of the period in which they are incurred.

(b) In some firms, an appropriate portion of overhead expenses relevant to the period in which the goods are manufactured are included in the closing inventories of such goods, on the ground that expenses related to the acquisition or production of goods unsold at the end of the accounting period should be carried forward and charged against revenue when they are sold.

The normal bases of valuation are:

(a) at cost;
(b) at the lower of cost or net realizable value;
(c) at the lowest of cost, net realizable value and replacement price;
(d) at cost less provision to reduce to net realizable value (or to the lower of net realizable value and replacement price).

The term 'cost' above means all expenses incurred directly in the purchase or manufacture of inventories, and bringing such inventories to their existing condition and location, together with such part, if any, of the overhead expenses as is appropriately carried forward in the circumstances of the business instead of being charged against the revenue of the period involved. This definition of 'cost', therefore, allows the divergence of treatment of overhead expenses which we noted earlier.

The term 'net realizable value' means the amount which it is estimated, as on the date of the Balance Sheet, will be realized from the disposal of the inventories in the ordinary course of business, either in their existing form or as incorporated in the product normally sold, after allowing for all expenses to be incurred on or before disposal.

The term 'replacement price' means an estimate of the amount for which, in the ordinary course of business, the inventory could have been, acquired or produced either at the Balance Sheet date or in the latest period up to and including that date. In a manufacturing business, this estimate would be based on the replacement price of the raw material plus other costs of the undertaking which are relevant to the condition of the inventories on the Balance Sheet date.

Current practices

The methods which are employed for calculating cost in connection with the valuation of inventories have already been discussed in Parts 2 and 3, but may be mentioned again briefly as follows:

(a) unit cost—in terms of which each article, batch or parcel is valued at its individual cost;

(b) First In First Out (FIFO), which assumes that goods sold or consumed were those which had been longest in inventory, so that goods in inventory represent the latest purchases;

(c) Average cost;

(d) Standard cost;

(e) Adjusted selling price, which is a method widely used in the retail trade. An estimated price is obtained by pricing the inventory at current selling price and deducting an amount equivalent to the normal profit margin and the estimated cost of disposal.

The usual rule in valuing inventories is that the reported value should be the lower of 'cost or market value'. The calculation of cost and market value for this purpose may be made in the following alternative ways:

(a) by considering each article separately; or

(b) by grouping articles in categories having regard to their similarity or inter-changeability; or

(c) by considering the aggregate cost of the total inventory in relation to its aggregate net realizable value.

As we mentioned in chapter 7 earlier with respect to the problem of uniformity, circumstances vary so widely that there is no single basis of valuing inventories which is suitable for all types of businesses, nor even for all undertakings within a particular industry. Unless the basis adopted is appropriate to the circumstances of the particular undertaking and used consistently from period to period, the financial report will not provide a true and fair view, either of the state of affairs of the undertaking at the date of the Balance Sheet, or of the trend of its trading results from period to period. The need to give a true and fair view—disputed though the meaning of this term may be—is the overriding consideration applicable to all firms.

Limitations of current practices

The most striking feature of current inventory valuation practices is the large diversity of alternative methods used. They fall within the ambit defined by 'generally accepted principles', despite the fact that each alternative method is likely to produce a different income measurement. The first four bases of valuation mentioned earlier—unit cost, FIFO, average cost, and standard cost—may be computed differently for partly processed and fully processed inventories. Cost may include prime costs only, or all variable costs, or variable costs plus a portion of fixed overhead costs. Moreover, in choosing between cost, net realizable value and replacement price, total inventories may be considered as single items, as categories or as aggregates.

Chambers has shown that given three bases of valuation, four cost methods, three methods of treating overhead expenses, and three for choosing the final figure, there are $3 \times 4 \times 3 \times 3 = 108$ methods of inventory valuation explicitly permitted under existing rules (Chambers, 1965). Moreover, if alternative ways of calculating overhead expenses were included in this arithmetic, the combinations would run into millions. This diversity of valuations permitted in practice is the weakest link in the measurement of accounting income (Underdown, 1971).

Research findings on current practices

Surveys based on questionnaires and interviews (Accountants International Study Group, 1968) have disclosed no logical correlation between types of firms and methods of treating costs. Hence, the argument that significant differences in circumstances affecting different firms justify different valuation procedures is not supported by empirical evidence. These surveys have also shown that one of the important factors affecting accounting methods is tradition, for the accountant's approach to problems tends to be influenced by his own past experience.

The surveys suggest also that failure to agree on the objectives of financial reporting is the most important single cause of differences among accountants in the realm of inventory valuation. They are more likely to agree on valuation methods if they are able to agree first on the major purposes for which these valuations are needed. The objective of financial reporting which is referred to by accountants is to present a 'true and fair view'. This in itself has turned out to be a confusing generalization: what is required is an illuminating analysis of financial reporting objectives. If the term 'true and fair view' is to be used in connection with a definition of a financial reporting objective, it should be accompanied by an analysis of what constitutes a 'true and fair view'. Recommendation 22 of the Institute of Chartered Accountants in England and Wales, for example, provides no guidance on this point.

Recommendations for reducing diversity

Given that the prime objective of financial reporting is to provide information which is useful for decision-making, two recommendations may be made;

(1) *Inventories should be valued using the value to the business criterion'*, which we discussed in chapter 6. This implies a valuation at replacement cost or net realizable value, whichever is the lower.

(2) *Inventory should be valued at variable cost for income determination.* Therefore, all fixed costs should be written off against the period.

The arguments in favour of providing variable costing information for assisting decision-making by external users are overwhelming. Some opponents of variable costing assert that it is incorrect to suggest that information which is useful for management decision-making is relevant for all business purposes, although it is difficult to accept the contention that variable costing information may be helpful to management but not to external users, for both management and investors are faced with the same task, that is, decision-making.

Both management and investors are concerned primarily with the future outcome of present decisions. Accountants who advocate the use of absorption costing for external financial statements deprive investors of a useful, analytical device and make the task of interpreting the results more difficult.

Variable costing emphasizes the behaviour of fixed and variable costs, which is of utmost importance to investors. Variable costing helps to predict cash flows in relation to volume changes; the isolation of fixed costs in the Income Statement permits more accurate forecasts of claims on cash in meeting current outlays on fixed expenses. Variable costing also helps to correlate fluctuations in cash flows with fluctuations in sales volume.

We argued earlier that management should not receive the credit for increasing the net worth of business before the critical event has occurred, and we conceded that in almost every case, the sale was the critical event. Since income should vary with a company's performance (which really means accomplishing the critical event) where income is related to sales, it is logical that there should be a direct relationship between the two. Variable costing should therefore be used in these cases. Absorption costing, being based on the product concept, does not provide this relationship between income and sales, because under this method, income variation is partly related to production.

Variable costing also permits more accurate income forecasts because net income will have a direct relationship with sales, instead of confusing the picture with the impact of the two activities of producing and selling.

A further advantage of variable costing is that it eliminates the need to assign to departments and products, costs which bear only an arbitrary association; hence, the need to make subjective judgments is further reduced. With regard to the recovery of fixed overheads, for example, it is quite feasible for a dozen independent accountants or engineers to find a dozen various versions of normal activity based on the same set of facts. In this connection, it is noteworthy that ED6 (1972) dismisses the differentiation of fixed and variable costs as a basis for valuing stocks on the grounds that it is 'too imprecise'. Yet, the same criticism may be levelled against the use of the 'normal level of activity', concept, and the apportionment of fixed factory overheads which the draft recommends!

The support for our recommendation that the use of variable costing be generally extended is provided in the Appendix to this chapter.

Appendix

The case for variable costing for inventory valuation

As we saw in Part 2, periodic income measurement and the matching principle form the core of financial accounting.

The importance of the matching principle to income measurement was emphasized by a committee of the American Accounting Association (1965) which affirmed that "appropriate reporting of costs and revenues should relate costs with revenues in such a way as to disclose most vividly the relationship between efforts and accomplishments". In accounting, costs constitute measures of business efforts while revenues represent accomplishments arising from those efforts.

Different methods of matching

The logic behind the matching principle springs from a desire to provide a rule which will secure uniformity in the preparation of Income Statements. Investors require uniformity in accounting practices if they are to be able to evaluate the performance of one firm against another. As far as the matching principle is concerned the problem is to develop suitable methods for matching costs to revenues. Two such methods have been developed: product costing and period costing.

(a) Product costing

Accountants long ago recognized the product itself as a convenient vehicle for matching costs with revenues. Product costing involves attaching all costs, whether direct or overhead costs, to the product. In measuring the cost of goods produced and sold to be matched against revenues from sales, product costing requires the inclusion of those manufacturing costs which are incurred irrespective of production. Thus, costs such as rent, insurance and rates which are incurred on a time basis rather than on the rate of production are recovered against the units produced.

The proponents of product costing as the only method of matching costs to revenues argue that all manufacturing costs are product costs, and that there is no such thing as a period cost because "ideally all costs incurred should be viewed as absolutely clinging to definite items of goods sold or services rendered.... The ideal is to match costs incurred with the efforts attributable to or significantly related to such costs" (Paton & Littleton, 1940). They argue, therefore, that manufacturing costs are incurred solely to make possible the creation of a product.

(b) *Period costing*

Period costing recognizes that certain costs are incurred on a time basis, and that the benefit derived from these costs is not affected by the actual level of production during a period of time. Since rent, insurance and salaries are items which are incurred on a time basis, their deteriorating effect on a firm's cash resources are not halted by the lack of revenue.

Period costing is a method of costing which conflicts with the traditional view of costing expressed by product costing, and has given rise to the variable or marginal costing controversy. The issue between the two schools of thought revolves round the question of whether fixed manufacturing costs, that is those costs incurred irrespective of production, should be charged as the costs of the product or charged against the income of the period. According to the supporters of product costing, who employ absorption or full costing, all manufacturing costs should be absorbed by the product. Variable costing assigns only the variable costs, that is the costs which vary with the level of production, to the products, and fixed manufacturing costs are written off each year as period costs.

One advantage of variable costing over absorption costing which is often advanced by its advocates is its superiority for management decision-making. Because the distinction between fixed and variable costs is 'built into' the accounting system, it assists profit planning, product pricing and control. However, the controversy which surrounds variable costing is whether or not it should be used for external reporting. The advocates of absorption costing argue that figures prepared on a variable costing basis for the use of management should be adjusted to an absorption costing basis before they are released to external users.

The treatment of overheads

As we noted earlier, the Institute of Chartered Accountants in England and Wales considered this problem in its Recommendation on

Accounting Principle N.22. The Institute did not recommend one method as preferable to another, leaving the choice of the most suitable method to management, but advised that once a method has been selected it should be adhered to (ICAEW, 1970).

The matter was subsequently considered by the Accounting Standards Steering Committee in 1972, whose mandate was to consider the problem of ways of reducing the diversity of practices. Exposure Draft 6 restated the traditional accounting view that the aim should be to match costs and revenues "in the year in which revenue arises rather than the year in which cost is incurred", cost being defined for this purpose as including "all related overheads, even though some of these may accrue on a time basis" (ASSC, 1972). The net effect of EDP 6 was to recommend the adoption of absorption costing.

Absorption and variable costing compared

Let us assume the following basic data:

Total sales and production over 4 years (500 units per year)	2000 units
Direct material costs per unit	£1
Direct labour costs per unit	£1
Variable overhead costs per unit	£0.5
Fixed overhead costs	£1000 p.a.
Sales price per unit	£6

Let us further assume that the volume of sales and of production are constant in time.

The volume of production, sales and the level of stocks in units is as follows:

Year	1	2	3	4	Total
Opening inventory (units)	40	40	40	40	40
Production (units)	500	500	500	500	2000
Sales (units)	500	500	500	500	2000
Closing inventory (units)	40	40	40	40	40

The results under the two forms of costing would appear as follows:

Year	1	2	3	4	Total
Variable costing	£	£	£	£	£
Sales	3000	3000	3000	3000	12,000
Costs of goods produced	1250	1250	1250	1250	5000
Add: opening inventory	100	100	100	100	100
Available for sale	1350	1350	1350	1350	5100
Less: closing inventory	100	100	100	100	100
Cost of goods sold	1250	1250	1250	1250	5000
Contribution margin	1750	1750	1750	1750	7000
Fixed overheads	1000	1000	1000	1000	4000
Net income	750	750	750	750	3000
Absorption costing					
Sales	3000	3000	3000	3000	12,000
Cost of goods produced	2250	2250	2250	2250	9000
Add: opening inventory	180	180	180	180	180
Available for sale	2430	2430	2430	2430	9180
Less: closing inventory	180	180	180	180	180
Cost of goods sold	2250	2250	2250	2250	9000
Net income	750	750	750	750	3000

The above example illustrates the effects on income of using absorption and variable costing methods for a firm in which everything stayed exactly the same in four consecutive years. Therefore, sales and levels of production are constant in each period and both opening and closing inventory remain unchanged. Under these conditions income figures for each year remain the same under both methods of calculating income.

In reality, the effect on production of shortages of materials, or the effect on sales of credit squeezes and changes in indirect taxation distorts the relationship between sales and production and inventory levels act as buffers. Inventory levels, therefore, are not stable; they are in fact very volatile. Moreover, modern methods of production require a constant rate of production not only to maintain the efficiency of operations but also to prevent lay-offs and so assist in the preservation of good industrial relations. Flexible inventory level standards are normally established for the purpose of planning for a reasonably uniform level of production.

We shall now examine the different results obtained under variable and absorption costing under the following circumstances:

(i) where sales fluctuate but production remains constant
(ii) where sales are constant but production fluctuates

Results where sales fluctuate but production is constant

As soon as the rate of sales begins to differ from the rate of production the use of different methods of allocating overheads to costs of production start to affect profit calculations. Let us take the figures given in the earlier example, but keeping the level of production constant against varying levels of sales as follows:

Year	1	2	3	4	Total
Opening inventory (units)	40	140	340	240	40
Production (units)	500	500	500	500	2000
Sales (units)	400	300	600	700	2000
Closing inventory (units)	140	340	240	40	40

The results under the two methods of costing would appear as follows:

Year	1	2	3	4	Total
Variable costing	£	£	£	£	£
Sales	2400	1800	3600	4200	12,000
Cost of goods produced	1250	1250	1250	1250	5000
Add: opening inventory	100	350	850	600	100
Available for sale	1350	1600	2100	1850	5100
Less: closing inventory	350	850	600	100	100
Cost of goods sold	1000	750	1500	1750	5000
Contribution margin	1400	1050	2100	2450	7000
Fixed overheads	1000	1000	1000	1000	4000
Net income	400	50	1100	1450	3000
Absorption costing					
Sales	2400	1800	3600	4200	12,000
Costs of goods produced	2250	2250	2250	2250	9000
Add: opening inventory	180	630	1530	1080	180
Available for sale	2430	2880	3780	3330	9180
Less: closing inventory	630	1530	1080	180	180
Cost of goods sold	1800	1350	2700	3150	9000
Net income	600	450	900	1050	3000

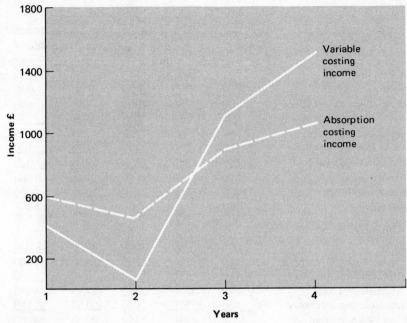

Fig. 4.1

It becomes evident why there is a controversy between the two schools of thought as regards the measurement of profit for the purpose of financial reporting for under the circumstances outlined above wide differences appear in net income figures. These differences may be illustrated graphically (Fig. 4.1), and it may be seen that the income profile fluctuates more widely when overheads are excluded, as they are under variable costing, than when they are included as under absorption costing.

Results where sales are constant but production fluctuates

Let us now keep the figures for sales constant, and compare results under the two methods of costing when levels of production vary.

Year	1	2	3	4	Total
Opening inventory (units)	40	140	340	240	40
Production (units)	600	700	400	300	2000
Sales (units)	500	500	500	500	2000
Closing inventory (units)	140	340	240	40	40

The results under the two methods would be calculated as follows:

Year	1	2	3	4	Total
Variable costing	£	£	£	£	£
Sales	3000	3000	3000	3000	12,000
Cost of goods produced	1500	1750	1000	750	5000
Add: opening inventory	100	350	850	600	100
Available for sales	1600	2100	1850	1350	5100
Less: closing inventory	350	850	600	100	100
Cost of goods sold	1250	1250	1250	1250	5000
Contribution margin	1750	1750	1750	1750	7000
Fixed overheads	1000	1000	1000	1000	4000
Net income	750	750	750	750	3000
Absorption costing					
Sales	3000	3000	3000	3000	12,000
Costs of goods produced	2700	3150	1800	1350	9000
Add: opening inventory	180	630	1530	1080	180
Available for sale	2880	3780	3330	2430	9180
Less: closing inventory	630	1530	1080	180	180
Cost of goods sold	2250	2250	2250	2250	9000
Over or (under) absorbed overhead	200	400	(200)	(400)	—
Total cost of goods sold	2050	1850	2450	2650	9000
Net income	950	1150	550	350	3000

In order to simplify the calculations under the absorption costing method we have assumed a normal level of production of 500 units a year. Since total fixed cost is £1000 per year, a recovery rate of £2 per unit is used. We have assumed also, that selling prices and costs remain unchanged over the four years. By using a normal overhead rate for recovering fixed overhead the value of opening and closing inventory per unit remains constant at £4.5 (£2.5 variable + £2.0 fixed). In the first two years the normal output level is exceeded by 100 and 200 units respectively, with shortfalls in the last two years. The cost of goods sold is adjusted by the over or under recovery of fixed overhead resulting from those differences in deriving income under absorption costing.

In this example, where sales have remained constant but production has fluctuated, we note that income results obtained under variable costing remain constant, but those based on absorption costing show wide fluctuation—£1150 in year 2 and £350 in year 4.

Variable and absorption costing: their impact on income summarized

The various examples which we have considered enable the following generalizations to be made on the impact on income of these two different methods of costing:

(i) where sales and production levels are constant through time income is the same under the two methods;

(ii) where production remains constant but sales fluctuate, income rises or falls with the level of sales, assuming that costs and prices remain constant, but the fluctuations in net income figures are greater with variable costing than with absorption costing;

(iii) where sales are constant but production fluctuates, variable costing provides for constant income, whereas under absorption costing, income fluctuates;

(iv) where production exceeds sales, income is higher under absorption costing than under variable costing for the absorption of fixed overheads into closing inventory increases their value thereby reducing the cost of goods sold;

(v) where sales exceed production, income is higher under variable costing. The fixed costs which previously were part of inventory values are now charged against revenue under absorption costing. Therefore, under absorption costing the value of fixed costs charged against revenue is greater than that incurred for the period.

The variable costing controversy

We have seen in this chapter how income may be affected by the manner in which costs are matched against revenues, so that the selection of one accounting procedure rather than another may, according to prevailing circumstances, affects the outcome of profit plans. Advocates of variable costing base their case on the superiority of this method for planning and control purposes. It does so by clarifying the relationship between costs, volume and income by identifying the contribution margin, that is the excess of sales revenue over variable costs of production, linking income to the level of sales which is the most critical event affecting a firm's financial performance.

The variable costing controversy arises not so much because there is disagreement about the need to distinguish the behaviour of fixed and variable costs, but because there is a question of its theoretical propriety for external reporting purposes. In the United States, variable costing has not been approved as a method of valuing inventory for external reports, and it has only been accepted as such in the United Kingdom since the Duple Motor Bodies Case of 1960.

Some accountants have been concerned by the fluctuations which are imported in income measurement by the exclusion of fixed costs, and to secure a certain stability in income, advocate the retention of the absorption costing method of valuing inventory. A further controversy arises from the effects of variable costing on the Balance Sheet of omitting fixed factory overheads from inventory values. The real argument on this issue is whether the Balance Sheet should show inventory at actual cost or at a value to the current period of the resources transferred from the period just ended. Variable costing is said to have an 'Income Statement emphasis', whereas absorption costing is said to have a 'Balance Sheet emphasis'.

The need for a definition of assets

The variable costing controversy stresses the need in accounting theory for a comprehensive definition of assets. Assets are not usually defined, and where they are, the definition is restricted to a vague description. Instead, considerable time is spent on discussing the classification of assets, and how one type of asset may be distinguished from another. Classifications which do not specify the tests to be applied in identifying assets are inadequate for an understanding of their basic nature.

Recently, there have been attempts to define assets as 'rights to service potentials' or 'rights to future benefits'. There remains the problem of interpreting these definitions, and some have taken the 'service potential' of an asset to mean its capacity to contribute to revenue-earning in the future. If one distinguishes unexpired and expired costs, according to whether or not they will contribute to revenue in the future, such a definition of assets would imply adherence to an absorption costing method of valuing assets.

A more recent interpretation of 'service potential' is one which considers assets as having a service potential to the extent that they avert the need to incur future costs. This 'cost obviation' interpretation has led some to believe that the variable costing method of valuing inventories is superior to the absorption costing method for the purposes of measuring inventories in terms of future benefits. The most detailed discussions of the cost obviation concept approach the problem of inventory valuation from the standpoint of relevant costs. Relevant costs are those which differ when two or more courses of action are contemplated, and they are those costs which will be avoided by not undertaking a given alternative. Irrelevant costs are those which have no influence on a decision because they remain the same under all the alternatives considered. The concept of relevant costs is not a new one. This text considers the concept fully when dealing with decision-making. This concept should be applied to asset valuation because the main purpose in providing accounting measurements is to influence decision-making. Therefore, inventories should consist only of costs that will influence future results.

Summary

Accountants are more likely to agree on the nature of measurement if they agree on the purpose of accounting. If the central purpose of accounting is to make possible the periodic matching of costs and revenues, and if the matching principle is the 'nucleus of accounting theory', then clearly the absorption costers are correct in their view. But if, as we argue in this book, the prime objective of accounting is to provide information which is useful for decision-making, then the case for variable costing seems to be very strong.

References

1. AAA Committee Report on the Matching Concept, *Accounting Review*, April, 1965.

2. ASSC Proposed Statement of Standard Accounting Practice: Stock and Work in Progress, May, 1972.

3. Chambers, R. J., Financial Information and the Securities Market, *Abacus*, Vol. 1, 1965.

4. ICAEW, *Recommendations on Accounting Principles*, N.22, 1970 edn, pp. 96–97.

5. Johnson, C. E., Inventory Valuation: The Accountant's Achilles Heel, *Accounting Review*, January, 1954.

6. Paton, W. A. & Littleton, A. C., *An Introduction to Corporate Accounting Standards*, Monograph 3, American Accounting Association, 1940.

7. The Accountants International Study Group, *Accounting and Auditing Approaches to Inventories in Three Nations*, 1968.

8. Underdown, B., Logical Principles Needed for Stock Evaluation, *Management Accounting*, July, 1971.

9
Interpreting and Comparing Financial Reports

Financial reports are combinations of facts and personal judgements both of which are influenced in the manner of presentation to users by accounting conventions. In attempting to interpret the meaning of the information disclosed, it is necessary to be aware of the limitations imposed by accounting conventions and methods of valuation, which, as we have noted in previous chapters may seriously distort the basic underlying events of importance to investors.

Ratio analysis is the most widely-used technique for interpreting and comparing financial reports. Ratios are useful because they can be used to summarize briefly relationships and results which are significant to an appreciation of critical business indicators of performance, for example, the ratio of net income to assets employed. Moreover, ratio are particularly useful for the purpose of comparing performance from year to year, and the performance of different companies, given that aggregate figures are always of differing orders of magnitude.

The collection of ratios on a systematic basis allows trends to emerge, and throws into relief the significance of changes indicated by the analysis of current events. Since the future is uncertain, the analyst has to rely substantially on past behaviour for predicting future changes. In this respect, the trends indicated by systematic ratios are very useful for making predictions. For example, it is not known which soccer team will win the championship next season. Hence, in making any predictions in this respect, one has to rely on the performance of all the clubs in previous seasons.

The function of ratio analysis, therefore, is to allow comparisons to be made which assist in predicting the future. In this connection, it should be stressed that the knowledge that the Alpha Co. has a ratio of net income to assets employed of 10% in the year 19X0 is meaningless by itself. To be meaningful, that ratio must be compared with the ratios obtained from the results of previous years, and may be made even more meaningful by comparing it with those of its competitors. In this respect, inter-firm comparisons were facilitated in the United Kingdom when the Centre for Inter-Firm Comparisons Ltd, a non-profit making organization, was established in 1959 by the British

Institute of Management in association with the British Productivity Council. This organization obtains confidentially from subscribers a large amount of management accounting information, computes therefrom a battery of ratios, and reports these ratios to the subscribers, together with the 'best' and 'worst' and the 'average' of all subscribers within a given industrial class. By contrast, the external analyst is confined to the information disclosed in published financial reports, and he tends to rely on such other information as he is able to obtain from other sources in assessing the performance and prospects of individual firms.

The nature of ratio analysis

Numerous ratios may be computed from financial reports and from other sources, notably Stock Exchange share prices. In this chapter, we shall limit our discussion to a number of important ratios which focus on two critical areas, namely, the ability of the firm to survive and grow, and the efficiency of its financial performance.

From the investor's viewpoint, these particular ratios are related directly to the two central issues, which we postulated in chapter 1 to be the focal points of a normative theory of financial reporting. We argued that the maintenance and increase of the value of the capital invested was the first consideration, and that the second consideration was the level of income which investors expected to derive from the invested capital. Clearly, both these considerations are inter-related and inter-dependent.

The maintenance of the value of the capital invested depends in the last analysis on the ability of the firm to survive, for shareholders, and particularly Ordinary shareholders, bear the burden of risk if the company should fail. Solvency is the most important criterion of the firm's ability to survive. Solvency is the ability of the firm to meet its debts as they come due for payment, and it is a question of both fact and law. If a creditor presses his claim for payment of the sum which is due to him, and the firm is unable to pay, its inability so to do is a question of fact. The firm may have substantial assets which may not be realizable. Its future prospects may not be necessarily bad—what is crucial, however, is that it has insufficient liquid resources, that is cash or near cash, to meet an individual claim, and, moreover, has no futher credit facilities available. Solvency becomes a question of law by the formal process in which the creditor seeks the recovery of debt through a court of law, and upon a direction by the Judge that the firm has defaulted upon a payment of a debt ordered by the Court, the firm is declared insolvent. The legal procedure for the firm's liquidation by winding-up ensues under a Liquidator appointed by the Court. Solvency is related, therefore, to the problem of liquidity in relation to the size of current obligations in favour of creditors, and to available credit facilities.

The level of income which investors expect to derive from their investment is related in the first instance to the firm's current financial performance, and in the next instance to its future growth prospects. We mentioned in chapters 3 and 4, that the income of shareholders may be seen as consisting of a stream of dividend flows. Dividends tend to be related to the level of current earnings, that is, realized income, and this in turn is reflected in the market value of the shares. Ratio analysis enables views to be formulated about the efficiency of current financial performance by relating net income to such indicators as net assets or share prices, and as far as the investor is concerned by relating dividends to corporate net income and to share prices. In the case of quoted shares, current financial performance does influence share price, and in this sense affects the value of investor's capital. Ratios of financial performance, therefore, affect economic income, which we argued, was the best criterion of income for decision-making by investors.

The analysis of solvency

We mentioned earlier that solvency was a question of fact in the first instance. Given the nature of financial reports, it follows that ratio analysis may make only a limited contribution to assessing solvency for the following reasons:

(a) The Balance Sheet statement of the firm's total current liabilities and total current assets at the end of the last accounting period may indicate that its financial stability is precarious, but solvency happens in the present and not in the past. In this respect, a firm may be perfectly solvent on the last day of the accounting period, and may now be insolvent by reason of the sudden withdrawal of a large credit facility upon which it relied.

(b) The Balance Sheet does not reveal sources of credit which the firm may tap, nor the willingness of current creditors and investors to see the firm through a difficult period.

Given these limitations, we may say that the usefulness of ratios of solvency lies as indicators for predicting insolvency (Beaven, 1966; Altman, 1968; Glautier, 1971). The financial stability of an enterprise in the short-term is the central concern in the analysis of solvency.

Nevertheless, investors are also interested in the analysis of longer-term implications of the current financial position. For this reason, we propose to discuss both short-term and long-term solvency.

Short-term solvency

Although shareholders bear the ultimate risk of losing their capital in the event of insolvency, unsecured creditors likewise run the risk of financial losses. In the face of a deteriorating financial situation, long-term creditors, such as debenture-holders, may either attempt to realize their security by selling specific assets mortgaged under the debenture instrument, or they may be willing to hold their hand if a viable rescue operation is mounted. Short-term creditors such as trade creditors are generally not willing to allow credit to a firm which is running into financial difficulties, and action from creditors is usually the precipitating cause of an act of insolvency.

Small firms in difficulties perish quickly: large firms, however, bring losses to many around them, not only to short-term creditors but to financial institutions which have supported capital expenditure programmes and granted credits. Indicators of short-term financial stability are particularly important, therefore, in respect of larger firms whose shares are publicly quoted, for if action is needed to prevent losses early signs are required to enable such action to be taken. There are two classes of ratios which are useful in this respect:

(a) Ratios which relate current assets to current liabilities, and indicate an imbalance between the burden of immediate debts in relation to the firm's ability to meet such debts.

(b) Ratios which indicate the rate at which short-term assets are liquidated, thereby affording a measure of the elasticity with which they are transformed into cash.

(a) Ratios of current assets to current liabilities

Two ratios in common use are:

(i) the current ratio;
(ii) the acid-test (or quick) ratio.

(i) The current ratio is the ratio of current assets to current liabilities expressed as follows:

$$\frac{\text{Current Assets}}{\text{Current Liabilities}}$$

For example, if a firm has current assets valued at £4000 and current liabilities amounting to £2000, the current ratio is 2:1. It will be recalled that the surplus of current assets over current liabilities also measured working capital, that is, the funds conventionally regarded as being available to finance current operations.

A number of problems stem from the use of the current ratio as a predictor of financial stability. First, since current assets include inventories, trade debtors as well as cash, an element of subjectivity is introduced into this ratio by methods of valuing inventories and by the assessment of the likelihood of bad debts. Second, an efficient business may be able to reduce inventories and debtor levels without affecting its financial stability, which is secured by a high rate of funds flowing from current operations. Hence, its current ratio may conceivably be less than 2:1, for example, and it will still be a viable concern. By contrast, a firm with a high current ratio represented by high levels of inventories, debtors and cash may be a very inefficient firm, and the current ratio may conceal a poor rate of funds generation, and hence a very unstable situation. For this reason, Glautier (1971) has argued that the current ratio is not a useful indicator of solvency from a theoretical viewpoint. Nevertheless, it should be said that what is a normal current ratio is particular to given industries, and financial analysts tend to look for current ratios falling within acceptable limits.

The Acid-test ratio applies where the inclusion of inventories in the current ratio means that as a measure of solvency it includes current assets which are not immediately realizable, such as inventories, debtors and prepayments. Thus, a firm could have a current ratio, which on the face of it is healthy by conventional standards, which may include a preponderance of inventories of raw materials and finished goods, which in the light of prevailing economic conditions may be difficult to realize in cash. The acid-test ratio excludes inventories and gives a sharper focus on the assets which are more readily convertible into cash. It is calculated as follows:

$$\frac{\text{Current Assets—Inventories}}{\text{Current Liabilities}}$$

For example, if current assets are valued at £4000 including inventories valued at £2000 and current liabilities amount to £2000, the acid test ratio would be 1:1, thereby indicating a coverage of current liabilities by cash or near cash current assets.

Whilst the acid-test ratio is a stricter indicator of solvency, it suffers from the same disadvantages which affects the current ratio, that is, it ignores the importance of cash-flows from current operations and by emphasizing cash and debtor balances tends to put the less efficient firm in a more favourable light.

(b) *Ratios of the cash-elasticity of current assets (i.e. activity ratios)*

Given that current assets normally consist of cash, debtors and inventories, the firm's ability to meet current liabilities depends upon the rate at which cash flows into the firm from current operations. Since sales is the critical event in this respect, the rate at which inventories are sold is clearly crucial. Where a substantial proportion of sales are on credit terms, the rate at which debtors settle their accounts is also crucial. For these reasons, the following ratios are good indicators of the cash-elasticity of current assets:

   (i) average inventory turnover

   (ii) collection period of trade debts.

   (i) The average inventory turnover is calculated by the following formula:

$$\frac{\text{Cost of Goods Sold during the period}}{\text{Average Inventory held}}$$

Example

If the firm's gross sales at cost during the accounting period amounted to £900,000 and the opening and closing inventories are £110,000 and £90,000 respectively, the average inventory turnover is as follows:

$$\frac{£900,000}{(110,000+90,000)/2}$$

i.e.,
$$\frac{900,000}{100,000}$$

$$= 9 \text{ times.}$$

This ratio means that the average length of time that inventory is held before being sold is $\frac{365 \text{ days}}{9}$, that is, 41 days.

The average inventory turnover ratio is only a crude measure of the rate at which inventories are sold for the purpose of comparing the cash-elasticity of inventories of different enterprises. Different marketing situations face different industries and trades. A butchery will clearly have a much higher inventory turnover rate than a firm selling luxury goods. Methods of inventory valuation will also distort the significance of inter-firm comparisons.

Nevertheless, the average inventory turnover may give a useful indication of trading difficulties facing a particular firm by comparing it with the average inventory turnover for previous periods. A fall in the average inventory turnover may indicate stiffening competition, adverse marketing circumstances or a degree of obsolescence in the firm's products. At the same time, firms operating in similar markets may be expected to have roughly similar average inventory turnover ratios, so that even as a crude ratio of comparability, it may be a useful indicator for investors. In fact, since cost of sales are not disclosed, analysts use sales figures as the numerator in this ratio.

(ii) An important measure of the cash elasticity of debtor balances may be obtained from the average collection period of trade debtors. The first stage is to establish the average amount of credit sales per day, which may be obtained by the following formula:

$$\text{Average Credit Sales per day} = \frac{\text{Total Annual Credit Sales}}{365}$$

The average collection period may be determined as follows:

$$\text{Average Collection Period} = \frac{\text{Trade Debtors as per Balance Sheet}}{\text{Average Credit Sales per day}}$$

$$\text{or} \quad \frac{\text{Trade Debtors as per Balance Sheet} \times 365}{\text{Total Credit Sales}}$$

Example

Given that total annual credit sales in the year 19X0 amounted to £1,460,000 and that total trade debtors at the 31st December, 19X0 were £160,00, the collection period for debtors may be calculated as follows:

Average credit sales

$$\frac{£1,460,000}{365}$$

$$= £4000$$

Average Collection period

$$\frac{£160,000}{£4000}$$

$$= 40 \text{ days}$$

These calculations show that 40 days is the approximate time required to collect trade debtors outstanding at the 31st December, 19X0. By applying this ratio, analyst expect to establish if the average collection period for debtors is too slow. A rough rule of thumb which is sometimes used by credit agencies is that the average age of trade debts should not exceed $1\frac{1}{3}$ times the net credit period. If a firm gives 30 days credit for the settlement of debtor accounts, the average collection period should not exceed approximately 40 days.

(c) *Other factors affecting short-term solvency*

In addition to the ratios mentioned above, other factors which should be taken into account when evaluating short-term solvency include:

(i) The size of operating costs. Neither the Income Statement nor the Balance Sheet reveal the cash required to meet current operating costs such as payroll, rent and other expenses, except where these are shown as outstanding on the Balance Sheet. Where a firm has very little current debt in its favour on the Balance Sheet, and it is faced, for example with large payroll obligations, it may be extremely short of cash.

(ii) Bank credit. A firm which has sufficient credit facility at the bank may, as we mentioned earlier, have lower current and acid test ratios.

(iii) Seasonal patterns of trade. Where firms normally expect seasonal patterns of trade, there will be distortions in the solvency ratios arising from seasonal build-up of inventories, trade debtors and cash depletions during the time interval across the peak season. Where such seasonal patterns of trade exist, they should be taken into account when making inter-firm comparisons.

Long-term solvency

We defined solvency as the ability to meet current liabilities as they fall due for payment. The long-term financial stability of the firm may be considered as dependent upon its ability to meet all liabilities, including those not current payable.

Two ratios which are considered important in this respect are:

(a) External claims against total assets expressed as a percentage (non equity)

$$\frac{\text{Long-term Debt} + \text{Current Liabilities}}{\text{Fixed Assets} + \text{Current Assets}} \times 100$$

(b) the interest coverage ratio.

(a) *The shareholders' equity ratio*

This ratio is considered by many analysts to be equal in importance to the current ratio as an indicator of financial stability. It is computed as follows:

$$\text{Shareholders' Equity Ratio} = \frac{\text{Shareholders' Equity}}{\text{Total Asset}}$$

It is generally felt that the larger the proportion of the shareholders' equity, the stronger is the financial position of the firm. This is related to the notion of 'gearing' which we discussed in Part 2 chapter 9. By increasing long-term borrowing, the firm may increase its current assets thereby creating a more favourable current ratio. At the same time, however, it reduces the shareholders' equity, signalling a possible over-dependence on outside sources for long-term financial needs. This creates problems associated with high levels of gearing, namely, where net income tends to fluctuate, the burden of fixed interest payments will greatly distort the dividend payable to shareholders and will, by that fact, affect the share price.

Although no explicit rules of thumb exist regarding desirable shareholders' equity ratios, financial analysts may have a general idea of the appropriate financial structure of a particular company by considering the stability of its income. The nearer a company comes to having a stable and assured income, the more it may safely use long-term credit.

(b) *Interest coverage ratio*

The ability of a firm to meet its debt service costs out of current earnings is a rough indicator of its long-term solvency. Long-term loans which are usually in the form of debentures carry interest charges which must be paid regularly. The inability to meet such interest charges places the firm's solvency into jeopardy. The interest coverage ratio is calculated as follows:

$$\text{Interest Coverage Ratio} = \frac{\text{Income Before Interest and Tax}}{\text{Periodic Interest Charges}}$$

Generally speaking, a firm which can cover its debt service costs several times over by its operating income even in a poor year would be regarded as a satisfactory risk by long-term creditors.

The analysis of financial performance

There are two aspects of a company's financial performance of interest to investors. First, its financial performance may be assessed by reference to its ability to generate income. Ratios of financial efficiency in this respect focus on the relationship between income and sales and income and assets employed. Second, its financial performance may be assessed in terms of the value of its shares to investors. In this sense, ratios of financial performance focus on earnings per share, dividend yield, and price earning ratios.

The analysis of efficiency as earning power

The overall measure of earnings performance for purposes of comparison is the ratio of return on capital employed. This ratio is made up of several components, two of the most important of which are the asset turnover ratio and the return on sales ratio.

The ratio of return on capital employed

There are several ways of expressing this ratio, and care must be taken in making inter-firm comparisons that the basis used is the same. The ratio of return on capital employed may be expressed as follows:

(1) Net income/Shareholders' Equity (i.e., share capital + reserves)

(2) Net Income + Interest/Equity Capital + Long-term Liabilities

(3) Net income/Gross Tangible Assets

The main problem with this ratio lies in the diversity of generally accepted principles applying to the measurement of net income and values. In selecting the appropriate denominator, for example, there is also a choice as indicated above. When considering the firm's efficiency in generating income, it is more appropriate to use total assets, that is net fixed assets plus current assets, as the denominator. Investors, on the other hand, would be more interested in relating net income to the value of the shareholders' equity. In this section, we shall assume that we are seeking a measure of the firm's internal efficiency in the generation of income, and use the ratio of net income to total assets.

The factors which affect the ratio of return on capital employed may be broken down into the following ratios:

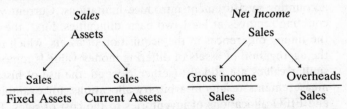

These ratios may be further subdivided, for example, by a closer analysis of the components of current assets, that is inventories and debtors, and the elements of direct and overhead expenses.

The ratio of return on capital employed is generally expressed as follows:

$$\text{R.O.C.E.} = \frac{\text{Sales}}{\text{Capital employed}} \times \frac{\text{Net Income}}{\text{Sales}} \times 100$$

(i) *The asset turnover ratio*

This is the first component of the formula for calculating the R.O.C.E. is an asset utilization ratio. It is intended to reflect the intensity with which assets are employed. Thus, if the firm has a low ratio of sales to assets, it is implied that some substantial under-utilization of assets is occurring, or alternatively that assets are not being efficiently employed. This ratio focuses, therefore, on the use of assets made by management. Because it is a measure of past managerial efficiency in this respect, it is thought to provide a reasonable basis for forecasting management's future efficiency. It is considered to be a prime determinant of the level of future income flows.

(ii) *The ratio of net margin on sales*

This is the second component of the formula for calculating the R.O.C.E. It seeks to assess the profitability of sales, that is, the efficiency of sales as a critical event in generating income.

The ratio of net margin on sales varies widely from industry to industry, so that it should be used solely for comparing similar companies in the same industry, or in comparing the performance of the same company over a period of time. Some companies may operate in an industry which is characterized by low profit margins and high levels of turnover, for example, manufacturers and distributors of foodstuffs.

In considering the relevance of ratios of performance, conventional accounting measurement introduce limitations. Current value accounting removes at least two basic difficulties. First, the effect of the timing differences in the acquisition of assets, which results in the aggregation of assets of differing money value is removed, and similar values are added together. Second, the use of historic cost measurements results in arbitrary allocations, for example, LIFO and FIFO allocations of inventories to the cost of sales. Replacement cost accounting increases the usefulness of ratio analysis by providing uniformity in cost allocations, since all costs are allocated at their replacement price.

The analysis of the efficiency of investment decisions

In buying the shares of a particular company, the investor is seeking to make the best allocation of his investment funds. Although the earnings efficiency of that company is very important to him, it has to be related to its shares. For this reason, several ratios are used by investors to appraise the performance of companies in terms of share prices and yields.

(i) Ratio of earnings per share

Since Stock Exchange prices are quoted on a share basis, it is considered useful to interpret a company's financial performance in terms of earnings per share. For Ordinary shares the ratio is calculated as follows:

$$\text{E.P.S.} = \frac{\text{Net income after tax—Preference dividend requirement}}{\text{No. of Ordinary shares}}$$

This ratio is significant only for Ordinary shareholders in the majority of cases, since Preference shareholders usually have the right only to a fixed dividend.

It is generally acknowledged that the market value of Ordinary shares is closely related to the earnings per share. Hence, this ratio is used as a basis for predicting the future value of Ordinary shares, and may assist also in formulating forecasts of future dividends. The problems of income measurement which we discussed in earlier chapters are not eliminated by the expedient of translating accounting income into earnings per share. This ratio does not, therefore, provide a reliable tool for comparing the financial performance of firms.

(ii) Dividend yield

The dividend yield focusses closely on the value of the declared dividends to an investor. It is calculated as follows:

$$\text{Dividend yield} = \frac{\text{Ordinary dividend per share}}{\text{Market price per Ordinary share}} \times 100$$

$$\text{or alternatively} = \frac{\text{Nominal dividend rate} \times \text{Nominal value of share}}{\text{Market price per share}}$$

Investors interested in seeking high yielding shares are able to compare the dividend yield of alternative share investments, and select for purchase those shares with the highest yield.

(iii) *Dividend coverage ratio (or pay-out ratio)*

The ability of a company to continue to pay current dividend levels in the future may be forecasted by the dividend coverage ratio, which may be calculated as follows:

$$\text{Dividend coverage} = \frac{\text{After tax earnings}}{\text{Total gross dividend}}$$

Where the dividend coverage ratio is, for example, three times the current gross dividend to Ordinary dividend, it may be taken as a good indication that the present dividend level will be maintained in the future since the company has an ample margin of earnings to make its current dividend declaration.

(iv) *Earnings yield*

The earnings yield expresses the dividend yield in relation to the market price of the share. It is calculated as follows:

$$\text{Earnings yield} = \text{Dividend coverage ratio} \times \text{Dividend}$$

$$\text{or alternatively} = \frac{\text{After-tax earnings per share}}{\text{Market value of the share}} \times 100$$

(v) *Price earnings ratio*

This ratio seeks to related earnings per share to the current market price of the share. It is the reciprocal of the earnings yield. It allows an investor considering the purchase of Ordinary shares to obtain a more accurate view of the return on investment implied by current earnings. In effect, it is a capitalization factor. The price earnings ratio is calculated as follows:

$$\text{P.E. ratio} = \frac{\text{Market price per share}}{\text{Earnings per share}}$$

Example

If the earnings per share in the Zebrox Co. is £10 and the Stock Exchange share price on the date of publication of this result is £25 per share, the price earnings ratio is 2.5. This ratio may be used to compare several share purchase alternatives in making a decision to invest.

Summary

Ratio analysis provides the most commonly used indicators to assess and compare the financial performance of companies, both over time and as between different companies. However, unless ratios are collected in a systematic and uniform manner, comparisons may be very misleading. For this reason, they are most useful when collected and developed by such organizations as the Centre for Inter-Firm Comparisons.

It is very important that external users of financial reports should understand the limitations of ratios based on conventional accounting measurements, otherwise their analyses will not be sound nor their interpretations valid. The conclusion which may be drawn from our examination of ratio analysis is that its general usefulness and relevance to investors would be enhanced by increasing the uniformity of financial reporting practices and adopting current value accounting.

References

1. Altman, E. I., Financial Ratios, Discriminant Analysis and the Prediction of Corporate Bankruptcy, *Journal of Finance*, 1968.

2. Beaver, W. H., Financial Ratios as Predictors of Failure, *Journal of Accounting Research*, No. 4, 1966.

3. Dev, S., Ratio Analysis and the Prediction of Company Failure, in *Debits, Credits, Finance and Profit*, Edey, H. & Yamey, B. S. (eds) Sweet and Maxwell, 1974.

4. Glautier, M. W. E., Towards a Reformulation of the Theory of Working Capital, *Journal of Business Finance*, Spring, 1971.

Increasing Financial Information

10
Increasing Financial Information

The deficiencies in current financial reporting practices which have become apparent in recent years, and the continuing controversies over what kind of information should be included in financial reports, have led many writers to advocate an expansion in the amount of information which is given in these reports. It is argued that such an expansion of information would allow users of financial reports a greater opportunity to select information considered to be relevant to their own particular purposes.

In this chapter, we conclude our analysis of financial reporting by examining four methods which have been advocated for increasing financial information, namely:

(a) Events accounting
(b) Multiple value reports
(c) Disclosure of budgets
(d) Cash-flow accounting.

Events accounting

The problem of specifying the decision models employed by users of financial reports has led to the suggestion that accountants should provide all the information about relevant economic events, thereby allowing particular users to generate their own information inputs to their decision models.

According to the proponents of events accounting, the main problem with current practice is its excessive concentration on the aggregating of information. Aggregation, it is argued, involves a loss of information in that the resulting information may be composed of many different components. For example, the disclosure of operating results in the form of net operating income, supplemented by the figure of the sales turnover, is virtually a total aggregation of all the important events which constitute the nature of the firm's operations. It conceals the firm's performance in different geographical areas and in different product lines, as well as many features which would provide a useful insight into the firm's prospects.

The difference in the conceptualization of the financial reporting process, which events accounting reflects, has been stated by Sorter (1969). According to Sorter, two schools of financial reporting may be distinguished. The first, defined as the value school, visualizes the purpose of financial reporting as providing measures which will allow users to make decisions which will optimize income and capital values. The second, defined as the events school, places the purpose of financial reporting at one level removed from the decision-making process, and deplores the loss of information which is occasioned by aggregation, and which would be considered relevant and useful to that process.

The proponents of events accounting suggest that the loss of information caused by aggregation and the valuation by accountants of such items as inventories and other assets, is greater than any benefits which are gained from the aggregation and simplification of masses of data by the accountant. Whilst agreeing that weights and values attached to such items by the accountants should be communicated, they insist that they be communicated in a disaggregated form. The Balance Sheet, for example, would be so presented that users would be able to reconstruct the events that occurred during the accounting period. Plant and machinery would be separated into categories, and for each category would be given opening values, acquisitions and dispositions.

The major problem in events accounting lies in deciding how far disaggregation should go. The events school has failed to establish a limit on the volume of data which should be reported. Significant cost implications are involved in storing and communicating data for the purpose of events accounting. Moreover, as we noted in Part 1, information theory indicates that the marginal utility of information is reduced as information is increased. By being overburdened with masses of data, the user of financial reports under events accounting may find himself making less effective decisions. Hence, it would be necessary to set some limit on the data communicated by relating its costs with its associated benefits. Clearly, great problems are implied for this type of analysis in that it requires measurements of user utility functions for information and means of allocating the cost burden of providing information.

Multiple value reports

Events accounting seeks to expand information by limiting each account classification to a single type of event, that is, by attaching a separate description to each facet of an activity. An alternative suggestion for expanding the supply of information is the multiple value report, which reflects the different values produced by alternative accounting measurements. Thus, the multiple value report would disclose replacement cost and net realizable value measured alongside historic cost measurements. These would be shown in a columnar form, with the effect of differentiating the effect of alternative measurements and allowing users to select the measurement which they consider appropriate to their own needs. Although we have argued that replacement cost measurements are more generally relevant to users' needs than historical cost or realizable value measurements, some users require these alternative measurements. In this sense, creditors may find realizable value measurements more appropriate than replacement cost for the purpose of establishing the value of their security, if any. As yet, taxable income is based on historic cost measurements, so that taxation authorities would wish to use historic cost income as a tax base. The general acceptance of replacement cost accounting for this purpose would lead, of course, to the redundancy of historic cost measurements.

Disclosure of budgets

Many writers concerned with the problem of increasing the supply of information to investors have argued that budget plans prepared for management purposes should be published for external users. The disclosure of budget plans would involve:

(a) publishing budgeted Income Statements, Balance Sheets and Funds-Flow Statements, detailing the company's projected results at the end of the next accounting period;
(b) publishing the actual results with critical comparisons between budgeted and actual results (Cooper, Dopuch & Keller, 1968).

Supplementary budgetary information in the form of long-range forecasts and capital budgeting plans would also be required for placing a proper perspective on the budget proposals.

The disclosure of budgetary information is clearly in keeping with the argument that financial reporting should be concerned with the provision of information which is relevant for decision-making by investors. Empirical research into the information needs of investors has indicated that they are concerned with obtaining information about the future and about expectations about the future. In this connection, research by Baker & Haslem (1973) into the importance attached by a sample of investors to different types of information revealed the following ranking in importance of the six top types of information:

(1) the future economic outlook of the company;
(2) the quality of management;
(3) the future economic outlook of the industry in which the company is located;
(4) the expected future growth in sales;
(5) the financial strength of the company;
(6) the expected future percentage growth in the company's earnings per share.

As a prescription for financial reporting, this type of research evidence goes very much beyond the idea of disclosing budget information. Nevertheless, the disclosure of budget plans would make a contribution to the supply of information allowing investors to make more realistic forecasts of the risk attached to their investment.

Commenting on the problem of budget disclosure, the American Accounting Association (1966) agreed that such disclosures would be highly relevant to investors, but stated that "accountants generally refrain from reporting budgets relating to future periods to external users on the grounds that the information is not sufficiently verifiable... Failure to observe the standards of verifiability to a minimum would place the accountant, in some cases, in the role of a forecaster and would reduce the confidence of the user and thereby diminish the usefulness of accounting reports." This statement clearly reaffirms the accounting dilemma between relevance and objectivity, which lies at the root of the problem of financial reporting.

Implied in the disclosure of budgets is an effective system of budget auditing designed to secure a degree of reliability in budget forecasts released to external users. According to Ijiri (1968), a set of generally accepted budgeting principles and procedures should be developed, together with a set of generally accepted auditing standards and procedures to enable firms and auditors to have some framework to rely on in preparing budgets for disclosure and their audit.

The problems stemming from the need to verify budgeted disclosures are not susceptible to easy solution. Budgeting comprises three types of activities—forecasting, co-ordinated planning and control, and performance evaluation. The verification of budget disclosures implies:

(a) an audit of the forecasting procedures used;
(b) a check of the routines involved in the budget process to ensure that the whole plan is properly co-ordinated and is internally consistent;

(c) a comparison of budgeted figures against results. When actual results vary from budgeted forecasts by a significant margin, explanations of the variances should be provided.

Verification presents the greatest difficulty as regards an audit of the forecasts themselves. It could be argued that although the accountant should have knowledge of forecasting techniques, it does not follow that the accountant should have an expertise in forecasting. Moreover, forecasting is not simply a question of handling techniques: it requires an expert knowledge of the industry and the markets in which the firm is located. Tomkins (1969) has suggested that a solution to this difficulty lies in the accountant obtaining a second opinion on budget forecasts from individuals other than the company's officials. Experts in the field of business forecasting outside the firm could be employed to provide such second opinions. Consequently, the auditor would not be legally liable for the forecasts and would be responsible merely for verifying the opinions of the experts concerned.

The problem of verification becomes more complex when forecasts covering several years are involved. Budget forecasts for the year immediately ahead merely provide an extended view of current achievements. Ideally, investors would need to be provided with forecasts covering a longer period. There would seem to be no reason why five-year rolling forecasts should not be adopted as a framework for budget disclosure, thereby enabling investors to appraise current performance and plans in relation to the firm's attainment of long-term goals. It would be difficult, however, to propose standard procedure which would ensure the required objectivity for audit purposes, for in the face of an increasing time-span, there could be a very wide divergence of opinion between management and expert forecasters of the forecasts formulated for budget disclosure purposes. For this reason, some writers have argued that there is little point in verifying these forecasts (Briston & Fawthrop, 1971).

Cash-flow accounting

In chapter 1, we argued that investors were primarily interested in the size and timing of future cash-flows. We suggested, therefore, that the purpose of income measurement is to enable investors to predict future cash-flows, for such measurement allows the size of future dividends to be estimated and future share values to be gauged, on the assumption that profitability is the main long-term determinant of share values. Hence, it may be asserted that investors may conceive the objective of financial reports to be the provision of information enabling investment decisions to be made by reference to the acceptability of expected future net cash-flows.

Contents of cash-flow reports

As we saw in Part 2 chapter 8, cash-flow statements provide information about cash inflows and outflows during an accounting period. Cash-flow analysis enables the sources and applications of cash to be identified. An important aspect of the analysis of the sources of cash inflows is the relative proportion of cash generated from operations and that injected from external sources. The analysis of cash outflows indicates how much has been applied to the maintenance and expansion of the income-earning structure, and how much has been distributed to investors by way of return on their investments. It also allows the cash-burden of taxation on company funds to be assessed.

Cash-flow reports may take two forms:

(a) Historic cash-flow statements, which explain differences between the opening and closing cash balances of the accounting period reported on.

(b) Cash-flow forecasts for the next accounting period, which have the objective of informing the investor of the total cash inflows and outflows which are expected to result from operations, and allow him to estimate future dividends. At the same time, cash-flow forecasts inform the investor of the cash requirements of investment plans, and the extent to which these requirements are to be financed from both internal and external sources of finance. Cash-flow forecasts also enable investors to judge the adequacy of working capital in relation to the firm's operating needs.

In Part 2 chapter 8, we discussed cash-flow statements in terms of cash balances and sources and applications of cash. To be useful for financial reporting purposes, cash-flow reports should be presented in a format convenient for analysis by investors. Lee (1972) has suggested that published cash-flow reports should distinguish the following elements:

(A) Manufacturing and/or trading transaction flows—giving details of revenues and expenditure relating to the operations of the firm. This information would exclude exceptional or non-recurrent items.

(B) Exceptional or non-recurrent transaction flows—giving details of those cash transactions connected with the firm's operations which can reasonably be described as either exceptional or relatively non-recurrent.

(C) Financial transaction flows—giving details of cash flows between the company and its shareholders, lenders and bankers, but excluding dividends and interest payments.

(D) Capital transaction flows—giving details of cash flows resulting from the acquisition and disposal of capital assets such as land, plant, investments etc., as well as expenditure on research and development.

(E) Taxation transaction flows—giving details of tax payments and tax refunds.

(F) Dividends and interest transaction flows—giving details of interim and final dividends paid to shareholders as well as interest payments to lenders.

In the example given by Lee (1972), these transactions flows are shown as follows:

		Statement of total cash-flows								
		19X0		19X1		19X2		19X3	19X4	19X5
Cash-flow		F	A	F	A	F	A	F	F	F
Cash retained b/f		±	±	±	±	±	±	±	±	±
Operational transactions	A	±	±	±	±	±	±	±	±	±
Exceptional ”	B	±	±	±	±	±	±	±	±	±
Financial ”	C	±	±	±	±	±	±	±	±	±
Capital ”	D	±	±	±	±	±	±	±	±	±
Taxation ”	E	±	±	±	±	±	±	±	±	±
Net distributable flows		±	±	±	±	±	±	±	±	±
Dividends and interest F		−	−	−	−	−	−	−	−	−
Cash retained c/f		±	±	±	±	±	±	±	±	±

Note. 'F' stands for forecasted cash-flows; 'A' stands for actual cash-flows; '+' stands for cash inflow; '−' stands for cash outflows.

From the foregoing cash-flow statement, the cash-flow forecasts for the years 19X0, 19X1 and 19X2 are compared with the actual cash-flows in those years, and any significant variance would have to be explained to investors. The reliability of forecasts would be assessible by reference to the size of any individual variances and the explanations given by management to investors. Forecasts for the next three years are also given, and in accordance with our earlier remarks on the verification of budget disclosures, these forecasts would require supporting opinions from forecasting experts.

Example

The following cash-flow statements of Greenhall, Whitely & Co Ltd reflect the practicality of Professor Lee's model, and its usefulness for financial management purposes.

Greenhall, Whitley & Co. Ltd

Statement of total cash-flows of group–year ending:

Cash-flows	Appendix	29.9 1972 £'000	28.9 1973 £'000	27.9 1974 £'000	26.9 1975 £'000
(1) Bank & cash balances brought forward		(4)	(2581)	(2551)	(3243)
(2) Operational Transactions flow	A	6120	8579	7570	9000
(3) Exceptional Transactions flow	B	66	27	(20)	7
(4) Financial Transactions flow	C	693	(495)	193	(72)
(5) Capital Transactions flow	D	(6102)	(4880)	(4831)	(4518)
(6) Taxation Transactions flow		(1241)*	(899)*	(1548)	(1394)
(6*) Cash-flows during year 2+3+4+5+6		(464)	2332	1364	3023
(7) Net distributable flow		(468)	(249)	(1187)	(220)
(8) Interest and dividends	E	(2113)	(2302)	(2056)	(1788)
(9) Undistributed bank & cash balances		(2581)	(2551)	(3243)	(2008)

* estimated.

Greenall, Whitley & Co. Ltd

Appendix A—Statement of Operational Transactions Flow

Cash Flows £'000	1972	1973	1974	1975
Sales	41,039	47,371	52,220	69,460
Cash Expenses	34,718	39,922	44,741	60,676
	6321	7449	7479	8784
Investment Income	184	181	285	289
Cash arising from operations and investments	6505	7630	7764	9073
Accrual Adjustments				
(Increase)/decrease in debtors	(813)	(412)	(890)	(1326)
(Increase)/decrease in stock	(640)	190	(1325)	(1308)
Increase/(decrease) in creditors	1068	1171	2021	2561
Adjusted cash movements	6120	8579	7570	9000

Appendix B—Statement of Exceptional Transactions Flow

Cash Flows	1972	1973	1974	1975
	£'000	£'000	£'000	£'000
Surplus on disposal of bulk wine & spirits	75	30	—	—
Losses on non-trading subsidiary	—	(40)	—	—
Net surplus on disposal of subsidiary companies	—	29	—	—
Sundry expenses and receipts	44	(4)	(20)	—
(Increase)/decrease in loans to employees	(53)	12	—	7
	66	27	(20)	7

Appendix C—Statement of Financial Transactions Flow

Cash Flows	1972 £'000	1973 £'000	1974 £'000	1975 £'000
Redemption of debentures	(70)	(262)	(49)	(62)
Released/(held) by debenture trustees	(45)	(233)	242	(10)
Issue of shares & debentures taken over on subsidiary	808	—	—	—
	693	(495)	193	(72)

Greenall, Whitley & Co. Ltd
Appendix D—Statement of Capital Transactions Flow

Cash Flows	1972	1973	1974	1975
Purchase of fixed assets:	£'000	£'000	£'000	£'000
Land & buildings	(2898)	(4320)	(2907)	(2102)
plant, mach., casks & vehicles	(2444)	(1697)	(1929)	(3004)
Trade furnishings	(640)	(718)	(676)	(574)
Hire of plant rentals	(86)	(135)	(167)	(233)
Sale of fixed assets	1839	1561	1360	1319
Deposits received re: sale of land & buildings	—	1002	62	—
Net cost of acquiring physical resources	(4229)	(4289)	(4257)	(4594)
Purchase of investments:				
In subsidiary	(21)	—	—	—
Other	(1674)	(250)	—	—
Sale of investments	∅	∅	—	183
Trade loans less repayments	(178)	(341)	(574)	(107)
	(6102)	(4880)	(4831)	(4518)

∅ assumed nil

Appendix E—Statement of Interest & Dividend Flows

Cash-flows	1972 £'000	1973 £'000	1974 £'000	1975 £'000
Dividends paid during year	(1173)	(1208)	(888)	(581)*
Interest on loan capital	(795)	(749)	(755)	(740)
Bank interest	(145)	(345)	(413)	(467)
	(2113)	(2302)	(2056)	(1788)

* a stock dividend was also paid.

The case for cash-flow reporting

The case for cash-flow reporting is argued from several standpoints. Some advocates of cash-flow reporting believe that there can be no objective 'correct' measure of income and of the financial position of a firm which result from conventional financial accounting procedures. Heller (1969), for example, states that "businesses do not earn profits; they earn money". Consequently, "the figure called profit is an abstraction from the true underlying movement of cash into and out of the company." For this reason, conventional financial reports should be replaced by cash-flow reports.

Lee (1972), by contrast, whilst advocating cash-flow reporting on the grounds of objectivity, would prefer not to abandon conventional financial reports. These should be published in addition to cash-flow statements "not so much for decision-making but more as information for an entirely different purpose—that of stewardship". Lee makes the particular point that cash-flow reports in their historic form as well as in the form of forecasts are far less subjective than conventional accounting measurements.

Lawson (1971) gives a different reason for his advocacy of cash-flow reporting. According to Lawson, investors seek to optimize the cash-flows they derive from their investments. The objective of financial reports, therefore, should be to inform investors of the dimensions of the company's cash-flows, thereby providing them with a realistic standard of reference by which to judge the adequacy of its dividend policy. The failure of conventional financial reports in this respect lies in financial accounting procedures for allocating against current income non-current expenses such as depreciation. As a result, accounting income is substantially less than cash-flow income. Lawson would abandon conventional financial reporting completely in favour of cash-flow reports.

An interesting variant proposed by Rayman (1971) is to segregate the subjectivity introduced by valuation in financial reports from the objectivity which lies in cash-flow reporting. Conventional financial reports would, under this proposal, consist of two elements—the effects of valuation on income measurement, and the effects of cash flows, both of which would be segregated so that their effect on reporting income might be clearly seen.

From a theoretical viewpoint, it may be argued also that although sunk costs, in the form of capital expenditure, represent an enduring benefit to the firm, they cannot be realized in another form with ease and should be written off as expenses in the year acquired. This notion goes very much against the accounting tradition of income measurement which seeks to match accomplishments with efforts. Nevertheless, it is true that the impact on the firm's financial resources are felt in the year of expenditure, and that if the major decision-criterion is the cash-flow, then sunk costs should be written off as incurred to allow investors to formulate a clear view of the firm's financial situation.

Advantages of cash-flow reports

The advantages of cash-flow reporting for decision-making are as follows:

(a) Cash is more objective than income, since its measurement is free of subjective valuations. It is also more easily verified than historical cost or current value accounting measurements, for receipts and disbursements are evidenced by means of source documents.

(b) The problems associated with distinctions between capital, revenue, income and expenditure, or of allocations of costs between a series of arbitrary time periods, do not arise under cash-flow accounting. Hence, although forecasts of either cash-flows or of income flows are subject to uncertainty, cash-flow forecasts are more objective than forecasts of income flows.

(c) Comparability between firms is enhanced since a common measure is applied, that is, cash, to all the elements of the financial report. The problem of uniformity which we discussed in chapter 8, therefore, disappears.

(d) Cash is crucial to the survival and progress of an enterprise. The problem of solvency is necessarily tied to the availability of cash to meet current liabilities, whereas conventional accounting treats the problem of solvency as of secondary importance by focusing primarily on income measurement. Many enterprises have shown book profits up to the day when a liquidator has been appointed, and equally, many enterprises have survived despite accounting losses owing to the availability of cash.

(e) Accounting systems based solely on cash-flows treat all receipts and payments automatically at their current value. Hence cash-flow reports approximate closely to current value accounting. Nevertheless, since cash-flow reports are focussed on monetary items, and since these items are affected by changes in price levels, cash-flow reports do not eliminate entirely the effects of inflation.

(f) As we have already argued, forecasts of future cash-flows form the basis for both corporate and investor decisions. Hence, in accordance with our normative theory of financial reporting discussed in chapters 1 and 2, cash-flow forecasts approximate the central criterion of such a theory more closely than any other methods of financial reporting.

Disadvantages of cash-flow forecasting

The Sandilands Committee (1975) considered the case for cash-flow forecasting and concluded:

> "We doubt whether such a proposal is practicable, at least in the foreseeable future. Many companies by the nature of their business would find it difficult to forecast their cash requirements with sufficient accuracy. Moreover, the proposal would require companies to disclose forecasts of their future position which could be damaging to their prospects. In general, we do not think it reasonable or practicable to require predictions about future events to be disclosed as part of a company's published accounts... We doubt whether such a fundamental change would be acceptable to British companies at the present time."

In making this statement, the Sandilands Committee revealed the attachment to sentiment which afflicts the question of financial reporting. Each sentence in the above paragraph is a denial of fundamental points which we have examined in this Part. To assert that firms are unable to make sufficiently accurate forecasts of their cash requirements is to deny the usefulness and, indeed, existence of cash budgeting as a central tool of management. To proceed to assert, by implication, that firms do make cash forecasts but their disclosure would be damaging to its interest exposes the weakness of the first assertion, and is a plea for secrecy and for discrimination in information supply. The third assertion, that it would not be reasonable or practicable to require predictions to be disclosed is a rejection of our basic premise—that the relevance of financial reports is to be found in information which allows predictions to be made about future events. The fourth assertion is really the substance of the case against cash-flow reporting—that the sentiment of management is against the disclosure of information which would expose managerial decisions to more stringent criteria of efficiency.

Summary

Concern with the problems of financial reporting has expressed itself in dissatisfaction with conventional financial reporting methods in a number of ways. In this chapter, we have examined four different proposals offering alternative methods of financial reporting.

The events approach seems a possible solution in reporting economic events rather than values. Valuation results in aggregation, whereas events reporting would involve disaggregation, thereby allowing investors to prepare their own information from the data contained in financial reports.

Multiple value reports overcome the need for choosing general purpose measurements by making available alternative accounting measurements such as replacement cost and net realizable value for different reporting objectives.

Advocates of budget disclosures argue that investors require information about future income and the future financial position. The main problem lies in the verification of budget disclosures.

Finally, cash-flow reporting appears to satisfy the central criterion of our normative theory of financial reporting by focussing on the disclosure of future expected cash-flows, which we argued to be the rational basis for decision-making by investors.

References

1. American Accounting Association, *A Statement of Basic Accounting Theory*, p. 27, 1966.

2. Baker, H. K. & Haslem, J. A., Information Needs of Individual Investors *Journal of Accountancy*, November, 1973.

3. Briston, R. J. & Fawthrop R. A., Accounting Principles and Investor Protection, *Journal of Business Finance*, Summer, 1971.

4. Cooper, W. W., Dopuch, N. & Keller, T., Budgetary Disclosure and Other Suggestions for Improving Accounting Reports, *Accounting Review*, October, 1968.

5. Heller, R., When is a Profit not a Profit? *The Observer*, 16th November, 1969.

6. Ijiri, Y., On Budgetary Principles and Budget Auditing and Standards, *Accounting Review*, October, 1968.

7. Lawson, G. H., Cash-Flow Accounting, *The Accountant*, 28th October, 1971.

8. Lee, T. A., A Case for Cash-Flow Reporting, *Journal of Business Finance*, Vol. 4, No. 2 Summer, 1972.

9. Rayman, R. A. Accounting Reform: Standardization, Stabilization or Segregation?, *Accounting and Business Research*, Autumn, 1971.

10. Sandilands Report: *Inflation Accounting*, Report of the Inflation Accounting Committee, p. 62. H.M.S.O. CMND. 6225, 1975.

11. Sorter, G. H., An "Events' Approach to Basic Accounting Theory, *Accounting Review*, January, 1969.

12. Tomkins, C. R., The Development of Relevant Published Accounting Reports, *Accountancy*, November, 1969.

Selected Further Readings

Accounting for Changes in the Purchasing Power of Money, Provisional Statement of Standard Accounting Practice 7, May 1974 (Published by each of the main professional accountancy bodies in the United Kindom).

American Accounting Association, *A Statement of Basic Accounting Theory*, 1966.

American Institute of Certified Public Accountants, *Report of the Accounting Objectives Study Group*, (Trueblood Report), 1973.

American Institute of Certified Public Accountant, *Reporting the Financial Effects of Price-Level Changes*, Accounting Research Study No. 6, 1963.

Andersen, Arthur and Co., *Objectives of Financial Statements for Business Enterprises*, Arthur Andersen and Co., 1972.

Backer, M. (ed.), *Modern Accounting Theory*, Prentice Hall, Englewood Cliffs, N.J., 1966.

Baxter, W. T. & Davidson, S. (eds), *Studies in Accounting Theory*, Sweet and Maxwell, London, 1962.

Bedford, N. M., *Income Determination Theory: An Accounting Framework*, Addison-Wesley, New York, 1965.

Bedford, N. M., *Extensions in Accounting Disclosure*, Prentice Hall, Englewood Cliffs, N.J., 1974.

Bird, P., *Accountability: Standards in Financial Reporting* Accountancy Age Books, London, 1973.

Chambers, R. J., Accounting, Evaluation and Economic Behaviour, Prentice Hall, Englewood Cliffs, N.J., 1966.

Edwards, E. O. & Bell, P. W., *The Theory and Measurement of Business Income*, University of California Press, 1961.

Garner, P. & Berg, K. B., *Readings in Accounting Theory*, Houghton Miflin, Boston, 1966.

Glautier, M. W. E. & Underdown, B., *Accounting in a Changing Environment*, Pitman Publishing, London, 1974.

Gynther, R. S., *Accounting for Price-Level Changes: Theory and Procedures*, Pergamon Press, Oxford, 1966.

Hansen, P., *The Accounting Concept of Profit*, North-Holland Publishing, Amsterdam, 1962.

Hendriksen, E. S., *Accounting Theory*, Richard Irwin, Homewood, Illinois, 1970.

Inflation Accounting, Report of the Inflation Accounting Committee (Sandilands Report) H.M.S.O. Cmnd. 6225, 1975.

Jaedicke, R. K., Ijiri, Y. & Nielsen, O., *Research in Accounting Measurement*, American Accounting Association, 1966.

Lee, G. A., *Modern Financial Accounting*, Nelson, London, 1973.

Lee, T. A., *Income and Value Measurement: Theory and Practice*, Nelson, London, 1974.

Lee, T. A., *Financial Reporting: Issues and Analysis*, Thomas Nelson & Son, London, 1976.

Macdonald, G., *Profit Measurement: Alternatives to Historical Cost*, Accountancy Age Books, London, 1974.

Macdonald, D. I., *Comparative Accounting Theory*, Addison-Wesley, New York, 1972.

MacNeal, K., *Truth in Accounting*, Scholar Book Co., New York, 1970.

Myer, J. N., *Financial Statement Analysis*, Prentice Hall, Englewood Cliffs, N.J., 1969.

Parker, R. H. & Harcourt, G. C. (eds), *Readings in the Concept and Measurement of Income*, Cambridge University Press, 1969.

Peasnell, K. V., *Accounting Objectives:—A Critique of the Trueblood Report*, International Centre for Research In Accounting, University of Lancaster, 1974.

Revsine, L., *Replacement Cost Accounting*, Prentice Hall, Englewood Cliffs, N.J., 1973.

Salmonson, R. F., *Basic Financial Accounting Theory*, Wadsworth, London, 1969.

Sterling, R. R., *Theory and Measurement of Enterprise Income*, University Press of Kansas, 1970.

Sterling, R. R., *Asset Valuation and Income Determination—A Consideration of Alternatives*, Scholar Book Co., New York, 1971.

Vangemeersch, R. G. S., *Accounting: Socially Responsible and Socially Relevant*, Harper and Row, New York, 1972.

Zeff, S. A. & Keller, T. F. (eds) *Financial Accounting Theory 1: Issues and Controversies*, McGraw Hill, New York, 1973.

Part 5

Social Responsibility Accounting

Part 5 SOCIAL RESPONSIBILITY ACCOUNTING

Introduction 673
References   675

1 Business Accountability in a Changing Society 676
The Consumer Protection Movement 676
The Ecology Movement 677
The Egalitarian Movement 677
The Public Interest Movement 677
Externalities 678
Dealing with social costs 678
Determining the extent of corporate social responsibility 679
    Net income contribution 680
    The human resource contribution 682
    Public contribution 682
    Environmental contribution 683
    Product or service contribution 683
Planning for social objectives 683
    The social audit 684
    The analysis of the social audit 685
    Evaluating and selecting social programmes 685
    Integrating social and business programmes 685
Measuring social outputs 686
Cost-effectiveness analysis 686
    Stages in cost-effectiveness analysis 687
Summary 688
References 688

2 Corporate   Reporting   and   Social   Responsibility
    Accounting 690
Financial and social stewardship 690
The development of corporate social reporting 690
Problems in corporate social reporting 695
Communicating information about social contributions 695
    Methods of communication 695
    The nature of the message 696
    The understandability of the message 697
    The role of accounting conventions 697
    Criteria for new accounting conventions 698
    Corporate social reporting and social auditing 699
Corporate social reporting: an example provided by the
    Quaker Oats Co 699
    The commitment to the concept of corporate social
        responsibility 700
    The company's definition of its social role in terms of
        its activities 700

The attempt to explain the company's social policy 701
The attempt to identify the company's social contributions 701
The attempt to integrate social and financial reporting 701
The practical problems of communicating information about total performance 701
Summary 702
References 702
Appendix: The Quaker Oats Company Annual Report 1973 703

3 Accounting for Human Resources 717
The development of human resource accounting 718
Comparison of fixed asset accounting and human resource accounting 719
Applications of human resource accounting measurements 720
Methods for determining the value of human assets 721
Replacement costs 721
Competitive bidding method 721
Capitalization of salary 722
Economic value method 723
Return on effort employed 724
Behavioural variables method 726
Financial and human resource accounting: R. G. Barry Corporation 727
Human resource accounting and corporate social responsibility 729
Corporate social responsibility and industrial relations 730
General information 730
Manpower 731
Financial 731
Prospects and plans 731
Summary 732
References 733
Selected Further Readings 733

Index 735

Introduction

In recent times, social problems have tended to move to the centre of political debate, and the search for solutions to social problems has been accorded an urgent importance. The interest in social responsibility accounting is a response to this development. It widens the scope of conventional accounting by considering the social consequences of decisions as well as their economic effects, and requires new measurements for defining social objectives and assessing the progress towards social goals. At a macro-level, for example, there is a considerable interest in defining relevant and useful social indicators. At a micro-level, social goals are being given an increasing importance in organizational strategy, and there is a recognized need for measurements which will be useful in the decision-making process.

Increasingly, management is being held responsible not only for the efficiency of operations as expressed in profitability, but also for what is done about an endless number of social problems. Business enterprises have been compelled to recognize their social as well as their economic responsibilities. As a result, there is a growing concensus that traditional measurements of performance derived from Income Statements and Balance Sheets are too narrow to reflect what many companies are trying to do.

In spite of much debate, however, there is as yet no generally accepted concept of the social responsibility of business enterprises. Almost everyone agrees that they should be socially responsible, though it may be argued that such a view is merely an extension of the universally accepted doctrine that individuals, either single or in groups, should weight the impact of their actions on others.

Three approaches to the concept of corporate social responsibility may be distinguished:

(a) The first approach originates in classical economic theory as expressed in the hypothesis that the firm has one and only one objective, which is to maximize income. By extension, the objective of a corporation should be to maximize shareholders' wealth. It is asserted that in striving to attain this objective within the constraint of the existing legal and ethical framework, business corporations are acting in the best interests of society at large. This classical interpretation of the concept of corporate social responsibility has been advocated by Milton Friedman (1962) in the following terms:

".... there is one and only one social responsibility of business—to use its resources and engage in activities designed to increase its profits as long as it stays within the rules of the game, which is to say, engages in open and free competition, without deception or fraud... Few trends could so thoroughly undermine the very foundations of our free society as the acceptance by corporate officials of a social responsibility other than to make as much money for their shareholders as possible".

(b) The second approach developed in the 1970s, and recognizes the significance of social objectives in relation to the maximization of income. In this view, corporate managers should make decisions which maintain an equitable balance between the claims of shareholders, employees, customers, suppliers and the general public. The corporation represents, therefore, a coalition of interests, and the proper consideration of the various interests of this coalition is the only way to ensure that the corporation will attain its long-term income maximization objective.

(c) The third view regards income as a means to an end, and not as an end in itself. In this view, "the chief executive of a large corporation has the problem of reconciling the demands of employees for more wages and improved benefit plans, customers for lower prices and greater values, shareholders for higher dividends and greater capital appreciation—all within a framework that will be constructive and acceptable to society" (Committee for Economic Development, 1971). Accordingly, organizational decisions should be concerned with the selection of socially responsible alternatives. Instead of seeking to maximize income generally, the end result should be a satisfactory level of income which is compatible with the attainment of a range of social goals.

The change from the second to the third approach to social responsibility is characterized as a move from a concept of the business corporation based on shareholders' interests to one which extends the definition of 'stakeholder'. The former concept views the business enterprise as being concerned with making profits for its shareholders, and treats the claims of other interested groups, such as customers, employees and the community, as constraints on this objective. The latter concept acknowledges that the business enterprise has a responsibility to all stakeholders, that is, those who stand to gain or lose as a result of the firm's activities.

In this Part, we are concerned, therefore, with the concept of total responsibility and with a broader analysis of corporate objectives. The debate is whether this viewpoint may replace the traditional view of the social role of the business enterprise as being concerned purely with economic activity, by one which attaches a much greater significance to the broader social contributions of business firms in improving the quality of life.

A note of warning should be sounded, however. At present, social responsibility accounting is an undeveloped subject. Serious obstacles impede its development. Not the least of these obstacles is the definition of social objectives which would be relevant to defining the nature and scope of social responsibility accounting. In addition, there are two further major obstacles which lie in the way of developing accounting information which would be useful in such a context. First, there is an apparent inability at this stage in time to develop measurements of performance which everyone will accept. In this sense, the uncertainty as to the meaning and extent of corporate social responsibility may be seen as impeding agreement on dimensions of the measurement problem as a first stage in the search for appropriate measurements. Second, there is an apparent inability to make creditable cost-benefit and cost-effectiveness analyses to guide decision-makers. This problem may be seen as related to the two previous problems, for if the objective of measurement is unclear, measurement standards cannot be developed and analyses cannot be conducted.

Despite these difficulties, we have included this Part in our book because we believe that social responsibility accounting is an area of accounting which will be of growing concern for the accountant.

References

Committee for Economic Development, *Social Responsibilities of Business Corporations*, p. 22, New York, 1971.

Friedman, M., *Capitalism and Freedom*, University of Chicago Press, p. 133, 1962.

1

Business Accountability in a Changing Society

Few topics in recent years have aroused more attention than the interrelationship between business and society. Through its ability to respond to technological change, business has affected the social values and expectations of society. In turn, these changed social values and expectations have been influential in affecting business conditions. Previously, economic growth was viewed as the source of all progress, social as well as economic. In recent years, however, a shift has taken place in the way society views the balance between economic progress and social progress, that is, between the available level of goods and services and the quality of life generally. This shift had led to the indentification of some of the unpleasant consequences of economic growth. The concern for the quality of life in an industrial society has found its most vocal expression in a number of movements, which have attacked the conventional values held by industrial society. In the United States and in Western Europe, the following movements have contributed in diverse ways to this debate.

The Consumer Protection Movement

In Great Britain, the Consumers' Association was founded in 1961 to test goods and services and to publish their results in the monthly magazine "*Which?*". More recently, the British Government has established bureaus to deal with consumer complaints. In the United States, Ralph Nader has been an effective force in documenting defective products.

In addition to consumer dissatisfaction with the quality of goods and services, there has been a strong consumer reaction to the manipulation of demand by means of advertising. Consumer protection movements have campaigned for truth in advertising, the consumer's right to be informed, the right to freely choose among products, the right to safety in products, the right to have their complaints heard, and the right to redress in respect of unsatisfactory product performance.

The Ecology Movement

This movement has been concerned with the environmental effects of industrial activity, and in particular with the pollution of air and water, solid waste disposal methods, oil spills, the despoilation of land and landscape.

The Egalitarian Movement

A feature of modern times is the concern for equality of opportunities among people, regardless of religion, race or social background. In particular, long-standing discriminatory practices against women have been attacked, and the women's liberation movement has achieved major victories in many Western countries. In Great Britain, the Sex Discrimination Act of 1975 made it illegal to discriminate against women in such matters as employment opportunities and financial rewards. As a result, wage and salary differentials between men and women have been made illegal.

The Public Interest Movement

The close affinity of interests between various movements is reflected in this movement, which in Great Britain has found its expression in the Public Interest Research Centre, which was established in 1971. Its purpose is to improve Government and corporate responsiveness to the public. Its publishing arm is Social Audit Limited which published the magazine '*Social Audit*' for the first time in 1973. The aim of this movement is basically to improve the democratic process by increasing the flow and improving the quality of public information. It recognizes that those who wield political or managerial power seek to avoid any challenge to their use of this power by witholding information. It recognizes also that this tendency has been an important factor in public dissatisfaction with Government and business activities.

As a result of these various pressures, many businessmen have altered their view regarding their social responsibilities, and this change has paralleled and partly reflected the changing expectations and priorities of society at large about the social functions of business enterprises. The idea underlying corporate social responsibility is the recognition that the activities of business enterprises have social implications which are both internal and external to individual enterprises. First, the enterprise may accept a responsibility for improving the social effectiveness of its internal processes, and this may be defined as its internal social responsibility. Included in this area of social responsibility would be the problems associated with the management of the human organization, such as employee selection, training, promotion and reward, as well as employee participation in decision-making as a means of providing a more cohesive framework of relationships within the firm. It also includes the provision of good physical working conditions, and the efficient use of physical resources from a social viewpoint. Second, the enterprise may accept a responsibility for the effects of its activities on stakeholders who are external to the firm. The debate about corporate social responsibility has been focussed on the external effects of corporate activities, and these are often referred to as 'externalities'.

Externalities

Externalities occur whenever a firm's activities have a positive or negative effect on society. Thus, a social benefit is an external benefit which society, rather than the owners of the firm, enjoys. A social cost is an external cost which society must bear, rather than the owners of the firm. Consider, for example, a firm which manufactures detergents. The firm's costs are related to the production and sale of detergent: the firm's benefits stem from the revenues derived from the sale of detergent to customers. The production of detergent results in the discharge of effluent, and dealing with the presence of this effluent, either in rivers or in sewerage systems is a burden which usually falls on the local community. Hence, the costs associated with the disposal of effluent need not be taken into account by the firm in deciding whether or not to produce detergents or in assessing the profitability of this activity.

Public concern has tended to focus on the external social costs of enterprise activity, rather than on the external social benefits. The most obvious social benefit is the provision of employment. Much of the debate about the social costs is addressed to two questions:

(a) how to control and reduce the undesirable by-products and effects of enterprise activity;

(b) how to calculate the financial costs involved with a view to determining the responsibility for these costs.

Ideally, social costs should be identified and internalized into the total enterprise costs of production. By bringing such costs to the knowledge of management, the information relevant to enterprise decisions is broadened to include financial and social costs.

Dealing with social costs

Social costs, as well as social benefits, are a function of society's perception of what is bad and good about business activity. As a result, the nature of corporate social responsibility is not a static concept. Rather, it is concerned with moving targets many of which are the subject of government action. Such action may take three forms:

(a) Legislation which outlaws undesirable social activities. Many examples exist of public concern with undesirable features of business activity, and of legislation to suppress such activities. One early example in the United Kingdom was the legislation relating to child labour in the 19th century which was made illegal.

(b) Licensing systems may be employed to limit the extent of activities which are useful to society, but present a potential social problem. The licensing of lorries, for example, has been made the subject of certificates of road-worthiness, and attention is now paid to the control of exhaust emission. Thus, licensing may be qualitative as well as quantitative.

(c) It has been argued that taxation is a convenient manner of internalizing external social costs of activities having negative effects on society. The objective is to impose taxes on the firm equal in magnitude to the damages sustained by society from the firm's activities. The obvious purpose of such taxes would be to encourage firms to abate the effects of such activities, or alternatively to finance public programmes for controlling these effects. According to some advocates of the taxation approach to dealing with social costs, business firms would be free to choose between abating the social nuisance and avoiding the tax, or continuing as before and paying the tax. According to other advocates of this approach, there should be a tariff of taxes designed to encourage firms to locate in areas where their method of production do least harm to the environment. Many environmentalists would probably argue, however, that such by-products as pollution do harm wherever they occur, and that suppression through legislation is the only appropriate course of action for society to take.

Determining the extent of corporate social responsibility

From the foregoing discussion of the nature of externalities and the role of government in solving social problems, it is apparent that corporate social responsibility is difficult to define. The question may be asked—to what extent should business enterprises be responsible for dealing with all social problems left unsolved by government? Should they concentrate on solving some of these problems? Or should firms merely operate within a strict interpretation of the letter of the law, and if so, would this adherence to the letter of the law frustrate any claim that their behaviour towards externalities could be anti-social?

In the absence of a clear definition of corporate social responsibility by legislation, individual firms must decide for themselves the nature of their social responsibility as a management concept and constraint. The only guidelines available to this firm in this respect is legislation on the one hand and public opinion and pressure on the other. Subject to these constraints, it is evident that corporate social responsibility may be broadly or narrowly defined, and that individual firms have a fair margin of choice as to the standard of corporate social responsibility which they may be willing to accept.

The social responsibility of a business enterprise is a concept which implies a broadening of the scope of corporate objectives as well as a broadening of the social unit by which these objectives are established. Since society is composed of many different social groups, socially responsible objectives should emerge from a more comprehensive social process than that provided by joint consultations between owners or shareholders and managers. To facilitate an analysis of business accountability, Brummet (1973) has identified five possible areas in which corporate social objectives may be found:

(1) Net Income Contribution
(2) Human Resource Contribution
(3) Public Contribution
(4) Environmental Contribution
(5) Product or Service Contribution.

The term 'contribution' includes both benefits and costs associated with an organization's activities.

Net income contribution
The growing attention which other social objectives are receiving does not reduce the importance of the income objective. A business organization cannot survive without an adequate financial surplus; and as we saw in Part 3, long-range planning includes calculating the minimum return to shareholders. The recognition of the importance of other social objectives does not diminish the importance of the income objectives. On the contrary, it adds meaning to the significance of corporate net income by drawing attention to the circumstances under which it has been produced. In this sense, there is a clear correlation between income and other social objectives. The failure to recognize a social problem may well affect the organization's income performance either in the short-term or the long-term. Thus, excessive hours of work under bad working conditions may damage the ability of workers to maintain the level of output. The failure to pay adequate attention to

the quality of the product and customers' reactions to poor product quality may ultimately affect sales and income.

Indeed, the failure to plan and attain social objectives will be reflected in the failure ultimately to attain the income target. For this reason, many would argue that the income objective is the complete test of business efficiency, both as regards financial and social goals.

In addition to those statements currently presented, the Corporate Report recommends the publication of a Statement of Added Value,

Statement of Added Value				
		19X0		19X1
		£m.		£m.
Revenue	£m.	90.0		100.0
Materials and services acquired		55.0		60.0
Value added		35.0		40.0
Applied as follows:				
To employees		27.0		30.0
To pay suppliers of capital				
interest on loans	0.9		1.0	
dividends to shareholders	0.8	1.7	1.0	2.0
To pay Government		3.3		4.0
To provide for maintenance				
and expansion of assets				
depreciation	0.9		1.0	
retained profits	2.1	3.0	3.0	
Value added		35.0		40.0

that is, the value added to materials and services acquired by the firm's activities. According to the Corporate Report, such a statement provides "the simplest and most immediate way of putting profit into proper perspective vis-a-vis the whole enterprise as a collective effort by capital, management and employees".

Value added may be defined as the wealth the reporting entity has been able to create by its own and its employees' efforts. The Statement of Added Value would show how value added has been used to pay those contributing to its creation. The example above shows the format of such a statement.

The human resource contribution

This contribution reflects the impact of organizational activities on the people who constitute the human resources of the organization. These activities include:

Recruiting practices
Training programmes
Experience building—job
   rotation
Job enrichment
Wage and salary levels
Fringe benefit plans
Management-union relations
Employee skills
Employee knowledge
Employee attitudes
Employee self-actualization
Congruence of employee and
   organizational goals

Mutual trust and confidence
Job security, stability of work
   force, lay off and recall
   practices
Transfer and promotion
   policies
Occupational health
Freedom from undue stress
On the job physical
   environment
On the job safety

The behavioural implications of managerial decisions have already been considered in Part 3. As yet, the development of a human resource accounting method which can cope successfully with measuring the impact of organizational decision on human asset values is experimental. The social implications of this development have yet to be debated. We shall discuss the development of human resource accounting in chapter 3.

Public contribution

This area considers the impact of organizational activities on individuals or groups of individuals generally outside the corporation *per se*, for example:

General philanthropy—contributions to educational, cultural, or charitable organizations.
Financial or manpower support for—public transportation, health services, urban housing, day care centres, minority business, community problem solving, minority group programmes and general volunteer community activities.
Equal opportunity employment practices.
Training and employment of handicapped persons.
Taxes paid.

The contribution which corporate enterprises make towards the public good tends to be overlooked in the debate about what they ought to do. It ought to be stated, for example, that the creation of jobs and the provision of employment are important public contributions, as well as the development of local services which often accompanies corporate expansion into a community. The training and employment of handicapped is an important corporate social contribution.

Environmental contribution

This area involves the environmental aspects of production, covering the use of resources, the production process and the product itself, including re-cycling and other positive environmental activities. Attention has been drawn in recent years to the negative aspects of organizational activities, such as the pollution of air and water, noise, and the despoilation of the environment. Moreover, industrial activities lead to a net use of irreplaceable resources and a net production of solid wastes.

Corporate social objectives are to be found in the abatement of these negative external social effects of industrial production, and in adopting more efficient technologies to minimize the use of irreplaceable resources and the production of waste.

Product or service contribution

This area concerns the qualitative aspects of the organization's product or service, for example, product utility, product life-durability, product safety, serviceability as well as the welfare role of the product or service. Moreover, it includes customer satisfaction, truthfulness in advertising, completeness and clarity of labelling and packaging. Many of these considerations are important already from a marketing point of view. It is clear, however, that the social responsibility aspect of the product contribution extends beyond what is advantageous from a marketing angle.

Planning for social objectives

Once a firm has determined the extent of its commitment to social objectives, plans may be considered for attaining these objectives. The integration of social and economic goals in the planning process provides, in our view, the best basis for understanding the interdependence of social and economic goals. In particular, such an integration allows the social implication of economic goals to be more adequately considered in the fusion of these goals in coherent long-range and annual operating plans. Admittedly, the integrated analysis of social and economic goals implies a reform of the planning process.

Bauer & Fenn (1972) recommend a four stage approach for planning social programmes:

(1) making an inventory of all corporate activities having a social impact;

(2) analysing the circumstances necessitating these activities;

(3) evaluating as best possible the type of social programmes which would be most relevant to the firm's activities;

(4) assessing the manner in which these social programmes match the corporation's own objectives and those of society at large.

The social audit

The first stage is an extension of the 'position audit' which we discussed in Part 3 chapter 3. The position audit in this analysis becomes a 'social audit' or social inventory. As in the position audit, similar questions are asked, such as "what are the company's strengths, weaknesses, opportunities, and threats?" in relation to a range of social problems associated with internal and external circumstances. Commenting on the process of conducting a social inventory for General Mills, Hunt (1974) wrote: "In developing items to be inventoried, it was decided to pinpoint "What does society expect of General Mills?" Two possible examples would be high quality products and good taste in advertising. Areas where General Mills could have a significant impact were placed high on the list. These included charitable giving, equal employment opportunities, employee safety, product quality, and food research. Conversely, areas where General Mills had lesser skills or potential, such as public transportation were de-emphasized. Finally, current topics which consumer advocates tend to emphasize were also covered. These areas included hiring of minorities and women, open dating, packaging and labeling, and children's advertising.

The following are some of the things that were eventually included on the list of items to be inventoried. They were divided into three major sectors covering most of the Company's resoonsibilities. They included: (1) the public, (2) consumers of our products, and (3) our employees. Included in the public sector were charitable giving, recruiting of women and minorities, and ecology. In the consumer sector, items such as advertising and consumer complaints were listed. Also, adequate attention was given to product safety, packaging, and labeling. Finally pay and fringe benefits were part of the employee sector, but also included were employee safety and responding to the employee voice (i.e. for job enrichment).

The analysis of the social audit

The analysis of these activities in relation to such internal and external circumstances sheds further light on the nature of the social problems to which the corporate social policy should be directed. This analysis is a pre-condition to considering the type of social programmes which may be required.

Evaluating and selecting social programmes

The selection of social programmes will be influenced by the firm's current performance and views about that performance. One approach to this problem is to carry out 'attitude surveys' (Worcester, 1973). This allows the firm to monitor, and possibly to forecast changes in attitudes among employees, customers, shareholders, government officials and public bodies about the firm's current social programmes. This technique has been used, for example, by General Electric for the purpose of analysing social priorities (Wilson, 1974). First, the major demands of various pressure groups were listed. Next, these demands were ranked in accordance with their intensity, that is, the emphasis which they were given by each pressure group. This method of developing a long-range social policy has led one writer to define social responsibility in terms of "social responsiveness, that is, the ability of the company to respond constructively and opportunely to changing societal needs and expectations" (Wilson, 1974).

Integrating social and business programmes

The final stage in the evolution of a long-range social policy is to translate plans into social action programmes. These programmes provide a means of allocating corporate resources to the attainment of particular social goals, and through control procedures to ensure that such goals are achieved efficiently. The use of such techniques as budgetary control enable social and business programmes to be jointly implemented.

Although we have expressed the view that the planning process, and implicitly the control process, should be reformed to allow social and economic goals to be considered in an integrated analysis, it is not possible at the present stage of the development of social responsibility accounting to effect such an integration. Hence, the proposals put forward by Bauer and Fenn must be seen as providing a theoretical blue-print for future research in developing tools of analysis in this field. In particular, their suggestion that there should be a matching of corporate social objectives with those of society at large poses very complex problems. At best, corporate managers will be able to place their own interpretation on the objectives of society at large. These objectives are not all known and often appear as part of a shift in public opinion, they are multiple, they often conflict and frequently overlap.

Measuring social outputs

The analysis of corporate social programmes pose the further problem in that most social objectives cannot be stated precisely, or in relevant, quantitative terms, that is, the output of such programmes may be gauged only in subjective and qualitative terms. It is difficult, therefore, to devise indicators for assessing the potential of alternative programmes and to measure the success or failure in attaining the desired social goal. Nevertheless, even without quantitative performance standards, output criteria are required, particularly for the following purposes:

(a) to relate outputs to the input of corporate resources devoted to social programmes;

(b) to monitor the efficiency of use of these resources.

Corporate resources have an opportunity cost, and the analysis of the desirability of particular social programmes implies that social goals will be attained at minimum cost. Hence, the absence of performance standard would seem to be a real stumbling block in implementing social programmes.

Cost-effectiveness analysis

Business enterprises may learn from the experience of Government in dealing with problems of planning and controlling social programmes. Cost-effectiveness analysis is directed to the analysis of programmes where outputs cannot be evaluated in terms of market prices. It is a technique which has the following purposes:

(a) finding the cheapest means of attaining a defined objective;

(b) finding the most effective manner of utilizing given resources.

Much of the early development work in CEA was conducted in the United States in the study of defence programmes. Defence is a field of administration which is very costly, but where there is no means whatever of evaluating benefits. These benefits are judged in political terms only, that is, in relation to defence needs established by political judgements. One may compare the production of defence goods with consumer goods in order to explain the nature of the problems to which CEA is addressed. It is assumed that the volume of consumer goods produced and sold on the market reflects the utility which the community derives from these goods. As regards the production of defence goods, however, there are no means of assessing how much should be spent on defence because there is no market by which to assess the utility attached by the community to defence goods. Defence objectives are determined by political decisions, and CEA assists in the making of such decisions by disclosing the most economical way of achieving these objectives.

Stages in cost-effectiveness analysis
Cost-effectiveness analysis involves three stages, as follows.

(a) Defining the objectives of a programme
The first stage, as in all the other forms of decision analysis which we have examined, requires the determination of the objectives to be achieved in terms which make an analysis of the problem possible. For example, a regional health programme may begin with the broad objective of 'improving the health of people living in the region'. This has to be interpreted in terms of goals, such as 'reducing the infant mortality rate in the region to the same rate that occurs in the general population, within a period of 5 years'.

(b) Identifying measures of effectiveness
Once goals have been defined, it is necessary to identify indicators which may be related satisfactorily to these goals and which will be sufficiently reliable as measurement standards for the purpose of assessing the effectiveness with which these goals are being attained. The selection of appropriate measurements is a central problem in all the areas of accounting responsibility which we have examined in this text, and it is none the less so in the selection of measurements of cost-effectiveness. We mentioned in Part 1 the necessity of selecting measures which will reflect programme goals without ambiguity, and we gave as an example the experience of a Soviet Nail Factory. Niskasen gives a further example which relates particularly to the problem of social responsibility, and concerns the manner in which Federal buildings are erected in the United States. According to Niskasen (1967), "the contracts for most Federal buildings are let on a fixed price, competitive-bid basis, primarily on the basis of cost per square foot. As a result, this had led to prison-like structures, with minimal outside window space and huge rooms inside—generally a depressing environment".

(c) The analysis itself
This is the process of considering the several alternative ways of attaining the desired goals of a programme. As a rule, very few social programmes may be evaluated by means of a single measurement.

Usually, several measurements are needed. In some cases, some measurements may overlap in the sense that they measure the same effect in a different way. In such cases, some overlap will occur. An American Accounting Association Committee on Non-Profit Organizations (1975) commented that ". . . four related concepts concerning programme outputs may require identification: (i) work completed; (ii) products produced; (iii) benefits achieved; and (iv) impact achieved. In the case of an educational programme, the courses given the students taught are examples of work completed. Students graduates may be considered as the product produced. The benefits asccomplished are the increased knowledge, improved skills, and increased earning power of the direct beneficiaries of the programme. The final indicator would be the impact these students have on society as a consequence of their educational experience."

Summary

In this chapter, we have explored the idea of corporate social responsibility, and have paid particular attention to the external social effects of business activities. These external effects are in the form of social benefits and social costs. Public attention has been focussed on the problem of controlling social costs. We noted that the extent of corporate social responsibility is the subject of debate. It is possible, however, to identify the nature of corporate social contributions, though planning for social goals presents serious accounting problems since social outputs are difficult to measure in quantitative terms. Cost-effectiveness analysis is a technique which offers a partial solution to the problem of planning and controlling social programmes where outputs cannot be evaluated in conventional market terms.

References

1. Abt, C. C., The Social Audit Technique for Measuring Socially Responsible Performance, in Anshen, M., (ed.) *Managing the Socially Responsible Corporation*, Collier Macmillan, London, 1974.

2. Accounting Standards Steering Committee, *The Corporate Report*, 1975.

3. American Accounting Association Report of the Committee on Non-Profit Organizations, *Accounting Review* Supplement to Vol. XLX, 1975.

4. Bauer, R. A. & Fenn, D. H. Jnr., *The Corporate Social Audit*, The Russell Sage Foundation, 1972.

5. Brummet, L. R., Total Performance Measurement, *Management Accounting* N.A.A., November, 1973.

6. Niskasen, W. A., Measures of Effectiveness in *Cost-Effectiveness Analysis*, Goldman T. A. (ed.), Praeger Publishers, New York, 1967.

7. Wilson, I. H., Reforming the Strategic Planning Process: Integration of Social Responsibility and Business Needs, *Long-Range Planning,* October, 1974.

8. Worcester, R., Monitoring and Forecasting Public Opinion about Business, *Journal of General Management,* Vol. 1 No. 1, Autumn, 1973.

9. Hunt, S. M., Conducting a Social Inventory, *Management Accounting* NAA, October, 1974.

2
Corporate Reporting and Social Responsibility Accounting

Financial and social stewardship

Corporate social responsibility implies that evidence of the pursuit of social policies should be made available to the public at large. Corporate social responsibility implies, therefore, that the concept of stewardship accounting, which has served accounting theory so well and for so long, should be restated. This concept lies at the root of financial reporting which we examined in Part 4. It is our thesis that the concept of stewardship accounting provides the link which unites financial accounting and social responsibility accounting in an unbroken chain of historical development. Accordingly, the concept of stewardship accounting should be interpreted to mean that the managers of business corporations have a responsibility to society as stewards of the social assets entrusted to them. Social stewardship implies an obligation to disclose information which will allow informed judgements to be made about the quality of the social management of these assets, which we may define as the management of assets for the benefit of society.

Corporate social responsibility extends the debate about financial reporting which we examined in Part 4, by widening the context in which the problem of financial reporting should be considered. The theoretical problems which we discussed in Part 4 are not thereby altered. The need for a theory of social reporting, for measurement and disclosure standards and for a degree of comparability between corporate social reports, is as relevant to the discussion of the problem of social reporting as it is to financial reporting. The only difference lies in the fact that the demand for corporate social reporting has not yet been properly articulated, its problems have been barely investigated, and a commitment to legislation in this area has not even been formulated in most countries, with the exception of France.

The development of corporate social reporting

Although the discussion of the important role of business corporations in modern society has been going on for many years, the accounting

690

implications of this role have only recently been the subject of debate. An impetus towards corporate social reporting was provided by the Trueblood Report in 1973, which we have already mentioned in Part 4. Discussing the objectives of financial reports, it stated that "an objective of financial statements is to report on those activities of the enterprise affecting society, which can be determined or measured and which are important to the role of the enterprise in its social environment."

In addition to the formal recognition of a corporate social reporting responsibility provided by the Trueblood Report, an informal acceptance of this responsibility is shown in the experiments currently being conducted by a number of companies in reporting on their social performance. Beresford (1974) has carried out surveys in the United States and has found that social disclosures have increased dramatically in recent years. These surveys showed that the most commonly used methods of presenting social data were as follows:

(i) separate sections in annual reports which were usually described as 'social reports';

(ii) separate sections in the President's letter to shareholders, very often addressed to 'shareholders and employees';

(iii) coverage of social matters as part of major topics of interest in reports.

Example

The Scovill Manufacturing Company produces a separate social report which is described as a Social Action Report. As may be seen from Exhibit A below, the Social Action Report of this company for the year 1972 is a four part report covering the following areas:

Employment opportunities

Environmental controls

Community involvement

Consumerism

In every case, it may be noted that a Balance Sheet framework is used to portray the assets and liabilities associated with each class of social responsibility. However, no attempt is made to determine whether the assets are greater than the liabilities, nor indeed is an attempt made to measure the financial implications of the information disclosed.

Exhibit A

A Social Action Report: This is an admittedly imperfect attempt to report on our corporate social action. We have used the balance sheet method of reporting—not because it is possible to attach monetary values to all of the things we are doing or should be doing, but aren't—but because it allows for brevity in highlighting strengths and weaknesses in this area. We will welcome comments on the contents and on whether to continue this report.

Employment Opportunities

Assets	Liabilities
Company expansion has provided approximately 10,000 new jobs since 1963.	Fluctuating employment levels still a problem at some plant locations.
One of first members of Plans for Progress (3/17/64) a voluntary program to provide more job opportunities for minorities.	Need more upgrading of minority employees into higher labor grade jobs.
Minority employment has grown from 6% in 1963 to 19% in 1972.	Need more upgrading of women employees into higher labor grade jobs.
Women now constitute about 40% of total employment.	Closing of Waterbury work training center after Scovill investment of $33,000 State & Federal grants to support it were terminated.
Established National Alliance of Businessmen training program which resulted in hiring of 280 disadvantaged and 170 veterans in last 18 months in Waterbury area.	
Began first major pre-retirement counseling program for employees with U.A.W. in 1964.	
Established one of first effective alcoholism control programs for employees in 1954 (now includes drug control program)	

Environmental Controls

Assets	Liabilities
$3,500,000 Waterbury water treatment plant completed Nov. 1972.	Problem of disposing of semi-solid sludge from new Waterbury water treatment plant still being researched for a solution.
$3,000,000 air filtering systems for Waterbury mills 80% completed.	New brass chip dryer ($700,000) installed one year ago to reduce air pollution in Waterbury must be modified to comply with new state standards.
$55,000 water treatment facility for Canadian plant completed March, 1972.	
$1,100,000 water treatment facility 70% completed at Clarkesville, Ga. plant.	New OSHA (Occupational Safety and Health Act) standards may require additional expenditures.
All 10 new plants added since 1959 were built with all necessary pollution control equipment.	Intermittent nitrogen dioxide emissions from Waterbury plant a problem requiring further research.

Community Involvement

Assets	Liabilities
Scovill charitable contributions averaged 1.2% of company pre-tax net income over past 5 years (1972 contributions were 8% of common stock dividends).	Programs to provide more low income housing have not been productive enough for time and money expended.
Local non-profit group to which Scovill contributed $163,000 has sponsored 174 units of subsidized housing.	Not enough rehabilitation of inner city neighborhoods.
Scovill partnership with minority business-man is rebuilding 12 vacant apartments and 4 storefronts to demonstrate benefits of rehabilitating deteriorating neighborhoods.	Still much to be accomplished in revitalizing core cities, controlling drug addiction, extending educational opportunities to the disadvantaged, etc. . . .
Support other such community projects as alcohol & drug control centers, inner city parks, recreational programs, public safety committees. . . .	Failure of programs to help youth groups establish minority owned businesses after Scovill investment of $20,000.
Employee participation in such community activities as selectmen, state representatives, school board members. . .	
Scovill loaned executives to federal, state and local governments in 1972.	

Consumerism

Assets	Liabilities
Corporate programs utilizing more effective quality control procedures throughout the company have upgraded product performance.	New and improved procedures to upgrade quality and service to insure customer satisfaction not foolproof—problems still occur and are corrected as soon as possible.
"Dial NuTone" established—a nationwide telephone network to speed up service and customer communications.	Improper use of products despite more informative product tags and installation instructions.
NuTone added over 100 authorized service stations to its national network in the past year—and expanded its Parts & Service Dept.	Pending or future legislation which may impose more stringent standards for quality and performance.
NuTone simplified its product installation books and added a new Consumer Assurance Laboratory.	
Hamilton Beach made its product tags more informative and simplified and clarified its warranties.	
Hamilton Beach established new nationwide service organization—trained factory personnel contact independent service stations weekly to insure warranties are enforced.	

According to the AAA Committee on Social Costs (1975), "many companies are presently involved in social accounting frameworks of different varieties, and it appears that these companies have progressed substantially further than the literature." Beresford (1974) analysed the reporting of 'social measurement' information by the Fortune 500 Industrial Companies, and found that the majority disclosed social measurements which could be classified as follows:

Environmental controls
Equipment and related operating costs to abate pollution
Improvement of products to reduce their pollutive effects
Recycling of waste materials

Minority employment
Hard core minorities employment
Training minorities for advancement
Minority purchasing programs, including bank deposits

Responsibility to personnel
Personnel counseling (alcoholism, etc.)
Assistance to displaced employees in locating new employment
Employee training

Community activities
Donation of cash or employee services to community welfare organizations
Public health projects, including drug addiction control
Aid to education and the arts

Product improvement
Safety
Quality (nutritional value, etc.)

The AAA Committee also mentions a comprehensive survey conducted by Steiner, Corsan and the Committee for Economic Development on the efforts made to develop measures of corporate social performance. This survey involved the despatch of a questionnaire to 800 corporations, of which 244 replied. Over 76% of the respondents indicated some attempted inventory of their social impact, and the AAA Committee notes in this connection that the substantial importance of the Steiner survey is "the response to the question "what do you see as the most important obstacle to the development of social audits?". Ranked as first and second in importance were the "inability to develop measures of performance which everyone will accept" and the "inability to make creditable cost/benefit analysis to guide company actions." Both these surveys show a willingness to provide information about corporate social contributions, and at the same time indicate the type of problems which business corporations are experiencing in attempting to communicate such information. The function of accounting theory at this stage of development would appear to be, first, to identify the nature of these problems, and second, to conduct research in the development of methods of reporting which will be useful and relevant to the solution of these problems.

Problems in corporate social reporting

An examination of the attempts made to portray the social contributions associated with corporate activities within the framework of current financial reporting methodology reveals a number of problems, as follows:

(i) how should the social contributions be identified?
(ii) how should the social contributions be measured?
(iii) how should the social contributions be described in a significant manner so that informed judgements may be made about these contributions?
(iv) how should the social contributions be related to the conventional financial information expressed in corporate financial reports?

Communicating information about social contributions

In Part 3, chapter 1, we examined the major components of an information system. These components provide a framework for discussing the problem of communicating information about social contributions to those social groups deemed to have beneficial interests in business corporations.

Methods of communication

Much of the debate about corporate social reporting focusses on the utilization of existing financial reporting methods for the purpose of communicating information about corporate social contributions. Two schools of thought may be discerned. The first consists of those who regard financial and social stewardship as two distinct accounting responsibilities, and would insist on their segregation by means of separate reports. The second consists of those who regard corporate social responsibility as integrating financial and social objectives, and would insist on corporate reports in which these aspects are fully integrated.

According to Arthur Andersen and Company (1972), "the information necessary for proper ethical enforcement and accountability to these broader social goals (of corporations) should not be integrated with information needed for economic decisions. Accountability in these other areas should be established by separate reports designed especially for these social responsibilities."

We have selected this statement because it encapsulates all the conflicts of views and sentiment about the nature and purpose of corporate social reporting. Let us analyse the implications of this statement in some detail.

First, the view that a distinction between financial and social objectives should be made runs contrary to the manner in which we defined corporate responsibility as integrating financial and social objectives.

Second, the view that the distinction should be made between financial and social information prevents correct interpretations of the financial results. Whether we assume that social goals act as constraints on financial goals, or that financial goals act as constraints on social goals, the fact remains that financial performance cannot be assessed in isolation. For example, if during the accounting period the firm has undertaken a programme aimed at reducing pollution—and this activity was voluntary undertaken—the costs involved in this programme will have reduced the firm's net income for that year, and will not necessarily have yielded the prospect of future financial benefits.

Third, the accounting practice of treating all expenses as immediately related to the income-earning process conceals the efforts (costs) made by the enterprise in making the social contributions, which we argue, form part of its set of policy objectives. Hence, this practice inhibits a valid assessment of managerial performance over the total range of corporate goals.

Fourth, informed judgements about a corporation's total performance cannot be made, unless an integrated analysis is conducted of all the elements by which performance is to be judged. The fundamental proposition of a theory of corporate social reporting is denied if the manner in which information is communicated makes it impossible for users to understand the significance of the inter-dependence of various organizational objectives.

The nature of the message

The foregoing discussion points to the complex nature of the message to be communicated, for the inter-dependence of the sum of organizational objectives, as well as their ranking in the enterprise's policy, must be perceivable in the message. These requirements imply the following characteristics in the message:

(1) It must reflect organizational objectives. This requires the sender of the message, namely the organization's management and its accountant, to provide information about the organizational goals set for the accounting period reported upon. As we mentioned in chapter 2, some of these goals might only have been stated in quantitative terms, for example, the income goal, whereas other goals, such as some of the social goals, will have been expressed in qualitative terms. Hence, the disclosure of organizational goals, which is the substance of the message, suggests the need for a multiple form of reporting framework.

(2) It must reflect the order of priority established by the organization's management for the attainment of the various social goals. This implies a full disclosure of the key points of its policy in relation to organizational objectives.

The understandability of the message

The basic proposition underlying the communication of information is that both the sender and the receiver of information should understand the nature of the message and what it is intended to convey. In a nutshell, this is the central issue in many of the problems which we have discussed in this text. A brief review of these problems will assist in throwing light on the very difficult problem of ensuring the understandability of the message.

The role of accounting conventions

It is appropriate at this stage of development to discuss briefly the influence of financial accounting conventions on the understandability of the information to be communicated.

It is evident that the process of change is a constant force breaking down such conventions as impede progress. At the same time, many conventions evolve because they are found to be useful. Difficulties occur at the point of friction between the needs created by new situations and the inertia inbuilt in established procedures. For this reason, the problem of corporate social reporting requires a reappraisal of the accounting conventions which we discussed in Part 2.

Churchill (1974) has already indicated the need to revise three conventions if information useful for social accounting purposes is to be produced. These are the entity convention, the realization convention and the matching convention. According to Churchill, the entity convention restricts the treatment of the effects of corporate social activities in that the efforts (costs) involved in these activities are treated as financial costs, whilst the benefits which they produce cannot be recorded in favour of shareholders, since they are mostly external social benefits. In his view, social accounting calls for a broadening of the entity convention so that all social costs may be matched against the benefits which they yield. Similarly, the realization and matching conventions become irrelevant to the treatment of social benefits. We have defined social benefits as resulting from actions taken to improve the quality of the condition of society, not actions designed to maintain existing conditions of life. Hence, Churchill argues, social benefits should be recognized in the accounting period when they are attained—once attained these benefits form part of the normal pattern of expectations, and they cease to be defined as benefits. In this sense, Churchill implies a distinction between financial and social benefits with which we would not agree. Nevertheless, what he is saying in effect is that the accrual convention, which supports the realization and matching conventions, is in itself unsuitable for corporate social reporting.

Once we are launched into a critical analysis of the relevance of financial accounting conventions, many of the conventions which we discussed in Part 2 chapter 1 become redundant to the objectives of this process. Our definition of social costs, for example, is an entirely different concept to the historic cost convention, whilst at the same time both social benefits and social costs go beyond the money measurement convention.

Criteria for new accounting conventions

At the heart of many financial accounting conventions is the desire that such information as is communicated should satisfy the criteria of objectivity and verifiability. These are rightly considered to be essential safeguards for ensuring that information be distinguished from opinion, and that the veracity of information be open to proof. These criteria are confused in current accounting theory since they are assumed to be the same thing. Thus, the realization convention is deemed to ensure objectivity, and verifiability is linked to the evidence of the rights and liabilities created by transactions.

The criteria of objectivity and verifiability particularly affect the process of valuation in accounting. This process is made much more difficult and complex in corporate social reporting, for as we have seen, money measurements serve more limited purposes whilst social values provide the standards of reference for defining social costs and social benefits. Hence, the selection of appropriate social indicators becomes a critical factor in providing a degree of objectivity, and verifiability requires a re-definition of the auditing process. This is an area in which a great deal of research is needed.

Corporate social reporting and social auditing

The term 'social audit' has acquired different meanings in the literature. In one sense, it refers to the assessment of corporate social contributions and the provision of information for this purpose for internal management use and for external reporting. In another sense, it refers to the process of attesting the veracity of this information (Bauer, 1973). We have used the term 'social audit' in the first sense in chapter 1. In a strict sense, however, we should use the term 'social audit' to mean the "process of examination and verification of information to give added credibility to such information (Brummet, 1973).

The audit of corporate social reports presents new challenges to the auditor. According to Brummet, "the auditor must know what it is he is auditing, so until a reasonable degree of proficiency is developed in social-performance detection and measurement systems, it will be difficult, if not impossible to see where the audit function, as accountants think of it, can be involved. However, when there has been further progress in the field of social accounting, the auditor's concern for fairness, verifiability, and freedom from bias will stand him in good stead to add credibility to social performance information".

Corporate social reporting: an example provided by the Quaker Oats Company

We conclude our discussion of the problem of corporate social reporting by an analysis of the annual report of the Quaker Oats Company for the year ended 30th June, 1973. We have selected this example for the following reasons:

  (a) It shows a commitment to the concept of corporate social responsibility as we have analysed it.

  (b) It attempts to define the nature of the company's social role in terms of its activities.

  (c) It attempts to explain the company's social policy.

  (d) It attempts to identify the company's social contributions.

  (e) It attempts to integrate social and financial reporting.

  (f) It illustrates the practical problems of communicating information to permit informed judgements to be made about the company's total performance.

The Quaker Oats Company made available to us its reports for the three years to 30th June, 1975. These reports show continuing improvements in presenting information about the company's total performance in a significant manner. In many senses, the 1974 and 1975 reports are superior in this respect to the 1973 report. The particular appeal to us of the 1973 report is the clarity of the message communicated about the policy of the company, and its commitment to the

concept of corporate social responsibility. Accordingly, we have preferred to reproduce selected parts of the 1973 report in the Appendix
to this chapter. We trust that the following analysis of this report does
justice to the effort which this company has made to be informative
about its social contributions.

The commitment to the concept of corporate social responsibility

The Report reflects the company's interpretation of corporate social
responsibility in the following ways:

(i) It is addressed to shareholders and employees, thereby recognizing that shareholders, employees and management all
share in the fortunes of the company.

(ii) It contains an implicit extension of the coalition to include
consumers and the public at large in its discussion of its
policy.

(iii) It contains a statement of the social goal theory in these terms
"business ... has an obligation to be useful to society in ways
beyond producing good products, providing employment and
paying taxes. It has long been our goal to be among corporate
leaders in public responsibility."

(iv) It describes how it attempts to realize this aim. "Many
Quaker progams have that specific purpose, and it is part of
our objective in everything we do. The Public Responsibility
Committee of the Board of Directors reviews these matters
regularly".

The company's definition of its social role in terms of its activities

The presentation of the report emphasizes the company's activities by
placing the activity report at the beginning, and leaving the financial
analysis of their results in the latter section. For example, it provides a
brief but well-presented, analysis of both activities and financial performance. This is followed by a detailed analysis of each of the product
divisions. The clearness of the message communicated in the use of bar
charts and the corresponding analysis may be seen from the company's
Report contained in the Appendix to this chapter.

The attempt to explain the company's social policy

In addition to the statements contained in pages 4 and 5, the company
defines its social policy in the inset to the front cover in the following
terms: "... we strive to maintain an environment for personal development and advancement that provides stimulation, satisfaction and
reward ... we shall continue our emphasis on good compensation and
incentive profit-sharing plans, on safe and pleasant work environments,

on equal employment opportunities, on assistance to employees in achieving educational objectives, and on benefits that assure a good income for retirement and security in the event of injury, illness or death."

As regards the community, the social policy is explained as follows: "... Quaker's people are encouraged to work within their communities and occupational fields, to participate in all levels of government, be active in school and church affairs and to join in many company programs aimed at improving the quality of life."

The attempt to identify the company's social contributions

The 1973 report is a very clear statement of the company's social contribution in which emphasis is given to people and products. Indeed, the first half of the report is concerned essentially with the human resource contribution, the public contribution, the environmental contribution and the product or service contribution. Although all these contributions are mentioned, either expressly or implicitly, it is evident that the company finds greater ease in dealing with the product contribution, and finds it less easy to deal with the other social contribution. One sees in the 1974 and 1975 reports of the company an awareness of the communication problems in these respects. Care is taken to provide sufficient information to understand the implications of the income contribution as may be seen from the notes which precede the financial statement.

The attempt to integrate social and financial reporting

The manner in which social and financial information is ranked in the report shows the desire to relate them in a significant way. The social contributions are first dealt with and they are followed by the income contribution. The analysis of the product contributions, in particular, is helpful to an integrated analysis of the relationship between the product and the income contributions. Once again, it is in the other areas of contribution that difficulties are experienced in the process of integration.

The practical problems of communicating information about total performance

Critics of the attempts to disclose information about corporate social objectives would not hesitate to suggest that the efforts of companies such as the Quaker Oats Company are merely attempting to put a fine gloss on what are essentially business activities. We do not take this view, and we trust that we have adduced enough evidence from the report to refute such criticisms. Nevertheless, the need to support statements by objective and verifiable evidence is not an easy one to satisfy. It is the function of accounting research to develop measurements and indicators which will be useful for achieving the type of reporting objectives which, clearly, the Quaker Oats Company has adopted. The company's continuing experiments in the 1974 and 1975 reports to improve the content and quality of information communication testify to its good faith in setting high standards of information communication. As we have noted, however, the 1973 report does show that difficulties lie in providing objective measurements of some of the social contributions. Moreover, the Report shows that the problem of integrating social and financial information in the manner which we consider to be theoretically desirable is not possible of solution at this stage of accounting development. Hence, informed judgements of the company's total performance over the range of its policy goals cannot be made. This is a measure of the gap in knowledge and method which must be closed in the process of developing corporate social reporting standards.

Summary

In this chapter we have examined the implications of corporate social responsibility in terms of corporate reporting. We have considered the problems involved in corporate social reporting, and in particular the problem of communicating information about social contributions. We have stressed that the central issue in this area lies in developing a theory of corporate social reporting. Postulates, principles and standards are required, and conventions need to be developed for the particular needs of this new area of accounting activity. A discussion of the accounts of a well-known company which is attempting to develop a corporate social reporting format reveals the difficulties which lie in the way of communicating information to permit informed judgements to be made about a company's total performance.

References

1. A.I.C.P.A., *Report of the Accounting Objectives Study Group* (Trueblood Report), p. 68, 1973.
2. Arthur Andersen and Co., *Objectives of Financial Statements for Business Enterprises*, Chicago, 1972.
3. Bauer, R. A., The State of the Art of Social Auditing, in *Corporate Social Accounting*, p. 14, Dierkes, M. & Bauer, R. A. (eds) Praeger Publishers, New York, 1973.
4. Beresford, D. R., How Companies are Reporting Social Performance, *Management Accounting*, August, 1974.
5. Brummet, R. L., Nonfinancial Measures in Social Accounts, in *Corporate Social Accounting* Dierkes, M. & Bauer, R. A., (eds), Praeger Publishers, New York 1973. p. 345.
6. Churchill, N. E., Towards a Theory for Social Accounting, *Sloan Management Review*, Spring, 1974.
A.A.A. Report of the Committee on Social Costs, *Accounting Review*, Supplement to Vol. XLX, 1975.

Appendix

The Quaker Oats Company
Annual Report 1973 (extracts from)

Quaker's People

A few of Quaker's people are shown on the covers of this Annual Report—men and women who represent their fellow employees worldwide. You see them with the Quaker products they know best, the brand names they work with every day. We can't introduce you to all Quaker's people, but we would like you to meet these 25. Some are your neighbors; many make products you buy and use every day; all are important to you as shareholders, employees and others with an interest in the company. Please see the inside back cover to meet these 25 representatives of Quaker's people.

The Asset That Doesn't Show on the Balance Sheet

The single dimension that cuts across all others in judging the future of Quaker is our people—more than 23,000 men and women around the world.

It's true, of course, that the Company's strong, established brand names, financial resources, manufacturing and distribution capabilities, and research centers are all essential to success. But all of these are only tools until the talent and ability of Quaker's people put them to work.

The people of Quaker dedicate their working lives to the progress of our company—for the benefit of shareholders and consumers, as well as for themselves. So that we may continue to deserve people of integrity, ability and ambition, we strive to maintain an environment for personal development and advancement that provides stimulation, satisfaction and reward.

The quality of excellence of our people would tend to indicate that we have done this successfully. To be certain that this situation remains and is strengthened where possible, we shall continue our emphasis on good compensation and incentive profit-sharing plans, on safe and pleasant work environments, on equal employment opportunities, on assistance to employees in achieving educational objectives, and on benefits that assure a good income for retirement and security in the event of injury, illness or death.

Superior performance is a constant reminder that the qualities of people who contribute most to success in our businesses extend to personal concern about the issues of our times and the needs of others. So it is that Quaker's people are encouraged to work within their communities and occupational fields, to participate in all levels of government, be active in school and church affairs, and to join in many company programs aimed at improving the quality of life. Just a few examples from thousands around the world:

Bruce Donelson, a production manager at the Omaha chemicals plant, who with his wife edits publications for the Garnett-Green Perceptual Motor Training Center—which aids children who have minimal cerebral dysfunction that inhibits educational social and physical development.

Jose De Leon, an audio-visual operator in Chicago, who is investing substantial amounts of his own time to upgrade his employment skills, with the aid of the Company's tuition-reimbursement program. Jose also devotes many hours a week to working with young children and their families in the company's tutoring program.

Lura Kilmer, an assembly supervisor at the Fisher-Price plant in East Aurora, who—as service unit director of the Buffalo and Erie County Girl Scouts—puts in almost another whole 40 hours a week supervising the troop leaders for 579 Scouts in five communities in Western New York State.

James Wells, a bulk cereal utility helper at the Cedar Rapids, Iowa, plant, who was recently returned by the voters for this third term in the Iowa House of Representatives.

Ralph Woodhull, now production manager of La Azteca in Mexico City, who—on a previous assignment in Cali, Columbia—worked with his wife to build and help sustain a school in the nearby barrio of Bellavista.

Sandra McNeil, a brand manager in the Cereals and Mixes Division at Company headquarters, who shares with many Quakers—and with her husband, who heads one of Chicago's major urban community action groups—a strong commitment to equal rights and opportunities for all people, and spends her energies accordingly.

Eric Ross, a weigher-mechanic with Quaker Oats Limited at Southall, just outside London in the United Kingdom, who as a member of St. John's Ambulance Brigade gives freely of his time to conduct first aid classes, assist with patient care in hospitals and help attend the injured in accident and other emergency situations.

With Quaker Cereals
Rita Maher, administrative assistant, holding Cap'n Crunch; *Earl Carr*, shift foreman, holding Instant Quaker Oatmeal; *Ross Wilson*, plant superintendent, holding traditional Quaker Oats—from the Cedar Rapids, Iowa, plant, which last year celebrated its centennial.

With Fisher-Price Toys
Jean Eichler, injection molding press operator at the Holland, New York, plant, holding the Crib & Playpen Cuddly Cub and the traditional Snoopy Sniffer; *John Slack*, senior industrial engineer at the Medina, New York, plant, looking at the Fisher-Price Movie Viewer.

With Ken-L Ration Dog Food
Jack Korinke, kennelmaster at the Barrington, Illinois, kennels, holding a lively dachshund puppy and standing next to both regular and cheese-flavored varieties of Ken-L Ration Burger.

With Aunt Jemima and Celeste Frozen Foods
Albert Currie, maintenance apprentice at the Jackson, Tennessee, frozen foods plant, with Aunt Jemima Original and Blueberry Frozen Waffles; *Phyllis Lewis*, production and sanitation worker at the Rosemont, Illinois, Celeste plant, with new Pepperoni and De Luxe Pizzas.

With Quaker Products in Canada
Gilbert Howson, shipper, with Croque Nature de Quaker (Quaker Harvest Crunch) ready-to-eat cereal; *Karen Northfold*, laboratory technician, with Quaker Bran Muffin and Sugar Drop Cookie Mixes and Aunt Jemima Frozen Blueberry Waffles (Gaufres); *Ingo Trautman*, cat food sales representative, with four varieties of new Puss'n Boots Flavour Morsels (Bouchés de Choix)—at the Peterborough, Ontario, Plant.

With the Chemicals Division
Carl Fields, Jr., foreman at the Cedar Rapids chemicals plant, with a drum of Q0 Furfural.

With Marx Toys
Mahlon Hirsh, toy design engineer, with the 727 Marx Jet; *Richard Rastetter*, package designer, alongside the Marx Big Wheel and holding the Square Shooters and Baseball Bagatelle games—at the Erie, Pennsylvania, Marx plant.

With Quaker Products in the United Kingdom

Winston Haisley, foreman, with Felix Complete Cat Food, Chunky Minced Morsels for dogs, and canned Felix and Chunky pet food; *Arthur Smale*, puffing machine operator, with Quick Quaker Oats and Sugar Puffs ready-to-eat cereal-at the Southall, England, plant of Quaker Oats Limited.

With Magic Pan Restaurants

Margaret Elder and *Wilke Harrison*, who serve delicious crépe entrees and desserts at the Walton Street Magic Pan Créperie in Chicago.

With Burry Cookies and Crackers

Guillermo Cott, mechanic, with Euphrates and Milk Lunch crackers; *Eola Tiggit*, packer with Girl Scout Cookies (Chocolate and Vanilla Cremes); *Irmgard Michaels*, product development technician, with Amandel and Scooter Pie cookies—from the Elizabeth, New Jersey, Burry plant.

With La Azteca in Mexico

Francisco Nuñez Toro, night shift foreman, with Express powdered chocolate beverage and Presidente candy; *Josefina Figueroa Arteaga*, candy making machine operator, with Abuelita, Morelia Presidencial and Tres Coronas beverages and Carlos V candy—at the Mexico City La Azteca plant.

With Needlecraft Products

Mark Zimmerman, mill mechanic, with the Ripple Afghan Kit; *Veronica Cudahy*, machine operator, with the Americana calendar kit and Wintuk synthetic yarn—at the Grafton, Wisconsin, plant of Needlecraft Division.

The Grocery Products Group

The Grocery Products Group, the largest factor in Quaker's business, set new sales and profit records in fiscal 1973. Grocery sales in the U.S. and Canada were $528.1 million, up 9.1 percent, while operating income increased significantly, up 17.5 percent, despite price controls and higher commodity costs. Very good sales increases and some reduction of marketing expenses toward the end of the fiscal year aided the earnings improvement. Most important, Quaker's grocery brands continued to show fine vitality.

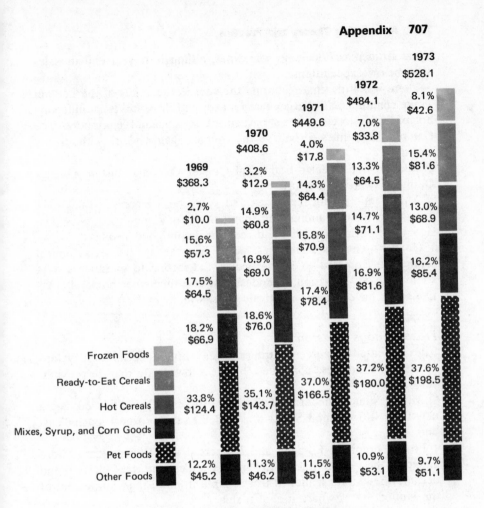

Sales in Millions of Dollars

Cereals and Mixes Division

Quaker's ready-to-eat cereal business had excellent growth during fiscal 1973, with sales up 27 percent, reflecting good market-share improvement at a time when industry sales were also up significantly. Quaker 100% Natural Cereal, a distinctively new and different product introduced in 30 percent of the United States last fall, has been very well accepted by consumers.

The Cap'n Crunch line of ready-to-eat cereals achieved its highest sales and market share. A new flavor, Cinnamon Crunch, is being introduced nationally.

Life cereal progressed very well, aided by new advertising that emphasizes the appeal of this nutritious product to children. King

Vitaman increased volume somewhat, although at year-end its sales were below expectations.

There was little change during the year in the status of the Federal Trade commission's charges that Quaker and three larger manufacturers of ready-to-eat cereals participate in a shared monopoly. The Company continues to believe the charges against it are without any merit.

Sales of hot cereals—traditional Quaker Oats and Instant Quaker Oatmeal—were off slightly.

Aunt Jemima pancake mixes and syrup both increased sales over prior year by maintaining their shares of expanding industry sales. The significant business in grits and corn meal continued strong.

Quaker's Cereals and mixes, which have always been economical foods, are expected to be particularly attractive to consumers as a source of good nutrition at modest cost at a time when some alternative foods have become relatively expensive.

Frozen Foods Division
Sales increased 26 percent during the year. Investment in the development of this business continued, but at a lower rate than in previous years.

Aunt Jemima Blueberry Waffles were successfully introduced, and a new flavor—Cinnamon Swirl—was added to the Frozen French Toast line.

Frozen prepared Lasagna and Pepperoni and Deluxe Pizzas were added to the Celeste line of Italian specialities, and the Celeste brand became the market leader in frozen pizza in more than 50 percent of the United States where it is available.

Pet Foods Division
Ken-L Ration semi-moist dog food products, which had strong market-share gains were the main contributors to record sales—up more than 10 percent. The Ken-L Ration brand of canned dog food increased sales and continues to lead the maintenance canned dog food market.

Sales and market share of Puss'n Boots cat food declined in fiscal 1973, reflecting a lack of new products during the year. Every effort is being made to correct this deficiency.

Strong research and development programs in both dog and cat food are under way at the Company's pet food research facilities in Barrington, Illinois, in order to support the Ken-L Ration and Puss'n Boots brand franchises with innovative new products.

Canada

The Quaker Oats company of Canada Limited performed very well in fiscal 1973. Strong growth in pet foods and good cost control across all operations combined to produce the best year in the Canadian company's history.

Several important new products were successfully introduced, including Harvest Crunch similar to Quaker 100% Natural Cereal in the U.S.—and Puss'n Boots Flavour Morsels, a semi-moist cat food. Blueberry Waffles were also added to Aunt Jemima line of frozen, prepared products.

Group Outlook

As pointed out in the President's letter there are a number of factors related to international food demand and U.S. economic policy that raise some uncertainties about the Group's results in the 1974 fiscal year. There will be problems in both the cost and availability of raw materials and difficulties in increasing prices to recover costs. Yet, despite this short-term problem, the fundamentals of the business are very strong, as demonstrated in fiscal 1973.

Financial Information

Growth in Earnings Per Share:

Since 1969 it has been Quaker's financial objective to improve per-share earnings an average of at least 10 percent a year over any five-year period, and this objective has been achieved. The reason for stating the goal as a five-year moving average is that the business is managed principally for long-term results. Most individual years should be more than 10 percent ahead, but this approach also contemplates that some years may be below it. Five-year averages (restated for the merger with Needlecraft) are:

5-Year Periods Ending June 30	5-Year Average Per-Share Earnings Improvement
1969	12.8%
1970	11.6%
1971	11.5%
1972	13.0%
1973	13.0%

This chart shows actual earnings-per-share data and dividends declared for the last ten fiscal years:

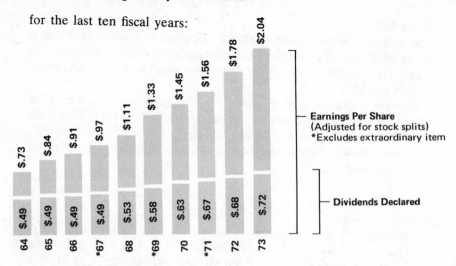

Earnings Per Share
(Adjusted for stock splits)
*Excludes extraordinary item

Dividends Declared

Stock Split and Dividend Increase:

The company's common shares were split 3-for-2, effective September 22, 1972. The quarterly common share dividend was increased to 18 cents a share, effective with the payment on October 20, 1972.

Sales and Operating Income by Groups:

There were significant upward trends in all four operating groups, as discussed in the respective Group sections earlier in this report. Particularly important is the planned improvement in the Grocery Products businesses. Actual data is:

Year Ended June 30	Millions of Dollars		
	1973	1972	1971
Sales*			
Grocery Products Group	$528.1	$484.1	$449.6
International Grocery Products Group	133.9	106.7	87.0
Toys and Recreational Products Group	224.7	116.8	81.9
Industrial and Institutional Products Group	104.1	87.6	83.4
Total	$990.8	$795.2	$701.9
Operating Income*			
Grocery Products Group	$51.1	$43.5	$43.2
International Grocery Products Group	6.8	5.3	5.2
Toys and Recreational Products Group	31.9	22.8	13.6
Industrial and Institutional Products Group	6.7	5.6	4.3
Total	$96.5	$77.2	$66.3
Less interest expense (net)	11.0	6.6	5.5
Income before income taxes	$85.5	$70.6	$60.8

*Prior years' data is restated to reflect the 1973 shift of organizational responsibility for industrial and government cereals business from the Industrial and Institutional Products Group to the Grocery Products Group, and refinements in the allocation of certain costs betwen groups.

Financing

The Company continues to maintain a strong, flexible financial condition. Quaker policy is to make aggressive use of borrowing and, at the same time, maintain the ability to take full advantage of unforseen investment opportunities. In accord with these concepts, the Company expects its debt ratio will be maintained between 25 and 35 percent. The chart below shows shareholders' equity and long-term debt at the end of each of the last five fiscal years. At June 30, 1973, long-term debt was 28.4 percent of the total.

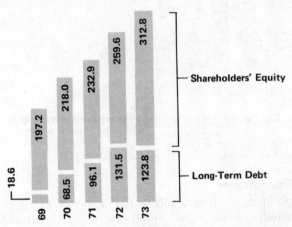

Early in the fiscal year, the Company sold 600,000 shares of additional common stock, thus adding an additional $22.6 million of equity to the permanent capital base for use in financing future working capital and fixed asset requirements. Also, in January, a $20.2 million, seven-year financing transaction was arranged to provide for the anticipated needs of foreign operations.

In addition to its permanent capital requirements, the company also incurs short-term borrowings from banks and in the commercial paper market, primarily in connection with seasonal working-capital requirements. In fiscal 1973, these domestic seasonal working capital requirements reached a peak of $42 million in October, were reduced to £4 million in January, and increased again to $49 million at June 30.

Return on Shareholders' Equity

The company recognizes that return-on-investment goals must be basically long-term in nature, and that the results of new investments are often unfavorable on short-term earnings. Overall, however, Quaker expects that its diversified businesses should be able to support a regular flow of substantial new investments on which long-term returns are favorable. This concept is reflected in the table below, which shows the after-tax return on shareholders' equity during each of the past five years.

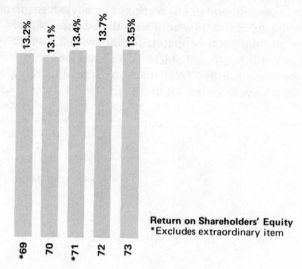

Return on Shareholders' Equity
*Excludes extraordinary item

Capital Expenditures

Quaker continues to invest substantial amounts to support future growth. Excluding acquisitions, capital expenditures in fiscal 1973 were $52.6 million, and have increased at an average annual rate of about 18 percent during the last five years. Principal spending last year was for new facilities to manufacture toys, pet foods, fozen foods, chemicals and ready-to-eat cereals.

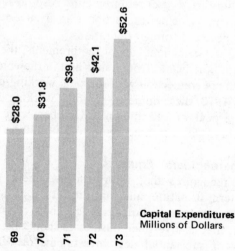

Capital Expenditures
Millions of Dollars

Research and Development

Technical research expenditures were $14 million in fiscal 1973. This represents scientific research and development, the creation of new products and improvements of current products, and the centralized coordination of quality assurance. The figures do not include market research nor the bulk of quality assurance expenditures, which occur at divisional and plant levels.

Quaker continues a heavy emphasis on technical research, seeking those products that will possess lasting, distinctive consumer benefits as well as new applications of specialty chemicals. These expenses have increased at a rate of more than 19 percent a year over the last five years.

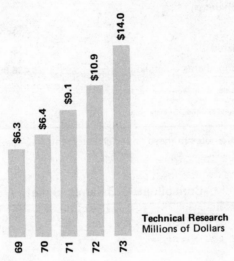

Technical Research
Millions of Dollars

The Quaker Oats Company and Subsidiaries
Consolidated Statement of Income and Reinvested Earnings*

Year Ended June 30	Thousands of Dollars 1973	1972
Revenues:		
Net sales	$990,767	$795,240
Other income—net	1,818	1,702
	992,585	796,942
Costs and Expenses:		
Cost of goods sold	692,723	545,783
Selling, general and administrative expenses	201,460	172,409
Interest expense	12,853	8,194
	907,036	726,386

Consolodated Statement (Continued)

Income before income taxes	85,549	70,556
Provision for income taxes	43,426	34,942
Net income	42,123	35,614
Reinvested Earnings:		
Balance beginning of year	187,561	162,805
Needlecraft Corporation	—	2,632
	187,561	165,437
Dividends—preferred stock	(452)	(484)
—common stock	(14,711)	(13,006)
Transfer to common stock re stock split	(29,911)	—
Balance end of year	$184,610	$187,561
Per Common Share: (A)		
Net Income	$2.04	$1.78
Dividends Declared	$ .72	$ .68
Average common shares outstanding	20,465,855	19,759,856

(A) Adjusted for stock split on September 22, 1972.

See accompanying notes to financial statements.

*The explanatory notes to these financial statements have been omitted by us from these extracts.

Consolidated Balance Sheet

Assets	Thousands of Dollars	
June 30	1973	1972
Current Assets:		
Cash	$ 3,038	$ 8,009
Marketable securities, at cost which approximates market	23,316	15,326
Receivables (less allowances of $3,546,000 and $2,613,000 respectively)	111,218	91,468
Inventories	169,607	126,732
Prepaid expenses	6,631	6,173
Current assets	313,810	247,708
Other Receivables and Investments:	6,903	5,575
Property, Plant and Equipment, at cost:		
Land	7,276	7,092
Buildings and improvements	113,284	101,544
Machinery and equipment	253,564	234,526
	374,124	343,162

Less accumulated depreciation (including reserve for estimated losses on plant dispositions of $4,020,000 in 1972)	102,047	99,234
Properties (net)	272,077	243,928
Intangible Assets:		
Excess of cost over net assets of acquired businesses	30,004	27,747
Patents, trademarks, designs, less amortization	7,276	7,751
	$630,070	$532,709

See accompanying notes to financial statements.

The Quaker Oats Company and Subsidiaries

Liabilities and Shareholders' Equity	Thousands of Dollars	
June 30	1973	1972
Current Liabilities:		
Notes payable to banks	$ 21,685	$ 14,558
Commercial paper	44,208	21,550
Current maturities of long-term debt	3,447	4,285
Accounts payable and accrued expenses	78,050	67,511
Income taxes payable	6,501	5,337
Dividends payable	3,823	3,449
Current liabilities	157,714	116,690
Long-term Debt, less current maturities:		
$3\frac{1}{2}$% Notes, $2,000,000 due annually through 1977	6,000	8,000
Revolving credit notes, due 1979	14,200	37,000
Note payable, due 1980	20,188	—
$6\frac{1}{2}$% Note, $1,250,000 due annually from 1975 through 1994	25,000	25,000
7.70% Sinking fund debentures, $1,800,000 due annually from 1977 through 2001	50,000	50,000
Obligations of subsidiaries	8,433	11,521
Long-term debt	123,821	131,521
Other Liabilities:	6,090	2,270
Deferred Income Taxes:	29,650	22,613
Shareholders' Equity:		
Preferred, $50 par value, $3 cumulative convertible, authorized 153,897 shares; issued 148,165 and 158,899 shares, respectively	7,408	7,945
Common, $5 par value, authorized 35,000,000 shares; issued 20,892,858 and 20,131,533 shares, respectively	104,464	67,105
Additional paid-in capital	22,359	3,350
Reinvested earnings	184,610	187,561
	318,841	265,961
Less treasury common stock, at cost	6,046	6,346
Shareholders' equity	312,795	259,615
	$630,070	$532,709

Consolidated Statement of Changes in Financial Position

Year Ended June 30	Thousands of Dollars 1973	1972
Source of Working Capital:		
Operations:		
Net Income	$42,123	$35,614
Depreciation and amortization	21,114	15,587
Deferred income taxes	7,037	6,210
Total from Operations	70,274	57,411
Issuance of 600,000 shares of common stock	22,622	—
Proceeds from long-term borrowings	20,188	37,000
Increase in other long-term liabilities	3,820	1,300
Sales of properties	3,904	1,926
Common stock issued under stock option plans	3,848	4,337
Total provided	124,656	101,974
Uses of Working Capital:		
Additions to properties	52,576	42,071
Cash dividends declared	15,163	13,490
Decrease in long-term debt	27,888	2,168
Excess of cost over working capital of acquired businesses	2,673	22,253
Other—net	1,278	1,623
Total used	99,578	81,605
Increase in Working Capital:	$25,078	$20,369
Consisting of:		
Cash and marketable securities	$ 3,019	$(11,879)
Receivables—net	19,750	26,293
Inventories	42,875	35,363
Prepaid expenses	458	(1,975)
Notes payable to banks	(7,127)	6,222
Commercial paper	(22,658)	(21,550)
Current maturities of long-term debt	838	(1,781)
Other current liabilities	(12,077)	(10,324)
Net increase	$25,078	$20,369

See accompanying notes to financial statements.

3

Accounting for Human Resources

It seems fitting to conclude this study of accounting with a chapter about accounting and people. It is no coincidence, however, that we should bring this text to a close where the study of accounting should find its focus on the importance of people.

Throughout this text, we have sought to relate the study of accounting to its changing socio-economic environment as a means of discovering and understanding the objectives of the accounting process. Accounting developed originally as a means of controlling wealth. At no stage in its early development did it concern itself with human welfare, and except where people might exist as property rights, for example as slaves, their existence and their needs were not regarded as being of accounting concern. Wealth was linked to ownership rights in property and the employment of those rights in agriculture, commerce or industry. This remains to this day the basic philosophy of financial accounting. People can no longer be owned as property, so the price paid for human labour is treated as an expense and charged against periodic income. An examination of financial accounting information in Part 2 mentions wages and salaries as the only direct evidence of people in the accounting process.

The accounting process begins to be aware of people with the development of management accounting, and the need to ensure the efficient use of all resources. Hence, we noted the development of standard costs and the application of such costs to the measurement of labour used in the calculation of unit costs of production. The discovery that human behaviour is a significant factor affecting business efficiency was an important landmark. It is noteworthy, however, that this discovery only occurred after the Second World War and coincided with the expansion of the social sciences and an emphasis on human welfare. Accounting information for organizational planning and control purposes remains focussed on the problem of the efficient allocation and use of resources in the attainment of organizational goals.

This analysis of the transition from wealth to people in accounting presents us also with the dilemma as to where we should locate a chapter on accounting for human resources. We should point out that human resource accounting has not, itself, developed out of a concern with people as such, but rather out of a concern with wealth. Indeed, the genesis of human resource accounting lies in the recognition in the 1960s of the need for human asset measurements for decision-making in the context of a managerial philosophy aimed at maximizing business income. Hence, we could have related it to the problem of organizational planning and control. Equally, we could have mentioned human resource accounting in the context of financial reporting, since shareholders and investors are interested in all the relevant factors associated with corporate income. We believe that social responsibility accounting implies a welfare concern with employees—as people—and for this reason, we consider that human resource accounting is concerned with providing information relevant to the social management of organizations, and with the measurement of human resource contributions.

The purpose of this chapter is to examine the concept of human resource accounting as it has evolved in its rather short history, and to touch upon the problems implied in its tentative proposals.

The development of human resource accounting

It is fair to say that the mainstream of thought regarding human resource accounting sees the significance of this development in terms of the effective use of human assets represented as financial costs. This is reflected in the definition of human resource accounting which have featured in the literature.

Two early contributors to thinking on HRA, Likert and Bowers adopted a broad view of the definition of 'human resources', and by implication, a broad view of the scope and objectives of HRA, in the following definition:

> "These resources include the value of all such assets as a firm's human organization, its customer loyalty, shareholder loyalty, supplier loyalty, its reputation among the financial community, and its reputation in the community in which it has plant and offices." (Likert & Bowers, 1968.)

This broad definition was quickly abandoned by subsequent writers, doubtless because it presents conceptual and measurement problems from an accounting viewpoint.

Flamholtz, perhaps the most prolific writer in this area, adopted a much more practical definition of HRA which was focussed essentially on 'accounting for people as organizational resources'. This view is echoed in the 1973 report of the American Accounting Association

Committee Report on Human Resource Accounting, where HRA is defined as "the process of identifying, measuring and communicating information about human resources to decision-makers." Such a definition covers a potentially wide field, notwithstanding its focus on the human element in organizations. Flamholtz (1973), therefore, emphasizes the relatively narrow scope of HRA in his view, as follows:

> "It involves measuring the costs incurred by business firms and other organizations to recruit, select, hire, train and develop human assets. It also involves measuring the economic value of people to organizations."

Such a definition of HRA led Flamholtz to identify the main areas of research interest in HRA as being:

(1) The determination of the value of individuals to organizations.
(2) The determination of reliable and valid measures of value and cost.
(3) The design of operational systems for these measures.
(4) The determination of the effects on decision-makers of the availability of HRA.

Comparison of fixed asset accounting and human resource accounting

The foregoing statement by Flamholtz of the main areas of research interest in HRA has much in common with the objectives of fixed asset accounting as conventionally understood. Indeed, in many senses much of the work which has been done in HRA so far represents the translation of traditional accounting objectives and techniques to this new accounting concept. Thus, many of the earliest contributors to HRA research took as their starting point the frequently encountered statement in corporate financial reports that the organization's employees were the most important asset of the business. The 1973 Annual Report of the Quaker Oats Company, which we discussed in chapter 4, begins with the statement "the asset that doesn't show on the Balance Sheet" (see Appendix). The implication of this statement is that the true value of organizational assets is not reflected in conventional accounting reports, when employees are only shown in terms of wages and salaries.

The need for HRA was also identified with managerial objectives of seeking the most efficient employment of all organizational resources.

In fact, the major concern of researchers in this area has been with the management aspects of human asset utilization rather than with the problem of financial reporting. The costs associated with the human element in organizations constitutes a substantial proportion of total costs. The quality of this element also has a deterministic influence on profitability. The significance of these factors has now been fully recognized in accounting, and the importance of HRA lies in the possibility offered for the development of a method which will assist management to make better decisions on investments in human assets and better decisions on the use and allocation of these assets.

The profit maximization concept, as applied to human resource accounting, required measurements of value which would allow human resources to be brought into an accounting framework, that is, they would provide for the integration of human and non-human assets.

Applications of human resource accounting measurements

Giles & Robinson (1972) have listed the possible uses of human asset values as follows:

(a) measuring the return on capital employed on total organizational assets, including the value of human assets;

(b) planning the use of resources, taking into account the valuable human resources in considering the use of financial and physical resources;

(c) examining the disposition of resources, for by allocating relative human asset values to different job grades, the location of organizational investments in human resources would be highlighted. This would have significance for management, and for established personnel policies and expenditure;

(d) examining personnel expenditure and re-appraising expenditure on personnel services and training;

(e) preparing organization and personal profiles, so as to plan the desired amount and disposition of human assets;

(f) valuing businesses, where the human asset value becomes a relevant factor in mergers and takeover decisions;

(g) industrial relations problems, where human asset values may, if accepted, provide a rational basis for discussing reward structures;

(h) integrating human asset values with financial accounts for reporting purposes.

Methods for determining the value of human assets

Several procedures have been proposed for valuing human assets, but as with other methods used for valuing assets, no one method is suitable for all purposes.

Replacement costs

The historical cost of human assets is compatible with the traditional accounting treatment of assets, and requires collecting the costs involved in recruiting, hiring and training human resources. The use of replacement costs has the advantage of adjusting the human value to price level changes and can assist the process of manpower planning by providing estimates of the costs involved in obtaining labour for different positions. By providing such information it is possible to make decisions about the quality of personnel to hire and the training programme they should follow. For example, would it be more feasible to employ less qualified personnel and to train them internally for positions, rather than hiring highly qualified personnel?

Accounting for human assets assists in a better allocation of resources. By treating labour costs as expenses an important part of the investment base is ignored. The use of an incorrect investment base yields an incorrect estimate of return on investment. Therefore, when comparing competing investment projects human resources should be included in the calculations if a realistic comparison is to be made. The same argument may be applied to external reporting; assuming that funds seek the highest rates of return, the exclusion of human assets from the investment base of companies causes an imperfect allocation of resources within the economy. Some writers assert that trends in the ratio of investments in human assets to total assets (the human asset investment ratio) may be a useful predictor of future profit performance. They contend that there is evidence to indicate a degree of meaningful correlation between profitability of organizations and their expenditures on acquisition, training and retention of human resources. This suggests that firms with a high human asset ratio will ultimately generate high profits, while firms with a low ratio may experience profit declines.

Replacement costs can be used to develop standard costs of recruiting, hiring, training and developing individuals. Such standards are used to compare actual results with those planned.

Competitive bidding method

The replacement cost method suffers from two deficiencies. First, management may have some particular asset which it is unwilling to replace at current cost, but which it wants to keep using because the asset has a value greater than its scrap value. Secondly, there may be no similar replacement for a certain asset. Some have suggested a possible solution to these difficulties lies in using the opportunity cost concept, that is the value of an employee in his alternative use, as a basis for estimating the value of human resources employed by the organization. The opportunity cost value could be established it has been suggested by competitive bidding within the organization, so that, in effect, managers must bid for any scarce employee. A human asset, therefore, will have a value only if it is a scarce resource, that is, when its employment in one division denies it to another division. The division or department with the highest bid would win the particular human resource and would include its price in its investment base.

Although the competitive bidding process provides an optimal allocation of personnel within the firm and a quantitative base for planning and developing the human assets of the firm, it suffers from several drawbacks. One disadvantage is that it makes serious omissions of certain asset values. It excludes employees of the type which can be hired readily from outside the firm, so that the approach seems to be concerned with only one section of a firm's human resources, having special skills within the firm or in the labour market.

Capitalization of salary

Another method which has been suggested is the valuation of a firm's labour force by aggregating and averaging the earnings profile of homogeneous groups of employees. The earnings profile of an individual is a mathematical presentation of the income stream generated by a person, and this of course is his productivity to the firm. After initially increasing due to the benefit of experience, productivity is assumed to be associated with age. As a person ages, productivity declines because of technological obsolescence and health deterioration, a fact which is expressed by a decrease in annual earnings. Hence, the value to the firm of human capital embodied in a person of age r is the present value of his remaining future earnings from employment calculated as follows:

$$V_r = \sum_{t=r}^{T} \frac{I(t)}{(1+r)^{t-r}}$$

where:

V_r = the human capital value of a person r years old
$I(t)$ = the person's annual earnings up to retirement
    represented by the earnings profile
  r = a discount rate specific to the person
  T = retirement age.

By extension, it is possible to arrive at a value of the total human capital associated with the firm based on average earnings data of a homogeneous group of employees. This approach, it is suggested, allows two values to be attached to the firm's labour force; a 'general' value based on overall census data, and a 'specific' value derived from the specific wage scale of the firm. The discount rate which is used is the cost of capital as used in capital budgeting decisions.

The derivation of a firm's human capital value in this way would permit the formulation of a new set of financial ratios. The first being the ratio of human to non-human capital values to indicate the degree of labour intensiveness. However, in accounting the reported values of non-human assets is not based upon the earnings profile of those assets, and therefore unless non-human assets are valued in a similar manner a ratio of human to non-human assets would not be very meaningful. Secondly, this method would provide information about changes in the structure of the labour force. The point here is that the ageing of a firm's labour force may account for a slower rate of growth as against another firm with a younger labour force. This information might well be useful if certain assumptions were correct about the methods of determining wages and the correlation between age and productivity. Certainly, in the United Kingdom the wages of white collar workers tends to 'increase' with age up to a ceiling, and there is no evidence to support the assertion that their productivity is less than younger workers. With increasing automation, it would seem that the level of productivity may well depend on other factors than age. Reporting the 'general' and 'specific' values of human capital may also usefully throw light upon the firm's recruiting and wage policy.

Economic value method

One criticism that may be advanced against the capitalization of salary method is the assumption that the earnings profile of the labour force should be the basis on which the labour force should be valued. In essence, the method adopts a 'cost based' approach to the valuation of human capital, and the only difference from conventional accounting is that it employs a 'future estimated cost' as against 'historic cost'.

A 'cost based' approach ignores such considerations as age, seniority, bargaining skills and known value to other employers, which may override considerations affecting an employee's real value to his company. According to economic theory, the value of an asset to a firm lies in the rate of return to be derived by the firm from its employment. Therefore, an individuals's value to an organization may be defined as the present worth of the set of future services he is expected to provide during the period he is expected to remain with the organization.

The economic value method focuses on the individual's value to a specific organization for two reasons. First, individuals are a central focus for much organizational decision-making, and secondly, measures of individual value can, in principle, be aggregated in order to value larger units of people. Beginning with the premise that the value of a resource should be defined as the present worth of its expected future services, the economic value method suggests that an individual's value to an organization should be conceptualized and measured as the present worth of his expected services. But the valuation of these services should take account of the individual's mobility through a set of organizational roles over time, so that an individual's value to an organization is a function of the total value of the services he will provide as he moves from role to role during his productive life. At any given time, the state occupied and hence the services derived cannot be predicted with certainty, but must be estimated probabilistically.

Accordingly, to measure an individual's worth to an organization, it is necessary to estimate the time interval during which the individual is expected to render services to the organization and assess the services expected to be derived from him during this period of time.

One limitation of this method of valuation arises from the narrow view taken of an organization. Since the analysis is restricted to individuals, it ignores the added value element of individuals operating as groups. Furthermore, advocates of this method have not suggested means by which a value may be arrived at in practice. As we saw earlier in chapter 7, the economist's method of valuation is fraught with difficulties of measurement, and for this reason replacement cost methods are usually more acceptable alternatives.

Return on effort employed

One method of accounting for human resources involves the measurement of effort employed on various functions—buying, manufacturing and selling. This kind of information may lead to a more efficient allocation and use of human resources.

Factors which distinguish the quantity and quality of effort expended, may be used to rate the contribution made by individuals. Such factors are:

(a) Level, or grade, of work done

Firms are obliged to distinguish between different grades of jobs for the purpose of developing wage structures. The following factors may be applied to job grades:

Job Grade	Factor
10 (e.g. director)	10
7 (e.g. sales manager)	7
4 (e.g. salesman)	4
1 (e.g. typist)	1

(b) *Effectiveness with which the individual performs his job*

Personal Assessment	Factor
Very good	1.5
Satisfactory	1.0

(c) *Experience, which increases, up to a point, the efficiency of job performance*

Years of Experience	Factor
0–1	1.0
1–2	1.1
2–3	1.2
2–4	1.3
4–5	1.4
Over 5	1.5

These factors are then multiplied together in determining a measurement of effort employed for each individual. For example, a very good sales manager with over five years' experience would score $1.5 \times 7 \times 1.5 = 15.75$ for effort employed. When all the calculations for every individual are aggregated, we obtain a figure which represents the total effort employed in an organization.

If the primary functions of an organization are buying, manufacturing and selling, and there are three business areas, it is possible to relate the profit of these areas to the effort involved in producing the profit:

Business Area	Measurement of Effort Employed Buying	Manu- facturing	Selling	Total Effort	Total Profit	Total Profit ÷ Total Effort
1	150	900	350	1400	£140,000	£100 per unit of effort
2	80	1000	120	1200	£24,000	£20 per unit of effort
3	100	2000	400	2500	£500,000	£200 per unit of effort

These calculations show wide divergencies between business areas and the return of effort expended. Area 3 gives a return of £200 per unit of effort expended as against £20 only for area 2. This kind of information leads management to question why such differences exist and whether it is possible to improve the performance of less effective areas. As in financial accounting where we consider return on investment, in human resource accounting we consider the return on effort expended, and ask whether it is satisfactory. This process leads to a more effective allocation of human resources. It is also possible to consider the ratio of *profits* to the effort employed in each of the three separate functions—buying, manufacturing and selling, and to thereby question the existing allocation of resources between these functions.

Behavioural variables method

One problem not adequately covered by the previous measures is that information is needed about the effectiveness with which an organization maintains the condition of its human resources. Traditional accounting measurements deal with such factors as costs, sales and *profits*, with the result that managers may be encouraged to dissipate valuable human assets and are even rewarded for doing so. This arises from the fact that managers can exert pressure on employees in order to increase short-run performance. In the long run, however, such tactics can be a serious cost to the organization, because a fall in the quality of human resources can have unfortunate effects on long-run performance.

The logic of decentralization calls for new measurements to prevent short-run liquidation of human assets. The R. G. Barry Corporation, a world pioneer in human resource accounting, identified five key result areas for which each manager is responsible within his unit. These areas are: profit, solvency, physical resources, human resources and customer loyalty resources. Rensis Likert contends that we need to measure such factors as loyalty, motivation, confidence and trust in order to determine changes in the quality of the human organization. He cites the findings of a research project which was conducted in a large company whereby two divisions were re-organized on a centralized, dictatorial, pressure-oriented basis and two on a decentralized, participating basis. The study concluded that putting pressure on employees could yield substantial increases in productivity, but only at a cost on the human assets of the organization. "In the company we studied the cost was clear: hostilities increased, there was greater reliance upon authority, loyalties declined and motivations to produce decreased while motivations to restrict production increased. In other words, the quality of the human organization deteriorated as a functioning social system." (Likert, 1967). Had this company had a human resource accounting system, it would have shown their value to be less at the end of the experiment than at the beginning. In increasing productivity, human assets may have been liquidated; if so this cost should have been quantified and charged against the increased output.

According to Likert, there is only one solution to this problem and it does not lie in more precise accounting data. The solution is to obtain periodic measurements of the character and quality of the human organization. A similar argument can be applied to customer goodwill. Increasing short-run profits by producing and selling inferior products is detrimental to the long-run position of the company. We need, therefore, a measure of consumer attitudes if goodwill is to be maintained.

The variables which need to be measured to maintain the quality of human assets involved such factors as loyalty to the organization, level of motivation of members, degree of confidence and trust among members, amount and quality of teamwork and aptitude scales of members. Certainly Likert believes that progress in social sciences in recent years enables any company which so desires to obtain measurements needed for adequate appraisal of the quality and performance capacity of its human organization. Instruments to measure many of the variables are now available; for those variables for which measuring instruments are not now available, the basic methodology now exists to develop the necessary tools.

Financial and human resource accounting: R. G. Barry Corporation

Despite the difficulties associated with the measurement of human asset values, a number of interesting experiments have been made in developing operational human resource accounting systems. The R. G. Barry Corporation is the most celebrated example of the attempt to derive human asset values from existing financial accounting data, and to integrate human asset values in a conventional financial Balance Sheet.

The R. G. Barry Corporation's approach was to capitalize the outlay costs of recruiting, acquiring, training, familiarizing and developing management personnel only. In accordance with the accounting conventions relating to the definition of assets, only outlays having an expected value beyond the current accounting period were treated as investments. These investments in human resources were amortized over the expected useful life of the investments.

The objectives of the Barry Corporation in developing a Human Resource Accounting Information System were to find answers to the following questions:

(a) What is the quality of profit performance?
(b) Are sufficient human capabilities being acquired to achieve the objectives of the enterprise?
(c) Are they being developed adequately?
(d) To what degree are they being properly maintained?
(e) Are these capabilities being properly utilized by the organization?

By kind permission of the R. G. Barry Corporation, we reproduce below the Statement of Income and the Balance Sheet for the year 1973. (Publication of this Statement for shareholders was thereafter abandoned whilst the Corporation continued their development of HRA for internal management purposes. Nevertheless we include the 1973 accounts as examples of the type of work being conducted by the Corporation.)

'THE TOTAL CONCEPT' R. G. Barry Corporation and Subsidiaries Pro-Forma (Conventional and Human Resource Accounting)

Balance Sheet		
	1973	1973
Assets	*Conventional and Human Resource*	*Conventional Only*
Total Current Assets	$18,311,713	$18,311,713
Net Property, Plant and Equipment	3,500,227	3,500,227
Excess of Purchase Price over Net Assets Acquired	1,285,829	1,285,829
Deferred Financing Costs	173,278	173,278
Net Investments in Human Resources	1,964,243	—
Prepaid Income Taxes and Other Assets	213,500	213,500
	$25,448,790	$23,484,547
Liabilities and Stockholders' Equity		
Total Current Liabilities	3,909,083	3,909,083
Long Term Debt, Excluding Current Installments	6,970,000	6,970,000
Deferred Compensation	143,150	143,150
Deferred Income Tax Based Upon Full Tax Deduction for Human Resource Costs	982,122	—
Stockholders' Equity:		
Capital Stock	1,902,347	1,902,347
Additional Capital in Excess of Par Value	5,676,549	5,676,549
Retained Earnings:		
Financial	4,883,418	4,883,418
Human Resources	982,121	—
	$25,448,790	$23,484,547

'THE TOTAL CONCEPT' (Cont.)

Balance Sheet (Cont.)

Statement of Income

	1973 Conventional and Human Resource	1973 Conventional Only
Net Sales	$43,161,564	$43,161,564
Cost of Sales	28,621,050	28,621,050
Gross Profit	14,540,514	14,540,514
Selling, General and Administrative Expenses	10,783,922	10,783,922
Operating Income	3,756,592	3,756,592
Interest Expense	598,846	598,846
Income Before Income Taxes	3,157,746	3,157,746
Net Increase in Human Resource Investment	184,293	—
Adjusted Income Before Income Taxes	3,342,039	3,157,746
Income Taxes	1,615,147	1,523,000
Net Income	$1,726,892	$1,634,746

Human resource accounting and corporate social responsibility

It can be argued that, far from being an isolated development in accounting, human resource accounting is merely one aspect of wider-ranging developments in the social sciences. Glautier (1976) has suggested that the genesis of HRA is to be found in the application of behavioural science concepts to the business organization and its management. Once the business enterprise is accepted as a complex social unit, whose components react upon each other in complex ways, rather than an institution within which productive resources are combined in a mechanistic manner, the deficiencies in information about the human organization become apparent. Similarly, once a range of organizational objectives become discernible, rather than a single profit objective, the management problem becomes the optimization of overall organizational performance. The link between the behavioural view of the organization and HRA is perhaps best seen in the seminal work of Likert (1967) and Likert & Bowers (1968) which highlighted the need for information about the human element in organizations.

HRA has a particular role to play as regards the concept of corporate social responsibility. If we define the social effectiveness of organizations as being reflected in the quality of the social relationships which they determine, any improvement in these social relationships should be reflected in benefits accruing both to the organization and to its members. These benefits are the non-financial rewards accruing to employees in the form of job satisfaction, and to the organization in the added element of organizational effectiveness attributable to this factor.

The quality of organizational relationships implies a great deal more than simply greater job satisfaction or employee motivation. It implies the consideration of the range of social contribution to employees in the form of increased monetary and non-monetary benefits, participation in management and improved industrial relations.

Corporate social responsibility and industrial relations

Many would judge corporate social responsibility towards employees as imposing an obligation to foster good industrial relations, thereby adding to the value of the organizational contribution to employees. From the organization's own point of view, it is evident that the financial value of human resources depends to a considerable extent on the quality of industrial relations. The term 'industrial relations' refers to the whole spectrum of points of contact between the organization and its employees. Though the wage bargain is often the central focus of debate, it is fair to regard the wage bargain as the apex of a complex set of relationships implied in the recognition of the firm as a social unit.

The disclosure of information to employees and their Trade Unions is of critical importance to good industrial relations. The attitude of employees will be determined in part by what they know about the organization which employs them, and conversely, the attitude of management will be influenced by how much they know about their employees. Moreover, the negotiation of the wage bargain may be improved by the extension of the information base available to the negotiators.

The consideration of the information requirement for collective bargaining led the Trades Union Congress Report (1970) to detail the type of information which would be useful in this respect. The list was as follows.

General information

A description of the Company's activities and structure: details of holding companies and subsidiaries; organizational managerial structure; outside contracts.

Details of ownership: Directors and shareholders in the company and in holding companies; beneficial control of nominee shareholdings.

Manpower

Numbers of employees by job description; rates of turnover, short-time, absenteeism, sickness and accidents; details of existing provisions for security, sickness, accidents, recruitment, training, re-deployment, promotion and redundancy.

Financial

Sales turnover by main activities: home and export sales; non-trading income, including income from investments and overseas earnings; pricing policy.

Costs: distribution and sales costs; production costs; administrative and overhead costs; costs of materials and machinery; labour costs including social security payments; costs of management and supervision.

Incomes: directors' remuneration; wages and salaries; make-up of pay-negotiated rates, payments by results, overtime and bonuses.

Profits: before and after tax and taking into account Government allowances, grants and subsidies; distributions and retentions.

Performance indicators: unit costs, output per man, return on capital employed, value added etc.

Worth of company: details of growth and up to date value of fixed assets and stocks; growth and realizable value of trade investments.

Prospects and plans

Details of new enterprises and locations; prospective close-downs; mergers and takeovers.

Trading and sales plans; investment plans, including research and development.

Manpower plans: plans for recruitment, selection and training; promotion, regrading and redeployment; short-time and redundancy provisions.

The foregoing specification of required information is interesting in a number of respects. It indicates the type of information relevant to employees and Trade Unions as a group whose objective needs are different from those of shareholders. It may be noted in this connection that the Industry Act, 1975 and the Employment Protection Act, 1975 recognized the special information needs of employees in their provisions for information disclosure. The TUC list also indicates the desirability of widening the range of conventional accounting disclosure to include both financial and non-financial information, where users' needs cannot be satisfied by purely financial reports. It highlights the growing importance of manpower planning and utilization, and in this respect underlines the potential functional usefulness and social relevance of human resource accounting. It repeats the urgency of developing non-financial measures of effectiveness to supplement standards of performance based on financial measures.

Summary

The foregoing considerations have a number of implications for human resource accounting. Techniques and measurement are required which will allow behavioural and social problems to be considered. Whilst it is true that accounting has a focus on monetary data, it is also true that this focus has impeded the flow of information about activities which cannot effectively be expressed in monetary terms. There has become apparent a need for non-financial measures of effectiveness which will reflect the behavioural and social aspects of organizational activities. Such indicators as rates of absenteeism, labour turnover, duration of employment, internal promotions, are all readily available indicators for these purposes.

The concept of the corporation as a social unit suggests that emphasis should be given to improving the internal organizational and social relationships in organizations in developing HRA systems. Glautier & Taylor (1975) have suggested that many of the difficulties associated with attempts to value people or identify costs associated with people implied in the attempt to integrate HRA into a conventional accounting framework might be avoided if attention were focussed on tasks rather than task-holders. The appropriate techniques for this purpose are found in job evaluation. Hence, according to Glautier and Taylor, substantial progress in the developing of HRA information systems may be possible by integrating personnel, financial and cost accounting information. We would warn, however, that absolute limits exist to the development of HRA. First, the cost of generating information will be a constraint. Second, not all the relevant dimensions of managerial or employee performance can be included in accounting reports, since neither accountants nor other specialists have developed comprehensive measures and standards (Hopwood, 1974).

We began our analysis of the development of HRA in the context of a search for means of improving the efficiency of asset utilization. We concluded our analysis with a brief analysis of the implications of HRA for improving the effectiveness of business organizations viewed as complex social units.

References

1. American Accounting Association Report of the Committee on Human Resource Accounting, *Accounting Review* Supplement to Volume XLVIII, pp. 169–185, 1973.

2. Flamholtz, E., *Human Resource Accounting*, p. 3, Dickension, Encino, California and Belmont, 1973.

3. Giles, W. J. & Robinson, D., *Human Asset Accounting*, pp. 24-26, Institute of Personnel Management and Institute of Cost and Management Accountants, London, 1972.

4. Glautier, M. W. E., Human Resource Accounting: A Critique of Research Objectives for the Development of Human Resource Accounting Models, *Journal of Business Finance and Accounting*, Summer, 1976.

5. Glautier, M. W. E. & Taylor, P. J., *Human Resource Accounting: A Framework for the Social Management of Human Assets*, paper presented to the Workshop on Designing Adaptive Information Systems, European Institute for Advanced Studies in Management, Cologne University, 19–21 March, 1975.

6. Glautier, M. W. E. & Taylor, P. J., *H.R.A.: A Task-Oriented Model for the Management of Human Assets*, Department of Economics, University College of North Wales, Bangor, 1975.

7. Glautier, M. W. E. & Underdown, B., Problems and Prospects of Accounting for Human Assets, *Management Accounting*, March, 1973.

8. Hopwood, A., *Accounting and Human Behaviour*, pp. 106–107, Accountancy Age Books, London, 1974.

9. Likert, R., *The Human Organization: Its Management and Value*, p. 102, McGraw-Hill, New York, 1967.

10. Likert, R. & Bowers, D. G., Organizational theory and human resource accounting, *The American Psychologist*, pp. 585–592, September, 1968.

Selected Further Readings

Accounting Standards Steering Committee, *The Corporate Report*, London, 1975.

American Accounting Association Report of the Committee on Non-Financial Measures of Effectiveness, *Accounting Review* Supplement, Vol. XLVL, 1971.

American Accounting Association Report of the Committee on Environmental Effects of Organizational Behaviour, *Accounting Review* Supplement, Vol. XLVIII, 1973.

American Accounting Association Report of the Committee on Human Resource Accounting, *Accounting Review* Supplement, Vol. XLVIII, 1973.

American Accounting Association Report of the Committee on Human Resource Accounting, *Accounting Review* Supplement, Vol. XLIX, 1974.

American Accounting Association Report of the Committee on Measurement of Social Costs, *Accounting Review* Supplement, Vol. XLIX, 1974.

American Accounting Association Report of the Committee on Social Costs, *Accounting Review* Supplement, Vol. XLX, 1975.

Anshen, M. (ed.), *Managing the Socially Responsible Corporation* Collier Macmillan, London, 1974.

Bauer, R. A. & Fenn, D., *The Corporate Social Audit*, Russell Sage Foundation, New York, 1972.

Caplan, E. H. & Landekich, S. *Human Resource Accounting: Past, Present and Future*, National Association of Accountants, New York, 1974.

Dierkes, M. & Bauer, R. A. (eds) *Corporate Social Accounting*, Praegers Publishers, New York, 1973.

Estes, R. W. (ed.) *Accounting and Society*, Melville Publishing Co., Los Angeles, California, 1973.

Goldman, T. A. (ed.), *Cost-Effectiveness Analysis*, Praeger Publishers, 1967.

Livingstone, J. L. & Gunn, S. C., *Accounting for Social Goals: Budgeting and Analysis of Non-Market Projects*, Harper & Row, New York, New York, 1974.

Luthans, F. & Hodgetts, R. M., *Readings on the Current Social Issues in Business*, Macmillan, New York, 1972.

National Association of Accountants Report of the Committee for Corporate Social Performance, *Management Accounting* N.A.A., September, 1974.

Seidler, J. L. & Seidler, L. L. (eds). *Social Accounting: Issues and Goods*, Wiley/Hamilton, 1975.

Steiner, G. A., *Business and Society*, Random House, New York, 1971.

Wolfe, J. N. (ed.), *Cost Benefit and Cost Effectiveness*, Allen and Unwin, London, 1973.

Index

Absorption costing, 417–18, 468, 626
  v. variable costing, 629, 630–36
Accidental damage
  losses by, 127
Accountability (*see* Social responsibility)
Accountant
  difficulties facing, 7–8
  financial planning, 317–18
  information systems design, 524–5
  model building, 33
  role of, 615
Accounting
  alternative methods, 606, 612–13, 618, 656
  as a social science, 2–7
  as an art form, 76
  as an information system, 10–24
  changes in, 1, 2, 7
  concepts of income and value, 570–72
  decision-making and, 2, 7
  definitions, 1–2
  education, vii, 7
  events, 654–5
  financial (*see* Financial accounting)
  for depreciation, 138–40
  for sale or disposal of assets, 140–41
  information (*see* Information)
  machines, 91
  management, 5–6, 51
  mechanization, 89–95, 97–8
  non-financial aspects, 97
  not an exact science, 7
  objectives, viii, 2, 11, 34
  process, 51
  rate of return, 329–30
  research on, 554
  responsibility, 342, 435–51
  social responsibility (*see* Social responsibility accounting)
  stewardship, 3, 4, 161, 538, 540–42, 543, 571
  systems approach, 21–3
  technological developments and, 22
Accounting conventions
  accounting information defined by, 12
  comparability and, 52, 73–4
  criteria for new conventions, 698
  financial reporting and, 76, 161–2, 542, 547
  nature of, 56–7
  purpose of, 52
  social reporting and, 697–8
  standardization and, 618
  types
    fundamental, 58–62
    entity, 58–60, 102, 559, 697–8
    money measurement, 35, 60–62, 698
    procedural, 62–75
    accrual, 68–9, 115–26, 618, 698

    conservatism, 74–5, 127, 142, 144, 162, 166, 168, 172, 618
    consistency, 73–4, 162, 618
    cost, 64–6, 74, 150, 161–2, 163, 164, 570–71, 698
    going-concern, 62–4, 162, 570, 594, 598, 618
    matching, 69–71, 134, 137, 146, 167, 293, 628, 698
    materiality, 276
    periodicity, 71–3, 112, 298
    realization, 66–8, 74, 123, 174, 571–2, 591, 698
Accounting income
  comparison with replacement cost income, 593–5 *passim*
  components of, 592–3
  economic income and, 570–77
  effects of cost convention, 570–71
  effects of realization convention, 571–2
  purpose of, 592
Accounting standards (*see* Standardization)
Accounting Standards Steering Committee
  groups having right to information, 543–4
  mergers, 240–42
  objectives, 57, 74, 547, 616
  overheads treatment, 630
  work of, 616–18
Accounting theory
  deductive approach, 27
  foundations, 25–40
  inductive approach, 26–7
  need for normative theory, 26
  (*see also* Accounting conventions)
Accounts
  adjustments for accruals, 116–25, 149
  as descriptions of transactions, 104–5, 561
  'interlocking', 103
  opening, 59
  personal, 105
  real, 105
  T form, 99–107
  accrual convention, 68–9, 115–26
Accruals
  adjustments for, 116–25, 149
  expenses, 117–2
  income, 116–17
Acid-test ration, 642
Acquisitions (*see* Mergers and acquisitions)
Activity levels, 286–8, 289, 292, 468
Activity ratios, 643–5
Actual costs, 292, 293, 337
Added value statement, 681
Adjustments
  accruals, 116–25, 149
  defaulting debtors, 141–5, 151
  depreciation, 127–40, 151
  loss in asset values, 150–51
  periodic measurement, 113, 115–26, 148–51
  price-level changes, 579–89

selling price, 624
Administrative costs
  allotment to product costs, 288, 289
  control of, 477–8
  definition, 277
  forecast, 349
Advertising expenditure, 325, 482–3
  valuation, 171, 172
Advice note, 81
After-sales service, 174
Aggregation and information loss, 654–5
Allocation of costs
  depreciation as, 73, 129–30
Allocation of resources
  accounting information and, 19–20
Analysts and advisers, 543
Annual plan (see Budgetary planning)
Articles of Association, 187, 202, 541
Aspiration levels, 503–4, 522
Asset Realization Account, 140–41
Asset Realization Reserve Account, 597
Asset turnover ratio, 648
Assets
  accounting for sale or disposal, 140–41
  appropriation between divisions, 449
  as capital, 560
  current, 156, 162, 164–8, 641–2
  definitions, 163, 636
  fictitious, 128
  historic cost of acquisition, 64–6, 74, 150, 161–2, 163, 164,
        564, 570–71, 582, 584–6, 587, 648, 656
  human (see Human resource accounting)
  intangible, 169–72
  long-term, 156, 162, 325
  losses in values of, 127–46, 150–51
  monetary and non-monetary, 582–6
  non-financial, 65
  replacement cost, 564
  shown on Balance Sheet, 59–63
  turnover, 446–7
  utility of, 129, 561, 562–3
  utilization of, 648
  valuation (see Valuation)
  (see also Fixed assets)
Associated companies, 617–18
Attitude surveys, 685
Auditors
  relationship with management, 615–16
  Reports, 539, 566
Audits, 157, 309–10, 657–8
Authorized Capital, 188, 194, 198–9
Average collection period of trade debtors, 644–5
Average cost, 624
Average inventory turnover, 153, 643–4
Average lifetime investment, 329–30

Bad debts, 127, 141–3
  provision for, 143–4, 156
Balance sheet
  bad debts shown on, 142
  budgeted, 357–8
  company, 203–6
  consolidated, 209–27 passim, 228, 232, 233, 239, 243, 244
  contingent liabilities as footnotes, 174
  contrasted with Income Statement, 155–6
  disaggregated form of, 655
  effects of variable costing, 636
  fixed assets information shown on, 138, 151
  form, 59–63
  formal presentation of, 158–9
  function, 4
  goodwill excluded from, 171
  historic cost v. replacement cost, 596–7

inflation adjusted, 586
  integration of financial and human assets in, 727–9
  inventory valuations distorted under LIFO method, 581
  investments and intangible assets shown on, 169–70, 172
  legal requirement, 541
  loan capital presentation on, 199–200
  preparation, 112–26, 155–9
  proposed dividend shown on, 202
  purpose, 4
  share capital shown on, 197–9
  social reporting, 691–3
Balances
  collecting and classifying, 156–7
  extraction of, 105–7
  verification of 157, 309–10, 657–8
Banks
  credit, 645
  Reconciliation Statement, 86, 157–8
  secret reserves, 65
Bearer shares, 188
Behavioural aspects
  decision-making, 20–21
  information systems design, 520–22
  performance evaluation, 497–508
  predictions of behaviour, 29–30
Behavioural variables method, 726–7
Bonus shares, 194–5
Book value, 139, 140, 163, 169, 228, 245, 571
Book-keeping (see also Double entry book-keeping)
  development of, 97–8
  origin of, 3, 97
  preparation of inventories, 559
Break-even analysis (see Cost-volume-profit analysis)
Break-even chart, 386–9
Break-even point, 383–96 passim
Budgetary control, 341, 373, 482
Budgetary planning, 340–59 (see also Cost-volume-profit
      analysis)
  Budget Committee, 342, 344
  Budget preparation, 350–58
    Budgeted Balance Sheet, 357–8
    Budgeted Direct Labour Costs, 353
    Budgeted Income Statement, 357
    Capital Expenditure Budget, 344, 355
    Cash Budget, 356–7
    Closing Inventory Budget, 355
    Cost of Goods Sold Budget, 355
    Direct Materials Purchase Budget, 352
    Direct Materials Usage Budget, 352
    Overhead Costs Budget, 353–4
    Production Budget, 351
    Sales Budget, 350
    Selling and Administrative Expenses Budget, 355
  Co-ordination of activities, 340, 342, 343–4
  determination of key factors, 342–3
  disclosure of budgets to external users, 656–8
  effects of budgets on people, 500–502
  evaluation of proposals, 358
  flexible budgeting, 462–5
  long-range planning and, 340, 344, 355, 434–5
  nature and function, 340–41
  need for flexibility, 341
  outline of steps in, 342–4
  preliminary information, 346–50
  probabilistic budgeting, 370–73
  rolling budgets, 341
  sales forecasting, 344–6, 347
  sales plan, 469
  simulation for 373–4
Budgeted Balance Sheet, 357–8
Budgeted costs, 344
  direct labour, 353
  standard costs and, 453–4

Budgeted Income Statement, 357
Buildings, 131, 132
  valuation, 163–4
Business contacts
  information needs of, 543
Businesses (see Companies)
By-product costing, 291

Capacity levels, 287–8
Capital
  account, 59, 102–3, 157, 559
  assets as, 560
  income and, 564–5
  nature of, 558–60
  valuation (see Valuation)
Capital budgeting
  analysis of proposals, 325–6
  appraisal methods, 327–36
    accounting rate of return, 329–30
    discounted cash flow methods, 330–33
      comparison of DCF methods, 334–6
      Internal rate of return, 333, 362
      net present value, 332, 564
    pay-back period, 327–9
  certainty equivalent method of risk appraisal, 365–8
  cost of capital, 336–8
  decisions, 324–5
  definition, 324
  human resources in, 721
  Monte Carlo simulation method, 374–5
  opportunity costs, 337, 418–19
  sensitivity analysis and risk measurement, 361–5
  taxation and, 336
Capital clause, 187–8
Capital employed
  problems in measurement of, 447–8
Capital Expenditure Budget, 344, 355
Capital expenditure planning (see Capital budgeting)
Capital gains, 314, 315–16
Capital investment decisions (see Capital budgeting)
Capital maintenance
  current cost accounting, 608
  current operating income, 597
  current purchasing power, 582–9, 608
  economic income, 572
  historical cost accounting, 582
  replacement cost income, 598
  solvency and, 639–40
Capital Reserves, 175, 199, 200, 201
Capital structure
  accounting procedures, 194–200
  companies, 190–94 passim
  gearing, 192–4, 315, 320, 337–8, 646
  projection, 320–21
  subsidiaries having complex structures, 230–31
Capital transaction flows, 660–62
Capitalization of salary, 722–3
Cash
  account, 102–3, 105
  at bank, 86, 156, 157–8
  Book, 86–7, 91, 92, 102–3
  Budget, 356–7
  expenditure, 349–50
  in hand, 156
  optimal balances, 357
  payment and receipt of, 67–9, 116
Cash in Transit Account, 232–3
Cash-elasticity of current assets
  ratios, 643–5
Cash-flow accounting, 658–66
  advantages, 664–5
  case for, 663–4
  contents of cash-flow reports, 659–63

disadvantages of cash-flow forecasting, 665–6
  inflation and, 665
Cash-flow statements
  contrasted with Income Statements, 178
  definition and nature, 177–8
  financial analysis, 179–80
  form and content, 178–9
  historic, 659–63
Cash-flows
  importance of, 306–7
  net cash inflows, 327–30 passim, 332–5 passim, 364–8 passim, 378
  net investment outlays, 327–30 passim, 332–6 passim, 378
  projection of, 319, 349, 553, 659–66 passim
  variable costing and, 626
Certainty equivalent method, 365–8, 377–8
Classical theory of organizations, 507, 508
Clerical work study, 454, 478
Closed system, 10–11
  double entry book-keeping as, 102–3
Closing Inventory Budget, 354
Commodity markets, 413
Communication (see also Information)
  basic function, 266–8
  restricted flow, 501–2
  social contributions, 695–9
  theory, 53
Companies
  Acts, 4–5, 57, 72, 209–12, 234, 540, 541, 580
  associated companies, 617–18
  capital structure, 190–94 passim
  financial accounting implications of status, 189–90
  financial accounting information for, 186–207
  groups of companies, 208–27
  gearing (see Gearing)
  groups
    consolidated accounts, 209–27 passim, 228–45
    Cost of Control, 215–16, 220–21, 224–5, 227, 228–9, 231, 238, 239, 240, 244, 245
    disclosure of information, 209–10, 211–12
    inter-group transactions, 231–4
    nature of, 208–9
    subsidiaries (see Subsidiary companies)
    treatment of dividends, 218–21
    treatment of minority shareholders, 221–6
  importance in financial accounting, 186
  information disclosure of small companies, 552
  issue of shares, 194–9
  limited liability of, 60
  loan capital, 190–94 passim, 199–200, 338
  nature of, 187–9
  payment of dividends, 202–3
  periodic income procedures, 200–202
  property, 588
  public and private defined, 187
  published statements, 203–6
  separation of functions of accountant and secretary, 189–90
Comparability of information, 52, 73–4, 548, 552, 598, 605, 612–18 (see also Standardization)
Competitive bidding method, 721–2
Completed jobs
  cost value, 298–300
Completeness
  corporate reporting information, 552
Computers, 22, 23, 431
  influence on information systems design, 522–3
  simulation methods, 373–5, 485, 517–18 (see also Data processing; Mechanization of Accounting)
Conservatism convention, 74–5, 127, 142, 144, 162, 166, 168, 172, 618
Consistency convention, 73–4, 162, 618

Consolidated accounts, 209–27 *passim*
  problems, 214–18, 228–45
Consultative Committee of the Accountancy Bodies in the
  United Kingdom and Ireland, 604, 605, 607, 608
Consumer protection movement, 676
Contingency theory of organizations, 507–8
Contingent liabilities
  valuation, 174
Contracts of sale, 67–8
Contribution margin
  cost-volume-profit analysis, 382–3, 385–6, 390–96 *passim*
  dropping a product line, 420, 481
  product-mix and profitability, 426–7, 429–31 *passim*
  sales variances, 469–72 *passim*
  short-term tactical decisions, 415–18, 424
  transfer pricing, 444
Contribution pricing method, 411–12
Control
  basic function, 264–6
  cycle, 434–5
  definitions, 14, 271
  extended meanings of, 271–2, 505
  'in-the-large' and 'in-the-small', 271, 400
  management, 269–70, 271, 434, 518
  measurement in, 272
  operational, 269–71, 274, 434–5, 518
  organizing for, 434–51
  planning and, 264–5, 434–5, 461–2
  standards, 435
  theory, 272
Controllable and non-controllable costs, 439–40, 462, 480,
  482, 500
Conversion cost, 276
  pricing, 408–10
Copyrights
  valuation, 170
Corporate reporting (*see* Financial reporting)
Corporation tax, 200, 201, 338, 566
Corporations (*see* Companies)
Cost accounting (*see* Costing)
Cost centres, 270, 278–81, 301–2, 436–7, 438
Cost control
  assigning responsibility, 435–40
  human aspects, 500–503
  non-manufacturing costs, 477–83
  standards, 453
Cost convention, 64–6, 74, 150, 161–2, 163, 164, 570–71,
  698
Cost obviation, 636
Cost of capital, 336–8
Cost of Control, 171, 215–16, 220–21, 224–5, 227, 228–9,
  231, 238–40 *passim*, 244, 245
Cost of Goods Sold Budget, 355
Cost value, 129
Cost-based transfer pricing, 443–5
  full-cost, 443–4
  variable-cost, 445
Cost-effectiveness analysis, 686–8
Costing
  absorption, 417–18, 468, 626, 629, 630–36
  basic framework, 274–304
  definitions of 'allocation' and 'apportionment', 278–9
  historical cost accounting systems, 293, 303
  job order, 294–300
  period, 629
  process, 300–303
  product, 628–9
  purposes of, 274
  standard (*see* Standard costing)
Costs (*see also* Expenses)
  accumulation, 275, 278–81, 449
  actual, 292, 293, 337
  administrative, 277, 288, 289, 349, 477–8

advertising, 171, 172, 325, 482–3
appropriation between divisions, 449
average, 624
behaviour, 286–7, 382–3
budgeted, 344, 353, 453–4
by-product, 291
classifications, 275, 286
completed jobs, 298–300
consciousness of, 454–5
controllable (*see* Controllable and non-controllable costs)
conversion, 276, 408–10
delivery, 288 (*see also* Marketing costs)
depreciation as allocation of, 73, 129–30
differential, 415, 416
direct labour, 276, 282–3, 297, 299, 301, 302, 348, 353
direct materials, 275–6, 297, 299
discretionary (*see* Non-manufacturing costs)
fixed (*see* Fixed costs)
flows, 293–8, 301–2
full product (*see* Full product costs)
future, 292, 414–15
historic costs of acquiring assets, 64–6, 74, 150, 161–2,
  163, 164, 564, 570–71, 582, 584–6, 587, 648, 656
implementing income measurement, 568
improvement, 132
joint products, 290–91
maintenance, 130, 137, 138, 164
managed (*see* Non-manufacturing costs)
manufacturing, 275–6, 293, 349
marketing (*see* Marketing costs)
mixed, 286
network activities, 493–5
non-manufacturing (*see* Non-manufacturing costs)
operating, 645
organization cost valuation, 170–71
overhead (*see* Overhead costs)
performance levels, 504
period, 277, 288
pricing decisions, 401–3 *passim*, 404–5
prime, 275–6, 279, 286
raw materials, 296–7
reductions, 454
relevant, 414–15, 416, 418, 419, 423, 636–7
repair, 130, 132, 133, 137, 138
replacement, 132, 133, 134, 200, 201
research and development, 71, 171, 172, 344, 478–9
running, 130
sales, 298, 300, 349
savings (*see* Holding gains)
social, 678–9
standard (*see* Standard costing)
sunk, 414, 416, 664
total asset costs and depreciation, 137–8
total product, 275, 277–8, 289–90
unit, 277, 285–8 *passim*, 623
variable (*see* Variable costs)
warehousing and storage, 289
work-in-progress, 298–300
Cost-volume-profit analysis, 381–99
  applications, 381–2
  assumptions and limitations, 397–8
  contribution margin, 382–3, 385–6, 390–96 *passim*
  cost behaviour, 382–3
  equation method, 384–5
  graph method, 386–90
  profit planning examples, 391–6
  relevant range, 397
Crash time and cost, 494
Credit
  bank, 645
  collecting and classifying balances, 156–7
  definition, 100–101
  sales, 644–5

Creditors
  definition and use of the term, 104, 105
  information needs, 16–17, 534, 541, 549
  short-term solvency and, 641
Credit-worthiness, 17, 93, 94, 567
Critical path analysis, 491–5
  costs of activities, 493–5
Critical success factors, 515–16
Cumulative Preference Shares, 191
Current assets, 156, 162
  ratio of current assets to current liabilities, 641–2
  valuation, 164–8
'Current cash equivalent', 600
Current cost accounting, 604–9
  features of, 604
  monetary items, 605–6
  non-monetary items, 607–8
Current cost value, 167–8, 564, 570–71, 581, 602–4
Current liabilities, 157, 172, 173–4, 202, 641–2
Current purchasing power accounting, 581–9
  appraisal of, 587–9
  v. current cost accounting, 604–8
Current ratio, 641–2
Current value accounting, 591–609, 648
  cash-flow reports and, 665
  realizable value accounting, 599–602
  replacement cost accounting, 592–9, 648
Customers
  information needs, 18–19
Data
  definition, 11
  flows, 79–81
  generation, 78–95
  information and, 11
  simultaneous posting, 88–9
Data processing (see also Computers; Mechanization of
            accounting)
  advantages, 92
  development, 87–95
  double entry book-keeping and, 97–109
  example of use, 93, 95
  influence on accounting, 22, 78
  information systems, 517
  program development, 92
Day Books, 85
Debentures, 190–94 passim, 199–200, 231, 545, 646 (see
            also Loan capital)
Debit
  definition, 100–101
Debtors
  definition and use of the term, 104, 105
  losses through defaulting, 141–3
  treatment of bad debts, 143, 156
  treatment of doubtful debts, 144–5, 156
Debtors' Ledger, 89, 93, 95
Decision models, 32–3, 373–5, 485, 517–19, 552–3, 554,
            654
Decision theory, 30, 32
Decision trees, 368–73
Decision-making
  accounting and, 2, 7
  behavioural aspects, 20–21
  centralization, 270, 278–81, 301–2, 436–40, 726
  decentralization, 270, 436, 440–51, 516, 726
  divisional profit performance and, 501
  dropping a product line, 419–21
  effect of alternative accounting methods, 612–13
  elements of, 31
  financial reporting concept, 542–3
  income as guide to socio-economic decisions, 567
  information for, 11, 14, 19-20, 34, 52, 268-71,
            542–3
  limiting factors, 423–5

linear programming and, 425–31
make or buy, 422–3
non-programmed models, 518–19
operating v. leasing assets, 421–2
optimal, 19
prediction and, 31–2
problem-solving and, 30–31
programmed models, 517–18
selling or further processing, 421
short-run tactical decision, 414–32
special orders, 382, 416–17
value and, 562–3
Decreasing balance depreciation method, 135–8
Deductive theory, 26–7
Deferred liabilities, 118, 120–21, 156, 174–5, 205
Deferred shares, 192
Deficits
  Cash Budget and, 356
  long-range financial plan, 319, 320
Delivery costs, 288 (see also Marketing costs)
Delivery note, 81, 83
Demand
  elasticity of, 394–5
  pricing and, 401
Departments, 262–4, 437–40 passim (see also Responsi-
            bility centres)
  self-centredness, 502
Depreciation
  accounting concept, 130–31
  accounting for, 138–40
  adjustments, 127–40, 151
  as a fall in price, 128
  as a fall in value, 129
  as cost allocation, 73, 129-30
  as deferred maintenance, 129
  as physical deterioration, 128–9, 131
  asset costs written off against income, 65
  buildings, 131, 164
  measurement, 131–7
    ascertaining useful life of an asset, 132–3
    determining residual value, 133–4
    identifying the cost of an asset, 132
    methods, 134–7
      decreasing balance method, 135–8
      straight-line method, 135, 137–8, 205
  nature of, 128–31
  Provision for Depreciation Account, 139–40, 141
  rate, 136–7
  recovery in accounting rate of return method, 329
  replacement cost accounting, 595–6
  total asset costs and, 137–8
Descriptive theory, 25, 40
Deterioration
  depreciation as, 128–9, 131
  rate of, 132–3
Differential costs, 415, 416
Direct costing (see Variable costing)
Direct expenses, 153, 154, 622
Direct labour costs
  accounting for cost flows, 301, 302
  basis for overhead rates, 282–3
  budgeting, 353
  definition, 275–6
  factory costs forecast, 348
  periodic profit measurement, 299
  standard costs, 456, 458–9
  treatment in accounts, 297
Direct labour hours
  basis for overhead rates, 283, 285
Direct labour variances, 458–9
Direct materials
  costs, 275–6, 296–7, 299
  Purchase Budget, 352

treatment in accounts, 296–7
Usage Budget, 351–2
variances, 456–8
Direct overhead costs, 279–80, 301
Directors, 4, 188–9, 200–204 *passim*, 538–9, 541, 613
Report, 538–9
Discount
debentures issued at a, 199
shares issued at a, 195
Discount rates, 330–36 *passim*, 577
adjustment for risk, 361
salary capitalization, 723
Discounted cash flow methods, 330–33, 362
internal rate of return, 333
net present value, 332, 564, 572, 574–7 *passim*   comparison of methods, 334–6
Discounted net value
liabilities valuation, 173–4
Discretionary costs (*see* Non-manufacturing costs)
Disposal or sale of assets, 140–41
Distribution channels, 382
Distribution costs (*see* Marketing costs)
Dividend Equalization Accounts, 175, 200, 201
Dividends
accounting procedures, 202–3
and interest transaction flows, 660–61, 663
as current liabilities, 172
calculation of, 315–16
dividend coverage ratio, 650
earnings yield, 650
forecasting, 553
income as dividend policy guide, 567
ratio analysis, 640
shareholders' rights to, 172, 188
treatment for groups of companies, 218–21
paid by parent, 218
paid by subsidiary, 218–19
paid out of pre-acquisition income, 219–21
yield, 649–50
Double entry book-keeping (*see also* Book-keeping)
as a closed system, 102–3
comprising 'interlocking accounts', 103
cost flow accounting, 296
data processing and, 97–109
infinite capacity of, 103
mathematical implications, 105–7
nature of, 99–101
origin, 3, 27, 98–9
periodic measurement and, 112–26
Doubtful debts
provision for, 144–5, 151, 156
Dropping a product line, 419–21, 481

Earning power, 549–50
Earnings per share ratio, 649
Earnings yield ratio, 650
Ecology movement, 677
Economic factors in sales forecasting, 345
Economic forecasting, 309
Economic income
accounting income and, 570–77
capital valuation and, 572–3
ex-ante, 574–5
ex-post, 575–6
subjective nature, 576–7
Economic Order Quantity, 487–9
Economic theories of pricing, 402–4
Economic value
assets, 129
human assets, 723–4
'Effectiveness' *v.* 'efficiency', 19–20
Efficiency
income as measure of, 565–6

Egalitarian movement, 677
Electronic data processing (*see* Data processing)
Embezzlement
losses through, 127
Empirical theory, 27–8, 553–4
Employees
information for, 5, 15, 52, 534, 543, 730–32
organizational objectives and goals for, 308, 309
participation in management, 189, 503–4, 508
personal initiative, 502
personal needs and goals, 499–500, 504–5
subordinates and organization structures, 508
valuation methods, 721–7
Entity convention, 58–60, 102, 559, 697–8
Entry values, 599, 602, 603
Environment, business, 261–2, 309, 508, 514, 515–16
organization structure and, 508
planning and information, 261–2
Environment, natural, 677, 683, 694
Equity capital (*see also* Share capital)
definition, 210–11
Equivalent completed units, 302–3
Errors, 108
Esteem value, 129
Events accounting, 654–5
Ex-ante income, 574–5
Exceptional transaction flows, 659–62
Exchange value, 129, 161, 561–2
Exit values, 601–2
Expense centres, 436–40
Expenses
accrual of, 117–21
contrasted with total product costs, 277
definitions, 69, 114–15
difference between fixed assets and current operating
expenses, 130
direct, 153, 154, 622
effect of adjustments, 122
identification of 113–15
indirect, 153–5 *passim*
matching with revenues, 69–71, 112–13, 123, 628–9, 630,
637
periodic, 622
prepayment of, 118, 120–21
(*see also* Costs)
Exponential smoothing, 346
Ex-post income, 575–6
Exposure drafts
accounting standards and, 616–18
depreciation, 618
inventories, 627, 630
mergers, 240–42, 617
overheads treatment, 630
External audit, 309
External users
information for, 52, 53, 65
Externalities, 678, 679

Factory costs
forecast, 347–8
overheads (*see* Overhead costs)
Feasibility
implementation of replacement cost accounting, 598
income measurement criterion, 568, 591
FIFO, 165–6, 581, 624, 648
Financial accounting, 3–5, 51 (*see also* Accounting)
information for companies, 186–207
groups of companies, 208–
method, 56–109
purposes of records, 62
Financial Accounting Standards Board, 5, 57, 548, 616
Financial (long-range) planning, 317–21
Financial objectives and goals, 308

Financial reporting (*see also* Balance Sheet; Income Statement)
  accounting conventions and, 76, 161–2, 542, 547
  characteristics of corporate reports, 551–2
  comparability (*see* Comparability of information)
  concepts, 539–43
    decision-making, 542–3
    general user, 543–4
    stewardship, 540–42
  concern about, 7–8
  current cost accounting, 604
  decision model approach, 552–3, 554
  increased information in, 654–67
  integration with human asset reporting, 720, 727–9
  integration with social reporting, 695–6, 701
  internal and external reporting, 533
  interpretation and comparison, 638–51
  legal requirements, 72, 162, 533, 538, 539, 542
  management influence, 615–16
  multiple value reports, 655–6
  need for standards, 547–8
  normative theory, 544–5, 554
  objectives, 71, 538–45, 549–51, 625, 691
  purpose and framework, 548–52
  role of judgement in, 614–15
  scientific method and empiricism, 553–4
  use of variable costing in, 635–6
  value and events schools, 655
  yearly, 72
Financial transaction flows, 660–62
Financing plan, 320
Finished goods
  Account, 299–300
  inventories, 486
Fixed assets
  accounting for losses, 128–40
  cost allocation over time, 73, 129–30
  cost identification, 132
  depreciable and non-depreciable, 131
  differentiated from current operating expenses, 130
  fixed asset accounting compared with human resource accounting, 719–20
  government indices, 598
  replacement of, 200, 201, 595–6, 598
  revaluation, 580
  shown on Balance Sheet, 138, 151
  total costs and depreciation, 137–8
  types of, 131, 156, 162
  useful life of, 132–3, 134
  valuation, 162–4
Fixed costs, 286, 289–90, 348
  allocation over time, 73
  as relevant costs, 415
  changes in, 391
  cost-volume-profit analysis, 382–94 *passim*, 396, 397
  dropping a product line, 420
  need to distinguish from variable costs, 290
  overhead costs, 348, 353–4, 463–4, 465
  pricing decisions and, 405–8
  profit planning and, 382–3
  sales volume changes and, 407–8
  short-term invariability of, 462
  special orders and, 416
  variable costing, 626, 629, 635, 636
Fixed overhead rate, 286–8
Flexible budgeting, 462–5
  advantage over fixed budgeting, 464–5
  marketing costs, 482, 483
Forecasting
  behaviour, 29–30
  budgets, 658
  cash-flows, 319, 349, 553, 659–66 *passim*
  decision-making and, 31–2
  dividends, 553
  economic and technological, 309
  profits, 501
  raw materials requirement, 348
  sales, 344–6, 347
Foreign market strategy, 382
Forms sets, 88
Franchise valuation, 170
Fraud, 161–2
Freehold land, 163
Full product cost, 275, 278, 281–4 *passim*, 293
  limitations of calculations, 289–90
Full-cost pricing, 405–8
Full-cost transfer pricing, 443–4
Fundamental conventions, 58–62 (*see also* Entity convention; Money measurement convention)
Funds-flow statements, 179–84
  definition of 'funds', 180
  methods of measuring changes, 181–4
  sources and applications of funds, 181
Furniture and fittings, 131, 164
Future costs, 292, 414–15

Gains
  holding, 67, 592–8 *passim*, 601, 604, 605, 607
  on monetary items, 588, 605–6
  operating, 67, 592–5 *passim*, 597, 598, 604
  unrealized, 66–7
Gap analysis, 310–12
Gearing, 192–4, 315, 320, 337–8, 646
General Reserve, 200, 201
General user concept, 543–4
Generalized purchasing power, 587
Goals
  divisional, 436, 437, 503–6 *passim*
  long-range planning, 307, 308–9, 310–11, 313–17
  organizational, 307, 308–9, 310–11, 317, 434, 469, 497, 505–7 *passim*, 516, 550
  personal, 499–500, 504–5
  profit, 308, 310–11, 313–17, 506
Going-concern convention, 62–4, 162, 570, 594, 597, 598, 618
Going-rate pricing, 412–13
Goods Received Note, 83
Goodwill (*see* Cost of Control)
Governments
  information needs, 16, 534, 543
Gross income
  calculation, 152–3
  definition, 151–2
Gross Profit ratio, 152–3
Gross Trading Income, 152–3

Historic cost convention (*see* Cost convention)
Historic cost of acquiring assets, 64–6, 74, 150, 161–4 *passim*, 564, 570–71, 582, 584–6, 587, 648, 656
Historic valuation of liabilities, 173–4
Holding gains
  current cost accounting, 604, 605, 607
  definition, 67
  realizable income, 601
  replacement cost income, 592–8 *passim*
  types, 596
Human relations theory of organizations, 507
Human resource accounting, 65, 325, 717–30
  comparison with fixed asset accounting, 719–20
  definitions, 718–19
  development of, 718–19
  example (R.G. Barry Corporation), 727–9
  human resource contribution, 682
  integration with financial accounting, 720, 727–9
  investment projects, 721
  methods, 721–7

behavioural variables, 726-7
capitalization of salary, 722-3
competitive bidding, 721-2
economic value, 723-4
replacement cost, 721
return on effort employed, 724-6
ratios, 723
social responsibility and, 729-30
uses of human asset values, 720
Hypothesis testing, 28, 29

Improvement
costs, 132, 164
gap, 311
Income
accounting (see Accounting income)
accrual of, 116-17
as creditworthiness guide, 567
as dividend policy guide, 567
as investment guide, 566
as managerial effectiveness indicator, 566
as measure of efficiency, 565-6
as socio-economic decisions guide, 567
as tax base, 566
capital and, 564-5
current operating income, 592-5 passim, 597, 598
definitions, 64, 565, 572-3
economic (see Economic income)
gross (see Gross income)
importance to shareholders, 544-5
net (see Net income)
replacement cost (see Replacement cost accounting)
undistributed retained income, 175, 188, 200, 201, 315, 316, 319
Income measurement, 64-5 (see also Periodic measurement; Profitability)
bad debts and, 142
cost information and, 274, 293
effects of absorption and variable costing, 631-6
effect of cost convention, 570
effect of periodicity convention, 73
historic costs v. replacement cost, 594-6
objectives, 565-7
problems in measurement of profit and capital employed, 447-8
selection criteria, 567-8
Income Statement
bad debts shown on, 144
Budgeted, 357
company, 203-6
consolidated, 209-27 passim, 233, 234-7, 238
contrasted with Balance Sheet, 155-6
contrasted with cash-flow statement, 178
doubtful debts shown on, 145
formal presentation, 154-5
function, 4
inflation adjusted, 586
preparation of, 112-26, 147-55
Projected, 318
provision for depreciation, 139, 151
variances shown on, 461
Indirect costs (see Overhead costs) Indirect expenses, 153, 154, 155
Inductive theory, 26-7
Industrial democracy, 189, 503-4
Industrial relations and social responsibility, 730-32
Industry
influence on the locality, 18, 694
Inflation
effect on accounting rate of return method, 329-30
effect on money standard of measurement, 35-6, 62
effect on rate of return, 315

effect on valuation of long-term liabilities, 174
historic cost valuation and, 570-71
Inflation accounting, 113, 579-89, 591-608 (see also Current cost accounting; Current purchasing power accounting; Current value accounting)
adjustments for general price-level changes, 581-9
monetary and non-monetary items, 582-6
alternative accounting methods compared, 606
partial adjustments for price-level changes, 579-81
LIFO method of inventory valuation, 580-81
revaluation of fixed assets, 163, 580
Information (see also Communication)
alternative sources, 606, 612-13
channels of, 519
comparability of, 52, 73-4, 548, 552, 598, 605, 612-18 (see also Standardization)
corporate reporting information, 551-2
data and, 11
disclosure (see Information needs)
efficient use of, 37
'exceptional', 266-7, 270, 454, 456, 473
feedback, 264-6, 434, 435, 437, 454, 493, 521, 540, 543
for decision-making, 11, 14, 19-20, 34, 52, 268-71
importance in prediction, 31
information generation process, 78
'inside' information, 62
losses through aggregation, 654-5
marginal cost of production, 38-9
marginal utility of, 38-9
merging of accounting and non-accounting information, 22, 524
monopolistic and competitive contexts, 613
predictive ability of, 542
production of, 37-9
quality of, 16, 22
reliability v. usefulness, 75-6
resource allocation and, 19-20
special meaning of accounting information, 11
theory of, 37-9, 655
value of, 39
Information needs,
analysts and advisers, 543
business contacts, 543
creditors, 16-17, 534, 539, 541, 549
employees, 5, 15, 52, 534, 543, 730-32
governments, 16, 534, 543
Inland Revenue, 52
investors, 5, 52, 72, 75, 172, 533, 539, 541, 543, 544-5, 549, 566, 577, 656-8, 659-66
loan creditors, 539, 543, 545
local community, 18, 534, 543
managers, 14, 51-2, 516-19
shareholders, 4-5, 52, 71-2, 75, 161, 203-6, 209-10, 211-12, 533, 538-45 passim, 547, 553, 577
trade unions, 52, 730-32
Information system (see also Management Information Systems)
accounting as an, 10-24
boundaries of, 11-13, 52
formalization, 22
importance of the accounting system, 21-2, 512, 513
input data for, 12
objective, 19
output of, 13
'total systems approach', 22
users' needs, 12, 13, 14-19
Inland Revenue
information for, 52, 175
Innovation objectives and goals, 308, 309
Institute of Chartered Accountants in England and Wales, 622, 629-30
Insurance
prepayment of, 120-21, 156
Intangible assets

valuation, 169–72
Interest and dividends transaction flows, 660–61, 663
Interest coverage ratio, 646
Inter-firm comparisons, 73, 74, 548, 638–9, 647, 648
'Interlocking accounts', 103
Internal audit, 309–10
Internal rate of return, 333, 362
  comparison with net present value method, 334–6
International Accounting Standards Committee, 548, 616
Inventories
  adjustments, 123–5, 150, 233
  average inventory turnover, 153, 643–4
  classification, 621–2
  closing, 123, 124, 125, 150, 156, 165, 351, 354, 599, 622–3
  control, 485–91
  cost of, 165–622, 623
  finished goods, 486
  historical note, 559
  holding and ordering costs, 487–9
  levels, 485–6, 631
  manufacturing, 621
  merchandise, 621
  opening, 124, 125, 150
  raw materials, 486
  recording at standard cost, 454, 457, 460–61
  re-order point, 490–91
  replacement costs for, 598–9
  safety levels, 490
  size, 620–21
  valuation (see Valuation)
  work-in-progress, 486
Investment appraisal (see Capital budgeting)
Investment centres, 446–51
  Residual Income method of appraisal, 450–51
Investments
  efficiency of decisions, 649–50
  income as a guide to, 566
  valuation 169
Investors (see also Shareholders)
  information for, 5, 14–15, 52, 72, 75, 172, 533, 541, 543,
    544–5, 549, 566, 577, 656–8, 659–66
  ratio analysis and, 640
  risk-aversion of, 375–8
Invoices
  sales, 81, 88, 89, 91, 92
  supplier's, 83
Issued capital, 188, 194, 198–9
Italian Method (see Double entry book-keeping)

Jenkins Committee, 211
Job order costing, 294–300
Joint product costing, 290–91
Joint Stock Company, 3–4, 15, 538, 540–41, 559
  Act, 4
Journal, 84–5

Key tasks, 518–19

Labour costs
  direct, 276, 282–3, 297, 299, 301, 302, 348, 353
  indirect, 276, 297
  salary capitalization, 722–3
Labour efficiency variance, 458–9, 472
Land, 131
  valuation, 163, 583
Law of requisite variety, 272
LCM, 166–8, 205, 603, 624
Leadership styles, 498–500, 501–2, 504, 505, 516, 518
Leases
  land classified as asset or expense, 163
  use of straight-line depreciation method, 135
Ledger
  Debtors', 89, 93, 95

  definition, 78
  punched cards and, 91–2
  subsidiary books and, 84–6
  writing boards and, 88
Ledgerless book-keeping, 89
Legislation
  companies, 4–5, 57, 72, 209–12, 234, 540, 541, 580
  information disclosure, 731
  undesirable social activities, 679
Liabilities
  current, 157, 172, 173–4, 202, 641–2
  monetary and non-monetary, 582–6
  shown on Balance Sheet, 59–63
  valuation, 172–5
    methods, 173–4
Licensing systems, 679
LIFO, 166, 219, 580–81, 648
Limited Liability Act, 4, 541
Limiting factors, 423–5
Linear programming, 425–31, 474–5
Liquidity
  conflict with profitability, 357
Loan capital (see also Debentures)
  accounting treatment, 199–200
  capital structure, 190–94 passim, 338
Loan creditors, 539, 543, 545
Local community
  information needs, 18, 534, 543
Logic
  inductive and deductive, 26–7
  theory and, 26–7
Long-range planning
  budgeting and, 340, 344, 355, 434–5
  continuous review and updating of plan, 313
  definitions, 269, 306
  financial planning, 317–21
    accountant's role, 317–18
    capital expenditure forecast, 320
    capital structure projection, 320–21
    financing plan, 320
    projected cash flow, 319
    projected income statement, 318
  formulation of strategy, 310–12, 518–19
  long-range objectives, 306–9, 321, 340
  management information systems, 269–70
  position audit, 309–10
  preparation and implementation of plan, 312
  pricing policy and, 401
  revenue objectives and goals, 469
  role of information feedback, 265
  stages, 306–23
Long-term assets
  definitions, 156, 162, 325
  valuation, 162–4
Long-term borrowings, 157, 173, 174
Losses
  accidental damage, 127
  in asset values, 127–46, 150–51
  made by subsidiaries, 229–30
  of information through aggregation, 654–5
  on monetary items, 588, 605–6, 607
  on non-monetary items, 607
  provision for, 74–5
  through defaulting debtors, 141–4
'Lower of cost or market rule' (LCM), 166–8, 205, 603,
  624

Machine hours
  basis for overhead rates, 283
  product-mix, 424–5, 426–30 passim
Maintenance
  costs, 130, 137, 138, 164
  depreciation as deferred maintenance, 129

inadequate standards of, 500
Make or buy, 422–3
Managed costs (*see* Non-manufacturing costs)
Management
accounting, 5–6, 51
aspiration levels, 503–4, 522
by exception, 266–7, 270, 454, 456, 473
by objectives, 504–7
control, 269–70, 271, 434, 518
financial reports and, 615–16
functions, 14
income as indicator of managerial effectiveness, 566
information needs, 14, 51–2, 516–19
leadership styles, 498–500, 501–2, 504, 505, 516, 518
ownership and, 188–9, 307
personal goals, 504–5
personality and decision-making, 522
personality and organizational structure, 508
processes, 260–68
reactions to budget pressure, 500
responsibility, 307
Management Information Systems (*see also* Information
system)
design, 512–25
accountants and, 524–5
behavioural aspects, 520–22
computer influence on, 522–4
criteria, 519–20
stages in, 514–19
designing channels of information, 519
determination of 'critical success factors', 515–16
devizing organizational structure, 516
establishing information needs, 516–19
specifying objectives, 514–15
systems approach, 512–14
function, 79, 269, 512
Managers (*see* Management)
Manufactured assets
capitalization of construction costs, 132, 164
Manufacturing account, 293–300 *passim*
Manufacturing costs, 275–6, 293
direct labour costs, 276
direct materials costs, 275–6
overhead costs, 276
Manufacturing transaction flows, 659–61
Margin of Safety Ratio, 388–9
Marginal costing (*see* Variable costing)
Marginal pricing, 411–12
Market objectives and goals, 308, 407
Market value, 134, 135, 137, 162–3, 169, 624
different meanings of, 167–8, 564
joint products, 291
replacement costs, 599
Market-based transfer pricing, 442–3
Marketing
business sectors, 479
functions, 479
pricing and, 407, 411–12, 413
Marketing costs, 277
classifications, 479–81 *passim*
control, 479–83
definition, 277
direct and indirect, 480, 481
order-filling, 481, 483
order-getting, 481–2
sales territory profitability, 480, 481
uses of analysis, 480
Mark-up, 405–11 *passim*, 446, 447, 648
Matching convention, 69–71, 134, 137, 146, 167, 293, 628, 698
Material price variance, 457–8, 472
Material usage variance, 458, 472
Materiality convention, 276

Materials costs
direct, 275–6
indirect (*see* Overhead costs)
Materials requisition, 82
Mathematical methods
control of variances, 473–4
decision-making, 425–31, 517–18
risk analysis, 363–79 *passim*
sales forecasting, 345–6
Measurement
dimensions of unit of, 35–6
in control, 272
object of, 34–5
standard of, 35
valuation and, 36–7
Measurement theory, 33–7
Mechanization of accounting, 89–95, 97–8
(*see also* Data processing)
Memorandum of Association, 187, 195
Mergers and acquisitions, 208–27, 228–45
City Code, 221
definition, 240–41, 617
Exposure Draft, 240–42, 617
Message
communication system, 266, 267
Minority employment, 694
Minority shareholders, 221–6
acquisitions and creation of minority interests, 222–6
calculating cost of control, 224–5
calculating purchase price, 223–4
recording minority interest, 225–6
consolidated Income Statements, 235, 236, 237
inter-group transactions, 233–4
losses made by subsidiaries, 229–30
subsidiaries having complex capital structures, 230–31
sub-subsidiary relationship, 238–9
Mixed costs, 286
'Mixed economy', 16
Models (*see* Simulation)
Monetary and non-monetary items, 582–6, 605–8
Money
time value of, 328–32 *passim*, 335, 576–7
utility function of, 375–9
Money measurement convention, 35, 60–62, 698
Monte Carlo method, 374–5
Motivation, 268, 498–9, 502, 504
Motor vehicles, 131–7 *passim*, 164
Multi-copy stationery, 88
Multiple subsidiaries, 228
Multiple value reports, 655–6

Negotiated pricing, 445
Net cash inflows, 327–30 *passim*, 332–5 *passim*, 364–8 *passim*, 378
Net income
appropriation procedures, 200–202
calculation, 153–4
contribution to social goals, 680–81
definition, 151–2
fluctuation in, 193–4
Net investment outlays, 327–30 *passim*, 332–6 *passim*, 378
Net margin on sales ratio, 648
Net present value, 332, 564, 572, 574–7 *passim*, 602–3
comparison with internal rate of return method, 334–6
Net realizable value
as market value, 167
definition, 564
inventory valuation and, 623, 624, 626
value to the business and, 602–4
Network analysis, 491–5
costs of activities, 493–5
New product, 325, 369–70, 501
'Noise' in communication system, 267

Non-manufacturing costs
  allotment to products, 288-9
  control, 477-83
  definition, 276-7
  marketing (*see* Marketing costs)
  research and development, 71, 171, 172, 344, 478-9
Non-programmed decision models, 518-19
Non-recurrent transaction flows, 659-62
Normal capacity, 287-8
normative theory
  accounting and, 25-6, 40
  definition, 25
  financial reporting to investors, 544-5, 554

Objectives
  financial reporting, 71, 538-45, 549-51, 625, 691
  long-range planning, 306-9, 321, 340, 514
  organizational, 261, 307-8, 310, 321, 434, 469, 505, 514, 521, 563, 697, 729
  performance evaluation, 497-8
  social, 680-1, 683-6, 687
Objectivity
  corporate reporting information, 552, 657
  historical cost valuation, 571
  income measurement criterion, 568, 591
  social reporting and, 698
  synonymous with verifiability, 36, 66
  tradition of, 37
Obsolescence, 129, 131, 133
Open system, 10-11, 102
Operating costs, 645
Operating gains, 67, 592-5 *passim*, 597, 598, 604
Operating or leasing assets, 421-2
Operational control, 269-71, 274, 434-5, 518
Operational research, 22-3
Operational transaction flows, 659-61
Opportunity costs
  dropping a product line, 420-21
  employee value, 722
  investment project appraisal, 337, 419
  make or buy, 422-3
  operate or lease, 421-2
  realizable value accounting, 599
  selling or further processing, 421
  social programmes and, 686
  useful life of an asset, 133, 134
  variances, 474-5
Opportunity value, 602
Ordinary shares, 191-8 *passim* (*see also* Shares)
  issued at par, 196
  issued at a premium, 196-7
Organization costs
  valuation, 170-71
Organization theory, 507-8
Organizations
  adaptive behaviour, 521-2
  objectives and goals, 261, 307-9, 310-11, 313-17, 321, 434, 469, 497, 505-7 *passim*, 514, 516, 521, 550, 563, 697, 729
  profit and welfare types, 14
  structures, 21, 262-4, 438-9, 440, 507-8, 516
Organizing
  basic function, 262-4
  definition, 14
  for control, 434-51
Output volume
  relevant range, 397
Overhead costs
  allotment to production cost centres, 278-81
  allotment to products, 281-6
  Budget, 353-4
  control of, 461-4
  cost flow accounting, 297-8

definition, 276
direct, 279-80, 301
end-of-period balance, 300
fixed, 348, 353-4, 463-4, 465, 468
full-cost pricing, 406-7
indirect, 276, 280-81, 297, 301, 302
indirect marketing, 480, 481
Institute consideration of, 629-30
inventory valuation, 622, 623
per unit, 278, 463
raw materials, 297
variable, 348, 353-4, 463-4, 465, 466-8
variable costing and, 629-30, 632-6
variance analysis, 465-8
Overhead rates
  based on direct labour costs, 282-3
  based on direct labour hours, 283, 285
  based on machine hours, 283
  fixed, 286-8
  plant-wide *v.* departmental bases, 284-6
  variable, 286-7
Ownership and management, 188-9, 307

Par
  debentures issued at, 199
  shares issued at, 195-6
Participating Preference Shares, 191
Participation, 189, 503-4
Patents
  use of straight-line depreciation method, 135
  valuation of, 169-70
Pay-back period, 327-9
Pay-out ratio, 650
Performance evaluation
  behavioural aspects, 497-508
  objectives, 497-8, 503
  quantitative and qualitative measures, 503
  standards of performance, 505-6
Performance reports, 438-40
Period costing, 277, 288, 629
Periodic expenses, 622
Periodic income (*see* Periodic measurement)
Periodic measurement, 112-84 (*see also* Income measurement)
  accounting procedures, 200-202
  accrual convention and, 115-26
  double entry book-keeping and, 112-26
  flow of manufacturing costs, 298-300
  income calculation, 114-15, 151-4
  losses in asset values and, 127-46
  problems in, 112-13
Periodicity convention, 71-3, 112
  effect on flow of manufacturing costs, 298
  effect on income measurement, 73
Personal accounts, 105
Personnel
  responsibility to, 694
P.E.R.T., 491-5
  costs of activities, 493-5
Petty cash, 87
Physical deterioration (*see* Deterioration)
Planning
  annual (*see* Budgeting planning)
  capital expenditure (*see* Capital budgeting)
  control and, 264-5, 434-5, 461-2
  cost information and, 274
  definitions, 14, 26
  environmental information and, 261-2
  integration with control, 434-5
  kinds of, 262
  long-range (*see* Long-range planning)
  project (*see* Capital budgeting)

short-term (*see* Budgetary planning; Cost-volume-profit analysis)
stages of, 261
Plant and machinery, 131, 132, 139–40, 141
plant layout, 382
valuation, 164
Pollution, 678, 679, 694, 696
Position audit, 309–10
Positive theory, 25, 40
Predetermined overhead rates (*see* Overhead rates)
Preference shares, 191–9 *passim*, 230–31
Premium
consolidating accounts of subsidiaries' acquired at a, 214–18
debentures issued at a, 199
shares issued at a, 195, 196–7
Prepayments, 118, 120–21, 156, 174
Present value (*see* Net present value)
Pressure groups, 676–8, 685
Price earnings ratio, 650
Price elasticity of demand, 394–5
Price-level change accounting (*see* Inflation accounting)
Pricing, 400–13
changes in selling price, 393–5 *passim*, 400, 446, 579, 588
classical economic theory and, 401–4
conversion cost pricing, 408–10
costs and, 401–3 *passim*, 404–5
'dumping', 412
effect of competition, 405
'fair' prices, 405, 408
full-cost pricing, 405–8
going-rate pricing, 412–13
influences on pricing theories, 401–2
marketing and, 407, 411–12, 413
nature of the problem, 401
policies, 18–19, 344, 400–401
price discrimination, 411
price-makers and price-takers, 405
return on investment pricing, 410–11
standard cost determination of selling price, 454
transfer pricing and, 441
variable cost pricing, 411–12
Prime costs, 275–6, 279, 286, 298
Private companies, 187
Probabilistic budgeting, 370–73
Probability
risk analysis, 363–79 *passim*
Problem-solving and decision-making, 30–31
Procedural conventions, 62–75
Process costing, 300–303
calculation of actual output, 302–3
Product costing, 628–9
Product costs (*see* Full product costs; Total product costs)
Product or service contribution, 683
Production
Budget, 351
constant, 632–3, 635
fluctuating, 633–5
new product line, 325
objectives and goals, 308
Order, 82
Production cost centres
allotment of costs to products, 281–6
allotment of overhead costs to, 278–81
Products
allotment of non-manufacturing costs to, 288–9
allotment of production costs centre costs to, 281–6
alternative, 382
dropping a product line, 419–21, 481
improvement, 694
mix, 381, 395–7, 409–10, 424–5, 425–31, 446, 470–72
profitability, 480–81, 482
selling or further processing, 421

Profit
centres, 270, 440–46
forecasts, 501
margin, 405–11 *passim*, 446, 447, 648
maximization of, 402–3, 404, 426–7, 429–30, 431, 562, 720
measurement (*see* Income measurement)
sharing, 15
Profit objectives and goals, 308, 310–11, 313–17
divisional targets, 316–17, 501, 506
Profit planning
cost-volume-profit analysis and, 382–3, 391–6
use of equation and contribution margin methods, 386
Profitability (*see also* Income measurement)
conflict with liquidity, 357
over-emphasis on short-term profitability, 500
products, 480–81, 482
sales, 648
sales territories, 480, 481
Profit-volume chart, 389–90
Programmed decision models, 517–18
Project control, 491–5
costs of activities, 493–5
Project planning (*see* Capital budgeting)
Projected cash flow, 319
Projected Income Statement, 318
Property companies, 588
Proprietary theory, 559
Public companies, 187
Public contribution, 682–3
Public interest movement, 677–8
Public need for information, 18, 534, 543
Punched card systems, 90–92
Purchase order, 82–3
Purchase requisition, 82, 93
Purchases Day Book, 85

Quick ratio, 642

Rates of return (*see* Capital budgeting; Return on Capital Employed)
Ratios
acid-test, 642
activity, 643–5
analysis, 638–51
asset turnover, 648
average collection period of trade debtors, 644–5
average inventory turnover, 153, 643–4
current, 641–2
dividend coverage, 650
dividend yield, 650
earnings per share, 649
earnings yield, 650
function and nature of analysis, 638–40
gearing, 192–4, 315, 320, 337–8, 646
Gross Profit, 152–3
human to non-human assets, 723
interest coverage, 646
Margin of Safety, 388–9
net margin on sales, 648
price earnings, 650
profits to effort employed, 726
Return on Capital Employed, 313, 315–16, 647–8
shareholders' equity, 645–6
Raw materials
costs, 296–7
standard costs, 455, 456–8
inventories, 486
requirement forecast, 348
Real accounts, 105
Realizable value accounting, 599–602, 656
case for, 599–600
components of realizable income, 600

limitations of exit values, 601–2
Realization convention, 66–8, 74, 123, 174, 571–2, 591, 698
Realized gains, 600–601
Realized holding gains, 596, 597
Receiver
communication system, 266, 267
Redeemable Preference shares, 191
Register of Shareholders, 188, 189, 196, 202
Registered shares, 188
Relevance
corporate reporting information, 551, 591, 657
income measurement, 567, 591
performance ratios, 648
Relevant costs, 414–15, 416, 418, 419, 423, 636–7
Reliability
corporate reporting information, 551–2
Rent, 116–20
underpayment, 118–20
Re-order point, 490–91
Repair costs, 130, 132, 133, 137, 138
Replacement cost accounting, 592–9, 656
components of replacement cost income, 592–6 *passim*
evaluation of, 598–9
historic and replacement cost Balance Sheets compared, 596–7
income measurement by historic cost *v.* replacement cost, 594–6
ratio analysis and, 648
treatment of holiday gains, 597
'value to the business', 602–4
Replacement cost measurement of human assets, 721
Replacement cost valuation, 167–8, 564, 570–71, 581, 602–4, 623, 626
Replacement costs, 132–4 *passim*, 200, 201, 595–6
Reporting (*see* Financial reporting; Responsibility reporting; Social reporting)
Research and development
costs, 71, 171, 172, 344, 478–9
project, 325
reductions in, 500
Reserves
Capital, 175, 199, 200, 201
General, 200, 201
mergers and acquisitions, 214–17 *passim*, 219–21 *passim*, 240, 241–3, 244–5
Revenue, 175
Residual Income method, 450–51
Residual value, 133–4
Resource allocation
accounting information and, 19–20
Resources availability, 514, 515
Responsibility accounting, 342, 435–51
Responsibility centres, 436–51 (*see also* Departments)
division, 436–7
cost centres, 270, 278–81, 301–2, 436–7, 438
expense centres, 436–40
investment centres, 446–51
profit centres, 270, 440–46
variances, 472–3
Responsibility reporting, 438–40
Retail Price Index, 582, 583, 587–8
Retained income, 175, 188, 200, 201, 315, 316, 319
Return on Capital Employed
analysis of financial performance, 647–8
importance of, 313
limitations of, 449–50, 647
measuring divisional performance, 446–51
targeted, 315–16
Return on effort emp! ~d, 724–6
Return on investment pricing, 410–11
Revaluation of fixed assets, 131, 163, 580
Revenue(s)

break-even sales revenue, 385, 386, 391, 393
control of, 468–72
definitions, 68, 114
effect of adjustments, 122
effect of price changes on sales revenue, 393–5
identification of, 113–15
matching with expenses, 69–71, 112–13, 123, 628–9, 630, 637
Reserves, 175
sales revenue curve, 387–8, 397, 398
margin of safety ratio, 388–9
Risk analysis, 360–79
aversion to risk, 375–9, 521
certainty equivalent method, 365–8, 377–8
decision trees, 368–73
discount rate adjustment, 361
role in planning, 312
sensitivity analysis and, 361–5
simulation, 373–5
uncertainty and information, 39, 360–61
utility theory, 375–9
Rolling forecasts of budgets, 658
Running costs, 130

Salary capitalization method, 722–3
Sale or disposal of assets, 140–41
Sales
Budget, 350
constant, 633–5
costs, 298, 300
forecast, 349
credit, 644–5
Day Book, 85, 88, 89, 91, 92
fluctuating, 632–3, 635
forecasting, 344–6, 347
methods, 345–6
invoice, 81, 88, 89, 91, 92
mix, 381, 395–7, 409–10, 424–5, 425–31, 446, 470–72
new product sales probability, 369–70
order form, 81–2
policy, 344
profitability of, 648
receipts, 349
territory profitability, 480, 481
Sales variances, 468–72
mix, 470–72
price, 469–70, 471
volume, 470, 471
Sales volume
changes in, 390–95 *passim*, 407, 446
variance, 470, 471
Salvage value, 328
Sandilands Report, 580, 587, 588–9, 598, 604–8, 665
Scientific method
and empiricism in financial reporting, 553–4
elements in, 28
social science and, 28–30, 40
Search process
decision-making, 521
investment projects, 311–12
Seasonal trade, 645
Secret reserves of banks, 65
Securities and Exchange Commission, 5
Selling and Administrative Expenses Budget, 355
Selling or further processing, 421
Selling outlets
operating *v.* leasing, 421–2
Selling price
adjusted, 624
changes in, 393–5, 400, 446, 579, 588
standard cost basis for, 454
variance, 469–70, 471

Sender
  communication system, 266
Sensitivity analysis, 361–5
  limitations of, 363
Service cost centres
  allotment of costs, 279–81
  definition, 278
Service potential, 636
Share capital, 190–99 (*see also* Equity capital)
  accounting procedures, 194–9
  information provision, 197–9
Shareholders (*see also* Investors)
  calculating returns to, 315–16
  information needs, 14–15, 52, 71–2, 75, 161, 203–6, 533,
      538–45 *passim*, 547, 553, 577
  limited liability of, 4
  minority, 221–6
  ratio analysis, and, 640
  register of, 188, 189, 196, 202
  rights and powers, 172, 188, 191–2, 307
  social responsibility accounting and, 674
Shareholders' equity
  ratio, 645–6
  valuation of, 175–6
Shares
  Authorized and Issued Capital, 188, 194, 198–9
  Bearer, 188
  bonus, 194–5
  Deferred, 192
  earnings per share ratio, 649
  earnings yield, 650
  issue of, 194–9
  nominal value, 188, 195
  'of no par value', 195
  Ordinary (*see* Ordinary shares)
  Preference, 191–9 *passim*, 230–31
  price earnings ratio, 650
  prices, 314–15, 321
  Registered, 188
  transfer of, 189–90
  valuation, 169
Short-run tactical decisions, 414–32
Short-term assets, 156
Short-term liabilities, 157, 172, 173–4, 202, 641–2
Short-term planning (*see* Budgetary planning; Cost-volume-
      profit analysis)
Simplex Method, 431
Simulation
  budget models, 373–4
  capital investment appraisal, 374–5
  decision models, 32–3, 373–5, 485, 517–19, 552–3, 554,
      654
  inventory models, 485
  P.E.R.T., 491–5
Social audit, 18, 534, 684–5, 699
Social benefits, 678, 686–8, 698
Social costs, 678–9
Social output measurement, 686
Social programmes, 683–6
  cost-effectiveness analysis, 686–8
Social reporting
  accounting conventions and, 697–8
  communication methods, 695–6
  development, 690–95
  examples
    Quaker Oats Company, 699–716
    Scovill Manufacturing Company, 691–3
  integration with financial reporting, 695–6, 701
  nature of the message, 696–7
  social auditing and, 699
  surveys of practice and attitudes, 691, 694–5
  understandability of the message, 697
Social responsibility

company commitment to, 677–8, 700
company influence on the locality, 18, 694
determining the extent of, 679–83
government action, 679
human resource accounting and, 729–30
industrial relations and, 730–2
planning for social objectives, 683–6
social objectives, 680–1, 683–6, 687
Social responsibility accounting, 673–732
  concepts of social responsibility, 673–4
  development, 6–7
Social science
  accounting as, 2–7
  scientific method and, 28–30, 40
  value judgements and, 7
Social stewardship, 690
Sole trader
  appropriation of net income, 200
  legal liability of, 59–60
Solvency
  capital maintenance and, 639–40
  ratio analysis, of, 640–46
    long-term solvency
      interest coverage ratio, 646
      shareholders' equity ratio, 645–6
    short-term solvency
      acid-test ratio, 642
      average collection period of trade debtors, 644–5
      average inventory turnover, 153, 643–4
      current ratio, 641–2
Source documents, 79–85, 88, 95
  related to purchases, 82–3
  related to receipt of goods, 83
  related to sales, 81–2
Special orders, 382, 416–17
Spending variance, 466–7, 473
Split-off point, 290, 291
Stakeholders, 674
Standard costing
  applications, 454–5
  budget and, 453–4
  cost-based transfer pricing, 443
  definition of standard cost, 292
  direct labour, 456, 458–9
  inventory valuation, 624
  overheads, 461–2, 465–8
  raw materials, 455, 456–8
  sales, 468–72
  setting cost standards, 455
  variance analysis and, 453–75
Standard deviation, 365–8
Standard hours, 466–8 *passim*
Standardization (*see also* Comparability of information)
  accounting profession, 616–18
  arguments against uniformity, 613–14, 615
  European and American developments, 5, 547–8, 616–18
  government needs, 16
  legal enforcement, 618
  need for, 547–8
  views of Trueblood Report, 550–51
Statements, 81, 88, 89
Statements of Standard Accounting Practice
  associated companies, 617–18
  stock and work-in-progress, 618
Statistical analysis in sales forecasting, 345
Statistical control charts, 473–4
Stewardship accounting, 3, 4, 161, 538, 540–42, 543, 571
  social stewardship, 690
Stock Exchanges, 175, 187, 188, 191, 193, 202, 314
Stock forecasts, 349
Stocks and shares valuation, 169
Straight-line depreciation method, 135, 137–8, 205
Strategic gap, 311

Strategic planning (see Long-range planning)
Subsidiary books, 83–7
Subsidiary companies, 208–10 passim, 213–27
    acquisition at less than book value, 228–9
    acquisition during an accounting period, 231
    complex share capital structures, 230–31
    definition, 210–11
    disclosure of information, 209–10, 211–12
    inter-group transactions, 231–4
    losses made by, 229–30
    mergers and acquisitions, 240–45
    multiple subsidiaries, 228
    sub-subsidiary relationship, 237–9
Sundry creditors balance, 350
Sunk costs, 414, 416, 664
Supplier's invoice, 83
Surpluses
    Cash Budget and, 356
    long-range financial plan, 319
    reinvestment of cash surpluses, 335–6
Synergy, 312
System
    definition, 10
    open and closed, 10–11, 102–3
Systems approach
    information systems design, 512–14
    study of accounting, 21–3

T accounts, 99–107
Takeovers (see Mergers and acquisitions)
Targets (see Goals)
Taxation
    capital budgeting and, 336
    corporation tax, 200, 201, 338, 566
    deferred liabilities, 175, 205
    effect of tax changes on rate of return, 315
    historic cost income as tax base, 656
    income as tax base, 566
    social costs and, 679
    transaction flows, 660–61
Technological developments
    accounting and, 22
    replacement costs and, 599
Technological forecasting, 309
Technology and organization structure, 508
Theft
    losses by, 127
Theory
    empirical, 27–8, 553–4
    logic and, 26–7
    nature of, 25–6
    normative, 25–6, 40, 554–5
    positive, 25, 40
    Theory X, 498–9, 501–2, 505
    Theory Y, 499, 516, 518
Timeliness
    corporate reporting information, 552
Timing of transactions, 67–8
Tools and sundry equipment, 131, 164
Total product costs, 275, 277–8
    limitations of calculations, 289–90
Trade
    seasonal, 645
Trade creditors, 641
Trade debtors, 127, 141–5, 156, 642, 644–5
Trade unions
    information needs, 52
    social responsibility and, 730–32
Trade-Mark valuation, 170
Trading transaction flows, 659–61
Transactions
    accounts as descriptions of, 104–5, 561
    cash-flow accounting, 659–66 passim

    timing of, 67–8
Transfer pricing, 441–6
    advantages, 445–6
    cost-based, 443
    full-cost, 443–4
    variable-cost, 445
    criteria for, 442–3
    market-based, 442–3
    negotiated, 445
Trial Balance, 105–8, 114–15
    adjustments for accruals, 115–26
    Balance Sheet preparation, 156–7
    errors not revealed by, 108
    Income Statement preparation, 147–50 passim
Trueblood Report, 548–51, 691

Uncertainty (see Risk analysis)
Understandability
    corporate reporting information, 551
    income measurement, 568
    social reporting, 697
Undistributed retained income, 175, 188, 200, 201
Uniformity (see Standardization)
Union Européenne des Experts Comptables, Economiques
        et Financiers, 616
Unit costs, 277, 285–8 passim, 623
Unrealized gains, 600–601
    holding, 596, 597
Unsecured notes, 191, 199
Use value, 129
Utility
    of assets, 129, 561, 562–3
    of inventory, 167–8
    theory, 375–9

Valuation
    advertising costs, 171, 172
    assets, 62–4, 74, 128, 161–72, 563–4, 570–71, 599, 601
    buildings, 163–4
    copyrights, 170
    current assets, 164–8
    fixed assets, 162–4
    franchises, 170
    goodwill, 171
    intangible assets, 169–72
    inventories, 76, 164–8, 205, 293, 298–300, 620–27
        at cost, 165, 623
        at cost less provision to reduce net realizable value, 623
        authors' recommendations for reducing diversity, 625–37
            passim
        current practices, 623–5
        effect of inaccurate measurement, 621
        FIFO, 165–6, 581, 624, 648
        importance of, 620–21
        Institute recommendation, 622–3
        LIFO, 166, 580–81, 648
        'lower of cost or market rule' (LCM), 166–8, 205, 603,
            624
        lower of cost or net realizable value, 623
        lowest of cost, net realizable value and replacement price,
            623
        realizable value accounting, 599
        SSAP on, 618
        Weighted Average Cost, 166
    investments, 169
    land, 163, 583
    liabilities, 172–5
    measurement and, 36–7
    natural resources 164
    organization costs, 170–71
    patents, 169–70
    plant and machinery, 164
    research and development costs, 171, 172

revaluation of fixed assets, 131, 163, 580
shareholders' equity, 175–6
stocks and shares, 169
trade-marks, 170
Value
  capital and income, 564–5
  decision-making and, 562–3
  definitions, 129, 560–61
  depreciation as a fall in, 129
  exchange, 129, 161, 561–2
  importance to shareholders, 544–5
  losses in asset values and periodic measurement, 127–46,
    150–51
  to the business, 602–4, 626
Value judgements
  social sciences and, 7
Variable costing, 626–7, 629–37
  advantages, 626–7, 629
  comparison with absorption costing, 629, 630–36
    effects of inventory valuation on Balance Sheet, 636
    fluctuating production but constant sales, 633–4
    fluctuating sales but constant production, 632–3
    impact on income, 635
    variable costing controversy, 635–6
  fixed costs and, 626, 629, 635, 636
  overhead costs and, 629–30, 632–6
Variable costs
  as relevant costs, 415
  changes in, 391–3, 462
  cost-volume-profit analysis, 391–7 passim
  definition, 286
  inventory valuation, 622, 626–7
  need to distinguish from fixed costs, 290
  overheads, 348, 353–4, 463–4, 465
  pricing decisions and, 405–6
  pricing method, 411–12
  transfer pricing based on, 445
Variable overhead rate, 286–7
Variances
  analysis of, 456–75
  direct labour, 458–9

direct materials, 456–8
  disposition of, 459–61
  investigation of, 473–4
  labour efficiency, 458–9, 472
  material price, 457–8, 472
  material usage, 458, 472
  opportunity cost, 474–5
  overhead costs, 465–8
    fixed, 468
    variable, 466–8
  responsibility for, 472–3
  sales, 468–72
  spending, 466–7, 473
  volume, 468, 473
  wage rate, 458–9, 472
Venture concept, 570
Verifiability
  budget disclosure to investors, 657
  corporate reporting information, 552
  historical cost valuation, 571
  social reporting and, 698
  synonymous with objectivity, 36, 66
Volume of output
  relevant range, 397
Volume variances
  overhead, 468, 473
  sales, 470–1

Wage bargaining, 730
Wage rate variance, 458–9, 472
Warehousing and storage costs, 289
Weighted Average Cost
  inventory valuation, 166
  of capital, 337
Women's liberation movement, 677
Work study in the office, 454, 478
Working capital, 320, 642
Work-in-Progress, 294, 295, 297–300 passim, 302, 486,
    618
'Write-it-once' principle, 88–9
Writing boards, 88–9